THE LONG ROAD TO SOCIAL SECURITY

THE LONG ROAD TO SOCIAL SECURITY

Assessing the Implementation of National Social Security Initiatives for the Working Poor in India

edited by

K.P. Kannan
Jan Breman

UNIVERSITY PRESS

OXFORD
UNIVERSITY PRESS

Oxford University Press is a department of the University of Oxford. It furthers the University's objective of excellence in research, scholarship, and education by publishing worldwide. Oxford is a registered trademark of Oxford University Press in the UK and in certain other countries

Published in India by
Oxford University Press
2/11 Ground Floor, Ansari Road, Daryaganj, New Delhi 110002, India

First Edition published in 2013

ISBN-13: 978-0-19-809031-1
ISBN-10: 0-19-809031-5

Typeset in Galliard 10/12.5
by The Graphics Solution, New Delhi 110 092
Printed in India by Thomson Press (India) Ltd.

CONTENTS

TABLES, FIGURES, AND BOXES

TABLES

FIGURES

BOXES

PREFACE

This book is the outcome of a long and continuing conversation and collaboration between us. While a large number of social science scholars, political and social activists, and some concerned policy makers and media persons have ardently highlighted the wretched conditions of work and life of an overwhelming majority of workers in India, state intervention at the national level to address this issue by providing a measure of social security has been minuscule, if not completely absent. Intervention by the sub-national state governments have not been much more effective, except with the notable examples set by Kerala, and then by Tamil Nadu. Some selected initiatives in a few other states notwithstanding, the general picture is one of hopeless existence for the vast majority of the working poor in India.

It is in this background that the first United Progressive Alliance (UPA) government, prompted by its own election manifesto, appointed a National Commission for Enterprises in the Unorganized Sector (NCEUS) in 2004 headed by the Late Arjun Sengupta. The reports of this Commission not only gave a systematic statistical profile of the working poor employed in the informal sector, both in the so-called unorganized and organized sectors of the economy, but also estimated them at around 92 per cent of the total work force. This was, in a way, shocking for an India that was celebrating its 'shining image', with aggregate economic growth moving from 6 to 8, and even 9 per cent per annum since the initiation of neoliberal economic reforms in the early 1990s. More shocking was the revelation of the NCEUS that around 80 per cent of the informal workers could be classified as poor and vulnerable, while the overall estimate for the entire population was around 76 per cent.

Such a scenario prompted the Government of India to initiate two important national social security measures. One was the National Rural Employment Guarantee Act (NREGA) of 2005, well known by now, and the other was the Unorganized Workers Social Security Act of 2008, a considerably watered down version of the proposal made by the NCEUS, and endorsed fully by a Parliamentary Standing Committee. When one of us—K.P. Kannan—returned to the Centre for Development Studies after completing his term as a Member of the NCEUS, Jan Breman proposed that detailed studies on the functioning of these two important national schemes be undertaken. This book is the result of the evolution, expansion, and execution of this proposal. We were very fortunate to have the collaboration of a number of scholars who agreed to undertake such studies in their respective states. The process was an interactive one where all the participating scholars met during three workshops conducted at different points of time, supplemented by visits to selected study areas by the two of us in addition to our own field level studies. We want to take this opportunity to thank all our fellow scholars who made this project a success.

Studies also require finance and a sponsor who shares empathy to the subject matter. We were fortunate to have the Humanistic Institute for Development Cooperation, The Hague, The Netherlands (HiVOS) readily agreeing to our request for sponsoring the study. We would like to record our thanks to HiVOS and to their team incharge of the Knowledge Generation Programme, headed by Josine Stremmelaar, who were in close contact with us at every stage of our study. Institutional support to the study was provided by our respective institutions—the Centre for Development Studies in Thiruvananthapuram and the Amsterdam Institute for Social Science Research in Amsterdam—and we take this opportunity to record our appreciation for their support.

Oxford University Press, New Delhi, deserves a special word of thanks for their speedy processing of our manuscript and putting in extra effort in publishing the book within a short period of time.

K.P. Kannan
Jan Breman

September 2012

ABBREVIATIONS

AABY	Aam Aadmi Bima Yojana
ADS	Area Development Society
ADS	Atta-Dal Scheme
AHC	Ayurvedic Health Centre
AIADMK	All India Anna Dravida Munnetra Kazhakam
AMC	Ahmedabad Municipal Corporation
APL	Above Poverty Line
APNA	AP-NGO Alliance
ASHA	Accredited Social Health Activist
BJP	Bhartiya Janata Party
BMS	Bandhkam Majdoor Sangathana
BPL	Below Poverty Line
CBO	Community Based Organization
CDS	Community Development Society
CHC	Community Health Centre
CHIAK	Comprehensive Health Insurance Agency Kerala
CHIS	Comprehensive Health Insurance Scheme
CMCO	Chief Minister's Camp Office
CMRF	Chief Ministers Relief Fund
CMSA	Community Managed Sustainable Agriculture
CMSLB	Cloth Market and Shops Labour Board
CPI	Commznist Party of India
CPI(M)	Communist Party of India (Marxist)
CPIAL	Consumer Price Index for Agricultural Labourers
CWWB	Construction Worker's Welfare Board
DISH	Department of Industrial Safety and Health
DLO	District Labour Officer
DPC	District Project Co-ordinator
DRDA	District Rural Development Agency
DSP	Deputy Superintendent of Police

DSSO	District Social Security Officer
E-MMS	Electronic Muster Measurement System
FDI	Foreign Direct Investment
FGD	Focused Group Discussion
FKA	Field Key Authority
FLG	Fixed Labour Groups
GDI	Gender Development Index
GKM	Garib Kalyan Mela
GRS	Gram Rojgar Sevaks
GUWWB	Gujarat Unorganized Workers Welfare Board
HDI	Human Development Index
HRDC	Human Resource Development Centre
IAMR	Institute of Applied Manpower Research
IAY	Indira Awas Yojana
IGNDPS	Indira Gandhi National Disability Pension Scheme
IGNOAP	Indira Gandhi National Old Age Pension
IGNOAPS	Indira Gandhi National Old Age Pension Scheme
IGNWPS	Indira Gandhi National Widowhood Pension Scheme
IKM	Information Kerala Mission
IRDA	Insurance Regulatory Development Authority
ITI	Industrial Training Institute
JSBY	Jana Shri Bima Yojana
KSSP	Kerala Sastra Sahitya Parishad
LDF	Left Democratic Front
MACSA	Mutually Aided Cooperative Societies Act
MBPY	Madhu Babu Pension Yojana
MGNREGA	Mahatma Gandhi National Rural Employment Guarantee Act
MGNREGS	Mahatma Gandhi National Rural Employment Guarantee Scheme
MKSS	Majdoor Kisan Sangharsh Samiti
MMS	Mahila Mandal Samakhya
MNC	Multinational Corporation
NAUW	Non Agricultural Unskilled Workers
NCEUS	National Commission for Enterprises in the Unorganized Sector
NGO	Non-governmental Organization
NIC	National Informatics Centre
NIMS	Nizam's Institute of Medical Sciences

NMSS	National Minimum Social Security
NREG	National Rural Employment Guarantee
NREGA	National Rural Employment Guarantee Act
NREGS	National Rural Employment Guarantee Scheme
NSAP	National Social Assistance Programme
NSS	National Sample Survey
OBC	Other Backward Class
PDS	Public Distribution System
PHC	Primary Health Centre
PPC	People's Plan Campaign
PRI	Panchayati Raj Institutions
RAMCO	Rajiv Aarogyasri Medical Coordinators
RAS	Rajiv Aarogyasri Scheme
RDO	Revenue Divisional Officer
RMP	Registered Medical Practitioner
RSBY	Rashtriya Swasthaya Bima Yojana
SC	Scheduled Caste
SEWA	Self Employed Women's Association
SGSY	Swarnajayanti Gram Swarojgar Yojana
SHG	Self Help Group
SNA	State Nodal Agency
SOR	Schedule of Rate
SSR	Standard Schedule of Rate
SSS	Shramika Shakti Sangam
ST	Scheduled Tribe
TCS	Tata Consultancy Services
TDP	Telugu Desam Party
TPA	Third Party Administrator
UCD	Urban Community Development
UDF	United Democratic Front
UID	Unique Identity Card
ULB	Urban Local Body
UPA	United Progressive Alliance
UWSSA	Unorganized Workers' Social Security Act
VLW	Village Level Worker
VO	Village Organization
ZMS	Zillah Mahila Samakhya

INTRODUCTION

UNTO THE LAST?

Jan Breman and *K.P. Kannan*

A WORKFORCE DEVOID OF PROTECTION AND SECURITY

India could rightly be characterized as one of the few large and growing economies with a vast informal sector, that is one dominated by a large number of very small enterprises consisting of the self-employed as well as hired labour without any employment and/or social security. The National Commission for Enterprises in the Unorganized Sector (NCEUS)—referred to as National Commission henceforth—set up by the Government of India in 2004 to take stock of the informal economy has drawn public attention to the pitiable plight of the labouring poor. The series of reports brought out until 2009 highlight the manifold problems of livelihood insecurity faced by an overwhelming majority of the people. The major findings can be summed as follows.

First, 86 per cent of the total workers are in the informal sector, accounting for half of the national output as on 2005. Given the fact that the formal sector has been growing at double the rate of growth of the informal sector, this share in national output could be around 45 per cent in 2010 while the share of workers has remained around 84 per cent (Table I.1). Of the remaining 16 per cent of workers, 46 per cent were employed as informal workers in the formal sector; this increased up to 51 per cent in 2009–10.

Second, self-employment is the dominant form of employment in the Indian economy where the main worker-owner is assisted by unpaid family labour, or by hired wage labour, hardly exceeding four to five workers. They usually toil for long hours since sizeable sections under this category are engaged as piece-rate workers based at home, or in small sweatshops.

Third, casual labour is the next largest category, that is those with irregular work and low wages. Given the irregular nature of

ABLE I.1 Employment in the Formal and Informal Economies of India

Year	*Informal Sector*	*Formal Sector*	*Total*
Informal Worker (in million)			
1999–2000	339.71	23.04	362.75
2004–5	393.47	29.14	422.61
2009–10	386.02	37.15	423.17
Formal Workers (in million)			
1999–2000	1.79	31.85	33.64
2004–5	1.43	33.42	34.85
2009–10	1.68	35.58	37.25
Total Workers (in million)			
1999–2000	341.50	54.89	396.39
2004–5	394.90	62.57	457.47
2009–10	387.70	72.73	460.42
Percentage Distribution			
Informal Workers			
1999–2000	93.6 (99.5)	6.4 (42.0)	100 (91.5)
2004–5	93.1 (99.6)	6.9 (46.6)	100 (92.4)
2009–10	91.2 (99.6)	8.8 (51.1)	100 (91.9)
Formal Workers			
1999–2000	5.3 (0.5)	94.7 (58.0)	100 (8.5)
2004–5	4.1 (0.4)	95.9 (53.4)	100 (7.6)
2009–10	4.5 (0.4)	95.5 (48.9)	100 (8.1)
Total Workers			
1999–2000	86.2 (100)	13.8 (100)	100 (100)
2004–5	86.3 (100)	13.7 (100)	100 (100)
2009–10	84.2 (100)	15.8 (100)	100 (100)

Source: For 1999–2000 and 2004–5, NCEUS (2009: 13) and for 2009–10, Kannan (2012).

Note: Figures in brackets represent percentage shares of informal and formal workers out of total workers in each sector.

their employment, this segment faces short and long periods of unemployment, especially in rural areas where work in the primary sector is often seasonal.

Fourth, close to 80 per cent of the informal sector workers belong to households who could be characterized as poor and vulnerable.

Apart from low wages, conditions of employment are often abominable due to absence of basic amenities, exposure to hazardous materials, and the employment of bonded and child labour in certain specific occupations in many, if not all, parts of the country.

Fifth, the incidence of informal sector work is much higher among women than men workers as well as among the Scheduled Castes (SCs) and Scheduled Tribes (STs) than others with pronounced wage disparities, compounded by a greater degree of illiteracy and low education, not to mention low level of skill.

Sixth, the absence of a labour contract, the non-implementation of basic labour laws (such as minimum wages), and their conditions of poverty demonstrate the weak bargaining power among informal workers, compounded by a lack of agency and representation.

The vulnerability is aggravated by the necessity to remain mobile. It means a never-ending search for employment in the local labour market, and leads to an occupational multiplicity which makes it necessary to continuously migrate across the various sectors into which the economy is split-up, or travel to destinations far from home for shorter or longer periods of time, to seek employment. The footloose nature of a large segment of the workforce exposed to the regime of informality is a consequence of the falling demand for labour in the primary sector of the economy. Households belonging to the landless and land-poor classes in particular are pushed out of agriculture, and the village economy, across the subcontinent of South Asia. Since this shift is not adequately monitored in macro-surveys, it is difficult to determine the size of this segment with any degree of reliability. The latest available data from the 64th Round of the National Sample Survey (NSS) conducted during 2007–8 shows that close to one-third of the Indian workers (140 million) work outside the place of their birth. But that is not saying much because it is not expected that everyone would be able to work in the place of their birth. What is important from our point of view is the rapidly growing category caught up in short duration seasonal/circular migration, which has been estimated by NSS at around 16 million. However, independent research reckons that this figure could be at least 40 million (Srivastava, 2011). In addition, Srivastava finds that another 40 million workers or so (in the permanent/semi-permanent category) were in the lowest three consumption quintiles, which could be treated as poor and vulnerable. This means that around 80 million migrant workers are poor and vulnerable. Of course, if we take the NCEUS threshold for poor and vulnerable (as those below the poverty line that was twice that of the official poverty line fixed in 2005), then the estimate of poor and vulnerable migrant workforce would exceed 100 million, that is a little more than one-fifth of the total workforce. Being pushed out from their place of origin, the problem these people face is that wherever they go, they do not find steady and somewhat secure employment. The fear of jobless growth has come to haunt us increasingly. This alarming perspective makes it all the more necessary to raise and solve the social question.

Not being paid enough for the work performed is a major cause of vulnerability, but that deficiency in economic status is compounded by a social identity which fixes the people concerned at the bottom of the heap. The labouring poor by and large hail from categories in the lower ranks of society: SCs and STs, members of the Muslim community, and other communities classified as Other Backward Classes (OBCs) in official statistics. Lack of schooling, of opportunities for acquiring a skill, and a dearth of social capital in general tend to hold them back from making their way up in mainstream society. From the marginal positions they occupy both in economy and society, these people lack voice and agency to move up the occupational ladder.

If this is the shape then what is the size of the segments clubbed together as the labouring poor? India's total workforce in 2010 was estimated around 460 million adults and minors, of which the overwhelming majority depend on the informal economy for their livelihood. According to the Planning Commission (2012), the ability to spend Rs 22.5 per day per capita or Rs 673 per month in early 2010 was the cut-off point to decide if members of a household in the rural economy are above or below the so-called poverty line, while those of a household residing in the urban economy would require six rupees more, that is Rs 28.5 per day per capita or Rs 860 per month. Since these figures are far below the minimal cost of basic needs, however defined, this official arithmetic cannot be accepted to classify people as poor or non-poor. In fact, when this issue was taken to the Supreme Court of India, it pulled up the Central Government for putting such a cap.[1] It is essentially an exercise carried out for policy and political expediency, to suggest that the ambit of economic growth does benefit all and sundry, eventually, if not immediately.

When the NCEUS classified the population according to various poverty bands or groups, it reported that in 2005 around 76 per cent of Indians lived below a poverty line that was twice that of the then official poverty line, that was also equivalent to the international poverty line of two dollars (at Purchasing Power Parity) per day per capita. A recent exercise using the same threshold found that this came down to 69 per cent in 2010 (Kannan, 2012).

Figuring out the complexity of the informal–formal dichotomy, the National Commission earlier referred to considered the prevalence or absence of social security benefits to be of critical and even definitional importance.

> Unorganized workers consist of those working in the unorganized enterprises or households, excluding regular workers with social security benefits, and the workers in the formal sector without any employment/social security benefits provided by the employers. (NCEUS, 2009: 12)

The statement leads to the conclusion that having a job does not automatically exempt workers from belonging to the vast army of the labouring poor. The employer may allow them to work more regularly, notwithstanding no or underutilization of their labour power, with somewhat higher incomes, but they are otherwise as unprotected and insecure as the thoroughly casualized workforce in their terms of employment. It means that it is not regularity versus irregularity which is responsible for the divide in the workforce, but the contrast between formality and informality. Thus the informal workforce at large, the National Commission argues, does not enjoy *employment security* (no protection against arbitrary dismissal), *work security* (no protection against accidents and health risks at the workplace) and *social security* (maternity and health benefits, pension, etc.) In the Commission's final report the on-going trend towards informalization of India's workforce, even in the formal sector, was highlighted. Recent employment data confirms this trend, resulting in a majority of workers in the formal sector ending up as informal workers as the figures below show. In 2010, 51 per cent of workers in the formal sector can be classified as informal workers, whereas this was 47 per cent and 42 per cent in 2005 and 2000 respectively.

Certainly, not all among the hundreds of millions at work in the informal economy suffer the kind of precariousness associated with the labouring poor. A small fraction is even quite well-off and manages to live in greater or lesser comfort of assets and earnings which do not show up in formal statistics. On the downside of this protracted and diffuse spectre of informality are the more numerous ultra-poor, the class of people so destitute that they survive or die in a condition of pauperism. Taking into account the wide differentiation that exists, our point of departure is that of the total workforce of close to half a billion, less than one-tenth enjoys the blessings of formal employment. Among the remaining majority of workers, massing up to a plenitude of 425 million, we would include around 300 million to be situated within the brackets of the labouring poor or vulnerable to sliding down to that predicament.

A precondition to improvement in the plight of the labouring poor is lowering the scale of multiple vulnerabilities which account for their misery. For that objective to succeed, the National Commission has outlined what it calls a 'levelling-up' strategy. This constitutes a list of proposals in favour of decent employment practices and focus on the promulgation of a 'social floor' of labour rights and standards that include introduction of a national minimum wage, minimum conditions of work and the provision of social security. While making a case for a more promotional agenda of rights (including food security, child welfare, the right to proper shelter and the granting of an unemployment allowance), the National Commission commented critically on the absence of protective security. Drawing attention in one of its reports to deficiency and adversity as characteristic for the treatment meted out to the labouring poor, the argument was that the most important issues to be considered here include cover for ill-health, accidents/death and old age. The Commission advocated the urgent implementation of the proposed set of interventions. If executed, 'this scheme will go a long way towards correcting the imbalances manifested in a situation whereby a high rate of economic growth and prosperity of a section of its population co-exists with poverty, deprivation and adversity among vast masses of workers in the informal economy' (NCEUS, 2006: 13). Clearly, in the Commission's considered opinion, more is at stake than mere poverty alleviation. Addressing and solving this social question requires a fundamental reappraisal, one which allows for a closure of the huge and still growing gap between the well-to-do and the deprived masses. It means a turnaround from a code of conduct, driven by a spirit of inequality, to a mindset which puts a premium on equality. What has been the political and policy response to the plea for the construction of a social safety net?

STATE INITIATED INTERVENTIONS

As part of a strategy of 'levelling-up', three schemes in particular were placed high on the agenda, namely, (i) the provision of employment in public works, (ii) a package of contingent social security, including insurance against failing health, and (iii) social benefits for the non-labouring poor. As observed above, a comprehensive social safety net would have to include remedial action on a broad front, to seek redress for the wide range of vulnerabilities to which the labouring poor are exposed in their day-to-day work and life. But there is little doubt that interventions which generate employment, facilitate health care, and deal with the problems arising from disability would go a long way in reprieving the worst misery of the people stuck at the bottom of the economy. Of course, the outcome of these measures depends on the sincerity and commitment with which they are carried out. Reaching a verdict of the attempts made requires a short summing up on the substance of these schemes.

The first major programme pursued was a National Rural Employment Guarantee (NREG), which in 2005 became the flagship initiative of the National Common Minimum Programme launched by the United Progressive Alliance (UPA) government when it came to power in 2004. But the draft submitted for enactment to parliament had become so watered down that it defeated the purpose of a legally enforceable employment guarantee. Due to a strong campaign by civil activists to repair the bill, the final version reinstated the promises made: guaranteed employment for applicants (100 days per household), universal coverage, time-bound extension throughout rural India, assured minimum wages and full transparency of the records kept. Still, the bill passed in 2005 met with a strong backlash in the course of the legal and political process that ensued.

> While it would have been very difficult for any Member of Parliament to oppose the Act in public, there was a great deal of 'behind the scenes' opposition to the Act in the corridors of power, notably from the Finance Ministry. Further, this opposition was organically linked to a powerful 'anti-NREGA' lobby, very vocal in the corporate-sponsored media and related forums. (Khera, 2011: 8)

The policy makers also retracted from the earlier commitment to extend the coverage of the programme to the urban economy. Neither was the promise effectuated to compensate prospective workers financially in case their application for employment was turned down. Finally, public works came to be understood as employment on infrastructural projects—land levelling, digging of bore wells, construction of irrigation canals and rural roads, bunding and building of check dams—meant to raise production and add value to already existing assets. These were to be undertaken in public owned land (such as by panchayats) or community-owned collective properties such as tanks and ponds. Subsequently, this extended to lands of small and marginal farmers, beginning with those owned by SCs and STs. However, upgrading the slum settlements inhabited by them—house construction, building of access roads, street lighting, sanitation via construction of sewers, arranging for tap water, garbage disposal—tended to be looked upon as outside the ambit of public works. This illustrates why more than half of the rural poor still have to go to the open fields around their tenements for defecation and why the most denigrated castes 'beyond the pale' are still involved in manual scavenging. Care for babies and infants, or for the aged and disabled, has never been considered for inclusion in the scheme of guaranteed employment.

Research conducted shows that the cost of health care is a major burden to the budget of the labouring poor; to the extent that seeking medical assistance to recover from illness or injuries is forfeited. The expenses which have to be incurred for recuperation of the labour power are often beyond consideration. The high morbidity in this milieu is caused not only by income deficiency—leading to under- and malnourishment and a recurrent lack of means required to gratify other basic needs—but also related to the abominable conditions of employment which have a debilitating effect on their well-being. An insurance scheme to attend to adversity arising out of low or failing health can therefore be an extremely important intervention to meet medical exigencies, which would otherwise remain unsolved. For the realization of this objective, a national social health insurance scheme called the Rashtriya Swasthaya Bima Yojana (RSBY) has been forefronted. Launched in late 2007, it has become the prime national insurance initiative for reducing vulnerability of the labouring poor who are in dire need of hospital care for serious health problems. In contrast to the Mahatma Gandhi National Rural Employment Guarantee Act (MGNREGA), which remained limited to the rural poor, the RSBY facility also covers the labouring poor in the urban slums. The support, only extended to those recognized as officially poor (called those Below Poverty Line or BPL), covers the cost of hospitalization for operation or in-door treatment up to a maximum of Rs 30,000 per annum for a household consisting of five members. The scheme includes maternity benefits and takes care of the cost of childbirth. Promoted as a public–private partnership, the premium of Rs 750 is paid to handpicked private- and some public-sector insurance companies, shared between central and state government in a 75 : 25 ratio.[2] A smart card carrying the name of the head of household and a maximum of four other family members has been issued to beneficiaries with which they can secure admission in an empanelled hospital of their choice. Largely located in urban areas, such empanelled medical institutions are heavily loaded in favour of private hospitals, which account for 70 per cent of the total number. The irony of such selection seems to be quite puzzling when we find that in West Bengal (ruled by a Left Front Government till mid-2011), only one public hospital was empanelled as against 483 private hospitals. On the other hand, the Government of Tripura (where a Left Front Government continues to rule) ensured that all empanelled hospitals were public institutions (see Chapter 2 by Kannan and Jain). Such a public–private partnership, even in a pro-poor social security scheme, would no doubt bring cheer to the private sector as a model to be emulated, given the fact that the real meaning of PPP turns out to be 'Private Profit at Public expense'. Another point of criticism concerns the supposed portability of the smart card. Although the card holders are entitled to avail of hospital services throughout the country, for themselves and the enlisted family members, their claim for treatment is not acknowledged when they are away from home. In general, a substantial part of the workforce which is at drift in the wider economy has no or marginal access to whatever social security arrangements have been introduced.

Helpful as it no doubt is, the RSBY card only gives access to health care when hospitalization is required, and even then, to a limited extent only. But most of the diseases and afflictions from which the labouring poor suffer temporarily or chronically are dealt with at home. It usually takes the form of self-care in the early phase. Not going for work is, in their experience, less costly than spending money to hasten recovery from failing health. If the problem persists, and in most cases it does, a lowly qualified medical practitioner is consulted who provides relief with an injection or a dose of medicine. The labouring poor, accustomed to live in a weak and deteriorating health condition from a young age, tend to consider the afflictions to which they are prone as beyond cure, and results in a debility which has to be endured, simply because they can not afford the cost of recovery. To raise their level of well-being would require a first-line approach rather than waiting until the ailment has progressed to a stage when hospitalization is resorted to as a last hope. But in the current regime of neo-liberalism, medicos and medicines have become private business, leaving whatever remains of the former system of public health care fighting a rearguard battle.

RSBY became one of the schemes included in the Unorganized Workers' Social Security Act (UWSSA) mandated by Parliament in late 2008. Although aimed at the workforce not covered by social security arrangements applicable to employees in the formal economy, the various schemes clubbed together in this bill remain restricted to segments acknowledged as belonging to the labouring poor. Informality and poverty are the dual principles for being eligible or not for access to state-provided social welfare allowances. The UWSSA basically seeks to bring a modicum of relief for people at the bottom of the economy, unable to take care of their own subsistence since they lack the means (property, assets) to do so and, in addition, have lost their labour power either temporarily or indefinitely. Thus, whatever support made available is targeted on the non-labouring poor who should actually be classified as destitute. The idea was to establish a National Social Security Authority, consisting of a Board, equipped with central funding, from which the benefits granted would be dispensed, to administrations and agencies, operating at state or sub-state level. A nation-wide organizational structure has not materialized due to sheer unwillingness in the policy and political circuit to do so. Early on, the aim to set up a national framework charged with the task to provide basic social security for the workforce in the informal economy was defeated by a strong coalition of forces, dead-against fixing a floor of labour rights and labour standards. Nor are the provisions stipulated in the 2008 Act mandatory to be granted at the state level. Consequently, the authorities have a lot of leverage in deciding what to do and how to go about it. The benefits scheduled are a mixture of already existing entitlements to which a few new ones were added, while others have been withdrawn. The result is a large variation in the nature, magnitude and spread of social security schemes. In its final report, the National Commission vented sharp criticism on the shortfall between what it recommended but was not conceded.

> The Act does not provide for a 'national minimum social security' for all unorganized (informal) workers. It also does not provide for an empowered body at the national and state levels nor a dedicated fund for financing the proposed national minimum social security. The economics of inclusion is yet to catch up with the politics of inclusion. The disconnect between the dominance of neoliberal orthodoxy in economic policy and the yearning of the vast majority for a life of work with dignity and security is getting increasingly glaring in a fast growing India. (NCEUS, 2009: 152)

The huge gap between the National Commission's proposal and the UWSSA has also been noted by scholars who scorned the final bill as an act of political expediency just before the 2009 Election (Dutta and Pal, 2012). Scaled down in the core objective to contribute to the welfare of the massive workforce at large in the informal economy, the UWSSA had to get its impetus from the schemes focusing on specific categories. The Act obligates the Central Government to introduce programmes on issues concerning health and maternity benefits, old age protection, life and disability cover, and other benefits reducing the vulnerability of the targeted beneficiaries. The progress made with the registration of informal workers at the state level, so as to facilitate implementation of schemes for particular occupations, has been very uneven; neither has a National Social Security Board been set up to streamline and coordinate the various interventions made. The *modus operandi* has been to fall back on an earlier initiative, the National Social Assistance Programme, dating back to 1995, launched with the intent to protect the poor and destitute in events of insecurities due to old age, death of the main breadwinner in the household, and maternity. While the last mentioned benefit on maternity was superseded when incorporated in other schemes later on (first as a safe motherhood intervention, then in the Janani Suraksha Yojana (JSY) under the National Rural Health Mission in 2005, and subsequently within the scope of the RSBY), the other two were given nation-wide coverage.

The first one, known today as the Indira Gandhi National Old Age Pension Scheme (IGNOAPS), stipulates that the beneficiaries should be 65 years old (reduced to 60 years in mid-2011) and living below the poverty line, without adequate means of their own, and not receiving family support. Earlier on, the monthly pension amounted to Rs 75 per person, but at the end of 2007 the allowance was increased to Rs 200, with equal contribution from the states. The benefit is disbursed through bank account or money order to be collected from the local post office. The state agencies in charge of the scheme are held responsible for the identification of eligible beneficiaries and have to open up their records to public scrutiny in doing so.

Much smaller in size and outlay—although for beneficiaries targeted naturally, of no lesser importance—is the National Family Benefit Scheme, providing financial support to households below the poverty line in case of death of the primary breadwinner. The age of the deceased should be between 18 to 64 years at the time of his/her demise and Rs 10,000 is paid in cash to the most senior surviving member of the household. This benefit is closely related to the Indira Gandhi National Widowhood Pension Scheme (IGNWPS), which since early 2009 grants a monthly allowance of Rs 200 to widows between 40–64 years and living below the poverty line.

Finally, and also introduced in 2009 under the National Social Assistance Programme, there is the Indira Gandhi National Disability Pension Scheme (IGNDPS), which aims to support persons below the poverty line and aged between 18–64 years who due to severe or multiple disabilities are prevented from providing for their own sustenance.

The schemes listed above have been amalgamated in the UWSSA, but eligibility is restricted to the most vulnerable contingent among them, the non-labouring poor. In addition, there is a mishmash of occupation-related benefits (for fishermen, handloom weavers, handicraft artisans) as well as a scheme for life insurance, and disability cover for a large number of rural and urban occupational groups. They are entitled to payment of a cash indemnity if in the age bracket of 18 to 60 years, and with the usual proviso of having incomes below the poverty line. Under the name of Jana Shri Bima Yojana (JSBY), it replaced an earlier initiative, the Social Security Group Insurance Scheme, which was of significance for agricultural labourers in particular. The handling of this scheme is in the form of a public-private partnership, in this instance entrusted to the Life Insurance Corporation of India. The state concerned contributes half of the premium of Rs 200 per member while the other half is collected from the beneficiaries or any nodal agency (such as Self Help Groups or SHGs). In the interest of construction workers, a sizable segment of the informal workforce throughout the country, an umbrella legislation has come into existence which provides a number of social benefits, including health care and life insurance, paid out of the Welfare Fund generated by charging employers a 1–2 per cent levy on construction works, while additional contributions for this purpose are made by state or central government agencies.

What has been the impact of the social security schemes on the targeted segments of the workforce in the informal economy at the national level? This is the question taken up in subsequent chapters of this volume. It will come as no surprise that the answers show a good deal of variability. This is largely due to interventions not having been uniform throughout the country. States were given a free hand to add or expand on the core welfare benefits prescribed by the central government. Further, provisions have not been implemented with the same commitment, rigour and zeal throughout the country. At the onset it has to be emphasized that the lack of standardization and how to deal with it from a common perspective already pre-empts any attempt to reach conclusions which can be generalized beyond the context of investigations. Rather than ending our overview in an overall verdict, we want to draw attention to the diversity in welfare, and the ill fare which exists and problematizes it. We have already clarified how policy makers and politicians colluded in watering down the core objectives of social benefits meant for the labouring poor in the preparatory phase. But did at least the implementation of whatever provisions became legally mandatory meet with less indifference, bordering on unwavering resistance? We shall deal with this question subsequently.

But before doing that, one major comment has to be put on record. So far the account has been on interventions to which the state has committed itself. What has not been discussed is the absence of capital as a stakeholder in the informal economy. Apart from the Welfare Funds constituted by a few states—prominently Kerala and Tamil Nadu—covering a large segment of informal workers and a few others covering specific segments, capital in the informal economy is not taxed for the reproduction cost of labour fairly and proportionally. Moreover, capital should be held responsible for refusing to abide by an employment regime that acknowledges the human dignity of the workforce. Our contention is that as long as this crucial omission is not repaired in legal, financial and administrative terms, the quest for a resolution of the 'social question' will, in all probability, be met with setbacks of one kind or another. Such a pessimistic conclusion is inescapable given the fact that the neoliberal policy regime, promoted by the executive arm of the Indian government, has been systematically shedding even the 'intermediate regime' (Kalecki, 1964) character of the state by blatantly positioning itself on the side of corporate capital. Neither the legislative nor the judicial arm of the state has been able to provide any effective course correction except to moderate the sharp edges of such a policy regime in bringing out some of the massive corruption cases involving government functionaries and corporate capital, or say, in questioning the abysmally low poverty line that are ultimately intended to limit public provisioning for the labouring poor. Repairing the moral hiatus, so strongly articulated by the Father of the Nation, is required with greater urgency than ever before.

THE RECORD OF INDIAN STATES INPRACTICING SOCIAL WELFARE

How to monitor the implementation of the various social security schemes? From the very onset of our project, which lasted from the middle of 2010 until the first quarter of 2012, our aim has not been to focus on topics and sites of research which somehow would lead us to findings which can be generalized across the board. Rather than making a spurious attempt in our enquiries to represent the total setting, we wanted to highlight the wide diversity that exists. With that point of departure in mind, the first priority was to decide on which states to select for our research. The funding received allowed us to focus on five states, sufficiently distinct from each other in their political, economic and social configurations, and situated in different parts of the country. The shortlist on which we agreed included Punjab, Gujarat, Odisha, Andhra Pradesh and Kerala. A major consideration in this selection was that the participating members of our research team belonged to the state on which their contributions would elaborate. They brought to the table their multi-disciplinary based research expertise, highly relevant to the *problematique* under study, and a keen interest in the theme of our project. We did not insist on a uniform research design and encouraged latitude in order to avoid becoming entrapped in a standard operational frame which would hide—instead of expose—contrasting methods of intervention and their outcome. At the same time, however, the favoured approach had been a combination of macro- and micro-level queries, arising from the need to confront secondary data as reported in official statistics, with quantitative and qualitative data sets collected by either conducting surveys or in the format of more localized case studies. We have not differentiated our investigations along the rural-urban divide. Most local-level reports included in this volume relate to rural settings. While one could argue that the thrust of deprivation is within the countryside, this should never be an excuse to ignore the deprived residing in and around towns and cities. Finally, and in addition to the state specific contributions, three participants were commissioned to write analytical papers appraising the legal status of labour rights, the social fabric of the labouring poor and the regime of informality in the political economy. Much to our regret, their essays could not be included in this volume, due to lack of space.

Our first round of comments specify a number of shortcomings reported for each of the three clusters, which jointly aim at increasing social welfare for the workforce in the informal economy: employment on public works, health insurance, and disability to gain income. Following up on these deficiencies as they have become apparent in the separate schemes, we shall draw out, from the findings presented in the subsequent chapters, some imposing features which are, in our opinion, characteristic of the way in which the state machinery operates in the realization of its proclaimed objective: social protection and security for the masses of underprivileged. Ending our synthesizing chapter, we shall reflect on the preconditions that should be in place to accomplish more than paying mere lip service to the politics of inclusion.

The NREGA, as it is known in popular parlance, is the only welfare scheme which is based on self-selection. It does not exclude participation in public works of people not officially identified and registered as having a BPL status. This intervention seems to have been implemented with a higher degree of success in the two southern states of India, studied as part of this research project. While the impact in Odisha and Gujarat leaves much to be desired, our reports show that performance in Andhra Pradesh and Kerala has been much more positive, particularly in creating greater space and agency for women as stakeholders, as well as a stimulus for collective action (Reddy, Chapter 3, and Kannan and Jagajeevan, Chapter 6 in this volume). Such best practices should certainly be put on record. In Punjab, a relatively prosperous state, the need for an employment guarantee is no less than elsewhere, as has been observed by Gill *et al.* (Chapters 12–13) in this volume. While the overall performance of the state is quite unimpressive, the field based study of villages show that there indeed exists demand for more work especially in agricultural labour households of SCs. With an incidence of poverty largely concentrated in the bottom segment of the population, it is hardly surprising that their participation rate in the employment scheme is more than 74 per cent. While women's share in employment has been low, ranging from 23–33 per cent, the field report suggests that young women are eager to participate in this public employment scheme since their parents are reluctant to send them for work in privately owned lands of the farmers. Workers also report some decrease in the arrival of migrant labourers from Eastern Uttar Pradesh, leading to a raise in the local wage rate, especially for women. It is also heartening to find that the Punjab study reports attempt at mobilizing workers into trade unions and articulation of demands such as increase in wages, work, crèche facility for children and so on.

Based on an analysis of the secondary data, the scheme has been able to provide, on average, only around 48 days of employment per participating household during the first five years with only 8 states achieving between 50–70 days. The average days of employment created works out to only half the ceiling of 100 days a year. A recurrent complaint concerns payment for the work done lower than the statutory minimum wage and, moreover, settlement of these urgently required earnings much later than the regulations stipulate. While the issue of job cards seems to have covered all those demanding it, wherever the news on the implementation of this scheme was adequately spread, there were instances where it has not been adhered to when the applicants were from the socially weaker sections such as the SCs, as has been noted by Kumbhar in Chapter 10 of this volume, in the Odisha Panchayat. There have also been instances of muster rolls kept that fail to provide reliable testimony in calculating the number of man-days worked; in not a single instance ever reported has an unemployment indemnity been shelled out, as per the regulations, to job seekers because of lack of public works.

In his commendation of the employment guarantee scheme, Jean Dreze has described how the redundant workforce in the countryside is driven out in the slack season. Looking back on his journey for the right to work (Rozgar Adhikar Yatra), he wrote as follows:

Everywhere we went, the rural economy looked like a graveyard and unemployment was the people's main concern. Seasonal migration (to distant brick kilns, tea gardens or urban sweatshops) was their lifeline at that time of the year. At times, the local railway stations looked like a flashback to the days of partition—crammed as they were with desperate people on the move, with haggard looks, heavy loads on their heads, and scruffy children in tow. The predicament of casual labourers did not seem fundamentally different from slaves, except that they were driven by economic necessity instead of physical coercion. (Khera, 2011: 3)

Is this acute observation on the precariousness which prevailed a recall from the recent past, a state of affairs which belongs to yesteryear? The suggestion that rural labour has become less footloose because of NREGA would, in our view, overstate whatever the scheme has managed to accomplish. There may of course be some local level reduction in distress migration, as reported by Reddy (Chapter 3) and Gill *et al.* (Chapters 12–13) in this volume, but to generalize the case, especially in light of the meagre average days of employment created, may be stretching the story too far. Migration, or ongoing circulation, to reduce lack of work and income in the lean months is still increasing, rather than decreasing, throughout the subcontinent. Most studies on mobility tend to focus only on the economic dimension—income generated, savings made, remittances to the people left behind—while neglecting the political and social cost of trying to find a niche of sorts, away from home. The idea that labour migration is a win-win for all stakeholders, as the World Bank would have it (2009), overlooks the losses incurred with the household breaking up and able-bodied adults and minors going off, sometimes in different directions, while members without labour power stay put and cope as best as they can. Is this a temporary setback, an option only resorted to for the duration of a season? In her essay, Sujata Patel (2012) has pointed out how the informal work regime has torn apart the social fabric by compelling wives to live separately from their husbands and parents away from their children. To the extent that social security benefits have become statutory—for example food rationing for BPL card holders—the assumption implied in the rules is that of a nuclear family which is and remains sedentary. Clearly, this is not how work and livelihood is structured in the lower circuits of the economy. Commoditization does not acknowledge the cementing of social ties and is blind to bonds along lines of gender, age and conjugality, let alone pay respect to multi-generational cohabitation.

The introduction of the main health insurance scheme has been very uneven and eclectic. While some states leapt ahead, others were rather slow in deciding how to proceed. It took time to draw up a list of empanelled hospitals, agree on the cost of treatment for a variety of ailments, demarcate zones for dividing the insurance contract between private companies selected as stakeholders and finally, identify beneficiaries and equip them with proof of their eligibility. For that purpose, the insurance company in charge issued a smart card with name and photo of the head of household. The implementation of the RSBY operation already derailed badly at this preparatory stage. The studies included in this volume reveal that the consultancy firms that were entrusted with the job of registration sent out teams to collect the information required. These investigators hired for the task failed to instruct beneficiaries to turn up on a particular day for the photo session, and were unable to contact many of them due to lack of familiarity with the locale. On the other hand, they accepted in the course of their visitation, carried out in a hit-and-run manner, details of households that did not meet with the criteria set for inclusion, because they had to complete the quota given to them. The distribution of the smart card became a messy affair; more so because the eventual recipients were often not informed how to utilize this facility. Finally, in case of hospitalization, the holders have no control over what is being done to their card and have to accept, in good faith, what transpires between the hospital and the insurance company. It is a joint venture that can easily lead to fake transactions and complicity, on one or both sides, which, with the connivance of state officials, is not difficult to cover up. The Kerala study in this volume, by Kunhikannan and Aravindan (Chapter 5) stands apart from other studies for its relatively higher level of political commitment and more inclusion through additional contribution by the state government. In addition, the relative success here can be attributed to the higher level of education, even among poorer sections of the population, an active panchayat, as well as the organization of rural women known as *Kudumbasree*. Yet, even in this best practice case, there are some notable drawbacks, especially in the under coverage of people belonging to the minority community in the field area.

Given the RSBY's rather poor record, we have included a study by G. Vijay on the functioning of another health insurance scheme called *Rajiv Aarogyasri* in Andhra Pradesh (Chapter 4). Initiated in

2007 by the Government of Andhra Pradesh, it covers 85 per cent of the population who hold a White Ration Card (BPL households as per the state list) or 70 million people, which is only marginally lower than the coverage under the RSBY spanning the entire country. It provides an insurance coverage of Rs 2 lakh, which is nearly seven times the coverage under the RSBY. However, the insurance is only for specified health problems requiring surgical interventions associated with tertiary level health care. As in the RSBY, this scheme is also heavily loaded in favour of private insurance companies and private hospitals. A major drawback is the non-coverage of out-patient care as well common diseases that often compel poorer families to spend on health care that are beyond their capacity. The scheme is quite popular and it also points, in our opinion, to the importance of ownership by a state government with consequent flexibility in implementation.

Finally, there are state benefits doled out to overcome the improvidence to which the disabled are prone. As it happens, many of them do not find ready access to such entitlements. An aged woman or man with an adult son is automatically disqualified from these benefits, as is a widow who is similarly blessed. They also would have to provide written evidence that their annual income is below a certain level, depending on the state in which they is located. Physically or mentally disabled persons older or younger than the age limit set (18–60 or 64 years), and still 'able' in body and mind for more than 20 per cent, are also exempted from receiving any cash allowance. These criteria indicate that the onus for support befalls on the immediate family as the first source of reprieve. Only if that safety net happens not to be in place does the state step in to provide to a modicum of care, and even then not enough for the individual(s) to be redeemed from destitution. It is the kind of logic which completely disregards that non-labouring poor are, by and large, related to households belonging to the labouring poor, who may not even have enough to satisfy their own basic needs. Of course, the parsimoniousness practiced is meant to scale down the packet of state provided social benefits to the lowest possible level.

The same purpose is served by forsaking the instruction which says that that the responsibility belongs to the agency of the state to identify and register the labouring poor in need of support. The potential beneficiaries are obliged to find out for themselves what is due to them, and when, where or how to try and get it. In their effort to do so they are handicapped in many ways. Firstly because of their illiteracy and lack of other social capital with which to seek access to these entitlements. Interaction with the state is not coveted at the margins of mainstream society, and if it occurs at all, chances are that the gist of the encounter has more to do with attempts to escape from punishment for breaches of the law than in laying claims to benefits reluctantly granted. Forms have to be filled up but where are these available and at what price? Papers have to be gathered as proof of identity, such as certificate of birth or death, BPL card, photo, residential permit, composition of household, status of indigence, etc. and all that in more than one copy. Submission of these documents is tedious and risky business. Whom to confide in and how to make sure that the file reaches the eyes of the official in charge? And, of course, money has to be spent and greasing the palms of the 'higher-ups' is costly business. It explains why applicants drop out or even don't bother to register their case.

No doubt, the state has to be held responsible first and foremost for throwing up a major threshold by scaling down the provision of social care benefits (RSBY) to the labouring poor fortunate enough to be registered with a BPL status. As has been widely reported, that exercise is fraught with errors of wrong inclusion and exclusion (discussed by Breman and Joshi in Chapters 7 and 9 respectively in this volume). Having critiqued before the way policy makers have construed this divide—the fixation of a standard which is close to destitution—the allowances paid out are far below the minimum required for bare survival. Investigations carried out in the vast landscape inhabited by the labouring poor testify to the arbitrariness with which households have been classified as living above or below the poverty line. Discretionary in design and execution, the handling of the schemes is further flawed by the highhanded, non-responsive and indifferent style with which officials tend to treat their clientele. That sullied performance is compounded by downright malfeasance in both the higher and lower echelons of the state agencies involved. Once again, the rich diversity that exists has to be emphasized. Best and worst cases can be found at a short distance from each other. Having said that, the last ones seem to outclass in some states the first ones by far. In the villages located in the central plain of south Gujarat, Breman found that NREGA is either not in operation, because the powers that be won't have it, or has become a total scam—a division of the spoils between village leaders, officials and district-level politicians. In contrast to these findings, Joshi is more positive on the generation of employment and income for the labouring households in the tribal belt. But at his research sites, public works have been converted into private contracts and officials take their cut from the budget. They pocket money from the budget as if it were their birth right. Where countervailing power exists, as in Andhra Pradesh and Kerala, such malpractices happen to be less prevalent.[3] The problems beneficiaries have with RSBY and UWSSA benefits are similar in nature. Apart from being doled out in scant quantity and rather haphazardly, the illegal procurement of speed money, bribes and fraud are part of the repertoire of deductions that recipients of care benefits have to face if they manage to become endowed at all. Mahadevia has signalled in her contribution, the sustained unwillingness of the municipal authorities to distribute the Welfare Fund accumulated for construction workers in Ahmedabad. The story is no different in cities situated in other parts of the country. Although the large-scale corruption exposed at the commanding heights of the economy seem to attract more public scorn and convulsion, the magnitude of malfeasance at the administrative bottom creates equal distrust in the business of state and politics at the grassroots. It is common practice to have a bounty being deducted from the total budget set aside for social protection and security—not by any means a huge fund—which is charged to the poor as gratuity by their benefactors.

SOCIAL SECURITY AS POOR RELIEF

With the state failing to reach out to its target in need of social care, and the people not knowing where and how to access their entitlements, mediation is of the essence to break through the impasse. In bridging this gap, civil society could be of crucial importance. Indeed, in many regions of the country a wide range of Non-governmental Organizations (NGOs) are active in providing assistance for the needy. Advocating in favour of social protection and security for the workforce in the informal economy, the NCEUS has taken stock in one of its reports of the role played by the voluntary sector in the business of care. Some best practices are discussed, such as the initiatives taken by Self Employed Women's Association (SEWA) to cover female workers against a variety of adversities—a pension scheme, maternity benefit, health insurance—and to enable them to get a fair return on their savings made in order to cope with future related expenditure.[4]

The Gujarat-based Self Employed Women's Association (SEWA) plan for social security is widely regarded as one of the more successful ones in this field. SEWA has established a bank daily collection initiative that brings a collection post to women on a daily basis. These are women who work between 14 and 16 hours a day, and cannot therefore find time to travel to the local bank and make deposits. Most members of the social security scheme earn less than Rs. 100 per day and do not have any formal education. SEWA Bank initially guaranteed a nominal return of 12 per cent and upon maturity, the money was returned as either a lump sum or in an annuity format to the beneficiary. As of 2002, SEWA initiated a new plan offering only 7 per cent return with lower minimum contributions and the removal of early withdrawal options. Already SEWA Bank has over 5,000 accounts managing almost Rs. 7.5 million. The SEWA Bank serves as an example worth emulation for many Self Help Groups (SHGs) across India. (NCEUS, 2006: 46)

The same report also pointed out that social security schemes undertaken by NGOs account for only a tiny fraction—about 1.5 per cent in 2005—of initiatives for the workforce in the informal economy. In other words, their reach, spread, and impact among the labouring poor should not be exaggerated. One of the explanations for their modest contribution is the unwillingness of the bureaucratic and political apparatus in many states to allow what is called the 'voluntary sector' to operate independent from official surveillance. SEWA finds itself sanctioned and curtailed by a state government anxious to exercise close control over civil society. While states do not provide what they should, they also do not tolerate intrusion of other stakeholders into the terrain which they consider their own prerogative.

Non-institutionalized mediation is much more common. It comes in two varieties, of which the first consists of voluntary support provided by facilitators close to the milieu of claimants. These comprise teachers, social workers, and members of the local panchayat, petty officials, and also earlier recipients of benefits, who have learnt which forms are required, where to get them, how to fill them up, and ensure that they reach the proper department of the sub-district or district administration. They are able to find their way in the administrative corridors and know how much to pay to whom. Their services are rendered either free of cost or paid for with a small commission. The second form of non-institutionalized mediation is structured along lines of verticality. It is interlocution which rests on the willingness of bosses and, more generally, persons of higher rank in the caste and class hierarchy, to use the social capital and political clout they have for the benefit of the labouring poor, who lack voice and agency to qualify for their entitlement. The price paid for that intercession is allegiance to the code of subalternity.

Having come to the end of our introductory essay to the volume, we want to reiterate what our objective has been to highlight the variance in state-initiated efforts to provide better protection and security for the labouring poor. This diversity does not remain limited to regional variation, but is also structured in terms of social identity. It basically boils down to the conclusion that the most vulnerable segments among the labouring poor—those without assets, skills, and social capital within the ranks of the SCs, STs, and the main religious minority—lag behind in accessing the social security arrangements that have been introduced. The recommendations made by the National Commission have been our point of departure. The strategy outlined in their reports stipulated the creation of a social floor guaranteeing, for all citizens handicapped by various degrees of vulnerability, access to adequate food (to end malnutrition), sufficient employment (to cope with lack of work), fair wage and steady income (to be reprieved from a life of poverty), social security (to be protected against adversity), housing, healthcare and education.Initially it suggested a return to the basic needs approach promoted by the International Labour Organization during the 1970s, but then gave up under strong pressure by powerful donor-members of this agency. Has the political climate in India become more conducive of late? No doubt, there are definite signs of hope. As far as access to food is concerned, there has been steady pressure emanating from various civil society organizations because of which the government is currently considering a Food Security Bill. However it must be pointed out that this electoral promise of 2004 has taken almost eight years, and continues to elude a consensus among policy makers as far as its coverage is concerned. But a stage has now come that the government can no longer delay the introduction of this crucial bill. The provision of public housing is rather understated, but our impression is that the national housing scheme for the poor, named the Indira Awas Yojana, has been making steady, even if slow, progress in a number of states. Its counterpart for the urban areas has come in only recently in the form of new scheme called the Rajiv Awas

Yojana. Here again we have to single out the performance of Kerala, where the agenda had been taken up much before the national government thought of it as a priority policy issue. With regard to access to education, a national legislation was passed in 2011 called the Right to Education Act, guaranteeing access to free education to all children between the age group of 6 to 14. A number of states had endeavoured to enhance enrolment of children, especially from the labouring poor, for quite some time. The recent national legislation is perhaps an extension of this effort for those states which are still lagging. But the emerging challenge in school education is not merely the access, but the ability of children from poorer households to complete at least ten years of school education, and this is predicated on their ability to come out of the situation of poverty.

In all these areas, we have to take into account a wide variety of conditions prevailing in different parts of the country. Three factors in particular are of vital significance in determining the nature of achievement: the presence of social activism propelled by civic society; commitment of government machinery to implementation of pro-poor policies; and due representation, along with effective participation, of the targeted beneficiaries in the welfare schemes. The assertion for inclusion into mainstream society of the labouring poor will depend on a further strengthening of the democratic policies at the grassroot level. Jointly, these preconditions seem to be operative in the best cases, which happen to be mainly located in the three southern Indian states taken up, namely, Andhra Pradesh, Tamil Nadu, and Kerala, with the last one showing a marked improvement by far. Already two decades ago, Guhan (1992: 211) pointed out that Tamil Nadu, along with Kerala, have pioneered in welfare programmes with a high social security content. Also, Drèze and Sen (1995: 51–6), commented on the stark contrast between Uttar Pradesh in North India, where social security arrangements were absent and the presence of such provisions in Kerala in South India. We should be aware that this divide did not materialize overnight but was the outcome of struggles and movements in the past or the absence of such concerted action along horizontal lines. While in some regions there was a groundswell of assertion, in other parts of the country the subaltern classes remained captivated in dependency.

In contrast to the progress made in South India, there is a continuation of stark poverty and destitution on the other side of the spectrum. The high growth rate in recent years has not resulted in any wealth redistribution. The gap between the haves and the haves-not has further widened. Rather than being able to detect a trend towards progressive inclusion, the economic and social policies practiced reflect sustained exclusion. More is amiss than just a slow, piecemeal, and reluctant expansion of attempts made by the government, to alleviate the precariousness so strikingly visible in the habitat of the labouring poor. What boils down to informalization of governance is a prominent feature of the administrative machinery, leading to widespread leakage of funds, lack of coordination, accountability and transparency between the various echelons in the bureaucratic hierarchy, and denial of legal entitlements. Rather than facilitating the requests made for benefits, the applications are examined in a spirit which comes close to distrust and suspicion of the claimants' good faith. The various schemes have a highly populist flavour and are subjected to bureaucratic or political manipulation. Whatever the government does to improve the plight of the underprivileged classes is frustrated by the indifference of the local authorities and overt or covert sabotage from more well-to-do quarters. The eligibility of the poor for state-provided benefits is compromised by the absence of horizontalized representation and forms of collective action. Their concerns and complaints are not made manifest in their ability to establish a platform and close ranks. Instead of standing united, their strategy is to rely on help from higher ups, to plead their case. Unaware of, or even misguided about the mismatch of social welfare schemes that have been enacted, the targeted categories often fall back on vertical relationships of dependency to qualify for what otherwise would remain beyond their reach.

The huge masses, with little or no resources of their own, constitute a fragmented workforce without the collective bargaining power required to redeem themselves from deprivation and insecurity. Following this line of thought could come dangerously close to suggest that to lag behind in welfare is a consequence of one's own failings. It basically means that inequality and inequity are justified on the notion that the classes held in exclusion get what they deserve. They do not possess enough resources or means to live with decency and dignity, but that degradation is of no concern to those who consider them to be an irritant to the public weal, a stigma on society. Rife in privileged quarters, such condemnation will not change until the written-off labour power, upgraded or as it is, gains in marketable value. Without that, the masses at the bottom of economy and society, which so far constitute a reserve army, will retrograde into permanent surplus to demand. It is at this juncture that we want to reiterate our opinion earlier stated that, with all due criticism on the doings and misdoings of the state, it is of utmost significance to keep in mind that capital cannot be exonerated from paying a proportionate share of the price which guarantees decency as well as dignity to the labouring poor. This exoneration is characteristic of the neoliberal orthodoxy that continues to reign, despite the recent and severe setbacks in the citadels of capitalism. But India does not enjoy the privilege of indulging in such exoneration when it has one of the worst records in tackling even the basic deprivations of its largely poor and vulnerable population despite its claim to be an emerging economy with unprecedented rates of economic growth during the past three decades. It is heartening to note that the pressure for entitlements to the labouring is building up in civil society and large numbers of informal workers have been demonstrating and waging democratic struggles. On the day we handed in our manuscript to the publisher of this book in early May 2012, a Pension Parishad was going on in Delhi, demanding for universal old age benefits.[5] In his seminal essay earlier referred to, Guhan demonstrated that it is feasible to implement a basic, affordable, and sustainable social security programme for the labouring and non-labouring poor in India's informal economy. He backed his well-argued case with a quotation from the 1991 UN *Human Development Report*, 'The lack of political commitment, not financial resources, is the real cause of human neglect' (quoted in Guhan, 1992: 227–8).

Given the urgency of ensuring livelihood security to the vast mass of labouring poor in India, which will empower them to acquire a measure of human dignity, we would like to highlight the following points, that should culminate in the setting of a national agenda for social security.

First, overt—and not covert—cognisance of the fact that the official poverty line, which has been subjected to public interrogation in recent times, is an abysmally low threshold and leaves out a larger segment that should be classified as vulnerable. Moreover, the official poverty line is not a sufficient indicator of deprivation since many other forms of deprivation—the outcome of an ingrained ideology of inequality—are alarmingly high, even compared to the record of other developing economies in Asia.

Second, social security provisions that have recently come into existence do not cover a majority of the poor and vulnerable. Moreover, provisions prior to the introduction of the rural employment guarantee and social health insurance schemes, as well as benefits covering the disabled, largely came about at the initiative of a few state governments over a long period of time.

Third, recognize the need for a macro-social policy, just as there is a macro-economic policy. The latter cannot be judged independent of the other or vice versa. Employment and its quality is a crucial and key link.

Fourth, recognize that there is a sense of urgency. The social security provisions now under consideration are meant to alleviate the intense misery that exists. To make work and life more decent and dignified, much more is required. We need to make a start with the formulation and enforcement of a national social floor encompassing, among other things, (i) fixing a level below which no minimum wage should be paid, (ii) minimum conditions of work, (iii) a national minimum social security to meet contingencies and eventualities for workers in the informal sector of the economy, and (iv) social security for the non-labouring poor, mainly consisting of destitute and the differently abled.

Fifth, recognize that restricting social security provisions only to the ultra-poor could end up in perpetuation of rent-seeking at lower levels of bureaucracy apart from its inherent inequity in dividing the poor. Universalization of social security provisions (obviously with the exclusion of the better off segment of the population) to the informal workers has been widely expressed and championed, which can avoid the problem of rent-seeking to a large extent, as well as the costs of enforcement.

Sixth, it is important to pay special attention to those informal workers who are on the move in search of work, especially the vast and growing army of seasonal migrants. Their numbers are rapidly increasing, but they largely remain outside the net of whatever meagre social security provisioning that exists today.

Seventh, there is an urgent need to reform and restructure the labour administration system, charged with the responsibility to implement the various labour legislations. The handling and processing of what are labour rights by state agencies shows appalling sloppiness, highhandedness and indifference wherever pressure from the targeted beneficiaries is lacking.

Eighth, social policy towards labour in general—and the informal labour in particular—cannot be the business of the state only. It also requires the active involvement of capital and cost sharing in the first place. At present, capital is exonerated in cost sharing, but enjoys the benefits in the form of casualization and contractualization of workers in the formal sector, and various forms of outsourcing and sub-contracting in the informal sector.

Ninth, there is a crying need for public agency, public space, and public institutions, especially in a democratic polity like India. It means engagement with the larger civil society in ways which does not make it a handmaiden of state or capital interests. The state, that is public governance, should distance itself from acting primarily in tandem with capital. In other words, the formula of public-private partnership that is currently loaded in favour of corporate capital should be critically addressed.

Tenth, there should be recognition of the significance of collective action for, and by, the labouring poor in a democratic polity like India. Giving shape to social policy cannot but imply creating space for social mobilization of the labouring poor. In such rare instances, where mobilization has indeed taken place, there has been a greater degree of access to basic entitlements as well as participation in the way that entitlements are delivered.

Finally, without in any way denying the salient features of state specific differences, we feel that a corporate authority at the central level needs to be set up for the implementation of a truly National Social Security Scheme. Only an overarching agency with a federated organizational structure will be able to do the job—that is, deliver security to people who are vulnerable because they are excluded from mainstream society. A National Board is required in order to keep the variation in state-level approaches under control, monitor experiences gained with best and worst practices, lobby for an agenda of social security in the corridors of political power and, last but not least, bargain with the owners of capital on their substantial contribution to the welfare of labour in the informal economy.

Notes

[1] On 29 March 2011, *The Statesman* newspaper reported: 'Seeking the government's rationale to cap the number of BPL card holders in the states,

a Bench of Mr Justice Dalveer Bhandari and Mr Justice Deepak Verma said: "We fail to understand the rationale and justification for the cap fixed by the Planning Commission." It asked Additional Solicitor General (ASG) Mr Mohan Parasaran, who appeared for the Centre, to "respond to the court on the rationality and justification of putting a cap"'.

[2]Out of 21 states for which data were available as on April 2012, the four public sector insurance companies were the sole insurer in the five states of Assam, Himachal Pradesh, Kerala, Manipur, Mizoram, and Tripura. In the remaining 16 states, except Meghalaya, public sector insurance companies were one of the insurers responsible for a limited region in the respective states. Eight private insurance companies, some of whom with very little previous experience, secured a lion's share of this public health insurance in 17 states.

[3] The widely diverse practices are documented in an anthology bringing together reports of investigations carried on the public works scheme operational between 2006 and 2012 in different parts of the country. This fact-finding collection has been compiled by N. Mann and V. Pande, edited by M. Shah and published under the auspices of the Ministry of Rural Development, Government of India.

[4] SEWA is currently engaged in the promotion of unconditional cash transfers as a means of social protection in rural Madhya Pradesh (communication provided by R. Jhabvala, 22 July 2012).

[5] See *The Hindu*, 12 May 2012.

References

Drèze, J. and A. Sen. 1995. *India, Economic Development and Social Opportunity*. New Delhi: Oxford University Press.

Dutta, T. and P. Pal. 2012. 'Politics Overpowering Welfare: Unorganized Workers' Social Security Act 2008', *Economic and Political Weekly*, 47(7), 18 February: 26–30.

Guhan, S. 1992. 'Social Security for the Poor in the Unorganised Sector: A Feasible Blueprint for India', in K.S. Parikh and R. Sudarshan (eds), *Human Development and Structural Adjustment*, pp. 203–31. Madras: Macmillan.

Kalecki, M. 1964. 'Observations on Social and Economic Aspects of "Intermediate Regimes"'. Reprinted in Selected Essays on the Economic Growth of the Socialist and Mixed Economy, 1972. Cambridge: Cambridge University Press.

Kannan, K.P. 2012. 'How Inclusive is Inclusive Growth in India?' *The Indian Journal of Labour Economics*, 55(1), January–March: 31–5.

Khera, R. (ed.). 2011. *The Battle for Employment Guarantee*. New Delhi: Oxford University Press.

National Commission for Enterprises in the Unorganized Sector (NCEUS). 2006. 'Report on Social Security for Unorganized Workers'. New Delhi: Government of India.

———. 2009. 'The Challenge of Employment in India: An Informal Economy Perspective'. New Delhi: Academic Foundation.

Planning Commission. March 2012. *Press Note on Poverty Estimates, 2009–10*. New Delhi: Government of India.

Srivastava, R. 2011. 'Labour Migration in India: Recent Trends, Patterns and Policy Issues', *The Indian Journal of Labour Economics*, 54(3), July–September: 411–40.

I

OVERVIEW PAPERS

1 HISTORIC INITIATIVE, LIMITED BY DESIGN AND IMPLEMENTATION

A NATIONAL OVERVIEW OF THE IMPLEMENTATION OF NREGA

K.P. Kannan and *Varinder Jain*

The one obvious uniqueness of the National Rural Employment Guarantee Scheme (NREGS) launched by the Congress-led United Progressive Alliance (UPA) that came to power in mid-2004 was that it was the first ever attempt to help the rural poor access public employment through legislation. There was a political backdrop to it as well, as the alliance's poll victory itself was hugely due to its electoral promise of taking the benefits of a fast-growing economy to rural India, where a little over two-thirds of the people lived in grinding poverty. The NREGA, enacted in 2005,[1] and subsequently named after the Father of the Nation, Mahatma Gandhi, and known as the Mahatma Gandhi National Rural Employment Guarantee Scheme (MGNREGS), was thus the fulfilment of this promise.

The implementation of the NREGA was sequenced in three phases; starting with the 200 most backward districts in 2006, another set of 130 districts was covered during 2007–8, and the whole nation was covered in the third phase beginning on 1 April 2008.[2]

Rooted in the 'rights-based framework', the basic objective of this Act has been to enhance the livelihood security of the rural poor through the provision of a legal guarantee for at least 100 days of employment in asset-creating public works programmes every year, at a stipulated minimum wage of agricultural workers to each rural household, provided its adult members volunteer, by application,[3] to undertake unskilled manual work.[4]

The implementation of this Act laid adequate emphasis on the Panchayati Raj Institutions (PRIs). It followed a three-tier structure of governance and involved planning at the village, block, and district levels. Another major objective of this Act has been to promote sustainable development of the rural economy through the generation of productive assets. The panchayats were authorized to plan, design and execute the projects. However, they needed to apportion their expenditure on materials and labour in a 40 : 60 ratio. The state governments were required to meet payments for one-fourth of the material cost, including the wages of skilled and semi-skilled workers, whereas the remaining expenditure on materials etc. and the whole expenditure on wage payments to unskilled workers were met by the Union Government. It also required the state governments to pay unemployment allowance in case it failed to fulfil the legal guarantee within 15 days of application. In order to encourage greater female participation, the Act gave priority to women by ensuring their share to be at least one-third among those who have registered and sought work. Accordingly, it made the provision of crèche for children[5] along with other facilities of shade, water, first-aid, etc. The Act also restricted the use of machines and contractors, along with providing the medical and accidental benefits to the NREGS workers.

The Act devised certain built-in mechanism to ensure transparency and accountability. It authorized Gram Sabhas within Gram Panchayats to conduct regular social audits of the projects undertaken. In order to ensure transparency in wage payments, this Act has actively engaged banks/post offices. Moreover, it also provided for grievance redressal through the institution of Ombudsman at the district level, although this is yet to be implemented. In the backdrop of the double burden experienced by the working poor in the form of employment irregularity and low wage payments, the enactment of this Act with such detailed features could be visualized as a major intervention for ameliorating the economic plight of the working poor in rural India.

By March 2011, this Act completed five years during which it covered the rural segment of all the districts (N = 614). As many as 73 per cent of the rural households were issued job cards, and of the total card holders, about 47 per cent were provided employment under the NREGA (Table 1.1). On the whole, the scheme had generated a cumulative total of 9,903.24 million man-days of employment, but the average annual days of employment generated per participating household remained around 48 as against the 100 days laid down in the Act. Many micro-level studies point out a contrasting picture

TABLE 1.1 NREG Performance in Rural India: An Overview of Initial Five Years

S. No.	*Indicator*		*Average for Period 2006–7 to 2010–11*
1.	Share of households with job cards in total rural households (%)		73.22
2.	Share of households given employment in total households having job cards (%)		47.48
3.	Average annual days of employment provided per participating household (Rs)		47.70
4.	Average daily wage received by a participating household (Rs)	Money	86.80
		Real	68.61
5.	Average annual money earnings of the participating household		751.44
6.	Average NREG earnings as % of rural poverty line		10.15
7.	Average share in total man-days (%)	Women	46.38
		SC	29.38
		ST	24.47
8.	NREGA participation vis-à-vis their population share	SC	1.18
		ST	2.04
9.	NREGA participation vis-à-vis their share in rural poor	SC	0.80
		ST	0.52

Source: Based on NREGA's official website: www.nrega.nic.in; Census of India (2001, 2011); Labour Bureau (2006–11); and GoI (2008).

of its relatively better implementation in a few states as compared to the poor performance in most others. It was important to note that most of the research effort on the assessment of the NREGA implementation remained micro in its scope. Despite the availability of district-wise disaggregated data in the official website of the Ministry of Rural Development, Government of India, there has not been a serious effort to build a national profile of the NREGS' performance through a comparative inter-state analysis.

Amid such a research gap, we provide a comprehensive performance analysis of its implementation over the past five years.[6]

First, we briefly discuss the key literature on implementation before presenting our own analysis in the discussion follows. Thereafter, the instrumental role of the NREGA in various spheres is highlighted. We then contrast macro-level performance with micro-level experiences through insights derived from state-level studies. Lastly, with issues related with the effective delivery of benefits under the NREGA and the final section provides our concluding remarks.

KEY LITERATURE ON IMPLEMENTATION OF NREGA

Given the historic nature of this national legislation to guarantee employment, albeit limited, to the rural working poor, social science researchers have shown a keen interest in examining its various facets so as to assess its impact, as well as to make other policy suggestions to strengthen the reach of this important Act. As a result, there have appeared numerous studies which could be classified into three broad categories: (i) those reflecting on the design and implementation related issues, (ii) those examining the outreach and impact of NREGA, and (iii) those attempting to build a national-level comprehensive profile of NREGA implementation.

Among the studies related to the first category, one of the initial attempts was made by Mehrotra (2008). Apart from highlighting lack of awareness, and lapses in monitoring and implementation, he also pointed out the missing distinctions among labour surplus and labour deficit regions in assigning 100 days of employment to a household. This raised issues related to the schedule of rates and wage rates, transparency in wage payments, asset creation on private land, and lack of professionalism in the NREGA. Besides being concerned with delays in release of funds, his work called for setting up a central employment guarantee council.

Similarly, Ambasta *et al.* (2008) raised concerns about understaffing and lack of professionals in implementing the NREGA. Along with the ineffectiveness of social audit, this work pointed out the inappropriateness of the schedule of rates. In a similar vein, based on the evidence derived from a survey of 11 villages and 15 NREG worksites in two blocks of Villupuram district in Tamil Nadu, Narayanan (2008) pointed out the absence of child care facilities.

Another set of studies belonging to the first category addressed governance and implementation related issues. The study, commissioned by the erstwhile National Commission for Enterprises in the Unorganized Sector (NCEUS), brought out the significant role of social and institutional factors in determining the NREG's relative success (in Rajasthan and Andhra Pradesh) and failure (in Bihar and Uttar Pradesh) (NCEUS, 2009).[7] Raabe *et al.* (2010), by using the process-influence mapping technique in the case of Bihar, pointed out the existence of inadequate transparency and accountability mechanisms, which enabled the elite to exercise power in the NREGA-priority areas. This study had also brought out cases of exclusion in issuance of job cards, misappropriation of funds, and lack of technical and professional capacities. Similarly, in a comparative analysis of Andhra Pradesh, Bihar and Rajasthan, Reddy *et al.* (2010) pointed out that the differences in institutional and governance capabilities had enabled the states to make the most of the NREG in Andhra Pradesh and Rajasthan, whereas lack of the same had resulted in the worst performance in Bihar.

The second category of studies focused on the experienced impact of the NREGA. Based on a pilot survey of three villages in Udaipur district of Rajasthan, Jha *et al.* (2008) found that the participation and targeting efficiency of the NREGA had been somewhat satisfactory, as there had been participation by large segments of disadvantaged groups, landless and the poor. Hanumantha and Durgaprasad (2008) found that the NREG programme had largely covered the poor, except in high poverty states of Bihar and Uttar Pradesh. Hirway *et al.* (2010a) went to the extent of working out the multiplier impact of various NREG initiatives undertaken in the village of Nana Kotda in Gujarat. Given the small size of the area covered, it was not surprising that the multiplier impact had been small due to the village's external dependence for its consumption.

Some of the studies had looked at the impact of the NREGA on women as well. Khera and Nayak (2009) pointed out that the NREG scheme has resulted in enhanced wage earnings of women workers, significantly contributing towards their increased food security, access to credit, and ability to cope with sickness. Pankaj and Tankha (2010) examined the impact of the NREG scheme on women's economic empowerment. They pointed out that the NREGS had broadened women's choices in two ways: first, by opening an entirely new avenue for paid employment, and, second, through expansion of choice set and reduction in economic dependence on other family members. They found Dungarpur (Rajasthan) and Kangra (Himachal Pradesh) performing better than Ranchi (Jharkhand) and Patna (Bihar). Similarly, Sudarshan *et al.* (2010) examined the reasons behind wide variations in women's participation across states, and based on the sample drawn from Sirmour (Himachal Pradesh), Palakkad (Kerala) and Sirohi (Rajasthan), found that women's participation in the NREG was shaped by numerous factors such as level and equity in wage rate, effective role played by women's organizations, traditionally determined gender roles, and availability of child care facilities.

There had not been much literature pertaining to the third category, especially in the district-level data being made available by the Ministry of Rural Development of the Government of India. In a major survey of 20 districts spread across India, a study by the Institute of Applied Manpower Research (IAMR) tried to provide an assessment of the NREG's impact on overall quality of life through the examination of household-earning levels, expenditure pattern, asset creation, and impact on reducing distress migration, among others (undated). Though informative, the findings of the study remained confined to 2006–7 only. As it was difficult to generalize the survey-based evidence, even at the state-level, it could not help much in providing a national-level profile.

The availability of data since 2006–7 from the Ministry of Rural Development made this exercise feasible. Two recent studies by Shariff (2009) and Hirway (2010b), have devoted attention to this prevailing research gap; but their effort had a major limitation—neither of them had factored in the phase-wise implementation of the NREGA in the country. As mentioned above, the NREGA had been implemented across the nation in three phases, covering selected districts from each state in each phase. In such a situation, an analytical exercise with appropriate phase-wise classification of districts was called for, to assess the effectiveness of implementation. So we aim to locate this phase-wise disparity in NREGA implementation, along with an analysis at the national and state levels. The scope of analysis included all the states in India, including the North Eastern region.[8] We have considered a period of the initial five years, that is, 2006–7 to 2010–11, and wherever considered relevant, we have assessed the NREGA's performance through five-yearly averages of respective indicators. Such a choice was made to offset the yearly fluctuations in the NREG performance.

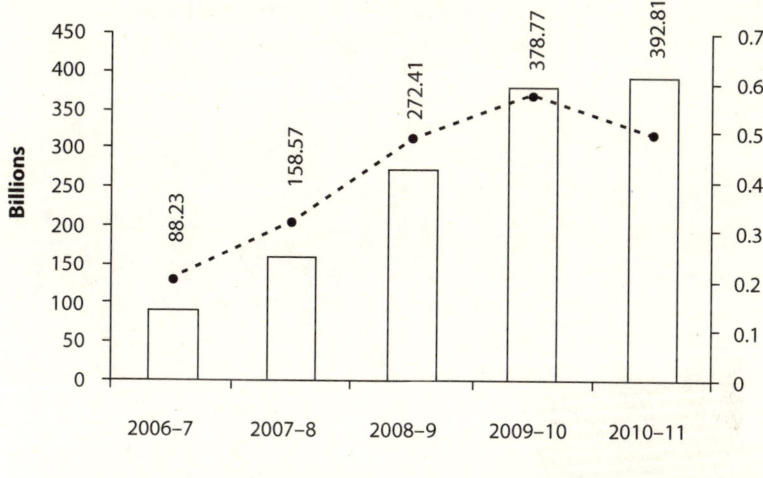

FIGURE 1.1 Trend of Annual Expenditure on NREGA

Source: Based on NREGA's official website: www.nrega.nic.in, and RBI's *Handbook of Statistics on Indian Economy*, 2006–7 to 2010–11.

Note: *GDP at market prices.

FIRST FIVE YEARS: AN ASSESSMENT

During the first five years, both the Union and State Government(s) incurred a cumulative expenditure of Rs 1,290.80 billion[9] for implementing the NREGA. Figure 1.1 depicts the trend in aggregate annual expenditure since 2006–7. It can be observed that the total expenditure incurred on the NREG Scheme (in absolute nominal terms) had increased continuously, over a period of time. This increase had been rapid during the initial four years, but it slowed down in the last year. Such a trend was also visible in the share of the NREGS expenditure in India's total GDP. The expenditure on the NREGS, as per cent of GDP, witnessed continuous increase over the initial four years, but recorded a deceleration in the fifth year. This raised concerns about the slowing down of efforts in implementing the NREGA.

In addition to this national-level scenario was the inadequacy of state-level efforts in the implementation of the NREGA. The state-level expenditure pattern when examined in relation to the state's burden of poverty did not reveal encouraging inferences (Table 1.2).

TABLE 1.2 Cumulative Expenditure Incurred on NREG Programme, 2006–7 to 2010–11

	Cumulative Expenditure Incurred (in Rs billion)		*Share (%) in All-India Rural Poverty**	*Expenditure-Poverty Comparison*	
	Total	*Share (%)*		*Ratio*	*Rank*
Andhra Pradesh	156.76	12.14	2.93	4.15	6
Arunachal Pradesh	1.06	0.08	0.09	0.91	17
Assam	40.46	3.13	2.47	1.27	15
Bihar	75.63	5.86	15.24	0.38	26
Chhattisgarh	64.62	5.01	3.24	1.55	11
Gujarat	18.82	1.46	2.87	0.51	22
Haryana	5.56	0.43	0.97	0.44	25
Himachal Pradesh	15.53	1.2	0.28	4.32	5
Jammu & Kashmir	7.25	0.56	0.17	3.38	8
Jharkhand	57.79	4.48	4.67	0.96	16
Karnataka	61.49	4.76	3.40	1.40	13
Kerala	14.74	1.14	1.47	0.78	18
Madhya Pradesh	156.81	12.15	7.95	1.53	12
Maharashtra	14.01	1.09	7.75	0.14	27
Manipur	12.67	0.98	0.17	5.76	4
Meghalaya	6.63	0.51	0.20	2.58	10
Mizoram	7.54	0.58	0.05	12.56	1
Nagaland	14.17	1.1	0.18	6.28	2
Odisha	44.2	3.42	6.87	0.50	23
Punjab	4.43	0.34	0.68	0.50	24
Rajasthan	172.95	13.4	3.96	3.39	7
Sikkim	2.05	0.16	0.05	3.16	9
Tamil Nadu	57.56	4.46	3.46	1.29	14
Tripura	21.08	1.63	0.28	5.83	3
Uttar Pradesh	177.76	13.77	21.41	0.64	20
Uttarakhand	9.43	0.73	1.23	0.59	21
West Bengal	69.81	5.41	7.84	0.69	19
All-states	1,290.8	100	100.00	1.00	

Source: Based on data released by NREGA's official website and Poverty Estimates for 2004–5, Press Information Bureau, Government of India, New Delhi, March (2007).

Note: *Based on Uniform Recall Period (URP) consumption; it refers to 2004–5.

Bihar, for example, accounted for 15.24 per cent of India's rural poor but the NREG expenditure was only 5.86 per cent. Similar had been the case of Odisha (formerly known as Orissa). The expenditure-poverty ratio remained below unity, indicating inadequate efforts by the state to launch this pro-poor programme. Such a pattern was visible in 12 states. In five other states, the expenditure-poverty ratio had remained marginally above unity.

Given the scenario, it was worth examining the performance of the NREGS through some of the vital indicators such as employment generation, wage receipts, and the consequent impact on poverty.

Employment Generation

During the initial five years of the NREGA implementation, 122.55 million rural households were issued job cards. Of these, 55.53 million households had demanded employment during 2010–11 (Figure 1.2).[10] There had been a generation of 2,563.60 million

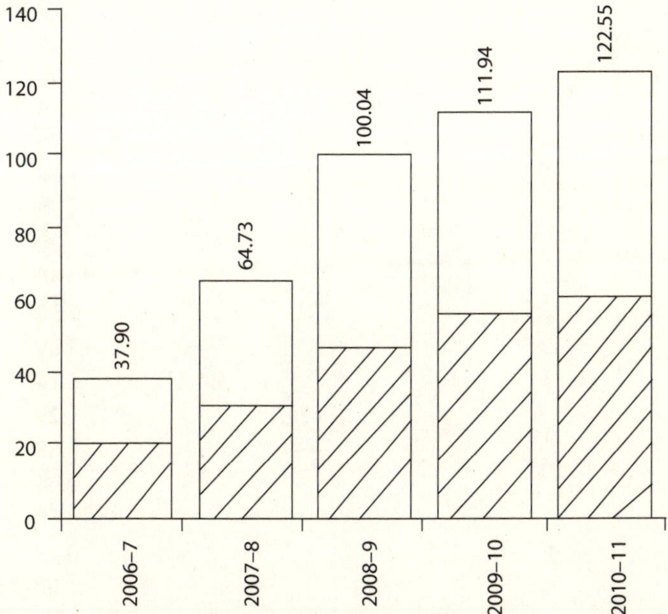

Figure 1.2 Households Issued Job Cards and Demanded Employment in Million

Source: Based on NREGA's official website: www.nrega.nic.in.

man-days of employment in 2010–11 as against 2,163.17 million in 2008–9—the first year of the NREGA implementation throughout rural India. However, in terms of man-days generated per participating household, the trend had not been encouraging as the NREGS generated the highest average of man-days (about 54) only in 2009–10; in all the other years, it had remained below 50. The average employment generated during 2010–11 had been even less than 2008–9 (Figure 1.3). From the point of view of the rural poor, such a trend was worrisome as the implementation of the NREGA was showing signs of weakening. The average man-days generated per household had remained only 47.70 over the last five-year period. Analysis across states revealed that only nine out of the 27 states[11] could generate average employment of more than 50 days—Nagaland performed best, followed by Mizoram, Manipur, Sikkim, Rajasthan, Tripura, Madhya Pradesh, Chhattisgarh, and Andhra Pradesh. Only six states registered an average employment of more than 60 days, and five of them were in the North East (Table 1.3).

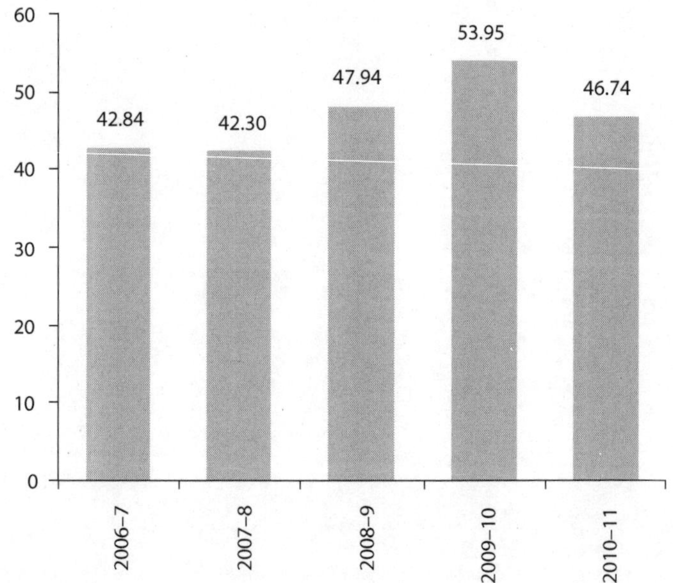

FIGURE 1.3 Average Man-days Generated per Participating Household

Source: Based on NREGA's official website: www.nrega.nic.in.

TABLE 1.3 Average Employment and Wage Performance of NREGA, 2006–11

	Man-days Generated per Household	*NREG Wages (in Rs)*		*NREG Wages as % of Stipulated Minimum Wages**	*Average Annual Per Capita Earnings (in Rs)*		
		Money	*Real*		*Money*	*Real*	*6 as % of 5*
	1	*2*	*3*	*4*	*5*	*6*	
Andhra Pradesh	51.2	90.30	70.15	113.17	1,039.68	807.68	77.69
Arunachal Pradesh	29.7	72.85	56.03	110.67	416.28	320.17	76.91
Assam	37.4	81.63	67.54	106.33	553.44	457.91	82.74
Bihar	28.4	90.39	73.91	114.85	422.64	345.58	81.77
Chhattisgarh	52.4	78.69	64.46	112.82	812.04	665.19	81.92
Gujarat	36.4	85.00	65.17	87.15	580.80	445.30	76.67
Haryana	40.6	138.39	102.32	100.99	953.76	705.17	73.94
Himachal Pradesh	48.6	105.86	88.37	107.24	1,029.12	859.09	83.48
Jammu & Kashmir	37.6	94.17	71.68	137.06	542.04	412.59	76.12
Jharkhand	44.3	91.77	76.75	101.97	721.44	603.36	83.63
Karnataka	48.3	100.76	69.85	125.46	937.32	649.78	69.32
Kerala	33.1	127.36	95.05	101.99	898.20	670.34	74.63
Madhya Pradesh	58.1	75.47	62.14	86.22	786.96	647.96	82.34
Maharashtra	43.7	93.71	75.99	139.77	825.84	669.68	81.09
Manipur	69.6	82.92	62.40	102.57	892.80	671.86	75.25

(*Cont'd*)

Table 1.3 (*Cont'd*)

	Man-days Generated per Household	*NREG Wages (in Rs)*		*NREG Wages as % of Stipulated Minimum Wages**	*Average Annual Per Capita Earnings (in Rs)*		
		Money	*Real*		*Money*	*Real*	*6 as % of 5*
	1	*2*	*3*	*4*	*5*	*6*	
Meghalaya	46.3	86.73	67.81	124.91	712.08	556.74	78.19
Mizoram	72.4	108.89	83.64	119.93	1,530.72	1,175.77	76.81
Nagaland	77.3	96.15	72.19	96.62	1,200.96	901.69	75.08
Odisha	44.4	83.65	66.75	134.49	790.32	630.65	79.80
Punjab	28.7	119.70	89.92	119.21	598.20	449.37	75.12
Rajasthan	68.0	79.58	62.80	81.62	881.40	695.55	78.91
Sikkim	69.1	96.11	73.24	96.28	1,422.36	1,083.90	76.20
Tamil Nadu	48.7	77.79	57.89	97.16	903.48	672.35	74.42
Tripura	65.4	92.44	77.24	117.03	1,221.84	1,020.93	83.56
Uttar Pradesh	49.6	97.22	78.33	100.43	746.28	601.28	80.57
Uttarakhand	37.8	92.83	73.97	129.07	672.48	535.85	79.68
West Bengal	28.8	89.57	68.84	121.79	504.12	387.45	76.86
All-states	47.7	86.8	68.61	101.19	751.44	593.97	79.04

Source: Based on data released by NREGA's official website: www.nrega.nic.in; Labour Bureau (2006–11); and Census of India (2001, 2011).

Note: *Refers to the period of 2007–11; minimum wages is the weighted average of district-level minimum wages; weight refers to the share of rural agricultural workers in respective state.

What was more worrisome in the state-wise analysis was the performance of poor states such as Bihar, West Bengal, Odisha, Uttarakhand, Assam, and Jharkhand. Bihar fared the worst with the lowest generation of average employment (28.4 man-days) over the five-year period.

A consideration of spatial disparity across states revealed further insights on weak implementation of the NREGA (Table 1.4) with about 53 per cent of the total districts providing employment of only 26 to 50 man-days per year during the first five-year period, and only 5 per cent of the districts generating more than 75 man-days over the same period. The pattern revealed that in the highest category of employment (>75 days), there was a large concentration of districts in states like Nagaland (64 per cent) and Mizoram (50 per cent). Similarly, there were a few states like Sikkim (100 per cent), Tripura (75 per cent), Rajasthan (67 per cent), Andhra Pradesh (59 per cent), Meghalaya (57 per cent), and Uttar Pradesh (54 per cent), where a high proportion of districts could generate more than 50 man-days. In Chhattisgarh, Karnataka, and Mizoram, about 50 per cent of the districts belonged to this category. It was also found that in 15 states, more than 50 per cent of the districts could generate an annual average employment of only 26 to 50 man-days. Such low generation of employment in states with low incidence of poverty was not very worrisome, but such was not the case with the poorer states as the average man-days, along with average wage rates, contribute to household income, and thus help reduce poverty. Any failure in this respect was bound to have severe implications on each household. It was observed that in states with high incidence of poverty like Bihar, Odisha, Chhattisgarh, Madhya Pradesh, and Jharkhand, there was a high concentration of districts generating low-level average employment.

Further insights into the intra-state spatial disparity were derived through phase-wise analysis of the NREGA implementation.[12] Here also, the analytical exercise corresponded to an aggregated analysis for five years (for Phase-I districts), four years (for Phase-II districts) and three years (for Phase-III districts), respectively. Despite the absence of significant disparity across Phase-I, II, and III districts at the aggregate level, there were significant variations at the state-level in both the absolute and the relative sense. The Phase-I districts of 16 states generated an average of less than 50 man-days over the last five-year

Table 1.4 Spatial Disparity in NREGA Performance across States during Initial Five Years

State	*Total Districts*	*Man-days per Household*			
		<25	*26–50*	*51–75*	*>75*
Andhra Pradesh	22 (3.58)	2 (9.09)	7 (31.82)	13 (59.09)	
Arunachal Pradesh	16 (2.61)	11 (68.75)	4(25)		1 (6.25)
Assam	27 (4.4)	8 (29.63)	15 (55.56)	4 (14.81)	
Bihar	38 (6.19)	10 (26.32)	28 (73.68)		
Chhattisgarh	18 (2.93)	1 (5.56)	8 (44.44)	9 (50)	
Gujarat	26 (4.23)	4 (15.38)	19 (73.08)	3 (11.54)	
Haryana	21 (3.42)	1 (4.76)	19 (90.48)	1 (4.76)	
Himachal Pradesh	12 (1.95)		8 (66.67)	4 (33.33)	
Jammu & Kashmir	22 (3.58)	3 (13.64)	15 (68.18)	3 (13.64)	1 (4.55)
Jharkhand	24 (3.91)		19 (79.17)	5 (20.83)	
Karnataka	30 (4.89)		15 (50)	15 (50)	
Kerala	14 (2.28)	1 (7.14)	13 (92.86)		
Madhya Pradesh	50 (8.14)	2 (4)	26 (52)	16 (32)	6 (12)
Maharashtra	33 (5.37)	10 (30.3)	16 (48.48)	7 (21.21)	
Manipur	9 (1.47)	1 (11.11)	1 (11.11)	4 (44.44)	3 (33.33)
Meghalaya	7 (1.14)		3 (42.86)	4 (57.14)	
Mizoram	8 (1.3)			4 (50)	4(50)
Nagaland	11 (1.79)			4 (36.36)	7 (63.64)
Odisha	30 (4.89)		24 (80)	6 (20)	
Punjab	20 (3.26)	7 (35)	12 (60)	1 (5)	
Rajasthan	33 (5.37)		5 (15.15)	22 (66.67)	6 (18.18)
Sikkim	4 (0.65)			4 (100)	
Tamil Nadu	31 (5.05)	2 (6.45)	17 (54.84)	10 (32.26)	2 (6.45)
Tripura	4 (0.65)			3 (75)	1 (25)
Uttar Pradesh	72 (11.73)		33 (45.83)	39 (54.17)	
Uttarakhand	13 (2.12)	2 (15.38)	10 (76.92)	1 (7.69)	
West Bengal	19 (3.09)	8 (42.11)	11 (57.89)		
All-states	614 (100)	73 (11.89)	328 (53.42)	182 (29.64)	31 (5.05)

Source: Based on NREGA's official website: www. nrega.nic.in.

Note: *Figures in parentheses denote percentage of districts estimated from the total districts in each respective state.

period, with the performance of Bihar and West Bengal being quite disappointing, to say the least. In relative terms, Phase-I districts of 20 states had performed better than Phase-III districts. Similarly in 16 states, the performance of Phase-I districts had been better than the Phase-II districts. Such a trend was encouraging, but the gap between the performance of Phase-I, Phase-II, and Phase-III districts was not that significant. In fact, given the poverty and economic backwardness of Phase-I districts, their performance ought to have been much more impressive, and any lack in this respect strongly suggested the persistence of systemic problems related to administrative and institutional bottlenecks in these districts.

Wage Receipts and Household Earning from NREGA

Following employment generation, we considered the indicator of wage receipts[13] so as to infer households' per capita earning. It was found that there had been an increase in the nominal unskilled wages received under the NREGA over the last five-year period—it had increased at the national level from Rs 64.48 in 2006–7 to Rs 100.02 in 2010–11 (Figure 1.4). An average for the 2006–11 periods was Rs 86.80 and there were 10 states where it had remained below the all-states' average (Table 1.3). It remained the highest in Haryana (Rs 138.39), followed by Kerala (Rs 127.36), Punjab (Rs 119.70), Mizoram (Rs 108.89), and Himachal Pradesh (Rs 105.86). On the other hand, it remained the lowest in Arunachal Pradesh (Rs 72.85), preceded by Madhya Pradesh (Rs 75.47), Tamil Nadu (Rs 77.79), Chhattisgarh (Rs 78.69), and Rajasthan (Rs 79.58). Bihar, which had performed badly in generating employment per household, had not fared that badly in providing average daily wages (Rs 90.39); in fact it was much better placed than the relatively high employment generating states of Rajasthan and Andhra Pradesh.

Under the NREGA, wages were fixed at par with the minimum wage rate for agricultural workers in a given state or region. However, due to the in-built mechanism for evaluating work performance, this system of wage payment had become like the piece-rate system where the wage payments were made after an assessment of work completed through pre-determined 'Schedule of Rates' (SORs).[14] Over 2007–11, the unskilled wages had remained below the stipulated minimum level. This was severe in Rajasthan, Madhya Pradesh, and Gujarat, whereas in about 20 states, it remained higher than the minimum wages

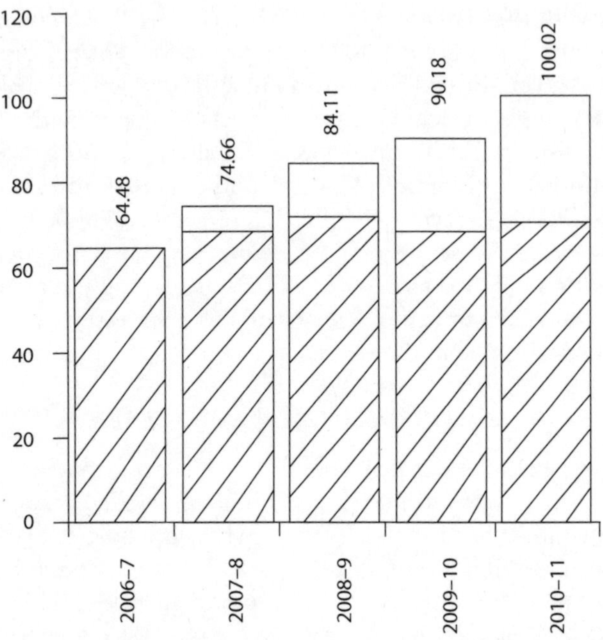

FIGURE 1.4 Average NREG Money and Real (Shaded) Wages (in Rs per day)

Source: Based on Data Released by NREGA's official website: www.nrega.nic.in; and Labour Bureau (2006–11).

(Table 1.3). Though such a trend, reflecting a relatively high proportion of the states providing average wages above the minimum was encouraging, its significance got reduced due to the fact that in a large number of states, the minimum wage rates were not revised periodically. As the revision of minimum wages was expected to maintain its real value that was prone to fall due to adverse impact of inflation, we examined the magnitude of inflation-neutral wages by deflating the received wages with the changes in consumer price index for agricultural labourers (CPIAL). The emerging results were not encouraging.

At the national level, the real average wages had risen continuously till 2008–9. Thereafter it recorded a decline, and by 2010–11, it had been a little above the 2006–7 base years (Figure 1.4). Though the annual growth in nominal wages had been 11.60 per cent, a large percentage of such districts were found in Arunachal Pradesh (19 per cent) and the surge in inflation measured by the growth in CPIAL had resulted only in a negligible rise in real average wages. Across states, Haryana reported the highest real average wages over 2006–7 to 2010–11 period (Table 1.3). It was followed by Kerala, Punjab, Himachal Pradesh, Mizoram and, interestingly, Uttar Pradesh. On the other hand, the real average wages had remained the lowest in Arunachal Pradesh, preceded by Tamil Nadu, Madhya Pradesh, Manipur, Rajasthan, and Chhattisgarh. In terms of spatial disparity, there was a large concentration of districts where the real average wages had been between Rs 61 and Rs 80 (68 per cent districts). What should be a matter of great concern was the fact that there were a few states where the real average wages had remained below Rs 50 over the five-year period. Similarly, the real wages had remained between Rs 61 and Rs 70 in a majority of districts in states like Meghalaya (100 per cent), Tamil Nadu (55 per cent), and Manipur (44 per cent).

Impact of NREGA on Poverty Reduction

Both the average wage and the average man-days of employment received by a household made up the annual earning that a rural household managed to derive from employment under NREGA. For analytical purposes, this average household earning is further normalized for the household size by way of estimating the household's per capita earning from NREGA.[15] Our estimates revealed that the average annual per capita money earnings from NREGA had been Rs 751.46 for the past five years. Sixteen out of 27 states had remained above average. Four of the North Eastern states—Mizoram, Sikkim, Tripura, and Nagaland—remained at the top level while Arunachal Pradesh, Bihar, West Bengal, and Jammu & Kashmir remained at the bottom level. Among the poor states, only Tripura managed to generate a relatively high level of per capita annual money earnings from NREGA (Rs 1,221.81); otherwise almost all the poor states remained either below, or slightly above, the national average.

In order to further diagnose the poverty alleviating impact of NREGA, we examined the NREG earnings as per cent of the rural poverty line.[16] It was found that over the last five-year period, NREG employment, on an average, could provide about 10 per cent of the income needed by a household to cross the new poverty line; however, the magnitude of NREG earnings remained below this average in 10 states (Figure 1.5).

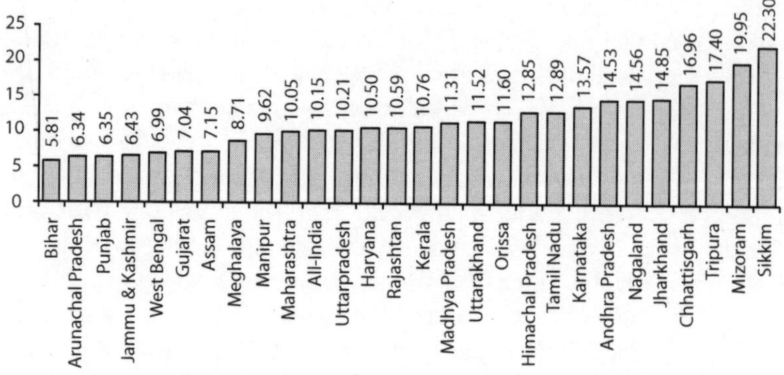

FIGURE 1.5 NREGA Earnings as Per cent of New Rural Poverty Line, 2006–11 Average

Source: Based on NREGA's official website: www.nrega.nic.in; and GoI (2009).

There had been sharp variations across districts in this respect. In about 7 per cent of the districts, NREG employment could contribute less than 5 per cent of the new rural poverty line. The districts belonging to Bihar, Arunachal Pradesh, Maharashtra, and Assam had high representation in this category. However, 42 per cent of the other districts could generate earnings equivalent to 5 to 10 per cent of the new rural poverty line; most of these districts belong to states with high incidence of poverty like Uttar Pradesh, Bihar, Madhya Pradesh, and Assam.

NREG seemed to have contributed to poverty reduction that was closer to its potential only in a few states. The potential impact would be 21.27 per cent if 100 days of employment per household was given. From this point of view, only two states, Mizoram and Sikkim, met the actual performance with the potential. Four other states, Chhattisgarh, Jharkhand, Nagaland, and Andhra Pradesh, were closer to the potential.

Given this state of the NREGA implementation over the first five-year period, it needed to be noted that in its analysis of the NREGA performance after two years of its implementation, Mehrotra (2008) lauded the magnitude of employment generation under NREGA vis-à-vis earlier employment generation programmes. Given the comprehensive design and scope of the NREGA, the scheme had been an improvement over earlier public works programmes; but it could not be termed as satisfactory as the average annual days of employment generated per household over the 2006–11 period had remained less than half of the stipulated 100 days per household. The Phase-I districts having large demand for the NREG work could not perform well—a worrisome inference hinting at the low organizational capacity, and bureaucratic and political commitment, in these districts. It was rational to expect that the poor households would have demanded employment for 100 days if they were to be honoured. But the existence of only about 11 per cent of such households in contrast to 41.8 per cent incidence of poverty in rural India suggested nothing but lapses in the implementation of the NREGA. Such was the observation of Shariff (2009) as well, who, based on a survey of 7 northern states, pointed out that the self-targeting mechanism under the NREGA had largely failed as the NREG jobs were appropriated mostly by relatively better-off households, with better bargaining capacity and awareness than the really deserving households experiencing food stress. Similarly, the surge in inflation during recent years had curtailed considerably the magnitude of real benefits to be gained from the NREG. A cumulative impact of both of these factors impacted the per capita earning from the NREG, which had remained only at 10.15 per cent of the new rural poverty line.

INSTRUMENTAL ROLE OF NREGA

Despite this dismal performance scenario, it was significant to note that the implementation of the NREGA over the last five-year period had played an instrumental role in many respects. It was important to highlight this lest the drawbacks pointed out here in its implementation were used by the neoliberal lobby to either denigrate it as 'wasteful', or allow it to have a slow death. We, therefore, discussed various facets of the NREGA's instrumental role as detailed below.

Contribution to Women's Economic Empowerment

The NREGA has certain in-built provisions[17] that have played a key role in stimulating increased labour market participation by women. At the national level, the share of women workers recorded an increase from nearly 40 per cent in 2006–7 to 48 per cent in 2009–10, but this declined marginally in the fifth year (Figure 1.6). Though 18

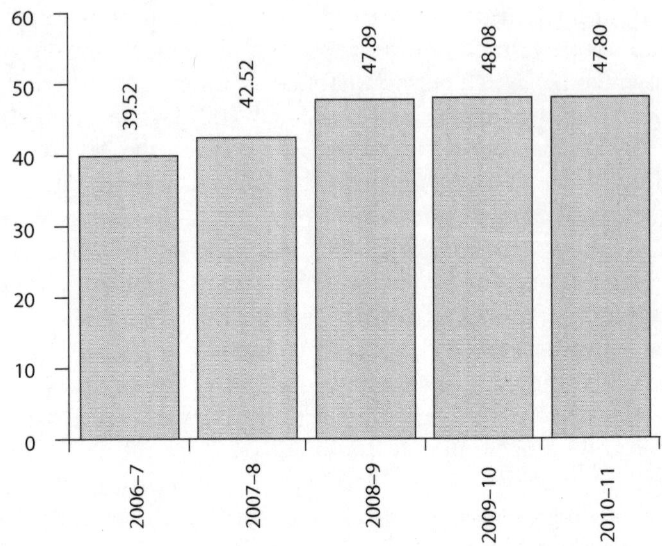

Figure 1.6 Share of Women Workers in Total NREG Employment

Source: Based on NREGA's official website: www. nrega.nic.in.

states could fulfil the norm of 33 per cent of women in total NREG employment over their five years of performance, there had been a varying pattern across states. In states like Kerala and Tamil Nadu, women's participation was more than 80 per cent. It was relatively high in Rajasthan (68 per cent) and Andhra Pradesh (58 per cent). In 14 other states, it remained below 50 per cent but above the stipulated norm of 33 per cent. Haryana and Jharkhand were just near this stipulated level of women employment, and the other near-norm states were Assam, Punjab, West Bengal, Bihar, and Arunachal Pradesh. In Uttar Pradesh and Jammu & Kashmir, the participation of women in NREG had been quite low, at 20 per cent and 6 per cent respectively (Table 1.5).

Social Inclusion

The implementation of the NREGA has led to increased social inclusion through the provision of employment opportunities to workers belonging to socially disadvantaged classes of SCs and STs. At the national level, the aggregate share of SC/ST workers in total NREG

TABLE 1.5 State-wise Women, SC, and ST Participation in NREGA over the 2006–11 Period

	Average Share in NREG Employment (%)			*Population Share*		*NREG Participation vis-à-vis Share in State's Population*		*NREG Participation vis-à-vis Share in State's BPL Population*	
	Women	*SC*	*ST*	*SC*	*ST*	*SC*	*ST*	*SC*	*ST*
Andhra Pradesh	57.61	25.64	14.29	26.89	9.54	0.95	1.50	1.67	0.47
Arunachal Pradesh	27.21	0.65	87.84	0.39	67.15	1.69	1.31		
Assam	28.67	10.11	35.49	10.14	14.31	1.00	2.48	0.37	2.52
Bihar	27.52	46.50	2.42	27.76	3.07	1.68	0.79	0.73	0.05
Chhattisgarh	45.66	14.89	40.30	18.86	33.98	0.79	1.19	0.46	0.74
Gujarat	45.60	13.44	45.16	11.88	21.75	1.13	2.08	0.62	1.30
Haryana	32.87	52.15		23.56		2.21		1.95	
Himachal Pradesh	41.87	32.96	9.11	28.32	7.59	1.16	1.20	1.68	0.61
Jammu & Kashmir	6.33	7.79	25.57	9.79	13.36	0.80	1.91	1.50	2.91
Jharkhand	30.58	17.88	41.52	26.38	26.44	0.68	1.57	0.31	0.77
Karnataka	42.02	19.04	10.44	23.20	9.47	0.82	1.10	0.60	0.44
Kerala	87.23	17.05	5.80	15.46	3.30	1.10	1.76	0.79	0.13
Madhya Pradesh	43.31	17.95	46.61	20.02	25.85	0.90	1.80	0.42	0.80
Maharashtra	42.63	19.49	37.74	18.45	13.47	1.06	2.80	0.44	0.67
Manipur	42.65	10.14	64.43	1.10	44.14	9.23	1.46		

(*Cont'd*)

Table 1.5 (*Cont'd*)

	Average Share in NREG Employment (%)			*Population Share*		*NREG Participation vis-à-vis Share in State's*			
						Population		*BPL Population*	
	Women	*SC*	*ST*	*SC*	*ST*	*SC*	*ST*	*SC*	*ST*
Meghalaya	42.50	0.44	93.30	18.06	82.12	0.02	1.14		
Mizoram	34.93	0.00	99.88	2.17	84.59	0.00	1.18		
Nagaland	38.00	0.00	100.0						
Odisha	37.26	20.79	39.76	25.20	25.43	0.83	1.56	0.41	0.53
Punjab	28.39	76.96		34.47		2.23		5.27	0.00
Rajasthan	67.50	25.53	28.34	18.99	18.60	1.34	1.52	0.89	0.87
Sikkim	45.27	9.40	42.92	5.80	21.00	1.62	2.04		
Tamil Nadu	82.11	58.53	2.26	28.51	2.84	2.05	0.79	1.88	0.07
Tripura	47.14	20.59	43.30	19.29	36.34	1.07	1.19		
Uttar Pradesh	19.66	54.87	1.92	30.87	2.65	1.78	0.73	1.22	0.06
Uttarakhand	39.42	26.54	4.17	22.25	3.80	1.19	1.10	0.49	0.10
West Bengal	28.22	36.79	14.41	33.51	9.85	1.10	1.46	1.25	0.34
All-states	46.38	29.38	24.47	24.86	11.99	1.18	2.04	0.80	0.52

Source: Based on NREGA's official website: www.nrega.nic.in; Census of India (2001, 2011); and GoI (2008).

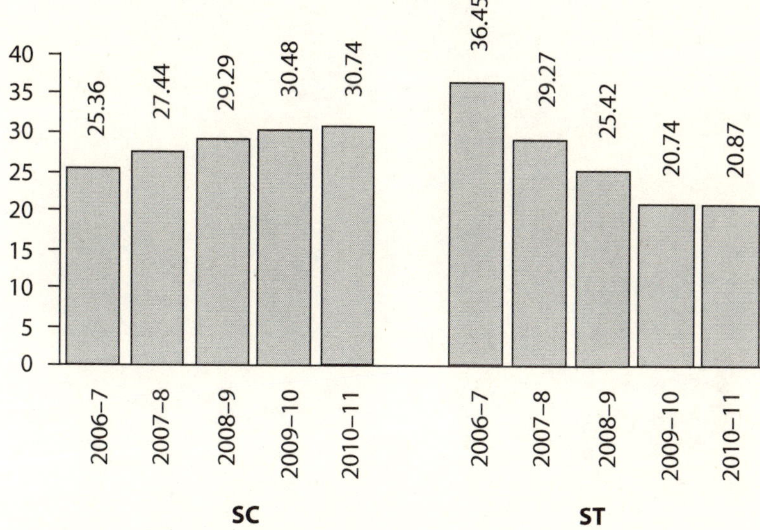

FIGURE 1.7 Share of SC and ST Workers in Total NREG Employment

Source: Based on NREGA's official website: www.nrega.nic.in.

has remained more than 50 per cent over the last five year period (Figure 1.7).

In terms of the five-yearly averages, in Punjab, SC workers accounted for about 77 per cent of the NREG employment. Next were Tamil Nadu, Uttar Pradesh and Haryana, with 59, 55, and 52 per cent respectively. In all other states, the share of SC workers remained below 50 per cent (Table 1.5). A consideration of phase-wise analysis revealed further that the performance had been better in Phase-I districts vis-à-vis Phase-II and Phase-III districts in this respect only in five states—Haryana, Uttar Pradesh, Bihar, Jharkhand, and Karnataka. Similarly, the share of ST workers had remained above 80 per cent in Mizoram, Meghalaya and Arunachal Pradesh.

One might argue that a mere representation of SC/ST in terms of their per centage share in employment would not reflect adequately the degree of their participation in NREG, so one must take into consideration the ratio of their share vis-à-vis their share in population. We estimated this indicator. It was found that the situation remained

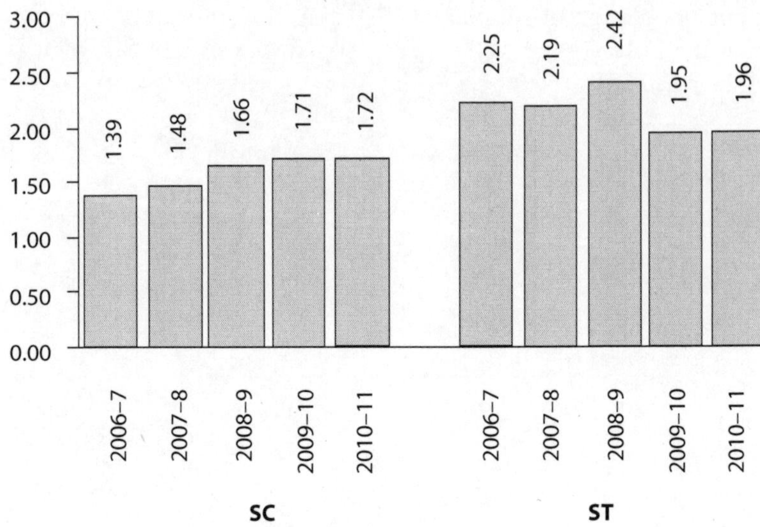

FIGURE 1.8 NREG Participation by SC and ST Workers vis-à-vis Their Population Share

Source: Based on NREGA's official website: www.nrega.nic.in; Census of India (2001, 2011); and GoI (2008).

satisfactory at the national level as the SC/ST workers continued to hold a relatively larger share of NREG employment vis-à-vis their population share[18] over the last five-year period (Figure 1.8). However, the pattern was not uniform across states.[19] A consideration of the last five-year period revealed that the SC workers got more NREG employment vis-à-vis their population share in 16 states—it was more than double in Manipur, Punjab, Haryana, and Tamil Nadu and more than 1.50 in Uttar Pradesh, Arunachal Pradesh, Bihar, and Sikkim. Similarly, in the case of ST workers, their participation in NREG had been more than their population share in 21 states. In Tamil Nadu, Bihar, and Uttar Pradesh, the share of ST workers in NREG employment remained lower than their population share (Table 1.5). These inferences, in light of their small population share and a high incidence of poverty, were significant.[20]

However, we would argue that this was still not an adequate indicator of a pro-poor scheme. The participation of SC/ST should be captured in relation to the share of poor SC/ST in the overall poor population of rural areas. By using this indicator, we found that the NREGA had done well in social inclusion of SC workers only in Punjab—their inclusion had been five times more than their share in the state's rural poor population (Table 1.5).[21] In seven other states also, the inclusion of SC workers had been more than their share in the state's rural poor population. In all other states, the situation had not been favourable and much more effort was needed to include SC workers in the scheme. The situation had been the worst in the case of ST workers. Only in three states—Jammu & Kashmir, Assam and Gujarat—had there been a relatively higher representation of ST workers vis-à-vis their share in the state's rural poor population.

Asset Creation in Rural Economy

The implementation of the NREGA had facilitated the creation of productive infrastructure in the rural economy. The Act stipulated the undertaking of eight types of works, such as:

- (i) water conservation and water harvesting;
- (ii) drought proofing, including aforestation and tree plantation;
- (iii) construction of irrigation canals, including micro and minor irrigation works;
- (iv) provision of irrigation facility to land owned by SC/ST families, or the beneficiaries of land reform—Indira Awas Yojana (IAY);
- (v) renovation of traditional water bodies including desilting of tanks;
- (vi) land development;
- (vii) flood control and protection works including drainage in water logged areas; and
- (viii) rural connectivity to provide all-weather access. It also provided for flexibility to add any other work by the Union Government after consulting with state government.[22]

In sum, the NREGA was concerned with capital formation in rural areas in terms of land and water resources management, and development and creation and maintenance of roads.

Out of the total works completed under NREG, the single largest in terms of numbers was rural connectivity in 2010–11, followed by water conservation and water harvesting, land development and

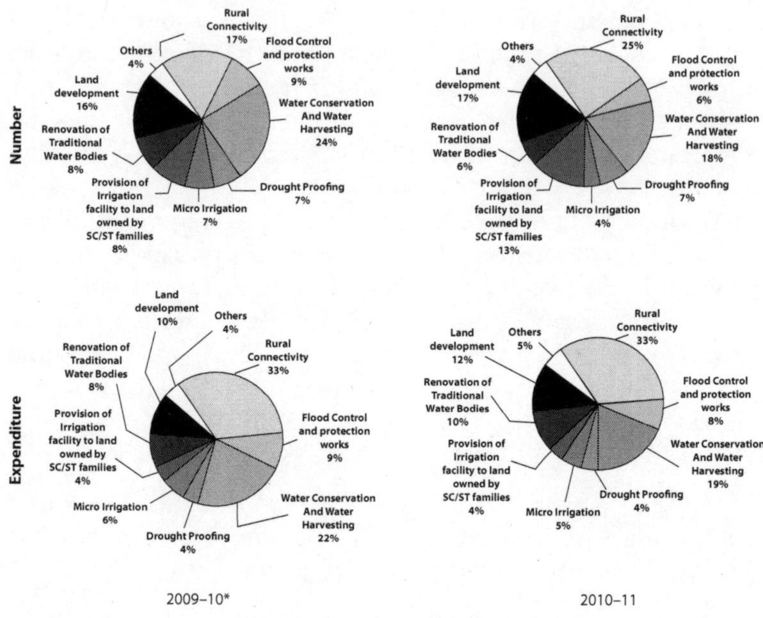

FIGURE 1.9 Distribution of Completed Works under NREGA

Source: Based on NREGA's official website: www.nrega.nic.in.

Note: *Asset Data for Odisha is not available for this year.

provision of irrigation facility to lands of SC/ST families (Figure 1.9). In terms of expenditure, rural connectivity occupied a share of 33 per cent followed by water conservation and water harvesting. Land development and the renovation of traditional water bodies incurred significant expenditure whereas the expenditure on the provision of irrigation facility to SC/ST families, micro-irrigation and drought proofing remained below 5 per cent in both the years under consideration. So, by a generic classification, it was fair to say that land and water resources development and management had accounted for more than 60 per cent of the expenditure.

Given the magnitude of efforts undertaken and the range of works brought under the ambit of NREG, there was no doubt that such an initiative would definitely lead to the sustainable development of the rural economy, though there might be a lag effect. It was observed by Tiwari *et al.* (2011) that the asset creation under NREG had brought ecological benefits; some reaction to these inferences was shown by Kumar *et al.* (2011). Besides such direct impact of asset creation under NREG, there had been attempts to capture the indirect impact of the expenditure undertaken. In a village study of Nana Kotda in South Gujarat, it was found by Hirway *et al.* (2010a) that the expenditure on various NREG works had generated multiplier impact on the rural economy, though the study did point out its low impact due to various leakages, which was not surprising given the linkages of the village economy to the larger regional economy.

There has been concern about the durability and quality of infrastructure works completed under the NREGS (Hirway, 2008). It was also argued that 'viewing the NREGS as a source of "crucial public investment" was romantic, but naïve. Regardless of the rationale advanced so far, NREGS was not a viable local infrastructure scheme and the bias against machinery only reinforced this weakness' (Kapur *et al.*, 2008: 87). However, the available evidence did not provide much weightage to this concern as the NCEUS commissioned study pointed out that as many as 83 per cent of the respondents had found the assets created under NREG productive. Similarly, the survey conducted by Singh and Nauriyal (2009) in six blocks belonging to Tehri, Champawat and Haridwar districts of Uttarakhand revealed that a majority of the workers perceived the quality of assets generated under NREG as 'good' and 'very good' (Figure 1.10).

Despite these subjective assessments about the quality and utility of infrastructural works accomplished under NREG, it cannot be denied that the in-built potential of NREGA for sustainable development of the rural economy was yet to be attained, and the lack of technical support for planning NREG works (through resource mapping exercises), as well as the shortage of technical staff in designing and supervising works, was acting as major roadblock in this endeavour (World Bank, 2011).

Support to the Disabled

The NREGA has been of some help to the disabled as the provision for group work and evaluation provides space for work to them. It became clear from the available information that as many as 2.04 lakh disabled workers had sought employment under the NREGA during 2008–9. This increased to 2.95 lakh in 2009–10 and then remained at 2.94 lakh in 2010–11. It was also interesting to note

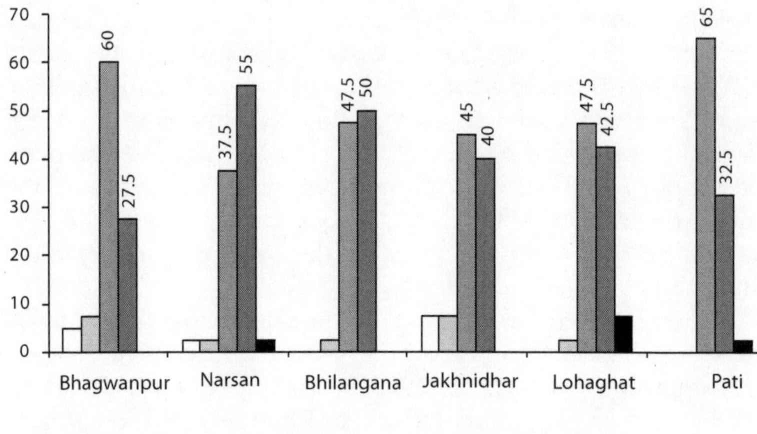

FIGURE 1.10 Quality of Asset Generated under NREGA as Perceived by Workers in Uttarakhand

Source: Singh and Nauriyal (2009: 98).

that a large proportion of these disabled beneficiaries belonged to the Phase-I districts, followed by the Phase-II and the Phase-III districts (Figure 1.11).

PROTECTION AGAINST DISTRESS MIGRATION

Though not its immediate objective, the NREGA has the potential to curtail 'distress' migration by providing employment opportunities at home. A set of studies showed that the beneficiaries saw this as a means to reduce the need for distress migration. These studies are summarized in Table 1.6. Similarly, a study in 2008 found that there had been a overall fall in migration, especially of women, owing largely to the direct impact of wage employment under the Scheme (ISWSD, 2008).

Indirectly, expansion in irrigation and other productive assets through the works undertaken, and the consequent increase in cropping intensity, as well as stabilization of farm incomes through availability of water, had also played a positive role. Similarly, there had been a marked reduction in the severity of push factors that had resulted in distress migration under adverse contracts, with debt and unemployment playing a lesser role in explaining out-migration.

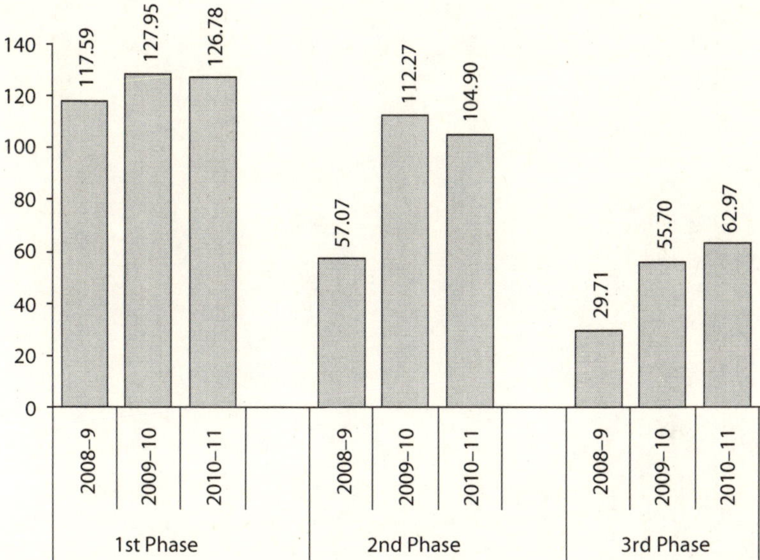

FIGURE 1.11 Employment to the Disabled under NREGA (000s)

Simultaneously, there had also been migration of males due to 'pull' factors such as wage differentials between rural and urban areas, and the prospect of continuous employment in sectors such as construction. Therefore, the evidence on reducing distress migration due to the NREG should be taken as a temporary and limited succour to segments of people who were often forced to migrate in search of work and income.

INCREASE IN THE RESERVE PRICE OF LABOUR

Besides these direct influences, there seemed to have been some impact on the wage pattern in the rural labour market. In order to arrive at a definitive conclusion in this regard, we made a comparison of average wages paid to the non-agricultural unskilled workers (NAUW) during the pre-NREG phase and the post-NREG phase. It needs to be noted that these workers were placed at the lowest rungs of the rural labour market. Our estimates suggested that in the pre-NREG scenario, the real average wages for male NAUW had declined significantly across all the major states except Karnataka, Odisha, Tamil Nadu and West Bengal. However, the introduction of NREG provided an

TABLE 1.6 NREGA Impact in Arresting Distress Migration, as Inferred from Selective Studies

Study Reference	*State*	*Survey Question*	*District/Block*	*Share (%)* *
Singh and Nauriyal (2009)	Uttarakhand	Implementation of scheme reduced migration of workers from your village?	Champawat	60.0
			Haridwar	42.5
			Tehri	82.5
Nayak *et al*. (undated)	Odisha	Did NREGA halt your family's migration to other villages?	Balasore	41.3
			Mayurbhanj	65.9
Kamath *et al*. (2008)	Andhra Pradesh	If NREGA work, will you migrate?	Anantapur	99.0
			Adilabad	91.7
			Gulbarga	88.9
			Raichur	88.7
IITM (2009)	Tamil Nadu	Household stopped migration after implementation of NREGA?	Cuddalore	37.8
			Dindigal	52.1
			Kanchipuram	57.4
			Nagai	34.6
			Thiruvallur	6.82
Panda *et al*. (2009)	Sikkim	Has NREGA helped in curbing migration from village to outside?	District Average	74.0
	Meghalaya		District Average	49.4

Source: Based on the inferences derived from various studies.

Note: *Respondents who consider NREGA arresting distress migration.

alternative opportunity to rural households. This led to an increase in their bargaining power and the consequent rise in wage rate. It was found that the growth rate of real wages for the NAUW had been positive across all the states. Almost similar was the case with female workers (Table 1.7).

An attempt was also made to understand the gender-wise variation in the NAUW wages vis-à-vis the NREG wages since 2006–7. State-specific graphs were drawn (Figure 1.12) which presented three main patterns across states. In the first category were Himachal Pradesh, Jammu & Kashmir, Kerala, and Rajasthan, where the NAUW wages remained higher than the NREG wages during most of the 2006–10 period. The second category depicted a pattern of convergence between the NAUW wage and the NREG wage in a number of states, which was definitely a positive outcome. This convergence had taken place in Andhra Pradesh, Tamil Nadu, Assam, Haryana, Punjab, Karnataka, Maharashtra, Uttar Pradesh, Bihar, and Odisha. What was worrying was the lack of convergence (third category) in Gujarat, Madhya Pradesh, and West Bengal, where the NAUW wages had remained consistently below the NREG wages.

PERSPECTIVES FROM MICRO-LEVEL STUDIES

Some of the major observations emerging from the above macro-level analysis of NREGA implementation hinted at its instrumental role in alleviating poverty, enhancing labour market participation of women, social inclusion, asset creation, and reduction in distress migration. Being vital outcomes of a pro-poor programme, they needed to be qualified further in the light of existing micro-level evidence, primarily to have a holistic picture of the NREGA implementation. These micro-level inferences were derived specifically from two types of studies: the first set belonged to the studies commissioned under a research project directed by the first author[23], and the second one referred to other key studies documenting the experience of the NREGA implementation in other states, some of which had already been referred to earlier.

An ultimate outcome of NREGA was its poverty curtailing impact. Khera and Nayak (2009), based on their field experience in Bihar, Chhattisgarh, Jharkhand, Madhya Pradesh, Rajasthan, and Uttar Pradesh, documented reduced hunger in two-thirds of the

TABLE 1.7 Real Average Wages (RAW) of Non-agricultural Unskilled Workers*

		Pre-NREG Phase				*Post-NREG Phase*					
		2003	*2004*	*2005*	*Gr (%)*	*2006*	*2007*	*2008*	*2009*	*2010*	*Gr (%)*
Andhra Pradesh	M	49.22	48.58	47.96	−1.29	47.81	50.38	58.62	62.36	71.9	10.29
	F	32.68	35.37	34.52	2.74	34.5	36.79	41.94	45.53	52.97	10.70
Bihar	M	49.77	50.36	48.87	−0.9	46.02	45.58	46.95	48.59	60.81	6.21
	F	45.26	45.27	44.2	−1.18	41.37	40.07	42.29	43.9	56.08	6.99
Gujarat	M	52.78	50.79	46.52	−6.31	44.64	46.47	49.22	45.55	45.7	0.26
	F	51.32	48.96	44.42	−7.21	42.81	44.69	47.79	44.47	44.17	0.57
Haryana	M	87.48	83.19	83.27	−2.46	81.01	80.57	84.59	86.12	105.97	6.03
	F	82.59	79.86	79.81	−1.71	77.92	75.2	80.52	85.77	101.01	6.50
Himachal Pradesh	M	100.28	104.24	100.3	0.01	97.26	98.37	100.4	96.44	108.41	1.97
	F	NA	NA	NA	–	NA	NA	NA	NA	NA	–
Jammu & Kashmir	M	103.15	105.13	102	−0.55	94.18	92.92	92.39	93.36	116.6	4.31
	F	NA	NA	NA	–	NA	NA	NA	NA	NA	–
Karnataka	M	44.95	45.51	46.8	2.01	45.72	43.74	45.77	45.74	54.11	3.81
	F	33.54	34.06	33.77	0.33	32.33	32.26	33.84	33.95	39.01	4.26
Kerala	M	143.16	141.56	141.54	−0.57	141.26	145.78	141.83	155.18	180.03	5.47
	F	100.89	104.01	109.43	4.06	110.84	113.52	104.82	115.05	128.62	3.10
Madhya Pradesh	M	37.77	36.88	35.45	−3.16	33.14	32.94	32.98	32.58	39.81	3.55
	F	31.92	31.17	30.34	−2.55	28.31	28.53	28.28	28.55	35.62	4.60

Odisha	M	46.18	46.06	46.4	2.35	45.69	44.73	45.16	47.52	60.62	6.25
	F	40.65	39.66	39.08	−1.97	38.17	36.79	37.82	40.42	54.32	7.99
Maharashtra	M	48.77	48.54	46.14	−2.77	45.39	45.6	45.82	43.74	53.06	2.70
	F	31.32	31.22	29.41	−3.15	28.7	29.5	29.38	28.59	34.95	3.62
Punjab	M	84.67	80.95	77.25	−4.58	73.65	77.16	78.28	78.43	95.63	5.38
	F	NA	NA	NA	–	NA	NA	NA	NA	NA	–
Rajasthan	M	70.38	66.79	61.31	−6.9	57.63	59.7	65.54	65.35	77.64	6.86
	F	61.21	59.82	54.62	−5.69	52.06	54.37	58.67	60.1	70.96	7.19
Tamil Nadu	M	71.46	73.2	74.29	1.94	74.92	75.32	77.33	80.83	102.78	7.02
	F	48.38	50.18	51.48	3.1	51.82	55.33	56.77	59.72	74.64	8.06
Uttar Pradesh	M	57.69	58.3	54.67	−2.68	51.9	53.28	56.47	57.7	69.23	6.55
	F	48.7	49.55	45.71	−3.16	42.85	44.33	46.5	46.58	56.11	5.88
West Bengal	M	51.33	49.85	51.42	0.08	50.8	50.51	50.41	47.77	56.19	1.45
	F	45.94	45.36	46.56	0.66	45.28	44.28	45.24	43.01	51.14	2.14
All-India	M	58.65	58.52	57.41	−1.06	55.58	55.84	57.52	58.11	69.59	4.89
	F	43.79	43.67	42.91	−1.01	41.49	42.16	43.54	44.35	52.93	5.37

Source: Based on *Indian Labour Journal*, 2004–5 to 2010–11.

Notes:

(1) *Implies base period 2003–4.

(2) Growth implies trend growth rate; real average wage is estimated by deflating nominal wage with consumer price index for agricultural labour, available from Labour Bureau, Ministry of Labour and employment.

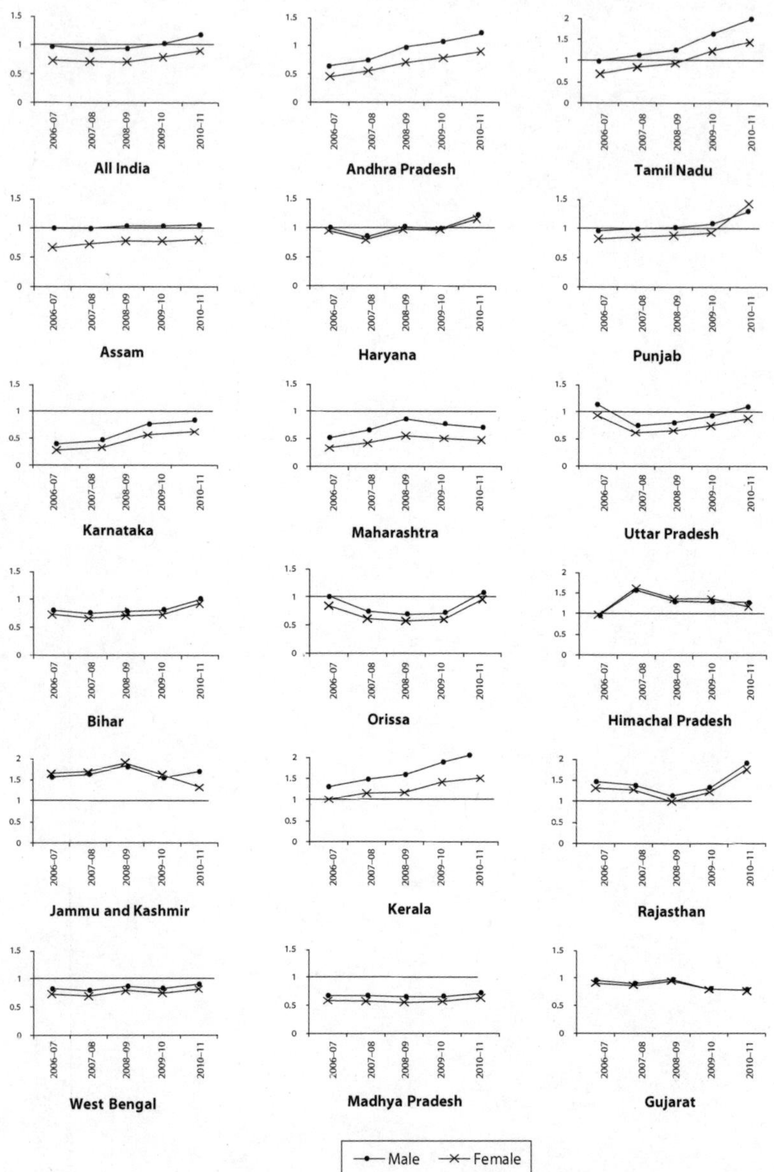

FIGURE 1.12 Trend of Rural NAUW Wage vis-à-vis NREG Wage

Source: Based on NREGA's official website: www.nrega.nic.in; and *Indian Labour Journal*, 2006–7 to 2010–11.

female respondents. It was pointed out that the NREG earnings improved food security in three ways: first, it enabled households to buy in large quantities, which often remained cheaper than buying on a daily basis; second, there had been a tilt towards diet-diversification from a cereal-dominated diet; and third, an improvement in access to credit, especially to meet food expenditures. In the case of Punjab, Gill *et al.* (2012) pointed out that the provision of additional employment under the NREGA to the SC landless families, especially during the lean seasons, had strengthened their livelihood security and protected them from the experience of poverty. Similarly, in the districts of Andhra Pradesh where the NREGA was better implemented, Reddy (2012) reported that due to enhanced earning, better functioning of PDS, and facilitation by self-help groups to buy foodgrains and other essential commodities in bulk, there was a complete turnaround in food deficit and hunger. But such experiences were not reported from regions where the NREG was inadequately implemented. Similarly, the Odisha experience reflected that the NREGA could not make much of a dent on poverty in the Sason Panchayat in Sambalpur District primarily due to the inadequate and erratic nature of employment, and irregular and delayed wage payments (Kumbhar, 2012).

In fact, the major routes by which the implementation of the NREGA could contribute to alleviating poverty had been the enhanced employment of women, inclusion of workers belonging to socially deprived communities, and construction of assets on the lands of poor families.

It would appear that owing to the in-built provisions relating to gender parity in wage rates and provision of worksite facilities, especially child care, there had been an enthusiastic participation by women in most, if not all, states. In addition, the perception of the NREG work as 'government work', with associated dignity and the absence of contractors, further stimulated the outcome. Various studies pointed out that the NREGA played an instrumental role in women's empowerment by opening up an entirely new avenue for paid employment by expansion of their choice set, even if limited, and the consequent reduction in economic dependence on others (Pankaj and Tankha, 2010). Based on the fieldwork in Kerala, Sudarshan *et al.* (2010) reported the upward revision of women unskilled (market) wages mainly due to the NREGA. Moreover, the enhanced earnings enabled women to send their children to school, buy them school uniforms and books, seek better healthcare, assist in repayment of small debts and the avoidance of demeaning and hazardous work (GBPSSI, 2009). In some cases, there had been an improvement in women's control over resources and the decision-making in spending of money. In places where scale of NREGA has been substantial, women bought productive assets with their earnings (Khera and Nayak, 2009).

Given the positive findings, there was further scope to bring women under the programme. However, as observed in our macro-level assessment, there were states which had not strictly followed the stipulated norm of 33 per cent participation for women. It was a reflection of numerous barriers such as tenacious social norms, presence of contractors, lack of child care facilities, SORs un-tuned as per women's needs, delayed payments and so on. GBPSSI (2009) also confirmed that the social dynamism in some of the states like Uttar Pradesh was such that the male relatives and gram functionaries showed resistance to women's participation; in certain cases, even their names were not written on job cards and some women, especially the single ones, were denied access to the programme.

Nonetheless, the implementation of the NREGA was instrumental in bringing workers from socially deprived castes into the ambit of the programme. The contribution of the NREGA in enhancing social inclusion was greatly acknowledged by a large number of studies (Mehrotra, 2008; and Mishra *et al.*, 2010). But, there was still further scope as these workers were not adequately included vis-à-vis their burden of poverty—an outcome much expected from a pro-poor programme.

There was still the prevalence of institutional bottlenecks. As reported by Kumbhar (2012) in the case of Sason Panchayat in Odisha, the process of issuing job cards remained biased and the card holders (generally belonging to the higher castes), with the connivance of officials, tried their best to keep the more economically challenged households without cards so as to extract commission by renting out the cards. The village-level politics in some cases acted as a formidable entry barrier. All this reflected nothing but the need for more socialy sensitive mechanisms for greater inclusion of the socially disadvantaged communities (Shariff, 2009). Another route by which the NREGA helped these sections of society was through the development of land belonging to marginalized communities.

Reddy (2012) reported that there was hardly any village in Andhra Pradesh where the NREG work on the lands of these marginalized sections was not undertaken.

In fact, the creation of assets under NREGA had been envisaged as one of the promising routes to sustainable development of rural India. State-level studies highlighted that the constructed assets had been productive in their nature and were expected to have a positive and sustainable impact on the growth of village economies where the NREGA had been implemented with some attention. Nonetheless, problems persisted in many cases. Lack of comprehensive and systematic planning in the selection of projects lowered the potential benefits of the scheme. Gill *et al.* (2012) pointed out that the selection of projects had remained largely ad hoc in nature. They related such an outcome to state's lack of experience in implementation of these mega schemes. Similarly, cases of mismanagement and the consequent leakages of resources had also been reported (Kumbhar, 2012).

There had been other associated problems of misreporting and corruption as highlighted by Joshi (2012) in the case of the Dangs district of Gujarat. Similarly Breman (2012), while examining the implementation of the NREGA in four villages of South Gujarat, reported that there had been *some* public work done under the NREGA—construction of a road—in only one of the villages, while there was an overall absence in others. Even in the limited project work undertaken in one village, there was a selective discrimination against *Halpatis* who were generally landless and earned their livelihoods from within the village. This study also highlighted the underlying practices of delay as well as under-payments, along with various other forms of rent-seeking and corruption by officials.

Curtailment of distress migration was another desirable outcome of the NREGA implementation. Gill *et al.* (2012), based on the experience of Punjab, which has significant dependence on migrant labour for both its agricultural and industrial operations, reported a decline in the arrival of migrant workers from poor states like Uttar Pradesh and Bihar. However, Joshi (2012) reported, based on his experience of the NREGA implementation in the tribal district of Dangs in Gujarat, that there had not been any perceptible decline in distress migration—to South Gujarat for sugarcane cutting—attributable to the NREGA because of inadequate implementation in this region. There had been, nonetheless, other factors such as the overall improvement in agricultural production, enhanced earnings due to overall increase in milk production and milk cooperatives, forest policy change permitting more earning to tribals from tree cutting etc., which emerged as the most probable reasons for decline in distress migration in the region. Reddy (2012) also did not find any evidence of distress migration in the case of Andhra Pradesh.

There have been some other related effects of NREGA implementation. The NREGA has played a large role in generating awareness among workers. Now workers at large are somewhat aware of the basic provisions of the Act, though there were still gaps, as pointed out by Kumbhar (2012) and Joshi (2012), through improper muster rolls, wrong job card entries, job demand and job card mismatch, non-receipt of unemployment allowance etc. in the cases of Odisha and Gujarat. Gill *et al.* (2012) reported that the NREGS had brought the workers together at one place and helped in fostering a community feeling among fellow workers, found to be discussing their common problems while recognizing the benefits of unity. But such was not the experience in Odisha as the workers reported no improvement in their bargaining power, primarily due to two reasons: first, most of the workers worked on job cards of others, thereby being excluded from the legal entitlement and, second, the non-continuity of work kept them scattered. In such a situation, even the feeble efforts of collective action got muffled by the elite panchayat officials (Kumbhar, 2012).

Besides enhancement of collective bargaining and strength, there has been an augmentation of workers' banking capabilities. With the introduction of the NREGA wage payments through banks, the NREG workers got introduced to banking operations. While they were assisted by intermediaries in certain cases, they remained, by and large, self-owners of their bank accounts which provided them a secure place for keeping money. They were found to be operating their own bank accounts, withdrawing money whenever needed, and saving the rest for their most pressing needs (Sudarshan *et al.*, 2010).

Amid all these positive outcomes, it was nonetheless difficult to deny the seriousness of the issue of wage payments. The procedure for calculating wages remained largely elusive with all sorts of measurement related problems, often linked with the piece-based method (Reddy, 2012). In the case of Rajasthan, it was pointed out that the payment was linked to the tasks completed and the workers were paid as per the simple formula of the value of work completed divided by the number of workers. It was disadvantageous and contributed to uncertainty on at least two counts: the first was related to the lack of information about the work that should be completed for earning the minimum wage, and the second emerged due to the fake entries on the muster rolls of persons who, in fact, were not present at the worksite (Sudarshan *et al.*, 2010). Similarly disappointing had been the inferences emerging from the group measurement experiment in the Jalor district of Rajasthan. It was reported that in the group measurement system, the workers could earn up to the limit of minimum wages whereas they often ended up with earning much below the minimum wages (Khera, 2011a).

Similarly, the issue of late wage payments had been perennial and pervasive, no matter what approach was used for distributing wages. This delay forced workers to opt for non-NREGA work, which was often oppressive and exploitative in nature (Kumbhar, 2012). The situation had been grim for single woman workers having access to no other form of social security. The delays in wage payments caused hardships to the workers who had to adopt low-paying or exploitative employment, which in some cases contributed to distress migration (Khera, 2011b). Nonetheless, the situation was somewhat better in a few states like Andhra Pradesh and Tamil Nadu, as wage payments were made with least time gaps (Reddy, 2012; and Khera and Muthiah, 2011). In fact, Andhra Pradesh took the issue of wage payments very seriously and pitched in effectively through systematic revision of 'schedule of rates' with proper work-time-motion studies, proper measurement, and the adoption of payment method through biometric smart card system operated by an independent agency (Reddy, 2012). However, the issue of wage payments remained a controversial and pressing one. There were even instances when lobbies of industrialists, farmers' unions (particularly a BKU group), and other local forces inimical to labour attempted to scuttle the move for raising the minimum wage applicable on NREG works (Gill *et al.*, 2012).

Another serious issue had been the limited generation of man-days under the programme. Despite being demand-led in nature, it turned out to be a supply led scheme. With an implicit 'top-down model,' this scheme could not effectively translate the entitlements into benefits. The access to employment, rather than being a right, remained conditional on the availability of work, which remained further dependent on various procedures like designing, requesting and sanctioning of work, and all this involved considerable period of time. Shortage of staff at various levels of NREGA implementation was another major roadblock in generation of adequate employment. The startling examples were Odisha and Gujarat, where the number of staff was too less to effectively implement the scheme. Dreze *et al.* (2011) reported that in Odisha, there was a severe shortage of staff from top to bottom. *Gram Rozgar Sewaks* and technical staff, such as junior engineers, often remained in short supply. Owing to this, there was no regular monitoring of works, which provided a temptation to rely on contractors to fill the gaps. Information asymmetry at various levels was another major factor that discouraged demand for work under the scheme (Joshi, 2012). Similarly, the wrong campaigning about the scheme (as in the case of Punjab), involvement of contractors (as in the case of Odisha), a nexus between politicians and bureaucrats (as in the case of Gujarat) were a few other factors that led to restricted demand under the scheme. Even in the better performing states like Himachal Pradesh and Tamil Nadu, understaffing emerged as the major debilitating factor that moderated NREGA outcomes considerably (Siddhartha and Vanaik, 2011; and Khera and Muthiah, 2011).

In four out of the five states focused on our study project (except Andhra Pradesh), it was found that the president of the village panchayat, often known as *Sarpanch*, played a large role in the effective implementation of the Act. The ability of the Sarpanch, in terms of his education and capacity to liaise with the officials, was found to be a major impetus, especially in the case of Punjab and Gujarat. It was also found that the Sarpanch and other elected officials often used their position to serve only their own people. Similarly, in states like Punjab, where the ruling SAD-BJP coalition was not very enthusiastic to effectively launch a programme sponsored by the Congress Party-led UPA Government at the national level, the rural politics dominated by big and medium-level farmers played a key role in slowing down the scheme. The absence of civil society organizations had been another debilitating factor in the poor performance in Punjab.

Contrasting was the experience of Andhra Pradesh, where despite the weakness of PRIs, the NREG could perform well. Tamil Nadu also provided a good example of a success story. With a long history of launching pro-poor programmes, the State could effectively launch this scheme for the welfare of its working masses. There has been an increase in the scale of employment, high share of women's employment, timely and corruption-free wage payments and the involvement of Gram Panchayats in the implementation of the scheme (Khera and Muthiah, 2011). Similarly, in Kerala the planning and implementation of the NREGA has been largely free from rent-seeking behaviour. The educated workforce have also demonstrated their capacity to deal with their bank accounts, as well as to work as groups organized by the Kudumbasree, instead of acting as individual workers. However, the problem of delayed payments due to a lengthy process was, again, a major source of worry for women workers. The indirect effects contributing to the empowerment of poor women have been a striking feature noted by the Kerala study.

***

Our assessment[24] of the implementation of the NREGA suggested that it has considerable potential for enhancing the livelihood security of the working poor in rural India. However, there were a number of issues that needed to be addressed for realization of its full potential.

First, the NREGA was limited in its design as well as implementation. The fact that the entitlement for manual work was limited to a maximum of 100 days per household would translate itself into around 60 days per annum per working member in a rural household. Ideally speaking, no such limit was really called for because the demand for work was confined to manual work that would attract only the poorer households. Even if a ceiling was needed on the grounds of availability of financial resources, it could have been applied as a state average which would have permitted provisioning of more employment days within state areas where the demand was higher.

Second, limited implementation resulting in about half the maximum permissible days of employment was a clear pointer to either a lack of strong political commitment, or weak implementation machinery, or a combination of both. Had these 100 days of employment been attained, it would have meant a transfer of income equivalent to one-fifth of the official poverty line to every participating household.

Third, one of the common complaints reported in most of the studies related to the delay in wage payment. Although it was known that workers participating in the NREG came from poorer households and did not have the required staying power to meet their daily expenses until their wages were received, the official machinery was not sensitive to this need. It was, therefore, imperative to reduce the delay between the completion of work and payment of wages. In this connection the idea of paying part of the wages as advance after completing a few days work needed to be seriously considered. Such a poor-friendly mechanism would augment a sense of trust among the participating workers on the system.

Fourth, various studies suggested that the NREGA had helped in capital formation in rural areas, howsoever small that might have been. Given the fact that 60 per cent of the expenditure under the NREGA was meant for wage payment, it would have been desirable to converge them with other rural capital formation projects, to realize a greater degree of synergy, thereby enhancing the process of capital formation, especially in the spheres of land and water resource management and development.

Fifth, there were advocates who did not see any merit in providing public employment, and instead argued for conditional cash transfers as a mechanism to not only increase income, but also enhance the reserve price of labour. However, various studies showed that the NREG had led to the creation of a number of tangible and intangible positive externalities, such as strengthening the Panchayat Raj, empowerment of rural workers, and realization of the potential for local level development.

Sixth, our assessment suggested that financial resources had not been a constraint in the implementation of the NREGA. What ought to be a concern was the slowing down of an otherwise historic initiative. Proper planning and availability of adequate staff was required at the Village, Block and District Panchayat levels for more effective implementation of the programme. By strengthening the tax collection system, it should be possible to channelize a much higher share of the budget of the Government of India to this programme than what was currently made available.

Seventh, we found that the political commitment at the state-level also was conspicuous by its absence. Although the NREG was a national programme sponsored by Government of India, there ought to have been enough flexibility to accommodate the specific characteristics and the context of different states, so that they could take ownership of the programme, leading to its more effective performance.

Last but not least, the NREGA had enabled the creation of an official machinery, working in conjunction with the Panchayati Raj system. Enhancing the capability of PRIs ought to have received special attention so that timely planning for project identification, selection and execution was put in place. Simultaneously, there should be a mechanism to not only provide, but also arrange for imparting training to the so-called unskilled manual workers. It was often not recognized that particular skills were required in works such as bunding, landscaping, designing and digging water bodies, canals and so on. Equally important were skills required for book-keeping and other organizational matters related to the execution of projects. Given the fact that a good proportion of workers were illiterate, or with very low levels of education, the NREG programme also provided opportunities for functional literacy classes, which could combine literacy with skill formation and upgradation.

If there was one conclusion that we needed to highlight, it would be the need to continue the programme with a greater degree of political commitment and effective implementation, given the pervasive nature of poverty and vulnerability among the working poor in rural India.

Notes

[1] Prior to the UPA-I initiative, there was a whole range of struggles faced by the working poor in India. However, the Bill to enact NREGA was introduced in the Lok Sabha on 21 December 2004. Following the criticisms for it being a dilution of UPA-I's National Common Minimum Programme promises, it was referred to the Standing Committee on Rural Development for a detailed scrutiny, and based on its recommendations, it got passed in both houses of Parliament on 23–24 August 2005. After getting President's assent on 5 September 2005, it was promulgated on 7 September 2005.

[2] On 1 April 2007, 113 districts were notified under this Act, and on May 1, 2007, an additional 17 districts of Uttar Pradesh were notified under this Act.

[3] There was a provision for advance application. The Act also provided for multiple applications by the same person, subject to the non-overlapping of the periods over which employment is sought.

[4] The employment programme under this Act mainly catered to the provision of wage employment. For promoting self-employment in rural areas, there was another programme called *Swaranjayanti Gram Swarozgar Yojna*.

[5] In case the number of children below the age of six years is five or more, the Act deputed one woman worker to look after the children; this women worker is paid the wage rate.

[6] Recognizing the availability of district-wise data about various indicators on a monthly basis, we've derived the annual aggregates by considering the financial year from 1 April to 31 March. We have also observed some discrepancies in data relating to man-days and wage payments for some districts. As we've corrected them in our estimates by taking into account respective

district's performance in preceding/succeeding months, our estimates may not match strictly with those reported by NREG website due to their being based on some incorrect district-wise figures.

[7] NCEUS stand for the 'National Commission for Enterprises in the Unorganized Sector'. This Commission was set up by the UPA-I Government on 20 September 2004 under the chairmanship of Prof. Arjun Sengupta to act as an advisory body for recommending measures on various aspects related to output and employment in India's informal economy.

[8] It is noteworthy that most of these states, except Assam, were generally left out of the analysis. But, we attempted to include them in this national-level assessment. We have used some proxies in a few places, where the respective data is not available.

[9] One billion = 100 crore.

[10] This amounts to 36.30 per cent of the total rural households in India.

[11] There are 29 states in India. However, Delhi and Goa were not considered due to non-implementation of NREGA in these states, as they did not have any rural segment.

[12] There were two motives for such phase-wise analysis. The first related to the fact of NREGA implementation in a phase-wise manner and the second assumed that the early start of some districts (like Phase-I districts) will provide them a better opportunity to derive maximum benefits out of NREGA due to their learning and adaptation to the Act vis-à-vis others starting subsequently.

[13] We focused on unskilled wage only. It was derived through the division of total unskilled wage expenditure with the total man-days generated during the time period under consideration.

[14] Concerns about the implicit exploitation in adopted SORs were also raised by Shah (2007), Mehrotra (2008), and Ambastha *et al.* (2008).

[15] Here, the household size was derived from the 2001 Census district level data on population and the number of households.

[16] With the acceptance of the recommendations of the Tendulkar Committee Report (GoI, 2009) by the Planning Commission, the New Poverty Line estimated at Rs 446.68 during 2004–5 has been in vogue. This poverty line was adjusted for subsequent years by taking into account the growth in CPIAL. Average level of this new rural poverty line for the last five year period was estimated at Rs 616.

[17] Some pro-women provisions were: i) priority to women workers by way of ensuring their 1/3rd share among total workers who have registered and requested for work; ii) absence of gender discrimination in remuneration mechanism; iii) provision of worksite facilities like crèche; iv) absence of contractors; and v) group work.

[18] At the time of writing this paper, the Census of India 2011 had not released population data for SC and ST. So, we estimated their population

based on their population share in 2001. Based on population growth rate for 2001–11 periods, the population for respective years is estimated.

[19] We did not go into further disaggregated analysis of this aspect at the district level (phase-wise analysis) because about 50 new districts were formed since 2001. This increase in the number of districts reflected merely the reconstitution of the districts as the geographical area of the state remained almost the same. As any data adjustment for phase-wise analysis might result in spurious estimates, we preferred to avoid the phase-wise analysis of this aspect.

[20] Hirway (2010b: 115) reported the incidence of poverty among ST population in Bihar, Tamil Nadu and Uttar Pradesh as 59.3, 47.3, and 42 per cent respectively.

[21] This could be due to the fact that the standard of living of the non-SC population in Punjab did not made this low wage public employment scheme attractive.

[22] From 2010–11 onwards, 'Rajiv Gandhi Sewa Kendra' was added to this list. For this analysis, we've merged it with others so as to maintain comparability with the 2009–10 period.

[23] In order to assess the implementation of NREGA at state-level, a total of five studies were commissioned under the project. These studies examined specifically the implementation of this pro-poor programme in the states of Punjab, Gujarat, Andhra Pradesh, Kerala, and Orissa.

[24] The authors would be happy to share a number of detailed tables giving the phase-wise performance of the NREG Scheme with those who are interested.

References

Ambasta, P. *et al.* 2008. 'Two Years of NREGA: The Road Ahead', *Economic and Political Weekly*, 43(8), 23 February: 41–50.

Breman, J. 2012. 'Poor Relief in Rural South Gujarat', Commissioned Study under CDS-ASSR Project on Social Security. Netherlands: the HiVOS.

Dreze, J. *et al.* 2011. 'Orissa: Ten Loopholes and the Silver Lining', in Reetika Khera (ed.), *The Battle for Employment Guarantee*, Ch. 10, pp. 187–200. New Delhi: Oxford University Press.

GBPSSI (2009), as quoted in NCEUS. 2009. *The Challenge of Employment in India: An Informal Economy Perspective*, Vol. I: Main Report. New Delhi: National Commission for Enterprises in the Unorganized Sector, Government of India.

Gill, S.S. *et al.* 2012. 'Functioning of NREGS in Punjab', Commissioned Study under CDS-ASSR Project on Social Security. Netherlands: the HiVOS.

GoI. 2008. *Eleventh Five Year Plan (2007–12)*, Vol. 2. New Delhi: Social Sector, Planning Commission, Government of India.

———. 2009. *Report of the Expert Group to Review the Methodology for Estimation of Poverty*. New Delhi: Planning Commission, Government of India.

Hanumantha, R. K. and P. Durgaprasad. 2008. 'Rural Poverty Alleviation in India: Contribution of NREGS', *IASSI Quarterly*, 27(1–2): 15–30.

Hirway, I. 2008. *NREGA: A Component of Full Employment Strategy in India*. Paper presented at International Conference on Employment Opportunities and Public Employment Policy in Globalising India, 3–5 April 2008, Trivandrum, Kerala, India.

Hirway, I. *et al.* 2010a. *Employment Guarantee Programme and Pro-Poor Growth: The Study of a Village in Gujarat*. New Delhi: Academic Foundation.

Hirway, I. 2010b. 'NREGA After Four Years: Building on Experiences to Move Ahead', *The Indian Journal of Labour Economics*, 53(1), January–March: 113–35.

IAMR. (undated). *All-India Report on Evaluation of NREGA: A Survey of Twenty Districts*. New Delhi: Institute of Applied Manpower Research.

ISWSD. 2008. *Impact of National Rural Employment Guarantee Scheme on the Living and Working Conditions of Women in Rural India*. New Delhi: Indian School of Women's Studies Development.

Jha, R. *et al.* 2008. 'Reviewing the National Rural Employment Guarantee Programme', *Economic and Political Weekly*, 43(11), 15 March: 44–8.

Joshi, S. 2012. 'Monitoring the Implementation of Social Security Schemes in Tribal Areas of Gujarat: With Reference to Dangs District', Commissioned Study under the CDS-ASSR Project on Social Security. Netherlands: the HiVOS.

Kapur, D. *et al.* 2008. 'More on Direct Cash Transfers', *Economic and Political Weekly*, 43(47), 22–28 November: 85–7.

Khera, R. 2011a. 'The Group Measurement Experiment in Jalore', in Reetika Khera (ed.), *The Battle for Employment Guarantee*, pp. 162–74. New Delhi: Oxford University Press.

———. 2011b. 'Wage Payments: Live without Pay', in Reetika Khera (ed.), *The Battle for Employment Guarantee*, pp. 250–6. New Delhi: Oxford University Press.

Khera, R. and K. Muthiah. 2011. 'Tamil Nadu: Slow and Steady', in Reetika Khera (ed.), *The Battle for Employment Guarantee*, pp. 233–8. New Delhi: Oxford University Press.

Khera, R. and N. Nayak. 2009. 'Women Workers and Perceptions of the National Rural Employment Guarantee Act', *Economic and Political Weekly*, 44(43), 24 October: 49–57.

Kumar *et al.* 2011. 'Employment Guarantee and Its Environmental Impact: Are the Claims Valid', *Economic and Political Weekly*, 46(20), 20 August: 69–71.

Kumbhar, R. K. 2012. 'Structural Legacy, Inefficacy and Weakening Social Securities in Odisha: A Study of NREG in a Panchayat', Commissioned Study under CDS-ASSR Project on Social Security. Netherlands: The HiVOS.

Labour Bureau. 2006–11. *Consumer Price Index for Agricultural Labour*. New Delhi: Labour Bureau, Ministry of Labour, Government of India.

Mehrotra, S. 2008. 'NREG Two Years On: Where Do We Go From Here?' *Economic and Political Weekly*, 43(31), 2 August: 27–35.

Mishra, P., B. Behera, and N. C. Nayak. 2010. 'A Development Delivery Institution for the Tribal Communities: Experience of the National Rural Employment Guarantee Scheme in India', *Development Policy Review*, 28(4): 457–79.

Narayanan, S. 2008. 'Employment Guarantee, Women's Work and Childcare', *Economic and Political Weekly*, 43(9), 1 March: 10–13.

NCEUS. 2009. *The Challenge of Employment in India: An Informal Economy Perspective*, Vol. I: Main Report. New Delhi: National Commission for Enterprises in the Unorganised Sector, Government of India.

Pankaj, A. and R. Tankha. 2010. 'Empowerment Effects of the NREGS on Women Workers: A Study in Four States', *Economic and Political Weekly*, 45(30), 24 July: 45–55.

Raabe, K. *et al.* 2010. *How to Overcome the Governance Challenges of Implementing NREGA Insights from Bihar Using Process-Influence Mapping*. IFPRI discussion paper 00963, Development Strategy and Governance Division, International Food Policy Research Institute.

Reddy, D.N. 2012. 'Functioning of National Rural Employment Guarantee Scheme (NREGS) in Andhra Pradesh', Commissioned Study under CDS-ASSR Project on Social Security. Netherlands: The HiVOS.

Reddy, D.N. *et al.* 2010. 'National Rural Employment Guarantee as Social Protection', *IDS Bulletin*, 41(4), July: 63–76.

Shah, M. 2007. 'Employment Guarantee, Civil Society and Indian Democracy', *Economic and Political Weekly*, 42(45/46): 43–51.

Shariff, A. 2009. 'Assessment of Outreach and Benefits of National Rural Employment Guarantee Scheme of India', *The Indian Journal of Labour Economics*, 52(2), April–June: 243–68.

Siddhartha and A. Vanaik. 2011. 'Himachal Pradesh: Assessment and Outlook', in Reetika Khera (ed.), *The Battle for Employment Guarantee*, pp. 201–19. New Delhi: Oxford University Press.

Singh, S.P. and D.K. Nauriyal. 2009. *System and Process Review and Impact Assessment of NREGS in the State of Uttrakhand*. Roorkee: Indian Institute of Technology.

Sudarshan, R.M. *et al.* 2010. 'Women's Participation in the NREGA: Some Observations from Fieldwork in Himachal Pradesh, Kerala and Rajasthan', *IDS Bulletin*, 41(4), July: 77–83.

Tiwari *et al.* 2011. 'MGNREGA for Environmental Service Enhancement and Vulnerability Reduction: Rapid Appraisal in Chitradurga District, Karnataka', *Economic and Political Weekly*, 46(20), 14 May: 39–47.

World Bank. 2011. *Social Protection for a Changing India*, Vol. I. Washington D.C.: The World Bank.

2 NATIONAL HEALTH INSURANCE FOR THE POOR

A REVIEW OF THE IMPLEMENTATION OF RSBY

K.P. Kannan and *Varinder Jain*

In December 2008, the Indian Parliament passed a legislation called the Unorganized Workers Social Security Bill that mandated the Central Government to 'formulate, from time to time, suitable welfare schemes for unorganized workers'. As part of this legislation, a schedule was attached that included two new schemes; one, the Rashtriya Swasthya Bima Yojana (national health insurance scheme), and the other, Aam Aadmi Bima Yojana (life insurance for the common man). In this chapter, we undertake a review of the former, known by its acronym RSBY. While this particular scheme constitutes the single largest contingent social security measure initiated so far by the Government of India, it is important to keep in mind the background and the circumstances under which such a scheme was introduced. This we do very briefly.

The incumbent political coalition in power at the national level in India, called the United Progressive Alliance (UPA), led by the Indian National Congress, contested the general election of 2004 (when it was in opposition) with an election manifesto that promised a number of welfare measures to India's *aam aadmi* (common people) against the backdrop of the campaign by the then incumbent political coalition led by the Bhartiya Janata Party (BJP), proclaiming a 'shining India' with its high rate of aggregate economic growth. The election manifesto of the UPA expressed its resolve as follows:

> The UPA government is firmly committed to ensure the welfare and well-being of all workers, particularly those in the unorganised sector who constitute 93 per cent of our workforce. Social security, health insurance and other schemes for such workers like weavers, handloom workers, fishermen and fisherwomen, toddy tappers, leather workers, plantation labour, beedi workers, etc. will be expanded.

As a sequel to its promise, the newly elected UPA Government constituted a national commission called the National Commission for Enterprises in the Unorganized Sector (NCEUS) to review and recommend measures for growth and development of the unorganized sector along with a 'review [of] the social security system available for labour in the informal sector, and make recommendations for expanding their coverage'. The NCEUS, in its first report, *Social Security for Unorganised Workers* (2006), recommended a national minimum social security (NMSS) for the 300 million plus unorganized workers. This was followed by another report, *Conditions of Work and Promotion of Livelihoods in the Unorganised Sector* (2007), wherein, apart from the NMSS, a national minimum wage and a national legislation on minimum conditions of work were also recommended. The idea was to provide a 'social floor' below which no worker should be allowed to fall, thus providing a modicum of security to the country's *aam aadmi*, who were estimated at 76 per cent of the population and classified as poor and vulnerable.[1] A draft bill was also provided to the Government.

A Parliamentary Standing Committee, while examining a Government draft bill, not only endorsed the proposed NMSS recommended by the NCEUS, but went to the extent of including the 'unpaid family labour' estimated at close to 90 million workers (mostly women), and also suggested that no contribution should be sought from the workers besides a nominal registration fee. To cut a long story short, none of these recommendations, including that of the Parliamentary Standing Committee, was accepted by the UPA-led Government and instead it got its own version of the bill passed by parliament. By doing so, the Government opted for a piecemeal approach to the fundamental problem of lack of social security among the unorganized sector workers in India, accounting for 86 per cent of the country's workforce.[2] By limiting eligibility, the Government did not accept the principle of universal coverage and the need for suitable organizational systems as well as a dedicated fund for the purpose. Instead, the Unorganized Workers Social Security Act (UWSSA) of 2008 provided a list of the schemes that the Government intended to implement. Except two schemes mentioned earlier, all the others were existing schemes with limited coverage applicable to either occupation-specific or age-specific groups. Elsewhere, one of us has dealt with this background in some detail.[3]

It is important to keep in mind this background as one may lose sight of the larger picture of poverty and vulnerability in an otherwise fast growing India, and the long road that it has to traverse if the country has to ensure a measure of social security to its predominantly working, poor population. Despite such a formidable challenge, one should not mistake the enthusiasm of the poorer sections of the population to welcome any measure, however limited and piecemeal in nature, which could alleviate their situation of poverty and vulnerability. This scheme had been launched by the Government of India in 2007, although the national legislation came about only towards the end of 2008. What this did was give the scheme a legislative backing through its inclusion in the schedule attached to the Act.

The RSBY has been welcomed by the state governments since the idea of social security to the poor is an attractive one from an electoral point of view. As the name suggests, the scheme is an insurance cover against sickness. The attractive features of the scheme ensured that:

(i) it gave insurance cover not only to the person in whose name the registration was done, but also to his/her family, up to a maximum of five members;
(ii) the beneficiary did not need to pay any premium, since that would be provided by the central and state governments in the ratio of 75 : 25;[4]
(iii) it provided cashless insurance cover up to Rs 30,000 per annum on a family floater basis; and
(iv) it took care of migration through the smart card system, which would entitle the beneficiary to avail hospital services across the country.

However, some limiting features of this scheme cast serious doubts on the objective of 'inclusion' propounded by the Government. It is important to keep them in mind. These include:

(i) the RSBY is limited to those families that are officially recognized as Below Poverty Line (BPL) families by the Government of India;
(ii) given an average family size of around five, the per capita insurance cover works out to be Rs 6,000, which is equivalent to recently revised per capita annual poverty line accepted by the Government of India;

(iii) the insurance cover is only available for in-patient treatment, thus excluding a large number of out-patient treatment frequently required by the working poor due to their poor working and living environments; and
(iv) the insurance cover is valid only in empanelled hospitals, which are few in number and thereby reveal a very low hospital-card holder ratio.

These limiting features are important from the perspective of the working poor. The eligibility being limited to BPL households means that only 73.32 million households or 32.20 per cent out of a total of 227.72 million households would be eligible as per the current official poverty line. This means that only the 'very poor' within the larger universe of poor and vulnerable would be eligible for coverage. Thus, while there is some 'inclusion' due to the introduction of this scheme, there is an equal proportion of 'exclusion'. A small number of state governments, mostly in the south, have sought to overcome this by extending coverage on their own, which will be highlighted later in this volume. The other major limiting factor is the exclusion of out-patient treatment as the most poor working families are prone to diseases of poverty, many of which require only out-patient treatment. Timely out-patient treatment is vital in preventing such cases from developing into in-patient treatment scenarios, thus saving not only on the insurance cover, but also on the wages and incomes forgone due to lost ability to perform work. As for the empanelment of hospitals, there are both advantages and disadvantages. Empanelment is based on the facilities and capacity of the hospitals, irrespective of whether they belong to the public or private sector. Given the paucity of reasonably functioning health care institutions, especially in rural areas, in many states the hospitals empanelled are few and far between. As we shall see later, this acts as a constraint on the ability of the working poor to access the services of hospitals within reasonable distance.

COVERAGE IN A NUTSHELL

The RSBY launched on 2 October 2007 became operational only from the financial year beginning with April 2008. Out of a total of 29 states and 6 Union Territories, 25 states and 1 Union Territory are implementing this scheme at present. A district-wise perusal points out that out of a total of 505 districts (in the RSBY implementing states),[5] 82.4 per cent or 416 districts have been covered so far (March 2012). But the real test of coverage lies in the number of people actually enrolled. Out of the estimated 66.80 million officially poor households, 28.20 million have been issued the smart cards (as of March 2012). It works out to 42.22 per cent coverage within a period of about four years.

DESIGN FEATURES

The salient features to be noted are the following:

1. The scheme is implemented by the respective state governments through a designated nodal agency.
2. The state government concerned enters into an agreement with an insurance company to provide the health insurance cover.
3. Eligible persons are registered under the scheme by way of issuing of a smart card that stores information of family members, subject to a maximum of five persons. Being based on a biometric system, such smart cards minimize possible fraudulent practices.
4. The scheme is based on a cashless insurance cover for which Third Party Administrators (TPAs) are appointed by the insurance companies to verify the rates charged by the hospitals.
5. The empanelled hospitals belong to both public and private sectors. Of course, there is always the possibility of the problem of moral hazard, especially for private hospitals whose objective is to maximize profits.

Along with all pre-existing diseases, the RSBY covers more than 700 in-patient procedures related to 15 disease categories, thus, covering most of the diseases (with least exclusions) (see Box 2.1). The health benefits under this scheme cover all expenses related to hospitalization, including maternity benefit and such services of a surgical nature which can be provided on a day-care basis.[6] It provides for pre- and post-hospitalization expenses for one day prior, and five days post-hospitalization. It also provides for transport allowance (with a maximum limit of Rs 100 per visit),

Box 2.1 Other Prominent Features of RSBY

Least formalities at initial end: The RSBY is an immaculately designed scheme having least formalities at the initial stage. The smart card issued to the beneficiary household, being biometric in nature, includes all relevant information about the beneficiary members, which reduces the possibilities of fraud and malpractices to a large extent.

Business model: This scheme is conceived as a business model by appropriately keeping in mind the issues of competence and sustainability. It is based on the principle of public-private partnership. In fact, this is for the first time that the government has collaborated on such a large-scale with the private sector to provide health insurance cover to the poor masses. Besides the Central Government, this scheme actively involves the state governments, who besides other roles, appoint nodal agencies to facilitate the implementation of the scheme. The nodal agency further selects the insurance company through the procedure of competitive bidding.

No age limit: This scheme is free from age limit as it automatically covers senior citizens. It also covers infants and new-born babies with their mothers (for the remaining policy period).

National coverage: This smart card is valid throughout the country in any of the network hospitals. Provision in the smart card facilitates portability of benefits which, in effect, alleviates the constraint of existing medical conditions and the beneficiary is free to make the choice of hospital. Besides providing the beneficiary a choice of hospital, the possibility of operability across states enhances its utility for the migrant workers. It needs to be noted that unlike earlier government-sponsored schemes where the beneficiary did not have the option to select the service delivery point, the RSBY empowers the beneficiary to choose hospitals from a list of network hospitals (that includes private hospitals as well) to seek medical treatment. It also has the provision for the issuing of split card in which an additional card is provided to worker which he/she can carry along with at the workplace.

Source: Authors (on the basis of information from official sources).

within an overall limit of Rs 1,000 per annum, to be paid out of the insured amount.

EXPANDED ELIGIBILITY: OVERLAPPING AND AD HOC

One of the major problems that the implementers of the RSBY face is the absence of clear eligibility. Eligibility has been shifted from time to time and has, *inter alia*, resulted in overlapping. To begin with, in 2007, eligibility was based on the poverty status—official BPL status to be precise. Two years later, in 2009, the scheme was extended to construction workers. The following year, in 2010, the eligibility to enrol in the RSBY was extended to rural workers who worked at least 15 days under the National Rural Employment Guarantee Scheme (NREGS). Simultaneously it was also extended to a sub-set of three groups of informal workers. These are 'to all licensed railway porters, vendors, and hawkers who are from Unorganized Sector *and are socially challenged* (emphasis added)' (Budget Speech of the Railway Minister, 24 February 2010: 14). While this gave the impression of extension of the RSBY to each of these segments of informal workers, it was limited to the socially challenged. However, in October 2010, the Government of India decided to extend the eligibility to street vendors as well (PIB, 2010). It also decided to extend the scheme to the accredited social health activists called ASHA workers,[7] and by the end of 2010, the RSBY was also extended to domestic workers.

It needs to be noted that the workers in many of these categories also belong to BPL families, and hence their further 'inclusion' has no practical meaning. The real beneficiaries are those who would not have qualified under the 'official BPL' standards, but are nevertheless poor and vulnerable if one goes by the definition of the NCEUS. In some cases, there could be beneficiaries who may not be either 'officially poor' or 'poor and vulnerable', but being informal workers—a qualified plumber or electrician—they could qualify for inclusion under this eligibility criteria. What we find, therefore, is a plethora of eligibility criteria and a process of selective inclusion without a consistent logic or even a political reasoning. On the inclusion of domestic workers, the problem of a lack of proper identification could pose itself as a major hurdle unlike other categories that might have some valid identification such as membership of Construction Welfare Board, railway licence for porters, municipal identification for street vendors, job cards or identity cards for NREGS workers and ASHA workers. One is, therefore, left to wonder whether there is any underlying logic in the extension, either in terms of eligibility criteria, or in the sequencing of groups of workers. It is hard to desist from the view that this has been more a case of ad-hoc decision-making on a crucial subject of extending social security than one borne out of a consistent planning.

OPERATIONALIZATION OF THE RSBY

The scheme, as it is designed at present, has a number of stakeholders. At the top is the Government of India, represented by the Ministry of Labour and Employment, followed by the state governments represented by a nodal agency. The other stakeholders are the insurance companies, empanelled hospitals, TPAs, and finally, the enrolled members in the scheme. Depending on state level policies, local government institutions such as the Panchayati Raj institutions, especially at the village level, have also emerged as indirect stakeholders, especially in assisting the potential members to access the scheme.

A pictorial representation given in Figure 2.1 provides an idea of the main stakeholders in the scheme. The central government, which introduced it as a national scheme, decides on various parameters and guidelines like benefits package, empanelment criteria, BPL criteria, setting up of rate schedules for services and reimbursement rates, and any other policy-related issues. It also facilitates overseeing all operations, and tracking and monitoring of information at the national level. It bears the major financial burden and provides the financing of annual premium on a shared basis between with the state government

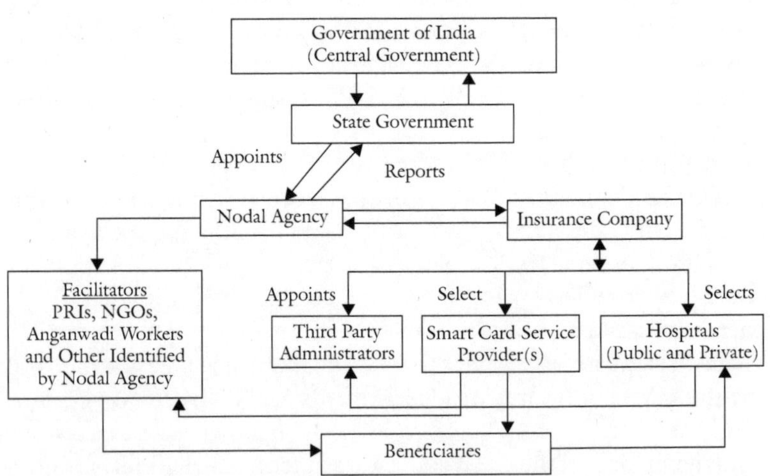

FIGURE 2.1 Schematic Presentation of the RSBY's Operationalization Process

Source: Authors.

concerned in the ratio of 75 : 25, except for special category seven states of the North East and Jammu & Kashmir for whom the ratio is 90 : 10. The maximum annual premium for the central government is fixed at Rs 750 per beneficiary. The central government's share of premium is released on the basis of number of smart cards issued. It also bears the cost of smart cards at the rate of Rs 60 per card.

At the next tier comes the concerned state government, which, if interested in implementing the scheme, commits the payment of its due share of annual premium, and any additional premium beyond the stipulated Centre-State ratio. It sets up an inter-departmental task force consisting of at least the Labour, Health, and Rural Development Ministries of the state. It also sets up an independent state nodal agency (SNA) for implementation of the scheme. As per guidelines, this must be a separate legal entity, under the control of the state government. It decides upon the number and identification of districts to be covered.

The nodal agency, which constitutes the third tier (though within government), prepares the BPL data in a prescribed format in conformity with the Planning Commission specifications for each project district. After getting the internal consistency check from the Government of India, it is allowed to advertise tenders for selection of insurance companies (both public and private) for each of the identified districts. It constitutes a committee for technical and financial bid evaluation and, following a process of competitive bidding, selects an insurance provider. It can select different insurance providers for different districts. Besides managing the contract with the insurance companies, it assists them in the enrolment of beneficiaries. It tracks and monitors utilization of resources, keeps record of patient information, and submits updates of the same to the central government for the national database.

Table 2.1 reveals that the Department of Labour has been the nodal agency in 44 per cent of the RSBY implementing states. The National Rural Health Mission and the Department of Health and Family Welfare have been the nodal agency for another 24 per cent of the states. In a few states, the Department of Rural Development and the Directorate ESI also remained the nodal agency for RSBY implementation. A separate nodal agency has been created in only two states—Himachal Pradesh and Mizoram.

At the fourth tier of the scheme is the insurance company which selects the empanelled hospitals and gets them approved by the nodal

TABLE 2.1 Nodal Agency for RSBY Implementation

Names of States	*Number of States*	*Nodal Agency*
Delhi, Goa, Jharkhand, Karnataka, Kerala, Maharashtra, Manipur, Nagaland, Odisha, Tamil Nadu, Tripura	11	Department of Labour
Arunachal Pradesh, Uttar Pradesh	2	Department of Rural Development
Assam, Uttarakhand	2	National Rural Health Mission
Bihar, Haryana, West Bengal	3	Directorate ESI
Chhattisgarh, Gujarat, Meghalaya, Punjab	4	Department of Health and Family Welfare
Jammu & Kashmir	1	Directorate of Family Welfare
Himachal Pradesh	1	HP Swasthya Bima Yojana Society
Mizoram	1	Mizoram State Health Care Society
All States	25	

Source: Based on RSBY's official website: www.rsby.gov.in.

agency (as per central guidelines). It sets up call centres, mobile enrolment stations, and kiosks to reach potential beneficiaries. It issues them smart cards with a validity of one year[8] and receives the annual premium (contributed by both the centre and state) from the nodal agency according to the number of smart cards issued. It processes claims and makes payments to the empanelled hospitals. It also monitors district-level utilization and patient information, and sends updates of the same to the nodal agency.

At the fifth tier comes the empanelled hospital whose prime responsibility is delivery of service. It has to provide quality service, charge for the treatment, and be transparent in transaction. It must not indulge in any malpractice as by doing so, it may face de-empanelment.[9] At the time of discharge, it must also provide the patient the stipulated amount towards transport.

Besides this five-tier operationalization of the scheme, a key feature related to the implementation of RSBY is the use of ICT services on such a large-scale for the first time. The adoption of technology has helped in making this scheme fool-proof to a large extent. In order to ensure that the card is not misused, the biometric data of beneficiaries is stored in the smart card. When a beneficiary visits the hospital, his finger print is matched through biometric devices installed in the hospital prior to the admission of patient for treatment. Similarly, in order to ensure that only the authorized persons record the transactions at the hospital, hospital authority cards are issued to the staff assigned to the task.

REGIONAL VARIATIONS

Given the fact that the subject of social security is included in the Concurrent List of the Indian Constitution, both the Union and state governments have the power to legislate and implement schemes as per such legislations. While a national legislation will supersede an existing state legislation, the state can go beyond the scope of the national legislation, if it so desires. As in many other cases, in the case of the RSBY as well, there are some state-level variations in both the scope and manner of implementation. As of now, two implementation models have emerged. One relates to those states where the national scheme has been extended to provide cover to a larger universe of poor and working poor households as along with enhanced insurance cover. Some states, such as Kerala, have extended the scheme to non-poor households in what is referred to as the inclusive model, provided such households pay the prescribed premium. In contrast, states where the scheme is implemented within the parameters set by the Government of India's RSBY are referred to as limited inclusion model. However, there are a few states that have not yet shown any willingness to even implement the centre-sponsored RSBY. The details are given in Table 2.2.

Given the political willingness of four states—Kerala, Andhra Pradesh, Tamil Nadu and Himachal Pradesh—to enlarge the scope and/or benefits of the national health insurance scheme, it is pertinent to briefly describe the main features of their respective schemes. These are the states that follow what we call the 'inclusive model' as far as the implementation of the RSBY is concerned.

Table 2.2 Implementation of RSBY across Indian States (as of December 2011)

State Type	*State Name*	*RSBY Details*
Extended RSBY	Kerala	In addition to Central Guidelines State BPL list is used; Extended to Above Poverty Line (APL) and other selected non-BPL Families; additional benefit of Rs 70,000 for specific diseases.
	Andhra Pradesh	State runs its own health insurance scheme, namely Rajiv Aarogyasri Yojana covering 85 per cent of the population.
	Tamil Nadu	Extended to welfare boards; Insurance benefit of Rs 1 lakh for four years.
	Himachal Pradesh	Additional insurance cover of Rs 1.71 lakh for critical care is provided by topping-up premium.
	Haryana	State BPL list is used which covers a higher proportion of population than the Government of India.
RSBY	Arunachal Pradesh, Assam, Bihar, Chhattisgarh, Delhi, Goa, Gujarat, Jammu & Kashmir, Jharkhand, Karnataka, Maharashtra, Manipur, Meghalaya, Mizoram, Nagaland, Odisha, Punjab, Tripura, Uttar Pradesh, Uttarakhand, West Bengal	In terms of scope and benefits, the RSBY is implemented as per Central Government's guidelines.
	Rajasthan	Introduced but later on discontinued in the wake of its own *Mukhya Mantri Jeevan Raksha Kosh*.
	Madhya Pradesh, Sikkim	Scheme not introduced yet.

Source: Based on RSBY Tender Documents (2010–11) of various state governments.

Kerala

Kerala has perhaps emerged as a pioneer state in extending the scope of the RSBY beyond central guidelines. It has not limited RSBY benefits to the 11.79 lakh BPL families (as per Planning Commission estimates); rather, it extended its coverage to another 10 lakh families identified by the state government—the premium for the latter is paid by the state. Moreover, the state has also allowed the extension of these benefits to APL (above poverty line) families, provided they bear the entire premium amount. In the second year of RSBY implementation, the state, in addition to BPL families, extended the coverage of the scheme to (i) SC/ST families, (ii) fishermen families, (iii) *Ashraya* families,[10] (iv) agricultural workers, (v) all workers belonging to beedi, handloom, coir, khadi, bamboo, kattuvalli, small plantations, and other unorganized sectors, (vi) cashew workers (pensioners), (vii) *anganwadi* workers and helpers, (viii) tailoring workers, (ix) Pensioners of building and other construction workers' welfare board, Headload Workers Welfare Board, Kerala Motor Workers Welfare Board and Kerala Abkari Workers Welfare Board, (x) NREG workers (with at least 15 days of work under the scheme), (xi) ASHA workers, and (xii) domestic workers. In terms of benefits as well, Kerala State has made an addition to central guidelines. Till 30 November 2010, it limited the RSBY benefits to Rs 30,000; but from 1 December 2010 onwards, it has provided an additional benefit of Rs 70,000 to RSBY beneficiaries for treatment of serious diseases related to kidney, heart, cancer etc., under a scheme called Comprehensive Health Insurance Scheme (CHIS) Plus. As in the case of the Union Government, the eligibility here is also an overlapping one in most cases, along with a non-overlapping one of being a worker in the unorganized sector, without any reference to his/her poverty status.

Andhra Pradesh

Rajiv Aarogyasri Yojana is an Andhra Pradesh state government scheme initiated on 1 April 2007, in a phase-wise manner, to treat critical medical conditions involving hospitalization among poor households (holders of White, Annapoorna and Anthyodaya Anna Yojana Card).[11] Under this scheme, the state government pays the premium to insurance companies, which in turn pay the medical bills for treatment thus sought at empanelled hospitals. It covers around

85 per cent of the population. In comparison to the RSBY, it has many interesting features like (i) it does not provide any separate card; rather it treats the 'White Card' as the insurance card; (ii) it is not restricted entitlement to five members in a family; rather all the members whose name and photo appear on the card are eligible under this scheme; (iii) the list of diseases covered is quite large; (iv) annual health insurance benefit per family goes up to Rs 1.50 lakh, and it provides an additional buffer of Rs 50,000 to take care of expenses exceeding the original sum.

Tamil Nadu

In keeping with the populist political image of the state, the RSBY scheme was launched in Tamil Nadu on 23 July 2009 under the title, 'Chief Minister Kalaignar [The Learned CM's] Insurance Scheme for Life Saving Treatments'. A very prominent feature that distinguishes this scheme from the RSBY implemented elsewhere is that this scheme was implemented across the entire state in one go.[12] By this step, the state facilitated the process for all deserving families to avail the benefits of the health insurance scheme from the very first day without any inter-district disparity in terms of waiting period, which is usually the case with other states where the RSBY is implemented in a phase-wise manner. The second distinguishing feature from the RSBY is related to its provision for high-cost treatments. Overall, it provides specialist treatment for 51 life threatening diseases, classified under 14 sub-headings, namely, (i) cardiology and cardiothoracic surgery, (ii) oncology, (iii) nephrology/urology, (iv) neurology and neurosurgery, (v) orthopaedic surgery, (vi) ophthalmology, (vii) vascular surgery, (viii) gastroenterology, (ix) plastic surgery, (x) ENT, (xi) gynaecology, (xii) thoracic, (xiii) haematology, and (xiv) others. It identifies more than 600 surgical procedures and treatments. The third feature is related to the provision of emergency or critical care, with eligibility proof to be submitted within 48 hours. Any family with an annual income below Rs 72,000 can become a beneficiary of this scheme. It is also open to unorganized sector workers, belonging to 25 Welfare Boards. Under this scheme, each eligible family gets the insurance benefit of up to Rs 1 lakh for a period of four years. One may opine that as per the RSBY, the total benefit over the four years would amount to Rs 1.20 lakh as compared to Rs 1 lakh under this scheme. That impression is partly mistaken, as by this scheme, the beneficiary is enabled to seek tertiary care, demanding huge resources, which is not an option under the usual RSBY.

With the change of government in June 2011, whereby the hitherto opposition party—the All India Anna Dravida Munnetra Kazhakam (AIADMK)—came to power, a new version of the health insurance scheme emerged. Tamil Nadu Chief Minister, Ms Jayalalithaa announced an improved health insurance cover in July 2011, under which a family can seek a maximum benefit of Rs 4 lakh in four years. The list of diseases covered also expanded from 642 to 950. It also contains provision of Rs 1.50 lakh for some specific diseases, besides covering expenses on certain tests, both prior to and after surgery. Moreover, it seeks to strengthen the capacity of public hospitals by way of creating special wards.

Himachal Pradesh

Himachal Pradesh is another state where the RSBY was introduced across the entire state in a single phase, between February–May 2010. With an aim to benefit around 2.98 lakh BPL families, the state extended the limit to Rs 1.75 lakh, in addition to the central guideline of Rs 30,000 insurance cover, by topping-up the premium and bearing the cost of the entire premium (GoHP, 2010).

VARIATIONS IN COVERAGE

By the end of March 2012, 26 (out of 29) states successfully provided health insurance cover to its poor population. Among these states, Andhra Pradesh took up this initiative on its own by launching its state-run scheme, namely, Rajiv Aarogyasri Yojana (Rajiv Health Welfare Scheme), named after the late Prime Minister, Rajiv Gandhi. All other states (25), in addition to the Union Territory of Chandigarh, followed the Union Government's initiative (in the form of the RSBY) on the provision of health insurance cover to their poor population. Yet, three States—Rajasthan, Madhya Pradesh, and Sikkim—are yet to follow suit. In fact, Rajasthan started implementing this scheme during the first half of 2008 in the form of Rajasthan Swasthya Bima Yojana and Swasthya Bima Yojana through the Ministry of Labour, GoI and the State Plan and NRHM funds respectively. Based on the experience that 'in the absence of adequate private accredited institutions, health insurance through a private insurer is likely to result in very poor number of claims against the premium transferred' (GoR, 2010). So, it launched the scheme on 1 January 2009, as Mukhya Mantri BPL Jeevan Raksha Kosh, with direct funding to Medicare Relief Societies of Public Health Institutions. Under this scheme, free OPD and IPD care is provided to BPL families. Moreover, the state government provides assistance to poor families with an annual income below Rs 40,000, for the treatment of serious diseases related to the heart, kidney, cancer, etc. The health benefits are limited to either 40 per cent of the total cost or Rs 60,000, whichever is higher—it is further extendable, subject to the Chief Minister's approval.

On the question of extent of coverage, what we find is a high degree of variation in coverage across the states, both in terms of districts as well as eligible persons and households. These and related statistics are provided in Table 2.3. Some explanation is called for in interpreting these calculations. As evident in Table 2.3, only 10 out of 22 states have implemented the scheme in all districts. The reluctance of a majority of the states to give full spatial coverage is difficult to understand, as there is no policy—unlike in the case of implementation of the National Rural Employment Guarantee Act, 2005—to implement the RSBY in a phased manner. Except the states of Jharkhand, Maharashtra, Nagaland, and Uttarakhand, which are close to giving full spatial coverage, the remaining eight states have a long way to go as per information available up to March 2012.

But a more important indicator of coverage is the number of persons and households who have been registered with the issuance of smart cards for use under the scheme. In the ten states where the spatial coverage is full, the performance of all, except Punjab, vary from 36 per cent to about 200 per cent of estimated poor households as per the poverty estimate released by the Planning Commission recently (GoI, 2012). The fact that Himachal Pradesh and Kerala show more than 100 per cent coverage means the inclusion of poor households not recognized by the Government of India, but by the respective state governments as well as some other categories (workers in the unorganized sector) who may not be officially recognized as poor by either the centre or state governments. Nagaland and Tripura also show a similar pattern owing to lack of further information, it is difficult to comment further.

With partial spatial coverage, five states—Jharkhand, Arunachal Pradesh, Meghalaya, Uttarakhand, and West Bengal—have more than 50

TABLE 2.3 Percentage Coverage under the RSBY across States (as of March 2012)

	RSBY Covered Districts out of Total Districts (%)	*Number of Cards Issued (in '000)*	*HCR*		*Total Poor Household (in '000)*		*Cards Issued as % of Total Poor Households (3 as % of 6 and 7)*	
		March 2012	*2004–5*	*2009–10*	*2004–5*	*2009–10*	*2004–5*	*2009–10*
1	2	3	4	5	6	7	8	9
		States with Overall District Coverage						
Bihar	38/38 (100)	7,184.46	54.4	53.5	8,041.22	8,850.55	89.35	81.18
Chhattisgarh	18/18 (100)	1,384.68	49.4	48.7	2,158.72	2,360.07	64.14	58.67
Gujarat	26/26 (100)	1,826.2	31.6	23	3,292.84	2,616.60	55.46	69.79
Haryana	21/21 (100)	584.68	24.1	20.1	968.23	886.66	60.39	65.94
Himachal Pradesh	12/12 (100)	235.13	22.9	9.5	293.79	128.78	80.03	182.58
Kerala	14/14 (100)	1,748.47	19.6	12	1,372.85	876.85	127.36	199.40
Mizoram	8/8 (100)	43.26	15.4	21.1	28.36	43.49	152.52	99.48
Punjab	20/20 (100)	220.49	20.9	15.9	959.78	778.93	22.97	28.31
Tripura	4/4 (100)	258.4	40	17.4	283.78	133.42	91.06	193.68
Uttar Pradesh	71/71 (100)	4,145.93	40.9	37.7	11,398.6	11,510.92	36.37	36.02
		States with Partial District Coverage						
Arunachal Pradesh	10/16 (62.5)	39.62	31.4	25.9	70.53	64.96	56.17	60.99
Assam	5/27 (18.52)	204.55	34.4	37.9	1,793.29	2,136.53	11.41	9.57

(Cont'd)

TABLE 2.3 (*Cont'd*)

	RSBY Covered Districts out of Total Districts (%)	*Number of Cards Issued (in '000)*	*HCR*		*Total Poor Household (in '000)*		*Cards Issued as % of Total Poor Households (3 as % of 6 and 7)*	
		March 2012	*2004–5*	*2009–10*	*2004–5*	*2009–10*	*2004–5*	*2009–10*
1	2	3	4	5	6	7	8	9
Jammu & Kashmir	1/22 (4.54)	13.01	13.1	9.4	220.09	174.55	5.91	7.45
Jharkhand	23/24 (95.83)	1,143.78	45.3	39.1	2,327.29	2,223.35	49.15	51.44
Karnataka	20/30 (66.66)	815.17	33.3	23.6	3,654.78	2,788.61	22.3	29.23
Maharashtra	32/33 (96.96)	2,178.04	38.2	24.5	7,946.81	5,484.19	27.41	39.71
Manipur	2/9 (22.22)	31.92	37.9	47.1	141.67	196.76	22.53	16.22
Meghalaya	5/7 (71.42)	67.55	16.1	17.1	70.96	84.81	95.2	79.65
Nagaland	10/11 (90.9)	77.87	8.8	20.9	31.07	74.93	250.63	103.92
Orissa	17/30 (56.66)	1,210.59	57.2	37	4,628.85	3,200.09	26.15	37.83
Uttarakhand	12/13 (92.3)	302.63	32.7	18	560.3	337.69	54.01	89.62
West Bengal	15/19 (78.94)	4,490.15	34.2	26.7	5,722.58	4,769.81	78.46	94.14
All-India	384/473 (81.18)	28,206.57	37.2	29.8	76,701.02	66,804.96	36.77	42.22

Source: Based on data provided by RSBY's official website: www.rsby.gov.in; Census of India (2011); and GoI (2012).

Note: The All-India estimate does not include Andhra Pradesh, where state government provides health insurance to the poor through a scheme other than RSBY; it also does not include the states of Tamil Nadu, Delhi, and Goa as no information is available for these states on the RSBY's official website; Similarly, it does not include the states of Madhya Pradesh, Rajasthan and Sikkim, where the implementation of RSBY has not yet started.

per cent coverage. What this suggests is a much higher coverage in the districts where the scheme is being implemented, because the coverage statistics is based on the estimated poor households for the entire state.

Even after the completion of about four years, the fact that eight states have achieved coverage of less than half the estimated poor should have been a matter of concern both to the states as well as the Union Government. The worst performers in this group is Assam, whose performance is close to or less than ten per cent coverage—Jammu & Kashmir, though being low, is not a cause of concern yet as it has started implementation process very recently. The case of Punjab should also be mentioned here because, despite full spatial coverage, the cards issued to persons and households works out to only around 28 per cent of the estimated poor. The reasons for non-implementation in Madhya Pradesh and Sikkim need to be investigated as we are currently not in a position to assess whether any alternative schemes are in operation in these states.

PHYSICAL ACCESS TO HOSPITALS

Physical access to hospital treatment is one of the crucial aspects of the assessment of RSBY. Card holders are entitled to get in-patient treatment only in empanelled hospitals, and such empanelment is supposed to be based on objective criteria such as capacity of the hospitals and its readiness to participate in the scheme. Some basic data pertaining to the availability of hospitals for the scheme are given in Table 2.4.

There are some important, as well as interesting, insights that could be gleaned from the information provided in Table 2.4. Both public and private sector hospitals are entitled for empanelment under the scheme. In a way, this gives an opportunity to the public hospital to generate additional revenue by way of reimbursement of costs of in-patient treatment. However, only 8 out of 22 states show a higher number of empanelled public hospitals than private hospitals. Interestingly, the state of Tripura, ruled by a Left Front Government, empanelled only public hospitals, while West Bengal, ruled by a similar Left Front Government (until May 2011 for a continuous period of 34 years), empanelled only one public hospital out of a total of 484 hospitals. It could be that the capacity of the public hospitals in West Bengal does not meet the standard set for empanelment or the fact there are not many hospitals in rural areas. However, it is difficult to believe that only private hospitals (including Kolkata) have the required capacity for empanelment under the RSBY.

Table 2.4 RSBY Hospital Empanelment by Type (as of March 2012)

State	*Empanelled Hospitals (number)*			*Share of Public in Total Hospitals (2 as % of 4)*	*Hospital Coverage*	
	Public	*Private*	*Total*		*Empanelled Hospitals as per 10,000 RSBY Cards*	*Empanelled Hospitals as per 10,000 Poor Households*
1	*2*	*3*	*4*	*5*	*6*	*7*
Arunachal Pradesh	2	0	2	100.00	0.50	0.28
Assam	22	27	49	44.90	2.40	0.27
Bihar	37	767	804	4.60	1.12	1.00
Chhattisgarh	453	302	755	60.00	5.45	3.50
Gujarat	412	1,134	1,546	26.65	8.47	4.70
Haryana	58	658	716	8.10	12.25	7.39
Himachal Pradesh	170	38	208	81.73	8.85	7.08
Jammu & Kashmir	0	3	3	0.00	2.31	0.14
Jharkhand	262	239	501	52.30	4.38	2.15
Karnataka	317	425	742	42.72	9.10	2.03
Kerala	153	200	353	43.34	2.02	2.57
Maharashtra	15	1,181	1,196	1.25	5.49	1.51
Manipur	0	4	4	0.00	1.25	0.28
Meghalaya	65	8	73	89.04	10.81	10.29
Mizoram	74	13	87	85.06	20.11	30.68

Nagaland	1	7	8	12.50	1.03	2.57
Odisha	284	116	400	71.00	3.30	0.86
Punjab	165	354	519	31.79	23.54	5.41
Tripura	29	0	29	100.00	1.12	1.02
Uttar Pradesh	676	1,392	2,068	32.69	4.99	1.81
Uttarakhand	75	88	163	46.01	5.39	2.91
West Bengal	1	483	484	0.21	1.08	0.85
All-India	3,271	7,439	10,710	30.54	3.80	1.40

Source: Based on data provided by RSBY's official website: www.rsby.gov.in; Census of India (2011); and GoI (2012).

Note: The All-India estimate excludes Andhra Pradesh, where State Government provides health insurance to the poor through a scheme other than RSBY; it also does not include the states of Tamil Nadu, Delhi, and Goa, as no information is available for these states on the RSBY's official website. Similarly, it does not include the states of Madhya Pradesh, Rajasthan and Sikkim, where the implementation of RSBY has not yet started.

In general, private sector hospitals, with a share of 69 per cent in total empanelled hospitals, have been the major beneficiary in this state-sponsored and funded national health insurance scheme for poor households. One of the main reasons for this could be attributed to limited outreach of public hospitals in rural areas, which suggest another dimension of failure of the Indian state in providing for appropriate institutional arrangements in ensuring health care of its people that should be counted as a basic socio-economic security.

The absolute number of empanelled hospitals is not sufficient condition to gauge the physical access to in-patient treatment. There are many other details that need to be marshalled to make a proper assessment, some of which can only be gathered through case studies. At the same time, we have worked out the number of empanelled hospitals per ten thousand RSBY cards and per ten thousand poor households (estimated on the basis of 66th Round NSS) in different states. Barring Punjab and Haryana, three small states of Mizoram, Himachal Pradesh, and Meghalaya have the best outcomes in both indicators of hospital coverage. Among others, the worst performers are Arunachal Pradesh, Nagaland, West Bengal, Bihar, Tripura, and Manipur (w.r.t. 1st indicator) and Jammu & Kashmir, Assam, Arunachal Pradesh, Manipur, West Bengal, Odisha, Bihar, and Tripura (w.r.t. 2nd indicator), with all-India average of 3.80 hospitals by former indicator and 1.40 hospitals by latter indicator. Such a picture is indeed not something that could be construed as a favourable indicator in accessing hospital care for the insured members or households under the RSBY. By all accounts, this could well limit access, given the concentration of hospitals in urban and semi-urban areas. While there is a provision for reimbursing transportation costs, it also assumes easy availability of such transportation facilities from the rural areas, which is not uniform across states.

INTER-DISTRICT VARIATIONS: LOCATING BACKWARD DISTRICTS

Having found the inter-state variation in the implementation of the RSBY, it is worth exploring whether the 'backward districts' received any priority from the state governments from the point of implementation of the scheme. In order to assess such an outcome, we locate the backward districts in comparison to the non-backward districts. The backward districts refer to the set of 200 districts identified by the Ministry of Rural Development for implementing Phase-I of the National Rural Employment Guarantee Act (NREGA) of 2005 on 2 February 2006.[13]

Owing to data limitations and non-uniform spread of the RSBY over the whole of India, we could include, by the end of March 2012, only 473 districts in our analysis of RSBY's district-wise performance. These districts are spread in a ratio of 35 : 65 across backward and non-backward districts (Table 2.5). An analysis of these districts confirms our doubts to a large extent. The states have not largely considered

TABLE 2.5 District-level Summary Status of RSBY Implementation (by the end of March 2012)

	Backward Districts	*Non-backward Districts*	*All Districts*
Total Number of Districts (in RSBY implementing states)	156 [33.0]	317 [67.0]	473
Districts Covered Under RSBY	133 [34.6]	251 [65.4]	384
Districts Yet to be Covered	23 [25.8]	66 [74.2]	89
Districts with 1st Year of Policy	30 [31.6]	65 [68.4]	95
Districts with 2nd Year of Policy	77 [39.5]	118 [60.5]	195
Districts with 3rd Year of Policy	26 [30.2]	60 [69.8]	86
Districts with 4th Year of Policy	0	8 [100.0]	8
Total BPL Households (in millions)	25.69 [47.0]	31.18 [53.0]	56.87
BPL Households Enrolled (in millions)	13.16 [46.8]	15.04 [53.2]	28.20
Enrolment Rate (%)	51.24	48.23	49.59
Share of Public Empanelled Hospitals	33.53	29.06	62.59
Average Premium (Rs)	455.82	502.14	485.95

Source: Based on RSBY's official website: www.rsby.gov.in.

Notes: The figures in brackets refer to the percentage share in respective total.

The district-level summary excludes Andhra Pradesh, where state government provides health insurance to the poor through a scheme other than RSBY; It also does not include the states of Tamil Nadu, Delhi, and Goa as no information is available for these states on the RSBY's official website; Similarly, it does not include the states of Madhya Pradesh, Rajasthan, and Sikkim where the implementation of RSBY is not yet started.

'district backwardness' as the criteria for prioritizing the districts for implementation of RSBY. Our analysis reveals that none of the backward districts got covered in the first year of RSBY implementation, that is, there is no district in its 4th year of this policy. It was only in the second year when about 17 per cent of the backward districts got covered and finally, over the last four years, about 85 per cent of the backward districts were covered under RSBY, which reflects that a large chunk of the backward districts was covered only recently, with about 15 per cent of them still remaining. A large number of backward districts yet to be covered belong to Manipur (100 per cent), Jammu & Kashmir (100 per cent), Assam (71 per cent), Karnataka (60 per cent), Meghalaya (50 per cent), Orissa (42 per cent), and West Bengal (20 per cent).

It needs to be noted that the backward districts, by definition, have a relatively large proportion of SC/ST population as well as poor households. The district-level summary status, as depicted in Figure 2.2, indicates that the enrolment rate in these districts remained at par with non-backward districts. However, one cannot term this outcome as uniform owing to inter-state variations in this respect.

A further look at the enrolment rate across districts reveals that the BPL households of the backward districts are relatively better covered

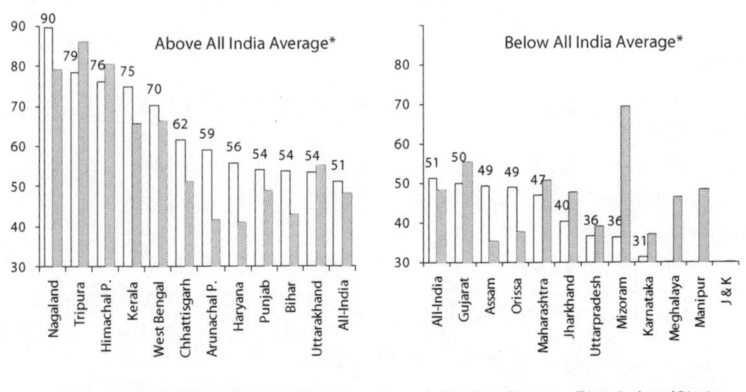

FIGURE 2.2 Enrolment Rate across States (%)

Source: Authors.

Note: *With respect to backward districts.

in ten states—Nagaland, Kerala, West Bengal, Chhattisgarh, Arunachal Pradesh, Haryana, Punjab, Bihar, Assam, and Odisha. In all other states, the enrolment rate has been high in non-backward districts.

FUNCTIONING OF RSBY: INSIGHTS FROM MICRO-LEVEL STUDIES

As our above macro-level assessment of the RSBY implementation does not shed much light on the actual functioning of the scheme at the ground level, we will briefly summarize some important insights from the field-based studies undertaken as part of a research project.[14] In addition, we also refer to other available studies that have seriously examined the implementation of this scheme at ground level.[15]

It is clear from the field-level studies that the selected states are at different stages of RSBY implementation. Some have followed a systematic procedure for implementation, whereas others reflect a sheer absence of the same.

As RSBY is a scheme fully financed by the Union Government, it does not bring any financial obligation to the state. Nonetheless, some states like Karnataka showed initial reluctance to the scheme as the ruling (BJP) party wanted to implement its own version—*Vajpayee Arogyashree*—and it was only after considerable pressure from the centre that it implemented RSBY in some of the districts. But, the implementation process remained marred by serious problems such as delays in issuing of smart cards, poor knowledge generation about the merit of the scheme, inadequate infrastructure at the hospital end, and various reimbursement related problems (Rajasekhar *et al.*, 2011).

In other states as well, the state governments did not perform more than their customary role of identifying the insurance company on the basis of competitive bidding and the provision of BPL list for registration purposes. Only the state of Kerala went beyond its customary role. It facilitated the registration process by way of entrusting the mobilization work to the *Kudumbasree*[16] volunteers for a fee to be paid by the insurance company. These workers performed a range of tasks associated with spreading information about the enrolment dates, timing and place, identification of BPL households and the distribution of smart cards, etc. (Kunhikannan and Aravindan, 2012).

In fact, the implementation procedure of the scheme is such that it does not involve Panchayat Raj institutions (PRIs) and this remains a major weakness, hindering effective implementation of this scheme.

Without assigned role and inbuilt incentives, even the elected representatives remain indifferent to the registration and implementation of the scheme. Das (2012) quotes that the Panchayat Sarpanch in his field area refused to distribute the cards when TPA officials asked him to do so. In the case of Kerala as well, the PRIs do not play any significant role. Based on their experience with RSBY implementation in Kerala, Kunhikannan and Aravindan (2012) ponder if certain activities like provision of suitable place for registration, crowd management, standby arrangement against power failure, late delivery of smart cards, etc., could be handled by the panchayats. Similarly, Gill *et al.* (2012), based on their experience of RSBY implementation in Punjab conclude that 'Sarpanch, Members of PRIs/ULBs and other government functionaries associated with village/urban life should be involved in preparing the smart cards'.

It emerges from field-level experience that the registration process could not ensure the full coverage of all BPL households—a factor strongly impacting sustainability of the scheme. A foremost debilitating factor in this respect has been the tying up of the scheme with the BPL list, which remains outdated and largely erroneous, as pointed by almost all the field studies. The BPL list is also found to be seriously mis-representing the households in certain cases, owing to which deserving households often remain excluded from the scheme (Kunhikannan and Aravindan, 2012; and Das, 2012). The inflexibility of registration timings remained another major factor for non-coverage of a large number of BPL households who could not turn up at the stipulated time and place.

Mahadevia (2012) depicts another serious problem of urban construction workers who have no basic documents to prove their residence since a majority of them are migrant workers in Ahmedabad city, where the field study was conducted.

All these studies report a serious moral hazard on part of the insurance companies. There exists an information gap and very little is done to raise the awareness levels of the masses about the scheme. The case of Punjab is aptly reported by Gill *et al.* (2012) when it is reported, 'most of the BPL families which the study team met did not know the benefits of (the) RSBY'. While studying the implementation of RSBY in Ahmedabad (Gujarat), Mahadevia (2012) points out that the insurance company has not done much to publicize the benefits of the scheme, leading to lack of awareness. Moreover, only the names of empanelled hospitals along with their phone numbers were provided, with no mention of the address, due to which card holders found it difficult to locate the nearby hospital. It has also not revealed clearly the coverage of medical conditions and the related expenses to the card holders. Similarly, Das (2012) reports the narrative of a Sarpanch of his study village in Orissa as, 'although people have received the card, they did not know how to use this card. Similarly, they did not have any information about the hospitals empanelled under the RSBY scheme and how money was to be claimed using this card.' Owing to this information gap, there has not been effective translation of benefits. Das provides two examples to illustrate the unawareness levels of the beneficiaries. In the first case, the card holder could not get benefits simply because the hospital to which he was rushed for treatment was not an empanelled one and in the second case, only part of the benefits could be refunded as the smart card lost its validity in course of treatment.

The registration process has remained mechanical in nature. The insurance companies have sub-contracted the registration work. In most instances, these are external agencies with little familiarity of local names and addresses, and being in hurry to accomplish the task, they have left large number of discrepancies in names, address etc. Owing to this, it often became difficult for the card holder to claim the benefit. Also, there is no procedure for rectifying the errors (Mahadevia, 2012). Such negligence on part of the registration agency contributes finally to the exclusion of otherwise deserving BPL households. In fact, there is still a lot of ground work that needs to be done. A major weakness pointed out by Rajasekhar *et al.* (2011) relates to the absence of any incentive to the insurance company to ensure that card details are correct, that cards are issued without delay, and that beneficiaries know how and where to obtain treatment, or what hospitals are prepared and ready to receive patients.

Readiness of hospitals to accept RSBY patients is another important aspect having a bearing on access to benefits. Initially, the hospitals were found to be willing to accept RSBY patients, but subsequently they started displaying reluctance due to serious problems with reimbursement. Studying the implementation of RSBY in tribal areas of Dangs district in Gujarat, Joshi (2012) documents the narrative of one doctor, 'the scheme is very good but there are also a lot of practical difficulties. In 2009–10, I treated 2000 cases. Because of irregularities in Samarath Hospital at Ahwa, all payments were stopped. I am tired of this and next year I am not going to accept this.' Similarly, the study documents another medical doctor whose claims worth Rs 32 lakh have not been settled.

The state-level studies reflect that the RSBY scheme has provided a good opportunity to hospitals to raise funds. But at the same time, there are cases when such temptation has led to malpractices as well. In an otherwise well-performing state of Kerala, it is reported by Kunhikannan and Aravindan (2012) that there are instances when the hospitals have retained patients for unduly longer periods than is necessary to claim a higher amount. It is further pointed out, 'the practice of holding patient's card at the hospital is also prevalent. The hospital is free to manipulate the card till the transaction is completed in the system. Most hospitals do not inform the patient the amount availed of from the card and the balance, even though there is a provision for giving a print out of these details to the patients'. Some of the malpractices are a clear reflection of the irrational rates prescribed under the scheme. Kunhikannan and Aravindan (2012) provide a detailed account of the implicit irrationality in the suggested package rates. Similarly, they also report various examples to depict the rigidity in operation,[17] which is definitely a point worth worrying about in the effective implementation of this scheme.

Annual renewal of the contract is another major problem affecting regular access to health insurance and the woes increase manifold when the insurance contract is given to another company. As it happened in the case of Orissa, the state wasted a lot of time in getting a new company for the insurance contract, and once this new company was given contract for the second year, it had to repeat the whole enrolment process with all its due problems again and in the process, there was a wastage of time and the poor remained at the risk of non-coverage under health insurance. There seems to be a strong case for moving away from an annual contract to a long-term contract with insurance companies with a track record of good service. Such settlement will also take care of cases when the patient remains in the hospital but the card expired, as mentioned earlier by Das (2012).

***

Before we make any comments on the functioning of the RSBY as a national health insurance scheme for the poor households of

India, it is important not to forget the larger picture of poverty and vulnerability, and associated insecurity for majority of the population in India. As has been brought out in recent times, the emergence of India as a fast growing economy is also characterized by an overwhelming proportion (more than three-fourth in 2005 and close to 70 per cent as in 2010) of its population belonging to a category of poor and vulnerable if one goes by the international definition of poverty. To this, one should add India's HDI rank of 119 among a total of 169 countries, which conveys a sense of pervasive absence or inadequacy of basic socio-economic security (UNDP, 2010). It is in such a context that the need for a measure of health security has to be appreciated.

However, this raises a serious problem of identification of poor households. In both rural and urban areas, there is a significant proportion of people and households just above the poverty line. This has posed considerable dilemma to the state governments whose enumeration of poor households (based on identifiable criteria) always comes up with a much higher estimate of the poor. This, of course, is in addition to the problem of wrong exclusion (excluding the deserved) and wrong inclusion (including the undeserved) that is endemic in India in relation to not just the RSBY, but many other schemes and programmes that are targeted to the 'officially poor'.

For any state-sponsored scheme to function reasonably well at the ground level, there are many pre-requisites. One such requirement is the level of awareness, and the capabilities of persons who are entitled for inclusion in such schemes. One of the basic problems is the continuing existence of illiteracy and low level of education in both urban and rural areas, although the problem is more acute in the latter. Owing to this, the people often have not fully comprehended the meaning of health insurance. Consequently, they face many difficulties in accessing the benefits. Women are at a distinct disadvantage, given their higher rate of illiteracy, and low educational capability. Often illiteracy alone is portrayed as a major problem. In our view, low educational capability—not more than five years of schooling—makes hardly any difference when it comes to the ability to read and write, and access information. In fact, when documents have to be filled and read, even five years of schooling is inadequate. This pervasive problem is a major structural constraint in Indian society, despite its celebrated political democracy.

A specific but fundamental constraint in the functioning of RSBY is the inadequate health care facilities, particularly in rural areas. Of course, the supply side is sought to be addressed by such projects as the National Rural Health Mission, but the progress on this front is quite tardy, to say the least. This could come in the way of utilizing the scheme effectively as can be gleaned from the rate of hospitalization in different states. Neo-liberals would be quick to point out to the private sector health care facilities and the need to encourage them. In fact, going by the share of private sector hospitals, they now stand to benefit by the scheme. However, here again the bias could be more towards urban areas, although there are exceptions where private sector hospitals account for a larger share in rural areas, as in the case of Kerala.

In terms of entitlements under the scheme, the exclusion of out-patient care could reduce the potential benefit to the households to a significant extent. Many diseases of poverty, including accidents that may not need hospitalization, are now beyond the insurance cover provided by the RSBY. Whether there is a strong case for such exclusion is something that has not yet been made public. But, as the Andhra Pradesh Government has rightly recognized, it is as important to provide out-patient care to the working poor as it is to have in-patient care, whose incidence is likely to be much less than the former. The argument for inclusion of out-patient care arises from the occupational and living environments of the working poor who are exposed to a variety of unhygienic, hazardous, as well as arduous conditions of work and life, which make them vulnerable to various diseases, that could at times lead to hospitalization. Yet, their burden on household budget could not be ignored. One of the studies has brought out that the catastrophic health care spending pushes about 4 per cent of the households below the poverty line in Kerala in a year, of which 2.5 per cent are on account of burden of acquiring medical assistance (George, 2005). If this is the case in Kerala, with high level of human development and extensive public provisioning for various kinds of basic socio-economic security, the situation in many other states could very well be much more serious.

A whole host of operational problems of a day-to-day nature also call for serious attention and careful remedial action if the benefits of the scheme have to reach the intended beneficiaries. The problems in preparation and collection of smart cards, proper registration and information counters at the hospitals, transparency by hospital staff about the amount deducted, timely renewal of the card by the state-level nodal agency, and so on, have been reported from various parts of the country.

As with many other schemes, this one also has its problems arising out of its 'top down' character. It is a sad commentary on Indian states that, except a few, most have not shown much enthusiasm for providing a measure of social security to its working poor or poor households and persons. It is the example of the very few that have often acted as a propelling force for the Union Government to come out with national schemes and programmes. Therefore, 'bottom up' might be a good idea as it could take into account the local specificities, contexts and problems but in practice, the absence of such an approach often prepares the ground for a top down approach leading to a design of one size that fits, all.

Notes

[1] For details, refer to Sengupta *et al.* (2008).

[2] Of the total workforce in India, 86 per cent were found to be working in the informal sector. While the remaining 14 per cent were employed in the formal sector, 6 per cent (of the total workforce) of them was employed on an informal basis. See NCEUS (2007).

[3] For details, refer to Kannan (2011).

[4] In the case of the North Eastern states and Jammu & Kashmir, the Central Government contributes 90 per cent of the premium and the State Governments are supposed to contribute only 10 per cent.

[5] These include the 32 districts of Tamil Nadu.

[6] Though OPD facilities are not covered under the scheme, OPD consultation is free.

[7] ASHA workers are the honorary workers who work as health workers at the village level, visiting families to give them advices on selected health care issues under the National Rural Health Mission. These are mostly related to family planning and identification of families for immunization of children and pregnant women. In return for their 'voluntary services' they get a nominal amount as honorarium that would hardly average Rs 600 per month, which is equivalent to the current official poverty line. These are predominantly women from relatively poor families in villages. The irony of such poor women working in the field, with pitiable monetary return, while their official bosses draw comfortable salaries with adequate social security should not be lost sight of.

[8] The central government is considering the extension of validity period of smart cards to three years.

[9] As happened in the case of some hospitals in Uttar Pradesh. These hospitals were engaged in various malpractices.

[10] Denoting scheme for destitute.

[11] White Cards are the ration cards given to those families having an annual income below Rs 11,000. As on 22 December 2010, there are 179.16 lakh White Card holders, 15.57 lakh Antyodaya Anna Yojana Card holders and 0.93 lakh Annapurna Card holders (GoAP, 2011: 21).

[12] It needs to be noted that the state, in order to facilitate speedier coverage, has engaged more than 1,000 teams which travelled across the entire state to complete the process within the record time of four months.

[13] Out of the 200 backward districts included in Phase-I of NREGA implementation, the Government of India seemed to have selected 115 districts belonging to the most backward districts as identified by GoI (2003). For the remaining 85 districts, they do not seem to have strictly followed these criteria, but these districts mostly correspond to the index of backwardness prepared by this report.

[14] The commissioned state-level studies examine the implementation of health insurance for the poor. Specifically, implementation of health insurance is examined with respect to RSBY in all the states except Andhra Pradesh, where a state-run health insurance scheme—*Rajiv Aarogyasri Yojana* is in operation.

[15] To our knowledge, there is only one such study conducted by Rajasekhar *et al.* (2011) in the case of Karnataka.

[16] *Kudumbasree* is a women's organization operational in Kerala.

[17] Kunhikannan and Aravindan (2012) report that even the critically ill patients had to be brought to the counter for thumb impression. Similarly, the patients 'who were admitted late were unable to register, since the RSBY counters worked only from 8 a.m. to 8 p.m'.

References

Census of India. 2011. *Provisional Population Totals*, Vol. I, Registrar General and Census Commissioner. New Delhi: Ministry of Home Affairs.

Das, A. 2012. 'Implementation of Social Security Schemes in Odisha: A Study of Rashtriya Swasthya Bima Yojana', Commissioned Study under the CDS-ASSR Project on Social Security. Netherlands: The HiVOS.

George, A. Thomas. 2005. *Catastrophic Health Expenditure and Impoverishment in Kerala: An Analysis Based on NSSO 55th Round, 1999–2000*, Unpublished MPhil thesis. New Delhi: Jawaharlal Nehru University.

Gill, S.S. *et al.* 2012. 'Social Security Schemes in Punjab: A Blend of State and Central Schemes', Commissioned Study under the CDS-ASSR Project on Social Security. Netherlands: The HiVOS.

GoAP. 2011. 'Socio-economic Survey: 2010–11', Planning Department, AP Secretariat, Government of Andhra Pradesh, Hyderabad.

GoHP. 2010. 'Budget Speech, 2010–11', available at www.himachal.nic.in/finance/2010-11/BS_Eng.pdf (accessed on 14 May 2011).

GoI. 2003. 'Report of the Task Force on Identification of Districts for Wage and Self-employment Programmes'. New Delhi: Planning Commission, Government of India.

———. 2012. 'Press Note on Poverty Estimates, 2009–10'. New Delhi: Planning Commission, Government of India.

GoR. 2010. 'Medical and Health', in *Annual Plan 2011–12*, Jaipur.

Joshi, S. 2012. 'Monitoring the Implementation of Social Security Schemes in Tribal Areas of Gujarat: with Reference to Dangs District', Commissioned Study under the CDS-ASSR Project on Social Security. Netherlands: the HiVOS.

Kannan, K.P. 2011. 'The Long Road to Social Security: The Challenge of Universal Coverage for the Working Poor in India', Working Paper No. 2, HiVOS Knowledge Generation Programme. Netherlands: the HiVOS.

Kunhikannan, T.P. and K.P. Aravindan. 2012. 'Functioning of Contingent Social Security Schemes in Kerala: The Social and Institutional Context of Delivery at the Local Level', Commissioned Study under the CDS-ASSR Project on Social Security. Netherlands: The HiVOS.

Mahadevia, D. 2012. 'Monitoring the Implementation of Social Security for Urban Poor: A Case Study in Gujarat', Commissioned Study under the CDS-ASSR Project on Social Security. Netherlands: The HiVOS.

NCEUS. 2007. *Report on Conditions of Work and Promotion of Livelihoods in the Unorganised Sector*. New Delhi: Academic Foundation, Government of India.

PIB. 2010. 'Extension of Rashtriya Swasthya Bima Yojana to the Street Vendors, 20th October'. New Delhi: Press Information Bureau.

Rajasekhar, D. *et al.* 2011. 'Implementing Health Insurance: The Rollout of Rashtriya Swasthya Bima Yojana in Karnataka', *Economic and Political Weekly*, 46(20): 56–63.

Sengupta, A., K.P. Kannan, and G. Raveendran. 2008. 'India's Common People: Who are They, How Many Are They and How Do They Live?' *Economic and Political Weekly*, 43(11): 49–63.

UNDP. 2010. *Human Development Report 2010: The Real Wealth of Nations: Pathways to Human Development*, 20th Anniversary Edition. New York: United Nations Development Programme.

II

ANDHRA PRADESH

3 FUNCTIONING OF NREGS IN ANDHRA PRADESH

D. Narasimha Reddy

The National Rural Employment Guarantee Act (NREGA) is one of the most ambitious programmes to provide employment as a legal right. Though the NREGA and the guidelines are uniform for the entire country, the performance in terms of implementation of National Rural Employment Guarantee Scheme (NREGS) is bound to vary. Besides the involvement and ability of Panchayati Raj Institutions (PRIs), state-level political commitment, administrative initiatives, and institutional innovations are likely to make a considerable difference to the functioning of the scheme.

It is in this perspective that we have set the broad objectives of the present study, which are: (i) to situate the functioning of NREGS in Andhra Pradesh in relation to other states, in terms of certain broad indicators; (ii) to examine NREGS implementation initiatives in Andhra Pradesh in terms of the broader political context and related policy perspectives; (iii) to document the innovations and institutional initiatives by the state, and the efforts to institutionalize certain processes in implementing NREGS; (iv) to examine the role of civil society organizations, including self-help groups (SHGs), in the implementation of the scheme at the panchayat level; and (v) to assess the impact of the scheme on specific social groups.

The study combines quantitative analysis and qualitative observations based on field visits and interaction with various functionaries. Household sample surveys were conducted in two villages in Medak district of Andhra Pradesh. Primary data from another inter-state study, with which the author is associated, are also utilized to a limited extent. The observations also reflect field visits by the author to 12 villages out of 16 under the project in the State. Discussions were held with various functionaries from the village level to that of the state.

THE REGIONAL CONTEXT: POLITICS AND POLICY REFORM

In 2004–5, when the Congress Party replaced the Telugu Desam Party (TDP) in the state, agriculture remained the main source of livelihood for the people, with relatively slow growing industrial and service sectors not impacting the masses much in rural areas. Evidently agriculture played a decisive role, not only on the conditions of the people, but also on the fortunes of parties in power. Whichever government ignored this and neglected agriculture paid the political price, as experienced by TDP in 2004, after having ruled the state for nine years.

To unravel the factors that contributed to the new Congress regime, one may have to examine the earlier government's neoliberal policy reforms, which contributed hugely to the regime change. These developments are well documented elsewhere (Reddy, 2008). It is interesting to note that the aggressive neoliberal reforms, along with the equally strong commitment to social protection policies like NREGS, seem to have stemmed not as mere rational economic choices, but as strong political considerations.

The TDP, when it first came to power in 1983 breaking the monopoly of the Congress, was credited with having brought about a 'regime change'. This meant more political space for the backward communities and the 'new rich'. The TDP lost the 1989 elections due to failure to implement its election promises. But its leader N.T. Rama Rao (more commonly known as NTR), a popular film actor, rode back to power in 1994 with an overwhelming majority on the promise of restoring the subsidized rice scheme, introduction of total prohibition, and subsidized power to the farmers. However, within the TDP, a growing section was of the view that social sector expenditure was unproductive and unsustainable. To them, market-oriented, privatized public works like roads and flyovers, aggressive scouting for foreign direct investment (FDI)—especially in projects with quick gestation period like information technology (IT)—constituted 'development'. But none could dare oppose NTR at that time. They bided their time and discreetly voiced their position.

In September 1995, the coup within the ruling TDP resulted in NTR'S son-in-law, Chandrababu Naidu, usurping power from NTR. The leadership change was seen as a paradigm shift in policy from NTR's 'welfarist' regime to Naidu's 'developmentalist' regime, which was based on attracting industrial investments and outsourcing public works. The state's finances were in the doldrums and Naidu was in no position to implement his plans. He turned to the World Bank seeking assistance—even if it meant loans—to stabilize the state agenda and establish himself as a capable developmental leader. The World Bank, which had brought the Government of India on to the reform track, was eager to extend the reforms agenda to the states. With a coalition government at the Centre, and the state governments belonging to different political parties, the Centre's power to push for reforms at the state level was limited. So the World Bank was delighted to find a willing ally in Naidu to implement its reforms agenda at the state level. By October 1997, the World Bank announced a package of loans to the tune of $2 billion to Andhra Pradesh. While the Bank's agenda was to redesign the institutional structures of the state in favour of privatization, Naidu's 'development agenda' was a ploy at image-building as growth-oriented and market-friendly 'CEO' of the state.

Reforms Relating to Agriculture

The agriculture sector in Andhra Pradesh was in the throes of severe structural and institutional disabilities. Small and marginal farmers accounted for about 85 per cent of holdings and over 40 per cent of the cultivated area. There was severe shortage of institutional credit, especially to small and marginal farmers. There was virtual stagnation in the area under canal irrigation, and decline in tank irrigation. Dependence on groundwater resources was growing. The demand for improved seeds and fertilizers was on the increase, but prices were high and supplies limited. There was hardly any improvement in technology relevant to dry regions, and extension services were grossly inadequate. By the mid-1990s, the agriculture sector was in distress. Ironically, instead of coming out in support of the peasantry, the State launched a series of reforms in agriculture as a part of the economic restructuring project, which pushed agriculture and the peasantry further into crisis (Reddy, 2006; and Galab *et al.*, 2009).

Almost writing off the small and marginal agricultural sector, the Government's 'Working Paper' on agriculture called for a 'paradigm shift' towards export-oriented agriculture, which required 'large-scale investments, which can only come through an organized system of agricultural production, rather than existing system of fragmented and marginal production'.

Andhra Pradesh, which was considered to be a relatively progressive state agriculturally, was in a serious crisis by late 1990s. Any mild aggravation—the pressure from private moneylenders, inability to sell produce due to depressed prices, a prolonged drought, or failure to meet expenses for children's education or health emergencies involving private hospitals—could trigger stress beyond endurance, forcing many farmers to commit suicide.

The period between 1997 and 2004 saw 688 farmers' suicides recorded in the State. Between May 2004 and November 2005, 277 starvation deaths of weavers were reported (Kumar, 2005).

CHANGE OF REGIME

On the eve of the 2004 State Assembly elections, the wave of reforms and technological prowess on which the Naidu regime had planned their publicity ride was completely exposed. The Congress took full advantage of the discontentment among the farming community and the rural poor in its campaign. Investment in irrigation, farm debt relief, free power supply to agriculture, subsidized interest rates for women's SHGs, land distribution to the Scheduled Castes (SCs), legalized land rights for the Scheduled Tribes (STs), and the promise of legislation to guarantee right to work were brought on to the agenda of the Congress party's political campaign. When the Congress came to power, it put in action initiatives like setting up of the AP Commission for Farmers' Welfare, launching of a massive irrigation development programme, free power supply to agriculture, the 'pavala vaddi' (3 per cent interest) loans to the SHGs, the Indira Awas Yojana (housing programme for the rural poor) and, from 2006, the NREGS.

NREG AS A FLAGSHIP WELFARE SCHEME

The fact that the NREGS, a national programme of the Union Government, was launched from a dryland district of Andhra Pradesh on 2 February 2006 by the Prime Minister, assumes political significance. Before we analyze some of the initiatives of the State Government, we shall have an overview of employment generated and the expenditure incurred.

Table 3.1 provides some basic facts relating to the implementation of NREGS during the last four years in Andhra Pradesh. In the

TABLE 3.1 Implementation of NREGS in Andhra Pradesh

Coverage: Employment, Expenditure and Social Groups	*Phase I*	*Phase II*	*Phase III*	
	2006–7	*2007–8*	*2008–9*	*2009–10*
1. Number of Districts under NREGS	13	13 + 6 = 19	19 + 3 = 22	22
2. Number of Households Covered				
Households with Job Cards (lakh)	50.7	88.5	113	117
Households provided Employment (lakh)	21.6	48.0	57	62
3. Person-days of Employment Guaranteed				
Total (lakh)	679	2,010	2,735	4,044
Per Job Card	13	23	24	35
Per Household Employed in NREGS	31	42	48	65
4. Share of Marginalized Group in NREGS Employment (%)				
Women	55	58	58	58
Scheduled Tribe	13	13	13	15
Scheduled Caste	30	28	26	25
5. Expenditure on NREGS				
Total Expenditure (Rs crore)	–	–	2,964	4,509
Average Expenditure per District (Rs crore)	–	–	135	205
Average Expenditure per Person Day (Rs)	–	–	108	111
Average Wage Cost per Person Day (Rs)	–	–	83	92
Share of Wages in Total Expenditure	–	–	76	82

Source: NREGA's official website: nrega.nic.in and nrega.ap.gov.in (27.8.10).

First Phase (2006–7), 13 districts were picked for the programme. In the Second Phase (2007–8), 6 more districts were added, and in the Third Phase (2008–9), the remaining 3 rural districts were included. The programme was in operation in all the 22 districts by 2008–9. Though the first two years were not comparable with the later two years because of the coverage difference, the progress in terms of job card provision, work assignment, and person-days of employment per household had seen substantial increase. The average person-days of employment per household was very low, at 31 in 2006–7; but the increase in the following years, especially in 2009–10, was very steep. The inclusion of marginal groups had been substantially high from the very first year. With the expanding coverage, the absorption of resources had been phenomenal. By 2009–10, each district was able to spend Rs 205 crore, on an average, and 82 per cent of it was on wages. This was more than 3.3 times of the national average expenditure per district (Rs 62 crore). With an average daily wage cost of Rs 92 per person, and an average of 65 person-days of employment per household, the NREGS could add on an average income of Rs 5,980 to a working household.

What was the impact of this additional income on poverty reduction? Going by the officially accepted Tendulkar Committee estimates, the poverty line for rural Andhra Pradesh was Rs 671 per capita per month in 2009–10. For an average household of five, it works out to Rs 40,260. Thus the average additional earnings of Rs 5,980 under NREGS amounted to only about 15 per cent of poverty level household income. But, this could be seen to make a substantial difference to poor households in shoring up the demand for food and other essential items. Further, since considerable proportion of the poor were at the margins of the poverty line, it could also be seen to have a considerable impact in reducing overall poverty.

Just as there were wide variations in the implementation and coverage of the programme across the states, there were wide variations across the districts in Andhra Pradesh as well. Table 3.2 differentiates districts on the basis of their inclusion in different phases—13 districts of first phase, 6 of the second and 3 of the third. The first phase districts were obviously part of the 200 identified as the most backward districts of the country. In terms of all the basic entitlements, the performance of the first phase districts was substantially higher compared to the second or third phase districts. This could be because of two reasons: (i) the first phase districts had a head start in implementing the programme and the time factor could have helped in improving performance; and (ii) the first phase districts were more backward, with more poor willing to do physical labour while the later phase districts were relatively more developed, where the demand for physical work might have been less, resulting in the

TABLE 3.2 Phase-wise Districts and Performance of NREGS in Andhra Pradesh

	1st Phase		*2nd Phase*		*3rd Phase*	
	2008–9	*2009–10*	*2008–9*	*2009–10*	*2008–9*	*2009–10*
1. Households Covered						
Households with Job Cards (lakh)	69.2	71.0	31.7	32.5	12.5	13.7
Households Provided Employment (lakh)	35.4	39.2	16.5	15.5	5.0	6.8
2. Person-days of Employment						
Total (lakh)	1,880	2,728	756	988	100	329
Per Job Card	27	38	24	30	8	24
Per Household Employed in NREGS	53	70	46	64	20	48
3. Share of Marginalized Groups in NREGS Employment (%)						
Women	60	60	55	56	48	51
Scheduled Tribe	14	15	9	11	19	27
Scheduled Caste	26	25	27	25	26	21
4. Expenditure on NREGS						
Total Expenditure (Rs crore)	2,054	3,086	809	1,066	101	357
Average Expenditure per District (Rs crore)	158	237	135	178	34	119
Average Expenditure per Person Day (Rs)	109	113	107	108	101	109
Average Wage Cost per Person Day (Rs)	82	93	83	89	80	93
Share of Wages in Total Expenditure (%)	75	82	78	83	79	85

Source: NREGA's official website: www.nrega.nic.in (27.8.2010).

differential performance. Both factors may have worked in favour of better performance of first phase districts.

Yet, a closer examination of the difference leads to some fundamental questions relating to the very design of the NREGS. For instance, expecting all the poor households to be relatively less educated, without any skills, and looking only for physical labour might have entirely bypassed the poor who were relatively better educated, with preference for semi-skilled or service sector-oriented nature of work. So the question remains whether NREGS work ought to be modified to include persons with better exposure to education, or providing an alternative social protection measures, designed just for them. These problems could be addressed if NREGS is redesigned to provide not only physical work, but also work that needs some basic level of education while also providing for skill enhancement of the rural poor.

Process of Implementation: Awareness of Basic Entitlements

For successful participation in rights-based guaranteed employment on demand, at a certain assured minimum wage, the primary requirement is that the citizens who are potential seekers of work are aware of the basic entitlements. In a state like Andhra Pradesh, where the literacy levels are below the national average, mere gazette notifications or media advertisements would not suffice. The guidelines under NREGA identify Gram Sabha as the principal agency for creation of awareness about the scheme. In Andhra Pradesh, the functioning of panchayats is not adequate to bring everyone into the fold of Gram Sabha, and disseminate information on all aspects of the programme. So the role of other agencies like Non-governmental Organizations (NGOs) and Community Based Organizations (CBOs), like SHGs become very critical.

In Andhra Pradesh, SHGs have, over the years, emerged as institutions of social mobilization. The formation and capacity building of the women's SHGs is carried on at the behest of a quasi-government—but autonomous—institution, like the Society for the Elimination of Rural Poverty (SERP), of which the Chief Minister is the Chairman and a senior civil servant on deputation acts as the Chief Executive Officer. Initially, SERP was formed to promote women's SHGs as thrift groups, and was linked to the banks.[1] The State invested in building their capacity not only to promote savings, but also as a measure of social mobilization, to enable them to undertake income-generating activities by linking them with banks and the self-employment programme of the Government of India, Swarnajayanti Gram Swarojgar Yojana (SGSY). Over the years, under the aegis of the SERP and the direct government support, SHGs have emerged as a well-knit legal federation with 10 million members.

SHGs at each village formed into Village Organization (VO); VOs formed Mahila Mandal Samakhyas (MMS) at the mandal level, and into Zillah Mahila Samakhyas (ZMS) at the district level. At mandal and district levels, these are registered under the Mutually Aided Cooperative Societies Act (MACS).

Originally starting as thrift societies, the SHG federation now performs as many as 18 functions, including procuring and marketing of grain, managing the Janashree Bima Yojana, and old age pensions of the Central Government. Political parties realized the significance of the SHG movement in the state. When the Congress came to power in 2004, one of the early decisions of the Chief Minister was to announce credit to SHGs at 3 per cent interest rate. This has become one of the most popular schemes of the Government, called 'Pavala Vaddi' (3 per cent interest).[2]

SHGs played an important role in creating awareness of the scheme among potential workers. In fact, the VOs helped in the payment of wages in cash for NREGS works without any hitch in the initial period, when the institutional mechanism for payments had not been streamlined. SHGs are credited for their role in creation of a high level of awareness about most of the basic provisions of the NREGA in Andhra Pradesh, as shown in Table 3.3. Presently NREGS wages in the State are disbursed mostly through SHG functionaries chosen for the purpose, and trained to make biometric-linked, smart card based wage payments.

Besides the entitlements related to provision of work and wages, the NREGA is also a landmark in the sense of providing 'decent work', since it ensures certain basic entitlements with the aim of granting dignity to workers and providing them some contingency—related social security such as prioritizing participation of women workers, ensuring travel allowance in case work is at a location more than 5 km distance from residence, and monetary compensation in case of injury at the work site. Awareness of these other entitlements, with the exception of travel allowance is relatively high in Andhra Pradesh.

TABLE 3.3 Percentage of Households Having Awareness of the Following Rights/Entitlements/Provisions Related to MGNREGS

Basic Entitlements	*Andhra Pradesh*
Up to 100 days employment	94.4
Minimum Wages for MGNREGS	94.6
Equal wages for men and women	97.8
Wage payment within 15 days	75.2
Unemployment allowance in case employment not provided within 15 days of demand	5.9
One third of jobseekers be women	36.3
Travel Allowance for work	27.6
Free treatment in case of accident	82.2
Compensation for disability and death	81.7
Worksite facilities	
Crèche	51.1
Shade	46.3
Water	96.1
First aid	86.7

Source: Reddy *et al.* (2010).

But the need for shade and crèche at the work site is yet to sink in to the minds of workers, as most of them seem not to insist on it.

RIGHTS, ORGANIZATIONS OF WAGE SEEKERS, AND INSTITUTION BUILDING

The State Government took proactive measures to not only promote awareness about the programme among workers, but actively assert their rights. For this, the State Government promoted 'AP-NGO Alliance' (APNA), of which the Chief Minister is the Chairman, with the Minister for Rural Development being the Vice-Chairman, and a senior retired civil servant, the Executive Chairman. The alliance identified over 40 NGOs and earmarked the regions wherein they would work to fulfil the following objectives: to help form Fixed Labour Groups (FLGs), especially of SCs/STs; to train FLGs on rights and entitlements under the Act; to ensure each FLG is linked to works up to Rs 2 lakh; and to train FLGs to play observer role in social audit.

In November 2009, the Government established an Institution Building (IB) Unit in the Office of the Commissioner of Rural Development with dedicated staff at the state, district and cluster level (GO Ms No. 355 dt. 18.11.2009). The main function of the IB is to ensure group formation, provide continuous training, and lending support to the labour groups. The FLGs thus formed would function as pressure groups for demanding wage employment, so as to ensure 100 days work guaranteed under the Act. Box 3.1 contrasts the experience of Rajasthan and Andhra Pradesh in this regard.

The impact of APNA could be seen in the formation of an FLG in the form of Shramika Shakti Sangam (SSS) in many villages identifying two workers in each group as 'Mates' and providing training to them.

Orders from the state administration show clear instructions on the provision of work site facilities. As early as in June 2006, there

Box 3.1 Unionization of NREGS Workers: Experience in Rajasthan vs Andhra Pradesh

Rajasthan

When Majdoor Kisan Sangharsh Samiti (MKSS) formed Union of NREGS workers sought registration, the Registrar of Trade Unions in Rajasthan refused permission on the grounds that they do not qualify as workmen under the Industrial Disputes Act.*

The MKSS leader observed "We are only facilitating dialogue by organizing a Union. It is sad that the authorities are against an initiative to organize the poorest of workers". Labour departments in other states do not share the dilemma of the Rajasthan registrar's office.

Andhra Pradesh

The Trade Union of NREGA workers in Chittoor in Andhra Pradesh was registered without any difficulty, primarily because it was a zonal affair.**

Sources: * 'Rajasthan refuses to recognize NREGA Workers' Unions', Business Standard, New Delhi, 30 September 2010.

In Andhra Pradesh, the government has been proactive in promoting the initiative of workers to form community leased 'fixed labour groups' and 'wage seekers' unions' (Shrama Shakti Sanghas).

** i. Government Order No. 353 (PR&RD-RD-II) dt. 18-11-2009

ii. Government Order No. 339 (PR&RD-RD-II) dt. 7-11-2009

iii. Government Order No. 240 (PR&RD-RD-II) dt. 9-7-2009

were instructions to engage one person for every 50 workers, to supply drinking water. This was revised to two persons per 50 workers in summer. Similar was the case in providing shade at work sites. There were official instructions on the number of high duty polythene sheets to be purchased and the number to be allotted to each panchayat. There were instructions to get the first-aid boxes refilled with due process. But the implementation of providing tools was replete with bureaucratic processes and inadequate provision. All the materials had to be procured by the district or mandal level officials, and supplied to the Gram Panchayats. This smacked of lack of decentralization, even in operationalizing small facilities. As a result, inordinate delays and shortages became common.

Muster Rolls and Transparency

Studies on the process of obtaining job cards in some states revealed bribes of about Rs 20 per job card, or even for a photo, being collected by the issuing authorities. Our field visits showed no such practice in Andhra Pradesh. Similarly, there is transparency in the maintenance of muster rolls, and attendance is marked by taking signature or thumb impression of the workers.

Worksite Facilities and Grassroots Governance

There was an instance where the villagers showed us the crow bars supplied, which were not useful for their work. Spades were essential but were not in the central purchase list. The result is in many places, workers were asked to bring their own tools, and a daily allowance of Rs 3 was paid for it. But there were instances where the workers were turned away as they did not bring the tools, which affected the poor most. If work site facilities could not be taken care of by the Gram Panchayats, and for every water pot or shade sheet damaged if the Panchayat had to indent to the Mandal Officials, there was no way that there could be satisfactory worksite facilities. The dismal capacity, poor public image, and low official confidence in panchayats together acted as the Achilles heel for the grassroots administration of NREGS in Andhra Pradesh.

Choice and Prioritization of Works

However in some cases, top down orders appeared to be more progressive. One such case related to the choice and prioritization of works. According to the guidelines of NREGS, the Gram Sabha is supposed to be responsible for preparing a shelf of works, and get it approved by the Mandal Authorities for implementation. There have been directives and orders from the State Government on prioritization of works to be taken up. Of the nine broad categories of works permitted under Section I of Schedule I of the NREGA, the fourth category—'provision of irrigation facility, horticulture plantation and land development facilities on land owned by households belonging to the SC, ST, BPL households or beneficiaries of land reforms or beneficiaries under Indira Awas Yojana (IAY)'—has been the focus of prioritization by the State Government. There were repeated orders and guidelines to give top priority to land development, irrigation provision, and horticulture development on the lands of SCs and STs, followed by other categories listed above, as well as small and marginal farmers included by a later amendment to the Act.[3]

Development of Private Lands of the Poor

Given the fact that in Andhra Pradesh, about 12 per cent of the total landholdings are either assigned under land reforms or government land allotted to the poor, the significance of the State prioritizing works for the SCs, STs and other poor is far reaching. Much of the land assigned by the Government to the poor, or even the land owned by poor farmers, especially in dry areas, is degraded or over-grown by bushes. Most of it remained uncultivated, and is therefore unproductive. The State Government's orders prioritizing NREGS works on these lands of the poor has been a boon to them. For clearing one hectare of *prosafis juliflora* along with root stumps, the investment needed is about Rs 46,000, which no poor land owner could afford. Such investments are now made possible by state prioritization of NREGS works and most of the land of the poor, which was unproductive, has been turned into productive assets. The recent circular (No. 1192/EGS dt. 6.9.10) of the Department of Rural Development provides guidelines for implementation of new work strategy for development of the lands of SCs, STs and small-marginal farmers who have worked for at least 20 days in NREGS work. The guidelines lay down that land of this category of each farmer be treated as one project, and such land development in each village be completed to a saturation point. If the new guidelines are implemented, the quality of at least 40 per cent of the dry land is likely to improve, thereby not only improving the wage income of the poor, but also the productive asset base of a substantial section of the rural poor.

TABLE 3.4 Average Person-days of Employment and Households Completing 100 Persons-days in Andhra Pradesh

Year	*No. of Households Provided Employment (lakh)*	*No. of Households Provided*	*(3) as % of (2)*	*Overall Average Number of Days of Employment per Household*
		100 Days of Work		
1	2	3	4	5
2006–7	21.6	0.67	3.1	31
2007–8	48	4.11	8.42	42
2008–9	57	4.18	7.33	48
2009–10	62	13.93	22.47	65

Source: NREGAs official website: www.nrega.nic.in (27.8.2010).

Employment Entitlement

The basic entitlement of NREGS is provision of at least up to 100 days of work to a household on demand. Andhra Pradesh started with a relatively low level state average of 31 man-days of work per household in 2006–7. It became 42 in 2007–8 and increased marginally to 48 in 2008–9. 2009–10 saw a sharp rise to 65 man-days per household (Table 3.4). This was due to prompt action on repeated letters and memoranda to the District Collectors, to augment the shelf of works, to get quick ratification for Gram Panchayat resolutions, and to start adequate work during the off-season.

Wage Related Issues

Assured minimum wages and timely payment of the same are basic entitlements under NREGS. But it turned out to be a controversial issue because of the complexity involved. This is because of the mode of payment under NREGS. Except Himachal Pradesh, all states in the country are required to pay NREGS wages on a piece rate basis, not on time rate or daily wages. The assured minimum wage that is fixed under NREGS is to be realized through physically measurable equivalent of work. This leads to the second problem of acceptable Standard Schedule of Rates (SSRs). The third problem is timely measurement of work that is done. How frequently it should be done, who should do it and who should approve it are the questions often raised. Then, who should pay the wages? The implementing agency or an independent agency? How should these steps be integrated? And, at the end of it, how to ensure timely payment?

The Andhra Pradesh Government dealt with these problems systematically. Since the SSRs used in contract works involves machines, these rates are not comparable to solely manual work as stipulated under NREGS. The Engineering Staff College of India was commissioned by the State Government to make work-time-motion studies and suggest amendments to SSRs, to ensure minimum wages under NREGS. The results showed that, according to existing SSRs, even after a day's work, the wages would be only one-third to one-half of the stipulated minimum wage under NREGS. Based on the study, the State Government revised the SSRs for NREGS by reducing the physical quantity by one-third to one-half. In fact, this change was accepted by the Union MoRD and was recommended to other states to follow.

Still, there were complaints that there were no rates in SSRs for certain tasks like 'tank silt', jungle and bush clearance etc. The State Government took the help of NGOs to carry out further studies, particularly focused on women's tasks in NREGS works. Based on the results of these studies, the SSRs were further revised, reducing the load of work to match one day's work to minimum wages.

Table 3.5 shows the technical capability and potential speed with which wages could be disbursed; however in actual practice, there are still delays.

TABLE 3.5 Progress in Wage Realized and Timely Payment

Year	*Average Wage Rate (Rs) per Person-day*	*Percentage of Payments Generated Within Three Days**
2006–7	82	8.79
2007–8	84	31.17
2008–9	84	33.3
2009–10	90	66.98
2010–11**	97	76.94

Source: NGRGA's official website: nrega.nic.in, and nrega.ap.gov.in (27.8.2010).

Notes: *After closing of the weekly muster, normally the third day is fixed for generating payments. But there may be delays in actual payment because of local personnel problems.

**First six months only.

The second problem of measurement was solved by the twin approaches of 'single-pit', or appropriate marking of the work site, by fixing the visit of a technical assistant on a fixed day every week for each cluster, and logging the same in the muster. Recently, there had been further technological upgradation of the system by developing software to transfer measurements through cell phone.[4]

The third problem of payment was solved by opting post-offices and banks for payment by using latest technology including Biometrics. Presently, Andhra Pradesh has moved from payment through post-office to payment by Biometric Smart Card System, operated by O-Mass Agency. In each panchayat, the system is operated by a woman, sponsored by the VO of SHGs. Payments are made based on a biometric device, which is linked to a bank by a cell phone.[5]

MIS in Andhra Pradesh

While all other states use MIS designed and provided by the National Informatics Centre (NIC), Andhra Pradesh uses its own MIS, developed by TCS. Their MIS has been credited for effectively reducing instances of inefficient implementation and corrupt execution of NREGS[6] (Box 3.2).

The MIS for Andhra Pradesh differs from the NIC-based platform in three key ways: (i) transactions are computerized at every step of the implementation of NREGS; (ii) the wage-seeker is put at the centre of all operations; and (iii) the primary aim is to expedite measurement and wage payment cycles, to ensure correct and timely payment of workers.[7]

Transparency and Accountability: The Role of Social Audit

Though social audit as a tool of transparency and accountability began with the public hearing (or *Jan Sunvai*) in Rajasthan, it ultimately found its stronghold in NREGS implementation in Andhra Pradesh. The State Government established a state-level social audit unit with a senior civil servant heading it and several experts involved in training of social auditors at different levels. Social audit, besides bringing out the strengths and weaknesses in the implementation of the scheme, also helped the wage seekers become more aware of—and protect—their rights. Social audit had emerged as an important countervailing force against vested interests that tried to misappropriate NREGS funds (Raju, 2009; and Akella and Kidami 2007).

Box 3.2 MIS and Monitoring Wage Payments

In Andhra Pradesh, the MIS is designed to be an instrument to actively monitor the implementation of NREGS. This is particularly apparent when one looks at the procedures put into place to manage the payment cycle and monitor the timeliness of wage payments.

The AP-Software helps minimize delays in wage payments in two ways: (i) by tightly monitoring wage payments if they are delayed by more than 3 days; and (ii) by making use of a performance-based management tool.

Several features of the payment cycle are particularly noteworthy:

(i) Once work is on-going on a worksite, NREGA staff at the manual level is instructed to follow a tight schedule and enter Muster Roll and measurement data in the MIS by the end of every week.
(ii) Internal cross-checking procedures are automated to scan for inconsistencies and completeness of information in the pay orders.
(iii) Indicators are in place in the MIS to signal delays in the issuance of pay orders and cheques issued after 1–3 days.
(iv) Close monitoring ensues for wage payments delayed by more than 3 days, with indicators signaling whether wages were paid within 15 days, within 15–30 days, or are delayed by more than 30 days.
(v) All steps in the procedure of wage payment are computerized. In particular, pay slips given to workers and pay orders are automatically generated by the Manual Computer Center once muster rolls and measurement sheets have been entered in the MIS.

Source: Thi Minh-Phuong Ngo* 'Note on NREGA's Management Information System (MIS)', 7 March 2010.

Note: *A Vietnamese Visiting Scholar at Centre for Development Economics, Delhi School of Economics.

Under the aegis of the State social audit unit, teams provide training to village social auditors in each of the 1,100 mandals. Social audit in the State began with the first phase of NREGS, and has since been conducted regularly in all districts. The State Government has made it an institutionalized system (Box 3.3). It has incorporated certain special provisions under NREGS in favour of certain disadvantaged groups like the physically handicapped and bonded labour (Box 3.4).

Box 3.3 Social Audit of NREGS Experiences of Rajasthan and Andhra Pradesh*

The NREGA made social audit mandatory under Section 17, vesting these powers with the Gram Sabha. Section 13 of Schedule I (at the end of the Act) reiterated that 'even scheme shall contain adequate provisions for ensuring transparency and accountability at all levels of implementation'.

Rajasthan

At the behest of the Campaign for Right to Work and Right to Information (SR Abhiyan, a loose network of NGOs and activists in the state), Rajasthan had a head start in the process compared to many other states. Social audit in Bhilwara district in October 2009 was the first attempt by the Abhiyan (NGO network) and government to come together in a participatory mode and conduct an audit of each and every village in an entire district, which uncovered huge frauds, especially in the material component in the form of inflated expenditure. The intention then was to replicate this in every district of the state. But this brought powerful resistance by *Sarpanches* (Panchayat Presidents) and Gram Sewaks (Panchayat Secretaries), supported by opposition political parties. The adhoc arrangement of social audit, without proper institutionalization, made the process difficult. What started as a massive success at the behest of the NGO network failed to continue the momentum and social audit in Rajasthan faces an impasse, leaving the corrupt to get away. While the strength and awareness that the local people acquired by these one-off social audits was immense, it lacked an institutionalized mechanism to keep it sustaining and truly empowering.

Andhra Pradesh

'Andhra Pradesh (AP), which started Social Audits after Rajasthan, moved to a position where others could take a lesson on the benefits of institutionalization of the process. AP has put in place a system where an autonomous Society for Social Audit, Accountability and Transparency (SSAT), led by a social activist (and not a government servant), has institutionalized social audit of MGNREGA in such a way that it maximizes government support but minimizes its interference. Importantly, it has maintained a separation of the implementing and auditing bodies, and proved that ordinary labourers, when imparted with the right skills, can conduct effective social audits. Today, social audits are carried out regularly in all districts of AP. Social audit teams are selected from the villages, based on a randomized process, and trained by district resource persons, themselves selected and trained by SSAT. They are then allotted villages to conduct the social audits, thus avoiding the pitfalls of Gram Sabha selection, auditing in one's own village.'

'The effects, to say the least, have been dramatic. As of 30 June 2010, Rs 120 crores worth of misappropriated funds have come to light, of which around Rs 15 crores has been recovered; 33 field-level functionaries have been implicated; 3,842 staff have been dismissed based on the social audit findings and 1,430 suspended. A total of 548 FIRs have been lodged and 1,220 departmental enquiries have been initiated. All this has been made possible by 60,000 village social auditors (wage earners trained in social audit) trained by 700-odd district and state resource persons, largely drawn from civil society organizations and 22 technical resource persons. Nothing could establish with more clarity, the benefits of institutionalizing social audit in an open and participatory way. Andhra Pradesh's initiatives and its outcomes silence, in one stroke, all the opponents of social audit in the rest of the country. It is noteworthy that this approach to social audit is expounded in the 'NREGS-AP conducting of Social Audit Rules' adopted in 2008, based on the very recommendations of the MoRD working group, which is facing clandestine resistance at the central and other state levels'.

'In conclusion, it appears that the single most important ingredient missing in the social audit attempts in Rajasthan is the absence of a strong political and administrative will. Andhra has shown what a state can achieve with a strong resolve, versus a weak one'.

Source: Soumya Sivakumar 'No Guarantee Anymore', *The Hindu*, (Weekly magazine), 26 September 2010.

Box 3.4 Physically Challenged and Bonded Labour

The Government of Andhra Pradesh initiated special provisions relating to the physically challenged and bonded labour. The initiative Circular No. EGS/ dt. 30-4-2010 aims at organizing special groups of physically handicapped on the lines of Fixed Labour Groups (FLGs) and to ensure an income of Rs 15,000 by providing 150 days of work. Work provided to them would be 30 per cent less than normal work.

The Government also issued an order (GO Ms NO. 173, dt. 1-6-2009) for an intensive campaign in Mahabubnagar district to prevent labourers going into the fold of 'group masters' and ending up in bondage. It provides for giving work to freed bonded labour without limiting to 100 days per household. It also aims at bring women of freed bonded labour families under the fold of SHGs and providing them credit under 'pavala vaddi' (3 per cent interest) scheme.

However, there have been many failures too. Anomalies have been identified in the implementation process, including fudging of muster rolls, financial irregularities, poor maintenance of records, deviations in payment of wages to labourers, and non-existence of works shown as having been completed (Akalla and Kidami, 2007a). The State initiatives have been to overcome these deficiencies, but a systematic analysis of the degree of success in this direction is still to be made.

GRASSROOT ANALYSIS

As observed earlier, there has been wide variation in the performance of NREGS across the states. In a country of India's diversity, this may not be surprising. Despite consistent efforts to evolve appropriate systems of implementation by the Andhra Pradesh Government, there have been wide variation in performance across the districts; the overall performance has, nonetheless, been much better than several other states. Any aggregate account at the State level may not help in better understanding of its functioning. Hence, it was decided to have a grassroots analysis of the functioning of the NREGS at the village level in a district. Kuppanagar in Jarasangam Mandal, Medak district was chosen as a high-performing village and Makkarajpet in Chegunta Mandal in the same district as a low-performing one. Household sample surveys were conducted in both the villages. However, the focus of the following analysis was on Kuppanagar.

OVERVIEW OF NREGS IN KUPPANAGAR

Kuppanagar is a relatively large village with a population of 2,463 (Census of India, 2001). It is predominantly an agricultural village, with about 3,000 acres of cultivated land classified as dryland. About 15 per cent of land is irrigated by groundwater sources. Pulses, sugarcane, jowar, cotton, potato, jute are the main crops, and a wide variety of other crops like ginger, banana, mango, turmeric etc. are also grown to a smaller extent.

The social composition of the village shows that almost 80 per cent of the population is SCs and OBCs. Majority among the remaining population are Muslims, who are also largely dependent on agriculture. Table 3.6 provides an overview of the working of the NREGS in Kuppanagar over four years. What is interesting is that almost all households, cutting across all communities, and regardless of their

TABLE 3.6 Overview of Social Groups and Participation in NREGS Employment in Kuppanagar

Social Group	*2006–7*	*2007–8*	*2008–9*	*2009–10*
I. Households Registered and Working				
i) SC Registered	245	245	245	245 (100)
SC Working	83	121	120	130 (53.0)
ii) ST Registered	4	4	4	4
ST Working	0	1	0	1
iii) OBC Registered	316	316	316	316 (100)
OBC Working	14	50	60	128 (40.6)
iv) Others Registered	16	156	156	156 (100)
Others Working	0	13	30	55 (35.3)
v) All Registered	721	721	721	721 (100)
All Working	97	185	210	314 (43.6)
II. Individuals Registered and Working				
i) *Individuals Registered*				
Male	804	804	804	804
Female	804	804	804	804
Total	1,608	1,608	1,608	1,608

(*Cont'd*)

Table 3.6 (*Cont'd*)

Social Group	*2006–7*	*2007–8*	*2008–9*	*2009–10*
ii) *Individuals Working*				
Male	118	145	172	302
Female	127 (51.8)	210 (59.15)	238 (58.0)	335 (52.6)
Total	245 (100)	355 (100)	410 (100)	637 (100)
SC	211 (86.12)	256 (72.1)	268 (65.4)	293 (46.0)
ST	0	3	0	9
III. Average Days of Employment per Household	52	144	74	84
IV. Average Wage Rate per Day per Person (Rs)	126	93	95	110
V. Total Number of Households Completing 100 Days of Employment	13	93	54	121
VI. Average NREGS Earnings per Household (Rs)	6,535	13,368	7,062	9,240

Source: www.nrega.ap.gov.in (6.1.2011).

Note: Figures in parentheses are percentages.

actual readiness do physical work, are registered under NREGS and possess job cards. The process of registration and provision of cards were transparent. While all SC, ST, and OBC households registered in the very first year, the 'others' followed suit only in the second year. The households actually participating in NREGS work—though gradually increased over the years in number—were much lower at 43.6 per cent, even in the fourth year (2009–10). Women's participation was more than 50 per cent from the beginning, and their absolute number had increased from 127 (51.8 per cent) in 2006–7 to 335 (52.6 per cent) in 2009–10. The participation of SCs had been very high, and increased over the years, though their share had been declining because of increased participation by other communities' in NREGS work.

The performance of the village in terms of average man-days of employment, average wage rate, households completing 100 days or more of employment, and annual household earnings showed fluctuation during the last three years. But the fluctuation was relatively at higher levels of performance. The decline in 2008–9 appeared to be common for many parts of the State, though substantial improvement had been seen in 2009–10. What follows is a much more detailed analysis based on the household sample survey.

Table 3.7 presents the caste and class composition of the households selected for the sample survey in Kuppanagar. As mentioned earlier, special emphasis in the selection of works for implementation of the NREGS had been placed by the State Government on irrigation, land development and horticulture plantation on private lands of SC, ST, BPL households, assigned lands, lands of IAY beneficiaries and small-marginal farmers. Keeping this in view, the sample was designed in such a way that it provided adequate representation to all communities as well as all classes of landholdings among those participating in NREGS works.

Some of the pre-conditions for successful implementation of a rights-based employment programme—like the one under NREGA, with a primary role to PRIs—were related to the extent of awareness among the workers on their entitlements, the organization of workers to canalize not only their demand for work, but also for participation in the selection of works that would benefit them and the community as a whole. Making the procedures simple and implementation process transparent became part of successful implementation.

TABLE 3.7 Caste and Class (Size of Land Holding) Classification of Sample Households (Kuppanagar)

Caste	*Landless*	*Marginal*	*Small*	*Semi-medium*	*Medium*	*Large*	*All*
SC	9	6	14	13	8	Nil	50
OBC	2	3	4	5	5	–	19
Others	4	4	4	7	4	–	23*
All	15	13	22	25	17	0	92

Source: Household Sample Survey.

Note: *Twenty households of these 'others' belong to Muslim community, which is also mainly agriculture dependant. Upper castes under 'others' in the village constitute a very meagre proportion.

The Kuppanagar experience showed that there had been considerable effort by both the Panchayat functionaries and the community based organizations, like the VO of SHGs, in creating awareness about the entitlements under NREGS. But, most of them were still not aware that they were entitled to transportation charges if the work was beyond 5 km from their village, and that they were entitled to compensation if they were not provided work within 15 days from the date of their demand. This was probably because even those responsible for creation of awareness did not anticipate works beyond 5 km, or failure of provision of work.

PROCEDURAL AND PROCESS DIMENSIONS

Table 3.8 provides household responses relating to certain procedures and processes of implementation at Kuppanagar. Though, as per the rules of the Act and the guidelines, every household had to submit a written application demanding work, in practice, hardly any one did it. Here, demand for work was invariably an informal request to the Sarpanch on behalf of SSS.

There was a good rapport between the Sarpanch and the workers organized into SSS, also called FLGs. Each FLG consisted of 10 to 20 workers, and continued for at least two years. From each FLG, two persons were selected, one as 'Mate' and another as 'Assistant Mate', and were imparted two days of training at the Mandal level. The training afforded better awareness of their rights and commitment to get and complete as much work as possible. Wherever SSSs existed,

Table 3.8 Procedural and Process Dimensions of NREGS in Kuppanagar, 2009–10

	SC	*OBC*	*Others*	*All*
I. Mode of Seeking Work				
a. Written Application	Nil	Nil	4	1
b. Group/Individual Informal Request	100	100	96	99
II. Person/Agency Approached for Work				
a. Sarpanch	100	95	96	98
b. Ward Member	–	5	–	1
c. Field Assistant	–	–	4	1
III. Time Lag between Request and Provision of Work				
a. < 15 days	100	100	91	98
b. 15 to 30 days	–	–	4	1
c. Not sure	–	–	4	1
IV. Muster Roll Signature				
a. Daily	–	–	–	-
b. Weekly	100	100	100	100
V. Evidence of Days Worked				
a. Job Card	–	–	–	–
b. Muster Roll	100	100	100	100
c. Weekly Pay Slip	100	100	100	100
VI. Gap between Completion of Work and Payment				
a. Within a Week	–	–	–	–
b. Week to 15 days	14	63	91	44
c. > 15 days	86	37	9	56
VII. Availability of Worksite Facilities				
a. Drinking Water	100	100	100	100
b. First-aid Box (sometimes not found)	100	100	100	100
c. Tent/Shade (sometimes only)	98	100	91	97
d. 'Aya'/Creche/ICDS (sometimes only)	80	100	96	88

Source: Household Sample Survey.

Note: All numbers are given in per cent.

their performance in securing work for longer duration was noticed. In Kuppanagar, at the time of field work in January 2011, there were 37 SSSs of 20 members each. The rapport between the panchayat and the SSSs enabled the groups to get work within 15 days of demand.

The workers did not complain about certain minor deviations, like signing the muster roll weekly instead of daily, or depending on muster roll and pay slips generated as the proof for days of work instead of entries in the job card. But the wage payments continued to exceed 15 days in almost half the cases. Regarding workplace facilities, while drinking water was provided, first-aid was kept at house, and shade and crèche were hardly in evidence.

Panchayats and Participatory Process

Despite the general perception that performance of Panchayats in Andhra Pradesh is much below par, Kuppanagar proves an exception. Table 3.9 shows that the due process of representativeness in administering NREGS is largely evident in the panchayat. Ironically, the higher level of grassroots participation is due to the top-down approach in prioritizing works.

The State Government orders that all the lands of the farmers eligible for the 'Fourth Category' of NREGS works on private lands makes every poor farmer be present at the panchayat meeting, to

Table 3.9 Panchayat and Participation of at least One Member of Household in Gram Sabha in Previous 12 Months (Kuppanagar)

Community	*Attended Gram Sabha*	*Response of Those Attended*		
		Participated in Discussion	*Gram Sabha Discussed NREGS*	*Gram Sabha Discussed Selection of Works*
SC	70	20	100	100
OBC	53	70	100	100
Others	41	56	100	100
All	59	35	100	100

Source: Household Sample Survey.

Note: All numbers are given in per cent.

know when the turn for work on his land is due, and the kind of work that would follow.

Substantive Outcomes

The substantive outcomes on the basis of the performance of the NREGS include average number of man-days per household, average wage per person day, the improvements in land resources of the poor, the extent of reduction in consumption deprivation of the poor, and the overall improvement in the soil and water resources of the village. Table 3.10 provides details about the extent of average household employment provided, the average wage level and the average annual household earnings under NREGS.

Person-days of Employment per Household

Kuppanagar shows an abnormally high average of 161 man-days of employment per household, against 100 days guaranteed under the NREGA. This requires some explanation. First, there are several instances in Andhra Pradesh where household employment under NREGS has been in excess of 100 days per annum. Second, employment in excess of 100 days per household is observed in villages where the registered households are high and where the panchayats make labour budgets, and select a large number of works, with expectation of larger number of households. When the actual turn out of households falls short of these projected high estimates, those who turn out are

Table 3.10 Average Person-days of Employment, Wages per Day, and Household Earning under NREGS, 2009–10 (Kuppanagar)

Work, Wages, and Earning	*SC*	*OBC*	*Others*	*All*
1. Average Person-days of Employment per Person	163	159	163	161
2. Average Wages Per Person Day	104	99	102	103
3. Average Annual Earnings from NREGS (Rs)	16,973	13,472	16,522	16,137

Source: Household Sample Survey.

Note: All numbers are given in per cent.

allowed to complete the planned works. This is exactly what has been happening in Kuppanagar. There has been a third element in the year in question, when additional works were provided in Kuppanagar under Community Managed Sustainable Agriculture (CMSA).

Additional Worker and Additional Employment Effect

What would be the impact on agriculture if there were to be a substantial increase in employment under NREGS, as in the case of Kuppanagar? Would there be a shortage of labour for agriculture? Or decline in the area cultivated due to shortage of labour? The Kuppanagar experience suggests that though initially there were signs of shortage of labour, over the past three years there have been interesting developments in the working hours and the working day. Gradually, there has been a shift in the daily work schedule of NREGS works. It is increasingly tending to be confined to forenoon and workers are taking up either agriculture labour or working on their own farm work in the afternoon, thus earning NREGS wages in the forenoon and earning from agriculture in the second half of the day, thereby doubling their day into two earning days. This is a clear additional employment effect. The other is the inducement of relatively higher wages for women in NREGS compared to agriculture. Some of the women, who do not work in agriculture, are participating in NREGS work, which attracts them because, besides the relatively higher wages, it is 'government' work, not work for a private contractor or a landowner. Thus, the additional employment and additional worker effects together appear to keep labour supply at a manageable level, but definitely at a higher level of wages.

NREGS Calendar

Like in many other parts of the country, NREGS work is suspended here during peak agricultural season. Combined with the NREGS investment on the fallow and rain-fed lands of SCs and other poor farmers, Kuppanagar has witnessed an increase in the area cultivated in the last two years.

NREGS Minimum Wages

In the first phase of NREGS, the minimum wage was Rs 80 per day. It was increased in Andhra Pradesh to Rs 100 in 2009. Since the NREGS wage is calculated on the basis of work done at the schedule of rates, the minimum wage level is only indicative and could be higher or lower, depending on the turnover of work. But in Kuppanagar, the average wage level obtained has always been higher. Even when the minimum wage was Rs 80, Kuppanagar workers logged wages ranging from Rs 93 to Rs 126 (Table 3.6). The results of the household survey show the average rate of Rs 103 in 2009–10. In Kuppanagar, work is allotted to a group calibrating the quantity equivalent to the schedule of rates that would fetch minimum wage to each member. Often, some members of the group do not turn up but the others complete the allotted work, and this increases the average wage to a level higher than the indicated minimum wage. Average wages are paid equally to men and women. The average NREGS wages logged by Kuppanagar workers are higher than local agricultural wages, especially for women. The impact of NREGS wages are felt in two ways. First, overall agricultural wages have increased. Male wages in agriculture increased from Rs 80 before NREGS to Rs 100, and female agricultural wages increased from Rs 50 to Rs 80. The male-female wage gap has declined substantively. The hours of agricultural work also declined, and it is invariably half a day, or about five hours of work at the wages mentioned above. The net impact on agriculture is higher wage costs.

The responses in the group discussion revealed an interesting pattern. Regardless of the social group, most of the NREGS workers were also small-marginal farmers who felt the impact of rising agricultural wages, but only marginally. First, their earnings, especially those of women, from NREGS were substantial. Second, they had substantial gains by way of improved productivity of their land due to NREGS land development works undertaken. Therefore, the small-marginal farmers, and of course the landless workers, did not have much to complain about regarding rising agricultural wages. Their main complaint was about the steep rise in prices or inflation.

The response of relatively bigger farmers, normally non-participants in NREGS, was about the rising agricultural wages. Interestingly, they did not complain about the NREGS, since most of them benefited from water table increase in their wells and bore wells due to NREGS works, especially due to de-silting of tanks and ponds, and construction of a number of percolation tanks in the village. These farmers had been repeatedly making a plea that half of their agricultural work and wages could be shared as NREGS.

Household Earnings from NREGS and its Impact

As a measure of social protection, the NREGS is expected to provide certain minimum employment that would ensure food security and help in reducing the intensity of poverty. In Kuppanagar, the contribution of NREGS to average household income for the year of enquiry (2009–10) was comparatively substantial. It was partly because of the households obtaining more than 100 days employment under NREGS, and also because of clearing work to obtain more than the indicated minimum wages. Under NREGS, the SC households obtained the highest average household earnings of Rs 16,973, while for the sample households it worked out to an average of Rs 16,137 (Table 3.10). According to the Tendulkar Committee, the rural poverty line for Andhra Pradesh for 2009–10 was Rs 671 per capita per month. For an average household of five, the threshold poverty income worked out to Rs 40,260. The average household earnings under NREGS in Kuppanagar (Rs 16,137) through NREGS household employment (161 person-days) amounted to 40 per cent of poverty threshold income, thereby supplementing the income substantially. Assuming there are two working members, and if the household is depending solely on wage employment, to cross poverty threshold income, it should have an additional employment of another 115 days of work for each person at NREGS level of wages. Even for Kuppanagar, the results of the sample survey present the 'best' scenario of employment and earnings under NREGS, and is an exception. The average scenario for Kuppanagar, taking into consideration all 314 working households at a wage rate of Rs 110, the average household earnings worked out to Rs 9,240 for 2009–10, earned over an average level of employment of 84 man-days. At this level of earnings, the households could cross poverty threshold if only there was an additional employment of 290 man-days per household or 145 per working person from other sources at NREGS wage rate. What transpires is that in all drought-prone, rain-fed agricultural areas, there is need to raise NREGS ceiling of man-days of employment from 100 to 150 days, and that appears possible without affecting the supply of labour to agriculture, as the Kuppanagar experience suggests.

Under the best of conditions, the earnings under NREGS could supplement, to a substantial extent, other sources of household income and help move out of poverty. The purpose for which the earnings from NREGS is utilized would throw light on the income elasticity of expenditure and on the nature of priorities the relatively poor households have. Although it is difficult to separate NREGS earnings from the overall household expenditure, an effort was made to obtain information as to what difference would the earnings from NREGS make to the expenditure pattern of the sample households. Table 3.11 presents the pattern of utilization of NREGS earnings. What is revealing is that almost one-fourth of the earnings is used for additional consumption of food. This is a clear indication of widespread under-consumption of food in rural households. Food, together with other essential items like clothing, accounts for almost two-fifths of the utilization of NREGS earning. Next in order is expenditure on education and health, which together account for one-fourth of the utilization. That even the poor have to pay for education and health substantially is a reflection of the state of access to basic needs, and the growing privatization of these essential social sector services.

TABLE 3.11 Pattern of Utilization of NREGS Earnings (in Rs)

Items of Expenditure	*SC*	*OBC*	*Others*	*All*
Consumption Food Items	2,596 (16.08)	3,261 (25.9)	6,735 (43.04)	3,735 (24.32)
Other Essentials	2,183 (13.52)	2,368 (18.29)	2,506 (16.01)	2,300 (14.52)
Health	1,750 (10.84)	1,684 (13.01)	1,409 (9.00)	1,654 (10.77)
Children's Education	3,140 (19.45)	1,211 (9.35)	1,636 (10.45)	2,374 (15.46)
Prepayment of Debt	3,420 (21.19)	2,947 (22.77)	2,182 (13.94)	3,022 (19.68)
Purchase or Repair of Household Articles	1,560 (9.66)	1,474 (11.39)	1,136 (7.26)	1,440 (9.38)
Purchase and Repair of House/Land	1,240 (7.68)	Nil	Nil	681
Festivals/Ceremonies	54	Nil	46	41
Others	200	–	–	110
Total Expenditure	16,143 (100)	12,945 (100)	15,650 (100)	15,357 (100)

Source: Household Sample Survey.

Note: Figures in bracket show share in total.

It seems that all—or a bulk of—the achievements of providing guarantee of certain number of days of employment, and ensuring supplementary income should end up being utilized for obtaining provision of public goods like education and health facilities. Further, the fact of another one-fifth of additional earning going for repayment of high-interest informal loans shows the widespread indebtedness of rural households.

Hunger and Food Insecurity

The best of situations could have some deficiencies and differences in assessment, but one area in which there is near unanimity in Kuppanagar is the contribution of NREGS in overcoming hunger and food insecurity. Table 3.12 shows the widespread prevalence of hunger and food insecurity in Kuppanagar before NREGS.

This could also be evidenced from high proportion of NREGS earnings being used for additional consumption of food. But the major achievement of NREGS is that hunger has almost become a thing of the past in Kuppanagar, though 8 per cent of SC households still suffer from food deficiency. Though NREGS earnings are the key factor, the better functioning PDS, and the SHGs' intervention to enable bulk buying of foodgrain and other essential commodities facilitated the process of moving out of food insecurity.

Household Perceptions about NREGS Impact

The perception of the participating households on the overall impact of NREGS on their living conditions in Kuppanagar is elaborated in Table 3.13. Though there is general agreement that NREGS has made

Table 3.12 Incidence of Hunger/Inadequacy of Food, Before and After NREGS

Experience of Household Incidence of Hunger/Inadequacy of Food	*SC*	*OBC*	*Others*	*All*
Before NREGS	92	100	91	93
After NREGS	8	0	0	4

Source: Household Sample Survey.

Note: All numbers are given in per cent.

TABLE 3.13 Perception of Households about the Impact of NREGS on Living Conditions

Perception	*SC*	*OBC*	*Others*	*All*
1. A Lot of Change for Better	4	5	27	10
2. Some Change for Better	96	95	73	90
3. Hardly Any Change	0	0	0	0

Source: Household Sample Survey.

Note: All numbers are given in per cent.

a positive difference to their living conditions, most of them (90 per cent) still appear to feel that the change is not substantial enough.

And this is in the context of one of the best performing villages. Possibly there are rising expectations in rural areas, and programmes like NREGS could fulfil only part of these expectations.

NREGS AND PRIVATE LANDS OF THE 'POOR'

As pointed out earlier, of the nine broad categories of works to be undertaken under the NREGS, the fourth category—works on the private lands of certain social groups—is accorded special priority in Andhra Pradesh. These include provision of irrigation facility, horticulture plantation, and land development facilities on the land belonging to the SC, ST, and BPL households, or beneficiaries of land reforms, or beneficiaries of IAY and small-marginal farmers. The panchayat of Kuppanagar has a good record in undertaking community as well as private land-based works with focus on water conservation and land productivity. Table 3.14 shows the NREGS development works on private lands of SCs and others. Given the fact that SCs constitute almost one-fourth of the population of the village, and that most of them have some land, often dry and uncultivable, one of the lasting ways of improving their economic condition is to develop their land.

Table 3.15 shows the beneficiaries of NREGS works in private lands, and SCs get top priority in these works. Table 3.16 shows that beneficiaries include marginal to medium size farms. Table 3.17 shows that most of the sample households obtained the benefit of tank silt application to their lands. In fact, the visible results of tank silt

TABLE 3.14 NREGS Development Works on Private Lands under Progress in Kuppanagar during 2010–11*

Type of Work	*Community-wise Beneficiaries*				*Total Expenditure (Rs lakh)*	*Average per Household (Rs)*
	SC	*OBC*	*Others*	*All*		
(1)	*(2)*	*(3)*	*(4)*	*(5)*	*(6)*	*(7)*
1. Desilting and Silt Application	103	13	1	117	13.08	11,178
2. Deep Polishing in Hard Soil	100	16	7	123	2.21	1,800
3. Development of Fallow/ Dry-lands	103	–	–	103	61.12	59,337
4. Open Wells	4	2	–	6	2.48	41,358

Source: Mandal Computer Centre, Jarasangam, Medak District.

Note: *These works are approved and implemented by the panchayat for the years 2010–11 and 2011–12.

application by way of increased crop yields has created very high demand from the SC and other eligible households for this programme, and the panchayat responded by according high priority to the same.

THE CONTRAST OF MAKKARAJPET

There are also villages in Medak district where, unlike in Kuppanagar, the NREGS performance is much below par. Makkarajpet in Chegunta Mandal is one such village. The household sample survey conducted in Makkarajpet threw up many interesting facts, some of which are presented to highlight the contrasts. Table 3.18 presents basic differences in performance of NREGS in these two villages. Makkarajpet, like Kuppanagar, is a fairly large sized village. In Makkarajpet too, almost all households are registered under NREGS. One positive feature of Makkarajpet was a higher proportion (87 per cent) of registered households participating in NREGS in 2009–10, compared to Kuppanagar's participation (44 per cent). This feature of Makkarajpet may also indicate a higher need of the households for additional employment, leading to higher commitment for effective implementation of the NREGS. But the actual

Table 3.15 Households Benefiting from Private Land Development under NREGS

Community	*All Household*	*Landless Households*	*Households with Land*	*NREGS Private Land Improvement Work**	*Extent of Land Covered (acres)*	
					Total	*Average per Household*
SC	50	9	41	38 (93)	62	1.6
OBC	19	2	17	8 (47)	14	1.8
Others	23	4	19	8 (47)	14	1.8
All	92	15	77	54 (70)	89	1.6

Source: Household Sample Survey.

Notes: *Households with land benefiting from NREGS improvement of private lands.

Figures in parentheses are percentages to Households with land.

TABLE 3.16 Size-class of Holdings and Households Benefiting from Private Land Development

Size of Holdings	*Number of Households*	*Households under NREGS Private Land Works*	*Total Extent of Area Covered (acres)*	*Average per Household (acres)*
Marginal	13	7	6	0.9
Small	22	18	30	107
Semi-Medium	25	16	32	2.0
Medium	17	13	21	1.6
Large	–	–	–	–
All	77	54	89	1.6

Source: Household Sample Survey.

TABLE 3.17 Type of Work on Own Lands under NREGS

Type of Work	*Marginal*	*Small*	*Semi-Medium*	*Medium*	*All Total*
Tank Silt Application	7	16	15	10	48 (89%)
Levelling and Bunding	–	1	1	2	4 (7%)
Horticulture	–	–	–	1	1 (2%)
Other Works	–	1	–	–	1 (2%)
All Works	7	18	16	13	54 (100%)

Source: Household Sample Survey.

performance was dismal, with only 31 man-days of employment per household, earnings much lower than the minimum wage, and average annual earnings from NREGS being at a low level of Rs 2,781. This was less than 7 per cent of poverty threshold income of rural households in the State. Hardly 1 per cent of households completed 100 days of employment, and Table 3.19 shows that payment of wages takes more than 15 days in almost all cases. Though most of the households felt that NREGS made some difference to their living conditions, 12 per cent felt that there was hardly any difference (Table 3.20). Worst of all, 87 per cent of households reported that hunger was still a persistent problem.

TABLE 3.18 A Comparative Picture of Better (Kuppanagar) and Worse (Makkarajpet) Scenarios of NREGS in the Same (Medak) District of Andhra Pradesh, 2009–10

Indicators of Performance	*Kuppanagar (Jarasangam Mandal)*	*Makkarajpet (Chegunta Mandal)*
1. Households Registered	721	656
2. Households Working under NREGS	314 (43.55)*	572 (87.2)*
3. Average Days of Employment per Household	84	31
4. Average Wages per Person Day (Rs)	110	86
5. Average Annual Household Earning From NREGS (Rs)	9,240*	2,781
6. Households Completing 100 days of Employment	121 (38.54)**	4 (0.7)**

Source: www.nrega.ap.gov.in (26.1.2011).

Notes: *Percentage of households working under NREGS to total households.

**Percentage of households completing 100 days employment to total households.

It is very difficult to explain satisfactorily how there could be a Makkarajpet in the same district which had a star performer like Kuppanagar. Nonetheless, there were some tell-tale indicators. The panchayat in Makkarajpet did not seem to be cohesive. It reflected a less participative process. There was no evidence of rapport of the panchayat leadership with wage earning groups.

While the entire Kuppanagar approached the Sarpanch, the entire Makkarajpet went to the panchayat secretary, that too with formal written applications. These applications, often generated at the panchayat, could also be fabricated. Social audits revealed mismanagement as well as misappropriation at the village level. At the time of field work, there was no regular Field Assistant, a very key functionary at the village level. Two of the earlier Field Assistants were dismissed on charges of misappropriation.

It was not possible to get the list of SSS in Makkarajpet. So the best of the state-level administrative initiatives could not possibly yield matching results in the implementation of a grassroots governance-based programme like NREGS without the panchayats

TABLE 3.19 Comparison of Procedural and Institutional Aspects of Better (Kuppanagar) and Worse (Makkarajpet) Scenarios in the Same (Medak) District

	Kuppanagar (Jarasangam Mandal)	*Makkarajpet (Chegunta Mandal)*
1. Mode of Seeking Work		
a. Written Application	1	93
b. Informal Request	99	7
2. Person/Agency Approached for Work		
a. Sarpanch	98	1
b. Ward Member	1	–
c. Secretary	–	99
d. Rozgar Sevak	1	–
3. Time Taken to get Wages		
a. Within a week	–	1
b. Within 15 days	44	–
c. More than 15 days	56	99
4. At least one from Household Attended Gram Sabha	59	43
5. Gram Sabha Discussed NREGS	100	84
6. Selection of NREGS Works Discussed in Gram Sabha	100	84

Source: Household Sample Survey.

Note: All numbers are given in per cent.

acquiring capacities for better delivery through a transparent, participatory process.

AN ASSESSMENT OF IMPACT

The following is an attempt to assess NREGS as a measure of social protection in Andhra Pradesh in terms of its impact on employment generated, wages and earnings, agriculture and labour market, migration, hunger and food security, and productivity of the land of the SC, ST, and other small-marginal farmers. As pointed out earlier, it is based on household sample surveys in two villages, field notes, and focus group discussions in 16 villages (of which 12 were personally

TABLE 3.20 Incidence of Hunger and Household Perceptions of NREGS on Living Conditions in the Best and Worst Cases

Household Perceptions on NREGS on Living Conditions	*Kuppanagar (Jarasangam Mandal)*	*Makkarajpet (Chegunta Mandal)*
a. A Lot of Change for Better	10	7
b. Some Change for Better	90	81
c. Hardly any Change for Better	–	12
Household Incidence of Hunger/Inadequacy of Food		
a. Before NREGS	93	*
b. After NREGS	4	87

Source: Household Sample Survey.

Notes: All numbers are given in per cent.

*Not clear.

visited by the author) spread over two drought prone districts, among other secondary sources.

NREGS EMPLOYMENT, WAGES, HOUSEHOLD EARNINGS, AND FOOD SECURITY

A large survey of impact of NREGS in Andhra Pradesh (Galab *et al.* 2008) provided the author access to 45 Focus Group Discussion (FGD) reports, covering 45 villages in nine Mandals of seven districts. These reports showed that by mid-2008, agricultural wages increased in all the villages as a result of NREGS work. Male-female agricultural wages started narrowing. Female agricultural wages, which ranged from Rs 30–50 across the villages, increased to Rs 60–80 by 2008.

In most of the villages visited, there was a gradual increase in the man-days of employment from about 40 to about 70 by 2009–10. During 2010–11, at the time of the visits, in some of the villages the man-days of employment already exceeded 80 per household. And in the case of some job cards, it was noticed that it exceeded 100 days. This was common to many villages. The classic extremes were captured by Kuppanagar and Makkarajpet. One major change that was common to all the villages visited was that NREGS work fetched the beneficiaries wages ranging from Rs 80–100; in some cases it exceeded Rs 100, as in the case of Kuppanagar, but in most cases the range was Rs 90–100. Equal wages were paid to men and women participating in NREGS work.

The Andhra Pradesh experience of the high, average and low performance in NREGS employment, wage rates, and household earnings is highly instructive and worth presenting here as a summary statement (Table 3.21). While the relatively high average for the State as a whole could be attributed to state-level political and administrative commitment and initiatives, the high and the low observed at the grassroots level could be seen substantially as a result of the presence or absence of Participatory Governance at the panchayat level.

Hunger and Food Insecurity

The experiences of Kuppanagar and Makkarajpet show what difference effective implementation of NREGS could make to food insecurity in dryland areas. While Kuppanagar may show that hunger is a thing of the past, in Makkarajpet 85 per cent still feel that they have to suffer the privation. While there has been a marked improvement in the

Table 3.21 High, Average, and Low NREGS in Andhra Pradesh, 2009–10

Indicator	*Kuppanagar Village*		*State Average*	*Makkarajpet Village*
	Sample Households	*All Households*		
1. Average Person-days of Employment per Household	161	84	65	31
2. Average Wage per Person-day (Rs)	103	110	92	86
3. Average Annual NREGS Earnings per Household (Rs)	16,137	9,240	5,980	2,781
4. NREGS Earnings as percentage of Poverty Threshold Income (Tendulkar Poverty Line)	40.0	23.0	14.9	6.9

Source: www.nrega.ap.gov.in and Household Sample Survey.

consumption of food and reduced food insecurity, there is growing concern about rising prices. There are interesting instances reported in FGDs which reveal varying degrees of impact, depending on the local conditions and the performance of NREGS. For instance, five villages in Karimnagar district report that NREGS has no impact on food insecurity, meaning Karimnagar, being agriculturally prosperous, did have higher levels of employment, wages, and consumption of food, and hence NREGS did not make a marked difference. At the same time there is Adilabad, a relatively backward district, where NREGS does not make much difference to food insecurity either. It is because of poor implementation of the NREGS in the district, no assured employment, low earnings from the scheme, and continued migration which together perpetuate low levels of food consumption.

In contrast, in Khammam district, where there were villages with food deficit and hunger before NREGS, reports show a complete turnaround in food consumption and security because of better implementation of NREGS, more employment, earnings, and access to food. There is also change in food habits, and some households have reported that they consume 'tiffin' for the breakfast. There are instances of the poor whose income before NREGS were too meagre to meet their own consumption requirements, and therefore, neglected the needs of the aged members of the household. NREGS has enabled them to take better care of their aged parents. Some households reported that they provide pocket money to parents to buy toddy and beedis.

Education and Health

In most of the households across the State, education of children and health are of high priority, next only to food in their expenditure out of additional earnings accruing from NREGS employment. It is paradoxical that NREGS employment, in the name of social protection, should result in the earnings ending up paying for much more basic social provisions like education and health, which are increasingly being privatized.

Other Labour Market Changes

Group Work

There are important changes in the nature of work, duration of working hours, and attitude to group work. Almost all work under

NREGS is in the form of group work. The workers in many places, like in Kuppanagar, are organized into FLGs called SSS. The group formation, training imparted to 'mates' of the groups, and working together for over two years appear to promote better awareness, solidarity, and motivation to perform better. The majority of groups are of mixed castes. There was considerable mutual understanding and sharing of work, especially when old people and the physically disabled are part of the group, where the stronger individuals compensate by taking more load but are willing to share wages equally. In the perception of workers, there is also certain amount of dignity associated with NREGS, as it is government work.

Change in Working Hours and Transformation of Working Day

There have been interesting developments in the hours of work. In many villages visited during May–June 2010, the hours of work as per NREGS were scheduled between 7 am and 12 noon or 1 pm. This was partly due to the summer season, and partly due to the need to attend to farm work in the afternoon. An interesting development was that there were households which worked in the forenoon carrying out NREGS work, and attended to their own farm work, or took up farm work for wages, in the afternoon.

The other shift in agricultural work is from daily wage employment to piece rate or contract employment. This has resulted in a working day being split into two sessions—one session to take up NREGS work, and the other to work on agriculture either for wages or on own account—in some places. Overall, the households observed that NREGS has improved the bargaining power of agricultural workers. They not only demand and get better wages, but also set terms for reduced working days. There is less regimentation at the work place, better treatment, respect for labourers, and more flexibility.

Impact on Agriculture

As observed earlier, NREGS has had a definite impact on agricultural wages, especially women's wages. Since male wages were higher even before NREGS, there was no significant increase in wages of male agricultural labour, but female agriculture labour wages increased considerably. To meet the seasonal increase in the demand for agricultural labour, some farmers are paying advance wages to the labour.

To meet the rising wage costs, many farmers appear to be looking for agricultural wage subsidy as a part of NREGS.

Seasonal NREGS Calendar

One of the developments as a response to seasonal shortage of agricultural labour is the mutually acceptable calendar of NREGS work, confining it to agricultural lean season, and avoiding works in the peak season. The workers too favour it, as it increases their earning days in a year.

Migration

Of the two villages surveyed, Kuppanagar and Makkarajpet, migration was not seen to be too high, and commuting for casual work to nearby towns has come down after NREGS. The author's analysis of reports of FGDs from 77 villages of 8 districts in the State (Reddy, 2011) shows that there was no migration in 12 villages, before or after NREGS.

Of the remaining, in four villages there was not much change in the migration situation, even after the job scheme, and in six other villages there was no clarity in the information recorded. The rest of the 55 villages witnessed varying degrees of decline in migration. Most of the decline was in distress migration, but not as much in the emerging process of movement of towards higher paying, relatively high productivity non-agricultural, and often, rural to urban mobility.

The non-distress type of migration from these villages, which is not affected much by NREGS, is of three types. One is the migration of male members of the household for high paying non-agricultural work, for relatively longer durations. For instance, from the villages of Kurnool district, which borders Karnataka, male members migrate to Bellary to work in construction, mining, and other activities. The second type is rural to rural migration, from dryland areas to fertile areas for agricultural work. For instance, from Mandals like Aspari in Kurnool district, members of entire household migrate to Guntur district during June–August to work in the *mirch* (chilli) and tobacco fields, where each migrating couple make as much as Rs 500 per day. These families return to their own villages in September–October to work in agriculture, and some, even in NREGS. The third type is commuting to neighbouring towns. For instance, in Kurnool district, members of some rural households commute to neighbouring towns, like Allagadda, to work in shops and other establishments where the wages are high. Interestingly, some work in NREGS in their villages in the morning, and commute in the afternoon to nearby towns to work in odd jobs, including vegetable and fruit vending.

SOCIAL AUDIT

Social audit as a countervailing process to check the misuse of power, by the local political and official functionaries, is one of the evolving institutions in participatory management of public programmes. As mentioned earlier, in Andhra Pradesh, the State devoted considerable resources to institutionalize social audit process. Yet it appears a long way before it becomes universal in participation as much as it has become universal in implementation. Even in the early stages of implementation of NREGS in 2008, in many villages there was awareness of social audit, though the workers were not aware of its provisions and processes. After the framing of 'NREGS-AP conducting of Social Audit Rules' and adoption of the same in 2008, a team of 60,000 social auditors (wage earners trained in social audit) enabled stabilization of the process that was thereafter carried on regular basis. One of the contributing factors for the credibility of NREGS in Andhra Pradesh is the institutionalization of the Social Audit process (see Box 3.3).

ASSETS OF THE WORKING POOR AND THE COMMUNITY

One of the signature works of the Andhra Pradesh Government, as part of the NREGS, is the development of the lands of the SC and ST households in particular, and other categories of small-marginal farmers, in that order of priority. There is hardly any village where development work on the land of these marginalized sections has not been undertaken.

There was widely shared positive response on the water and land development works under NREGS. Desilting and strengthening the bunds of the tanks, clearing of main as well as field channels, construction of percolation tanks were perceived as productive and beneficial works. In some of the villages there was evidence of increased *ayacut* under tanks, augmented water table, and switch to irrigated crops. Desilting and silt application brought double benefit of better storage; percolation resulted in augmented groundwater resources on the one hand, and silt application resulted in increased soil fertility and better yields.

Andhra Pradesh has earned a reputation of being one of the leading states where NREGS is successfully implemented, despite the principal agency for the implementation—Gram panchayat—being relatively weak. Political commitment to the programme, and the reinforcing perception that the programme makes a difference to political outcomes, emerge as the clear pointers to the ownership of the NREGS by the Government of Andhra Pradesh. Although this may be a necessary condition, it is not necessarily sufficient to make it successful. Mobilizing grassroot support and administrative ability to reach out are the other conditions. This has been achieved to an extent through active involvement of the SERP-promoted SHGs across the state, and senior administrators of high integrity and commitment to the cause of the marginalized, without any political interference. Yet another important dimension is the institutionalization of certain critical processes of implementation, and effective adoption of IT solutions like Electronic Muster Measurement System (E-MMS), and cell phone-linked smart cards based on biometrics, to deal with difficult problems like work measurement and prompt wage payment. Further, there is clarity in the approach of Andhra Pradesh that though NREGA is a product of national legislation and is a centrally sponsored programme, its implementation success is bound by state-level readiness to initiate appropriate innovation and build institutions that sustain the programme. All these state-initiated measures could translate into exemplary results if, and only if, the panchayats match their performance, as is exemplified by Kuppanagar on the positive side and Makkarajpet on the negative.

Notes

[1] Originally, SERP was promoted by the World Bank aid to build up SHGs as thrift groups, which over a period of time would serve as credit institutions, with a capacity to borrow from the banks and lend to the members at commercial rates of interest, obviating the need for targeted lending involving low, and often subsidized, interest. Ironically, as SHGs evolved as institutions of social mobilization, governments realized their political significance and extended interest subsidies. Thus, the unintended consequence of World Bank assistance resulted in an entrenched institution of SHGs enjoying social clout and interest subsidies.

[2] The difference between the priority rate of lending of 7 per cent and the 3 per cent is borne by the state government. It is also administered in a novel way. The borrowers pay the usual rate (7 per cent) but the subsidy is sent by the state agencies by way of cheque to the Village Organization (VO) of the SHGs, which distribute the same among members.

[3] Para I of Schedule I of NREGA was amended on 18 June 2008 to include small and marginal farmers, as defined in the Agricultural Debt Waiver and Debt Relief Scheme 2008, as eligible for the works on individual land.

[4] It is called Electronic Muster Measurement System (e-MMS). Under this system the Village Assistant records measurement every day and transfers the 'e-muster' through a cell phone. The Technical Assistant takes the measurements every week and transfers the 'e-measurement' data to the Mandal by cell phone. The Engineering Consultant (two or three for each Mandal) makes 'e-check measurement' and the Mandal Programme Officer acts as the 'e-muster verification officer', with power to verify and consolidate the information.

[5] The person chosen is one of the Vice-Presidents of the VO of SHGs. Often she is also an NREGS worker. She is paid a commission of Rs 500 per Rs 1 lakh.

[6] See Pankaj Mishra. 2009. 'Andhra finds tools to Plug NREGA Loopholes', *The Economic Times*, 21 September.

[7] See Santhi Kumari. 2008. 'NREGA—AP Software', in Piyush Gupta, R.K. Bagga (eds), *Compendium of E-governance Initiatives in India*. New Delhi: Universities Press.

References

Akella, Karuna Vakati and Sowmya Kidani. 2007. 'Social Audits in AP: A Process in Evolution', *Economic and Political Weekly*, 24 November: 18–19.

Census of India. 2001. *District Census Handbook*, Medak District, Series 2. Hyderabad, Andhra Pradesh.

Galab, S. *et. al*. 2009. 'Farmers' Suicides and Unfolding Agrarian Crisis in Andhra Pradesh', in D. Narasimha Reddy and Srijit Mishra (eds), *Agrarian Crisis in India*, pp. 164–98. New Delhi: Oxford University Press.

Galab S., Pruthvikar Reddy, E. Revathi, and M. Ravi. 2008. *Evaluation Report on the Impact of NREGS in Andhra Pradesh* (Processed). Hyderabad: Centre for Economic and Social Studies.

Raju, K. 2009. *Social Audit Immersion Clinic*, Presentation made on 23 March, at World Bank, Washington, D.C.

Reddy, D. Narasimha. 2006. 'Half a Century of Travails of Agriculture in Andhra Pradesh' in R.S. Rao *et al.* (eds), *Fifty Years of Andhra Pradesh 1956–2006*. Hyderabad: Centre for Documentation, Research and Communication.

Reddy, D. Narasimha. 2008. 'Alliances of Opportunisim and People's Distress: The Story of Economic Reforms under N. Chandrababu Naidu in Andhra Pradesh', *Biblio*, November–December.

———. 2011. *Mahatma Gandhi Rural Employment Guarantee Scheme: Opportunities and Challenges to Indian Agriculture*, Working Paper, Institute for Human Development, New Delhi.

Reddy, D. Narasimha *et al.* 2010. *Institutions and Innovations in the Implementation Process of Mahatma Gandhi National Rural Employment Guarantee Scheme (NREGS) in India*, Working Paper presented at Social Protection Asia Programme, along with Institute for Human Development, 18–19 October 2010, New Delhi.

4 THE BUSINESS OF HEALTH CARE AND THE CHALLENGE OF HEALTH SECURITY

THE CASE OF RAJIV AAROGYASRI COMMUNITY HEALTH INSURANCE SCHEME IN ANDHRA PRADESH

G. Vijay

The main objective of this study is to analyse the functioning of the Rajiv Aarogyasri Community Health Insurance Scheme, a social health insurance scheme for the poor households, introduced in Andhra Pradesh in 2007.

Until the mid-1980s, state policy in India was free health care provision by public health care institutions, to any citizen seeking it. The private sector also catered to those who were prepared to pay for it. Over the years, there has been very low priority accorded to public health services. Paradoxically, despite great strides in the methods of treatment and improved availability of medicines at relatively lower prices, public health facilities have witnessed deterioration. Health care in the country failed to achieve equity in access and service provision. The condition worsened in the 1980s, and liberalization of the economy in the 1990s aggravated it further. The poor people were the worst hit and this necessitated a search for alternative models for providing health care through reforms in the health sector. Health insurance through public-private partnership has emerged as one of the leading alternative approaches under the neoliberal economic reforms that began in the early nineties.

Contextualizing the Origins

In Andhra Pradesh, the share of the State's budgetary expenditure on health care facilities declined from 5 to 3.7 per cent between 2000 and 2006, and the per capita public health expenditure in 2005–6 was less than Rs 150 (Ravi *et al.*, 2009). At the same time, in 2001–2, the expenditure on health in the State was 5.9 per cent of the gross state domestic product, one of the highest in the country. But, 73 per cent of this was private expenditure, again the highest in the country. Public expenditure on health accounted for only 18.5 per cent. According to the NSS 52nd round (2003), nearly 65 per cent of the extremely poor had to borrow, often at very high rates of interest, and another 21 per cent had to draw from whatever savings they had, to meet hospitalization expenses (Institute of Health Systems as quoted in Ravi *et al.*, 2009).

There was a growing recognition of the catastrophic nature of hospitalization. Poor families were drawn into a vicious cycle of ill-health, poverty, indebtedness and bankruptcy. When faced with serious ailments, they often had to sell their assets, or borrow large sums of money, to meet the cost of treatment and hospitalization (Rao *et al.* 2009). Along with the growing agrarian crisis, farmers' suicides, often linked to high indebtedness—which in some cases were linked to borrowing for medical treatment—made health care for the poor a critical political issue. For the Congress which came to power in the State in 2004, replacing the Telugu Desam Party (TDP), health care, especially for the poor, became one of the top priorities and a strong political commitment. And credit for this was given to the then Chief Minister, Y.S. Rajasekhara Reddy, who was himself a medical doctor. It was realized by the Government of Andhra Pradesh (GoAP) that there was a need for institutionalization of health care facilities to treat serious ailments and for hospitalization of the poorer sections. The result was the conceptualization of the Rajiv Aarogyasri (Community Health Insurance) Scheme (RAS) (Figure 4.1) to address the serious health ailments of those below poverty line (BPL).

Salient Features of Rajiv Aarogyasri Scheme (RAS)

The GoAP established the Aarogyasri Health Care Trust in 2006 to implement the new scheme. RAS was launched in April 2007, and extended to all 23 districts across the State in five phases. The first pilot phase was rolled out in three districts, and by July 2009 the fourth and fifth phases were completed and the entire State was covered. There are two parts to RAS; (i) Aarogyasri–I and (ii) Aarogyasri–II. Aarogyasri–I was launched in April 2007 and covered most of the categories mentioned in the schedule of medical or surgical conditions. Aarogyasri–II was launched in July 2008 and included certain

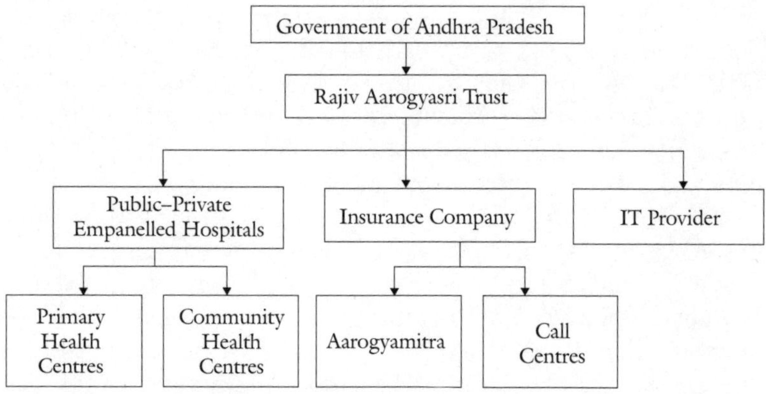

FIGURE 4.1 Institutional Structure of Rajiv Aarogyasri Scheme in AP

Source: Author (based on the Aarogyasri Trust official website: http:www.aarogyasri.org).

additional categories.[1] There was hardly any difference in the procedures adopted or treatment extended, except that under Aarogyasri–I, the expenditure was met from the budgetary allocations of the State, and in the case of Aarogyasri–II, the expenditure was met from the Chief Ministers Relief Fund (CMRF).

Objectives

The main objectives of the RAS may be summed up as follows: (i) to provide social protection by addressing the problem of growing indebtedness faced by the poor owing to burdensome health care costs; (ii) to monitor trends in diseases and treatment of ailments, to ensure that health care reached the grassroots; (iii) to provide health care security to the largest and the most disadvantaged segment of the population; and (iv) to improve overall health infrastructure for the well-being and betterment of all citizens.

Benefits and Coverage

The benefit per family was fixed at up to Rs 2 lakh in a year on a floater basis, that is a total reimbursement of Rs 1.5 lakh per annum could be availed of, individually or collectively, by members of a family, and an additional Rs 50,000 was provided as a buffer. In addition, the costs of cochlear implant surgery, with auditory verbal therapy, were reimbursed up to a maximum of Rs 6.5 lakh for each case by the Trust.

The total surgical and medical procedures covered were 938 by 2010. Most of these top-end, low frequency, tertiary surgical interventions involved high-cost hospitalization. These were broadly grouped into 32 categories, which were open to a further broad grouping into 19. The beneficiaries of this scheme were members of BPL families, as enumerated by the Rajiv Aarogyasri Health Card, or the BPL white ration card. The definition of BPL families in Andhra Pradesh is fairly flexible and differs from the one used by the Planning Commission. Hence, the coverage under RAS was vastly larger. According to a recent study by Reddy *et al.*, 2011:

> ... in 2009, approximately 20.4 million families and 70 million beneficiaries were covered by the scheme, which was about 85 per cent of the total population of the State. It is interesting to observe that a scheme, which was originally planned to be focused on BPL families, went ahead to cover almost the entire population of the State. This scheme certainly counts to be one of the pioneers in terms of achieving equity and universalization in a limited sense.

However, it is interesting to note that an independent estimate of the population which may be classified as poor and vulnerable (roughly living below PPP $2 per day per capita), was taken to be 65 per cent in 2004–5 (Kannan and Raveendran, 2011).

Institutional Set-up

The RAS was a unique community health insurance scheme, which was not community-based insurance; it did not involve any beneficiary contribution as it was considered that cost of collection of meagre premiums from the poor was likely to not be economical. It was entirely financed by the State budget, the CMRF, and a small proportion in the form of transport costs through National Rural Health Mission. The annual premium per registered family during 2008–9 was about Rs 297 (Reddy *et al.*, 2011). The scheme was implemented through the Star Health Insurance Company, selected on the basis of a competitive bidding. In order to operationalize the scheme, a public-private partnership was launched by a coalition led by Star Health Insurance—a private insurance company—and a network of empanelled private and public hospitals. The Aarogyasri Health Care Trust coordinated the activities of insurance company and involvement of all the sectors of the government that could help in the implementation.

Besides the Trust, insurance company, network hospitals, and district administration, the RAS has instituted yet another unique set of functionaries—the *Aarogyamitras*. Aarogyamitras, or 'friends of health,' were the health coordinators who assisted the patients in registration, admission, evaluation, pre-authorization, treatment, discharge and post-discharge follow-up. The organized structure of rural self-help groups (SHGs) in the State was effectively used to select and train these facilitators. Aarogyamitras were of two types: (i) Aarogyamitras with PHCs, AHCs, CHCs, District Hospitals—hired by the Mandal and Zilla Samakhyas; and (ii) Aarogyamitras with network hospitals—hired by the insurance company (Table 4.1).

Aarogyamitras were trained by the Trust and insurance company, with the training material prepared by the Trust. All the Aarogyamitras were connected via a closed user-group mobile network (www.oneworld.net, 2010).

The RAS also made use of the latest technologies. The ICT formed the backbone of the scheme. A dedicated real-time online workflow system was created by the Tata Consultancy Services (TCS), in collaboration with the Trust, to implement a decentralized and dynamic system.

Nature of Hospitalization under the RAS

An analysis of disease-wise distribution of hospitalization cases under RAS during 2007–10 showed an interesting pattern. The major thrust of the scheme was to target the top-end, low frequency, high cost surgical procedures. Table 4.2 shows oncology (20 per cent) and cardiology care (16 per cent) accounted for the major share of hospitalizations under the scheme. On the other hand, infectious diseases causing the maximum morbidity in India accounted for an insignificant number of cases.

RAS IN COMPARATIVE PERSPECTIVE

As discussed earlier, RAS was launched in April 2007. However, a national social health insurance scheme called the Rashtriya Swasthya Bima Yojana (RSBY) was launched as a centrally sponsored scheme a year later, in April 2008. The GoAP did not switch to RSBY, but continued with its own scheme because it considered RAS to be more effective in design and coverage. Even in some of the preliminary procedures, there were certain similarities between the RAS and the RSBY. In both cases, the enrolment was for a period of one year. In other words, the beneficiary needed to undergo the enrolment process every year. The responsibility of enrolment was on the insurance provider. Though in both cases the enrolment was the issue of programme-specific cards, in the RAS the mere possession of white cards or even

TABLE 4.1 Decision Makers and Their Responsibilities under Aarogyasri

Decision Maker	*Oversight of the Scheme*	*Financial Management and Planning*	*Package of Services*	*Selected Providers of Care*	*Monitoring and Evaluation*
Aarogyasri Trust	✓	✓	✓	✓	✓
Insurer			✓	✓	
Health Care Providers					
Aarogyamitras					
Decision Maker	***Contract with Insurer***	***Price Setting***	***Awareness of the Scheme***	***Enrolment***	***Claims Processing and Payment***
Aarogyasri Trust	✓	✓			✓
Insurer		✓	✓	✓	✓
Health Care Providers			✓	✓	
Aarogyamitras			✓	✓	

Source: Reddy *et al.* (2011).

TABLE 4.2 Distribution of Surgeries and Therapies under RAS, 2007–10

Surgeries and Therapies	*Percentage Share (%)*
Oncology	20
Cardiovascular Surgery	13
Poly-trauma	11
Genito-urinary	10
General Surgery	9
Neurology	8
Nephrology	5
Gynaecology and Obstetrics	5
Cardiology	3
Paediatrics	3
ENT	2
Others	11

Source: Reddy *et al.* (2011).

the white card number was sufficient to issue the Aarogyasri card on-the-spot; however, in the case of the RSBY, the smart cards were equipped with electronic chips that linked the card through a card-reading machine to the network that provided the information about the beneficiaries' insurance amount details. Therefore, the possession of the card was an absolute pre-requisite to access the scheme. Further, issue of the RSBY smart cards required the presence of the head of the household. This has been sighted as one of the reasons for low RSBY enrolment in certain regions.

Table 4.3 presents a summary of important features of the RAS and the RSBY. The striking feature of the former is its coverage. Across India, RSBY covered 22.7 million families, with a total number of 79.45 million beneficiaries. What the RSBY did for the country as a whole, the RAS did almost as much for one state, with 22.4 million families and 70 million beneficiaries. Regarding revenue-raising through insurance premium from the beneficiaries, while RSBY required the beneficiaries to pay Rs 30, RAS was completely funded by public revenues, without any contribution from the beneficiaries. Since the poor were the main beneficiaries, financing their health care through public revenues was a measure towards equity.

TABLE 4.3 Comparative Statement of Some of the Features of RAS and RSBY

Features Compared	*RAS*	*RSBY*
1. Insurance Coverage		
i. Unit of Enrolment	Family	Family
ii. No. of Families (million 2009–10)	22.4	22.7
iii. No. of Beneficiaries (million 2009–10)	70	79.45
2. Sources of Revenue		
i. Beneficiary's Contribution	Nil	Rs 30
ii. Subsidies	100% State	75% centre, 25% state
iii. Average Premium Rates*	Rs 267	Rs 440 to Rs 750
3. Type of Care		
i. Chronic Diseases	✓	✓
ii. Out-Patient	✓**	×
iii. In-Patient	✓	✓
4. Benefit Package		
i. Benefit Package	In-patient and out-patient secondary and tertiary care for listed diseases	In-patient, Secondary care only
ii. Number of In-patients Packages	938	1,100

(*Cont'd*)

Table 4.3 *(Cont'd)*

Features Compared	*RAS*	*RSBY*
5. Public-Private Hospitalization (2010)		
i. Distribution of Hospitals	97–Public (29%) and 241–Private (71%)	2,267–Public (32%) and 4,923–Private (68%)
ii. Distribution of Claims	Public (18%) and Private (82%)	NA
6. Premium and Coverage		
i. Average rates per family per year (Rs)	267	440 to 750
ii. Coverage Amount per family per year (Rs)	1,50,000 + buffer 50,000	30,000
7. Administrative and Hospital Expenditure		
i. Expenditure per	beneficiary (Rs) 128[a]	78[b]
ii. Expenditure per hospitalization (Rs)	27,848[a]	4,262
8. Coverage for Migrant Workers	Only Intra-State Migrants Covered	Inter and Intra State Migrants Covered

Source: Compiled from Reddy *et al.* (2011); and Kannan and Jain (2011).

Notes: *Per family per year.

**RAS free consultation and medical management for listed diseases for out-patients.

[a] For the first year.

[b] Does not include enrolment or admission costs (2009–10).

This depicts that if the states get their due devolution, especially from the growing direct tax revenues of the Centre, financing even an ambitious health care programme like the RAS—which is the right step towards universal coverage—should be possible in the future. What is interesting is that the RAS, which focused on high-end, tertiary health care, was able to secure a bargain premium of Rs 267 per person per year compared to Rs 440–750 in the case of RSBY, which largely focused on lower-end, secondary services. Further, the upper limit of the benefit was only Rs 30,000 under the RSBY in contrast to Rs 2 lakh under the RAS. The benefit package under the RAS (938) had high-end surgical procedures. In contrast, the package under the RSBY, though large (1,100), was limited to procedures that could be addressed by secondary level hospitals. In the case of claim settlements, the insurance company concerned was responsible, under the direction of RSBY, while RAS followed an elaborate pre-authorization process. In both the cases, transactions were paperless and with the exception of the initial Rs. 30 fee under RSBY, transactions were also cashless. RAS also had proper cost containment mechanisms like prior-authorizations, package-rates, surveillance, and medical vigilance teams and Aarogyamitras in the hospitals. Paying the hospitals promptly proved to be successful in terms of getting better rates from hospitals. In general, better negotiations with network hospitals based on mutual interest helped the scheme get better rates for beneficiaries (Reddy *et al.*, 2011).

Stakeholder participation was better designed in the case of RSBY; the role of stakeholders was clearly defined, which was both the strength and challenge of the scheme. In contrast, all stakeholders under RAS—including the insurer, the Aarogyamitras and the providers of care—seemed to be under the influence of the Aarogyasri Trust. This seriously restricted their freedom to act independently. It has been suggested that the Trust should appoint independent technical experts who would not only bring their expertise, but also the missing independence and integrity to the scheme's implementation and design (Reddy *et al.*, 2011).

DEMAND SIDE DYNAMICS OF RAS

This part of the study tries to answer the following questions:

(i) How far has the RAS been successful in addressing the health-related insecurities in Andhra Pradesh?

(ii) What is the impact of RAS on the development of:
 (a) different levels of the health care system
 (b) different types of hospitals

(iii) In the backdrop of concerns raised by the study of the Public Health Foundation of India (Reddy *et al.*, 2011), we tried to address the question of how the RAS can be made sustainable?

In order to address these questions, the study carried out household-level surveys in tribal-dominated—but not so remotely located—Chenchugudem village, and remotely located Appapur penta and Eerla penta[2] in Balmoor Mandal and Lingal Mandal of Mahabubnagar district, respectively. Household surveys were also conducted among different categories of non-tribal rural population in Mogiligidda village, and among different categories of industrial workers in Kothur town, also located in Mahabubnagar district. A structured purposive representative sample of 160 households was drawn to include: (i) households with different types of BPL cards;[3] (ii) poor households who did not have cards and non-poor households who had cards—to address exclusion and inclusion errors; (iii) poor households with different BPL cards but no Aarogyasri card, and (iv) households belonging to different socio-ethnic and religious groups, occupational groups, migrant[4] and non-migrant groups.

The household surveys included not only sample units drawn from the village, but also the patients and their attendants, admitted to different empanelled sample hospitals studied—Osmania General Hospital, Nizam's Institute of Medical Sciences (NIMS), and Care Hospital, Banjara Hills branch (Table 4.4).

Apart from the household-level survey, the study collected secondary data from different hospitals. In addition to the three hospitals already mentioned above, the PHC at Ambatpally, the Civil Hospital at Lingala in Mahabubnagar district, the District Hospital of Mahabubnagar, the ESI Hospital at Kothur, and a relatively small-sized private empanelled hospital—Shushrutha People's Hospital in Mahabubnagar—were also included. Apart from this, Aarogyamitras, Rajiv Aarogyasri Medical Coordinators (RAMCOs), and Administrative in-charges of Aarogyasri in different sample hospitals were also interviewed. The sample also included the superintendents of Government hospitals, and doctors, nurses and paramedical staff of all the sample hospitals. It also includes interviews with non-MBBS private rural registered medical practitioners (RMPs). And, finally,

TABLE 4.4 Location-wise Distribution of Sample Units

S. No.	*Name of the Area*	*Aarogyasri*	*Non-Aarogyasri*	*ESI and Others Migrant and Non-Migrants*	*Grand Total*
1	Osmania General Hospital	20	5		
2	NIMS Hospital	20	5		
3	Care Hospital	22	5		
4	Chenchugudem and Eerla penta	15			
5	Mogiligidda Village	32	1		
6	Kothur Town			35	
7	Totals	109	16	35	160

Source: Based on the data provided by the Aarogyasri Trust official website: http://www.aarogyasri.org.

the sample of respondents included some bureaucrats who have been associated with the health sector.

Structured questionnaires, interviews, and individual and group discussions were employed for primary data collection. The method of participant observation was adopted for recording details pertaining to ambience, facilities, beneficiary and service provider interactions, and for documenting patients' experiences and grievances.

SOCIALLY EMBEDDING THE ACCESS TO—AND EXPERIENCES WITH—HEALTH CARE SYSTEMS UNDER THE RAS

From the vantage point of demand side, especially from the households, what became evident was (i) *heterogeneity* among poor households and (ii) *asymmetry of access* for poor belonging to the same income groups due to the role of *other social mediations* determining access.

The public policy itself acknowledged and distinguished the poor into different categories who were eligible to access the Aarogyasri cards. Apart from these groups, the RAS also included certain lower income group categories, belonging to the non-BPL households, after a process of verification and approval by the Chief Minister's Camp Office (CMCO).

However, these classifications of households, firstly into poor and non-poor, and then of poor households as mentioned earlier, were insufficient to analyse and understand the dynamics of inclusion and exclusion from health security access. The well-known problem was that of wrong inclusions and exclusions. While we found that the wrong exclusions were more in remote[5] areas involving poor households whose nature of activity involved more mobility (for instance among hunting-gathering tribal households or circular migrant households), in the not-so remote areas such exclusions were minimal, and mostly transient as a consequence of separation of individual households from joint-families among the poor. The wrong inclusion errors, on the other hand, were estimated to be between 20–30 per cent. Even where the card distribution was accurate, access to health care could be asymmetric in the process. We have presented macro-data, as provided by the Aarogyasri Trust on its publicly accessible website,[6] to further elaborate on this issue.

Structures of Vulnerability and Access to the RAS

We have tried to answer the question whether there was any gender or social bias in the enrolment and care in RAS. Also there is a social analysis of the demand side, based on the gender and social composition of beneficiaries, which presents in social structural terms the inclusion and exclusion from accessing the Aarogyasri programme. This analysis was based on a sample of 30,000 beneficiaries drawn from the macro-data provided by the Aarogyasri's official website, which has over 1 lakh beneficiaries who sent feedback about their experience with the programme.[7]

From Table 4.5 it can be observed that of the sample of 30,000 people, about 90.5 per cent belonged to BPL households, 6.75 per cent to the poorest of the poor, and 0.023 per cent to the destitute households, while 2.72 per cent to those households which have received assistance on the recommendation of the CMCO. This clearly suggested that the relatively better-off within the poor have benefited more than the poorest of the poor or destitute families. This finding, however, needed to be calibrated on the basis of the fact that at the village-level we found that the poorest of the poor accounted for only 5 per cent of all the poor households, and the destitute families accounted for only 0.3 per cent of the total poor households. Considering this scenario, it may be contended that although the poorest

TABLE 4.5 Distribution of Beneficiaries According to Type of Card

Age Group	*WAP*		*YAP*		*CMC*		*AAP*		*Total*		*Total*	*%*
	Male	*Female*	*Male*	*Female*	*Male*	*Female*	*Male*	*Female*	*Male*	*Female*		
<1	321	196	28	15	11	9	0	0	360	220	580	1.6
									62	–38		
1–5	402	268	24	7	7	3	0	0	433	278	711	2.37
									–60.9	–39.1		
6–13	805	436	453	26	8	6	0	0	1,266	468	1,734	5.78
									–73	–27		
14 – 21	1,094	587	104	64	13	13	0	0	1,211	664	1,875	6.25
									–64.5	–35.5		
22–55	10,328	7,609	462	478	276	197	2	3	11,068	8,287	19,355	64.51
									–57.2	–42.8		
56–70	2,742	1,692	157	148	164	85	0	2	3,063	1,927	4,990	16.63
									–61	–39		
71–86	519	146	32	27	15	11	0	0	566	184	750	2.5
									–75	–25		
> 86	3	2	0	0	0	0	0	0	360	240	5	0.016
All	16,214	10,936	1,260	765	494	324	2	5	17,970	12,030	30,000	100
	–59.7	–40.3	–62.2	–37.8	60.3	–39.7	–28.5	–71.5				

(Cont'd)

TABLE 4.5 (*Cont'd*)

Age Group	*WAP*		*YAP*		*CMC*		*AAP*		*Total*		*Total*	%
	Male	*Female*	*Male*	*Female*	*Male*	*Female*	*Male*	*Female*	*Male*	*Female*		
% of total	54.04	36.45	4.2	2.55	1.64	1.08	0.006	0.016	59.9	40.1	100	100
Total (male–female)	27,150		2,025		818		7				30,000	100
Type of Card %	90.5		6.75		2.72		0.023				100	100

Source: Based on Sample drawn from Aarogyasri Feedback Forms data.

Notes: For details about WAP, YAP, and AAP, refer to *n* 2.

CMC refers to Chief Minister's Camp Office.

of the poor households might not have been under-represented, the destitute households have certainly been excluded from access to the programme.

Considering the gender representation across different types of poor households, we found that men had been better represented than women. So it could be concluded that gender representation for women was much worse in the poorest of the poor families than in the poor families. Taking into consideration representation based on age as a category, we found a striking over-representation of prime-working age category. Children below 15 years were under-represented, despite constituting about 28 per cent of the total population in Andhra Pradesh, and infant mortality in Andhra Pradesh was 53 per 1,000 children born.

The secondary data by Aarogyasri Trust provided district-wise information pertaining to all the medical camps, total people screened, cases registered, out-patients, in-patients, surgeries, therapies, and the total amount spent. The regional representation is one of the most debated aspects in Andhra Pradesh today. With the possibility of the State being divided into several states, this topic resurfaces in terms of access to the Aarogyasri programme, especially in relation to the Rayalaseema region. The former and the incumbent Chief Minister apparently belong to this region, which is the worst represented in terms of the total amount claimed/spent, followed by the Telangana region and Coastal Andhra (Figure 4.2). While the poor areas within Coastal Andhra, such as Srikakulam and Vijayanagaram were under-represented in terms of claims/amount spent on treatments, the rich areas within this region were the major beneficiaries of the programme. While we found that the grave lack of empanelled hospitals to cater to the BPL households was a general phenomenon, it was especially alarming in the backward regions. This reinforced the ongoing battle cries about regional injustice.

What we inferred from the above analysis was that the poor households were not a homogenous category. Apart from the classification of the poor into three categories mentioned earlier, there were errors of exclusion and inclusion in data collection. And added to all these problems, the above analysis showed that there was a significant role for social mediation. We found that different individuals from within the poor households with different attributes of gender, age, region, etc., could be in advantage or disadvantage in terms of being included or excluded from access, despite having the Aarogyasri cards.

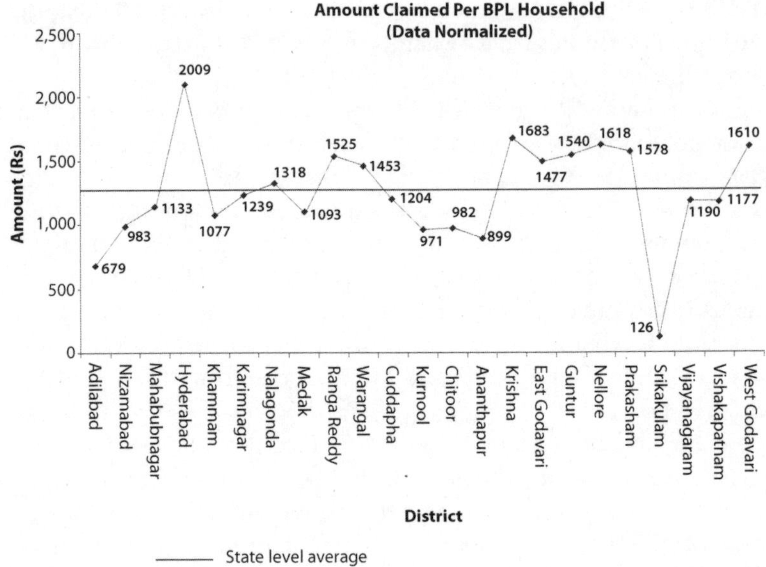

FIGURE 4.2 Regional Representation of Aarogyasri Beneficiaries

Source: Based on the data given on Aarogyasri website normalized using BPL cards data supplied by the Civil Supplies Department.

THE SOCIAL GRADATION OF HEALTH CARE

The interface between the structures of vulnerability presented above proved to be a formidable constraint to the stated objective of Arogyasri, of resolving the dualism of development of health care sector and the lack of access to it for poor households. The heterogeneity among poor households showed that there was a multi-pronged policy orientation to the problem of access. We present some profiles from different social contexts to clarify the point.

The Remoteness, Backwardness, and Mobility Constraint to Access

The Chenchu households, located deep inside the forests, have often been completely excluded from several social security programmes implemented by the ITDA and the Government. Aarogyasri was no exception. Both in Appapur penta and Erla penta (and especially in Erla penta), despite their poverty-ridden day-to-day living conditions, a large number of tribal households did not have white ration cards.

The reason for this, according to the officials, was that it was very difficult to visit these areas and if and when the officials visited, the tribals were usually not at home. Even if the officials made announcements before their visits, people often did not understand the calendar week days and dates. And they were just not around because they had to hunt for their survival. The consequences of under-development of a region could be very significant in determining access to the health care under Aarogyasri programme.

In the interior tribal areas, 108 mobile medical services visited the pentas on the fifth day of every month. They usually carried out medical check-ups and distributed routine medicines. For those suffering from more serious ailments, they provided referrals and advised the households to visit a hospital. However, while lack of White Cards was one limitation, sheer ignorance could also prove to be fatal. This clearly pointed to the failure of Aarogyamitras who were supposed to be in the local area, providing people with necessary information about the Aarogyasri programme.

Here is one instance: Nimmala Balamma, 70, a Chenchu tribal and resident of Erla penta told us that her husband Lingaiah, 80, had developed a tumor on the throat. For a very long time, it remained unnoticed. However, when he developed difficulty in swallowing, he was taken to Acchampet Civil Hospital where the doctor said an operation was necessary and that he must be taken to the District Hospital in Mahabubnagar. After being admitted there, he was told that several bottles of blood were required. The family could not arrange it. So Lingaiah, though being in a critical condition, was brought back and died soon after.

Remoteness of location often caused neglect of health problems and the ignorance about the programme led to lack of timely medical intervention, which aggravated minor health ailments into major problems. In regions that are remotely located, the Aarogyasri programme must have a supply driven orientation to access, rather than a demand-driven one. However, there was gross neglect of the lower-end segments of the health care system such as the Primary Health Care Centres, Community Health Centres, Area Hospitals, and District Hospitals. Every Primary Health Centre has one Aarogyamitra. The Ambatpally Primary Health Centre located in the region that serves tribal villages, for instance, was the only Primary Health Centre for 20 villages, serving a population of 22,000 people.[8] A supply driven approach to access required many more primary health centres, with many more Aarogyamitras, to take access closer to people who cannot reach the health care systems.

Shukla, A. *et al.* (2011) pointed to a model of having a family medical practitioner for every 400–500 families; an epidemiological station for 8000–20,000 population, with 5–20 beds; a basic hospital with general medicine, general surgery, paediatrics, obstetrics and gynaecology, orthopaedics, ophthalmology, dental services, radiology, and other basic diagnostic services with an ambulance for 50,000 population. Every such five basic hospital must have a multi-specialty hospital at the block or taluka level, to cater to 1.5–2.5 lakh population. These lower-end health care systems play a significant role which goes beyond mere pro-active supply driven access provisioning. This will be taken up for discussion subsequently.

The Constraint of Trust Deficit in Government Hospitals

Yet another dimension to the problem is the trust deficit in government hospitals among beneficiaries. We found from the data that the largest segment of poor households (83 per cent) actually visited different types of private health care systems rather than government hospitals when they fell sick. This included the non-MBBS practitioners like RMPs. The reasons ranged from lack of doctors, medicines and proper diagnosis, to poor attention and misbehaviour in government hospitals.

However, the poor related themselves to government hospitals in different ways.

(i) *Cost aversion strategy*: While the poorest of the poor preferred private hospitals for minor ailments, they considered these hospitals beyond their means if they had a major ailment. Such households often went to the government hospitals if they had any major ailment as part of a cost-aversion strategy.

(ii) *Risk aversion strategy*: The not-so poor among poor households usually went to government hospitals if they had minor ailments, but considered it a risk to go to a Government hospital if they had a major ailment. Such households preferred better quality health care, even if it cost a little more in private hospitals. Such households had a risk-aversion strategy in preferring private hospitals.

However, this did not undermine the importance of government hospitals. The argument that people lacked faith in government hospitals was not to say that people did not want them. Large sections of the poor felt their lives would be worse off without government hospitals. The most significant role the Government hospitals seemed to be playing was in the safe delivery of babies.

However, the fact that the poor in general have very little respect for and confidence in government hospitals has led to several problems, despite Aarogyasri. When poor people fall sick, they might choose private doctors in the first instance. Depending on what the ailment is, they could incur a low-to-very high expenditure; especially when the poor are not aware that Aarogyasri is applicable only in the empanelled hospitals, they might end up paying the bill themselves, although the particular ailment could have been covered under Aarogyasri. In such instances, although Aarogyasri's stated goal was a cashless transaction for the poor, they often ended up being treated under Aarogyasri with an empanelled hospital after having incurred costs in a non-empanelled private hospital.

The Diseases and Coverage

The focus of Aarogyasri programme was on ailments requiring surgical intervention, or medical management related to such diseases. The occurrence of the diseases covered under Aarogyasri among poor households seemed to be rare, although there was no denial that these procedures were expensive. Table 4.6 provides data based on village

TABLE 4.6 Mogiligidda Village Aarogyasri Coverage Profile, 2007–11

Category	*Number*
Total Population	10,000
Total Households	2,300
Total BPL Households	1,700
Total Number of Pre-authorizations	30
Total Out patients	20
Total In-Patients	10
Total Surgeries for type of Systems/Ailments	
Heart	4
Kidney	3
Brain	1
Uterus	2

Source: Field study data.

survey which suggests that for a BPL population of 7,650 (approximate) over the past four years, there have been only 10 beneficiaries in terms of those that underwent actual surgeries.

There were several reasons because of which the stated objective of cashless treatment under Aarogyasri for the poor households might not be delivered. Some of the scenarios are presented in the list provided in Table 4.7.

Table 4.8 provides details of the costs poor households incurred because of lack of faith in government health care facilities, but ultimately ended up with Aarogyasri treatment. The expenditures incurred were on different health care interventions, medication, diagnostic tests, and surgery.

Thus, even in the not-so remote areas, if the objectives of Aarogyasri were to be achieved, it was essential to ensure that poor people were secured against health care costs related indebtedness and poverty. While 82 per cent of the poor risked not being benefited by a cashless treatment objective, at least 31 per cent of such poor households incurred a debt of Rs 20,000–5,00,000; for such households, Aarogyasri as a source of circumventing poverty on account of health costs remained elusive. A revamping of lower-end government health care systems is pressing in the long run, so as to inspire confidence in the public health care systems addressing not only diseases involving surgical intervention, but all the diseases, especially those with a higher frequency of occurrence among poor households. However, in the short run, grassroot agencies and individuals, whose function is to provide complete information and to direct the poor to the empanelled hospitals, must be made more effective. This also required that each primary health care centre served a reasonable size of population. This needed to be worked out to correct a situation where one Aarogyamitra was left to serve 20 villages or 22,000 people.

The assumption that government hospitals were inefficient did not seem to be a general phenomenon. In the interviews with industrial workers, we found that although they were not very happy with the local ESI hospitals, they were full of admiration for the ESI hospital in Hyderabad providing tertiary care, including specialized surgeries. The inference was that a well-organized community of consumers could cause an improvement in the health care provisioning systems.

TABLE 4.7 The Gradations of Possible Exclusion from Cashless Treatment

Problem	*Solution Offered/Observation*
Poor household without white card	No Solution
Beneficiary with white card but photograph missing	MRO and Collector Office Clarification
Beneficiary with a white card but name wrongly recorded	MRO and Collector Office Clarification
White card holders with lost card	WAP, YAP or AAY number
White card holder without Aarogyasri card	WAP, YAP or AAY number
Aarogyasri card holder with photograph missing	MRO and Collector Office Clarification
Aarogyasri card holder with photograph but not properly visible	MRO and Collector Office Clarification
Aarogyasri card holder with name wrongly recorded (completely wrong or differently spelt from the one on white card)	MRO and Collector Office Clarification
Aarogyasri card holder with an unlisted disease	No Solution
Aarogyasri card holder with a listed disease but who has innocently entered non-empanelled private hospital and already paid exorbitantly	No Solution within Aarogyasri/ Chief Minister's Camp Office can be approached for some relief
Aarogyasri card holder with a listed code in an empanelled hospital but whose cost may exceed the package so is either asked to move on or informally agree to make partial payment	Grievance Mechanism/one rupee complaint registration phone service/complain as part of feedback
Aarogyasri card holder with a listed disease, in an empanelled hospital, operated free of cost but who has to pay for his own transport and/ or post-operative medical management and follow up	Grievance mechanism/one rupee complaint registration phone service/complain as part of feedback

(*Cont'd*)

TABLE 4.7 (*Cont'd*)

Problem	*Solution Offered/Observation*
Aarogyasri card holder with a listed disease, in an empanelled hospital, operated free of cost, and transport charges reimbursed, complete follow up and medical management expenses borne by hospital for the specified time	This best case scenario is very rare in actual practice

Source: Based on field study.

TABLE 4.8 Expenditures Incurred by Poor on Private Health Care

Health Expenditure Incurred (Rs)	*No. of Respondents*	*% in Total*
< 1,000	6	7
1,000 – < 5,000	22	25
5,000 – <10,000	19	21
10,000 – < 20,000	14	16
20,000 – < 50,000	19	21
50,000 – <100,000	5	6
100,000 – < 500,000	3	3
500,000 – > 500,000	1	1
Total	89	100

Source: Based on field study.

The Question of Wrong Inclusions

Several non-BPL households had white cards in the rural areas. It was often debated how the relevant agencies monitor wrong inclusions. The evidence that emerged as part of this study compelled us to differ with this dominant approach to the problem of 'wrong inclusions'. The fact was that several sections of the lower and middle-class belonging to the non-BPL households simply could not afford to pay the health expenses that were covered by the Aarogyasri. Although sometimes we came across narratives by the functionaries of sample empanelled hospitals that some of the Aarogyasri patients arrived by flight or in a luxury segment car and got admitted, the fact that

Aarogyasri patients were admitted only in general wards and not in independent luxury rooms was an in-built deterrent for the affluent classes. However, for the lower and middle-class, rural and urban non-BPL households, these social barriers were easily surmountable. In fact, there was a sense of social justification for this manipulation in the rural areas, and given the local dynamics, which sometimes occurred in collusion with the officials, it was impossible to monitor such wrong inclusions. Instead of spending on monitoring it, reduction in costs of Aarogyasri programme and cross-subsidization were more feasible and meaningful objectives to pursue in course of extending the programme than spending on monitoring to prevent wrong inclusions. This way the programme would provide for a universal coverage, and charge the existing premium to the non-BPL households, who would be more than willing to pay. To use BPL notion of poverty, we found, was inappropriate for health related poverty, as the two were distinctly different. The assumption that only BPL families could not afford health costs, and therefore lacked access to health care, was false.

The limitations and constraints of the programme were not limited to the demand side alone. There were several issues to be addressed on the supply side as well, affecting access and quality health care. We will now take up the supply side processes and issues.

SUPPLY SIDE DYNAMICS

Classification of Empanelled Hospitals

On the supply side, as already suggested, the Aarogyasri programme set some broad parameters which were pre-requisites for empanelling as network hospitals of the programme. When any hospital applied for empanelment, a team of experts from the Aarogyasri Trust and the insurer visited these hospitals, to ensure that the hospital fulfilled all the pre-requisites. Although a homogenous set of characteristics had been identified as minimal pre-requisites for empanelling hospitals, the empanelled ones actually presented heterogeneity of characteristics. This was of analytical significance for supply side dynamics.

Some of the differences among the empanelled hospitals could be drawn based on the following characteristics:

(i) *Organizational classification*: The empanelled hospitals could be classified, based on the nature of ownership, into:

a. Private-owned.
b. Autonomous (public-owned payment services).
c. Government hospitals (free medical services).

(ii) *Technical classification*: Based on technical characteristics, the empanelled hospitals can be differentiated into:
a. Empanelled hospitals with general specialization—usually catering to general surgery, poly trauma, etc.
b. Empanelled hospitals with super-specialty—nephrology, neurology, cardiology, cardio-thoracic, paediatrics, etc.

(iii) *Scale classification*: In terms of scale of fixed investments and activity, the empanelled hospitals can be differentiated into:
a. Small-sized hospitals: 50–100 beds.
b. Medium-sized hospitals: 100–300 beds.
c. Large-sized hospitals: over 300 beds.

In the scale of activity, these hospitals almost handled an equal number of out-patients per day. In terms of the relationship between the technical classification and the scale classification, it was observed that while general specialization was relatively scale-neutral, super-specialization was not scale-neutral. Depending on the specifics, while certain super-specialty services could be offered by medium-scale hospitals, certain super-specialty services could be performed only by large-scale hospitals because of the requirement of exorbitantly high-cost equipment to perform super-specialty services, which in turn requires a scale of activity to recover the fixed costs.

(iv) *Locational classification*: In terms of the location of the hospitals, we found that the empanelled hospitals could be classified into the following categories:
a. Rural hospitals: hospitals that were located in the sub-district level.
b. Semi-urban hospitals: hospitals located at the district level.
c. Urban hospitals: hospitals located in and around the twin cities, and the Greater Hyderabad municipality limits.

In terms of relating the technical and scale classification to the location classification, while the large-scale super-specialty hospitals had a strong urban bias, the medium-scale super-specialty could not move below the district-level; the general specialty had no location bias.

(v) *Activity classification*: Based on activity classification, the empanelled hospitals can be classified into:

a. non-teaching
b. teaching
c. higher education and research

Some of the teaching hospitals had been decentralized to district level as part of a drive towards increasing private medical colleges. The medical colleges in themselves had some prescribed minimal requirements that scale them up to medium-to-large-scale medical institutions. While the private medical colleges had moved to district level, the Government medical colleges, and higher learning and research institutions in medicine had an urban bias in their location.

The Significance of the Role of Different Hospitals

From the data provided in Table 4.9 we found that in terms of the proportion of Aarogyasri patients to the total beds in the hospital, private large-scale branded market leaders like Care Banjara contributed the least, while the not-so-well-known small- and medium-scale private operators contributed much more. The large-scale government hospitals absorbed more number of patients in proportion to the total patients in the considered sample compared to the private hospitals. However, at a macro-level the statistics showed that 80 per cent of the Aarogyasri patients got treated in private hospitals while the government hospitals catered to only 20 per cent of the total Aarogyasri patients. Based on the above evidence, we could infer that of this 80 per cent of patients treated in private hospitals, a larger proportion was being treated by small- and medium-scale hospitals rather than by large-scale hospitals.

However, when it came to the analysis of the Aarogyasri health services provided by different hospitals in terms of value, the per capita value of Aarogyasri received by different hospitals suggested that the hospitals under government administration got a much smaller value vis-à-vis the proportion of the patients they catered to when compared to autonomous Government hospitals such as NIMS (Table 4.9). And the large-scale private hospitals got a much larger proportion of value vis-à-vis the proportion of Aarogyasri patients they catered to in comparison with small- and medium-scale private hospitals. In the case of the private hospitals, a clear inference that could be drawn was that the large-scale private hospitals performed high-valued surgeries and, therefore, by performing smaller number of surgeries they got a larger proportion of value. In the case of small- and medium-scale

TABLE 4.9 Type of Hospitals and Share of Aarogyasri Treatment

Hospital	*Total Beds*	*Usual Status of Occupancy By Aarogyasri Patients*	*As a Proportion of Total Beds (%)*	*Average Aarogyasri Patients Treated Per Annum**	*As a Proportion of Total Number of Aarogyasri Patients Treated Annually by Sample Hospitals (%)*	*The Average Value of the Treatment Annually (Rs. lakh)*	*As a Per Capita Value*
Osmania General Hospital (Public)	1,140	400	35	8,367	53	1,029	12,298
NIMS (Public)	1,000	300	30	5,635	36	2,045	36,291
Care Banjara (Corporate)	380	41	11	1,175	7	926	78,808
Shusrutha People's Hospital (Private)	170	100	59	694	4	164	23,631

Source: Based on data provided by the hospitals.

Note: *The actual data is available for different time periods. The data provided at the hospital level has been used to derive annual averages to make the data comparable.

private hospitals, performing such high-value end codes was not possible, and they ended up getting a relatively smaller proportion of value, even if they had treated a larger number of patients. In the case of government hospitals, a deeper probe is required to find out why they ended up getting relatively smaller share in value in comparison to the proportion of patients they absorbed.

We found that each hospital had a very different understanding of what Aarogyasri programme had done to it. The large-scale, branded market leader, especially in cardiology, such as Care Banjara, had provided evidence which stated that the hospital had incurred a loss to the tune of Rs 6 crore on account of Aarogyasri. The Nizam's Institute of Medical Sciences had a peculiar problem of delayed payments of their claims. As a consequence, the hospital authorities felt that their finances had got clogged. The Osmania General Hospital benefited to a certain extent and bought new equipment using Aarogyasri funds. Shushrutha People's Hospital too benefitted immensely from Aarogyasri, and not only scaled up its in-take from 53 to 170 beds, it also diversified into a larger number of codes. Initially, it was empanelled only for general surgery, poly trauma, and gynaecology. It diversified into ENT and orthopaedics, and was building a super-specialty hospital with urology, neurology, paediatrics and plastic surgery. The small- and medium-sized hospitals were seen as institutions that could contribute to decentralization of super-specialty services. The reason for this variation in the experience of different hospitals with Aarogyasri programme requires a deeper analysis.

Varying Impact on Variety of Hospitals

The assessment and the relationship of different hospitals pertaining to Aarogyasri programme, as evidenced above, varied and with it the impact of the programme on developing health care security in health care systems could also be significantly different. As already pointed out, the general belief that Aarogyasri programme had benefited only private hospitals was only partially true. The crucial factors determining the relationship between different types of hospitals with the Aarogyasri programme and, in turn, the objective of developing health care security for poor households in health care systems included: (i) the value of packages; (ii) the process of empanelment and coding; and (iii) the administrative and infrastructural mechanisms.

Experience with the Packages: Getting the Prices Right, Wrong and Equal

In course of the formulation of the Aarogyasri Programme, a team of doctors had been constituted to design packages for different codes (medical/surgical treatment). Though the details of the basis on which these packages had been formulated were not known, they clearly seemed to be values which meant different balance sheet outcomes for different persons. And since these packages seemed to have been worked out by varied area specialists, there seemed to have been different structures of costs considered in the course of working out the average value of the package for each code. As a result, not all packages presented the same structure of benefit or loss for each type of hospital. Some packages offered for certain codes were offering a value above the average cost and some others were found to be offering a value below the average cost. Fundamentally, different hospitals differed in the average costs they incurred in the market.

Table 4.10 shows how the basic average cost of providing health service varied across hospitals, consequent to structural differences between the hospitals. Some of the indicators providing a clue to this difference are presented below:

Consultation fee and the cost of beds seemed to provide the benchmark for the cost difference across all other services provided

TABLE 4.10 The Average Cost Structures by Type of Hospitals

Hospital	*Outpatient Consultation Fee*	*General Ward Cost**	*Three Shared Room Cost**
Osmania General Hospital (Public)	Free	Free	Does not exist
NIMS (Public)	Rs 50	Rs 200	Rs 450
Care Banjara (Private Corporate)	Rs 250	Rs 1100	Rs 1600
District Hospital Mahabubnagar (Public)	Free	Free	Does not exist
Shushrutha People's Hospital (Private)	Rs 50	Rs 300	Rs 500

Source: Based on field study and hospital data.

Note: *Per day.

by different hospitals. While the Osmania General Hospital and Government District Hospital provided services free of cost, the NIMS was an autonomous body and thus had the administrative freedom to work out its own cost packages. We found that in the case of consultation fee, NIMS and Shushrutha People's Hospital charged Rs 50, which was five times lower than the consultation fee charged in Care Hospital. Care also charged a price for general ward per day, which was five-and-a-half times higher than that of NIMS (providing super-specialty services, including cardiology and cardiac surgeries) and almost four times higher than what Shushrutha People's Hospital charged. Thus, the health care costs could be brought down by five times if Aarogyasri focused on government hospitals, and by four times if small- and medium-scale private hospitals were given preference. In the long run, sustainability of the Aarogyasri policy will be dependent on reduction of costs—though the big private hospitals certainly do not provide much scope for optimism. However, in the short run it needs to be acknowledged that given the condition of the infrastructure and human resources, government hospitals by themselves were not geared up to cater to the entire demand of Aarogyasri. Therefore, it was the small- and medium-sized private hospitals that were the institutions with greater potential to make substantive contribution to the Aarogyasri programme.

Risk of Deviation from Scheduled Packages

In some packages, the insurer's rates differed from the average cost of the hospitals. So the hospitals adopted different strategies to overcome this problem. Hospitals tended to choose those codes that were beneficial, and avoided codes that involved higher risk. Part of the scope for circumventing a high risk package was provided by the Aarogyasri itself. In what follows, we present some of these processes and problems, innate to the structure of the Aarogyasri.

It is important to identify some of the risks involved and understand how it impacted the perception of the programme from the point of view of the hospitals. As already suggested, hospitals across the board were of the opinion that the packages of Aarogyasri covered the costs of the procedures on the whole. However, a lot of caveats came up while discussing whether the package amount was adequate. Despite there being other opinions, the dominant view of the hospitals was that if a patient was admitted, diagnosed and was found fit for surgery; if the surgery was for a specific code as mentioned in the Aarogyasri list; if the surgery was simple and straightforward as anticipated; if the accessories and support structures used were limited to those suggested by the codes; and if the patient post-operative recovery was normal, then the packages were sufficient and perhaps even beneficial (although with some exceptions).

However, the real experiences were very different from the model case-based packages. When a patient got admitted for a particular problem under a particular code, there was always a risk because: (i) the patient might be diagnosed either as normal, or might have a disease not in the list of codes of Aarogyasri (in which case costs were not compensated by Aarogyasri and the poor might not be in a position to pay); (ii) a patient might be positive on other high risk factors (obesity, diabetes, high blood pressure, etc., in a heart patient), these factors might eventually cause multi-organ failure; (iii) identification of new problems in the course of an operation, for instance requiring more implants than anticipated; (iv) the patient might develop problems because of which he might be found unfit for operation (blood pressure, boils, etc.); (v) the patient might have other problems, making him/her unfit to undergo treatment which might not be covered by the codes; (vi) the actual recovery time could be much longer than the average expected by the package; and (vii) there could be the use of certain equipment not permitted in the codes.

Although these were not exhaustive, they did present a dominant set of concerns about who would bear these costs? Under any of the above risk factors, the hospital incurred a cost which was either not compensated at all, or compensated inadequately, and the hospital ended up paying these additional costs. From the point of view of the Aarogyasri Trust, such costs had been taken into account in the packages itself or, it argued, were subject to a provision for enhancement (of the package) after it was scrutinized by a committee. However, the hospitals were skeptical or pessimistic about actually receiving these enhanced claims. The Aarogyasri structure divided itself into Aarogyasri–I and Aarogyasri–II and while regular claims went to the insurance company named as Aarogyasri–I, the enhancement claims went to Aarogyasri–II or to the Trust. Hospitals maintained that while Aarogyasri–I payments were prompt, Aarogyasri–II payments were kept pending for an uncertain period. Different hospitals had different strategies to cope with the risk.

They can be broadly classified into: (i) innovative strategies; (ii) coping strategies; (iii) segmentation strategies; (iv) aversion strategies; and (v) manipulative strategies.

In the innovative strategies, an organization might bring down its costs through bulk purchase of equipment, inputs and medicines, bringing down the average costs to a considerable extent. The coping strategies usually involved two sub-strategies of innovative methods of involving NGOs, or other donors, to raise funds to address the deficit. In the aversion strategies, delaying the procedures through medical management helped in streamlining the in-take of patients by spreading them over a period of time, keeping the in-take well within the pre-calculated break-even volumes.

A third strategy involved the use of local metallic implants instead of implants with high biological values, cheaper operation procedures rather than more advanced ones (like plastic surgeries), and poor quality post-operative care such as not keeping the patients in the intensive care unit, and instead placing them directly into general wards, being prescribed generic medicines, etc.

In the aversion strategies, the hospitals tried to avoid high-risk patients through strategic empanelment for codes which had lower risks. For instance, accident or poly-trauma, burn injury codes, were almost never preferred (government hospitals thus become dumping grounds); stringent screening and weeding out processes were put in place, either by informing the patients wrongly that a particular procedure did not fall under Aarogyasri programme, or by telling the patients that there were no vacant beds, or by making the patient travel long distances several times and making them wait without providing any facilities following which patients could incur high costs, or by telling the patients that the doctor or the paramedical staff concerned was on leave, or that they might have to make partial payment since some procedures were not included, and advising them to go to Government hospitals, where everything could be free of cost, etc.

And finally, the manipulative strategies involved faking patients and procedures, dodging systematically between high-valued codes for actual low-valued procedures, carrying out unnecessary procedures, holding the patients for a longer time, so as to claim higher amounts, etc.

Hospitals used a combination of these strategies to manage risk costs. The effectiveness of both strategies was contingent on the capabilities of the management and its ethical values.

The innovative strategies were being used by those hospitals that were scaling up. The coping strategy presented a more ethical alternative relatively speaking, which was resorted to only by those large-scale hospitals that had good social networks.

The segmentation, aversion and manipulative strategies were adopted by all the hospitals that were coded for high risk procedures. The segmentation strategies, for instance, could prove to be useful in cutting down costs, but they required robust regulatory systems. While some hospitals used these strategies to ensure that they did not make losses due to Aarogyasri, others used them to make 'misery profits'. Many private hospitals were found resorting to the most dehumanized forms of commercial exploitation of the Aarogyasri programme, performing surgeries where they were not necessary, and so on. There were several instances of such cases coming to light, and hospitals were de-empanelled by the Aarogyasri Trust as a penalty. But there could be several other hospitals that have managed to get away with these unethical practices.

The introduction of cheaper but good quality implants, and generics that have been authenticated for their quality could possibly emerge as a future strategy in promoting local pharmaceutical and surgical implants' manufacturers. Some of these actors have enjoyed a privileged status for promoting FDIs, and for earning foreign reserves by exporting their produce as sub-contractors for MNCs. Such actors could make substantial profits by supplying cheaper products to the segment of policy-driven health security systems in the national markets, and in turn could use these resources to invest in research and development, to promote their external markets. However, any slacking in the regulatory systems could lead to enhanced risk for the patients and the Aarogyasri programme, with government hospitals ending up with trust deficit, making people choose (safer) private medical care over a cashless transaction. Such a potential disaster embedded in the segmentation strategy must be avoided.

In the case of manipulative strategies, costs were usually borne by the Aarogyasri Trust, whereas in the case of the aversion strategy, costs were likely to be borne by the patients, and at an institutional level by the government hospitals, which they complained had been reduced to dumping grounds for all high risk, high cost procedures. It needed to be recognized that a voluntary empanelling for selective codes was bound to be against the usual logic of normal distribution of risk. This is completely irrational and this policy needs a review.

Alternatively, all the procedures that a private hospital sells in the market must be offered to the Aarogyasri patients if a hospital wants to be empanelled. There is no denial that certain private hospitals have been motivated by normative concerns and altruistic motives. Unfortunately they happened to be exceptions. The objective of maximization of profits had been the dominant motive. Although profit motive and cost reduction of the health care systems were in conflict with one another, an extensive, or even better, a universal coverage of population under health insurance and subsidized health care systems could be complementarities. As already suggested, Aarogyasri has played an important role in helping the small- and medium-scale private hospitals scale up, diversify and decentralize super-specialty services. However, unless competitiveness was preserved at the district level and below, we may not succeed in delivering a quality health care system at more affordable prices. The real success of the Aarogyasri programme would be not when the programme provided mere coverage to all, but when it succeeded in reducing the cost of quality health care itself, compelling the dominant large market players to move to the peripheries for their survival and provide quality health care at affordable prices, even to the non-poor households. In order to achieve this objective, the district and area level hospitals needed to be revamped. Area level hospitals should be promoted to perform general specialization-related services and the district level hospitals should offer super-specialization services in the diseases prevalent in the region of its location. If district hospitals were not promoted to super-specialty services, then the outcome of the current process would only be a decentralization, which might not lead to reduction in the cost of health care, but would segment the entire population of patients across different dominant players in the private sector.

Need for development of responsive health care security system

Finally, the development of the lower-end systems was not merely in the interest of preserving competitiveness and preventing monopolies at the district level as high valued health care services get decentralized; it was also to prevent the degeneration of high value-end services, provided by large-sized government hospitals in the major cities, and of the reproduction of quality human resources by the health care system.

In what follows, we have elaborated both these aspects. In the case of government hospitals, unlike in the private hospital system, the services assumed the structure of a chain. The primary health care centres, the community health centres, the area hospitals, and the district hospitals were inevitably connected to the tertiary and research institutions such as Osmania General Hospital and NIMS. In today's scenario, it was found that at the primary health care centres and area hospitals, there was a lack of, or effective use of, available infrastructure; there was grave negligence in posting doctors or, even if posted, of ensuring their presence. We have briefly presented some of the findings in different levels of the health care chain in the government hospitals (Table 4.11).

The PHC at Ambatpally, as already stated, was meant to cater to a population of 22,000. On an average, it was visited by 75 patients daily. The stock of syringes and needles available were sufficient for 20 days only and the patients were being asked to bring their own needles. There were two doctors during 2004–7. But at the time of this study in 2011, there was no doctor in this PHC. However, it would not be true to say that there has been no improvement in the conditions. The Ambatpally PHC was started in a rented building with two beds in 1996. In 2004, the PHC shifted to its own building. Currently it has 10 beds. In 2001, a microscope and in 2007 blood sugar and urine sugar testing equipment were purchased for the PHC. However, they have never been used for lack of disposable inputs.

According to the doctors, the existing conditions were not encouraging them to continue in the hospital for a long period. On the other hand, bureaucrats occupying high positions in policy-making stated that when the doctors at the PHC and up to the district-level hospitals were not present in the hospitals beyond the afternoon, and when the existing infrastructure itself was underused, why should more resources be spent on equipping these hospitals?

Some of the doctors had observed that 'the lower-end hospitals were squeezed of resources and were then being asked to compete at par with the private sector'. The district hospital authorities argued that they must be developed into model hospitals. Every district hospital should have physicians, general surgeons, gynaecologists, ENT surgeons, paediatricians, orthopaedic surgeons, ophthalmologists, and anaesthetists. Despite the revolving funds, district hospitals' infrastructure left a lot to be desired. For instance, in Mahabubnagar there was only one general physician for the entire district. The posting of doctors did not seem to have a rationale, with cardiologists

Table 4.11 An Overview of the Conditions of the Lower-end Hospitals Chain

<table>
<tr><th colspan="2">Village Level Equipment</th></tr>
<tr><td colspan="2">Weighing machine ANM/Multi-purpose health workers</td></tr>
<tr><th colspan="2">PHC Level</th></tr>
<tr><td>Medical camps for eye tests are conducted by Lions Club and L.V. Prasad Eye Institute
– Family planning surgery delivery equipment and injections for this purpose are there
– Mucus sucker, Umbilical Scissors, thread available also are available
– BP operator
– Stethoscope
– Weighing machine
– Microscope</td><td>– Disposable quantity supplied is less
– There is 50 per cent shortfall of injections
– No incubator or ventilator
– No blood bank
– Injection being used cannot even be sterilized because these are plastic injection. In the interior villages the old injections are still being used and the old system of sterilization and reuse of needles continues here</td></tr>
<tr><th colspan="2">Civil Hospital</th></tr>
<tr><td>– HIV testing kit available
– Oxygen cylinders available
– Blood bank available
– Lab microscope</td><td>– No ECG
– No X-ray
– Operations: Family planning, first-aid in poly trauma cases</td></tr>
<tr><th colspan="2">Area Hospital</th></tr>
<tr><td>– X-ray, HIV testing equipment
– CT scan
– ECG</td><td>– No Orthopaedic
– No Paediatric</td></tr>
<tr><th colspan="2">District Hospital</th></tr>
<tr><td>– Paediatrics, General Surgery, orthopaedics, Poly Trauma Equipment is available; however patients complain that there are no tests done at the district level
– Partly because of absence of doctors and because they are engaging in private practice,
– Operation theatre cables, rigid endoscopy, monitors, pulseocso meters, X-ray, CT scan, ultra sound.</td><td>– A doctor who was DGO has been suspended for negligence. Now owns a private hospital
– Scarcity of doctors- Radiology machine available but no radiologist posted
– Laparoscopic equipment was not available—purchased with the money given by the collector's office.</td></tr>
</table>

Source: Based on field study.

and qualified general surgeons sometimes being posted in the PHCs. Secondly, doctors who are MBBS and those who have super-specialty were both being paid the same salary. Further, the salary was being fixed on the basis of the district administration hierarchy and was not based on the value of the professional services. The district hospital superintendent, for instance, was equated in the district hierarchy with an RDO and a DSP and paid accordingly. Following such a mechanical bureaucratized structure of remuneration, there was no incentive for the doctors to join government hospitals. The doctors were also complaining about lack of proper residence or schooling facilities for their children if they opted to stay in rural areas. At present, they were commuting to their places of work, which partly contributed to their absence in the hospitals. Without having a systematic plan to attract high-valued services in rural areas, Aarogyasri programme might not self-sustain in the long-run, and could be monopolized by the private sector.

A comparison by these doctors with the payment structures in the private sector was a de-motivating factor, and causing bad practices such as using the government hospitals as fertile grounds for their private consultation. There was a move to make rural hospital service compulsory for the new doctors. This could help only if the infrastructure was adequately revamped. There was also a proposal to create health care clusters wherein some number of PHCs would be organized into a cluster with specialist doctors. This was meant to reduce birth-related deaths of women and children. But other issues might have to be addressed. This entire process has affected the functioning of hospitals such as Osmania General Hospital and NIMS, where the doctors and authorities complained about over-crowding and wastage of valuable time on simple cases. According to them, this was because several patients were coming to the secondary and tertiary institutions such as NIMS without proper primary level investigation and diagnosis. As a consequence, the average waiting time of patients to get an X-ray or an endoscope or CT scan, etc., increased, which eventually was inferred as neglect. This could, in turn, reduce the number of patients preferring to come to these institutions as a first choice. Thus, revamping of the lower-end services for proper filtering and streamlining of patients could improve the secondary and tertiary services.

Finally, the poor reputation of government hospitals could have an impact on availability of quality doctors. This is where the distinction between teaching and non-teaching hospitals becomes significant. Despite the rise of several private medical colleges, the government-run medical colleges still rank among the best institutions imparting medical education. With a large number of patients with serious illness preferring private hospitals, the initiation of medical students into surgery happens with a hydrosol or hernia. So, medical students are exposed to a less complex variety of diseases. Aarogyasri in its present form may prove to be advantageous to private hospitals, but this could be counter-productive for several government hospitals, which are also teaching institutions. On the other hand, because of shortage of staff in institutions like the NIMS, all the paper work was being done by the doctors and this eats into their teaching and research time. This could affect the high-valued services of extremely proficient doctors, and reduce them to medical clerks and accountants.

***

The Aarogyasri experience showed that commitment to equity and health care access to the poor was clearly visible, as it covered over 85 per cent of the State's population. Notes a comparative analysis of health care insurance: 'The realization among the top leadership for the commitment to cover nearly all of the population, despite their socio-economic status is quite commendable, since evidence clearly suggests that in India, it is not only the poor but a large section of above poverty line (APL) also ends up in catastrophic payments and faces impoverishment due to illness' (Reddy *et al.*, 2011).

However, the present study showed that the large-scale market-dominant private players were not likely to be very enthusiastic to continue the programme in the long run unless their markets were threatened. This could happen only by decentralizing the super-specialty services. Although the programme seemed to have succeeded in decentralizing the general and super-specialty services, there was a risk of it becoming unviable in the long run unless the costs of health care itself were reduced. There was a need to remove trust-deficit in government hospitals. Focus needed to be diverted to small- and medium-scale private players in the medium-term, but the long-term policy option was to strengthen government hospitals. To improve the Government hospitals at the secondary and tertiary level, there was a need to correct the entire chain of the health care system. Also, there was a need for adequate staff to carry out documentation without encroaching on the quality time of doctors. We have a historical context where the right discourse and the economies of bulk purchases, economies of locally driven production of implants and generic drugs, the economies of location, and the objectives of welfare and competitiveness have converged. In this context, how best the political wisdom moulded the economic pragmatism to take on the short-sighted 'misery profits/rents maximizing' rent-seekers, monopolists, and lobbyists remained to be seen.[9]

In spite of several structural and institutional constraints, Aarogyasri was a unique health care system which comprehensively addressed the high-end, low frequency medical needs of the poor. The very fact that 91 per cent of the beneficiaries were BPL card holders showed that hardly anyone would have been able to get this high-end medical care without getting caught in the economically catastrophic hospitalization and indebtedness. But at the same time, there was a widely shared view that the major weakness of the Aarogyasri was lack of provision for out-patient treatment of everyday illness which affected the working capacity of the poor. The focus on tertiary health care, to the exclusion of all other forms of medical assistance, would lead to an inefficient medical care model, with a low-level real impact on meeting the needs of health care and the health of the population (Shukla, R. *et al.*, 2011). Lack of attention to low-end but high frequency diseases would make the poor pay heavily on health care. It posed a paradox that a person of a poor household, with a serious ailment, was getting Aarogyasri treatment free, but others in the same household continued to incur high expenses on frequently occurring diseases, leaving the household on the margins of indebtedness. It is suggested that to improve the RAS delivery system, integration of all levels of the health care system to develop a more coherent and cohesive patient-centred system, needed to be considered; this was possible through integration of preventive, promotive, and curative services, to improve early detection and treatment, thereby reducing the load on tertiary care (Rao *et al.*, 2009). While the Aarogyasri experience showed too much of a bias in favour of high-end diseases and tertiary treatment, the RSBY was focused on relatively low-end diseases and secondary level treatment while catering to in-patient care for out-patient ailments. An ideal system of health care might be to move towards a cohesive and judicious mix of RAS and RSBY approaches, along with taking on board effective out-patient care.

Notes

[1] For further details see aarogyasri.org.

[2] *Penta* is the local term for a hamlet or settlement of a group of independent homes of Chenchus.

[3] There are different Public Distribution System Programmes for each of these categories as well.

- The *BPL families* having white cards coded as WAP, who receive 4 kgs of rice per person to a maximum (5 persons) of 20 kgs at Rs 2 per kg;
- The *poorest of the poor households* having Antyodaya cards coded as YAP, who receive 35 kgs of rice at Rs 2 per kg.
- The *destitute poor* having Annapoorna card coded as AAP, who receive 10 kgs of rice free of cost.

[4] The Aarogyasri programme is applicable to intra-state migrants but, it is not applicable to inter-state migrants. A proof of local residence is part of the requirement. However, there have been instances where some inter-state migrants have successfully procured the white as well as the Aarogyasri cards, through their local social networks they developed in the course of their long stay. In other instances, inter-state migrants have been helped by sympathetic social actors who have taken the initiative to write to the district collector's office and helped the migrants get compensation through the Chief Minister's Camp office on the recommendation of the district collector. Such instances are, however, rare.

[5] Remoteness, not only in terms of geographical location, but in terms of active presence of government administration.

[6] See www.aarogyasri.org.

[7] The very nature of this data at one level is likely to be biased if filling and sending feedback forms is considered as a relatively active category of respondents, but at another level this data in its very nature being random, it provides an important representative basis for analysis.

[8] Health sector reforms have been identified with:

(i) *Structural and functional reforms*: The focus is on inter-sectoral convergence, integration of existing services, strengthening of infrastructure, mainstreaming management initiatives, increased access to health services at the household level, etc.

(ii) *Finance-related reforms*: Focus is on social protection mechanism, insurance coverage, better management of human resources, supply chain management, drug procurement policies, etc.

(iii) *Governance-related reforms*: Focus on involvement of Panchayati Raj Institutions, decentralized management, monitoring and planning mechanisms, etc. (Ravi *et al.*, 2009).

[9] It must be pointed out that the Principle Secretary of Health Mr Ramesh was shifted when he attempted at improving the conditions of district level government hospitals, supposedly at the behest of the private corporate hospital lobbies.

References

Kannan K.P. and Varinder Jain. 2011. *National Health Insurance for the Poor in India;* A Review of the Implementation of RSBY, Paper presented at the final workshop under CDS-ASSR-HiVOS project on the Monitoring of Social Security for the Working Poor in India's Informal Sector. Thiruvananthapuram: Centre for Development Studies.

Kannan K.P. and G. Ravindran. 2011. 'India's Common People: The Regional Profile', *Economic and Political Weekly*, 46(38): 60–74.

Mallipedi, Ravi, Harna Pernefeldt, and Sofi Bergkvist. 2009. *Andhra Pradesh Health Sector Reform; A Narrative Case Study*, Technical Partner Paper 7, Access Health Initiative and William A. Hosteline foundation for Medical Sciences and Arts. The Rockfeller foundation.

Oneworld.Net. 2010. *Rajiv Aarogyasri Health Insurance Scheme—Andhra Pradesh, Documentation of the Best Practices*, One World Foundation of India, October.

Rao, Mala *et al.* 2009. *A Rapid Evaluation of the Rajiv Aarogyasri Community Health Insurance Scheme—Andhra Pradesh*: A Report. Hyderabad: Indian Institute of Public Health.

Reddy, K. Srinath *et al.* 2011. *A Critical Assessment of the Existing Health Insurance Models in India*, (Sponsored under the Scheme of Socio-Economic Research, The Planning Commission of India), Public Health Foundation of India.

Shukla, Abhay, Anant Phadke, and Rakhal Gaitonde. 2011. *Towards Universal Health Access to Health Care in India*, Medico Friends Circle Bulleting, August 2010–January 2011.

Shukla R., Veena Shatrugna, and R. Srivatsa. 2011. 'Aarogyasri Health Care Model: Advantage Public Sector', *Economic and Political Weekly*, 46(49): 38–42.

III

KERALA

5 FUNCTIONING OF CONTINGENT SOCIAL SECURITY SCHEMES IN KERALA

THE SOCIAL AND INSTITUTIONAL CONTEXT OF DELIVERY AT THE LOCAL LEVEL

T.P. Kunhikannan and *K.P. Aravindan*

Kerala is one state with a long history in providing social security to a large section of its people. Most of the schemes, if not all, have also been institutionalized to meet conditions of 'deficiency' and 'adversity'. The former refers to poverty or inadequate livelihood security, and the latter refers to the absence of fall back mechanisms that take care of contingencies and eventualities (Kannan, 2007). Against this background of a historical evolution of social security measures in the State must be viewed the performance record of the national social insurance scheme for health care known as the Rasthtriya Swasthya Bima Yojana (RSBY). This study covers two village panchayats in the State and is part of a larger study of the national social security schemes for the working poor in India. The two Gram Panchayats selected for the purpose of the study are Naduvannur and Cheruvannur-Nallam in Kozhikode District. While Cheruvannur-Nallam forms part of an urban agglomeration, Naduvannur is purely rural, making possible an urban-rural comparison.

THE KERALA EXPERIENCE

Kerala's development experience is the outcome of the interplay of multiple factors, including social security. The important feature of the outcome is its commendable social and human development, even at low levels of per capita income. This peculiar situation, which is not in sync with conventional economic norms, came to be called the 'Kerala Model of Development'. As noted in the Human Development Report for Kerala 2005, a highlight of Kerala's development experience has been the rapid reduction in intra-state disparities and gender differentials in most indicators of human development (Government of Kerala, 2005).

Current Social Security Schemes in Kerala

Social security schemes in present-day Kerala are four fold: (i) insurance schemes, (ii) pension schemes, (iii) schemes of welfare fund boards (numbering around 32 as of 2011), and (iv) an integrated social security scheme called *Ashraya* to take care of the destitute in society. The agencies executing these schemes differ. They include the Central Government, Departments of State Government, Welfare Fund Boards and Local Self Government Institutions. Among the schemes, the present study focuses only on those which are implemented through Local Self Government (LSG) Bodies, specifically Gram Panchayats. An overview of the schemes is given below.

RASHTRIYA SWASTHA BIMA YOJANA (RSBY)

The RSBY is a health insurance programme launched by the Government of India in October 2007. This programme intends to provide health assistance to people living below poverty line (BPL). The beneficiaries are families of workers in the unorganized sector. The scheme provides cashless hospitalization benefit of up to Rs 30,000 in specified empanelled hospitals, for a family of five members. The eligible families are those included in the BPL list as per the criteria of the Central Government. Biometric smart cards with photographs and finger prints of the insured persons are issued to the beneficiaries. Unlike the general health insurance schemes, there is no age limit for enrolments in RSBY and all pre-existing illnesses are covered from day one. An insurance company, selected through a tender process by the State Government, is responsible for enrolling families to the scheme and settling claims. The insurer shall enrol the beneficiaries based on the soft data provided by the State Government.

The Salient Features and Financing of the Scheme

The salient features of the scheme are: (i) total sum insured is Rs 30,000 per family per annum; (ii) pre-existing conditions too are covered; (iii) cashless coverage of all health services in the insured package; (iv) provision for a smart card based system of beneficiary identification; (v) provision for reasonable pre- and post-hospitalization expenses for one day prior and five days after hospitalization; and (vi) provision for transport allowance (with a limit of Rs 100 per visit) but subject to an annual ceiling of Rs 1,000.

The financing of the scheme are as follows: (i) the annual premium per family is capped at Rs 750, of which 75 per cent is contributed by the Central Government, along with the cost of the smart cards (Rs 60 per card); (ii) 25 per cent of the annual premium is borne by the State Government; (iii) the beneficiary pays Rs 30 per card as registration/renewal fee; and (iv) any administrative and other related cost of the scheme in each state, not otherwise included in the premium cost, shall be borne by the respective governments.

Implementation Process in Kerala

The implementation of RSBY in Kerala was formally launched in October 2008 in Alappuzha District. Subsequently, the programme was extended to other districts and within a few months, the entire State came under the protection of this scheme. This programme has been operating successfully in the State for the last three years. The Labour and Rehabilitation Department is the nodal agency to administer the scheme. The actual implementation at the ground level is carried out by the Health and Family Welfare Department and the LSG Department. Given the local peculiarities, the State Government had brought in a few additions into the original scheme, with a view to extending its benefits to more families. For instance, the State Government had identified and brought in an additional 10 lakh poor families within the fold of the insurance scheme over and above the Planning Commission estimate of 11.79 lakh BPL families; the premium of the additional families was borne by the State. Any Above Poverty Line (APL) family in the State could also join the scheme provided the full premium was borne by the beneficiary himself. In order to extend the benefits of the scheme to the additional 10 lakh BPL families and the volunteering APL families, the Government had formulated a Comprehensive Health Insurance Scheme (CHIS) on the same lines as RSBY. A. separate nodal agency, namely, Comprehensive Health Insurance Agency, Kerala (CHIAK) was formed under the Labour Department for the implementation of RSBY and CHIS.

In the first year of the implementation of the scheme, 135 hospitals in the Government sector and 165 private hospitals (including hospitals in the co-operative sector) joined the scheme. In the former, all the five Government Medical Colleges, all District and Taluka Hospitals, and Community Health Centres were empanelled in the scheme. Private hospitals could enter the scheme by submitting an application. After assessment of the facilities available at the hospital, the insurance company would empanel the hospital and give clearance. A public sector insurance company, the United India Insurance Company, was selected as the insurer through a tender process.

Going by the available statistics, the State had issued the largest number of RSBY smart cards in the country. Both the Government and the insurance company were recipients of the Union Government award for the best implementation of the scheme (RSBY Connect, 2012). For 2011–12, the State has set itself an ambitious target of bringing 35 lakh needy families under the scheme. To this end, it has given a blanket eligibility to all SC and ST families, fishermen families, *Ashraya* families, agricultural workers, Welfare Fund members, and all other families whose monthly income, as recorded in the ration card, is not more than Rs 600, irrespective of whether they have been included in the BPL list of the Central or State Governments. The new entrants could register themselves at the various Akshaya Centres and the IT Mission centres of the State. The State budget for 2010 also announced an additional Rs 70,000 coverage for all RSBY beneficiaries for the treatment of all major illnesses relating to the heart, kidney and cancer, in specified major government hospitals. This scheme, titled CHIS Plus, is administered directly by CHIAK through non-insurance route.

In sharp contrast, the performance of RSBY at the national level seems quite slow in its progress. There is no sign of RSBY reaching all the poor by end of 2012. But Kerala and a few other small states have shown what could be achieved, given the needed commitment. It may be noted that since early 2006, a health insurance for the poor has become a political issue in the state (Narayana, 2010). Political leaders and social activists, including the present authors, were also active participants in the debate on health insurance in Kerala (Aravindan and Kunhikannan, 2006).

PENSION AND OTHER FORMS OF SOCIAL ASSISTANCE

There are more than 40 pension schemes, of which 20 are financed by the State itself. These pension schemes are implemented directly by the government departments, or through different Welfare Fund

Boards (Kannan, 2002). It is estimated that more than 59 lakh people are benefited by pension schemes (Government of Kerala, 2011). In the present study, based on a survey of two village panchayats, we evaluate six such schemes and assistances. They include pension for (i) agricultural workers; (ii) old people; (iii) widows; (iv) physically challenged; (v) unmarried women above the age of 50 years; and (vi) unemployment assistance.

Pension Scheme for Agricultural Workers

This scheme, instituted in the year 1980 by the State, is meant to provide financial assistance to agricultural workers who are above the age of 60. The beneficiary must be a member of the Agricultural Workers' Welfare Fund. Their family income per year should be less than Rs 20,000 in rural areas and Rs 22,375 in urban areas. The applicant should be a resident of Kerala for the last 10 years at the time of submitting the application.

Old Age Pension

This scheme was implemented by the State in 1995. The beneficiary of the scheme should be a permanent resident of Kerala for not less than three years. The applicant should be above 65 years of age (the upper age limit was reduced to 60 in the State Budget of 2011). Family income of the applicant per annum should be less than Rs 20,000 in rural areas and Rs 22,375 in urban areas. The applicant should not be a member of any of the geriatric care homes and should not be a beneficiary of any other social security pension.

Widow Pension

This scheme was instituted in Kerala in the year 1973. The beneficiary should either be a widow, or a woman separated from her husband, or a married woman whose husband's whereabouts are not known for the last seven years. No age limit would apply for widow pension. The family income criterion is the same as in Old Age Pension.

Special Pension Scheme for Handicapped

This scheme was introduced in 1982. The beneficiaries are those who have proven disability of 40 per cent and above. The income of the applicant should not be more than Rs 250 per month.

Pension for Unmarried Women above Age of 50 Years

This scheme came into effect in 2001 for unmarried women above the age of 50, with no other income. Family income of the applicant was similar as in Old Age and Widow Pensions.

Unemployment Assistance Scheme

The unemployment assistance scheme was introduced in 1982. Implemented through LSG institutions, the beneficiaries were unemployed persons in the age group of 21–35 years, who had passed SSLC (except for SC/ST and physically challenged) with a monthly family income limited to Rs 100. They should also have been registered as unemployed in the employment exchange for the past three years.

Ashraya

Ashraya was the first integrated programme for addressing the poorest of the poor, who lived at the margins of the economy and society. It was visualized as a sub-programme of *Kudumbasree* and implemented through community-based organizations of Kudumbasree. The LSG Institutions were the real planners of this project, with the State Government playing the role of an active facilitator. The destitute families are taken care of till they achieve a minimum standard of life. Thus *Ashraya* is not a one-time assistance, but ongoing till the objective is realized.

The dimension, extension, and impact of these schemes in the two panchayats surveyed are being analysed in the succeeding sections. Special emphasis is given to RSBY, since it is a new scheme introduced in India with wide coverage. Moreover, the RSBY is the first insurance-based social security scheme initiated in India.

THE SELECTED VILLAGES

Cheruvannur-Nallam and Naduvannur were the two panchayats selected for study. The former was an independent Gram Panchayat till 2010 but was later incorporated into Kozhikode City Corporation. The latter is a first grade panchayat. Cheruvannur-Nallalam is situated 12 km south of Kozhikode city, and falls in Kozhikode Taluka. Naduvannur village is nearly 27 km north of Kozhikode and is part of present Koyilandy Taluka. Naduvannoor was, at one time, the headquarter of Kurumbranadu, an old territory of the Malabar region. Before the re-organization of the State in 1956, Nallalam and Cheruvannur were separate villages, which later became part of the Beypore panchayat. In 1963, the two villages Cheruvannur and Nallalam were unified and formed the Cheruvannur-Nallam Gram Panchayat.

One of the reasons for selecting these two panchayats for the present study was that they were periodically surveyed and analyzed for various development purposes and those data were readily available. First among these survey reports are the village study monographs produced as part of the 1961 census. In 1961, the major objective of the survey was to map out the socio-economic structure of the countryside, with a direction of change, and also to understand the social structure and social change (GoI, 1961; and Reddy, 2004). Cheruvannur-Nallam was included in the survey mainly to take stock of the living conditions of the tile-factory workers. Naduvannur at that time was a centre of multi-cottage industries like handloom, beedi, pot-making, coir-spinning, oil pressing, etc. We had purposefully selected these two areas for our present study, to contextualize it and relate places where some sort of database were available for the last three or four decades. It is against this background that the present study was pursued in these two Gram Panchayats. In our study, 932 households were covered; that included 530 from Cheruvannur-Nallam and 402 from Naduvannur.

Objectives and Methodology of the Study

The objectives of the study were

(i) to assess the extent of coverage and quality of delivery of:
   a. RSBY
   b. Ashraya
   c. Old-age and other important pension schemes
(ii) to delineate the variables associated with the effective (or otherwise) performance of the above mentioned programs

The study employed collection of three types of data namely, (i) direct data from the beneficiaries of RSBY, and the social security pensions collected by surveying two wards from two selected Gram Panchayats; (ii) focus group discussion among the stakeholders; and (iii) macro-data from the insurance company, relating to enrolment and payments.

The primary data were collected through sample surveys and questionnaires, from one ward each of the two panchayats. The Wards were randomly selected and all the households within the wards were fully covered.

The survey was conducted in October, 2010. The total number of households surveyed was 932. The total population covered in the survey stood at 4,660, of which Naduvannur occupies 1,687 and Cheruvannur-Nallam occupies 2,973. The average family size is five, which almost exactly corresponds to the state average. Four types of questionnaires were used for the survey. The first one was used for collecting the overall socio-economic status of the family. The other three were used to collect details of Ashraya, RSBY and other six social security pension schemes. While the data relating to socio-economic status were collected from all households, the other questionnaires were used only in those houses where at least one member was found availing of any one of the above mentioned social security pensions. The socio-economic classification that was followed here was the one developed by the People's Science Movement in Kerala, popularly known by its organizational name, Kerala Sastra Sahitya Parishad (KSSP) (Aravindan and Menon, 2010).

The KSSP classified the families surveyed on the basis of their socio-economic indicators, which were believed to be more realistic in the Kerala context. The four variables used were: (i) per capita income; (ii) per capita expenditure; (iii) ownership of consumer durables; and (iv) the physical features of the houses. We did not include education as a variable in this analysis since education directly influenced the formation of socio-economic status of a family and vice versa.

The variables noted above were assigned different weightages. After assigning the weightage, an overall composite index of each family was computed. Then, fixing a cut off score, the families were divided into four economic groups (EG1, EG2, EG3, and EG4). This classification and calculations were not arbitrary, but based on the judicious incorporation of judgments guided by the practical life experiences (Aravindan and Menon, 2010).

A preliminary draft of the report was presented at the Centre for Development Studies, Thiruvananthapuram, in November 2010 for a brainstorming session. Incorporating the suggestions emerging from the brainstorming session, we presented a redrafted version for discussion before a 28-member Focus Group (which included representatives of hospital managements, doctors, PRO's of RSBY, insurance companies, Kudumbasree, Third Party Administrators (TPAs) and social activists) at Kozhikode in January 2011. Their opinions, based on experience and observations, had also been taken into consideration while making the final report. A group discussion of *Ashraya* beneficiaries was conducted in the Cheruvannur-Nallam panchayat in which 14 beneficiaries participated.

Macro-level Data from Insurance Company

The data regarding receipts, payments, and loss for all the 14 districts of the State were obtained from the insurer—the United India Insurance Company. Detailed statistics regarding individual claims for Kozhikode District were also obtained.

RESULTS OF THE SURVEY

The beneficiaries under various schemes in the surveyed areas are indicated in Table 5.1. There is a little difference in the socio-economic

TABLE 5.1 Number of Beneficiary Persons and Families in the Surveyed Areas

S. No.	*Pension*	*Naduvannur*	*Cheruvannur-Nallam*	*Total*
1.	Pension for agricultural workers	42	7	49
2.	Unemployment benefit	4	0	4
3.	Widow pension	25	14	39
4.	Old age pension	7	7	14
5.	Pension to the physically challenged	9	11	20
6.	Pension to unmarried women above 50 years	0	4	4
7.	Other social pensions	6	5	11
8.	Sub total of social security pension (individuals)	93	48	141
9.	RSBY (family)	169	50	219
10.	Ashraya (persons)	69	45	114
11.	Total beneficiaries	331	143	474
12.	Total houses surveyed	402	530	932

Source: Based on data collected from field survey done as part of this study.

TABLE 5.2 The Sample by Demographic and Socio-economic Characteristics

Category	*Number*	%
Panchayat		
Naduvannur	402	43.1
Cheruvannur	530	56.9
Religion		
Hindu	327	35.1
Muslim	598	64.2
Christian	7	0.8
Caste		
Scheduled caste	76	8.2
Scheduled tribe	0	0
Others	856	91.8
Economic group		
Very poor (EG1)	122	13.1
Poor (EG2)	271	29.1
Lower middle-class (EG3)	374	40.1
Upper middle-class (EG4)	165	17.7

Source: Based on data collected from field survey done as part of this study.

profile of these two wards of the two Gram Panchayats (Table 5.2). For instance, while half of the population in Naduvannur could be categorized as 'very poor' or 'poor', in the semi-urban Cheruvannur this segment of poor accounted for only 36 per cent. Moreover, the population of the sample was predominantly Muslim, who constituted 64 per cent of the overall sample. This was much higher than the ratio of Muslim population in the Kozhikode District. SCs accounted for 8.2 per cent of the sample, which was somewhat reflective of their share in the State population.

The distribution of the sample in terms of economic group in the two panchayats is shown in Figure 5.1. As noted above, the division of the sample into four Economic Groups (EG) was adopted from Kerala Sastra Sahitya Parishad (KSSP). The population was classified into very poor (EG1), poor (EG2), lower middle-class (EG3), and upper middle-class (EG4). Economic stratification was needed in

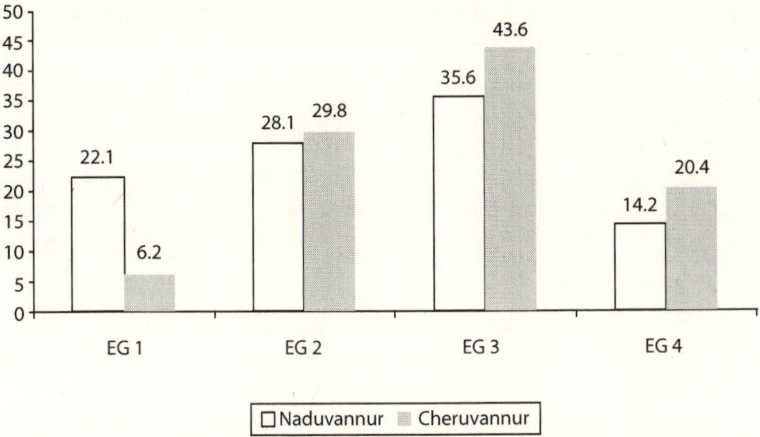

FIGURE 5.1 Distribution by Economic Groups in the Two Panchayats (%)

Source: Based on data collected from field survey done as part of this study.

the study for independent evaluation of the fairness (or otherwise) allocation of RSBY cards, and other pension benefits.

More than one-fifth of the households in these panchayats were RSBY beneficiaries, as seen from Table 5.3. It can be seen that 3 per cent of the population received some social security pension or the other.

RSBY SURVEY DATA

It has been the general experience in the State that enrolment is higher in rural areas, as compared to the urban. This was reflected in our sample, as shown in Table 5.4. In Naduvannur, the rural panchayat

TABLE 5.3 Beneficiaries of Social Security Schemes—Summary

Social Security Scheme	*Number*	%
RSBY beneficiary households	216	23.10
Social security pension—households	121	14.01
Social security pension—persons	141	3.02

Source: Based on data collected from field survey done as part of this study.

TABLE 5.4 Actual RSBY Enrolment in the Two Panchayats and District, 2010

Place	*Enrolment*	*Target*	*Achievement (%)*
Naduvannur	1,999	2,274	87.9
Cheruvannur	1,162	1,995	59.2
Kozhikode district	1,74,739	2,29,489	76.1

Source: Based on panchayat Data and district level data from the Insurer, United India Insurance Company.

showed definitely a higher enrolment in comparison to the semi-urban Cheruvannur.

Figure 5.2 shows our independent assessment of the fairness of the BPL list as existing in 2010. There has been a gradual decline from 47.5 per cent in EG1 to a low 4.8 per cent in EG4. So, the problem is less of the undeserving being enrolled than the under-enrolment of the really deserving. The EG1, or 'very poor' category, corresponds more or less to the BPL category of the Government of India. Even among these, only 47.5 per cent have been enrolled in the RSBY.

Figure 5.3 is further testimony of the overall fairness of the card distribution. No one with more than 7 consumer durables has been issued an RSBY card.

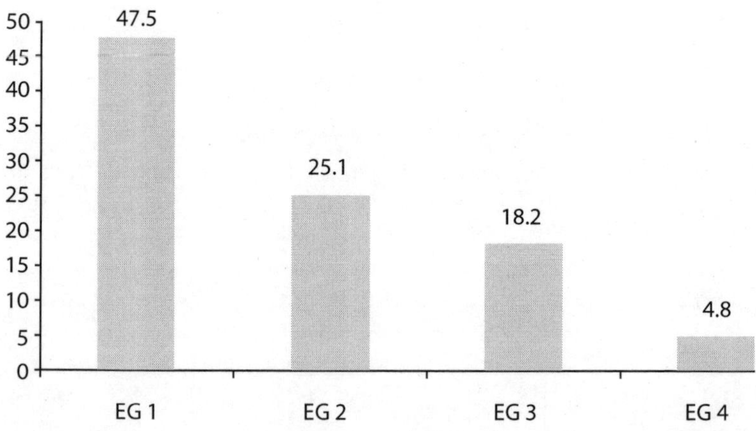

FIGURE 5.2 Enrolment in Each Economic Group in the Sample

Source: Based on data collected from field survey done as part of this study.

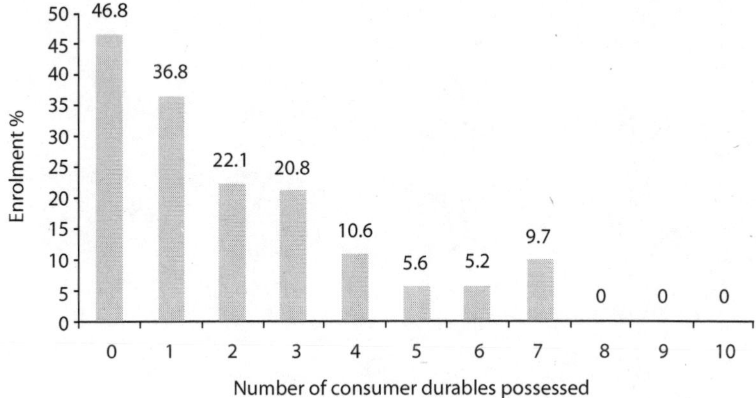

FIGURE 5.3 Enrolment and Possession of Consumer Durables

Source: Based on data collected from field survey done as part of this study.

Though enrolment among the SCs was 59.2 per cent, among Muslims it was even lower, at 9 per cent (Figure 5.4). Figure 5.5 shows that the reason for poor enrolment of Muslims is not because of the lack of poverty among them. Even among EG1, only 14.6 per cent Muslims had joined the RSBY. The reasons for this under enrolment have to be enquired.

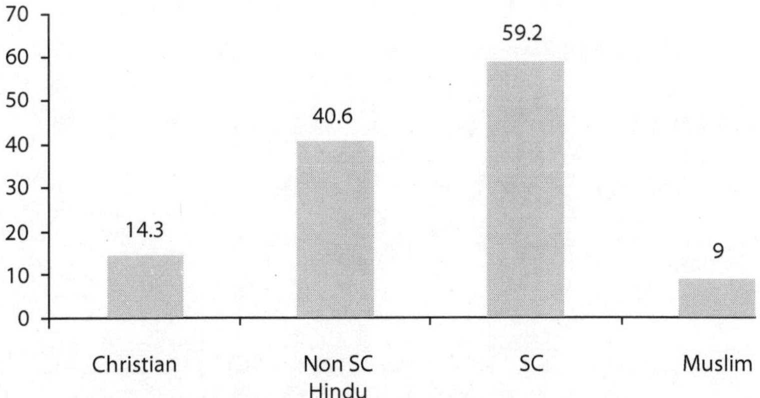

FIGURE 5.4 Enrolment by Religion and Caste (%)

Source: Based on data collected from field survey done as part of this study.

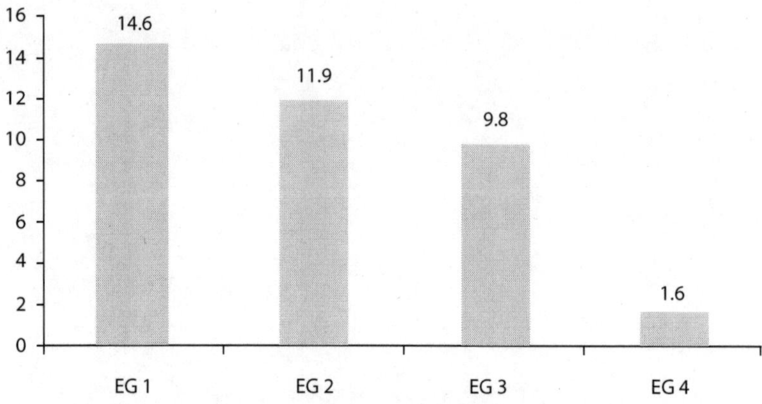

FIGURE 5.5 Enrolment by EG among Muslims (%)

Source: Based on data collected from field survey done as part of this study.

The main source of information regarding the RSBY beneficiary status were the Kudumbasree workers, and they were also predominantly responsible for educating the population about the scheme (Figures 5.6 and 5.7).

Figure 5.8 shows the main reasons behind the selection of the five beneficiaries. It is seen to be mostly a matter of convenience.

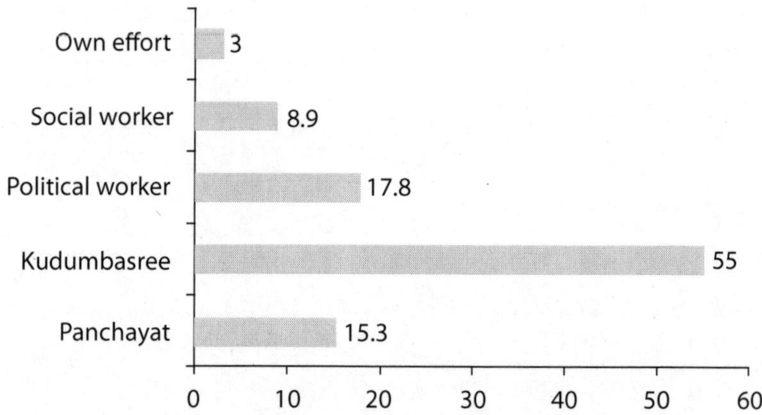

FIGURE 5.6 Source of Information Regarding Beneficiary Status

Source: Based on data collected from field survey done as part of this study.

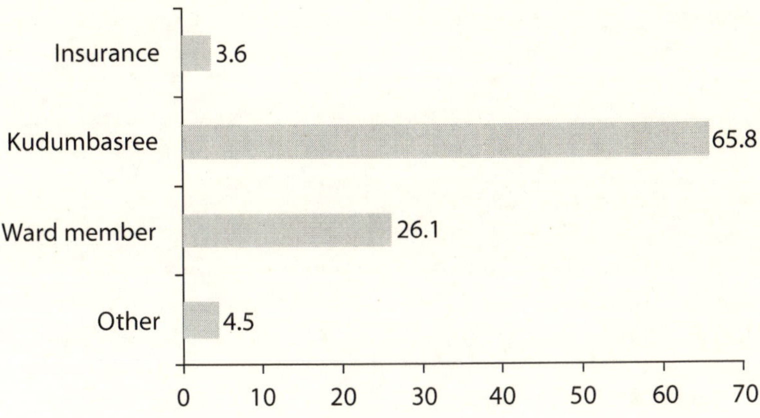

FIGURE 5.7 Who Explained About RSBY?

Source: Based on data collected from field survey done as part of this study.

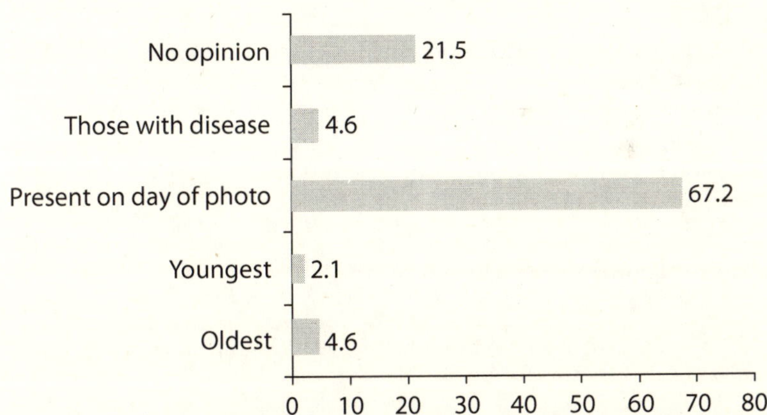

FIGURE 5.8 How Decision Regarding the Five Beneficiaries was Arrived at (%)

Source: Based on data collected from field survey done as part of this study.

Adverse selection or selectively enrolling those with disease is not seen to be a big problem.

Tables 5.5 and 5.6 show the responses to questions regarding enrolment, issue of cards, and service in hospital. Loss of wages for

TABLE 5.5 Questions Regarding Enrolment and Issue of Card (%)

Question	*Yes*	*No*	*Not Enrolled*
Did the enrolment procedure result in loss of wages (workers)	67.1	28.1	4.8
Did the enrolment procedure result in loss of classes (students)	47.1	47.6	5.3
Was the RSBY card received on the same day?	81.2	18.8	–
Was the information on the card correct?	97.1	2.9	–
Did anyone explain to you about RSBY?	57.8	42.2	–

Source: Based on data collected from field survey done as part of this study.

TABLE 5.6 Questions Regarding Service in the Hospital (%)

Question	*Yes*	*No*
Was completely free treatment provided in the hospital?	80.0	20.0
Were detailed instructions displayed in the hospital?	83.3	16.7
Were you asked to remain admitted longer than required?	11.1	88.9
Was the card returned during discharge?	84.2	15.8
Were you informed of the amount deducted from card at the time of discharge?	29.4	70.6

Source: Based on data collected from field survey done as part of this study.

workers and loss of classes for students was witnessed in many cases. More importantly, details regarding the scheme were not given at the time of enrolment in as many as 57.8 per cent cases. Also notable was the fact brought out in Table 5.6, that 70.6 per cent of the patients were not informed about the amount deducted from the card at the time of discharge from the hospital.

As per our survey, the claim ratio was 12.2 per cent of the sampled households. There is unanimity in the opinion that the RSBY scheme was useful (Table 5.7).

TABLE 5.7 General Questions Regarding RSBY

Question	*Yes*	*No*
Was a claim made in the past 1 year?	12.2	87.8
Should the same card be renewed every year?	75.7	24.3
Is the cover of Rs 30,000 adequate?	37.7	62.3
Is the RSBY program useful for the people?	98.1	1.9

Source: Based on data collected from field survey done as part of this study.

RSBY: Macro Data from Insurance Company

Information was sought from the Insurance Company (United India Insurance) and the TPA for Kozhikode District (Medsave) regarding enrolment, claims and pattern of diseases for which claims were made. These are presented in Tables 5.8, 5.9, 5.10, 5.11, and 5.12.

Although Government and private hospitals are nearly equal in number in Kozhikode District, the Government Medical College, which is one of the largest hospitals in the State, accounted for more than a third of the claims (Table 5.8).

Table 5.10 shows the claims in Kozhikode District in 2010–11 according to the type of hospital. The Government Medical College accounted for nearly one-third share. It is seen that three ophthalmic hospitals together accounted for more than 2,000 claims. These were mostly for cataract surgeries.

Tables 5.11 and 5.12 provide details regarding the diseases to which the claims were related. The general ward admissions accounted

TABLE 5.8 Information Regarding Empanelled Hospitals in Kozhikode District, 2009–10

Information	*Type of Hospital*		
	Government Health Service	*Government Medical College*	*Private Hospital*
Number of empanelled hospitals	15	1	14
Average claim (Rs)	3,230	4,147	3,063
Total claim (Rs crore)	1.2	2.8	2.7

Source: MedSave Healthcare (Third Party Insurance administrator).

Table 5.9 RSBY Claims, Kozhikode District, 2009–10

Claims (number)	19,159
Claim ratio	11. 0 %
Claim amount (Rs crore)	6.65
Average claim	3,474
Claim acceptance rate	86.30%

Source: MedSave Healthcare (Third Party Insurance administrator).

Table 5.10 Claims and Payment of RSBY in Kozhikode District, 2010–11

Type of Hospital	*Number*	*Number of Claims*	*Total Claims*	*Average Claim*
Government community health centre	9	1,793	4,51,0000	2,515
Government general hospital	5	5,212	1,68,41,373	3,231
Government medical college	1	10,971	4,13,71,110	3,771
Private eye hospital	3	2,037	1,24,73,213	6,123
Private general hospital	11	11,128	2,34,45,044	2,107
Private medical college	2	7,683	2,58,07,685	3,359

Source: MedSave Healthcare (Third Party Insurance administrator).

for nearly two-thirds of the claims. Cataract surgeries came next, followed by radiotherapy.

As per data available, the insurance company posted a loss of 88 per cent in 2010–11. There is a wide variation in the losses incurred by the insurance company, ranging from 0 per cent in Wayanad, to 220 per cent Thiruvananthapuram.

OTHER SOCIAL SECURITY PENSIONS

According to our survey data, 14.01 per cent of households, and 3.02 per cent of all individuals, received some social security pension or the other. Table 5.13 shows the break-up of these pensions. Pension

TABLE 5.11 Diseases/Procedures for Which Claims are Made in Kozhikode District

Disease/Procedure	*Claims*	%	*Average Claim*
General ward admission	25,502	65.7	2,451
Cataract with IOL	1,927	5.0	6,110
Radiotherapy—per sitting	1,714	4.4	1,457
Normal delivery	1,675	4.3	2,500
ICU admission	833	2.1	3,209
Caesarean delivery	784	2.0	4,499
Chemotherapy—per sitting	663	1.7	997
Closed reduction of fractures	546	1.4	1,689
D&C (dilatation and curettage)	416	1.1	2,500
Hysterectomy—abdominal	330	0.8	9,828
Hernioplasty	223	0.6	7,000
Open reduction internal fixation (large bone)	185	0.5	13,462
Cataract—unilateral	150	0.4	3,458
Ovariectomy	125	0.3	6,726
Appendicectomy	114	0.3	5,934
Drainage of large abscess	96	0.2	1,981
Thyroidectomy—total	94	0.2	16,000
Debridement and closure—minor	83	0.2	3,000
Others	3,364	8.7	6,952

Source: MedSave Healthcare (Third Party Insurance administrator).

for agricultural labourers forms the largest group, followed by old age pension.

It was seen that the likelihood of being a pension beneficiary was much higher (35.5 per cent) among the very poor (EG1), and decreases steadily to a negligible level among the upper middle-class (9.8, 3.4, and 1.1 per cent for EG2, EG3, and EG4 respectively).

The survey also revealed that the proportion of beneficiaries was markedly less among Muslims (1.51 per cent). The figure for Christians (11.1 per cent) might not be representative because there were only a handful of them in the sample. The Hindus constituted 6.22 per cent and SCs 5.15 per cent. Figures 5.9 and 5.10 show the sources of information, and the help received in obtaining the pension.

TABLE 5.12 Claims According to Medical Specialty, Kozhikode District

Specialty	*Number of Claims*	*Average Claim*
Dental	2	200
ENT	281	6,282
General ward admissions (majority in general medicine and paediatrics)	25,502	2,451
Gynaecology	3,586	4,063
ICU admissions	833	3,209
Neurosurgery	34	14,029
Oncology	663	997
Ophthalmology	2,225	5,906
Orthopaedics	1,502	6,192
Radiology	13	385
Radiotherapy	1,714	1,457
Surgery	2,297	6,644
Urology	172	9,303

Source: MedSave Healthcare (Third Party Insurance administrator).

TABLE 5.13 Break-up of Social Security Pensions Received by Individuals in the Sample (%)

Old age pension	27.7
Widow pension	9.9
Pension for disabled	14.2
Pension for unmarried women (> 50 years)	2.8
Pension for agricultural labour	34.8
Unemployment benefit	3.5
Unspecified items	7.1

Source: Collected from the records of the respective panchayats.

Political workers, including elected representatives, seemed to have played the most important role in this regard. Virtually no one had paid a bribe (Figure 5.11).

According to many, the frequency of receiving the pension was reportedly irregular. Majority of them received the pension by money

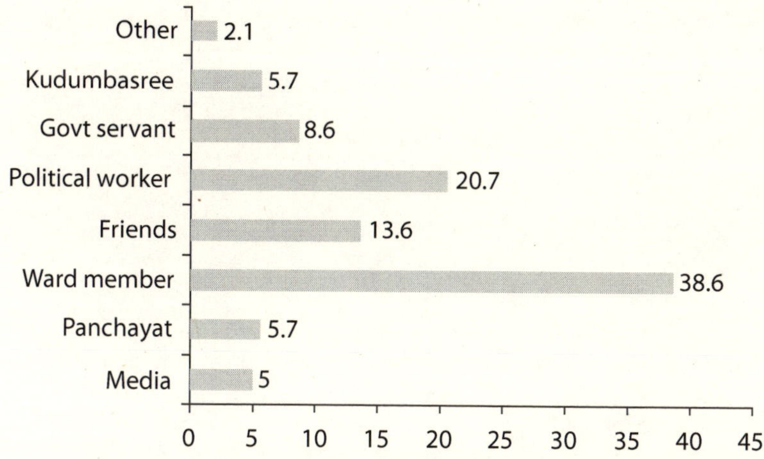

FIGURE 5.9 Source of Information about the Pension

Source: Based on data collected from field survey done as part of this study.

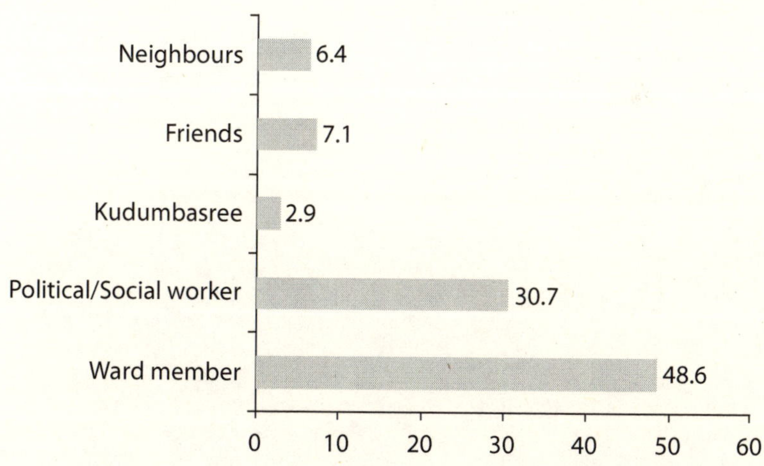

FIGURE 5.10 Who Helped in Obtaining Pension?

Source: Based on data collected from field survey done as part of this study.

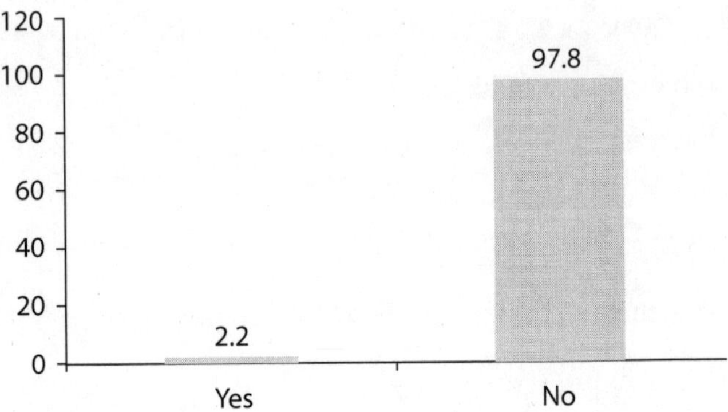

FIGURE 5.11 Did You Have to Pay Bribe?

Source: Based on data collected from field survey done as part of this study.

order, as that was the preferred mode of receipt (Figures 5.12, 5.13, and 5.14).

ASHRAYA SCHEME

The main beneficiaries (84.2 per cent) of the Ashraya scheme were found to be females. Table 5.14 shows the main reasons for being

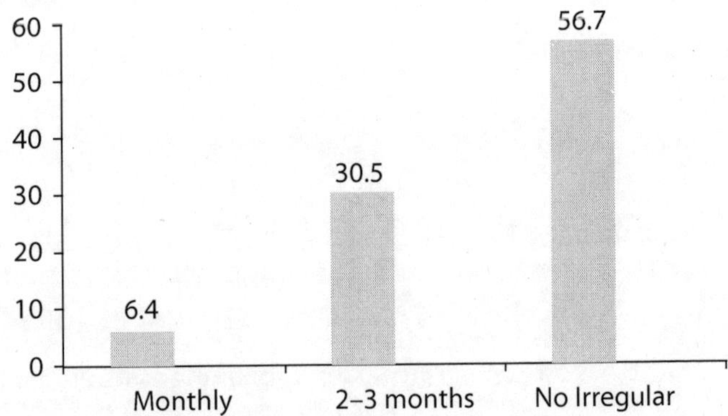

FIGURE 5.12 Frequency of Receiving Pension

Source: Based on data collected from field survey done as part of this study.

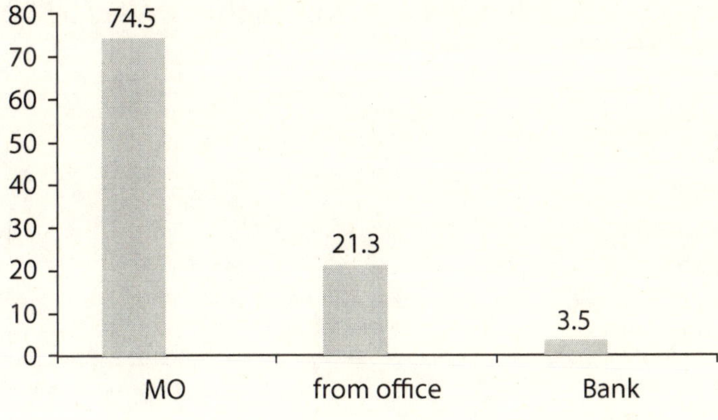

FIGURE 5.13 Mode of Pension Receipt

Source: Based on data collected from field survey done as part of this study.

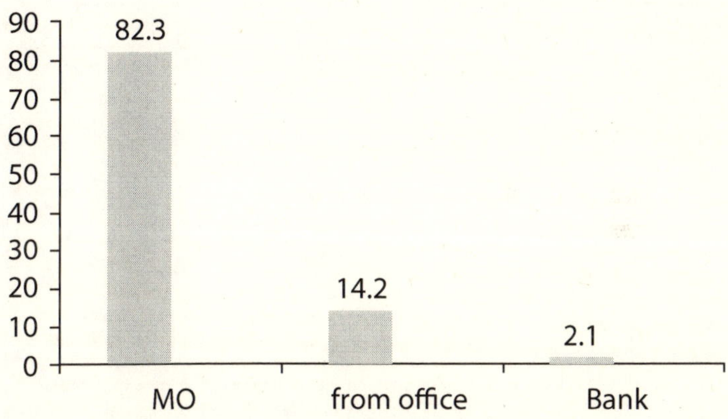

FIGURE 5.14 Which Mode do You Prefer?

Source: Based on data collected from field survey done as part of this study.

in the Ashraya scheme. As could be seen, widowhood and illness remained the most important reasons.

The various benefits demanded and supplied under the scheme are depicted in Table 5.15, the most sought after being food and medical aid.

All the beneficiaries perceived pension as useful, with 57.1 per cent among them saying that it was 'very useful' (Figure 5.15).

TABLE 5.14 Main Reason for Participating in the Ashraya Scheme

Reason	%
Disability	3.6
Illness	35.5
Widowhood	41.8
Lack of children	3.6
Accidents	0.9
Death of near ones	4.5
Other	10.0

Source: Based on data collected from field survey done as part of this study.

TABLE 5.15 Benefits Demanded and Supplied under the Scheme (%)

Item	*Demand*	*Supply*
Food	73.7	100
Medical aid	55.3	17.5
Clothing	32.5	100
Land	21.1	45.8
House	37.7	81.4
Drinking water	42.1	43.8
Self employment	30.7	5.7
Educational help	20.2	56.5
House repair	30.7	34.3

Source: Based on data collected from field survey done as part of this study.

While food and clothing were provided to all those who asked for them, and housing was provided to 81.4 per cent, medical aid lagged far behind with only 17.5 per cent. As with the social security pensions, it was political workers (50.6 per cent), followed by Ward members (35.1 per cent) and Kudumbasree (11.7 per cent) who informed and helped the destitute to obtain the benefits as per the scheme.

For 58.3 per cent of the beneficiaries, the benefits were obtained within six months of applying for it. For the rest, it took longer.

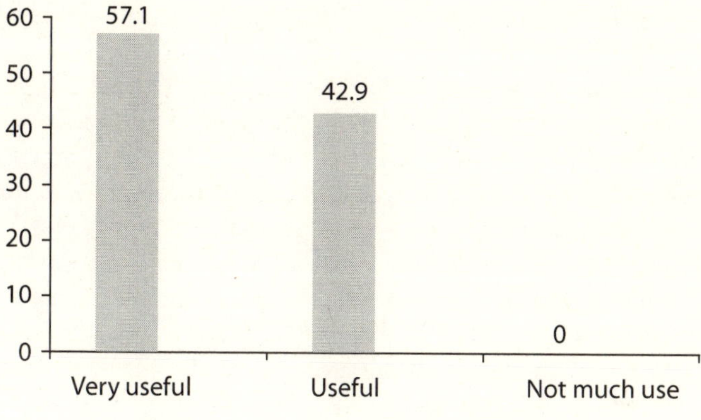

FIGURE 5.15 Usefulness of Pension

Source: Based on data collected from field survey done as part of this study.

EXPERIENCE AND VIEWS OF STAKEHOLDERS

As has been noted already, we conducted two focus group discussions. This was to enlist the views and experiences of actual stakeholders of RSBY and Ashraya programmes. These discussions helped us to reach conclusions and suggestions that had more practical relevance. 28 persons participated in the discussions on RSBY and 14 members on Ashraya.

The RSBY participants included activists of 'Kudumbasree' (3), doctors (4), representatives of hospital management (3), PROs of RSBY (7), officials of insurance companies (6), TPA (2), and social activists (3). A brief summary of the views expressed and issues raised are listed below.

To begin with, majority of field works like educating and mobilizing the beneficiaries, the task of enrolment, were carried out by the Kudumbasree activists. Even though Kudumbasree was not a direct agency in the programme, its activists were compelled to bear much of the field-level burdens. It was pointed out that they were not sufficiently informed about the details of the programme. And although cards were entrusted to them in bulk for distribution, many of the cards were illegible and some even had incomplete addresses.

It was also found that the insistence of the head of the family or spouse being necessarily enrolled was creating problems. Since the Kudumbasree activists were entrusted with the job of informing the beneficiaries of the enrolment, there was often a misunderstanding on the part of the public that the selection of beneficiaries was also carried out by them. As a result, they had to face the ire of the persons who had been excluded from the list. They also pointed out that the photos in many cards were not clear, thus creating additional problems in distribution.

For their part, social activists complained about the non-awareness of the scheme among hospital staff, and the absence of proper direction to the general public. Inadequacy of manpower to cater to the huge crowds in government hospitals, particularly in the Government Medical College hospital, created problems. Bystanders were forced to be at the kiosks round the clock. Even critically ill patients had to be brought to the counter for thumb impression. Those patients who were admitted late were unable to register, since the RSBY counters worked only from 8 a.m. to 8 p.m. It was further suggested that travel allowance (TA) should be paid from the ward itself, and that the number of RSBY counters be increased to cater to the rise in demand. Staff in Government hospitals were paid incentives from the amount collected through RSBY. This, it was pointed out, would lead to unhealthy trends like unnecessary billing, neglect of non-RSBY patients, etc.

The representatives of hospital management had their own tales of woe. They found RSBY counters, hospital cards and pharmacists inadequate, even in big hospitals. Both government and private hospitals raised the issue of non-settlement of claims properly and promptly. Errors in cards and software provoked people to agitate against hospitals. To block the cards for more than three days, the TPA's sanction was required, which usually never came in time. They pointed out the need to revamp the list of procedures and the rates, to include costly diagnostic tests. They complained against the poor response on the part of the TPAs in solving problems related to registration (especially of manual registration), reimbursement of travel expenses, etc. The amounts received from the TPAs were not sent with the reconciled list. This made it difficult for the hospitals to know what the claims were, how much of it was received, and how many pending. A common problem was with the 'hot listing' of cards, and their rectification with the TPAs. It was pointed out that in Kozhikode District alone, there were 14,000 such cards. Hospitals pointed out that submission of photocopy of voucher for reimbursement of TA was impractical. Another problem was that when patients were referred to another hospital, the first hospital was denied reimbursement.

Officials from the insurance company were very critical of the BPL list prepared by the Government. The software used was inflexible and insisted on the enrolment of the head of the family, or spouse. There was insufficient cooperation in the enrolment process from many of the Gram Panchayats. The Ward Members always found it difficult to agree on the BPL list. The insurance officials suggested that the per day rate of Rs 500 be reduced due to widespread misuse. Since many of the works of RSBY were entrusted to the TPA, the insurance company was not in a position to intervene in a timely fashion and rectify the issues. They also invited our attention to the stand of the Union Government of putting a cap on the chargeable premium at Rs 750. They said that the premium should be correlated with the claims settled. Government decision to increase other benefits of RSBY/CHIS had to be considered. They made a request to intend medicines in generic names.

The RSBY investigators observed that patients were kept for unduly long periods. They also pointed out that for BPL patients, sometimes it was better to avail of the benefits with BPL cards instead of opting for RSBY benefits.

The issues and concerns raised by different stakeholders in the focused group had been extensively discussed. Since a cross section of different agencies was present at the discussion, it was easy for them to share and understand the practical issues involved, and to make suggestions for improvement. The group reached the following general conclusions: First the social security cards should be issued on the spot. Second, members of the Gram Panchayat should be fully involved in the enrolment process and they should not evade responsibility. Pressure should be put on these officials by the District Collector and DLO to this end. The RSBY meetings should be held under the auspices of the Gram Panchayat, prior to enrolment. Crowd management should be the primary responsibility of the Gram Panchayat, along with providing provision for adequate facilities for enrolment. Third, in case of long hospitalization for chronic illnesses, the patients should be counselled on the loss of benefits to them. Fourth, the list of procedures in the package needs to be expanded, particularly to include costly diagnostic procedures. Fifth, the hospitals must be persuaded to cross subsidize their expenditure. It is not necessary to recover the full amount of expenditure from a particular patient himself. Sixth, the system of incentives might be avoided.

Focus Group Discussion: Ashraya

Ashraya scheme was designed to tackle the problems of destitute living on the margin of the economy. In the current study, besides the household survey of Ashraya beneficiaries in the two panchayats—Naduvannur and Cheruvannur-Nallam—the living conditions of the target groups in the latter panchayat had been observed and analysed. There were 45 Ashraya families in the panchayat. We visited 14 of them, and conducted personal interviews and a group discussion. The group included twelve women and 2 men. The discussions were mainly on: (i) the background or reasons for one to become an 'Ashraya' member; (ii) current benefits available to an Ashraya family; (iii) specific problems being faced by Ashraya beneficiaries; and (iv) their perceptions and suggestions for improvement.

During the discussion, a majority of the group pointed out that chronic diseases were the important reason for their deplorable condition. Nine out of fourteen suffered from chronic diseases. Three women became destitute due to separation from their husbands, and one each by accident and physical challenges respectively.

All the members reiterated that the scheme was highly beneficial for them. It was clear that the living conditions of these people were extremely poor. Very few had completed houses and own source of drinking water. Twelve families had incomplete houses and were dependent on public piped water supply system. Shortage of food and the burden of treatment were other major issues of the Ashraya members.

As for the benefits, each 'Ashraya' member was entitled to get 35 kg of rice per month, free of cost. In addition, they were provided a supplementary nutrition kit of sugar, pulses and green gram. An Ashraya family with one or two members would be given by a kit worth Rs 100 per month. Families having three or more members would get a kit worth Rs 150 per month. In Cheruvannur-Nallam, the kit was distributed from the Gram Panchayat office, on the eighteenth day of every month, at 2.30 p.m.

The burden of disease and the cost of treatment were the greatest problems they faced, according to their narration. The chronic patients among them did not get the RSBY benefits, unless they were treated as in-patients. Thus, the group demanded special attention to extend the RSBY benefits to Ashraya members who were admitted to hospitals. The group also requested for higher education facilities for their growing children by way of reservation, financial assistance, fee concession, etc. Concessions for travelling to hospitals for periodic check-up and priority to avail other schemes like widow pension, etc. were among their other demands.

AN ASSESSMENT

HEALTH INSURANCE—RSBY

The overall enrolment to RSBY in Kerala had been very impressive in relation to the target fixed by the Union Government. It managed to enrol 73.6 per cent of the BPL list and was second only to Chhattisgarh among the major states. The Kerala Government extended the list to others who were BPL, but would not have been entitled as per the criterion fixed by the Union Government. The benefit of this scheme was also extended to APL families, provided they were willing to remit the full premium amount.

The scheme had envisaged that the insurance company should be responsible for mobilization and enrolment of the beneficiaries. However, realizing that the insurance companies themselves could not effectively mobilize the target population, the State Government intervened by entrusting the mobilization work to Kudumbasree volunteers for a fee to be paid by the insurance company. In the second year, it also appointed a District Coordinator to coordinate various departments.

The beneficiaries of the scheme were enrolled on the basis of the BPL list issued by the Government for this purpose. There were, however, widespread complaints that the BPL list had excluded a large number of the really eligible sections, while several well-off families had found a place therein. On account of the anomalies in the list, the Kudumbasree volunteers and other local representatives had faced the ire of the public, which led to the Panchayat Members dissociating themselves from the scheme altogether.

The Enrolment Process

It is clear from Figures 5.6 and 5.10 that the Kudumbasree workers had played a very important role in enrolment process. First, the TPA intimated the date of enrolment to a panchayat and Kudumbasree. The latter circulated the messages among the members in each Ward of the panchayat. The place of enrolment, where the family photographs and finger prints were to be taken, was fixed by the panchayat. Usually there would be around five to six enrolment centres in each panchayat. An eligible BPL family had to come together to the enrolment centre, where the family photo and finger prints would be taken. This situation created a big rush in the mornings since all wanted to complete the enrolment before going for work or school. A large number of people preferred not to get enrolled for the same reason. People who were out of station on the day fixed for enrolment also lost the opportunity to get enrolled since the date of a particular panchayat was uploaded to the machine only the previous day.

Another issue with the BPL list was that the house name was not available in the list; only the door and Ward numbers were in the list. With frequent renumbering of houses and Wards, the only way to identify the families was with the names of the family members, who might be familiar to the Kudumbasree volunteers or the Ward Members. Again, a large number of families in the list was shown as 0 (zero) ward, with only the name of the head of the family. This had led to widespread confusion with several families turning up for enrolment. Since several enrolment centres were functioning simultaneously at a panchayat, several families got enrolled at different centres against the same family id. The duplication came to light only when the data were subsequently merged and the system threw up the errors. As we had noted already, in Kozhikode District alone there were more than 14,000 such cards. These cards created problems when the patients approached the hospital with a claim.

Crowd Management

It was pointed out that in most enrolment centres, the Panchayat Members had dissociated themselves from the scheme and the entire burden was placed on the TPAs, their team and the Kudumbasree volunteers. When the crowd got unmanageable, the enrolment staff, in an effort to disperse the crowd, took the photos and finger prints but did not issue the cards. They were later delivered to the Kudumbasree/panchayat offices, and not the actual beneficiary. This led to complaints of non-receipt of cards. The intervention of the local Panchayat Members would have gone a long way in sorting out such issues.

Power Supply

Erratic power supply had often resulted in the disruption of printing of cards. Even though the panchayats have been instructed to provide generators, the required number of generators are not always available.

According to the RSBY guidelines, cards need to be issued on the day photos and finger prints were taken. This proved time consuming and, consequently, working families had to forego their wages and students their classes. Sick persons were hit harder as, according to the guidelines, even they had to be present on the date and at the place prescribed to have their photos taken and fulfil other formalities. Bringing such patients was difficult enough, and in the event of TPAs changing the date of enrolment, they had to bear the burden of travelling again on another day. In such situations, the Panchayat Members and the Kudumbasree could request the enrolment team to complete the enrolment and issue the cards later.

Enrolment within the State was found uneven, with some districts enlisting nearly double the number of the centrally sanctioned list and others not even touching half. Kozhikode District got the highest rate of enrolment (186.4 per cent), while Malappuram the lowest (36 per cent). The picture was much the same for the State as a whole. This trend has to be studied in detail. Much depended on the level of local mobilization and the competence of the TPAs. Each district was assigned to a TPA and there was considerable difference in their performance. Involvement of Kudumbasree workers was crucial in local mobilization. Wherever the panchayats and the insurance company made real efforts to rope in Kudumbasree workers and give them guidance and supervision, enrolment had been high.

The part played by private hospitals also left a lot to be desired. Some even failed to install the necessary equipment and later opted out of the scheme, after having been empanelled. In such cases, the beneficiary came to know that the hospital had already opted out of the scheme only at the time of seeking reimbursement. There was no provision to enforce the agreement, or even to penalize these hospitals.

Empanelled Hospitals

Under the RSBY scheme, both public and private hospitals provide free treatment. States like Tamil Nadu, Delhi and West Bengal have only private hospitals in their list of empanelled hospitals. The reasons seem to be that the services of government hospitals are anyway free to patients belonging to the BPL category. It is assumed that any required treatment or diagnostic investigation for a particular disease can be made completely free in a government hospital. This assumption is rarely true. More often than not, patients have to buy drugs or do tests outside, or have to do with whatever is available. The reason is that funds available for government hospitals have not gone up, even with of the introduction of RSBY. States like Maharashtra and Gujarat also have very few government hospitals in their list. It has been pointed out that the greater reach of public sector hospitals would encourage the poor in remote areas to seek treatment, and the insurance claims will supplement government hospitals' earnings also.

States like Chhattisgarh, Jharkhand and Kerala, on the other hand, have a much larger proportion of empanelled government hospitals. Government hospitals get reimbursed for the treatment of RSBY in-patients, just like any other private hospital. The money thus earned can be added onto the government funds for capacity building of these hospitals. Empanelling government hospitals becomes imperative also in situations where there aren't enough private hospitals willing to be part of the RSBY programme. This is particularly true for the corporate or higher-tier hospitals, which are unwilling to enter into agreements for procedural reasons. In Kerala, it is the second-tier small hospitals that have joined RSBY. This has helped the revival of some hospitals facing closure due to severe competition from corporate hospitals.

Problems Faced by Hospitals

In our discussions, a doctor from a second-tier well-equipped private hospital said that 'income from RSBY is steadily increasing. Now it is around Rs 7 to 8 lakh per month out of a total monthly income of Rs 18 to 20 lakh. This income is presumed to go up in the coming months with more smart cards being issued, and commissioning of another 20 beds with ICU in our hospital'.

Irregular payment from the insurance company was an important problem raised by all the private hospitals. Regular payment was never ensured, and this created financial problems, particularly for small hospitals. According to the RSBY scheme, claims settlement has been entrusted to the TPAs and, as in the case of enrolment, they have proved to be the weak link in the process.

The RSBY package rates are irrational. Even private hospitals running the scheme successfully complain that the actual expense incurred is not considered while fixing the rates. For minor cases and surgeries carried out under spinal anaesthesia, the rates are acceptable. For cases done under general anaesthesia (GA), the rates are low. The actual cost of gases (oxygen, nitrous and isoflurane) for GA and post-operative medications (muscle relaxants, IV fluids) are very expensive. It is felt that unless the rates are rationalized, the scheme would fail.

However, it is to be borne in mind that according to the current RSBY package rates, there are many diseases and procedures in which the hospital can make a reasonable profit, even while there are others in which the hospital may lose money. For instance, for cases that require only medical management, the rate is Rs 500 per day, while for ICU cases it is Rs 1,000 per day, and much less for ordinary fever and minor ailments.

The problems faced by many of the private hospitals in the implementation of RSBY can be traced to the lack of awareness among doctors and medical administrators about insurance regulated medical practice. If the cost has to be within the package rate, the doctor has to use the minimum required investigations, medicines and consumables. They may have to resort to clinical judgment, generic medicines, low cost technology, local anaesthesia wherever possible, short hospital stay, and follow evidence-based protocols.

In unspecified surgical cases (cases not mentioned in the package list), double procedures and prolonged hospitalization, pre-authorization from TPA is required. A cumbersome procedure is involved to obtain pre-authorization for x-rays, CT scans, etc. A busy doctor may not take an active interest in all these formalities, or in responding satisfactorily to the queries of TPAs; for their part, TPAs also do not respond in time.

In case of government hospitals, particularly those attached to medical colleges, there is yet another problem. They cater to a very large patient base. Hence, they do not have enough staff to deal with the administration of the RSBY programme. More importantly, only one RSBY terminal is allotted to such a hospital. This forms a bottleneck when the patient load is very high, and the problem cannot be solved even by allotting more staff. The only solution is to make software alterations as needed, in order to enable the working of multiple terminals in large hospitals.

Problem of Hospital Fraud

A lot of fraudulent claims have been detected in hospitals. The scheme has a list of 750 surgical procedures for which a package rate is fixed, which includes all expenses of medicines, tests and doctors' fees. For surgical packages which are not in the list, special rates and pre-authorization have to be obtained from TPAs for the claim. In the case of medical management, a fixed amount of Rs 500 per day is payable to the hospital for ward patients and Rs 1,000 for ICU. It is often seen that the actual surgery expenses of the hospitals exceed the surgical package rate as per the scheme. A malpractice which is often resorted to is retaining patients in the hospital for a longer period than necessary, to claim the daily rate of Rs 500 or Rs 1,000, instead of the surgical package rate. This is also the case when diagnostic tests like MRI scan, which are not included in the package, are done.

There are also instances where hospital gives free treatment to the patients up to the package amount, and thereafter asks the patient to pay up. Patients are also asked to purchase certain outside items which are not part of the hospital supplies. Patients usually abstain from complaining against the hospital(s) and doctor(s) since they are reluctant to antagonize them. The practice of holding the card of the patient at the hospital, even after discharge, is also prevalent. The hospital is free to manipulate the card till the transaction is completed in the system. Most hospitals do not inform the patient the amount availed of from the card, or the balance, even though there is a provision for giving a printout of these details to the patients.

As much as 70.6 per cent of patients in our survey were not informed of the amount deducted at the time of discharge. Thus, the patients who were not aware of the package rates would not have an idea of possible fraud by misusing their cards. The hospitals are expected to give Rs 100 to the patient at the time of discharge, to meet his/her travelling expenses. But hospitals have discontinued paying travelling expense on the ground of the procedures being cumbersome. There is also the possibility of patients and hospital colluding together, particularly towards the end of the policy period, to avail of the unutilized balance in the card.

Actual Claims and Payments

During 2010–11, 18.7 lakh families were insured under RSBY in Kerala, and the premium accrued on this account to the insurance company was Rs 78.93 crore, with the premium rate being fixed at Rs 464. This rate was fixed by floating open tenders and selecting the lowest bid. The United India Insurance Company (UIIC), one of the four public sector general insurance companies, was selected to run the RSBY programme in Kerala. It is to be remembered that the Centre pays a subsidy of Rs 750 per BPL family. So in effect, Kerala was losing Rs 286 per family of the subsidy provided. The operating loss of the company with the premium being Rs 464 is 88 per cent, which is clearly unsustainable. If the premium is raised to Rs 750, the loss comes down to 5.4 per cent. It can be brought down further and the company could actually come out of being in the red with better management, prevention of fraudulent claims, etc.

If the insurance companies consistently incur losses, there would be no takers for the RSBY programme in the long run. In the interest of sustainability, it would be better to keep the premium fixed at the value of maximum subsidy offered by the Union Government. It would be better to choose a public sector company rather than one in the private sector, because of the former's operational scale. Better facilities are required to handle large number of beneficiaries. One among the four public sector companies can be chosen, based on technical considerations, or a consortium of the four companies may be set up to manage the RSBY program in the State.

There were 15 government hospitals and 16 private hospitals empanelled in the RSBY scheme in Kozhikode District. One-third of the total claim amount was accounted for by a single institution, the Government Medical College at Calicut. This was followed by two private medical colleges and 11 private general hospitals. The highest average claim of Rs 6,123 was for private eye hospitals. It is gratifying that the major ophthalmic hospitals in the private sector have joined the RSBY scheme and that large numbers of 'Cataract Surgery with Implantation of an Intraocular Lens' are being done.

General ward admission constituted 65.7 per cent of all admissions. Termed non-surgical (medical) treatment in the general ward, the package rate for daily hospital stay is to be negotiated by each state with the insurer. In Kerala this has been fixed at Rs 500 per day. The package rates include bed charges (general ward), nursing and boarding charges, fees of surgeons, anaesthetists, medical practitioner, consultants' fees, blood, oxygen, O.T. charges, medicines and drugs, x-ray and diagnostic tests, food to patient, etc. Expenses incurred for diagnostic test and medicines up to one day before the admission of the patient and cost of diagnostic test and medicine up to five days after discharge from the hospital for the same ailment/surgery, including transport expenses, are also be part of the package. This is to ensure that the package should cover the entire cost of treatment of the patient from the date of reporting (one day pre-hospitalization), to his discharge from hospital and post-operative care (five days after discharge) (RSBY website).

It is this provision of fixed daily charges for general ward patients that is misused the most. In many trivial cases such as fever, the hospital may have only minimum expenses and may yet keep the patient in the hospital for many days. Conversely, when an expensive investigation like an MRI scan or a costly immunological or endocrine test—not listed in the RSBY package—is to be done, the only way the hospital can recoup the money is by keeping the patient in the hospital for the requisite number of days.

The main problem is that the RSBY package list seems to have been drawn up with only surgical conditions in mind. The major omissions in the list include costly diagnostic tests and procedures like endoscope. The obvious solution would be to include all the costlier diagnostic tests and non-surgical interventions in the package, and simultaneously reducing the daily charges for general ward admissions from Rs 500 to something like Rs 150 or 200.

There are other problems too with the package list. On the whole, it seems to have been carelessly prepared by joining together lists submitted by many people, with no later scrutiny. For instance, there is a procedure called 'Breast Lump Left Excision' charged at Rs 5,000, which is the same for 'Breast Lump Right Excision'. Why left and right sides have to be mentioned separately is anyone's guess. There is another item 'Breast Mass Excision' costing Rs 6,250. What finer distinction is there between a lump and a mass in the breast is another moot point. There is yet another item—breast excision—with charges fixed at Rs 12,250. Presumably what is meant here is removal of the whole breast. But 'mastectomy,' as well as 'radical mastectomy,' which are more difficult surgeries, are both priced at Rs 9,000. So, a hospital doing a radical mastectomy has just to change the name for it to breast excision and they can claim Rs 3,250 more in the process. In another example, the charge for excising a spindle cell tumour is Rs 7,000, and that of a soft tissue tumour is Rs 4,000. Fact is, all spindle cell tumours are soft tissue tumours, and to a surgeon it is all the same till the finer distinctions between various soft tissue tumours are provided in the final pathology report.

Social Security Pensions

In the surveyed area, 13 per cent households and 15 per cent individuals drew some social security pension, distributed through Gram Panchayat. We focused our attention on seven types of pensions as noted earlier. Of these, pension for agricultural workers constituted the largest group (34.8 per cent), followed by old age pension (27.7 per cent). As expected, agricultural pensioners formed a larger proportion in rural Naduvannur as compared to the semi-urban Cheruvannur-Nallam. Nearly 15 per cent of pensions were accounted for by the physically challenged. This worked out to 2.1 per cent of the population. This is remarkable considering the overall disability rate in Kerala is 2.7 per cent, thus indicating good coverage. 10 per cent of the pension beneficiaries were widows. This is a growing problem in the State with the widening life expectancy between males and females. Considering the economic group of the beneficiaries, it is seen that 35.2 per cent of households in EG1 had some member or the other drawing a social security pension. This was only 1.1 per cent for EG4, an indication that showed no widespread misuse of pension schemes. The fact that more than one-third of the poor received some form of pension also highlighted the importance of this scheme in their livelihood, and legitimized its continuation. With regards to various community groups, the proportion of households among the Muslim population receiving pensions was seen to be abnormally low at 1.5 per cent compared to 6.2 per cent overall among Hindus and 5.2 per cent among SCs. Muslim beneficiaries were fewer in RSBY as well. The reasons for this require further probe.

Information about pension schemes and help for obtaining them came largely from the Panchayat Ward Members (38.6 per cent), followed by political/social workers (20.7 per cent). This indicated the influence and continued relevance of the grassroots political system in the delivery of pro-poor government schemes. It was also found that virtually no bribe of any kind was involved in obtaining these benefits. This underlined the primacy of the political system over the administrative at the village level.

On the flip side, only a very small section (6.4 per cent) got pensions regularly. For the majority, the frequency was far from regular. The Gram Panchayat authorities would do well to look into it, as all the seven pension schemes were being distributed by the panchayats. More than 80 per cent of the beneficiaries preferred money order as the mode of payment. All the beneficiaries revealed that they were benefited by the schemes and 58 per cent stated that pensions were highly useful to them.

Ashraya Scheme

This served the most vulnerable section of pension beneficiaries and majority among them were women (84.2 per cent). Widowhood and illness were the major reasons for one to become an Ashraya destitute. Data showed that the Ashraya scheme had worked fairly well in both the panchayats under the direct supervision of the Kudumbasree network. Noticeably, social and political workers and Ward Members helped the destitute and the vulnerable get access to the scheme, and obtain the benefits. Here also, delay and time lag were the most striking issues to be addressed.

SUMMARY OF FINDINGS AND LESSONS

The present study was conducted in two wards of two Gram Panchayats, whose number of households corresponded to that of a whole village settlement in other states. Thus, it was basically a village study. The areas of the present study were periodically surveyed for various development purposes. In our study, we made use of primary data collected by us, while secondary macro-level data came from insurance companies. We were also benefited from two focused group discussions on RSBY and 'Ashraya'. The scheme for division of sample was adopted from the KSSP study. A total of 932 households were studied—530 from Cheruvannur-Nallam and 402 from Naduvannur. The number of the very poor households (EG1) was more in Naduvannur Panchayat constituting 22 per cent, while it was only 6.2 per cent in Cheruvannur-Nallam. Our study focused mainly on the social security pension and insurance schemes being implemented through the Gram Panchayat, with an added emphasis on RSBY.

From the analysis, it was revealed that all pension and insurance schemes benefited the people in general, and the poor in particular.

Forty-five per cent of the households belonged to EG1 and EG2—very poor and poor—and they got some sort of a social security pension. This showed the extensive coverage of the schemes among the poor people. All the beneficiaries opined that the schemes were useful and more than half of them (58 per cent) specifically stated that the schemes were very useful to them. The Ashraya scheme was a comprehensive project to identify and eradicate the vulnerability prevailing in society. The demand for primary requirements like food and clothing were fully met by the scheme. Acute patients and widows constituted nearly three-fourth of the Ashraya beneficiaries. The RSBY also had wide acceptability among people at large, as a means to address the issue of increasing health expenditure.

On the basis of the analysis and discussions the following specific recommendations are made, with regard to RSBY and other pension schemes, with a view to improving their administration and delivery at the local level.

(i) Periodic updating of the BPL list must be ensured so that no eligible poor is left out of the RSBY or social security pensions.
(ii) Instead of TPAs, State Government must take responsibility for enrolment in RSBY as in election/census processes.
(iii) Review and revision of the package rates of hospitals must be undertaken. All foreseeable procedures and diagnostic tests must be included. The daily rates of Rs 500 and Rs 1,000, for the ward and ICU for medical management, should be reduced.
(iv) Reimbursement must be made directly by the insurance company rather than by TPAs.
(v) Software improvements, including common software for the entire country, are called for. TPAs need not develop their own software.
(vi) More involvement of the elected members and staff of the panchayats must be ensured in RSBY enrolment.
(vii) Renewability of the insurance card must be made possible.
(viii) Hospital fraud and misuse should be strictly prevented. There should be more RSBY counters in big hospitals.
(ix) All special incentives to doctors and hospital staff must be abolished.
(x) An Ombudsman may be appointed in each district to look into all complaints regarding RSBY scheme.

(xi) Monthly payment of social security pensions by money order must be ensured.

(xii) There should be a provision to meet the burden of chronic illness among the Ashraya beneficiaries.

Though official statistics show a steep fall in poverty in Kerala, there still exist pockets of poverty that require locally specific intervention strategies. This situation warrants improvements in the quality of delivery of all types of public schemes at the local level. We admit that social security pensions and health insurance are not a panacea for poverty eradication and socio-economic development. However, these schemes should act as a support to political interventions in the public sphere. Quality improvements in public education, health, food distribution etc, coupled with a prompt delivery and judicious implementation of social security schemes will help a lot in a state like Kerala, to attain a better level of living to the people at large.

References

Aravindan K.P. and R.V.G. Menon. 2010. *Snapshot of Kerala—Life and Thoughts of the Malayalee People*. Thrissur: Kerala Sastra Sahitya Parishad.

Aravindan K.P. and T.P. Kunhikannan. 2006. 'Arogya Insurance, Paranjathum Parayathathum', *Mathrubhoomi Weekly*, 83(5–1): 45–8.

GoI. 1961. *Village Study Monographs*. Kozhikode District: Census Department.

Government of Kerala. 2005. *Human Development Report—Kerala*, State Planning Board, Thiruvananthapuram.

———. 2011. *Economic Review 2010*, State Planning Board, Thiruvananthapuram.

Kannan K.P. 2002. *The Welfare Fund Model of Social Security for Informal Sector Sorkers—the Kerala Experience*, Working Paper 332. Thiruvananthapuram: Centre for Development Studies.

———. 2007. 'Social Security in a Globalizing World', *International Social Security Review*, 60(2–3): 19–38.

Narayana D. 2010. 'Review of the Rashtriya Swasthya Bima Yojana', *Economic and Political Weekly*, xlv(29): 13–18.

Reddy, D. Narasimha. 2004. An Overview of 1961 Village Survey Monographs and Other Village Studies in Andhra Pradesh, KRPLLD, Discussion Paper no. 1. Thiruvananthapuram: CDS.

RSBY Connect. 2012. Available at http://uhcforward.org/sites/uhcforward.org/files/RSBY_Connect_March2012_Issue_no.2.pdf, Ministry of Labour and Employment, Government of India, and German Development Cooperation.

6 BENEFICIARY AS AGENCY

ROLE OF WOMEN'S AGENCY AND THE PANCHAYAT IN IMPLEMENTING NREGA—A STUDY IN KERALA

K.P. Kannan and *N. Jagajeevan*

The emergence of *Kudumbasree* (roughly translated as light of family),—as a powerful organization of women from poorer households in Kerala—offers a promising *modus operandi* and *modus vivendi* to state-initiated schemes for poverty alleviation and social security. It had a modest beginning which over time grew into a significant socio-economic movement. Little wonder that the Kerala Government decided in the year of grace, 1998, to implement all its poverty alleviation schemes and programmes through Kudumbasree. Given the fact that Kudumbasree represents half the households in the State, it can safely be reckoned that it would comprise of the officially recognized poor (through the holding of a BPL card)[1] and those who consider themselves poor enough to join this organization, even without official recognition. In a recent exercise it was found that the percentage of 'poor and vulnerable' households in Kerala in 2010 was close to 48 per cent, which seemed to vindicate the membership ratio in Kudumbasree.[2] Accordingly, when the National Rural Employment Guarantee Act (NREGA) was implemented in the State in 2005–6, Kudumbasree emerged as a major player in the implementation process within the framework of the panchayati raj, whereby village panchayats assumed responsibility for local level planning and decisions relating to implementation. This study is therefore an attempt to understand the new implementation process through the study of a village panchayat located in the Trivandrum (also known as Thiruvananthapuram) district.

Thanks to the contiguous habitat pattern in much of Kerala, villages are not geographically separate clusters of settlements, as in most

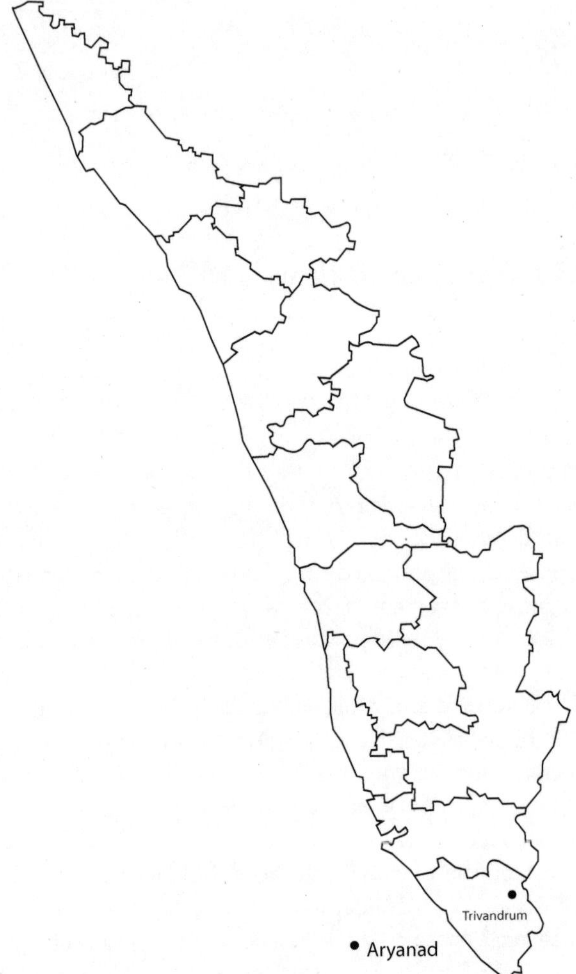

FIGURE 6.1 Location of Aryanad

Source: Government of Kerala, Public Relations Department.

other parts of India. Currently, the Aryanad panchayat has 18 wards (Figure 6.1), which may be approximately referred to as villages. The panchayat got into the public limelight when it was shortlisted as one of the 15 best-performing panchayats in a television presentation called 'Green Kerala Express', a social reality show, wherein panchayats and municipalities were invited to present their developmental activities and achievements, and submit themselves to an interrogation by a jury.[3] The first author, who chaired the jury, came into contact with the panchayat and its elected President in 2010 and visited the area in June 2010. During this time, he held discussions with the panchayat council, activists from the different developmental institutions sponsored by the panchayat, the Kudumbasree members, and a few local people, especially those associated with schools, child care centres, and farmer's organizations. In the course of the study, a few more visits were made with the second author, with a view to seeing the ongoing works under the National Rural Employment Guarantee Scheme (NREGS) and meeting with the Kudumbasree workers, panchayat officials, and households. The second author, who had known the President—Mr Viju Mohan—since 2001, organized a team of investigators who assisted in collection of the required data and conducted several meetings and interviews with the members of Kudumbasree. Mr Viju Mohan, who was re-elected for another term of five years in 2006, thus completing a 10-year tenure, had indeed played the role of a catalyst in the transformation of the panchayat administration, thus positioning it at the forefront of local-level development initiatives in the area. In the process, he also demonstrated the potential of democratic decentralization as a powerful instrument in ensuring people's participation in governance and development, giving them a new status as stakeholders. The new President, Mr Radhakrishnan, who assumed office in 2011 when this study was initiated, thus inherited a rich and favourable legacy. What we therefore want to emphasize here is the close interaction the authors had during the course of the entire study, arising out of their earlier familiarity with the main office bearers and the panchayat.

THE NEW PANCHAYATI RAJ

Before we dwell on the issues relating to the implementation of the NREGS in the panchayat, it is important to have an overview of the emerging panchayati raj in Kerala following the Constitutional amendment in 1992 (which came into force in 1993) at the national level, and the Kerala-specific legislation in 1994. While the former can be rightly characterized as a watershed in the recent history of democratic decentralization in India, the latter ensured its implementation through the creation of active local level-self governments. In the case of Kerala, it was the Left Democratic Front (LDF) led government that played a crucial role in the realization of such democratic decentralization in governance within the parameters set by the amendment. Its political opposition, the United Democratic Front (UDF), led by the Indian National Congress, was also bound to swear by it given the fact that it was its national leadership that brought in the Constitutional amendment. However, the LDF did gain considerable edge over the UDF since democratic decentralization had been core to its agenda since early 1980s. While a State-level legislation was brought in by the UDF government in 1994 two years after the Constitutional amendment was passed by the Centre, it was left to the LDF that came to power in 1996 to launch what was called, a 'People's Plan Campaign' (PPC) with a view to involving the citizens in the making of the new panchayati raj.

Much has been written on the PPC, but what is important from the point of this study is the involvement of the people in terms of consultation and deliberation in identifying developmental problems and solutions at the local level, and the preparation of a plan document for each panchayat with the involvement of knowledgeable persons invited by the panchayat. Simultaneously, the state government announced a financial devolution package under which nearly 40 per cent of plan expenditure was devolved to the panchayat bodies.[4] This gave an immediate push to the decentralization process because the panchayat bodies had to prepare a plan for spending the amount. They were also encouraged to enhance collection of own revenue, which had been an important source of income for panchayats in Kerala even before the decentralization process. Despite several problems of omission and commission during the first 3–4 years, and the political fallout, a political euphoria was created all over the State over the PPC with the devolution of financial resources, preceded by the devolution of functions; demand for deployment of government employees to panchayats; involvement of State-wide developmental movements such as the Kerala Sastra Sahitya Parishad (KSSP), along with a large number of other local level organizations; the media focus on critically monitoring the PPC; and last but not the least, a watchful but often a highly critical opposition (UDF). All these created a social and political ambience, drawing vast public attention on the panchayati raj. Several youths, already accustomed to work in various social, cultural and political organizations, were attracted to work for, and participate in, the panchayat; some of them were also opted to contest in elections and thus assume political office in the emerging panchayati raj.[5] The Sarpanch of the Aryanad panchayat, Mr Viju Mohan, was one such young political worker. When he was elected, he was only 36 years old and was working as an employee in a State-owned public sector company in Trivandrum city. His tenure of 10 years witnessed the release of a lot of youth energy in his native panchayat, backed by a large number of people from different walks of life.

But one should not overestimate the role of personality here; Kerala as a State had borne witness to the prior existence of a political and social history of mobilization and organization of the labouring poor as well as the peasantry, the high density emergence of civil society organizations that often had either explicit or implicit affiliations to political parties or their ideologies, the emergence of Kudumbasree as an organization of women from poorer households, the existence of a number of public service institutions of the state and, above all, the existence of not just literate, but a reasonably educated population, as is the case in most parts of Kerala. But personalities do matter when they are charged with a high degree of social commitment because they then become the much-needed 'catalysts' of socio-economic change.

THE SELECTED PANCHAYAT AND ITS GEOGRAPHY AND DEMOGRAPHY

Aryanad panchayat (Figure 6.2), formed in 1953, is located around 40 kms from Trivandrum city, the capital of Kerala. It's a large panchayat with an area close to 105 sq. km, and a population of 32,500 as of 2010, thus showing a population density of 310. The average is, however, quite misleading given the fact that 78 per cent of the area is under forests, vested with the government and managed by the Forest Department, with only limited access to the people to share its produce. So, the effective population density is 1,407 (as compared to 1,130 excluding the forest area and 859 including the forest area for the State as a whole), which is quite visible with its bustling market centres, rows of buildings and constant flow of people. In many respects, Aryanad is 'capsuled' Kerala. Being close to the mountains, its geography is undulating, separating Kerala with Tamil Nadu at the eastern end. A major river and several small canals make the area quite water abundant, almost through the year. The favourable

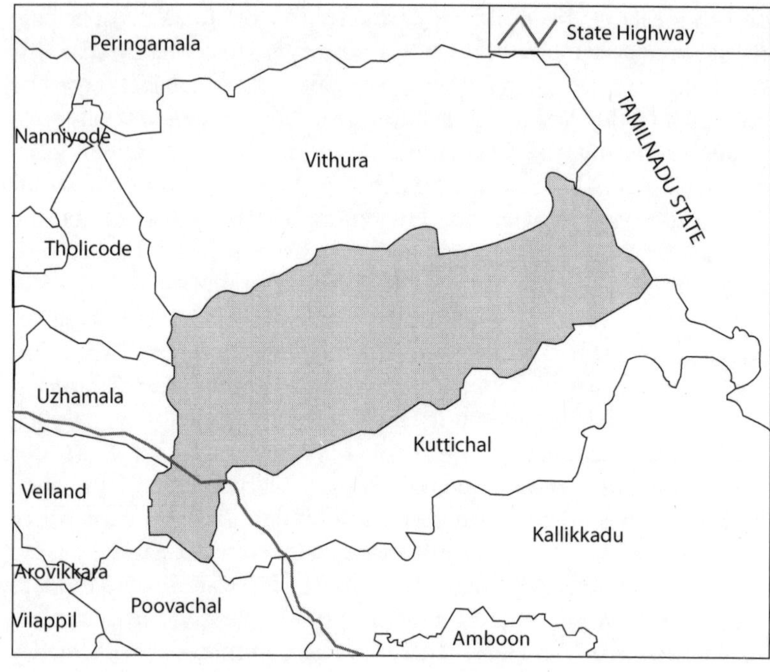

FIGURE 6.2 Aryanad Panchayat

Source: Aryanad Panchayat Office.

Note: Map not to scale.

female sex ratio of Kerala is also reflected in Aryanad. For every 1,000 males, there are 1,079 females as against the State average of 1,084. Hindus (including the SCs and STs) constitute around 70 per cent of the population, followed by 20 per cent Christians and around 10 per cent Muslims, as against the State average of 57, 19, and 24 per cent respectively. The SC population is around 20 per cent and the ST, around 1.8 per cent, as against the State average of 9 and 1 per cent respectively.

ECONOMY AND SOCIETY AND ITS ORGANIZATIONAL DENSITY

Though only a little more than one-fifth of the area is available for habitation and socio-economic activities, the people have made the best use of the favourable agro-climatic conditions by growing a number of crops that form the backbone of the local economy. It has also given rise to a number of non-farm activities. Topping this is the spread of education and a continuing process of acquiring higher educational qualifications by the younger generation, seeking secure employment and livelihood outside agriculture and also outside the local economy.

Rubber is the leading crop because it has suitable cultivation conditions on the slopes and also because commercially it is highly attractive, giving rise to a continuous income (at least on a weekly basis) when trees are ready for tapping after the initial gestation of around seven years. Of the nearly 2,000 hectare of land under cultivation, rubber cultivation accounts for around 45 per cent of the area largely covered by medium-size plantations owned by a few households outside the panchayat. A number of small and marginal farmers have also planted rubber in their small plots of land, thanks to its commercial attraction. The second major crop is coconut, accounting for 38 per cent of area, followed by banana cultivation in around 200 hectares or 10 per cent of the area. A number of other crops with areas ranging from 10 to 50 hectares account for the remaining crops, with rice cultivation gradually declining to just around 30 hectares due to its low profitability and, as the farmers say, lack of economic viability.

Other crops include tapioca, pepper, vegetables, roots, medicinal plants, and decorate flower plants. Animal husbandry such as cattle rearing, poultry and dairying, agro and food processing, some micro- and small-industries, and repair workshops represent other economic activities. Since a few individuals/households own large areas under rubber, land distribution is quite skewed. On an average, the 4,150 registered farmers have 0.30 hectare of cultivated land per household. Nearly one-third of the labour force may be counted as 'farmers'. Most of them are either the Forward Castes or the Other Backward Castes among Hindus and Christians. Some Muslim families may also be small and marginal farmers, but they generally tend to focus on non-agricultural operations such as trading, and other forms of self employment. Most SC households do not have any cultivated land, although ST households traditionally owned/had access to land. Hence the potential labour force for the NREG is largely from this pool of small and marginal farmers, and self employed and rural labour households. Significantly, there is a visibly large service sector

TABLE 6.1 Public Service/Developmental Institutions in Aryanad Panchayat

Within the Supervisory Control of the Panchayat	
Krishi Bhavan (Agricultural Office)	1
Primary Health Centre (PHC)	1
Sub-centres under the PHC	7
Homeo Health Centre	1
Ayurveda Health Centre	1
Veterinary Hospital	1
Office of the ICDS	1
Anganawadis under the ICDS	33
Village Extension Office	1
Office of the Assistant Engineer	1
Government Primary School	7
Public Libraries	3
Autonomous Institutions Sponsored by the Panchayat	
Socio-economic Development Centre	1
Human Resource Development Centre	1
Recreation Club for the Elderly	1
Children's Knowledge Centre	1
Jagrata Samiti (to report crimes against women)	1
People's Food Processing Unit	1
Processing and Marketing Centre for Agricultural Produce	1

Source: Enumeration of institutions carried out by the authors.

because of the demand for education, health care and other services (Table 6.1).

The panchayat is responsible for the management and functioning of a number of public service delivery institutions following the devolution of powers/functions by the State Government. These include an agricultural office called Krishi Bhavan, veterinary hospital, primary health centres, village extension office, office of the assistant engineer (roads), 33 child care centres called *anganawadis* under the National Integrated Child Development Scheme, and seven primary and four upper primary schools. In addition, as shown in Table 6.2, there are a number of educational, health and other public service institutions, mostly in the public domain. The panchayat had taken

TABLE 6.2 Other Public Service Institutions Outside the Control of the Panchayat, including Privately Owned Ones

Higher Secondary School (1 General, 1 Vocational) (G)	2
Upper Primary School (PA)	2
English Medium School (P)	2
Industrial Training Institute (G)	1
Information Technology Service (Akshaya Centre)	1
Pharmacy College (P)	1
Post Office	3
Banks (Co-op. 3, Public Sector 1, Private Sector 2)	6
Non-Banking Financial Institutions	5
Ration (PDS) Shops (G)	33
Government Fair Price Shop (Maveli)	2
Medical Store (G)	1
Office of the Rubber Board	1
Village Office (Revenue Dept)	1
Police Stations	2
Excise Office	1
Telephone Exchange	1
Road Transport Corporation Office	1
Electricity Board Office	1
Water Authority Office (Drinking Water)	1
Public Works Department Office	2
Office of the Sub-Registrar	1
Integrated Cattle Development Project Office	1
Soil Conservation Department Office	1
Liquor Retail Shop (G)	1
Financial Enterprise Office (Chit Fund)	1
NBFI (Gold Loan and Chit Fund)	2
Integrated Cattle Development Project Office	1

Source: Enumeration of institutions carried out by the authors.

Note: G Indicated Govt Dept/Public institution. P indicates Private sector. PA means private but funded by Govt.

initiative in sponsoring a number of developmental institutions at the time of the PPC. We will share more on this subsequently.

Traditional and modern institutions co-exist as well as co-habit vigorously in this village panchayat, as in the rest of Kerala, not to speak of the country in general. However, the Kerala scenario is noted for its greater density of socio-cultural as well as political and economic institutions that often cooperate as well as combat on ideological grounds. In the present day Kerala, the most vigorous institutions at all levels are the political parties and Aryanad is no exception. The two main political parties that have powerful local presence are the Communist Party of India (Marxist) CPI (M), which leads the LDF and the Indian National Congress, which leads the UDF; next is the Communist Party of India (CPI). Although other smaller parties do make their presence felt, no one has an elected member in the panchayat council. Youth organizations of these political parties also have a presence and they do participate, sometimes cutting along party lines, in the developmental activities within the village panchayat.

Local level units of major trade unions are also quite active, but confined to their areas of work such as wage bargaining (or even wage-setting), worker's welfare and social security. There are local units of the three women's organizations, loyal to the CPM, Congress and the BJP. In addition to these, there is what may be called politically-secular institutions, where ideology is not the basis of membership (Table 6.3). These are the village libraries, a common sight in all villages in Kerala. There are nine libraries in Aryanad with abundance of books, as well as facilities for reading. Three of them, the bigger ones, are directly under the supervision of the panchayat, while others are run on a voluntary basis. In addition, we counted 33 sports and arts clubs providing facilities and opportunities to the youth for sports as well as artistic performance. While membership is open to both young men and women, as is generally the case in Kerala, they are largely managed by young men who visit on a daily basis and participate in its activities. Young women are often members of the library and sometimes participate in special events organized by these clubs. In that sense, the intermingling of young men and women are along 'socially expected lines', that is, limited informal interaction. Clusters of households are also being organized into residents associations, a phenomenon that was, till recently, confined to towns and cities. Aryanad has seven such residents' associations.

Co-existing with them are the organizations of religions and communities. There are local level units of the Nairs (classified officially as a Hindu Forward community) called the Nair Service Society; of the Sree Narayana Dharma Paripalana Sangham (SNDP) of the Ezhava

TABLE 6.3 Civil Society Organizations in Aryanad

Secular Organizations	
Youth Organizations	6
Trade Unions	5
Women's Organizations	3
Kudumbasree Units	18
Co-operative Societies (milk and credit)	13
Farmer's Committees	18
Microfinance Agencies	5
Men's Self-Help Groups	2
Village Libraries	9
Sports and Arts Clubs	33
Residents' Associations	7
Charitable Institutions (including one old age home and one orphanage)	4
Religions Community and Caste Organizations	
Organizations of Communities	9
Hindu Temples	8
Christian Churches	6
Muslim Mosques	4

Source: Enumeration of institutions carried out by the authors.

community (classified as Other Backward Community or OBC); Vellala Sabha (an FC); Vishwakarma Sabha (Other Backward Community of carpenters); Nadar Sabha (who may be found in both Hindus and Christians); Pulayar Sabha (SC group), a Muslim Sabha and a *Jama-et* (both Muslim groups). Christian communities are organized according to their groups, represented by the church. Reflecting the religious composition of the population, we counted eight Hindu temples, six Christian churches, and four Muslim mosques within a 22 sq. km area where most people live.

DEVELOPMENT-ORIENTED INSTITUTIONS

It is also important for us to deal briefly with the specific initiatives of the new panchayat in giving shape to developmental organizations and social welfare activities that have a direct bearing on the local level development including the ability to plan and execute NREG works by Kudumbasree.

One of the first initiatives of the panchayat in early 2000 was the setting up of a Socio-Economic Development Centre. Our enquiries revealed that the motivation for such an initiative was the Karakulam panchayat, which is 30 kms away and had earned a reputation during the PPC as one of the leading model panchayats. With the help of the elected members of the panchayat, youth organizations and farmers in the area, the then panchayat President mooted this idea and gave leadership to its formation assisted by social activists, drawn from school teachers, retired officials and members of youth and political organizations. The main objective is to provide guidance and expert services in tackling problems in agriculture and rural development. It invited experts from both within, and outside, the panchayat to formulate a number of schemes and projects. Many issues and problems, and ideas to solve them emanated from the monthly meetings convened by the farmer's committees wherein panchayat council members and agricultural and other developmental officials participated. Shortage of labour for manual work in agriculture, low yields, lack of modern agricultural equipments, and absence of serious cooperation among farmers which resulted in low prices being received were some of the issues that needed to be dealt with. Ideas that were discussed in the larger debates across Kerala, on its development problems and solutions, found a positive chord in these meetings.

Many interesting initiatives came out of such interactions between farmers, elected representatives, government officials and the youth activists. For instance, a land bank was created to identify fallow lands as well as lands left uncultivated by farmers. On the basis of an agreement between the bank and owners of such lands, these were then leased to farmer's groups as well as Kudumbasree groups in exchange for payment of an annual fee. Similarly, a labour bank was created for those willing to work not only in farms, but also in other kinds of development work schemes, who could then register with the labour banks. The bank would, in turn, deploy workers in groups on the basis of demand for work in the area. Initially such a bank worked well, but over time the problem of retaining workers became a problem since many would migrate to other areas and occupations as and when they found employment that they considered better. The SEDC also started a seed bank for distributing high quality seeds and planting material to the farmers by giving a brand name. Using grants and other sources of income, the SEDC also started renting out modern agricultural machinery at reasonable rates.

We visited a marketing outlet created by the SEDC in the panchayat, which enabled many farmers to bring their produce to a specific centre in the market area. Buyers from outside, including Trivandrum city, visited the centre and procured good quality agricultural produce, which also enabled farmers to receive better prices than before since they no longer had to go to the selling point and sell the produce individually. Aggregation of their output and single point selling has proved to be economically more attractive. The SEDC has also promoted a couple of agro-processing units of tapioca, banana, coconut and paddy.

Another major initiative is the establishment of a Human Resource Development Centre (HRDC). Consequent on the PPC, issues relating to the capacity of the people in the area, for local level development planning, became a major topic. They were acutely aware of their dependence on outside expert knowledge, although there were a few persons within the panchayat with a level of education that could contribute to various initiatives of the panchayat. We were told that many discussions took place at Kudumbasree meetings, Gram Sabhas, as well as workshops organized for plan preparations. The ideas and suggestions from these meetings were given a concrete shape in the form of the HRDC. The panchayat assisted in the construction of a building for the HRDC; a management committee with bye-laws and working manuals was setup. An advisory committee, an academic committee, a facilitator's team consisting of teachers and other educated persons in the area, and theme-based subject committees were formed. The facilities included a reference library with a couple of thousand books, internet facility, reading room, language laboratory, children's corner, computer lab, science lab, information centre, and a conference hall. The library is open to all, but visited mostly by students and a few young men and women, as a centre to gain knowledge without travelling outside their residential area. A lot of youth use the library as a centre for career guidance by collecting relevant information. Often classes are organized for them to write competitive examinations. Counselling sessions are sometimes organized as well, to give guidance in studies and choice of employment. Some skill-oriented training programmes covering agricultural workers, construction workers, and health care workers had been undertaken. The HRDC often acts as a platform for the initial formulation of projects for the panchayat, including those under the NREG. The conference hall was the venue for many meetings and events, besides being let out to the residents for social functions. During one of our visits, a large meeting was organized in the conference hall in which Kudumbasree workers, ASHA workers, Anganawadi teachers, and various other functionaries and the public at large were invited. The discussions were alert and articulate, and the people did not shy away from pointing out drawbacks. Delays in the payment of wages for NREG workers and difficulties experienced by certain elderly persons in securing their social pensions were frequently aired. Our visit to the library turned out to be an enjoyable one when we saw young girls sitting and reading in the reading rooms; the shelves contained books by Amartya Sen and Noam Chomsky. The HRDC published 'Village Newspaper' is known by the same name in Malayalam, *Grama Pathram*.

Given the restricted scope of this study, we are not dealing with a whole lot of otherwise interesting initiatives, especially in the areas of health care and educational facilities and activities. But a mention of a few instances are important, to give an idea of the formal structure and office facility that has come up over a period of the last 15 years in the Aryanad village panchayat. We shall then discuss the emergence of Kudumbasree as a critical women's agency, which is currently involved in a number of activities with the support of the panchayat.

NEW PANCHAYAT AND ITS ORGANIZATION

Following the devolution of functions, finance and functionaries, beginning from 1996, village panchayats in Kerala have emerged as active local government institutions euphemistically referred to as 'local self government institutions.' Euphemistic because they are mainly confined to providing basic civic services, and a number of developmental activities, but not maintenance of local law and order, revenue record keeping and registration, revenue collection (except some specified items) and related governance functions. Aryanad had a total revenue of Rs 386 lakh in 2009–10, out of which 61 per cent was 'own revenue,' that is, taxes and other fees collected by the panchayat. The elected panchayat council consists of 18 members; this includes nine women. Six women representatives worked earlier as Kudumbasree members. There are four standing committees, according to areas of work, chaired by a member to oversee the various activities. The secretariat consists of a panchayat secretary and 13 other officials. Besides, the panchayat has recruited two persons on a contract basis for data entry and accounting work.[6] With the assistance and guidance of the Information Kerala Mission (IKM), an autonomous body set up by the state government to provide information technology services to local government institutions, Aryanad panchayat has computerized many services. Using the software(s) developed by the IKM, the panchayat prepares the Plan accounts, payment of social security pensions, registration of birth, death, marriage, and relates certificates to the citizens. It maintains a website (www.lsgkerala.in/aryanadpanchayat) where detailed information and guidelines are given about the various services and procedures.[7]

When we visited the panchayat, what struck us was the spacious front office that should be the envy of many of the state government offices. We saw a number of facilities such as chairs, a television, a notice board listing the various types of services, dates of meetings of various committees, a table for filling up applications, days when elected members were available for meetings with the public, attendance details of office staff, special facilities for women breastfeeding children, separate toilets for men and women, a complaint box, waste box, drinking water, counters for receiving and enquiring about applications. The office facilities included separate cubicles for staff and a records section for keeping records. Monthly meetings of office staff, chaired by the President, to discuss pending issues and other office matters were also held.

One of the highlights of the new panchayati raj in Kerala is the preparation of a Comprehensive Development Document in 1996. Aryanad has one such document. Besides, it has produced its Development Documents for the 10th and 11th Plans. We were also given a copy of the 'citizen's charter' published in 2010 by the Aryanad panchayat on its own initiative, which contains information on, among other things, various services and responsibilities of the panchayat.

The panchayat also supports the functioning of Kudumbasree. Attached to the panchayat office, there is a furnished office room for the use of the CDS and its chair person. Office facilities have also been provided to the ADS in every ward. Every neighbourhood group

(NHG) has been provided with two registers, one for membership details and another for recording their economic activities. A gender centre has also been allotted which is managed by Kudumbasree.

ROLE OF KUDUMBASREE AND ITS ROLE IN IMPLEMENTING NREG

Kudumbasree has been functioning in the panchayat since 2001, well before the launch of NREG (Box 6.1). By 2008, the Kudumbasree had made its presence felt in all the wards (17 in 2008, which expanded to 18 subsequently). It had 330 NHGs, with a membership of 5,475 women representing 84 per cent of total households. All the NHGs with a membership not exceeding 20 members in a given ward constituted an ADS with an elected chairperson and other office bearers. The total number of ADS, being equivalent to the total number of wards, constituted the CDS, with an elected chairperson and executive committee members. The CDS chairperson is the crucial link between Kudumbasree and the panchayat council.

The CDS basically acts as a conduit for disseminating information, facilitating registration and helping the ADS with the identification and planning of activities. As part of these activities, the CDS in Aryanad takes the initiative to convene special meetings of Gram Sabhas, as well as of ADSs at the ward level, and of the NHGs. It also arranges for facilities such as taking photographs and distributing job cards. Working through the ADS, the CDS also selects the number of Mates and arranges training through the Kudumbasree Mission. It also convenes the meetings of Mates once a month. In addition, it monitors the working of Mates as well as the ADS of its area, to ensure that there are no lapses in discharging their duties. Whenever workers come up with problems, complaints and suggestions, those are taken up with the panchayat from time to time.

The ADS acts as a link between the CDS and NHGs at the ward level by disseminating information, making available official application etc. At this level, ward campaigns and meetings are organized with the active involvement of the ADS. It has been given the responsibility to monitor the functioning of Mates and take remedial action as and when required. The ADS helps individual workers fill up their application forms for job cards, take photographs and demand work. Usually it ensures that the applicants are responded to by the

Box 6.1 Activities of the Kudumbasree in Aryanad

Efforts to initiate *Kudumbasree* activities in Aryanad were started in 2001 with the formation of NHGs, enlisting a membership of not more than 20 members per unit. As of 2010, 330 NHGs had been formed and they were brought under ADS in each ward/village. These included 13 per cent NHGs of SC households and 2 per cent of ST households. At the panchayat level, these ADSs were brought under a CDS. At the State level, a Poverty Alleviation Mission sponsored by the Government of Kerala provided guidance, training and financial assistance for selected activities to the members through the CDS.

The activities of Kudumbasree at the panchayat level may be divided into (a) organizing and implementing thrift and loan schemes, (b) self/group employment activities, and (c) acting as agency for delivery of poverty alleviation/social welfare schemes implemented by, and through, the village panchayat.

In Aryanad, the thrift fund of Kudumbasree was Rs 162 lakh in 2010, which was used to advance loans to needy members. In addition, they had also raised Rs 140 lakh as bank loans for various group activities. The district mission of Kudumbasree extended a grant of Rs 8.8 lakh for various activities. By using these amounts as investment, the various NHGs started 118 micro-enterprises by groups of women, besides 574 individual micro-enterprises. These ranged from cattle rearing, bee-keeping, horticulture, to various food-processing as well as some service sector activities such as diagnostic labs.

As part of its role as an agency in poverty alleviation schemes, Kudumbasree is responsible for carrying out NREG works, ensuring care to the destitute in the panchayat under the *Ashraya* scheme of the State Government, and supplying personnel for waste collection and other specific civic work. Kudumbasree runs the 'Gender Centre' sponsored by the panchayat.

With the support of the panchayat and the Kudumbasree Mission, the CDS in the panchayat has initiated a number of activities for and among the children. So far, 137 Child Forums (*Bala Sabhas*) have been formed. They are organized on a ward/village basis. A *Bala Panchayat* is organized by electing a girl and a boy from each *Bala Sabha* and they in turn elect a seven member body with a president, vice president and secretary. This *Bala Panchayat* meets every month and plans its activities. A Children's Knowledge Centre has been formed with assistance from the panchayat. In addition, the panchayat was persuaded to fund the purchase and distribution of a kit consisting of a dictionary, chess board, shuttle-badminton set and a notebook for writing minutes of meetings to all the *Bala Sabhas*. Vacation camps are organized and in these camps children are given the opportunity to interact with the panchayat and its various institutions, taken on study tours and conduct environmental activities. To help the children in their various activities, the CDS has appointed a member as a convener.

In all these activities, the district-level officials of Kudumbasree Mission provide guidance, training and arrange for financial assistance wherever available.

Source: Based on interviens with the CDS Chairperson and focus group discussion.

panchayat within seven to ten days. It also helps the workers link up with the bank for opening of new accounts. It identifies works at the ward level. It also helps in preparing estimates and prioritizes the works by preparing the work schedule.

Once sanction is accorded it convenes the meetings of the workers, and briefs them on the details of the work undertaken. As soon as a given work is completed, it prepares a muster roll and informs the Assistant Engineer, and undertakes the measurement of the work. The ADS is also responsible for ensuring basic facilities in the worksite, distribution of implements, and maintaining the work diary and the muster roll. This apart, it prepares the display board for installation at the work site giving the salient features of the work.

The ADS being in charge of the work undertaken monitors any accidents at the work site and ensures timely medical help. By collaborating with the Primary Health Centre in the panchayat, it also arranges for first aid and preventive health care facilities. The social audit is conducted with the help of the ADS by bringing together experts in the field, social workers, health workers as well as the NREG workers and ward member of the panchayat. At the panchayat's request, the ADS actively participate in the preparation of a watershed development plan in Aryanad. It organizes groups, in all four, consisting of seven members each, which includes some of their own NHG members, and collects information about water sources, soil and its quality as well as other bio-resources in their ward.

The primary unit of NHG has a secretary elected by the members. The information and notifications received from ADS and CDS are disseminated to the members. All their individual requirements are aggregated at this level, and transmitted through the ADS and CDS to the panchayat. The meeting of the NHGs also discusses beneficiary-oriented schemes of the Government such as the health insurance scheme and the housing schemes. The functioning of the three-tier organization of Kudumbasree at the panchayat level is supported and assisted by the State-sponsored Kudumbasree Mission through its district-level team of officials.

Implementing NREG

The NREG was introduced in the year 2008–9 as part of the Phase III of the national programme. At the initial stages, the panchayat officials did not have a clear idea on how to start the employment scheme by eliciting registration of people, based on their need for such employment. Only around 30 people in a panchayat consisting of roughly 12,000 to 13,000 workers came forward for registration. This led to a serious debate and discussion within the working groups in the panchayat, and finally it was decided to disseminate information through a campaign across the 18 wards/villages of the panchayat. It was at this point of time that the panchayat sought the involvement of Kudumbasree, not only for the campaign but also to implement the scheme, starting with distribution of job cards to demanding households.

Once it became its 'agenda' as well as a 'project', the Kudumbasree launched a campaign with the help of the panchayat. As part of the campaign, workshops were organized with the active participation of elected ward members and voluntary organizations within the panchayat. The Kudumbasree members were briefed through NHG meetings in which panchayat ward members interacted with them about the NREG and its implementation. Following this the Kudumbasree members visited each and every household in their respective ward and gave them notices detailing the NREG Scheme, and notified them of the decision to convene a special meeting of the Gram Sabhas. They also undertook a poster campaign as a matter of 'high visibility' publicity. Consequent to such a high profile campaign, meetings of the Gram Sabhas were convened under the chairmanship of the ward member in which the President and panchayat members, resource persons and representatives of Kudumbasree participated and interacted with the members of Gram Sabha.

It must be pointed out here that such close interactions and deliberations were part of the PPC throughout Kerala, arising out of a political decision implemented through the government machinery. Despite understandable drawbacks and partisan politics that were subject to criticism even by some of the members of the LDF, let alone the political opposition (the UDF), the PPC did create a sense of euphoria among social and development activists. That the highly organized trade unions, especially the white collar unions of government employees, hardly shared this euphoria and even became an obstacle in the Government's decision to deploy staff to the local government institutions is, however, another story.

Issue of Job Cards and Identification of Works

Following this campaign, the panchayat council noticed a rather dramatic increase in the demand for job cards, which led to a decision that job cards would be distributed through Kudumbasree. Distribution of application forms, and helping the applicants for filling up the forms were all undertaken by Kudumbasree as a matter of voluntary service. On its part, the village panchayat offered to take care of the cost of taking photographs and also setting up the facilities for it in every ward. It also took the initiative in contacting the local branch of Canara Bank, a large public sector national commercial bank, for opening individual accounts for the NREG workers but without success.[8] However, the President took initiative in negotiating with the local co-operative bank (Aryanad Service Co-operative Bank), which agreed to open the required accounts for the NREG workers that, in our view, made a point about the importance of local-level institutions with a stake in the local economy and society.

Identifying Works, Their Implementation, and Evaluation

What exactly is the process adopted for identifying specific projects under the NREGA? We were told that the potential work sites were identified jointly by the elected panchayat member and the ADS on a ward basis. These works mainly consisted of rehabilitation of derelict ponds and tanks, cleaning of canals, water harvesting sites, road repairs and construction, and later identification of lands belonging to small and marginal farmers, to carry out land preparation work for facilitating cultivation. Once they were identified, the information was passed on to the NREG Cell within the panchayat office, which consisted of an Assistant Engineer, an Overseer, and two data entry operators. The NREG Cell prepared the estimates, which were then discussed in 'project meetings' attended by the panchayat council.

Once sanctions were given for the estimates, the Kudumbasree and ADS were asked to implement the same.

Kudumbasree also convenes meetings of the members in which Mates are selected from among the relatively better educated members, who in turn prepare the muster rolls. The ADS and the Mate together are responsible for ensuring basic facilities for workers in the proposed work site. Once the work is over, intimations are given to the Assistant Engineer who undertakes the measurement of such work and prepares the wage bill and other formalities.

We were, however, told that out of the three years, not much progress was made in the implementation of NREG in the first, 2008–9. As the data entry system had not been established, we could secure reliable data only for the second and third year, that is, 2009–10 and 2010–11. What we found (Table 6.4) was that a number of works had been undertaken during the second year such as cleaning of drains, canals and roads, rehabilitation of water bodies, digging of water harvesting dredges, reclaiming fallow lands and some land preparation works in privately owned agricultural lands. However, in the third year much of the works undertaken were in the nature of land preparation in privately owned agricultural lands (93 per cent of total works and 84 per cent of expenditure). We were not able to secure a credible explanation for this, except the absence of adequate and feasible projects of a common nature. This could be partly due to the stringent conditions set by the State Government, that non-wage expenditure under the NREG should be discouraged resulting, in 93 per cent expenditure in the form of wage payments in the State as a whole.

However, the panchayat had recently initiated an Integrated Watershed Development Master Plan which is still in the making. Such a plan is expected to help prepare a shelf of projects for the next three to five years, the officials pointed out.

The panchayat has instituted a Vigilance and Monitoring Committee that includes, apart from the elected members and the chairperson of Kudumbasree, an Assistant Engineer, Overseer, and retired but knowledgeable officials who are not formally part of the panchayat or NREG Scheme. This committee gives guidance right from the identification stage of the work undertaken. There is a social audit mandated under the NREGS, and such a system functions through an annual meeting in which the elected panchayat member

TABLE 6.4 Work Status of Aryanad Panchayat—Completed

S. No.	*Type of Work*	*Number of Works*		*Expenditure (Rs in lakh)*	
		2009–10	*2010–11*	*2009–10*	*2010–11*
1.	Rural connectivity	18 (6)	0 (0)	6.82 (7)	0.07 (0)
2.	Flood control	126 (42)	3 (1)	53.02 (55)	5.74 (3)
3.	Water conservation and water harvesting	15 (5)	0 (0)	4.50 (5)	0.35 (0)
4.	Drought proofing	17 (6)	0 (0)	1.8326 (2)	0 (0)
5.	Micro irrigation	0 (0)	1 (0)	0 (0)	0.60 (0)
7.	Renovation of traditional water bodies	107 (36)	11 (5)	27.41 (28)	20.74 (12)
8.	Land development	15 (5)	204 (93)	3.55 (4)	144.31 (84)
9.	Rajiv Gandhi Seva Kendra	0 (0)	0 (0)	0 (0)	0 (0)
	Total	298 (100)	219 (100)	97.14 (100)	171.81 (100)

Source: Aryanad Panchayat Office.

Note: Figures in brackets are percentage to the total.

of the ward, local level social workers, ADS Committee, members of Kudumbasree are members. The statement of accounts, including wages paid, are presented and discussed in this meeting. However, on the basis of our interaction with Kudumbasree members, we felt that a more effective method of informing the workers of the scheme has been the meetings where the Mate of a team reads the muster roll once a week at the work site, which includes details such as number of participating workers, wages paid etc. During this time, workers also get an opportunity to check whether their individual details, such as number of days worked, are correctly entered in the muster roll. Each work under the NREG is subjected to a labour budgeting so as to decide in advance the wage bill. Such a labour budgeting is prepared by taking into account the number of person days required to complete a given project. During the two years for which data are available, we give below (Table 6.5) the details of employment demanded and the number of days of employment made available.

As can be seen from Table 6.5, although job cards were issued to all those who demanded, only 56 to 60 per cent of households were given employment. This worked out to 39 to 42 per cent of the total households. All those who demanded were given employment, although one should keep in mind that in practice, demand synchronized with preparation of project proposals that would indicate the man-days required (labour budget) for the works proposed to be undertaken. During 2009–10, a total of 95,022 days of employment were generated, which increased to 121,713 in 2010–11. It worked out to an average of 35 days and 48 days per household during 2009–10 and 2010–11 respectively.

We did pursue the question of low employment along with a set of other important ones. Our enquiry covered 30 NHGs consisting of 513 households. Our first question was the source of information about the NREGS, and the possibility of getting work on demand. 58 per cent reported Kudumbasree as the source of primary information either through the Mates/ADS, or through the NHG meetings, or through the CDS chairperson. Interestingly, 22 per cent reported the NREG Cell/Assistant Engineer as the source of information, while another 11 per cent reported media (mainly newspapers) and 6 per cent as elected ward member.

As for the low employment, majority of the NHGs reported personal and family constraints as the single most important factor

TABLE 6.5 Participation in NREG

Category	*Individuals*		*Households*	
	2009–10	*2010–11*	*2009–10*	*2010–11*
1. Registered Members	8,295	8,386	4,557	4,607
2. Job Cards received	–	–	4,556	4,599
3. Those demanded work	3,772	2,945	2,746	2,567
4. (3) as % of (2)	–	–	60.3	55.8
5. Those who secured work	3,750	2,935	2,739	2,558
6. (5) as % of Labour Force (at 40% of population)	29	23	–	–
7. Those who secured 100 days of work	–	–	32	34

Source: Aryanad Panchayat Office.

in accessing 100 days of work. Most of the women, being married, having young children and/or older parents to look after, found themselves unable to report for duty at the prescribed time of 8 a.m. after completing their household duties in the morning (Table 6.6). They all reported that household duties such as sending the children to school, preparing food, taking care of domestic animals in a number of cases, and similar types of responsibilities were just unavoidable.

Given the fact that most of these women belong to the poorer families, they found the opportunity to work in the NREGS quite attractive, if only some flexibility in the timing is possible. This brings us to the inherent lack of flexibility in such matters, as well as the absence of decision-making powers on these matters at the level of panchayat. This often results in straight-jacketing an otherwise highly beneficial scheme for the poor. This was not confined to a few panchayats, but was a common complaint that emanated from almost all panchayats, articulated through the members of Kudumbasree in various meetings. As a result of such a chorus of complaints, and backed by the State-level mission of Kudumbasree, the Government of Kerala changed, a few months ago, the NREG work timing from 8 a.m.–4 p.m. to 9 a.m.–5 p.m. Notwithstanding such a positive but marginal gesture, it is our view that it would be far more desirable to delegate to the village panchayats the power to fix the time schedule for such works. After all, the entire labour budget prepared by the

TABLE 6.6 Reasons for Not Getting Hundred Days of Work

Reasons Reported	*Number of NHG Responses*
Personal and family constraints especially the household and child care work in the morning	17
Inability of the Panchayat to plan in advance or undue delay in taking decisions	6
Lack of adequate and appropriate work within the Ward/Village that are listed in the NREG scheme	3
Too many workers demanding work or inadequate cooperation among workers	2
Officials do not show interest in planning for 100 days of work per household	2

Source: Based on focus group discussion.

NREG cell would have already fixed the total number of days of employment in a given work scheme, and hence it is far more desirable to allow flexibility in timings.

The second most important factor related to the inability of the panchayat to plan in advance, or the reluctance of officials in planning for 100 days of work, or inadequate work opportunities within the village.

Our expectation that the demand for work will be concentrated in a few months, showing some sharp seasonality, was belied, presumably due to the fact that it was women who demanded such employment. Although there was a greater degree of demand during the months from December to March as well as from July to August, there was a core demand that was fairly spread over the year (Figure 6.3).

There is very little seasonality in agricultural occupations in the panchayat because a major proportion of cultivation, such as rubber, coconut and banana, is under perennial or annual crops.

Another major complaint that came up in our interaction was the delay in the payment of wages. 30 per cent of women reported that it took them around 60 to 90 days to receive the wages after completion of work, whereas 8 per cent reported a delay of 30 to 60 days, and another 32 per cent reported a delay of upto 30 days. For reasons that could not be found out, 4 per cent reported a delay exceeding 90 days. Given such long delays, which would defeat the very objective

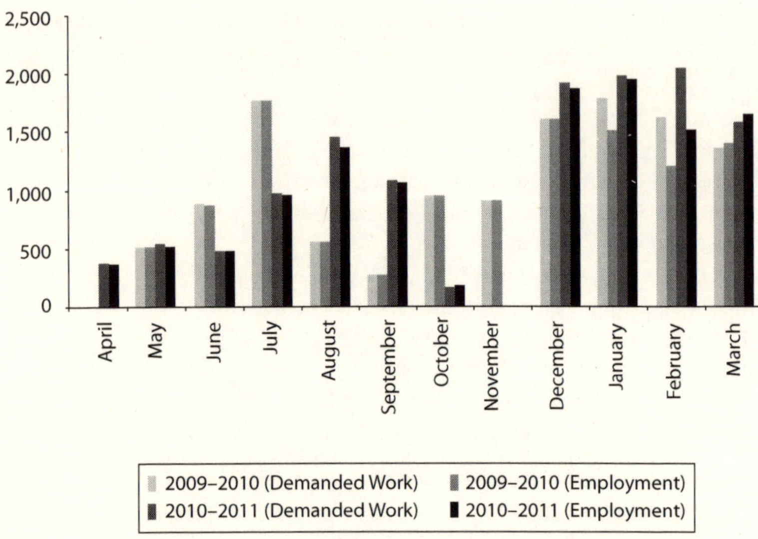

FIGURE 6.3 Month-wise Demand for Work

Source: Aryanad Panchayat Office.

of the NREGA (that is, income generating employment to the poorer households), it would only be appropriate if half the wages are paid immediately after completion of a given work (Figure 6.4).

With regard to the provision of basic facilities at the worksite, all our respondents reported that drinking water was available at all work sites, whereas 80 per cent reported availability of first-aid at the work site (Table 6.7). Only a little more than one-third reported some facility for resting in the form of a shed.[9] Distribution of implements for manual work was much less as also facilities for taking preventive injections while engaging in hazardous work such as cleaning and rehabilitating tanks, ponds and canals. Often infested with dense weeds, broken bottles, unhygienic wastes, not to speak of snakes and similar but dangerous living beings, the women leaders also admitted that many women workers were agnostic or plainly indifferent to taking injections before embarking on such work. Our own visits to the work sites convinced us that in such cases the ban on use of machinery was not a well thought out response. Many labour intensive works require some expenditure on materials such as granite, sand and cement, etc., or eco-friendly alternatives such as geo-textile or

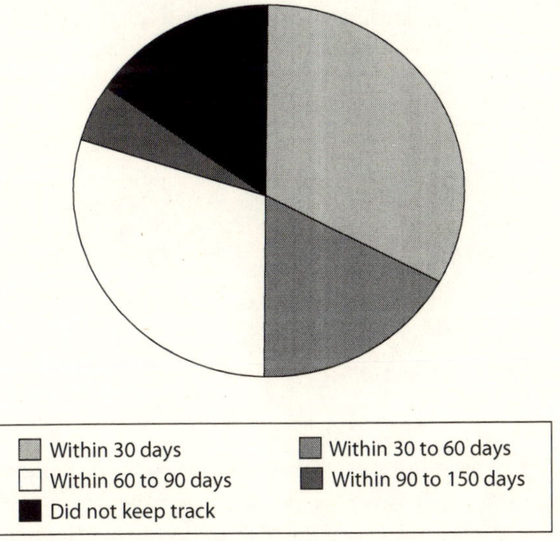

FIGURE 6.4 Periodicity of Payment

Source: Based on focus group discussion.

TABLE 6.7 Response to Basic Facilities in Work-sites

S. No.	*Facilities*	*Number of Positive Responses*	*Percentage*
1.	Drinking water	513	100
2.	First-aid	408	80
3.	Shed	182	35
4.	Preventive injection	20	4
5.	Implements for work	92	18

Source: Based on focus group discussion.

selected plants, which could act as binding material to the rehabilitated tanks and ponds, canals, as well as in various land development works. While 40 per cent of the expenditure had been earmarked for non-labour costs in the NREGS, the Government of Kerala did not allow such expenditure for fear of creating opportunities for leakages and various rent-seeking activities, such as corruption at the lower levels. We do realize that there is a dilemma here, but it can certainly be resolved through imaginative planning and supervision, facilitating

TABLE 6.8 Age, Status, and Employment in NREG, 2010–11

Status	*Registered Persons*	*Employed Persons*	*Employed as % of Registered*	*Percentage Share in Total Employed*
18–30	1,100	232	38	8
30–40	2,192	827	38	28
40–50	2,312	888	36	30
50–60	1,918	688	32	24
60 above	946	300	35	10
Total	8,468	2,935	35	100

Source: Aryanad Panchayat Office.

non-labour expenditure as required, especially in contexts where the social auditing process is vigilant and effective.

What is the age profile of the NREG workers? Of the total workers who participated in 2010–11, we found that 92 per cent were above 30 years of age, of which 58 per cent were between 30 to 50 years and the remaining 34 per cent above 50 years (Table 6.8). 10 per cent of the total workers were found to be above 60 years, which seemed to reflect that elderly women did seek public employment in rural contexts. Given the fact that women in this age group constituted around 15 per cent in Kerala, such a rate of participation either suggested the absolute nature of poverty in those households, or the attractiveness of public works as a means of some additional income arising out of relative deprivation of the elderly women in rural areas. Our respondents also pointed out that adoption of flexible time schedule for work would attract more women to demand for NREG work.

THE IMPACT OF NREG ON THE LOCAL ECONOMY AND THE WORKER HOUSEHOLDS

Has the NREG made any impact on the local economy? What about its impact, if any, on the worker households in general and the women in particular. It goes without saying that a public employment scheme such as the NREG could have made some impact, in one way or another, on the local economy as well as the local households. On the basis of the number of workers who participated, we found that it roughly worked out to 23 to 28 per cent of the estimated labour force in the panchayat. The total number of days of employment generated was between 95,000 and 1,22,000 per year. However, only appallingly few workers—less than 40—could get employment upto 100 days per year. We had already mentioned that the type of works undertaken by most of them was in the nature of land and water resource management, and development as well as land preparation in the lands of small and marginal farmers.

As far as the worker households are concerned, their average income worked out to Rs 4,336 and Rs 5,233 per annum in 2009–10 and 2010–11 respectively. While this was only an additional source of income to the households, it entirely came into the hands of the women members of the households. Most workers used such incomes for subsistence expenditure for their families. In households where the women did not work earlier, and depended entirely on their husband's income from casual work, reported that they utilized this income for their children's education, health, clothing and school accessories such as umbrellas, footwear, bags and stationery. As members of the NHGs of the Kudumbasree, they used part of this income to increasing their thrift fund. Some women workers said that they could leverage such thrift funds for getting higher amount of loan through Kudumbasree for starting micro-enterprises, house repairs and so on.

From our detailed interaction, we could elicit that participation in NREG along with their Kudumbasree activities led to perceptible changes in the form of (i) self awareness, (ii) self dignity, and (iii) enhancing self capability. Together they also brought a slow but steady change in the social profile and social status of these women workers. As for self awareness, it is indeed difficult to separate the role of these women from their participation in the NREG. There seemed to be a mutually reinforcing process of engaging in various Kudumbasree activities along with wage makers in the NREG scheme. The women said that in the initial stages, they were not sure of their ability to undertake responsibility for implementing specific works entrusted to them by the panchayat. They had to familiarize themselves with skills such as preparing work estimates, muster rolls, and also carrying out the work in trust. Many of them did not have much skill in works such as cleaning and rehabilitation of tanks and ponds and canals, as well as land levelling, shaping and related work. The few elder male workers working with them taught them such specific skills, which spawned a new relationship. The elderly men were in need of wage work offered by the scheme because their labour power no longer had a market due to age. In return, the women took care of these elderly men by giving them less tenuous work and more time for resting. While the older men imparted skills, the younger women reciprocated with care and empathy, leading to a mutually respectful relationship. Our interaction with the 30 NHGs revealed that as a result of such acquisition of skills, women started taking up works in groups whenever they were not employed in the NREG Scheme. We also realized that there was nothing like unskilled work and that every kind of work required a process of acquiring skills. It would be far more productive, in our view, if the NREG scheme provided for training programmes that imparted specific skills and thus, helped the labouring poor to enhance their productivity.

Another instance of capability acquisition related to their dealings with banks, in view of them having bank accounts. Many of them already had such an account through the micro-credit scheme of Kudumbasree. The organizational membership as well as the platform of Kudumbasree exposed these women workers to meetings and collective discussions and deliberations. Often they had to speak at such meetings, prepare short notes, and also interact with officials from the panchayat and other agencies. This gave them a sense of confidence in dealing with people with whom they had not had the opportunity to interact before.

All these instances and experiences did not mean that they had not faced any constraints and obstacles. Most of the women reported that apart from the constraints imposed by household responsibilities, other family members were not enthusiastic about their participation in the NREG, especially for those women who had not worked as casual manual labourers before. In the case of some women belonging to the Ezhava caste (officially classified as OBC), their households were engaged, till recently, in the manufacture of illicit liquor as a means to overcome their economic difficulties. In this they had to collaborate with their husbands, often becoming subjects of social ridicule, criticism and, sometimes, exclusion. The activities of Kudumbasree, reinforced by the support of the NREG, enabled many of them to leave such illegal activities and lead a life with work of dignity.

WOMEN'S PERCEPTION OF PARTICIPATION IN NREG

Women's participation in the NREGS in the Aryanad panchayat, like elsewhere in the state, accounted for 91 to 94 per cent. That could lead to a view that public employment as a felt need in Kerala is confined to women only. In our view this is not due to the absence of unemployment prevailing among men, but because of the nature of unemployment, as well as the emerging labour market dynamics for manual labour in Kerala. The market wage rate for casual workers engaged in manual work has been steadily on the rise in Kerala and it is nearly double that of the daily wage under the NREG when it was introduced, that is, Rs 250 per day. The gap seems to have widened across the State by as much as 2 to 3 times. In Aryanad panchayat, the market wage rate for men varied from 2.5 to 3 times for male workers and 1.5 to 2 times for the women workers during 2008–10 (Table 6.9). During December 2011 when the study was completed, the market wage rate for casual manual work for men varied from Rs 350 to Rs 550, depending on age and skill while it was between Rs 300 to Rs 350 for women. The significant difference between the wages

TABLE 6.9 Wage Rates for Men and Women Engaged in Casual Manual Work in Aryanad, 2010 (Rs per day)

Activity	*Men*	*Women*
Rubber tree tapping (skilled)	400 (Re 1/tree)	Not usually engaged
Latex collection from rubber tree	Not usually engaged	Rs100 (Re 0.25/tree)
Coconut tree climbing (skilled)	400–450 (Rs 10/tree)	Not done/engaged
Construction work like masons, carpenters, plumbers, concreting, etc. (skilled)	500	Not usually engaged
Forest dept plantations	375–400	250
Plant nursery assistants (unskilled)	300	150
General agricultural work (unskilled)	300	175–200
NREG scheme*	125	125

Source: District Kudumbasree Mission, Thiruvananthapuram.

Note: *In 2011–12 this was raised and is currently reported to be Rs 167 per day.

of men and women is also due to the high mobility of male workers. Given the connectivity to Trivandrum city and other places, many men work outside the panchayat as construction workers, auto rickshaw and taxi drivers, shop assistants, in hotels and so on. On the other hand, except a few educated women who work in the government and other establishments, most women are confined to their homes due to household responsibilities and the caring of young children and/or aged parents. It is therefore not surprising that male workers of working age are not attracted to work in the NREG scheme, even when they are unemployed, because they would simply not accept a wage rate lower than what they get while at other work.

Second, the emerging scenario of unemployment, especially among the younger age group of 18 to 35, is one of educated unemployment because most of them have acquired at least 10 years of schooling. Both among young boys and girls, there is a high premium attached for regular employment even at a lower wage (which they prefer to receive as monthly salary) because of the security and status such employment affords. The situation in Aryanad is no different. Women workers from rural labour households engaged in manual work have hardly any alternative sources of income except working as casual manual workers. For the educated youth, the NREGS is not an attractive option because of its low quantum of work-days as well as the irregular and delayed wage payment. Around one-third of the women workers engaged in the NREG work in Aryanad panchayat were found to be from households where women were not compelled to go out and work out of sheer poverty. Instead, they are from relatively poorer households characterized as vulnerable and hence an additional source of income is greatly valued. We tried to probe this further and found that 45 per cent of them came into the NREG scheme as a result of the group dynamics arising out of their membership in Kudumbasree. Another 38 per cent women we interviewed reported economic necessity, while 14 per cent reported the public character of the employment scheme as the motivation for demanding work under the NREG. It would appear that the role of the NREG in Kerala, going by the insights of this case study as well as the State-level statistics, has been instrumental in bringing out 'the hidden saving potential' of surplus rural labour, *a la* Ragnar Nurkse, that would not be easy to mobilize through the rural labour market.

We also probed as to why all women members of Kudumbasree demand work under the NREG. 35 per cent confessed their inability to demand work due to ill health, something that points to the extremely crucial role the health factor plays in one's individual and family welfare. Another 20 per cent reported that they were engaged in traditional occupations such as pottery and bamboo products making, from which it was not attractive to switch over to the once-in-a-while works under the NREG, even when their traditional occupation wasn't attractive enough from a wage/income point of view. Another 10 per cent reported that they were responsible for taking care of animal husbandry in the household, even though the income from such activities did not always accrue to them directly. Only 5 per cent attributed lower wage rate in the NREG as well as the delay in securing it through the bank channels as a factor for not demanding work. Only 10 per cent responded by saying that they were simply not interested in the NREG, presumably due to their relatively better household economic status. The remaining 20 per cent reported that the main reason for not participating in NREG was the objection from their family members, like mothers-in-law or elder brothers or their husbands.

One of the unintended consequences of women's participation in the NREG in Aryanad has been the new sense of confidence in undertaking manual work as projects for implementation by groups of women. This in turn helped them acquire new capabilities like working on land with which many of them were not familiar, skills in particular type of operations such as land shaping, construction of retailing walls, maintaining and entering registers, measurement of work, dealing with officials and so on. Since the average days of work under the NREG had been quite minimal, a number of women felt the need to continue to work for taking care of economic security of themselves and their families. Since they had already been working as groups, it occurred to them to form groups of like-minded women and canvas for different types of work that they could execute. They realized that there was demand for manual work in the private plots of farmers in the panchayat. This gave rise to formation of what may be called 'labour teams' and we found that 20 per cent of the women workers out of the 53 with whom we interacted were members in such labour teams, whose average membership was mostly between 5 and 7. This was indeed a novel idea that the women workers came up with, arising out of their participation in the NREGS as Kudumbasree workers, and the consequent group dynamic that was set in motion including a sense of solidarity.

One of the authors of this study, who was also a Programme Officer at the State-level Kudumbasree Mission, realized the potential of the 'labour teams' and discussed the matter with the Executive Director and other colleagues in the Kudumbasree Mission. The idea was quickly converted in the form of a proposal for replication in all the panchayats of the State. A guideline in the form of a booklet was also prepared, published and distributed throughout the Kudumbasree network in the State. The suggestion was positively received by many district-level Kudumbasree workers, and discussions are now on as to how best it can be implemented in their respective villages and panchayats. For our assessment of the economic impact of NREG on women workers, we tried to compile their responses in their own words, which are provided in Table 6.10.

Many of them gave multiple answers and what has been presented is a compilation of these into a manageable indicator. Either taken one by one, or in combination, these responses underline the distinct changes in their personal profile and capabilities.

TABLE 6.10 Description by Women, in Their Own Words, of the Changes in Their Personality

Type of Changes	*Number of Responses*
'Learned work/improved skills'	153
'Improved health status'	217
'Reduced financial problems in the family'	157
'Became self reliant/independent'	202
'Learnt Banking procedures'	43
'Got courage to interact with people'	148
'Self Confidence'	93
'Developed urge to work and earn money'	118
'Gained better interpersonal relationships'	86
'Started participating in social activities'	34
'Learnt to value mutual help'	30
Total responses	1,281(100)

Source: Based on focus group discussion.

Note: Responses from 513 women from 30 NHGs. Many gave more than one response.

What it conveys is the fact that a majority of them reported a lesser reliance on money lenders. For some others, they contributed to the expenditure on repair of their houses or buying household articles. The remaining people reported some personal gain in terms of their ability to meet their personal expenses, to buy some jewellery or to save some money for future. However, a more significant impact seems to have happened in their personalities and attitudes towards the larger society. The women workers were of the opinion that their participation in Kudumbasree activities in general, and NREG in particular, exposed them to an understanding of natural resources and its utilization in their local economy. They talked of the contribution they made in converting fallow lands into cultivable land. An overwhelming majority pointed to the improvement in public hygiene and sanitation. They realized their potential in contributing to the welfare of the community, which in turn helped them improve their economic status and social profile. There seems to be a greater degree of social awareness and positive outlook. They were earlier largely confined to the household affairs, with contact extending to their extended family members and a few friends. This has now changed, the women said, to a greater sense of understanding and mutual help through their participation in Kudumbasree. Now, they claim to have acquired a greater degree of hygiene, better awareness of environmental issues, and the ability to tackle these problems.

WEAKER SECTIONS AND THE NREG

The Aryanad panchayat is fairly large going by its geographical area (105 sq. km) as well as its population (32,500 in 2010). The SCs account for 20 per cent of the population, which is close to double their share in the State as a whole (9 per cent). As for STs, their share is around 1.7 per cent, as against the State average of just 1 per cent. While a good part of the area is mountainous, the ST population is located in the upper reaches of the mountains and largely confined to one ward spread over 8 hamlets. Educationally, their achievement is much lower than that of others and public service facilities are relatively limited in the areas they inhabit. Their livelihood is dependant primarily on forest resources, such as making products out of bamboo, animal husbandry, collection of fire wood and medicinal plants, and related activities.

As against this scenario, people belonging to the SC are spread over five wards/villages, extending across 14 colonies. Traditionally, they have been agricultural labourers, though some have some land of their own. Over time they experienced some occupational diversification but largely, if not wholly, have remained confined to the primary sector. While they are more connected to the other sections of the population compared to the STs, they also constitute the least economically and socially secured sections in the local economy and society.

According to the information collected by us and presented in Table 6.11, the share of SCs in the total number of workers in the NREGS worked out to 11 per cent in 2009–10, and 14 per cent in 2010–11. The share of STs was 2.3 and 3 per cent respectively. However, the average days of employment received was only 25 to 28 days for the SC and 30 to 32 days for the ST. This is considerably less than the average days of employment received by the other categories of the population, which is suggestive of some form of discrimination.

The lower number of days of employment has, naturally, affected the average income received from the NREG by the SC/ST households. Most SC workers have to walk 3 to 4 kms to the work sites. The women workers are often constrained to report to work at 8 a.m., having to take care of household duties, and at times other economic activity in and around the house. While many ST households owned land which made them eligible to carry out NREG work, they were not so successful, leading to their lack of enthusiasm in participating in the NREGS.

TABLE 6.11 SC and ST Participation in NREG

Year	*Number of Workers*	*% Share in Total Workers*	*Population Share*	*Average Days of Employment per Household*	*Average Wage Income (Rs)*
Scheduled Caste					
2009–10	417	11.1	20.0	25	3,099
2010–11	418	14.2	20.0	28	3,462
Schedule Tribe					
2009–10	87	2.7	1.8	32	3,941
2010–11	87	2.7	1.8	30	3,741

Source: Aryanad Panchayat Office.

While the formation of NHGs ensures some community homogeneity, the fact that these groups work together in worksites has created opportunities for social interaction between SC/ST workers and others. This has been pointed out to us as a refreshing experience. In addition, their interaction with banks, visits to health care centres, overcoming their fear about tetanus and other injections have imparted them a small but desirable changes in personal confidence, and the ability to interact with the people and institutions in their local milieu. Those who were confined to carrying out only their traditional occupations seemed to have realized the expanding, though limited, set of opportunities that the NREG has opened up to them. Those who were reluctant to interact with public institutions such as banks now talk of their capability for such transactions, as well as decisions making when children and family members need health care. Attending meetings of NHGs, Gram Sabhas, and those convened by ward members is said to have equipped them to go to panchayat and other government offices whenever required. As part of their collective deliberations and decisions taken, many women from the ST households led campaigns against illicit liquor manufacturing activities in their hamlets.

SOCIAL SECURITY PENSIONS

While this study's main focus has been the implementation of the NREGA, we have also tried to find out about the delivery of social security pensions in the panchayat. The computerization and digitization of the panchayat records (along with other local bodies) by the IKM has indeed imparted the much-needed transparency in such public services. The IKM maintains a dedicated website for information relating to social security pensions, which gives details for all local bodies from the ward level onwards, according to type of pension, gender, SC/ST, criteria for eligibility, amount entitled, and the date of delivery of the pension. This system was started in 2009–10. On the basis of information collected, we have also checked the data with the panchayat office. The details of the social pensions funded entirely by the State Government are given in Table 6.12. Many elderly workers in the unorganized sector, who are eligible for pensions through their respective Worker's Welfare Board (for which they make a contribution during the working years), are not included here.

Table 6.12 Persons Receiving Social Pension in Aryanad Panchayat, 2011

Type	*Total*	*Women*	*SC*	*ST*	*% of Women in Total*	*Amount per Month (Rs)*
Pension for Agriculture Labourer	792	341	NA	NA	43	400
Indira Gandhi National Old Age pension	595	273	NA	NA	46	400
Pension for mentally challenged	NIL	NIL	NA	NA	–	400
Pension for physically challenged	280	127	NA	NA	45	400
Pension for the unmarried women above 50 years	55	55	NA	NA	100	400
Pension for widow	1,199	1,199	NA	NA	100	400
Total	2,921	1,995	82	6	68	–

Source: www.lsgkerala.in/aryanadpanchayat/.

Note: The monthly pension till March 2011 was a measly Rs 250 and even the enhanced amount works out to around 52 per cent of the abysmally low but revised official poverty line for rural Kerala in 2010.

By the end of 2011, the total number under the two old-age pensions (for agricultural labourers and other old aged poor) works out to 1,387, which is roughly equivalent to one-third of the population above 60 years of age. However, there would be a segment of pensioners under other categories, especially among widow pensioners, who should be counted as old-age pensioners. If one takes, roughly speaking, one-third of the widows and unmarried women to be above 60 years,[10] the old age pensioners will work out to 41 per cent of the total estimated old population. Given the active interaction of the people with their representatives and the presence of Kudumbasree in disseminating information as well as the existence of various organizations of the farmers and workers, it is not surprising that there is fairly high coverage. While all of them may not be qualified by the severely restrictive criteria for entitlement, there is no doubt that they all belong to a broader group of poor and vulnerable households.

However, what is surprising are the unbelievably low shares of persons belonging to the SC and ST communities. We found that pensioners of all types in the SC category were just 82, accounting for a mere 3 per cent, while their population share is 20 per cent. The pensioners in the ST category were just 6 in number, accounting for a mere 0.2 per cent. Further enquiries did confirm that the number given is indeed as per the records. If this is the situation, then there is no doubt about the subtle exclusion that cannot but be social in our view. While overt social exclusion is difficult in the present-day socio-political milieu in Kerala, covert exclusions of the type that we have found here should indeed be a matter of concern to the Government. Earlier, we had mentioned about the low coverage of the NREG among these communities, but that has been largely, if not only, been due to high wage rate in the labour market as well as the availability of work for most part of the year.

SOME REFLECTIONS

Our study on the implementation of the NREGA in Aryanad panchayat threw up several lessons and issues for further reflection. First, we realized the critical importance of the larger socio-economic environment that makes it possible, or less difficult, to implement pro-poor schemes such as the NREG. The highly favourable initial condition in Aryanad is not an isolated one, but a larger phenomenon throughout Kerala. However that alone is not going to make a programme successful because, if that were the case, Kerala would have been in the forefront of the implementation of this scheme. The fact that it is not points to the specific local factors such as the quality of leadership and its ability to carry large sections of the local community of citizens, cutting across political and social categories. Further, the labour market dynamics in Kerala has changed so drastically that there is a shortage of labour for manual work especially among men, leading to an inflow of migrant labour from outside, largely from eastern India. However, there is the 'hidden saving potential' in the form of unutilized labour of women, whose participation in the labour market for manual work is contingent on several economic and sociological factors. But the emergence of Kudumbasree as a collective of women from poorer households has enabled the mobilization of their labour within the framework of public employment. We have noted that the implementation of NREG is only one of the activities of Kudumbasree, and that they have many other 'mutual help' programmes, which include caring for the elderly—known as Ashraya[11]—and young children, besides participating in women-specific social issues. All these have been made possible by a process of gendering by social mobilization, which was not the hallmark of earlier social and political mobilizations. The purely economic benefits of such a mobilization seem to be quite limited, but its unintended social and economic consequences have been, in our view, quite significant and will have a bearing on the socio-economic transformation from the point of women in the villages.

That Kerala's civil society has undergone significant transformations, which also worked as a favourable initial condition for these women, should also be kept in mind. We had noted the high density of political, social and cultural organizations in Aryanad that shows the highly organized nature of civil society, something that is also a Kerala-wide phenomenon. This evolving civil society has not only created an active and deliberative 'public space' for many initiatives of the new panchayat system, but has also given rise to public action of a developmental kind, which is rooted in an earlier era of asserting rights, bargaining for entitlements and working for socio-economic change. A distinguishing characteristic of this civil society is its 'home grown' nature, being organically rooted in local economy, society and culture. In a way, what we are witnessing, not just in Aryanad but in most villages in Kerala, is the role of organic intellectuals and their contributions in local socio-economic change. Such a picture of civil society is a far cry from the externally sponsored 'NGO phenomenon' that has gained much currency in international development circles.

Having said that, we have noted with concern that the socially weaker sections of SCs and STs continue to experience subtle forms of exclusion, as revealed in the coverage under social security pensions and declining rate of participation in the NREGS. At the time of finalizing this manuscript, we could get the statistics on NREG employment for the year 2011–12. While it shows an overall improvement in average days of employment (56 as against 48 the previous year); however in the number of persons who received 100 days of work, there has been a drastic decline in SC and ST participation—a mere eight households in the former and just one household in the latter category. This was explained away by the officials in terms of much higher market wage rate as well as regular demand for their labour; but it is difficult to deduce from that that there are not many women in SC households who might be in need of NREG work, but are not able to access it due to household or other responsibilities. Some ST households did complain that works on their land are not being undertaken, while several works are carried out in lands belonging to non-SC/ST community. We have also noted earlier that the share of SC and ST communities in the entitlement to social pension is far below their share in the total population. Despite the progress made by the SC and ST communities in Aryanad in the matter of access to schooling, health care, public assistance for housing and so on, the distance between them and the other communities is perhaps increasing given the faster pace of progress registered among the non-SC/ST communities, whose initial conditions were much better than the former. Such an increasing gap has been noted in the incidence of poverty and vulnerability in Kerala as a whole, despite its impressive performance in the overall rate of reduction (Kannan and Raveendran, 2011).

We think that the relatively low inclusion of SC/ST in public welfare schemes calls for a detailed investigative study by sociologists in a rural setting, which is otherwise active in social mobilization and public action.

Aryanad, as we mentioned in the very beginning, was judged as one of the well performing village panchayats in Kerala, and hence the findings cannot be generalized beyond a point. However, given our close association with the functioning of the panchayati raj, we have no hesitation in saying that it belongs to the 10 to 12 per cent of the similarly well performing panchayats in Kerala. In the context of this particular study, if we were asked to point out a striking feature we would, without hesitation, point to the changing profile of rural women who now occupy a visible public space, with new sense of identity and dignity along with a sense of quiet confidence for their own socio-economic upliftment. They seemed to be discovering the wider world as members of a larger collective organization, which has now made a mark in Kerala's public life.

Notes

[1] The definition of 'poor and vulnerable' in this exercise follows the threshold adopted by the National Commission for Enterprises in the Unorganized Sector, that is double the official poverty line as on 2005 that comes marginally above the international poverty line of two PPP dollars per capita per day. For details, see NCEUS (2007), and Kannan and Raveendran (2011), for the incidence of poor and vulnerable in Kerala and other states.

[2] In a short questionnaire survey among 617 Kudumbasree members in December 2010, who were attending a state-level conference in their capacity as chairpersons of Community Development Societies, we found that half of them possessed a BPL Card for their households.

[3] The jury consisting of public personalities, experts and reputed social activists. 140 village Panchayats and 12 Municipalities participated in this television social reality show broadcast in 78 episodes by the Doordarshan Malayalam Channel from 1 March to 21 June 2010.

[4] However, the actual disbursal was below this rate due to the limited absorptive of the panchayats.

[5] For a detailed account of the People's Plan written from the political perspective of the leading party in the LDF that is, the CPI(M), see Issac and Franke (2002). Given the absence of preparation, the first few years of the PPC elicited a lot of criticism (Kannan, 2000).

[6] Recognizing the importance of maintaining accounts in a professional manner, the state government has appointed, in 2011–12, professional accountants in all village panchayats in the state.

[7] All the local government institutions in Kerala (Panchayats and Municipalities) have their own websites, maintained and serviced by the IKM.

[8] The bank did not take much interest under the pretext that they did not have adequate staff. While the shortage of staff could be a factor, our understanding is that reluctance is due to more additional work involved in dealing with so many accounts with nominal amount, and hence the lack of profit from such activity.

[9] It is the general practice in Kerala that pre-school children in the age group of 3 to 5 years from poorer and lower-middle class families are sent to

the *anganawadis* and hardly taken to the worksite. Young children below 3 years are taken care of in their families and that acts as a constraint for their mothers from participating in the labour force, even if they need to. Moreover, pre-school children in the *anganawadis* return home by 3 p.m.

[10] Currently women's life expectancy in Kerala is 76 years; that is at least 12 years higher than for India as a whole.

[11] Ashraya is a scheme of the state government where the old, aged and destitute are taken care of by provision of essential food items, medicines for the sick, housing for the homeless, along with home visits by designated Kudumbasree volunteers.

References

Issac, Thomas and Richard W. Franke. 2002. *Local Democracy and Development: People's Campaign for Decentralized Planning in Kerala*. New Delhi: Leftword Books.

Kannan, K.P. 2000. 'People's Planning, Kerala's Dilemma', *Seminar*, January: 92–7.

Kannan, K.P. and G. Raveendran. 2011. 'India's Common People—A Regional Profile', *Economic and Political Weekly*, 46(38), 17–24 September.

IV

GUJARAT

7 THE PRACTICE OF POOR RELIEF IN RURAL SOUTH GUJARAT

Jan Breman

The findings reported on the implementation of the Informal Workers' Social Security Act (2008) relate to four villages in South Gujarat, which have been sites of my local-level research during the past half century. These localities are spread over three districts. While Bardoligam in the Surat district, and Chikhligam in the Navsari district, belong to the central plain, in which agriculture has continued to remain the central economic activity, Gandevigam in the Navsari district and Atulgam in the Valsad district are situated on the fringe respectively, in the middle of what is known as the 'golden corridor'. This is the zone of industrial-urban growth, stretching from north to south, bordered on one side by the railway line and on the other side by the national highway which connects Mumbai to Ahmedabad.

When I was given the opportunity to return to the region which I had frequently visited, 'the most deprived' became the theme of my new round of fieldwork. A slow but steady decrease in poverty due to an accelerated pace of overall economic growth is said to have marginally, if not significantly, reduced the vulnerability of people who have no other means of livelihood apart from their labour. In my earlier micro-level studies based on empirical research, I remained wary of accepting this claim. Next to a segment which managed to cross the poverty line because of better work and higher pay, there are numerous others who lagged behind and could not follow in the footsteps of those who managed to better their station. What about the non-working poor, the people who have lost, or never had, the capacity to provide for themselves? Their destitution has remained understated in the literature. State initiated attempts to redress the vulnerability of these infirm people should have led to a change for the better. Has the introduction of a National Social Security Bill—enacted in late 2008—meant for people living below the poverty line, resulted in adequate protection against adversity of the most deprived men, women and children? I have operationalized this question in the four villages of my recurrent fieldwork by collecting data on poverty ridden households which wholly or partially lack the labour power required to make a living—the old and aged; single women with or without children; and the physically or mentally handicapped of all ages.

The investigations were undertaken between August 2010 and February 2011, with a short break in between, and were conducted by both myself and by Kiran Nanavati, who was also my research associate in earlier spells of fieldwork in the region. In the first exploratory round, we focused on the inhabitants of the landless colonies in Gandevigam and Chikhligam, the two villages with which I had been closely associated since the early 1960s. Our survey was meant to identify *Halpati* households, where one or more members were possible beneficiaries of poor relief schemes managed by the state. With only a few exceptions, the households of this community of landless labourers are listed in the BPL category, which is the main selection criterion for granting government benefits. In Chikhligam, however, we decided to add a fair number of *Dhodia* households to our survey. The households belonging to this tribal caste of small and marginal farmers make up a large majority of the village population and the land-poor, or landless, among them are also ranked under the BPL classification. Being in a similar condition as most Halpatis, at the bottom of the village stratification, we included 17 of these Dhodia households, whose members are particularly vulnerable due to the lack of labour power, in our initial survey.

FINDINGS IN THE FIRST ROUND OF FIELDWORK

In the 101 households of our survey, we found 112 members altogether who hypothetically should have been recipients of social benefits because of old age, widowhood, or physical/mental disability (Table 7.1). Out of this total, only 29 were granted such benefits—22 members were granted an old age pension, 6 members a widowhood allowance, and 1 grant was given to a handicapped youngster. Much larger is the number, 83 out of 122, who were not able to qualify for these provisions despite having reached old age (30), having lost their male partner (25), or being either physically or mentally disabled (28). These findings alarmed us; to begin with were the problems the ultra-poor have to get entitled to their legal dues. Exclusion from statutory benefits, however meagre and irregular they may be, is a

TABLE 7.1 Destitute People Seeking Social Benefits in Chikhligam and Gandevigam

					Benefits			No Benefits		
	Households	*Male*	*Female*	*Total*	*Old Age*	*Widow*	*Handicapped*	*Old Age*	*Widow*	*Handicapped*
Chikhligam										
Village—proper	40	18	28	46	–	1	–	22	7	16
New settlement	27	14	14	28	19	1	1	–	1	6
Gandevigam	34	6	32	38	3	4	–	8	17	6
Total	101	38	74	112	22	6	1	30	25	28

Source: Author's village survey, 2010–11.

serious reality. It basically means that the working poor are supposed to take care of those who do not belong to households with earning members are. They have to provide for the livelihood of the non-working poor. Worse off are elderly men and women, and widows who run their own households, who are badly in need of outside support for their minimum requirements because of their inability to be gainfully employed. It also explains why for their sheer survival, handicapped people have no other option but to be members of a larger, income gathering household.

Our first round of data collection highlights how benefits are granted to a mere one-quarter of the poorest of the poor, who desperately need them for their bare subsistence, across the board. The distribution among various categories of the vulnerable is highly uneven. Although most men and women of old age do not get a pension, a fair share of them (22 out of 52) have managed to find access to this provision. Their inclusion, however, shows an enormous variation, even between localities situated at a short distance from each other. Indicative of the disproportionate distribution is the skewed spread in Chikhligam where in the new settlement—to which many Halpatis were deported two generations ago[1]—most of the elderly do get their pension. They were given their entitlements in 2009, when the local administration decided to register all old age persons who were residents of this village, below the poverty line. Apart from the Halpatis, the *Koli Patels* and members of various SC communities also benefited from this drive. All were brought to the civil hospital in the taluka headquarters to get their age certified and the collective processing of their papers resulted in 44 pensions, out of which 25 happened to be Halpatis living in this neighbourhood which was one of our research sites. The entitlement was all the more striking because in the nearby village of Chikhligam, which was one of our fieldwork locations, not a single one of them became entitled. Widow allowances in both villages were grossly under-represented (allotted to 6 out of 31), but handicapped youngsters or adults even more, since only 1 of them became eligible in the two villages. The total number is most probably still higher than the 29 which we identified, since several households are often reluctant to acknowledge the presence of disabled members in their midst.

Our tentative conclusion so far is that the provisions granted, although far from adequate to redeem the beneficiaries out of their state of pauperization, do constitute a meaningful contribution and give a modicum of relief, without which many of these lives would be even more miserable and intolerable than they are. What also struck us in our encounters with 'the fortunate ones' was that they viewed their allowance not as an entitlement meant to last, but rather as a stroke of luck, a windfall gain, which might end as unforeseen as it had come. Their attitude remains one of deep insecurity.

The findings were a major point of departure for pursuing our next round of investigations by extending our survey—with a somewhat different methodology—to all four villages of our research in South Gujarat. At this stage our leading questions differentiated between those who were admitted to receipt of benefits provided by government agencies as opposed to the far larger number who did not gain access to these social welfare schemes. Talking to those who became included, we wanted to find out what had made them eligible; how they had proceeded; who had helped them along; their experience with officials who handled their files; and the time and cost spent on becoming formally accepted as beneficiaries. As for those who remained excluded, our interaction with them concentrated on the reasons why they failed to become beneficiaries. Many of them seemed to have been completely unaware about the existence of these benefits, even if a neighbouring household had found access to them. Neither did they make any effort to find out whether they would qualify or not. At this point, we would like to observe that prolonged and intense poverty leads to isolation and absence of social capital in whatever form. Hearsay, as the main source of information in a milieu of illiteracy, falls short of concrete knowledge of what to do and where to go. Here it needs to be emphasized that the state does not come to the clients; the clients have to approach the state in a circuit alien to the poor, one in which they fear to tread because more often than not, they do not know how to find their way around. A lot of paperwork is required, which is beyond the reach of people unable to fill up forms, collect certificates and other documents testifying to their credentials (BPL card, photo of applicant, voter's card, Birth/Death Certificate, a school diploma, receipt for payment of house tax/electricity bill, and the most puzzling requirement of all, authenticated proof of their monthly or annual income). It is all formal evidence of their identity at the time of handing in their application. The social network in which the poor operate is a shallow one, and in most cases deplete of the kind of support and guidance, without which government offices remain out of bounds. All this explains why a large segment of the non-beneficiaries have not attempted to meet with the officials who need to authorize their application, and in the presence of whom they have to give their thumbprint by way of signature. But time and again informants told us that many costly trips had been made to the sub-district or district headquarters, that sets of papers, painstakingly brought together, had been submitted but to no avail. There are instances where unforeseen hurdles arise, too difficult to cross. For instance, how can a widow show proof that her annual earnings are less than Rs 2,400 or below Rs 4,500 for the whole household of which she happens to be part and parcel? Her saying so will have to be put in writing in an affidavit signed by her and accepted by an official, willing to be persuaded that her statement is correct. This leniency can, however, be bought for a couple hundred rupees, a lot of money, as well as an investment, with a high risk of non-delivery.

However, the high percentage of non-inclusion cannot be attributed mainly to the failure of the non-working poor to access to the social welfare schemes. The state is to be blamed much more for not reaching out to alleviate the plight of its poorest clientele; not merely because of lack of understanding of why the most vulnerable people are unable to access the enacted social protection provisions, but also because the government machinery has neither the efficiency nor the efficacy required for operating these schemes. Forms which need to be filled up in order to become eligible for one of the social benefits are not locally available, and need to be collected from government offices at the sub-district or district headquarters. On being widowed, women are entitled to an immediate, one-time allowance of Rs 10,000, post the demise of their husband. All such applications are processed at the sub-district level with the Mamlatdar as the authorizing agent. Forms for an old age pension allotted to men and women from the age of 60 years onwards (of monthly Rs 200 between 60–65 years, increased to Rs 400 above 65 years) have to be submitted to officials at the District Collectorate with the *Prant* Officer, who is second in command to the collector, as the sanctioning authority. The Social Defence Department at the district level handles applications for a regular widow allowance, amounting to Rs 500 per month, with a supplement for a child of Rs 80, up to a maximum of two children. The same agency is in charge of processing applications submitted by the severely handicapped. Deserving cases are entitled to a monthly allowance of Rs 200 for youth less than 17 years of age, increased to Rs 400 for the age bracket between 18–64 years. Between the various administrative echelons and the various departments involved at either the district or sub-district level, there is a lack of coordination and communication, which is counter-productive to the interests of the clientele. Follow-up is constantly required to keep the application alive, moving from one table to the next. Files do not only get stuck, but often get lost in interdepartmental transfers, resulting in an unacceptably high percentage of non-response to requests for severely needed entitlements. Adding to the confusion created in and by the government apparatus is the fact that the chain of officials handling the files are not instructed to report back on the action taken. This means that the *Talati*, who is in charge of the village administration, has no idea who the beneficiaries of these social provisions are, and neither does he receive information on applications submitted, pending or rejected.

What we found particularly remarkable was that many government officials were not familiar with the range of social provisions made available. The Talatis of both Gandevigam and Chikhligam had only a faint notion of the differential pensions for the old age, the first one of Rs 200 paid solely by the government of Gujarat for the elderly from 60 to 65 years, and the second one for men and women above 65 of Rs 400, out of a fund to which both the Government of Gujarat and the Central Government contribute Rs 200 monthly.[2] In Chikhligam only one widow had qualified for financial support and although in Gandevigam a few more were recipients of a regular allowance, the women in this category remained hugely victimized because no information was locally available on their entitlements. Even more striking was the emphatic denial of many officials that there were statutory benefits for disabled youngsters or adults. They were willing to concede that the severely handicapped might get a free bus and rail pass, or be provided with a wheelchair or an artificial limb, but no regular financial support whatsoever. When we insisted and referred to the Indira Gandhi National Disability Scheme (IGNDS), they remained firm in their opinion that this benefit did not apply in Gujarat.

In a setting where even the authorities are misinformed, it is hardly surprising that the large majority of people without labour power in the village—a pauperized segment which in my estimate adds up to about a quarter of the rural underclass of landless and land-poor households—remain deprived from their legal due. Receiving it or not is perceived as good or bad luck by them, something which they cannot claim as their right but which is a favour, one over which they have no control, and which can be withheld as arbitrarily as it has been granted.

CHANGES IN THE SITE OF INVESTIGATION

Digesting and reflecting on our findings from the first round of fieldwork, we started the second round with a change in research strategy. Our initial entry point had been to find out from the non-working poor we met in the landless colonies of Gandevigam and Chikhligam whether, in their search for survival, they had tried or not to qualify for state provided social benefits. We now decided to proceed from the opposite end of our investigations, by verifying how government agencies charged with the implementation of the Social Security Bill take cognizance of a pauperized clientele, bereft of the labour power required to maintain them. The BPL register in the four villages of our fieldwork became our point of departure in the operationalization of this research question, because without such a card no household is eligible to social benefits provided by the government.

It was not always easy to get hold of this list and in one instance we failed because the Talati of Maliadhera—the village which administers the new settlement, which is the abode of the Halpatis evicted from nearby Chikhligam—managed to avoid meeting us in her office. While the landless poor feel scared of paperwork and are apt to consider all cards and documents as an intimidation which might hamper their latitude and manoeuvrability, bureaucrats here consider official papers to be their prerogative and are wary to share their stock of capital with outsiders, afraid to be confronted by questions they find difficult to deal with. But in the end, we succeeded in securing the BPL lists of the four villages in South Gujarat which were the focus of our second round of investigations.

In an effort to clean up the public distribution scheme which had become too inclusive, a village-level count was held in 2002–3 to find out which households had struggled to make both ends meet. The heads of enlisted households received a card which specified the quantity of subsidized food items (mainly rice, flour, vegetable oil, and sugar) that they could buy in the local fair price shop once a month. The PDS distinguished two categories of the poor and the needy respectively. The latter, labeled *Antyodaya*, qualified for a larger food ration at a reduced price. Ranking in the BPL list depended on a number of key indicators: landholding and other means of production, occupation and schooling, quality of housing and ownership of durable consumer goods. In the report of my fieldwork carried out between 2004 and 2006, I gave details of a recount held in Gandevigam in order to bring down the number of BPL households:

I was able to observe this operation close up. It was entrusted, via the *Gram Sevak*, to a couple of Koli women who insisted resolutely that they had visited every house in the village and that it had taken only a few minutes for each of the household heads to fill in the forms. None of my informants in the landless colonies, however, remembered any such visit, and the questions on the form were certainly too difficult to answer in a few minutes. What probably happened, as it did on previous occasions, was that the village secretary decided who met the criteria and who didn't, and that the answers were filled in accordingly. This explains why in the records I was allowed to copy, every Halpati had the same income, exactly the amount specified to be eligible for a 'BPL' card. The cards are issued at the Sub-District Office and bear the stamp of the Mamlatdar. The Talati is informed of how many BPL cards have been issued, as is the local shopkeeper who is supplied with goods every month according to the number of cards. (Breman 2007: 101)

The forms filled in locally were sent to Gandhinagar, where the score for every household was fixed. The poorest ranked lowest, with scores from 0–16, while households which are a little better off were allotted scores from 17–20. Those above were removed from the BPL list and lost the PDS facility. The poverty classification and the subdivision in ranking was subsequently also used for distribution of other state provided benefits, for instance accommodation under the Indira Awas Scheme (IAS), of a one-room house built of brick, with plastered walls inside, a thin iron door, and a window with shutters. Inclusion in the BPL list has become more important over the years since those who are exempted stand to lose all government support for the poor and needy. The decision to be admitted or rejected has not been a matter of fair and careful administrative scrutiny, but has been reached haphazardly, and is affected by undue influence of stakeholders at the local level. Moreover, there is a constant pressure from above to restrict the number of beneficiaries under the pretext of getting rid of fake cases of inclusion. On the policy of adding a cap to the total figure put on record, I wrote up what I witnessed only a few years ago in one of the villages of my recurrent fieldwork:

> The day before I arrived in Gandevigam in January 2006, the Mamlatdar had paid a visit to inform the Village Council of the instruction he had received from the state capital Gandhinagar, to close the BPL register. After an earlier decision to clean up the register by removing households that had allegedly been given BPL status erroneously, this latest instruction announced that no names could be added to the current list. The state Chief Minister Narendra Modi had decided to remove poverty from the political field of vision, and there was, therefore, no room for new cases in the government accounts. (Breman 2007: 421)[3]

The moral of the story—which I bring up five years later—clarifies the finding that the poverty dynamics, the reported decrease in incidence, and the reduced intensity of deprivation is not borne out by factual and close monitoring of what is happening in the households at the bottom of the rural economy, but is more a fabrication, inspired by the political gambit of producing good news. As I summed up my earlier conclusion, policy reports and official statistics present a façade of wishful thinking which conceal a reality of deep and widespread poverty.

Distinguishing the poor from the destitute is an exercise that has turned out to be equally flawed by arbitrariness as well as bias. Though most of the households with a low score in the BPL list would have no problem in testifying to their urgent need for a wide range of state benefits, we found that many households who ranked higher in the BPL list were visibly not better off. So why they are not accepted as 'needy' rather than just poor? It seems that yet again, the quota of destitute is politically motivated, restricted at the higher bureaucratic echelons and not reflective of the scale of misery we encountered in the course of our fieldwork. As a high-ranking official at the sub-district level in Bardoli told us, it is only when a slot in the category of the ultra-poor falls vacant that he can decide to facilitate the choice of a substitute. These are rare occasions and he agreed that there is no dearth of candidates fitting the profile of being destitute. The outcome is that we have no alternative but to stick to the BPL list as provided, and also to the gradation of poor households made in it, but our hope is that the haphazard quality of the information provided has been well understood. New households cannot be added to the BPL register, nor can the included poor be 'upgraded' to the segment of destitute. In the wake of the 2011 population census, the government is now involved in a new count of BPL households, and in view of the verdict of policy makers and politicians that poverty is reducing in size and intensity, it is to be expected that the list saying so will be further trimmed down.

THE MAGNITUDE OF EXTREME VULNERABILITY

So where did this lead us for the next stage of our research? We conducted a random sample survey of BPL households in the four villages of our research in South Gujarat, to gather more factual data on the predicament of the non-working poor, and to reach an estimate on the frequency of vulnerabilities which make people in the landless colonies dependent on external support for their survival. We focused our investigations on the households to which men, women and children without labour power belong, but contextualized their presence in the wider setting of the habitat, on the outskirts of the villages in which the poor invariably reside. The selection of households was done from the BPL lists pertaining to all sites of our fieldwork: Gandevigam, Chikhligam, Bardoligam and Atulgam.

The number of inhabitants in the four villages amounted to 8,521 in the beginning of this century, spread over a little above 1800 households. A total of 855 BPL households means that close to half of all households had problems in making both ends meet, a figure which is in accordance with our earlier investigations in these localities.[4] The villages bear a striking difference in the proportion of households which are classified as BPL. As seen in Table 7.2, Atulgam

TABLE 7.2 Schedule of BPL Households

Village	*Total Number*	*Score 0–16*	*Score 17–20*
Gandevigam	71	31	40
Chikhligam	167	24	143
Bardoligam	161	26	135
Atulgam	456	246	210
Total	855	327	528

Source: Author's village survey, 2010–11.

has the highest percentage, and that is surprising given that the village is situated in the centre of the golden corridor, with non-local employment relatively easy to access. Many of the working poor commute to one of the neighbouring towns (Vapi, Pardi, or Valsad) or qualify for casual jobs in the Atul Industries, which are even closer by. Therefore, it comes as no surprise that the local wages are 20–25 per cent higher than in the other villages of our fieldwork. This finding suggests that rather than divergent levels of living, the classification of poor versus non-poor is not standardized, but dependent on the way in which indicators are weighed and methods of counting, which vary between the localities monitored. The same explanation accounts for the unequal distribution between the BPL households with scores between 0–16 or 17–20, much more disproportionate in Chikhligam and Bardoligam than in the other two villages. These contrasts do not reflect stark differences in levels of poverty in the localities under investigation. Our contention is that they are the outcome of various ways of administrative classification.

In drawing our random sample of BPL households, we gave priority to the 0–16 category in the assumption that the old aged, widows and handicapped would be concentrated in the segment registered as 'needy'. In Atulgam we opted for the selection in the 0–16 category only because those already contained 246 households, more than half in the BPL list. However, for reasons of representativeness, we also wanted to aim at a fairly equal spread of our respondents over the various localities inhabited by communities to which most of the poor belong. We expected that the same principle of selection would make sure that all tribal castes, invariably the poorest class in our research villages, stood an equal chance of getting included in our random sample. Only in Chikhligam we decided to select no neighbourhood other than those inhabited by Dhodia households, who constitute four-fifths of the village population. Halpatis here are a minority, covered adequately by us in our first round of investigations. Our data collection then took place mainly in the new settlement to which many of the landless households from Chikhligam had shifted, belonging to the territory of an adjacent village. Both in Bardoligam and Atulgam the majority of BPL households are Halpatis, as in Gandevigam; but in the first two villages they are clubbed together with members of other tribal castes—Naikas, Chodhris, and Dhodias in particular. Thus the random sample which was the base for our second round of fieldwork was stratified to the extent that more weight was given to households with a lower score (up to 16), while ensuring that in the process of selection all landless colonies (and by implication all tribal castes) were fairly even represented. Adding to the randomness of our sample, we were unable to identify about 10 per cent of the names in the BPL list of Chikhligam, Bardoligam and Atulgam. These villages have many landless colonies spread over the village territory, which is quite large, and the inhabitants of the different tribal caste neighbourhoods lack familiarity with colonies other than their own. The households we failed to find despite our best efforts—the names may have been nicknames or were those of a former generation—were substituted by households we blindly selected.

Table 7.3 shows that we collected information on the frequency and intensity of vulnerability of approximately one-third of all BPL households, a percentage which went up to over two-fifths of the households ranked in the lower scores of the BPL list, while somewhat less than one-fifth of the households with scores in between 17–20 were interviewed. In view of the arbitrary and biased way in which the BPL survey was carried out, and subsequently adjusted downwards for political reason, it should come as no surprise that there are many cases of vulnerability which escape formal registration. Having failed to get classified as 'poor', such people are incorrectly exempted from state provided social benefits. Our findings should therefore be considered as having measured, through the eyes of the government, the minimal size of 'the deserving poor'.

How many households formally acknowledged as being poor include members who are bereft of the labour power required for

TABLE 7.3 Random Sample of BPL Households

Village	*Total*	*BPL Households*		*Random Sample*		*Total*
		Score 0–16	*Score 17–20*	*Score 0–16*	*Score 17–20*	
Gandevigam	71	31	40	26	26	52
Chikhligam	167	24	143	12	40	52
Bardoligam	161	26	135	26	31	57
Atulgam	456	246	210	85	–	85
Total	855	327	528	149	97	246

Source: Author's village survey, 2010–11.

making a living? Somewhat less than half of the households included in our sample (109 out of 246) report that they have to manage their livelihood without receiving regular outside help. Of the total number of households, 137 (about 56 per cent) have vulnerabilities which should qualify for government support; in 15 cases, for more than one member. This finding seems to corroborate our supposition that not being able to work is indeed a feature that is particularly common in households classified in the bottom ranks of the BPL list.

Of the 152 potential beneficiaries, only 29 have been granted the allowance to which they are entitled, as shown in Table 7.4. This is not even one-fifth of the total, and less than the one-quarter we found in the first round of our investigations. The distribution among the three categories suggests that with one out of four, the elderly seem to have the best chance to qualify. However, this ratio has to be reduced, since three women who do receive an old age pension, owe their allowance to being widows of husbands who had a formal sector job (one a teacher, one a government peon, one a signalman at a railway crossing). Removing these cases brings down the number is recipients of state provided benefits under the social security bill to the average of 20 across areas being studied. At best one out of five women eligible to widow support do manage to get it. They have to produce a certificate of death, but are often unable to do so because the demise of their husband is not always officially registered. It also happens that their spouse is still alive but that they have split up, often due to marital quarrels leading to the wife returning to her native village to avoid being beaten up by her husband or in-laws, or because she is fed up living with a man who rather than contributing to the household budget, spends a major part of his earnings on liquor. But we also came across cases of women who have come back to the parental home to look after an aging father or mother, or when both have expired, to take care of minor siblings, too young to fend for themselves. Divorcees are entitled to widow allowance but how to prove that you have separated to set up your own household? And again, most pitiable is the condition of the handicapped of all ages since they very rarely qualify for what is their legal due. In our sample only one out of 16 we came across had managed to get access to a state benefit, but we are pretty sure that the total number of the disabled is strongly understated.

Apart from incorrect exclusion, according to our sample a huge and urgent problem, an issue which also needs to be addressed is

TABLE 7.4 Households with Members Who Qualify for Social Benefits

Village	*Households*	*Not Applicable*	*Receiving Benefits*				*Not Receiving Benefits*			
			Old Age	*Widow*	*Handicapped*	*Total*	*Old Age*	*Widow*	*Handicapped*	*Total*
Gandevigam	52	23	4	2	1	7	7	15	4	26
Chikhligam	52	23	–	1	–	1	9	13	6	28
Bardoligam	57	27	3	3	–	6	9	14	3	26
Atulgam	85	30	6	9	–	15	17	23	3	43
Total	246	109	13	15	1	29	42	65	16	123

Source: Author's village survey, 2010–11.

inclusion for the wrong reasons. A striking example is an elderly *Anavil* woman in Gandevigam who receives a widow's allowance. Although certainly not well endowed, her condition is not so bad that she can be considered a fitting case for state benevolence. Her name is not included in the BPL list, but belonging to a family of landowners, she receives a monthly stipend from the fund that the dominant caste has set up for needy members. In other words, there are other criteria for deciding on applications than the ones formally put on record. This also explains why applications submitted are processed on the basis of less, rather than more, destitution. In all four villages very few households have managed to become classified as Antyodaya—or the poorest of the poor—eligible for higher and still cheaper food rations as well as other government benefits. Cases submitted are decided on the basis of *olkhan*, or recommendation as a precondition for acceptance. That is how in Gandevigam several Koli Patel households have managed to qualify for old age and widow benefits, although only one of them has managed to become listed in the BPL register.

Who are the people mediating between the state and its clientele in the milieu of the poor? In a few instances it is relatives of the applicants, who are not afraid of the paperwork involved and familiar with where to collect the forms and submit these once filled up. A case in point is the sister of a widow in Atulgam, living in the nearby town of Valsad—the headquarters of the sub-district—herself a widow who had passed through the bureaucratic trajectory only a short while before. But in most cases the intermediaries are members of high castes, well acquainted with handling paperwork and experienced in dealing with government officials. They are willing to help because the applicants are known to them, directly or indirectly, as domestic servants or as labour in their business. Closer by are somewhat influential figures in the village such as members of the local Panchayat, primary school teachers, *Gram Sevaks* or social activists with the reputation of getting things done. If demanded in advance, applicants do not mind paying a reasonable price for such services, but in view of the unpredictable outcome, they may also decide to abandon their attempt to get their application to the stage of 'pending'. In Atulgam we were duly impressed by a compassionate high-caste woman from a neighbouring village who rushed to the support of widows wanting to avail of the one-time allowance of Rs 10,000 for themselves, paid after the demise of a husband, to cope with the sudden fall in income as well as with debts then incurred. She would immediately come to the house of the bereaved woman, get her thumbprint on the form that had to be filled in and returned some time later to pay out the benefit she had managed to encash. However, this sum would amount to much less than Rs 10,000; usually not more than Rs 2,000–3,000, with the empty promise that more might follow later on.

The money orders for what are meant to be monthly allowances are sent with long, variable intervals in between and this irregularity adds to the uncertainty that the benefits will continue to be disbursed. Recipients are not informed of the reason for why their entitlements are suddenly withdrawn. This may happen when a minor son reaches the age of 21 years and is hence supposed to take care of his widowed mother or aged parents. In other instances there is no good reason for abruptly stopping payment of the provision. Can this be attributed to a temporary problem, lack of sufficient expertise, which will be overcome once the agencies involved in making the remittances become better versed with what they have to do? The Indira Gandhi National Old Age Pension Scheme (IGNOAPS or Vayvandana Yojana) has been implemented from April 2008 onwards; the passing of time, however, does not seem to have overcome tenacious practices of inefficiency caused by bureaucratic incompetence, sloth and sloppiness. In my earlier study on the poverty regime in the same fieldwork villages, I narrated the misery of one woman in Bardoligam who was at her wit's ends to keep her household afloat. I wrote that what she narrated poignantly illustrated the impossibility of finding one's way in a labyrinth of obstacles and deliberate obstruction:

M's husband has not worked for many years because of illness, their only son died a few years ago, as did their daughter, who had returned home after getting divorced. M is now bringing up their 12-year-old granddaughter. She is in the last class of primary school and is an excellent pupil. The girl would like to go on to secondary school, but the costs are clearly too high. M is the only working member of the household, but a lack of income and the responsibility of taking care of her husband and grandchild is driving her to desperation. At the advice of the school head, she tried to get a benefit for people in her situation. With his help she filled in the forms and collected together all the necessary documents (the grandchild's birth certificate and registration of residence in the village). She received different amounts of money in the post on three occasions, and then nothing more. She went to the post office in Bardoli town, which is where the money orders come from,

> but to no avail. Twice she tried another office but that too proved to be the wrong address. She is illiterate and has no idea how the bureaucracy works, under what scheme she may be entitled to the benefit, who is responsible for it and how to find them. No one even seemed prepared to listen to her story. Eventually she gave up and went home, convinced that she would never get what others did, for equally incomprehensible reasons. (Breman 2007: 353)

This story on past failure can be backed up by many similar ones pertaining to the situation as it exists today. Nothing in the fabric of the bureaucracy seems to have changed. As borne out by our local-level survey, the incidence and frequency of poor people living in a state of acute vulnerability has remained unacceptably high in my sites of recurrent research in South Gujarat. When many potential beneficiaries do not even bother to file an application for one of the entitlements, it is not only because they do not know where to go and how to proceed. It is also because they have little faith of gaining access to what are their legal dues. The scepticism of this underprivileged clientele does not only concern the diffidence with which authorities accountable for the implementation of the social security bill handle their charge. It stems from a long experience which tells the working and non-working poor that their basic needs are downgraded by government agencies, who have always been, and will remain, unsympathetic to their problems. The attitude often encountered when walking the corridors of officialdom is one of non-interest in the problems of the downtrodden. Bureaucrats who have to deal with the underprivileged segments of the population seem to be lower in the pecking order than their colleagues who cater for the better-off classes.

INTERFACE BETWEEN THE STATE AND THE POOR

In the third round of our investigations, we have followed the trajectory of the applications for social benefits to government departments in the sub-district or district in which they are processed for acceptance or rejection. In the villages, we checked what successful applicants had done to get qualified and why the large majority of the non-working poor had remained deprived of their entitlements. Shifting our investigations to government agencies would enable us to gain information on the *modus operandi* of the officials involved. In that way we learnt how applications are screened, and when files get passed on or referred back to another department. Starting with meeting the local authorities at our fieldwork sites, we moved up or sideways in the bureaucratic agencies at the sub-district and district level, to find out more about the procedures followed in dealing with a clientele trying to gain access to state provided social benefits. From the Talati and the Village Headmen, we made occasional trips to the office of the Mamlatdar and his staff in the Talukas in which Gandevigam, Chikhligam, Bardoligam, and Atulgam are situated, and equipped with letters of introduction we also did the rounds of government departments in the district headquarters of Surat, Valsad and Navsari. Almost all offices were visited more than once, because there was little sense in making formal appointments in advance. We had to wait our turn, waiting in the corridors until either being admitted, or curtly being told to come back the next day because the person we wanted to see was in a meeting, on tour or just 'not available'. This time spent was not time lost since we were usually kept waiting with many others, and in exchange for sharing our business, we listened to what had brought them here. While petty bureaucrats make do with peons to barricade themselves from direct access, the High-Ranking Officials have Personal Assistants for handling the roster of the boss. Since a multi-layered chain of gate-keepers decide who is next, they have to be 'befriended' in order to gain admission. We came away from our expeditions in the official corridors with the strong feeling that the state and the poor belong to different realms, are caught up in separated circuits which do not share the same language, but also have a different script for getting the work done. The down and out do not know how to address the departmental staff, and are unsure of whether to respond or not to the instructions given to them. From their side, officials are by and large not highly concerned about the problems of their clientele, hold strong opinions about people unable to fend for themselves (their laziness, unwillingness to save up, lack of providence), and often do not bother to find out if the benefit claimed should indeed be facilitated. It was rather disheartening sitting next to a clerk ticking off what he found missing in the file, and then putting it aside with a note of rejection. Of the non-working poor, not many have the guts to venture into the offices mandated to take care of their needs, and often tend to be easily intimidated by their interlocutors. When they come unaccompanied it is mainly to get hold of the form required for making the application. They seek the help of a peon and are rarely seen interacting with somebody above that station. It is the start of a long trajectory in which applicants try, to the best of their ability, to collect the documentation with which to validate their claim. On turning 60, and thus becoming eligible for an old age pension, men and women have to submit a copy of their birth certificate, which should be made available from the Panchayat's Office. Not registering a new-borne child in the local administration, however, is a long-standing practice which still lingers. In such cases, a Medical Doctor of a public hospital has to certify that a person is indeed of 60 years of age or older. The problems involved, both time- and cost-wise, in getting it issued are such that many candidates abandon their efforts to pursue their application for benefits at this early stage. As discussed before, without *olkhan*—recommendation of a respectable person with social capital reaching up to the district level—the failure rate is quite high. But the additional presence of an intermediary is required at all stages, to bridge the gap between the state and the poor; somebody familiar with the spheres on both sides, savvy in translating the give and take from both sides, and willing to follow up with further action demanded in order to keep the file alive; a person who also knows whom to bribe, and at what price, and where to get hold of missing certificates/documents—for instance proof of place and year of birth—or if necessary, how to fabricate them. How can a widow prove that her annual income does not exceed Rs 2,400? Women from Atulgam who commute to work as domestic maids in middle-class households of Valsad town are paid Rs 150 monthly for each job they do (that is cleaning the house as well as washing clothes). Among them are widows and they are often employed in three houses a day, amounting to Rs 900 each month. The way out from having their application rejected is signing an affidavit saying that the information provided is truthful. She is made to put her thumbprint on the statement in the presence of the authorizing agent, and this occasion is the only chance she has to meet with such a senior figure in the bureaucracy. One of the Prant Officers whom we met told us that he goes out of his way to approve of claims for social benefits from the really needy falling under his mandate, and that he does not mind much when the papers have come in beyond the given time frame. Our first comment on his record of leniency is that one of his underlings pockets a couple of hundred rupees for passing on the prepared file with a green signal to his boss. Moreover, the very problem with leniency is that it can be arbitrarily shown or withheld. In other words, it is a matter of discretionary power, which seems to be decisive for granting benefits rather than entitlements which are legally binding.

It soon became clear that the various agencies mandated to handle the files of the poor are heavily understaffed. Officials transferred to other posts are often not replaced automatically, and certainly not immediately. We were told that this is the main reason why applications are not dealt with more promptly. It is not exceptional at all to grant or reject social benefits more than a year after the papers have been submitted. On making enquiries, which the poor seldom venture to do, they are fobbed off with meaningless information. Of course, such complaints can be heard about the bureaucracy at large, but it seems that departments which have to administer services to the poor excel in vacant staff positions, inefficiency and ineffectiveness. A striking defect of the government machinery is the lack of communication and coordination between the departments to or from which, in the process of screening, the files have to be transferred. Not only are the applicants confused about where and how to tackle this veritable labyrinth, but the bureaucrats themselves lose track of paperwork they are supposed to have handled. They were quite wary, and even worried, when we questioned them about how they handle the work-load and their liaison with other agencies, afraid to be criticized for inadequate efficiency and performance. 'Do tell us the application you are interested in and we shall see to it that it will get accepted', was a common reaction when we intruded into the official domains, usually fenced off from one another by boundaries too intricate for us to fathom. This sort of reply underlines again the significance of *olkhan* and the crucial role of the locally influential in the outcome of claims for benefits made. In case of lacking recommendation, the standard reaction to queries is to say that the application is still pending but that evasion may hold out for years. The problem is that the government does not acknowledge accountability for action taken to what are defined as outsiders, be they citizens or not. We have earlier pointed out that the large majority of disabled people, in particular, fail to qualify for benefits made available to them as part of the Social Security Bill. Our enquiries made at the local and sub-district level was often met with roundly denials that handicapped men, women or children could receive allowances for being deprived of their labour power. It was for this stout negation that we carried forms from the

District Social Defence Department with us to show to officials in lower or parallel echelons of the bureaucracy that such provisions were indeed statutory. There were a few exceptions to the dominant opinion that this sizable and extremely vulnerable category did not qualify for an allowance. One of them was the Prant Officer of Bardoli Taluka, who had taken the initiative to periodically organize in the territory under his jurisdiction camps for catering to the needs of BPL listed men, women and children with grave physical or mental disorders. One of the Accredited Social Health Activist (ASHA) in Bardoligam told us how some time ago she had gathered, with much difficulty from the landless colonies, an assortment of blind, polio-affected and deaf-mutes adults or children—bringing also the mentally retarded was beyond her power of persuasion—whom she had managed to get transported to the camp held in a village at some distance. There they would undergo medical examination in order to ascertain if their disabilities entitled them not only for equipment with aids and appliances to better handle their handicaps, but also classification on a scale of disorder. Those with an invalidity of more than 80 per cent may gain access to a regular disability allowance. On reaching the campsite, all who had come were made to wait for many hours, and ultimately had to leave without being attended to. As she was told later on, the doctors had failed to turn up. No further information followed and she does not know if a fresh effort would be made.

Such instances of miscommunication and failing coordination between various departments and agencies involved in the implementation of the Social Security Bill are anything but rare. Higher levels of authority have not remained completely unaware of the problems this creates, particularly for people at the receiving end, entrapped in a state of extreme vulnerability.

The Chief Minister of Gujarat himself has announced a scheme meant to improve the plight of the non-working poor. The welfare agencies have been instructed to arrange for camps at the sub-district level and present themselves there in order to facilitate the distribution of social benefits to the needy clientele in the villages around. Under the banner of *Garib Kalyan Mela*, this initiative is promoted with fervour in the regional newspapers and, in a short time, has become quite popular. Long before the event is going to take place, the local authorities are briefed to spread the word in the landless colonies and make sure that that the targeted beneficiaries are assembled and fetched to the Mela grounds. The idea is that the deserving cases are fixed on the spot, but that is difficult to realize because of the formalities which are required. It means that several files get duly prepared in advance, but that the successful applicants only come to know about their entitlements in the course of the festivity held. Narendra Modi is not shy to turn up himself on such occasions to read out the list of benefits granted. The impression created is that it is due to his benevolence and largesse that the non-working poor are blessed with endowments, even when the source of funding is not the state of Gujarat but the Central Government. Both in Bardoligam and Atulgam we met with a few men and women who had received their pension or allowance when a Mela was held nearby. But they also told us that they owed their windfall—because that was how they perceived their good fortune—to their own tedious efforts for many months, running around to collect all papers required rather than to the personal blessing of the man who has proclaimed himself as the saviour of all Gujaratis, until the very least and last of them.

COMING BACK TO WHERE WE HAD STARTED

We followed up to our investigations within the government apparatus by collecting data on the payments made to the recipients of benefits in the four villages of our fieldwork. This was done in order to check whether there was any discrepancy between the entitlements recorded in the official accounts and the cash the agents of the state were willing to hand out to the non-working poor. We collected the data from the Prant Officer at the district headquarters and verified whether the tally corresponded with the list kept by the Postmaster in Gandevigam, Chikhligam, Bardoligam and Atulgam. On it are the names of the beneficiaries, together with the amount due to them. It was not always easy to lay our hands on this information. Three of the postmasters were initially reluctant to allow us to write down the names and the one from Bardoligam insisted that no such list existed. He was only prepared to do the needful when we tackled him once again in the presence of his boss.

These records confirm that of all BPL households in the villages of our research, not even one out of six or seven qualify for social benefits yet, which should have been made available to them under the Social Security Bill. This implies that the large majority of the non-working poor are excluded from their legal dues. But more deprived from receiving entitlements than the old and aged and widows are the disabled, a substantial category who barely figure in the official statistics. The record is even more dismal than this because not all beneficiaries deserve to be included. In Gandevigam, one Anavil Brahmin and two Kolis receive old age pensions, although they are not listed in the BPL register; similar is the case in Atulgam, where two Anavil Brahmins are paid an old age pension. All said and done, however, wrongful exclusion is a much greater problem than incorrect inclusion. As we have pointed out before, the survey held in 2002–3 to identify vulnerable households ended up in denying many people from being classified as living below the poverty line. They are not necessarily less poor and less vulnerable than the recipients of benefits. This is not only our conclusion but also the opinion held in the landless milieu, and adds to the deep-felt sense of social injustice.

Our next comment concerns the lack of standardization in the remittances made. Although monthly allowances are provided, in three of the four villages they are transmitted every two months, and in Bardoligam village only once in three months. The interval between payments is long as well as irregular. The uneven flow of disbursements, further complicated by not combining the pensions paid by the state of Gujarat and those of the Central Government, sent in separate instalments for an amount of Rs 200 each, adds to the impression that the benefit comes as a favour which can be temporized at the discretion of the funding agency. The uncertainty created by the lack of regularity is compounded when no further money orders arrive. This may be because the household includes a son who has reached the age of 21, and is henceforth supposed to take care of his widowed mother or elderly parents between 60 to 65 years. But there are cases in which this rule is erroneously not adhered to; besides, from 65 years onwards the old age pension is independent of having an adult son or not. It is all very confusing, more so because the criteria for granting or withholding are beyond the comprehension of beneficiaries, resulting in an ambiguity that adds to the ample space for manoeuvre on the part of the bureaucrats responsible for the implementation.

Not all beneficiaries get the full amount of their entitlement because the Postmaster has to be given some commission when the clients come to encash the money order. The amount is not standard, and tends to be deducted in a haphazard manner from the full sum rather than as a gratuity voluntarily made by the recipient. More fraudulent seems to be the practice for settling the widow allowance. When granted a regular emolument (of Rs 500 per month plus Rs 80 for a child, with a maximum cap of two children), they are also allotted a financial account number in which the money is deposited monthly. Several widows, residents of different villages, told us that they had to hand over their passbook to the Postmaster instead of keeping it with them at home. When withdrawing money they were made to sign with their thumbprint. The Postmasters concerned told us that they needed the passbook for administrative reasons but their arguments were not very plausible, less so because the widows told us that they used to receive different amounts on each occasion. The corruption we came across may not be huge, but it is at the cost of very low budgets, where small amounts matter a lot.

The findings reported above lead us to conclude that the social benefits distributed by the government are in the nature of poor relief. What should have the character of a right gained in a process of empowerment has turned into a dole handed out in a haphazard fashion, with discretionary benevolence, and not on a scale adequate to provide a modicum of regularity, security and protection for people bereft from earning a livelihood. The schemes in operation do not address the magnitude, nor the intensity of misery found in the habitat where the non-working poor reside. According to the data provided by the local post office, the total number of 60 beneficiaries (consisting of old and aged, widows and only two handicapped) in the four sites of our local-level investigations are split up in a female–male ratio of 8 : 1. The main reason for the skewed distribution is the high mortality rate of men, not only at an advanced age, but also at an able working age. Death or disability at a fairly young age is often caused by hazardous and strenuous manual labour to which the unskilled workforce at the lower end of the rural economy is exposed. This also explains why widows of all ages are much more numerous than widowers. Men are more at risk than women to become vulnerable to premature loss of their labour power, resulting in increasing feminization at old age. There are not many couples in the landless colonies who have the good fortune to grow old together in reasonably good health; and even if there are, we have not come across a single case of both receiving an old age pension in the course of our fieldwork.

On what do the recipients of social benefits spend the cash allowance sent to them by money order? In most cases, it is spent on staple food, purchased at the local PDS shop. Some of them told us that they make use of their BPL card only every alternate month because they cannot afford to do it more frequently. The month they have to go without ration, their card is used by the household of a son or daughter who also live in the village. Often a large part of the money is set apart to buy prescribed medicines for the beneficiary or another member of the household. The problem which arises when the cost is higher than the budget tolerates is simply dealt with by not buying the medicines any longer. Men habituated to drinking liquor, which most of them do in order to escape from the misery of poverty and destitution, use their pension to buy their regular dose—a quarter a few times a week—with elderly women sometimes join in the indulgence. What else is there to do?

Well, actually a lot because the money received by way of benefit is certainly not enough to live on. The current level was fixed back in 2007, and prices have shot up since, reaching new heights during the last few years due to inflation. The paucity of cash among the non-working poor is such that although worn out and wasted in a cruel production process, they have to engage in economic activity to keep the body and soul somewhat intact. Women living alone with small children cannot afford to remain fully unemployed, although they have to hide what they earn when applying for a widow allowance. They cannot venture far from home but continue to work as casual agricultural labour, or become a maid in a landowning household. One woman told us that she went for domestic service, which does not yield much in terms of cash remuneration, because she could bring home the meal given to her at noon and share it with her small daughter, portioning it over two meals for both of them. Her story actually meant to convey the relief she felt when her application for a regular widow's allowance got sanctioned. For her it made the difference between far from enough and helpless to face adversities, to still not enough but make do. Ageing is an extensible concept. It basically means not voluntarily withdrawing into retirement but being told, sometimes brutally, that the labour power has become too weak for employability and does not stand up to the strength required to do a proper job. Then again, economic needs compel men and women at their old age, burdened with all kinds of ailments, to hang on and make themselves useful even for a pittance of a payment: the men grazing a few goats or cows, collecting firewood along the roadside, tending the standing crop and gleaning fields after the harvest; the women continuing as domestic maids and bringing back leftovers from the house of the boss, looking after babies and infants of neighbours or their own kin. It is common to take up chores in the nature of time pass, which are rewarded with mere scraps. Soliciting alms at temples, fairs and festivals, and begging house to house in villages are more exceptional, but not unheard of. Poverty pushes them to carry out all such tasks while keeping a low profile, afraid to become a burden to those who have the ability to work and are supposed to take care of the vulnerable in their midst. The worst affected are the elderly and single women living on their own, without any other source of income. They are somewhat better off as members of another household since the cash benefit they receive from the state, however meagre, may help to strengthen their bargaining position within that larger setting, redeeming them from their earlier status as free riders.

The neoliberal doctrine of self-reliance dictates that social security has to be provided by the poor themselves. It means making transfers from the working members of the households to the dependent ones. According to the World Bank, no public safety net is required because traditional solidarity mechanisms have remained intact and through their own efforts, people at the bottom of the economy manage to overcome adversities in their livelihood by levelling out spells of good and bad fortune. In the wake of the structural adjustment policy in the 1980s, which drastically ended the state's labour-friendly reforms, the Bank's World Development Report 1995 argued strongly against the introduction of public provisions to ease life somewhat for the most vulnerable categories:

> Financial help from relatives remains the principal form of income support and redistribution in developing countries. The extended family system is an important way of providing extra income and security to individual workers and their immediate household. Private transfers play an important insurance function in addition to reducing income inequality: they provide old age support and ameliorate the effects of disability, illness and unemployment. In most developing countries, especially in rural areas, older generations rely on the young to supplement their income. (World Bank 1995: 87)[5]

Solid evidence already available, pointing out the implausibility of this kind of wishful thinking was completely disregarded, in line with the standard practice of the World Bank to be very selective in substantiating its preconceived views. The Government of India has bought the hands-off credo with gusto. Not only has the Social Security Bill for the impoverished workforce in the informal economy taken a long time to be enacted, the way in which it has come about is also illustrative of the reluctance, if not outright aversion, with which the policy makers were forced to take the first few steps to tackle the social question, mainly for political reasons. Not motivated by an urge to empower the underprivileged, to make their lives decent and dignified, but more from the realization that any further delay in enactment would adversely affect the votes share required to remain in, or returning to, power. Restricting the benefits to BPL households and drastically cutting back the magnitude of this segment has been followed with instituting conditionality—such as age, length of residence, income and degree of infirmity—which exclude large numbers of poor and destitute people from at least somewhat mitigating the intensity of their misery.

Self-reliance is the motto with which the unproductive poor are encouraged to fend for themselves. For the old, aged and incapacitated with all kinds of ailments, this is clearly not an option, and they still do not qualify for an entitlement in case they have an adult son, who is responsible for looking after his parents. The assumption of filial support is not borne out by our findings in the colonies of the landless. As heads of their own households, men tend to default on the needs of their aging parents, particularly when living separately. Grown up daughters seem more prone to extend support and we have met married women who decided to return to their home village to take care of ageing parents, even at the cost of breaking up their own household. But generally economic and affective support related to filial piety seems to flow down to the next generation rather than up to the one before. The insistence on self-reliance also applies to widows. They may be entitled to an allowance, but only as long as they remain unable to earn their own livelihood. There is pressure on them to be trained in some craft, such as tailoring, and become an own-account worker, operating from home. Even the handicapped are expected to contemplate becoming micro-entrepreneurs. Those who are not certified with infirmities graded beyond 80 per cent—for instance those who are only missing one arm or leg—are referred to schemes under which they can be set up with a tea-stall or a cabin shop in their neighbourhood. If still able to walk around, they may be given a *larry* to set themselves up as street vendors. Of course, most handicapped are not equipped with any means to become petty businessmen, and even the few who are tend to fail miserably as self-employed. A Dhodia man from Chikhligam, who lost his leg in an accident while travelling to work, has found another escape. He has become a beggar at the Bilimora Railway Station. Once a week or fortnight he used to come home to hand over part of his earnings to his wife; but he stopped coming to the village when she died, and has now made vagrancy his life, cutting all ties with the village.

Of course, the vain efforts made by the government for the rehabilitation of the unproductive do not add up to much. They enable the authorities, however, to ward off most claims for entitlements under the pretext that the quest for social security and protection is best served if left to self-help. It basically means that even if not ensuring the welfare, at least the survival of the non-working poor is entrusted to the households sharing the same habitat with them, the working poor. The implicit notion is that in the countryside a fund of subsistence solidarity exists which motivates the coping poor to help the improvident segment in their milieu to keep going. Is that a fair and realistic proposition? Finding an answer requires us to comprehend the problem of destitution in the wider landscape inhabited by the rural proletariat. More pointedly, has the nature and level of poverty in the countryside of South Gujarat decreased in recent years? And if it has, does this upward trend manifest itself in a better spread of welfare all around, a slow but steady improvement in life standards for the lower classes which so far have lagged behind in the process of economic growth? In short, how do we understand the dynamics of poverty in the villages of our fieldwork?

PUBLIC WORKS

In the combat against poverty, schemes to reduce the vulnerability of the targeted population have to be accompanied by a variety of interventions. Employment generation, which helps to ease the problem of lack of adequate earnings on the income side, is of major importance in such a multi-pronged approach. Unfortunately taking care of the underutilization of labour at the bottom of the economy has only been understood as the execution of rural public works. As a matter of fact one can think of a wide range of public sector jobs which would make life for the underprivileged more decent and dignified. However, the Government of India has at long last decided to introduce a nation-wide programme to tackle the huge labour surplus in rural areas by the execution of public works. In Gujarat, the National Rural Employment Guarantee Scheme (NREGS) has become operative only a few years ago, somewhat later than in most other states. What has been the impact so far? In the margin of our investigations on the provision of social benefits, we have also collected data in the four villages of our fieldwork and enquired whether projects had been carried out and who benefited from participating in these works. We verified the information gathered in the localities by meeting staff in charge of this operation in the sub-district and districts offices. A wide range of officials are responsible for checking whether the proposals received from the Village Panchayats comply with the directives and the manual of instructions. In the final stage, the work done is sanctioned for payment by them. Our conclusion is that what is put on record as a successful programme deserves blame rather than praise, and is a far cry from the ground reality. The way in which the official administration is concocted boils down to fabrication of falsified information.

In order to substantiate this verdict, we shall report first on the absence of NREGS in three of the four localities under investigation. The job cards which should have been issued, required for registration at the work site, were never distributed. Only in Chikhligam was one country road found to have been built in 2009 under the NREGA banner, and the Village Head told us that more are to follow in the years to come. Why not in the other three villages? The answer invariably given to our local enquiries was that in view of the ample availability of work in the region there was no compelling need for generating more employment. That explanation has some validity in the case of Atulgam, where the larger part of the village workforce has access to employment outside the village and only a residual segment remains engaged in agricultural labour, which is to a large extent seasonal in nature. Commuters going off to urban-industrial sites nearby would not be tempted to go back to navvy work at Rs 100 a day. The Village Head of Gandevigam did not refer to a lack of interest for not initiating NREGA projects, but stated that there was no public land anymore in the locality which could qualify for infrastructural upgrading. According to him there is no further need for country roads, neither are there village ponds around which need to be cleaned or deepened. His is not a persuasive comment since the country road built in Chikhligam is on the land of the biggest landowner in the village, and has been constructed for no other reason than to make one of his orchards more easily accessible. In view of the huge underemployment we found in Bardoligam, the landless households in the village would be definitely interested in taking part in public works. According to our informants this does not materialize because the *Kanbi Patidars*, the dominant caste of landowners, do not tolerate any such interference in what they consider to be their domain. The District Development Officer we subsequently met told us that NREGA was being fully implemented in the area under his jurisdiction. When we asked for more details regarding the subdistrict in which Bardoligam is located, he had to concede on second thought that this applied only to four villages out of 86. No indeed, also not in Bardoligam. Why not? He gave the standard reply, which is that given the huge demand for labour in agriculture, for growing and harvesting sugarcane in particular, there is no need to start public works. In reaction to my comment that only migrants from far away can be found in the cane fields, and that their presence adds to the underemployment of the labourers born and bred in the region, this Senior District Official insisted that the influx of all these outsiders had to be attributed to the local landless deserting their traditional occupation. According to him the speed with which the rural underclass moves out of agriculture shows that employment in the region is abundantly available and, thus, no public works are required. The two Managing Directors of the Bardoli Cooperative Sugar Mill happened to be more forthright when we discussed with them the non-implementation of NREGA in the central plain of South Gujarat as well as in the hinterland from which the army of seasonal migrants hail. If these labour nomads would find enough employment in their home villages, they might decide to opt out of the brutal work regime which awaits them for the duration of the harvesting campaign, from end October until the end of May.

Halpatis—the caste which, as no other, is characterized by their landlessness—seem to have been excluded from involvement in NREGA projects throughout South Gujarat. In Chikhligam, the only village of our fieldwork research in which the name of the public programme rings a bell in some of the neighbourhoods, the labour gang recruited for laying the country road consisted only of Dhodia men and women. Why were no Halpatis allowed to participate? The Village Head, also a Dhodia, maintained that they showed no interest since they are engaged to Anavil landowners as farm servants. A factual misrepresentation, since we could on the spot give the names of households belonging to this tribal caste and earning their livelihood as daily wage earners roaming around inside and outside the village. Then another argument came up. Halpatis, as we were told, are only willing to work if they are paid at the end of the day and refuse to wait for wage settlement until later, as is standing NREGA prescription. The practice of instant pay cannot be denied but it stems from the cash need to buy commodities for the evening meal. The explanation given is a different one that the improvidence of these people said to be unable to balance income and expenditure beyond the span of a day. Behind the implied suggestion of financial mismanagement other reproaches are concealed—such as a lack of foresight, the total inability to save up for a rainy day. It is a stereotype which suggests that thrift and sobriety are alien to Halpatis, a judgment that finds support in the ease with which a sizable part of their earnings are spent in addiction to drinking liquor and chewing *gutka* (tobacco). These vices are said, by those who vent them, to be compounded by other negative traits such as an ingrained unwillingness to hard-working, bordering on indolence. The regrettable consequence is that what should be a solid eight-hour working day is half spent in idleness. Such an inadequate output should, so our high-caste informants claimed, certainly and righteously allow for payment of half of the minimum legal wage. Even Rs 50 a day is considered to be more than enough for the work done. The outright refusal to provide work to the landless and to pay them an amount required to keep their labour power valid is, in that line of argument, turned around to the charge that these pauperized proletarians are afflicted with defects for which they themselves are to blame. The case of the Halpatis belonging to the category of the non-deserving poor can be fabricated with other examples as well; for instance their mismanagement of micro-credit loans. The staff of the community health wing of a local hospital told us that out of 107 Self Help Groups (SHGs) set up in the surrounding villages, all 26 which consisted of Halpati members had failed. The explanation given was not their total absence of property, which excluded them from most forms of self-employment, but the urge ascribed to them to spend immediately whatever cash they get in hand. These people simply lack the habit to save, we were told. A high ranking bureaucrat, the District Development Officer of Surat, succinctly summed up of all that is wrong with the Halpatis: they are genetically defective. He made that statement towards the end of our conversation with him in which he had laid out the arguments one by one, all of them fake, why in Bardoligam NREGA projects are neither being planned nor executed.

Do the no-go sign to public works in most villages of South Gujarat mean that the budget made available for this programme is not spent? Absolutely not, as we found out when we contacted monitors commissioned to collect data on the implementation of the programme. It so happens that our research sites were situated in districts for which social auditors had been engaged by a Non-government Organization (NGO) in Ahmedabad, to find out how projects are initiated and executed. In our conversations with them, we were able to verify what we had been told by the staff of departments at the sub-district and district level responsible for getting the work started and completed. These officials used to be full of praise for the enthusiasm with which the rural proletariat had shown their readiness in making their labour power available for building country roads, digging ponds, making bore wells, levelling land, constructing check dams for minor irrigation purposes, etc. The District Development Officer of Navsari spoke to us about a veritable Green Revolution taking place in the zone of dry land on the eastern side of the district where, due to the large number of bore wells that were dug, the amount of arable land in many villages had expanded to the great and lasting benefit of both farmers and labourers. In short, a success story which he invited us to go and see with our own eyes.

These are all local initiatives for which prior approval of the Village Council is required. In the next stage, the projects proposed are assessed by officials on their technical merits, logistical format and financial feasibility. In the budget made, the quantity and cost of manpower is calculated for executing the project, and with authorization from officials at the district headquarters the Village Head is given the green signal to proceed. He assembles one or more work gangs which are supervised by a Mate. This is an educated young man who handles the administration—stamp job cards brought by the workers; keep a muster roll for daily attendance; measure the work done by each gang member and write down the payment to be made for it. A petty Engineer from the sub-district office checks on the progress made and collects the work-lists maintained by the Mate. The project administration report is sent to the district headquarters for sanctioning and should result in payment of the wages earned within a fortnight. The amount is deposited in a bank account which is opened for each card holder. The procedure sketched follows the official manual in minute detail. The impression created is that of a waterproof and fail-safe scenario, one with the greatest possible public transparency—with every project detail being accessible online, from beginning to end—with the strictest adherence to a bottom-up procedure, founded on the close and cordial collaboration of government, local authorities and the labouring beneficiaries.

This whole construction of the role of NREGS is a façade, a make-belief kind of theatre in South Gujarat, a pretence which is not difficult to deny. The discrepancy between official fancy and down-to-earth fact is borne out by the findings of the social auditors. A telling detail is that from a total of 81 projects reported by the authorities to have been successfully completed in the sub-district of Chikhli, the large majority (64) existed only on paper, although the budget for all of them was spent, sometimes even overspent. Local dignitaries either tried to threaten or bribe the social auditors to submit favourable progress reports, covering up the fraudulent practices. The abuses were manifold. The smaller corruption concerns the Village Headman and Mate, who only admit those labourers to the project who they themselves have selected. It means non-compliance with the right of participation, which should be enjoyed by all who are eager to work. Instead of issuing job cards to each and every household entitled to have it, the practice is not to distribute them. The Sarpanch is able to recruit any number of labourers at short notice. As local powermongers, many of them have a booming business as petty contractors. In collusion with the inspecting official who comes around to check on the project, much more work is reported than is actually carried out. And finally, direct payment in cash is given to labourers at the wage rate of Rs 50, but their thumb print is taken on the muster roll and the full amount of Rs 100 per day is pocketed, to be deposited in their account later on. By appropriating the pass books, or by not bothering to issue them individually, the Village Headman collects the remittance himself, a practice condoned by bank clerks or the postmaster in the village, for a price of course. That embezzlement remains unnoticed because the earnings made while working on the project are paid out not within a fortnight, as should be done according to the regulations, but after several months. As mentioned earlier, all these abuses fall in the range of petty fraudulent and corruptive practices. Much larger in scale is the swindle practiced by the departmental staff of the sub-district and district headquarters in collusion with many other stakeholders. This would largely explain the glee with which one of these officials told us about his full-time involvement in NREGA. Every day he travels a distance of 200 kms on his motorbike to visit project sites. The hectic schedule he keeps does not diminish his eagerness in the heavy workload he and his colleagues are burdened with—'we enjoy this programme like anything.'

> The social auditor commissioned to check the NREGS administration in Gandevi Taluka found that in one of the villages, gangs of Halpatis had been engaged for a project. He took their names from the muster rolls and went to meet them to come to know if the wages had been paid on time. It then came out that none of them had been called even for a single day and that the project only existed on paper. A copy of his report saying so went also to the TDO (Taluka Development Officer). This official, in charge of NREGA, first tried to threaten the social auditor, and then offered a bribe of Rs 15,000 which he refused to accept. The NGO which had engaged him sent all his progress reports to the Secretary, Rural Labour, in Gandhinagar. No action has been taken and the NGO has recently been informed that the contract for monitoring NREGA will not be renewed. (From author's fieldwork notes, 2010–11)

The fraud which we slowly came to know about in the course of our fieldwork, and the racket to which the social auditors had alerted us, was vindicated in a series of shocking reports published in the regional edition of *Diviya Bhaskar*, a leading newspaper in Gujarat, between end November and early December 2010. Bureaucrats, Bank Officials, Postmasters, Village Headmen and District Politicians had all teamed up to profit from a scam going on in the name of public works.

The record of NREGA is not only a dismal one in Gujarat but also in many other states, particularly in the Gangetic plain in the north. What has gone wrong? The design of this nation-wide public works programme rests on the assumption of a democratic framework at the local level. The village council is, in this line of thinking, the authority which mandates the infrastructural projects—construction of country roads, digging of bore wells, land levelling, check dams, etc.—selected for execution. The stakeholders, including all those who have no other resources than their labour power, are supposed to participate in the decision making process. A second misconception is the idea of a district and sub-district bureaucracy, which is committed to the public cause rather than to rent seeking behaviour of the officials in charge. Both assumptions are only correct in instances where the land-poor and landless have managed to build up political and social countervailing power in a sufficient quantity, to make their presence felt and see their interests attended to. These preconditions are not met in the case of Gujarat, nor in many other parts of the country.

DIFFERENTIAL DYNAMICS IN THE RANKS OF THE RURAL PROLETARIAT

Among the rural proletariat some segments are better off than others, and the more successful ones, although a smaller contingent, seem to have a higher visibility than the numerous lagging behind. The worst off are, of course, the households with no or hardly any labour power. Even when the disabled belong to other households with working members, their presence weighs heavily on the available budget, but they do share whatever is available, albeit often not proportionately. The destitution of the elderly (who have to maintain themselves) and of single women (living on their own) is visible for all to see. Even more vulnerable are the handicapped, not only because they require to be fed, but also because they have to be taken care of by other household members. At this point it is important to highlight that the stringent criteria which the government applies for acknowledging vulnerability enormously understates the volume of men, women and children who are in desperate in need of external support. In the milieu of the poor growing old starts already from 45 years onwards. The physical constraints of stoop labour or of hazardous work in industry, together with an inadequate diet and poor sanitation and hygiene have a debilitating impact, which disqualify these people from continuing to earn an income long before they turn 60. Striking also is the number of the decrepit and chronically ill individuals in their middle-age, who have lost the ability to move around on their own, leave alone to go for waged work. With an invalidity of even more than

80 per cent, they still do not qualify for any entitlements. Their never abating health problems find no redress and also home they may be accused of malingering, let alone that the medical authorities would take cognisance of such cases. Mental disorders remain unattended to, and in one of the landless colonies of Bardoligam we came across a young man tied to a pole and being beaten with a broom, clearly in a psychotic state. Such cases find some relief when they are seen by a *bhagat* or by a woman officiating as *devi*, to drive out the evil spirit. Going through our field notes we estimate that the non-labouring poor, condemned to living as paupers, constitute at least one-fifth of the rural proletariat in South Gujarat.

On the opposite polar end is the segment of the rural proletariat, in our estimate about one-quarter of all inhabitants of the land-poor and landless colonies, who have found access to informal sector jobs somewhat more skilled, and on conditions of employment a bit more decent, with the result that the household to which they contribute dispose of a budget around Rs 6,000 a month, or roughly Rs 1,250 per capita, for their upkeep. It is an amount which starts to set them free from an existence structured by acute and stark insecurity. The defining features of households thus privileged are a more steady flow of cash income and expenditure, a greater regularity in the daily rhythm of activity, protection against adversity not only based on actual savings made but also because of a higher credit rating, prior planning for life cycle events, investment in post-secondary education for the next generation, and in general a lifestyle showing greater providence. All the more fortunate are the happy few able to bring home earnings of Rs 10,000 a month or more, such as a Halpati who, certified with an ITI Diploma, has become Factory Supervisor, an experienced Diamond-Cutter-cum-Polisher, a petty contractor, or the most fortunate being those employed in a formal sector job, even as a peon. What stood out in our conversations with this advance guard was not only the quality of perseverance which helped them to overcome all obstacles on the long and winding trajectory accomplished, but also *olkhan* they received from higher up. The landowning castes have lost the local dominance which they used to exercise in the past.[6] But their social capital at the district level is beyond dispute and a source of recommendation which is solicited when deserving cases from further down the social ladder want to persuade employers with their credentials. It is also a fact that those who have become upwardly mobile, with only few exceptions, have not abandoned their rural habitat, but remain firmly embedded in their milieu of origin.

How do we rank the land-poor and landless that belong to the workforce and contrive to live on the sale of their labour power? The large majority of them, half or approximately that figure, have to be classified as the labouring poor. A substantial part of them continue to remain engaged in agriculture and are predominantly employed as daily wage earners. The number of working days and the income their activity yields clearly indicate that their life is one of unrelenting poverty. A growing segment, mainly consisting of the younger age sections, has managed to find non-agrarian jobs, usually outside the village. The defining features are lack the skills as well as the contacts to qualify for any other work than in the lower echelons of the informal economy in which low wages, long hours of work, lack of social provisions, absence of labour rights, frequent rotation around a variety of work sites and no upward mobility. They may have succeeded in getting redeemed from the sweat and toil of agricultural labour, but not from a life of poverty. Of course, those who stay on, working in the fields and the ones who have opted out of agriculture and the village do not constitute segments living in separation from each other. They tend to belong to the same household, the older and younger members, who may respectively be employed inside and outside agriculture; but their joint earnings—adding up to a disposable and consolidated household income amounting to about Rs 5,000 per month—attest to their sustained subsistence in deprivation. The following sketch, with which I ended my village study carried out between 2004 and 2006, pertains to the work and life of this majority among the rural proletariat:

> A reserve army of labour has accumulated in Rural South Gujarat, which can be deployed according to the demand of the moment, in or outside agriculture, in factories and workshops, in construction and the service sector, or to transport goods and people. These working men, women, and children, are sometimes needed in the towns and sometimes in the countryside. Sometimes they are put to work in the obscure and degraded landscape in between these two extremes: alongside the highways and railway lines, in agro-industrial enclaves, brick kilns, quarries, and saltpans, gathered together in temporary camps that arise where rivers are dammed, where earth has to be moved to dig canals or lay pipelines, where roads have to be laid or bridges and viaducts built, and so on. They live and work at these sites for as long as

the job lasts. The rest of the time they are confined in slum-like, sprawling settlements on the fringes of villages, squatting with no legal title, waiting for the next call to leave on another project. If the work is relatively close to home, they commute back and forth each day; if it is farther afield, they stay away longer, sometimes for whole seasons. But sooner or later the work is completed again and they return to their waiting-room that lies beyond the purview of politicians and policy-makers. Yet the fact that these people are hidden away from mainstream society in colonies and transit camps is no reason to label them as peripheral or marginal. They are an army of reserve labour that is at the heart of the predatory capitalism which emerged so virulently on the subcontinent of South Asia in the second half of the 20th century. (Breman 2007: 409)

My contention is that this profile written five years ago has not lost its validity.

It would be misconceived to assume that the differentiation made above within the ranks of the rural proletariat—the paupers (20 per cent), the somewhat better-off (20–25 per cent) and in between the labouring poor (55–60 per cent)—have crystallized into distinct sub-classes. The condition also of those who have leaped ahead is still too fragile to take for granted that the progress made is going to be consolidated in the next generation. All said and done, the rural proletariat constitute a reserve army of labour, partly inside and partly outside agriculture, hired and fired according to the need of the moment, and conditioned to a life which, for the large majority of them, is passed in excessive poverty.

Should that conclusion not be qualified by pointing out that in due course the trend also in South Gujarat is for non-agrarian employment to increase? After all, the starkest deprivation that we have found is of the workforce remaining behind in an agricultural economy that goes on to be ridden by a huge labour supply for which there is no steady demand, an imbalance which is further aggravated by a seasonal influx of footloose nomads circulating between the hinterland and plain. Is there hope for ever-more employment in the secondary and tertiary sectors of the economy for the masses pushed out of agriculture and the countryside? Among the younger generation from the land-poor or landless class in the four villages of our fieldwork, many commute to work sites away from home, mainly as low-skilled and low-paid labour in industry, transport, construction or the service sector. Their number may further increase and their wages may go up; but is that a somewhat optimistic prediction—optimistic since we do no comment on the horrendous terms and conditions of employment—borne out by factual evidence?

What finally needs to be emphasized is that while non-agrarian employment has steadily expanded, the rural landless have not departed from their colonies in the villages. In the four localities of fieldwork, only a tiny fraction of land-poor households more than landless ones opted to resettle in a town or city. The reason for staying put is, no doubt, the uncertainty of regular and secure employment in the bottom ranks of the urban economy. An additional hurdle is the high cost of urban housing and livelihood in general, together with the outright refusal by employers to pay a family wage which includes maintenance cost of dependents. Omitting payment of an allowance to provide for non-working members of the household to come along means that departure from the village becomes an option only when the budgetary capacity for changing the place of residence from rural to urban is ensured. Such cases are a rare exception in the habitat of the rural proletariat in South Gujarat. Labour goes off but also has to come back from where it is abundantly available, in the countryside. In addition to crowding, there is another danger looming large in the vast informal sector, which is switching to a less labour intensive mode of production. The booming of economic activity beyond regulation and control by the state is, as has been our argument, the consequence of a growth strategy based on keeping the cost of labour down to the lowest possible level. But what if owners of capital decide that the hunt for the reserve army, the constant hire and fire operation, the threat that these nomads change from a posture of docility to one of restiveness becomes a nuisance, which can no longer be tolerated? The management of Bardoli's Agro-Industry is pondering not whether, but when, to bring the combined harvesters to the cane fields and get rid of the seasonal migrants brought in from faraway. The Diamond-Cutting-and-Polishing Industry in Surat was badly affected when the Global Recession hit the city in 2008–9. The workforce clamoured for compensation and benefits which the atelier owners refused to provide. However, they reacted to this claim by speeding up the drive towards automation which was already going on (Hirway, 2009).[7] And when we left Bardoligam at the end of our fieldwork in February 2011, landless men from the village, employed in the textile industry which has come up in the township of Jolwa (along the road from Bardoli to Surat) told us about a strike going on in the power looms. Although they do not have the skills to be engaged as operators, they were also laid off until production could be restored. In the preceding months the same had happened in the Surat metropolis and industrial peace had not yet come back to the city. Once strikes were over—when the request was met for some hike in the piece rate to compensate for sky-rocketing food prices—they soon flared up again. An interesting phenomenon was that the signal to stop the looms and leave the worksite was not organized, but spread like wildfire. The industrialists frantically sought out the strike leaders, in order to reach a compromise that would be binding for all workshops, but these perpetrators could not be identified. The captains of business gave press conferences in which they vented grievances about the lack of pliability of the workforce consisting of out-of-state migrants, but also raised an alarm about the dwindling volume of new generations of these footloose workers from Odisha and Andhra Pradesh making their appearance. Why have they stopped coming? Is it because of infrastructural development in their home states, providing employment in construction work which was not available before or is it because NREGA has become a better alternative? Or is it because these labour nomads have grown tired of becoming worn out in a work regime cruel beyond sufferance? Whatever the cause of sabotage may be, the statements made indicate that the owners of capital in South Gujarat consider mechanization to be the way to fix the problem of consolidating and further expanding production. The likely consequence will be that what has been a huge reserve army so far will retrogress into an army increasingly made redundant.

Going back to the main theme of our fieldwork-based research, the urgent need for adequate and effective poor relief, our conclusion for the immediate future is that banking on the solidarity between the people with and without labour power is not a feasible proposition. Self-reliance cannot be the organizing principle for providing social security and protection at the bottom of the rural economy, especially when the working poor barely succeed to take care of their own basic needs, leave alone holding them accountable for looking after the non-working segment of the old and aged, single females and handicapped in their midst. Leaving the indictment of failing support to people without the wherewithal to be self-reliant is a policy of immorality. The question is not one of solidarity but of carrying capacity. To at least alleviate the misery in which both the non-working and working poor are entrapped in South Gujarat, the state has to be more forthcoming and forceful in extending social benefits and in generating public employment than it has been. But, is the state willing to do that and change the policy from exclusion to one of inclusion?

Notes

[1] For what led up to this event and on what happened in the aftermath, see Breman 2007: 167–71.

[2] In June 2011, the Central Government decided to lower the pensionable age to 60 years, which meant a doubling of the old age allowance for all men and women from 60 instead of 65 years onwards.

[3] In the same publication, I have elaborated on the problems the landless poor in Bardoligam face in holding on to their BPL card (Breman 2007: 351–3).

[4] For more details, refer to Breman (2007).

[5] For a more extensive critique of this policy document, please refer to the essay 'Labour Get Lost: A Late-Capitalist Manifesto' in Breman 2003.

[6] For more details, refer to Breman (1974, 1985, and 2007).

[7] For more details, refer to Hirway (2009).

References

Breman, J. 1974. *Patronage and Exploitation: Changing Agrarian Relations in South Gujarat, India*. Berkeley: University of California Press.

———. 1985. *Of Peasants, Migrants and Paupers: Rural Labour Circulation and Capitalist Production in West India*. London: Clarendon Press.

———. 2003. *The Labouring Poor in India: Patterns of Exploitation and Exclusion*. New Delhi: Oxford University Press.

———. 2007. *The Poverty Regime in Village India*. New Delhi: Oxford University Press.

Hirway, I. 2009. *Losing the Sparkle; Impact of the Global Crisis on the Diamond Cutting and Polishing Industry in India*, Discussion Paper, Lasting Solutions for Development Challenges. New Delhi: UNDP.

World Bank. 1995. *Workers in an Integrating World*, World Development Report. New York: Oxford University Press.

8 SOCIAL SECURITY FOR THE URBAN POOR

A STUDY IN GUJARAT

Darshini Mahadevia[1]

Social security literature in India largely focuses on the rural areas, primarily on account of the fact that 70 per cent[2] of the 1.2 billion still live there. Nonetheless, an estimated 377 million of the nation's population live in urban areas, of which 95 million would be BPL, taking the proportion of incidence of urban poverty officially estimated in 2004–5. Therefore, the urban residents are by no means in small numbers, although in 2011, just 31.8 per cent of the national population lived in urban areas. There is also an assumption that an average urban resident is richer than an average rural resident, again judged by the fact that the incidence of poverty in urban areas is lower than in rural areas. However, urban areas pose complex problems of delivering social security schemes, largely on account of continuous population influx into the cities. The rural-to-urban migration is an inherent part of the economic growth process, and hence delivery of social security schemes has to take into account the continuous migrant streams to urban areas. This paper brings to the fore these dynamics of urbanization in a high-growth and highly urbanized State of Gujarat on the basis of a study conducted in Ahmedabad city.

The methodology for research in this paper uses secondary data of the schemes, and their overall implementation from the government sources. The data was collected from the websites of the relevant organizations, as the records were not accessible at the concerned government organizations. The assessment of availability of social security schemes among the long-term migrants and urban poor is through primary surveys in the slums in Ahmedabad city alone, although the paper also dwells with overall urban Gujarat. Data were collected from 200 households in two wards of Ahmedabad, Odhav (industrial ward) and Sabarmati (low and middle income ward). These settlements were revisited after a year for focused group discussions (FGDs), to assess functioning of the Rashtriya Swasthya Bima Yojana (RSBY). Thereafter, case studies of seasonal workers were carried out through discussions with the brick kiln workers. The short-term migrants are tribal workers in the construction field. Their case studies have also been done from construction sites on the city's periphery. The data for the other construction workers were collected from four different types of construction sites in Ahmedabad.

HIGH GROWTH WITH HIGH DEPRIVATION

Gujarat is the fourth most urbanized state in India, with an urbanization level of close to 43 per cent in 2011; Tamil Nadu leads the tally at 48.5 per cent, followed by Kerala at 48 per cent and Maharashtra at 45 per cent in 2011 (Census of India, 2011).

Gujarat is among the fastest growing economies of the country, surpassing the national average for almost three decades. India has registered a high economic growth rate from 2004–05 almost up to 2009–10, the average rate being 8.4 per cent per annum. During this period, the average annual growth rate in Gujarat had been 10.1 per cent. That being said, Gujarat's economy is imbalanced and this is the first major issue in the state's development path. It has a very large presence of informal sector workers; 72.8 per cent in 2004–5 (NSSO 2007: 80). As per the Planning Commission's estimates of poverty (following a revised poverty line), Gujarat had 9.16 million poor people in rural areas (26.7 per cent of total population) and 4.5 million poor people in urban areas (17.9 per cent of total population) as in 2009–10.[3]

In the first human development report of the State (Hirway and Mahadevia, 2005), it was observed that (i) the agricultural sector, that employed half the population, had stagnated since early 1980s;[4] (ii) large parts of the state were drought prone; (iii) there was high urban-rural inequality; (iv) the state lagged behind in human and gender development, ranking 6th among the 15 large states of India in the human development index (HDI) and gender development index (GDI) in 2001.[5] Since 2001 however, the state's standing in health indicators, particularly regarding infant and child health, has deteriorated.[6] The hunger index in the state is alarming, ranking 13th among the 17 large states of India (Menon *et al.*, 2009). The 2011 National Human Development Report of India (Institute of Applied

Manpower Research and Planning Commission 2011) puts the state's rank in HDI at 11 among 23 states as compared to 10 in 2002 (Planning Commission, 2002). Gujarat's poor HDI ranking is on account of its poor performance in the health sector. In particular, it has a poor record in terms of functioning of the public health facilities; as a result, just 54.7 per cent children in urban and 40.1 per cent children in rural Gujarat have been vaccinated, as against 57.6 per cent and 38.6 per cent respectively in India in 2005–06 (Institute of Applied Manpower Research and Planning Commission 2011: 307). This is the state's context within which the implementation of the RSBY, and Construction Workers' Welfare Board's functioning is assessed.

URBAN CITIZENSHIP

Access to Social Security or Lack of It

Urban citizenship is a complex notion. It is attained through numerous ways, and there are levels of citizenship rights in a city. A legal address is the most acceptable way of attaining urban citizenship. A legal address is the one which is obtained when the premises in which the household is living has legal land title and development clearances from the planning agency. A household wanting to have legal right to a land needs to have the land registered in the name of at least one of the household members. Then, the development on the land needs to be approved by the planning authority. Generally, the urban poor and new migrants to the cities do not have legal identity and hence, access to urban citizenship is denied through residential security. Half or even more of the urban residents live in such conditions in the cities of India, as well as in Gujarat.

The urban poor do not get access to the legal space in the cities. Instead they begin their urban life by squatting on vacant land, which is either government land, or where the squatting is invited by private land owners.[7] They may also share a house with their relatives and friends from back home and pay rent to them. In the absence of citizenship status, through shelter security and land rights, they attain rights through the processes of electoral democracy. The initial settlements of the poor, called squatter settlements, are allowed because they have some political patronage, or are accepted by the local authority because there are no other options for housing the poor. But such informal settlements expand. A sizeable size of such settlement attracts the attention of the local politicians who strive to get the residents as their vote banks and get them electoral voter cards or voter identity (ID) cards. The larger the settlement the higher is its value as a vote-bank, and hence higher is their security against eviction and chances of getting ID cards. This card has a photograph of the individual and residential address, even though the housing may be illegal. The households then make arrangements to get a ration card using this card, which carries the names of all the members of the household. Political leaders, time and again, take up the cudgels to legalize the slum dwellers.

The local government if financially sound, which has been the case in the cities of Gujarat including Ahmedabad, extends basic services such as water supply, sewerage and storm water drains, roads and street lights to the settlements. Individual households can get electricity connection independently. In Ahmedabad, a private electricity company, Torrent Power, supplies power to the slum household on payment of a token amount (Mahadevia *et al.*, 2010a). Each such household gets an electricity bill, which carries its address. These households thus perceive a sense of security against demolition. This is called *de facto* tenure security status. Ultimately, slum settlements get legal status by acquiring land *pattas*[8] from the local government. However, this is possible only for slums on government land, where there is a legislation to give *pattas*.[9]

Lastly, there is the concept of cut-off date, which is announced from time to time for coverage under different subsidized government programmes. The cut-off dates are largely used for subsidized housing schemes, for which eligible households have to be identified. A cut-off date means that the households who can prove their residency in a city before such a date, would be considered eligible for the benefits under the scheme. The state announced Regulations for the Rehabilitation and Redevelopment of the Slums (2010) in March 2010, wherein, the beneficiary had to meet the following criteria (i) one who is 'not a foreign national, (ii) is the occupant of a hutment for a period of minimum 10 years, and (iii) has a domicile of Gujarat for 25 years or his descendant.'[10] For proof of occupancy, any two of the following documents were required (i) copy of ration card; (ii) copy of electricity bills; (iii) proof of being included in the electoral rolls; and (iv) any other proof as decided by the prescribed authority.[11] The key point here is a domicile of 25 years, which is a cut-off date of 1985. In Delhi, the cut-off date was 1998.

The processes discussed above illustrate how the new migrants to Ahmedabad city obtain their identity as an urban citizen, and then access various levels of identities so that they become eligible for social security and assistance schemes. All the current social security and assistance schemes are linked to a ration card in the BPL category, which is accessed as the last among the various ID proofs that they acquire. The first to be obtained is the election card, then follow other residential address proofs, and finally a BPL card for the urban poor household, as illustrated in Figure 8.1.

This process can be short-circuited by intervention of local politicians. In Ganeshnagar, an informal housing settlement in Odhav industrial area of Ahmedabad, we found that nearly all the residents had registered themselves as BPL households. Prior to the last municipal corporation elections, a booth was set up near their colony for registration as BPL households. The households had to give proof of their residence in this colony and they gave electricity bills for the purpose. Now, electricity connection is taken by only those who have some settled life in the city. The households residing in Ganeshnagar are migrants, but have been living in the city for more than 10 years. They were able to

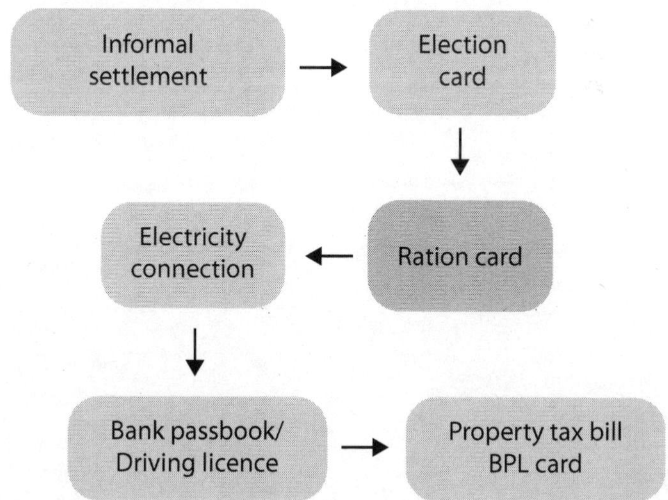

FIGURE 8.1 Process of Getting Eligibility for a Social Security Scheme

Source: Author.

get electricity connection, but not a ration card. They were also required to furnish their income certificate, which they obtained from their local councillor. All of them, therefore, got registered as BPL households. Their names are now in the BPL list. Ironically, the household has to be better endowed to access a BPL card.

The moot question is whether the project of Unique Identity Card (UID) would extend urban citizenship to the new migrants and the poor, who are disempowered and would have to go through the above mentioned process to obtain an identity, and then a citizenship in the city? The answer is obviously no. The UID process is asking the applicants to present a proof of their residence before registering them and providing a card. How can the UID card give identity to the urban poor, and in particular the migrants among them, if it is tied to existing identity proofs, procurement of which has been discussed at length in this section. It is erroneous to assume that the UID card would be better than the BPL card, as there would be as many problems and loopholes in the issuance of the former, as it is with the issuance of the latter. The urban systems are inherently biased against the poor and the migrants among them, to extend citizenship to the latter.

Possession of Various ID Proofs by Slum Residents

In our surveys in Ahmedabad and Surat, we found a very low proportion of households possessing BPL cards. In Amraiwadi ward, in the industrial part of Ahmedabad, only 14 per cent households had a ration card and 1 per cent a BPL card (Table 8.1), while in a middle

Table 8.1 Percentage Households Holding Different Identity Cards, Ahmedabad and Surat

Location	*Ration Card*	*BPL Card*	*Election Card*
Amraiwadi, Ahmedabad*	13.9	1.1	17.0
Vasna, Ahmedabad**	81.5	19.3	92.3
Surat***	56.8	10.1	82.4

Sources:

*Mahadevia *et al.* (2010b).

**Mahadevia *et al.* (2010a).

***Extracted from primary data by the author.

class ward of Vasna, 81.5 per cent households had a ration card, 19.3 per cent a BPL card, and 92.3 per cent an election card. In Surat, only 56.8 per cent had a ration card and 10.1 per cent a BPL card. Availability of even ration cards in the industrial ward of Amraiwadi and industrial city of Surat is low, probably on account of a large migrant population. But, this table also shows that in the other two locales, one member of the family has an election card. In other words, it is easier to get an election card. Vasna ward, in west Ahmedabad, had the intervention by NGOs in four of the six surveyed slums for either slum development or micro finance (Mahadevia *et al.*, 2010a), increasing the access to ration card at least, if not to BPL card.

The BPL cards are issued by the district administration. But, the BPL survey is undertaken by the Ahmedabad Municipal Corporation (AMC) and the Urban Local Body (ULB). The AMC undertook the BPL survey in December 2008. Then objections were invited and list correction process was undertaken.

When we first went for our survey in nine slums and *chalis* in two wards of the city, the BPL list was available on the AMC website. In fact, we used this data to select the urban poor settlements for our survey. There was a big time-lag between the survey and issuance of BPL cards. When we visited the research locales in early 2011, none of the listed household had received a BPL card. In the second visit after a year, they had received the cards. A total of 163 of the 200 households surveyed in early 2011 possessed ration cards and another 23 BPL cards (Table 8.2). About 185 had electricity connections and 190 had voter ID cards.

Seasonal Migrants and BPL Cards

It was not possible to carry out a systematic survey of the seasonal migrants. Hence, we have documented their case studies (Box 8.1). One profession where we found them in large numbers in Ahmedabad City was in the brick kilns located in the city's periphery.

The typical situation of the brick kiln workers is that of Asharam Verma, 28, from Pratapgarh district of Uttar Pradesh, who works in CR Bricks at Adalaj village, in the periphery of the city. He has been working in this brick kiln for the last three years; he works for six months and goes back to the village for agricultural work for six months. He was introduced to this employment by his parents. There are other workers from his home region working in the brick kilns as

TABLE 8.2 Various Identity Documents Held by Surveyed Population by Settlement

Settlement	*Ration Card*	*BPL Card*	*Electricity Bill*	*Voter ID Card*
1	20	1	26	24
2	22	1	25	22
3	16	7	21	18
4	13	6	12	16
5	17	6	18	19
6	17	2	20	20
7	3	0	1	10
8	11	0	14	14
9	43	0	47	47
Total	162	23	184	190

Source: Based on primary survey by the author.

well. He is single and earns about Rs 8,000 per month. The working conditions are harsh, as they do not have any protective gear or mechanized equipment for work, thus often burning of their skin in the sun and frequently falling ill. He can send only 50 per cent of his earnings back home, because of high expenses on treatment in private dispensaries. At home, his one *bigha*[12] of land is cultivated for self-sustenance and his wife, who is living in the village with the children, takes care of the farming. He lives in the open on the work site, which has discouraged him from bringing his family from the village. All his identities—the BPL card, election card and bank account—are in his home village and he does not have any identity card in the city. If he continues to work like this, he will never become a citizen of Ahmedabad, will never be part of the social security schemes in the city, or get subsidized treatment at the local government hospital.

There are small variations in the story. Some workers come along with their spouses, leaving children behind in the village with their parents. Mularam Meghvala, 39, from Nagor district, Rajasthan, also working in CR Bricks, has come with his wife, and both work in the same kiln. He has been following this routine for 18 years. The duo has no urban connect except getting food rations once a week, and visiting private dispensaries when either of them falls ill. Dhanjibhai

Box 8.1 The Case Studies of Accessing BPL Cards

We visited nine low income settlements. Of these, six were established settlements and one was a squatter settlement. The stories we could gather from each of the settlement is narrated below.

Harijan Vas na Chhapra (Bhangiwas), Odhav: This is a settlement of about 2,000 households. These are all *katchha* chhapras (hutments). But, only 250 households are in the BPL list of the AMC. On visiting these houses, we found that they had been given a BPL number on a slip of paper. We tallied that number with the name and number in the list and found them to be correct. But, they have not been issued new BPL cards. Some of them, however, had an APL ration card.

Shaktinagar, Odhav: Fifty per cent of the residents are migrant workers and construction workers. All of them had their names in the BPL list and had BPL numbers. But, they had not yet received any card. 20 per cent households, which should not have BPL cards, had one because the local councillor got them this card. There was one Mahila Housing Trust (MHT), SEWA member in the slum, who assisted two to claim widows' pension. They have assisted a few other such women to fill up the form and they are awaiting their pension claim.

Indiranagar, Sabarmati: This is a very clean and well developed *chawl*. The first house we visited was a bungalow, but, the household name was in the BPL list. Three people from the settlement had also been given something under the Garib Kalyan Mela. Two households received assistance of Rs 3,500 for constructing toilets and another person has received a sewing machine. None of the households here were under the BPL income.

Powerhouse slums, Sabarmati: These are scattered squatters on the road; they also reside below the Sabarmati bridge. They belong to Devi Pujak community. Their names are in the BPL list. When the roads were widened, half of them were displaced. They have moved away from this location and were not traceable at the time of our survey. This is a real issue in many cities, of displacement by infrastructure projects, and the people who were enumerated in the BPL list have shifted and are not traceable.

Kankumata ni Chali, Sabarmati: This slum is on the riverbank, below the railway bridge. In this slum, nearly all inhabitants had a BPL number, but no one has yet received a card. Many of them are migrants from Rajasthan.

Satkevalnagar, Sabarmati: This is a slum of ragpickers. Some of them had BPL cards earlier, which were converted into Antyodaya cards, and they are beneficiaries of the Antyodaya scheme. One widow was given a sewing machine in the Garib Mela.

Harekrishnanagar, Sabarmati: The situation is in line with the dwellers of Satkevalnagar. They also have Antyodaya cards.

Source: Field work.

Nayak, 42, from Pushkar district, Rajasthan, has brought his 14-year-old daughter and 10-year-old son, who hang around the kiln as he does not have parents to leave his children with in the village. His children do not go to the school in the city as they do not have any address to register the children in school with. Nor are they permanently residing in the city. There are no hostel facilities in the village to accommodate the children for six months. Living in the city is very expensive and hence they cannot save much.

Some migrants can get a foothold in the city if their employer is supportive. *Damor Dineshbhai Dalabhai*, 23, is a tribal from Santrampur Taluka, Panchmahals District, working as a security and maintenance person in a housing society on Sola Road, Ahmedabad. He has been living in the city since the age of 13, when he first came with his uncle. The housing society has given him a room to stay. He has joined a college and is a second year BA student. His mother and younger brother have now joined him and his father is living in the village to take care of their farm. His monthly income is about Rs 4,500, of which he sends half home. He has a bank account and a voter's ID card. He also got himself insured with the LIC. He plans to stay in the city permanently, but he still does not have a ration card or a BPL card.

He said that it would have been very difficult for migrants like him to find residential stability in the cities. He is grateful to the builder who helped him get the necessary documents. His father still lives in the village where they have some land, as they do not want to sell it. Thus, he and his family are holding full citizenship in the rural area, but a partial citizenship in the urban area. The documents that he holds would give him shelter and security, but not a social security scheme until he gets a new ration card for himself and then gets it converted into a BPL Card.

The problems of new migrants as well as short-term or seasonal migrants get compounded by the bias of the government officials. 'If you cannot afford the city, go back. Why have you come to Ahmedabad when you have land in the village?' Such statements are often heard from government officials. Seasonal migrants are seen more as a burden to the city than an asset. The city dwellers do not see that the migrant population keeps the wages in the overall economy low. And yet they do not want to pay for the welfare of these migrants. If the identity proofs are denied or made hard to access, the migrants will not settle or migrate to the city.

SOCIAL SECURITY IN URBAN GUJARAT

IMPLEMENTATION OF SOCIAL WELFARE SCHEMES

The social welfare schemes in Gujarat are implemented by the Social Justice and Empowerment Department. In rural areas, these schemes are implemented through the line departments at the district level and the District Development Office. In urban areas, however, the schemes are implemented by the ULB or the District Collectorate. The social welfare schemes in the state are for those holding a BPL Card. The BPL card listing is done by the Urban Community Development (UCD) Department. The UCD Department surveyed the households in slums and *chawls* in Ahmedabad in 2008 and prepared a provisional BPL list for the AMC area. According to that, of the 322,297 households living in the slums and *chawls*[13] of Ahmedabad, 167,796—or 52.1 per cent—were BPL households (Table 8.3).

At the outset, not all households living in the slums and *chawls* fall within the category of BPL. While 56 per cent households in the eastern zone of the city, which is the industrial zone, live in slums and *chawls*, only 53 per cent among them are identified as BPL. In

TABLE 8.3 Zone-wise Summary of BPL Households in Ahmedabad Municipal Corporation, 2008

S. No.	*Zone*	*BPL Households*	*Total Households in Slums and* Chawls	*% BPL Households to Total Households in Slums and* Chawls	*% Households Living in Slums and* Chawls
1.	Central	27,560	49,894	55.2	46.5
2.	East	44,871	85,007	52.8	55.7
3.	South	29,299	63,212	46.4	44.8
4.	West	24,457	47,468	51.5	33.4
5.	North	41,609	76,716	54.2	51.4
	City total	167,796	322,297	52.1	46.6

Source: Population data from census 2001, from http://www.egovamc.com/outline0506/T03P33.pdf (accessed on 31 March 2011) and BPL data from http://www.egovamc.com/bpl/SUMMARY_REPORTS/ZONEWISE.pdf (accessed 31 March 2011).

the western zone, which is the high income zone, only 33 per cent households lived in slums, but among them 52 per cent of dwellers had BPL cards. On the first look itself, it appears that there are inclusion errors in the west zone and exclusion errors in the east zone.

In all there are 121 social welfare and assistance schemes in Gujarat. Of these, 36 are being implemented in Ahmedabad city through either the District Collectorate or the AMC. In the last few years, the benefits of these schemes are distributed through Garib Kalyan Melas (GKM), and not by the concerned authority.

In Ahmedabad city, GKMs have been held for the residents of 10 wards—Odhav, Nikol, Vastral, Ramol, Gomtipur, Rajpur, Saraspur, Nava Naroda, Dani Limda and Behrampura—where 70 per cent of the BPL households are located. Two such Melas were held in Ahmedabad by the AMC, one on 16 February 2010 (organized by the District Collectorate), and another on 20 February 2010. A total of 4,439 beneficiaries were reached by the AMC and welfare assistance of Rs 4,268.53 lakh was distributed. The District Collectorate reached out to 1,586 beneficiaries (Table 8.4), with a total assistance of Rs 70.05 lakh. On discussions with the District Collectorate and AMC officials, we could gather that the social assistance was not being disbursed any more during normal times. Our studies showed that the Dr Ambedkar Safai Kamadar Avas Yojana had the highest allocation of Rs 4,416 lakh. This is a housing programme, which comes under the category of development programmes.

The household survey, mentioned in the previous section, revealed that eight schemes were being implemented in the city. These were (i) widows pension; (ii) free medical help; (iii) Sankat Mochan Scheme; (iv) Vidhya Laxmi Scheme; (v) Shehri Mahila Swa- sahaya Programme; (vi) Dikari Yojana; (vii) Garib Kalyan Mela; and (viii) others. The benefits of these schemes are now being distributed through Garib Kalyan Melas, attended by the Chief Minister or a state government Minister. The impression created was that the ruling party in general, and the Chief Minister in particular, was concerned about every individual in the state and hence, was doling out these benefits to them. This exercise was started with an eye on the local elections, which were held in October 2010, in which the ruling party swept the urban and rural local bodies.

Our survey showed that only eight households benefited from the GKM of the 200 surveyed (Table 8.5). This was just 4 per cent.

TABLE 8.4 Welfare Distribution through Garib Kalyan Melas by District Collectorate (upto 16 February 2010)

S. No.	*Office*	*Scheme Name*	*Aid Detail*	*Number of Beneficiaries*	*Total Disbursement in Rs (lakh)*
1.	District Welfare Office	Manav Kalyan Yojana	Tool kit of Rs 4,000	339	6.78
	Vikasati Jati Kalyan	Kuvarbai nu Mameru	Rs 5,000 cheque	10	0.50
	Department	Bankable Scheme	33% subsidy	9	0.36
		Gujarat Minorities Development and Finance Corporation	Upto Rs 40,000 for business loans	29	10.80
		Stitching Trainer's Tool Kit Aid	Rs 3,000 worth kit	17	0.25
		International High Education Loan Scheme	Upto Rs 10 lakh aid	1	5.00
		College Hotelier Students Scholarship	Scholarship of Rs 3,000 to Rs 6,000	428	21.70
		Merit Cum Means Scholarship	Scholarship of Rs 3,000 to Rs 20,000	64	7.74
2.	District Backward Class	Inter-caste wedding	Rs 50,000 aid	8	4.00
	Welfare Officer	Direct Loan Scheme	Rs 25,000 to Rs 5 lakh loan	20	5.00
		Post Metric Scholarship	Scholarship of Rs 1,900 to Rs 7,500	17	0.36
		Kuvarbai Nu Mameru	Rs 5,000 cheque	64	7.74
		Shop Loan Aid	Aid upto Rs 75,000	1	0.60

(*Cont'd*)

TABLE 8.4 (*Cont'd*)

S. No.	*Office*	*Scheme Name*	*Aid Detail*	*Number of Beneficiaries*	*Total Disbursement in Rs (lakh)*
3.	Assistant Employment Officer	Standing Conference of Public Enterprises (SCOPE) Yojana	Certificate	99	1.87
4.	District Social Security	Disable Tool Aid	Tool kit upto Rs 25,000	25	0.62
		Financial Assistance to Widows and Destitute Women	Assistance upto Rs 5,000	15	0.75
		Disable Free Travel ID card	Identity card	16	0.00
5.	ITI	Stipend to Student	From Rs 750 to Rs 1,500	116	1.16
6.	City Deputy Collector Office	Vayvandana	Monthly Rs. 200 aid	335	0.71
		Total		1,586	70.05

Source: From http://www.egovamc.com/garib_k_m/gkm.asp (accessed 1 May 2011).

TABLE 8.5 Extent of Welfare Distribution by the CWWB, Gujarat

	Welfare Scheme	*2009–10*		*2010–11*		*2011–12*	
		Number of Beneficiaries	*Amount of Benefit (Rs)*	*Number of Beneficiaries*	*Amount of Benefit (Rs)*	*Number of Beneficiaries*	*Amount of Benefit (Rs)*
1.	Children Education Assistance Scheme						
	Ahmedabad	2,001	3,299,910	19,981	5,232,302	207	782,185
	Vadodara	421	74,290	98	130,275	47	289,750
	Surat	759	1,069,833	397	701, 008	–	–
	Rajkot	2,548	4,096,885	1,449	5,299,075	425	1,706,103
	Total	5,729	8,540,918	21,925	11,362,660	679	2,778,038
2.	Accidental Death Benefit Scheme						
	Ahmedabad	2	400,000		3,299,910	2	400,000
	Vadodara						
	Surat						
	Rajkot						
	Total						
3.	Medical Assistance	The scheme is non operative because of multiplicity of schemes for health care					
4.	Maternity Benefit						
	Ahmedabad			2	6,000	4	12,000

(Cont'd)

Table 8.5 (*Cont'd*)

	Welfare Scheme	*2009–10*		*2010–11*		*2011–12*	
		Number of Beneficiaries	*Amount of Benefit (Rs)*	*Number of Beneficiaries*	*Amount of Benefit (Rs)*	*Number of Beneficiaries*	*Amount of Benefit (Rs)*
	Vadodara	1	3,000	1	3,000		
	Surat	3	9,000				
	Rajkot	20	60,000			4	12,000
	Total	24	72,000	3	9,000	8	24,000
5.	Funeral Assistance Scheme						
	Total	10	87,000	5	10,000	6	14,000
6.	Financial Assistance scheme for purchase of building or house	The Scheme has discontinued after the introduction of Indira Awas Yojana					
	Total		9,099,918		11,381,660		3,216,038

Source: From the files of the CWWB, Gujarat.

There was only one beneficiary of the widow's pension, free medical help and the Shehri Mahila Swa-sahaya programme, while six others benefited from social welfare schemes. The findings show very dismal picture as far as implementation of the social welfare schemes in Ahmedabad City is concerned.

SOCIAL SECURITY BOARDS FOR UNORGANIZED WORKERS[14]

On its own, Gujarat has set up one non-statutory board, the Gujarat Unorganized Workers Welfare Board (GUWWB), and one statutory board, the Cloth Market and Shops Labour Board (CMSLB), in Ahmedabad. The GUWWB was set up in February 2007 to provide a social security net to the urban unorganized workers (other than agriculture workers), and is operating in the municipal corporation areas Ahmedabad, Surat and Jamnagar. In Ahmedabad, nine trades are covered by the board (see Table 8.6). These are (i) agarbatti rollers; (ii) rag pickers; (iii) street vendors and hawkers; (iv) catering services; (v) kite makers; (vi) readymade garment makers; (vii) independent

TABLE 8.6 Occupation-wise Workers' Registration under GUWWB

S. No.	*Occupation*	*2007–8*	*2008–9*	*2009–10*	*2010–11*	*2011–12*
1.	Agarbatti rollers	3,686	3,117	755	785	462
2.	Rag pickers	4,058	2,971	718	1,482	468
3.	Street vendors and hawkers	3,786	5,682	3,599	2,408	1212
4.	Catering services	0	985	3,305	4,334	2057
5.	Kite makers	0	443	384	434	80
6.	Readymade garment makers	0	3,123	4,870	3,831	1951
7.	Independent sweepers	0	530	238	536	227
8.	Roadside stall holders	0	39	94	134	85
9.	Workers of mandap business	0	27	37	56	58
	Total	11,530	16,917	14,000	14,000	6,600

Source: Based on the data collected from the documents of the GUWWB.

sweepers; (viii) roadside stall holders; and (ix) workers of mandap (temporary structure erected for special occasions) business.

The workers are given identity cards and they have to register with the board every year. Hence the registrations are seen to fluctuate greatly year to year. Further, the registration does not happen without assistance from organizations such as SEWA or a trade union, on account of lack of awareness. A positive development is the registration of workers through some of the trade unions; however, without an address, the registration of any worker with the Board is not possible.

The registration in the GUWWB in Ahmedabad is very small as compared to the labour force. According to our estimates, there were a total of 21.05 million workers in Ahmedabad in 2009–10, of which about 16.34 million were in the informal or unorganized sector. Of this workforce, only 63,047 (0.38 per cent) were registered with the GUWWB in Ahmedabad. In addition, 2,609 workers were registered with CMSLB, taking the total registered workers with the welfare boards in Ahmedabad to just 65,656 or just 0.40 per cent of the total unorganized workers in the city. A total of Rs 25.6[15] million had been spent over these registered workers in the whole period since 2007, an expenditure of Rs 476.5 per registered worker.

The total achievements of the GUWWB in Ahmedabad are as below:

i) Total number of workers registered with the board: 63,047.
ii) Total tool kits distributed to workers: 11,075.
iii) Number of beneficiaries of training: 1,862.
iv) Total mediclaims approved: 874.

The schemes of the GUWWB were very limited and available to the card holder only (see Box 8.2). The benefits were not extended to their family members, making its scope even narrower. The benefits consisted of (i) skill development and training, whose benefit was enjoyed by 15,019 workers, and the amount spent was Rs 12.92 million between 2007–11, about Rs 860.4 per worker; (ii) assistance of a tool kit worth Rs 300 per worker in general, benefiting 19,947 workers in the same period, on whom a total of Rs 8.4 million had been spent, which was Rs 422 per worker; and (iii) medical aid of Rs 1,200 per hospitalization and health check up on which Rs 0.09 million had been spent for 722 workers. The benefits had been there but did not have a lasting impact on personal welfare of the workers.

Box 8.2 The Case Studies of Accessing Social Welfare Schemes

Shaktinagar, Odhav: In this slum, we found that a member of Mahila Housing Trust (MHT), SEWA, residing in the slum, assisted two widows to claim widows' pension. They had assisted a few other such women to fill up the form and they were awaiting their pension claim.

Satkevalnagar, Sabarmati: In this slum of ragpickers, one widow was given a sewing machine in the GKM.

Kashinath Ramkishore Tiwari of Ganesh Colony, Odhav: He has 10 members in the house. He and his son work as casual labour and earn about Rs 2,000 per month from irregular work. Another son is affected by polio. They somehow manage their expenses. His name is in the BPL list, but he has not yet received a card, and hence does not get any benefit, including medical assistance, from the government.

Pal Siaram Biharilal of Ganesh Colony, Odhav: He has a family of five. He lost one of his is legs in a factory accident, while working. He is trying to get medical help, and had approached the councillor. Although his name is in the BPL list, without the BPL card he is not been considered eligible for low cost medical help in the civil hospital. He had to incur the expenditure for treatment after the accident in the factory himself as his employers did not extend any help.

Lilavati Thakore of Ganesh Colony, Odhav: She is a widow and has four daughters. All are now married. There is no earning member in her house. She is eligible for widow's pension of Rs 200 per month but has received it only for one month.

Gangabhen Baldevbhai Vaghela of Ganesh Colony, Odhav: She is a widow. She has one married daughter and lives alone. She goes to work in nearby houses and earns about Rs 200 every month. She had applied for widow's pension eight months back, but has not yet received any amount.

Source: Field work.

Mostly, those who were members of some organization like SEWA had benefited. The board depends greatly on such organizations in reaching the target group. SEWA mobilizes the people concerned, informs then about the welfare schemes or any upcoming training programme. However, the Government has not developed any independent mechanism to identify and reach out to the target group. Consequently, without the presence of any organization, it is difficult for the benefits to reach the targeted group of workers (Box 8.2).

Under the skill development scheme, workshops are conducted to impart training in application of *mehendi* (henna), soft toys making or imitation jewellery making. The board could not provide all benefits to the registered members. Therefore, the members taking skill upgradation training were denied the benefits of a tool kit. The skill development scheme is applicable only to registered members, and is not extended to their families. Therefore workers busy with their existing work schedule find it difficult to make productive use of such training. In addition, the training programmes are not adequately supported to develop market linkages. So monetary cost, as well as the cost of making use of such newly imparted skills, usually turn out to be very high. The beneficiaries get the kit only once, even if the kit is perishable in nature. Such an intervention is reduced to a mere token gesture rather than one making a valuable difference in improving working conditions.

The CMSLB was set up under the Gujarat Unprotected Manual Workers Act, 1979, to regulate the employment conditions of unprotected manual workers in the specified employment. It is a very small board and covers only Ahmedabad city. It collects levy from the employers of the market at the rate of 8 per cent of the remuneration paid to the worker. A total of Rs 21 lakh was collected during 2009–11 (three years) and a total of 3,730 beneficiaries received assistance of either medical aid of up to Rs 2,000 per worker per annum, educational kit to the children of the registered workers and maternity benefit of Rs 500 for the first delivery, Rs 400 for the second and then Rs 250 after two children, for family planning operation to the registered female worker.

The board has been working to the satisfaction of the workers, but the coverage is very small. The geographical jurisdiction of the board is limited to the old municipal corporation limits as defined in 1981. There is no amendment till date to expand the coverage area. The cloth and textile market has grown manifold in Ahmedabad since then. However, all newly developed markets are not yet included under the board's jurisdiction. We learned from a SEWA worker that more than 3,500 women head-loaders are members of SEWA, whereas only 2,618 men and women are members of the board.

The main source of finance for the board is levy collected from the cloth merchants, which is 8 per cent of wages. The Bombay Cloth Market Board collects 28 per cent levy. The merchants have to pay the levy fortnightly. However, many merchants pay it only annually, that too after many reminders. The merchants often do not show workers' names on registers, to avoid paying the levy. The members also complained about the lax approach of inspectors in collection of the levy. The inspectors for the job are deputed from the Labour Commissioner's office.

IMPLEMENTATION OF RSBY

RSBY was implemented, phase-wise, in the state; five districts were covered in the first phase, another five in the second phase and then all the rest in the third phase. The third phase commenced in 2010. Of the total 1.99 million BPL families, 0.85 million (43 per cent) families had been enrolled by the end of August 2010. A total of 539 private hospitals and 258 public hospitals had been empanelled. The scheme is operational only in the rural areas of Gujarat as of now.

At the time of our first survey, the programme was not being implemented in the urban areas. This was because the BPL list, which had been prepared by the municipal corporation, had not reached the Health Department, the implementing agency of the programme. The Health Department then hands over the list to the insurance company for the issuance of the RSBY card. The process got delayed because there was a huge time-lag between the BPL survey and the finalization of the BPL list. Then there was a lag between finalization of the list and issuance of the BPL cards. The BPL list was displayed on the website in early 2011, after about two and a half years of the survey. The RSBY cards were then issued in November–December, 2011.

Seven of the nine settlements studied earlier were revisited in January 2012. In Kankumani Chali, while every household held a BPL number, only about half had received the RSBY smart card. Those holding the card had a list of empanelled hospitals in Ahmedabad district, but they did not know the utility of the card. In Shakti Nagar and Ganesh Colony, in the industrial suburbs of Odhav, while all households were in the BPL list, only three-fourths had received the RSBY card. Even one year after the survey in Harijan vas, no household had received a BPL card and consequently, no RSBY card. In the two settlements in Sabarmati area, Satkevalnagar (whose residents were rag pickers and holders of the Antyodaya card) and Harekrishnanagar (whose residents were also holders of Antyodaya card), only about half of the listed dwellers had received RSBY card, when all should have. The other half was awaiting their cards. Some households had missed out on getting the card because at the time of the issuance of the card, they were out of the city. Subsequently, they did not know how to get the card issued, as this was a one-off process.

For those who had received the RSBY card, there was total lack of awareness on what to do with it. People were under the wrong impression that the card was valid only for the public hospitals. Apparently the RSBY booklet given to them was providing insufficient information. The hospital list given had only names of the hospitals with contact numbers; the full address was not mentioned. So people were not able to locate the nearest hospital from their house. It seemed that the RSBY programme had not been well publicized by the State Government. The holders of the card were unaware of the medical conditions covered by the card, and were not clear about the coverage of expenses outside the hospital in case of further medical tests.

Despite holding the RSBY cards, some people opted to go to the nearby private health facility for treatment because (i) there was very little information about how the programme operated; and (ii) going to the empanelled hospital meant transport costs, and hence people felt that it was cheaper to go to a nearby doctor for minor ailment treatment rather than use RSBY card.

The card holders also faced some other difficulties such as their name being misspelt, or sex wrongly mentioned. There is no mechanism as of now to rectify these errors, because of which these card holders cannot use their cards. There were also problems in the final delivery of the benefits because of multiplicity of agencies involved in the RSBY programme. Five different agencies are involved in the delivery mechanism, whose coordination is essential in reaching the benefits to the targeted households. These are:

1. Government: The Government plays two roles; (i) it prepares the BPL list; and (ii) it pays the premium to the insurance company. If these cards are not used by the holders, then the company makes a neat profit.
2. Insurance Company: It collects premium from the Government and pays the bill of all the insurance claims.
3. Card Issuing Company: The insurer appoints a private company, which issues the biometric card to all the people having BPL numbers.
4. Third Party Advisory Company (TPA): It is appointed by the insurance firm, to approve the empanelment of a private

hospital, and verify all the insurance claims raised by the hospital.

5. Software Company: It is appointed by the insurance company, on the approval of the government, to develop the software that is installed across the state.

A visit to a public hospital to know about the issues of functioning of this programme showed that the card issuing company was a private company working on contract. Their employees were given daily targets, so they were working in a hurry and made many mistakes while entering the names. As the employees were not local, they were not familiar with local names and their spellings. Therefore the patients were often denied the benefits, as their names did not match with the ones written on the card, and the insurance company did not recognize the differences in names. There was no clarity on who would rectify the errors in data entry. In some cases, the cards were renewed by the card issuing company, but the software company did not correct the names in the list of beneficiaries that it held. So the system refused to recognize the patient as an enrolled beneficiary, and the patient was left without any benefit.

SOCIAL SECURITY FOR CONSTRUCTION WORKERS

The Overall Situation

This sub-section looks at the implementation of the Building and Other Construction Workers (Regulation and Employment and Conditions of Service) Act, 1996, and Building and Other Construction Workers' Cess Act, 1996. Gujarat Building and Other CWWB was set up as a statutory board. Up to September 2011, 54,697 construction workers had been registered and given identity cards from a total of 58,323 applications received. The board had collected a cess of Rs 1,90.29 crore up to January 2011. These figures are very low given that the Gujarat Government has been investing heavily into infrastructure, and hence is expected to have a large number of construction workers working in the state. According to Mr Vipul Pandya of Bandhkam Majdoor Sangathana (BMS), a union of the construction workers, there are about 15 lakh construction workers in the state. The total number of registered members is a cumulative figure since 2005. There is no clarity as to how many of them have renewed their registration, or how many are actually eligible for getting any benefit.

The registration of workers was very low because they needed to prove that they had worked for 90 days, and that proof had to be given by any one of the following: (i) the Talati/a Manrti; (ii) contractor; (iii) Rural Labour Commissioner; (iv) Labour Commissioner; or (v) Department of Industrial Safety and Health (DISH). The documents required for registration were (i) the certificate of continuous work of 90 days on construction work; (ii) residential proof; (iii) 3 passport size photographs; (iv) proof of age; and (v) domicile certificate of Gujarat.

There were a few non-operatives here, which were meant to exclude rather than include. First, no contractor would like to give the proof of a labourer working on his site for so long in order to avoid the labour legislation application. Second, the tenure of the worker differed for different types of work. The skilled workers did not have a long tenure, while unskilled workers did. Thus the former category of workers would not be able to show the proof of their work on a particular site for 90 days at a stretch. Third, the onus was on the workers to show proof of working on a site and register themselves; the State Government was not responsible for the same. Fourth, many of the contractors themselves were not licensed and hence they could not issue a certificate to the workers. Fifth, there was no workers' representative empowered to register the workers, or assist them in registration, and without such assistance the local bureaucracies were non-negotiable by the workers. Very often the construction workers were inter-state migrants and they were immediately disqualified on this count, as they would not be able to provide domicile certificate of Gujarat. Finally, as discussed at length later in the chapter, the urban poor, including the construction workers, did not have a legal address, or proof of it. By the very design of the eligibility criteria, a large proportion of construction workers get excluded. The domicile certificate requirement means that the workers had to possess ration cards of Gujarat. This was in contravention of the Supreme Court directive that all the construction workers should be mandatorily registered.

The state has not empowered the trade union to register a worker. However, for a short duration in 2008, this right was given to the trade unions; till 2008, only 750 workers had been registered (Box 8.3). After the trade unions were given this right, the registration of workers increased. For example, BMS itself had filled up 36,000 forms.

Box 8.3 PIL on Implementing Social Security Schemes in Gujarat

A news item appeared on 28 December 2009 in Indian Express (source below) that the Gujarat High Court had sought details from the State Government on the steps taken under the Unorganized Workers Social Security Act, 2008 and on any of the schemes framed under it. The High Court had also asked the State Government to furnish details of the State Social Security Board and the schemes under it. The HC order was pronounced recently by the division bench of Chief Justice S.J. Mukhopadhaya and A.S. Dave on a 2008 petition filed by an NGO, Bruhad Ahmedabad Adivasi Bhil Shikshit Yuvak Mitra Mandal. It sought direction to the State Government to implement various statutory schemes for the welfare of unorganized construction labourers.

The petitioner said lakhs of construction labourers were illiterate tribals, unaware of their statutory rights. Some of these were accidental benefit schemes, pension and retirement schemes, housing loans, group insurance, educational and medical schemes, maternity benefits and the like, under laws like Building and Other Construction Workers (Regulation of Employment and Conditions of Service) Act, and Building and Other Construction Workers' Welfare Cess Act, 1996. The money collected as cess from builders for the welfare of construction labourers was lying unutilized, contended the petition. It also stated that although there was a provision to punish the errant builders and contractors for not honouring legal provisions for the labourers, not many such instances were known in Gujarat.

The petitioner had also contended that although the Gujarat Building and Other Construction Workers Welfare Board had come into effect on December 2004, the board has not been performing many of its statutory duties. At the time of preparing this study, further hearing on this PIL was to continue.

Source: http://www.indianexpress.com/news/what-have-you-done-for-construction-labourer/560252/ (accessed 21 October 2010).

After that, even the government officials became pro-active and went to construction workers' sites to register the workers. Thereafter this provision was withdrawn. If the rule had continued, about 2 lakh workers could have been registered by now.

Besides the registration of workers, the other reason for low cess collection was a very low schedule of rates (SOR). The SOR forms the basis for estimation of project cost. Cess is 1 per cent of the estimated project cost of the total project. The SOR fixed in Gujarat in 2006 was derived by calculating Rs. 3,000 as an average construction cost per square meter. Cess at the rate of 1 per cent of construction cost turned out to be only Rs 30 per square meter. It has not been revised since, despite a huge rise in construction cost. The real construction cost per square metre in October 2011 was about Rs 12,000, four times higher than that estimated costs. As a result, according to Mr. Pandya, actual cess collected worked out to just 0.25 per cent of the actual construction costs. There was also a problem of monitoring the construction sites for collecting cess.

While the process of cess collection had been streamlined for public sector projects, the process of monitoring the private projects was very weak. In public sector projects, the contractors were given their due after deducting the cess. The Labour Department and DISH did not have adequate staff, nor did they have adequate budget to hire staff for the purpose. The labour department was unable to monitor short-term construction projects.

The board had been working with a single officer as against the required six. Due to lack of staff, the board depended on DISH for implementation of many schemes. There had been 155 deaths in the state at the construction sites in the last two years, 2008–9 and 2009–10, but families of only two were given compensation of Rs 2 lakh each. In Ahmedabad city alone, 14 workers die every year at construction sites according to Mr Pandya of BMS, and nearly no one gets any compensation from the CWWB. As of early 2011, the total welfare benefits given out by the CWWB, was only Rs 32.1 lakh, just 0.91 per cent of the amount collected as cess. The board had given education scholarship to 8,357 children, maternity benefits to 57 women, cremation aid to 10, and medical aid to none.

There were also problems with DISH. This organization has mechanical and chemical engineers as employees, but no civil engineers with technical expertise to oversee safety in construction projects. Also, DISH works for the entire state and it oversees safety issues in industries. In 2009–10, at the time of the study, the department was understaffed and the staff did not inspect the sites regularly.

The Directorate of Industrial Safety and Occupational Health, the organization in charge of enforcement of labour laws in both the organized and unorganized sectors, suffered from severe shortage of staff. The requirement of labour officers for only the factory sector in the state, as per ILO norms, was 232 (one labour officer per 150 factories, and there are 34,860 factories). Against this, the sanctioned posts were 154 (Class I and II) officers, which was two-thirds of the requirement. Of these, 46 posts (30 per cent of the sanctioned posts) had been vacant for the past year or more (2010). (Hirway and Shah, 2011: 61)

The short duration projects were less likely to be inspected than the long-term ones. In all, there were problems with the functioning of DISH.

However, the state had an innovative mechanism of collecting cess. The AMC and the Ahmedabad Urban Development Authority (AUDA)—the project plan passing authorities—were the cess collecting authorities. They collected the cess at the time of passing the plan. They then passed on the amount to the state treasury, from where the money was sent to CWWB. Box 8.4 presents the failure of the CWWB in individual cases.

Mr Pandya says that the ideal way would have been to create a separate account and transfer the cess collection directly to the account, instead of depositing it with the state treasury. Further, the CWWB gets the funds from the State Government as a grant-in-aid. This means that the cess collected for the construction workers does not come to their Board as workers' right, but as welfare from the Government. There is another problem in such a system. According to Government rules, an individual or a household can claim assistance from only one of social welfare schemes of the State Government. Thus, if a SC/ST has claimed assistance under another scheme—say a scholarship for his/her child—then that person cannot claim any benefit from the CWWB's assistance. A large proportion of construction workers are either SC or ST. The scholarship amount of the SC/ST board is only Rs 100 per child, whereas the CWWB can give minimum of Rs 250. The cess collected is workers' right and not a grant or favour to the workers. However, the manner in which the state is implementing this legislation has diluted greatly the spirit of the legislation. This subversion of the law has happened because all the builders of the state are close to the ruling party.

The scheme is weakly implemented because the CWWB is very weak. It was a one-man board till recently, and there were no representatives of the employees or no permanent staff on the board. Everyone had an additional charge, and hence no one was interested in working in the board. But now it has become a tripartite board.

The Gujarat legislation has also some drawbacks. The Central Act has prescribed a pension scheme, which has not been included in the Gujarat CWWB schemes. Also, there is a need to add a few more

Box 8.4 Individual Cases

We also visited the construction sites where we found tribal workers from North Gujarat, in particular from the Panchmahals and Dahod districts. Their stories show why they would not be able to benefit from the CWWB.

Damor Jaswantbhai Harjivanbhai, 38, is a tribal from Santrampur Taluka, Panchmahals. His story is typical of the tribal workers in the construction sector. He has five bigha land in his village. At the time of our survey, he was working on a construction site on Sola Road. They are five brothers, all married with children. Their land is rocky, and hence not very productive, and can only take one crop in the monsoon. To sustain their lives, they have to depend on other work, such as construction in the city. His elder brother brought him to Ahmedabad 10 years ago and he has been moving from one construction site to another ever since. At each site, he gets work for only 20–22 days a month and then he has to look for another site for work. This means that he cannot get benefits of the CWWB, as he cannot show continuous work of 90 days at one site. He lives alone; his family is in the village. He earns about Rs 150 daily. Half of it is saved and sent home to the family, his wife, two sons and two daughters. His children study in the village school. He holds an election card, APL card and bank account in his home village. He is living here all alone, and has not found any time to get information on the BPL card or any other card. He wants to settle down in the city, but, cannot do so on his own. The question is whether the local government is ready to extend any help.

Most of the tribals migrate with their spouses. **Bamaniya Somabhai Bhalabhai**, 25, who works with the same construction company, and moves from one site to another, is joined by his wife and 18-month-old daughter. His sister and brother-in-law are also on the same work site. Often, many members of the joint family migrate to the same site and live together.

The life of women construction workers living and working at the site is harder, as they do not get access to any facility. They have to keep their children in the open at the work site. They are not allowed to go and attend to the child. If they do so, their wages are cut. Same is the case with **Urmilabhen Lachhubhai Katara,** 28, from Fatehpura Taluka, Panchmahals, working on the same construction site. She and her husband have been working in the city for the last 15 years and moving from one site to another. They go back to home village only during the Diwali and Holi festivals.

Some tribal workers come to work in construction as a group. They are brought by the labour contractor to work on infrastructure projects, such as road and bridge construction, and they too move from one site to another. **Ramaben Nabirbhai Bhabhor**, a tribal woman from

Dahod District, was working on a construction site in Odhav area. She had come to Ahmedabad three months back, with her husband and a two-year-old son, along with about 80 people from her village.

Sometimes, a group of migrant workers from the same region who are brought to work on a construction site by the same contractor tend to share a living accommodation in a slum, on lease. **Kalubhai Bhurjibhai Sangada**, 23, from Zalod Taluka, Dahod district is living in Bharwad vas of Odhav village. He has been living with his wife and two children for the last six years. All their ID proofs are of their village. They also have a BPL card in the village. Hence, during his wife's pregnancy, she went to the village to get benefit from Chiranjeevi Yojana. He has a work card given by the employer and that is his only identity in the city. But that has not helped him to register with the CWWB. There are others from his village who go to the *kadia naka* or labour point in Odhav village to be picked up for work by a contractor. This means that they do not have a regular employer and regular employment site. Every morning they go to the kadia naka at 7.30 am to be hired by a contractor who then gives them transport allowance to go to the construction site. This means that they do not have the same employer every day, which would make it impossible for them to get registered with the CWWB. They take their kids along with them to work. They do not have any identity card and hence cannot benefit from any of the government schemes in the city.

All of them wanted regular employment which can help them live permanently in the city. There is also the other issue of shelter security, which is not provided for. These are their aspirations, which, it seems, would never be fulfilled.

Source: Field work.

schemes, such as assistance for marriage (similar scheme is there for the BPL households and is called Kuvarbai nu Mameru). Kerala's model could perhaps be adopted for the purpose. The health scheme does not cover skin and other occupational diseases, whereas diseases of prosperity have been included. Road workers are also prone to accidents and this category is not covered. Construction workers do not have unemployment benefit, which is important especially in times of lack of work during the monsoon season, natural calamities and riots.

Four large construction sites were visited by Toshniwal (2010), during 2009–10, when it was found that none of these had any worker registered with the CWWB. Only two sites had some basic facilities and even on the site where infrastructure construction by the public agencies was ongoing, there was no worker registered. The details of the sites studied, and working conditions there, are detailed out in Annexure A8.1. These sites are not all inclusive and were picked up randomly. But, the findings do not bring any credit to the CWWB.

These cases of migrant construction workers show that they do not have any identity in the city. They are casual labour and move from one site to another, and hence cannot be registered with the CWWB. Without an ID in the city, they are not entitled to a BPL card that would make them eligible for a social security scheme. Even if these workers have a domicile of Gujarat, they are not in a position to get registered with CWWB, or get a secure shelter in the city, which would eventually fetch them a permanent ID in the city.

There are also workers from other states who cannot fulfil the requirement of domicile of a certain period in Gujarat. If these workers were to be covered, new mechanisms of social security would have to be thought of.

In short, the CWWB is not very functional as the legislation has limited coverage when compared to the legislation of other states. It does not actively pursue the registration of the workers, and the onus of registration has been passed on to the workers themselves; and lastly, the eligibility criteria itself would exclude a large section of construction workers.

***

Gujarat is a typical capitalist state and its development ideology has never been pro-worker. It believes that economic growth will trickle down to benefit the poor and if not, the philanthropy, which is dominating public actions, would take care of the poor. The last two however have not taken care of the human development concerns of the state and the economic reforms regime has further strengthened and justified this anti-labour ideology. Hence, the challenge of reaching out the social security to the urban poor is in the specific context of a state which lags in human development, and lacks the will to implement schemes for the welfare of the working class.

The mandatory national level legislation, such as the BOCW Act, Building and Construction Workers' Cess Act, and Unorganized Sector Workers' Social Security Act, 2008, are being implemented under a Supreme Court order (as in case of the first two) or a High Court order (as in case of the last one). For construction workers, there is lack of interest in implementing them, coupled with subversion at the state level in implementing them. Hence, the progress is very poor and we do not find any worker on any construction site in Ahmedabad registered with the CWWB.

The state is among the last to frame the rules for implementation of the national legislation, the Unorganized Sector Workers' Social Security Act, 2008. The Gujarat State Social Security Board (GSSSB) was set up in the last week of December 2011. The rules that have been framed do not display seriousness of the State Government in addressing the issue of the social security of the unorganized workers. One important lacuna of the rules is there is no mechanism specified to ensure collection of large levy, and without funds the board may not be able to do much work. Besides, the board has left it to the District Panchayats, as well the ULBs, to evolve their own mechanism of registering the workers, which in essence would mean delay in registration on one hand and passing on the onus of registration to the workers on the other, who may not get registered on account of time and cost involved.

This study shows that lack of interest in workers' welfare and social security continues, as reflected in the shoddy implementation of the Construction Workers' Welfare Legislation, lack of enthusiasm in implementing the RSBY in the urban areas, and apathetic implementation of other assistance programmes. Amid such a dismal implementation of welfare and social assistance programmes in urban areas, the state has taken to distributing the welfare schemes and assistance through a unique approach called Garib Kalyan Melas, which the political observers feel is an attempt by the Chief Minister to take individual credit for benefits provided. In other words, the social welfare programme implementation has been transformed into an ad hoc mechanism to boost the image of a leader rather than treat it as a regularized State Government activity, providing poor households' and individuals' with certain entitlements.

In a state where there is poor public health care infrastructure and high dependency on private health care, the RSBY itself is a programme with many drawbacks. Lack of affordable health care hinders RSBY coverage. On account of sub-contracting every task, there are many operational issues in the programme. Thus, despite issuance of the RSBY Cards, we did not find any utilization of this programme in Ahmedabad. Clearly, the insurance companies are assured of a business, but there is no guarantee of increased health care coverage.

Besides, the programme is tied to the BPL list, which has taken a long time to be prepared for the cities in Gujarat. The BPL list in the urban areas is tied to the issue of identity; households have to establish that they are residents of a particular city and that is very difficult for the urban poor (who do not have shelter security), and for the migrants (who do not have identity cards in the city). This road to urban citizenship is becoming harder on account of land captures in the cities by the real estate groups. Hence, establishing urban citizenship is a significant challenge for the urban poor, posing a great obstacle in getting covered under any social security and welfare programme. The poor attain urban citizenship through electoral democracy, wherein the politicians have an interest in extending election cards to them to consolidate their vote-banks. Through this process, the poor attain a quasi citizenship by getting their name enrolled in the voters' list, and through their endurance in the city in the face of innumerable hardships, they obtain urban citizenship. Hence, the UID project would not fulfil the anti-poor urban systems, to ensure extension of the citizenship to the latter.

If social security has to be provided by the state governments, the high income states (which are the recipients of the migrant population) would resist, as we see in the case of Gujarat. Maharashtra also discriminates on the basis of language and regional identity. There is a need to reconsider two aspects of the current social security scheme implementation if all types of migrants to the urban areas have to be included (i) setting up of Central Fund for the mobile population; and (ii) delinking social security and the BPL card.

This paper raises two major issues with regard to social security of the unorganized workers in the context of a metropolitan city. First, it is a process through which the new worker in the low income category gets assimilated in a city and attains its citizenship. Till then, he/she is left to fend for himself/herself. If there is no proactive mechanism of identifying such workers, they and their families tend to remain outside of the social security net for many years. The hardest of all is to get access to a secure shelter and hence an address. Many, in fact, do not settle down and continue to remain as temporary or seasonal migrants on account of these difficulties of accessing shelter and citizenship. Second is the growth path selected by the State of Gujarat—which finds concentrated expression in the development dynamics of Ahmedabad—has not been sensitive to labour welfare and human development aspects. In such a situation, high growth or high level and rate of urbanization might not bring forward security for the unorganized sector workers in the state.

APPENDIX A8

TABLE A8.1 Summary of Case Studies

S. No.	*Parameters*	*Case Study 1*	*Case Study 2*	*Case Study 3*	*Case Study 4*
1.	Project Name	Safal Parivesh	Safal Profiteer	Gujarat National Law University (GNLU)	New Drainage line
2.	Project type	Residential	Commercial	Institutional	Infrastructure
3.	Project size	1,000 apartments	3.6 lakh sq built-up	Four storey building on 15 acres of land	250 m long line
4.	Developers	Private	Private	Law University	AMC
5.	Workers employed (approx.)	1,000	200	200	20
6.	Number of children on site	80–100	10–15	25–30	6
7.	Proportion of migrants	80%	30%	100%	100%
8.	Type of migrants	Intra-state	Intra-state and inter-state	Inter-state and intra-state	Intra-state
9.	Facilities on site	60–70 shelter, no toilets, borewell water stored in syntex tax, electricity, canteen run by a worker, crèche, and informal school managed by employer	Corrugated sheet shelter, two toilets, AMC water, no electricity, no canteen, and crèche and informal school managed by employer	Corrugated sheet and concrete blocks' shelter, no toilet, water available, electricity, no canteen, no facilities for children	No shelter and workers live under tarpaulin sheets, public toilet nearby but not by employers, no water and use nearby garden's tap, no electricity, no canteen, no facilities for children

(*Cont'd*)

TABLE A8.1 (*Cont'd*)

S. No.	*Parameters*	*Case Study 1*	*Case Study 2*	*Case Study 3*	*Case Study 4*
10.	Approval from DISH	No	No	Yes	No
11.	No of workers registered with CWWB	None	None	None	None
12.	Building and Other Construction Workers Welfare Cess Act	Applied	Applied	Applied	Applied
13.	Holding NREGS Card	Their parents hold one	Only a few	Yes	Yes
14.	Pension	No	No	No	No
15.	Life insurance	No	No	Yes	No

Source: Toshniwal (2010).

Notes

[1] The author would like to acknowledge the contribution of Tejal Patel and Kaushal Jhajoo of Centre for Urban Equity for research support.

[2] The 2011 Population Census Data has not yet put out the estimate of urban population in the total population. It is presumed to be 30 per cent at the time of writing this paper, although it may be more.

[3] See Planning Commission (2012), *Press Note on Poverty Estimates 2009–10*, Government of India, New Delhi.

[4] We have seen some revival in this sector, and in 2009–10, only 42 per cent workers depended on agriculture.

[5] Data in this paragraph are from Hirway and Mahadevia (2005), unless specified.

[6] See Mahadevia, D. 2007. 'An All Too Inhuman Index', *Tehelka Magazine*, 4(48), 15 December, http://www.tehelka.com/story_main36.asp?filename=Ne151207inhuman.asp.

[7] If the land is to be acquired for public purpose under the city's Master/Development Plan, and in the period of ULCRA as excess land to be notified for acquisition, the land owners sell-off the land parcels in the informal market and thereby invite squatting.

[8] *Patta* is a right to the land parcel.

[9] For a detailed discussion on land *pattas* and tenure levels, see Mahadevia (2010).

[10] For a detailed discussion, see http://www.indiaenvironmentportal.org.in/files/smPolicy.pdf (accessed 16 October 2012).

[11] Ibid.

[12] 1 hectare = 4.45 bhiga or 1 bigha = 0.225 hectare.

[13] A *chawl* is a low-income settlement with dwelling units laid in a row. It was the former industrial housing in the city, mostly now in a dilapidated status.

[14] Data in this section are from the labour department, Government of Gujarat taken from Ms A.A. Mehsania, Assistant Labour Commissioner.

[15] The figure is not adjusted for inflation.

References

Census of India. 2011. *Provisional Population Totals, Paper 2, Rural-Urban Distribution*. Registrar General & Census Commissioner, New Delhi, India.

Hirway, I. and D. Mahadevia. 2005. *The Gujarat Human Development Report, 2004*. Ahmedabad: Mahatma Gandhi Labour Institute.

Hirway, I. and N. Shah. 2011. 'Labour and Employment under Globalization: The Case of Gujarat', *Economic and Political Weekly*, 46(22), 28 May: 57–65.

Institute of Applied Manpower Research and Planning Commission. 2011. *India Human Development Report 2011*, New Delhi: Oxford University Press.

Mahadevia, D. 2010. 'Tenure Security and Urban Social Protection Links: India', *IDS Bulletin*, 41(4): 52–62.

Mahadevia, D. and H. Narayanan. 2008. 'Shanghaing Mumbai: Politics of Evictions and Resistance in Slum Settlements', in Darshini Mahadevia (ed.), *Inside the Transforming Urban Asia: Processes, Policies and Public Actions*, pp. 549–89. New Delhi: Concept Publishing Co.

Mahadevia, D., R. Sharma, P. Shah, and P. Ankinapalli. 2010a. *Tenure Security through External Agency Intervention—Case of Vasna*, Unpublished paper. Ahmedabad: Centre for Urban Equity, CEPT University.

———. 2010b. *Leaving Poor to Their Own Devices—Case of Amraiwadi, Ahmedabad*, Unpublished paper, Ahmedabad: Centre for Urban Equity, CEPT University.

Menon, P., A. Deolalikar and A. Bhaskar. 2009. *The India State Hunger Index: Comparisons Of Hunger Across States*, International Food Policy Research Institute, Welt Hunger Hilfe and UC Riverside. Source: http://www.ifpri.org/sites/default/files/publications/ishi08.pdf (accessed 1 November 2011).

National Sample Survey Organization (NSSO). 2007. *Informal Sector and Conditions of Employment in India, 2004–05, (Part–I)*, April, NSS 61st Round, (July 2004–June 2005), Report No. 519 (61/10/7). New Delhi: Ministry of Statistics and Programme Implementation, Government of India.

Planning Commission. 2002. *The National Human Development Report, 2001*. New Delhi: Planning Commission, Government of India.

———. 2009. *Report of the Expert Group to Review the Methodology for Estimation of Poverty*, November. New Delhi: Planning Commission, Government of India.

Press Information Bureau. 1997. *Estimate of Poverty*. New Delhi: Government of India.

———. 2007. *Poverty Estimates for 2004–05*, March. New Delhi: Government of India.

Toshniwal, R. 2010. *Evolving Social Security for Construction Workers: The Case of Ahmedabad*, Unpublished Master's Dissertation. Ahmedabad: Faculty of Planning and Public Policy, CEPT University.

9 SOCIAL SECURITY SCHEMES IN TRIBAL AREAS OF GUJARAT

A STUDY IN THE DANGS DISTRICT

Satyakam Joshi

When independent India's Constitution was drafted, social security was specially included in List III of Schedule VII, and it was made the concurrent responsibility of the Central and State Governments. A number of Directive Principles of State Policy (DPSP) relating to social security were incorporated in the Constitution. This was followed by a series of initiatives such as the Industrial Dispute Act (1947), the Employees State Insurance Act (1948), the Minimum Wages Act (1948), the Coal Mines Provident Funds and Miscellaneous Provisions Act (1948), the Employees Provident Fund and Miscellaneous Provisions Act (1952), the Maternity Benefit Act (1961), the Contract Labour Act (1970), Payment of Gratuity Act (1972), and the Building and Construction Workers Act (1996), which revealed official concern for social security for organized workers. However, the benefits were primarily meant for employees of the Central and State Governments, public sector establishments and organized private sector establishments.

The major security needs of the unorganized workers are in the fields of food, nutrition, health, housing, employment, income, and old age. In the last decade, many social security schemes had been initiated by the Union Government, like, the National Rural Employment Guarantee (NREG), the social health insurance scheme called Rashtriya Swasthya Bima Yojana (RSBY), Old Age Pension, and Widow Pension for the unorganized workers. This paper, divided into three parts, will try to analyse these schemes, in the tribal areas of Gujarat in general, and the Dangs district in particular.

PLIGHT OF THE TRIBES

Despite its economy growing by 10.3 per cent during the last decade, Gujarat records considerable regional and class disparities. Studies by

Indira Hirway (2009, 2010, and 2011) on globalization, labour and unorganized workers in Gujarat indicated that the benefits of growth had not been equitably shared. This resulted in the state slipping in poverty reduction, human development and hunger removal. As per recent statistics, the daily wage rate of casual workers in rural areas was Rs 69, and of casual female workers Rs 59 (Hirway and Shah, 2011).

Gujarat has a population of 60.3 million. The upper castes, including Patidars, comprise about 25 per cent of the population, Other Backward Class (OBC) around 52 per cent, Scheduled Caste (SC) around 7.5 per cent, and Scheduled Tribe (ST) around 15 per cent. The tribal population of around a million is concentrated in the eastern hilly track of Banaskantha, Sabarkantha, Panchmahals, Dahod, Vadodara, Narmada, Bharuch, Surat, Valsad, Navsari, and Dangs districts. The tribal settlements cover 15.01 per cent of the area, of which 56.86 per cent is forest area. There are about 30 tribal groups, the major ones being Bhils, Dubalas or Halpatis, Chaudharis, Dhodias, Gamits, Naikas and Kukanas. Forests cover 19,113 sq. km of the total area, of which 14,155 sq. km (71 per cent) is reserved forest, where tribals cannot enter.

As a result of the construction of various irrigation projects, a large number of tribals have been displaced from their native lands, forcing them to migrate to towns and cities in search of employment. Poor rehabilitation efforts by the state further affected the deteriorating socio-economic plight of the displaced families. According to a study by the Vadodara based Centre for Culture and Development, around 20 lakh hectares of land had been acquired by the Government between 1947 and 2004, for the construction of large, medium, and small irrigation projects; this displaced around 3.5 lakh families consisting of 8.8 lakh people, of which 77 per cent were tribals (Lobo and Shashikant, 2009).

Tribals are distinctly divided into different strata and class. Studies (Shah 1976, 1977; Bose 1978; Desai 1969; V. Joshi 1980; and S. Joshi 1993) show that there is a clear cut differentiation among the tribals in terms of resources. They are also equally affected by the processes of development, both planned and unplanned, and by the continuous structural and institutional shifts in rural India. They are stratified in terms of control over resources. (Further more, during the process of industrialization, major alterations in the pattern of stratification are inescapable. Old resources acquire a new significance, and new resources are to be managed and controlled effectively to survive in the severe competition over the control of resources. In this, a tribe cannot remain isolated any longer, and changing stratification is consequently appropriate in order to understand present day tribal society (Punalekar, 1997). In view of the above description of tribals of Gujarat, the most poverty stricken tribal district of Gujarat, that is, the Dangs, has to be located in terms of socio-economic and human development measures.

DANGS DISTRICT

Dangs is a tribal district located in southern Gujarat. It shares its border with Maharashtra and is covered by high hills and dense forests. The district headquarter is at Ahwa. The reserved forests in Dangs are among the richest in the state and cover 1,72,356 hectares, or 1,764 sq. km. The district comprises 311 villages, 70 panchayats and one Taluka. The total population, as per Census 2001 is 1,86,712, spread into 39,092 households. The tribal population is 1,75,079 (93.76 per cent). The total number of BPL families in the district is 33,968, which is 86 per cent of the total families in the district. Dangs is mainly inhabited by 13 different tribes, but the main ones are Konkana, Bhil and Varli, which constitute 51 per cent, 25.8 per cent and 14.7 per cent, respectively. The remaining tribes constitute 8.5 per cent of the total population.

The density of the population in the district has been steadily growing, from 43 per sq. km in 1961 to 108.3 in 2001. This is slightly higher than the state average. The sex ratio is 987 females per 1,000 males, considerably higher than the state and the national average (921 and 927 respectively).

Despite being one of the most backward districts of Gujarat, the literacy rate here is 60 per cent, much higher than the state average among tribals, of 42 per cent. There are 412 primary schools, and 32 secondary and higher secondary schools in the district. The Anganwadi, which is the primary service centre for integrated child development, has its presence in 210 out of 311 villages. There is one Government Arts and Commerce College, and an Industrial Trainsing Institute at Ahwa.

The workforce is around 50 per cent of the population. Majority of the population are dependent on agriculture for their livelihood.

Agriculture productivity, however, is quite low, with only 57,843 hectares (33 per cent) of the total geographical area under cultivation, and about 7.68 per cent of cultivable land under irrigation.

The average landholding per household in the district is 1.58 hectares. Major food crops and fruits produced in the district are rice, ragi, kharsani, tuver, groundnut, mangoes, and custard apple, to name a few. Due to very small holding and very low productivity of the land, most households have diversified pattern of occupations. Since no single activity provides sufficient resource to ensure livelihood, majority of the working population migrate during winter and summer in search of jobs.

OBJECTIVES AND METHODOLOGY

This study focuses on monitoring the implementation of social security schemes initiated by the Gujarat Government in the Dangs district, considered as one of the most backward tribal districts of the state. It specifically looks at two major objectives: (i) implementation of the social security schemes; and (ii) how far they have benefited the tribals.

We used both qualitative and quantitative research methods. In the qualitative research method we used research tools such as case study, group discussion and participant observation while in the quantitative research method, we used survey research technique through a structured questionnaire. To understand the ground reality of the implementation of social security schemes, we selected four of the 311 villages in the district—Borigavtha, Koshimda, Chokia, and Linga. The selection of the villages was based on their geographical location, inhabitation of various tribes, implementation of social security schemes, and infrastructural facilities. We randomly selected 25 households from each village for in-depth interviews. We also met and interviewed Sarpanches of the villages, village officials, village employment assistants called Gram Rojgar Sevaks (GRS), and five to seven Village Leaders (both political and social). Sarpanches of about 20 other villages in the district were also interviewed. For participant observation, we attended Gram Sabhas (Village Assemblies) of all sampled villages during the entire field work period.

At district and taluka levels, we carried out in-depth interviews with various officials, social activists, and media. One of the main challenges of this study was a high level of variation between the officials' and peoples' versions. Though this led us to further investigate the details, we were unable to grasp the complexities involved in the often conflicting perspectives about the schemes.

PROFILES OF STUDY VILLAGES

As mentioned in the methodology, we selected four sample villages. Each village is unique in terms of geographical location, and the basic amenities available. Demographic, socio-economic and basic amenities details of the villages, as we found it, are provided in Table 9.1.

The profile of the villages indicated that Borigavtha and Koshimda were better off in terms of socio-economic development. In both the villages, milk co-operatives were predominantly active. The plain terrain of north Dangs ensured plenty of water for drinking and irrigational purpose. This also helped agricultural production. Borigavtha had a very proactive, efficient, and committed Sarpanch. He managed to implement many development schemes in the village successfully. However, he could not do much in terms of providing continuous work to the villagers due to district level problems in allocating work and releasing pending payment to workers. The Sarpanch of Koshimda was comparatively not as proactive, but the village youth were very dynamic, and well informed about government schemes. Besides, availability of water is good, and the proximity to the nearby Tapi district is also advantageous to the village.

By comparison, the other two villages—Linga and Chokia—lying in hilly terrain, were found to be more backward. Linga, the former, was one among the five villages of the Dangs from where the Bhil king once ruled in the early 19th century. It is dominated by the Bhil tribes; since the Bhils were traditionally and culturally not accustomed to do settled agriculture, agriculture here was not developed. In Chokia village, the leadership was very weak, but the Sarpanch, who was from the nearby Pandva village, was very active.

NREGS IN DANGS

The National Rural Employment Guarantee Scheme (NREGS) was implemented on 2 February 2006, in Dangs. Under this scheme, all rural families were guaranteed upto 100 days of wage employment in a financial year. To be eligible for getting the benefit, the household needed to be registered in the Gram Panchayat. In the case of Dangs, the position of NREGS as on March 2011 has been detailed as below;

TABLE 9.1 Demographic, Socio-economic, and Basic Amenity Details of Villages Studied

Details	*Villages*			
	Borigavtha	*Koshimda*	*Linga*	*Chokia*
Total Population	1,102	1,800	1,172	309
Name of the group Gram Panchayat	Dungarda	Koshimda	Linga	Chokia
Number of villages under group Gram Panchayat	4	3	5	7
Type of tribes in the village	Kunbi, Varli, Bhil	Kunbi, Varli, Bhil, Gamit, Kotvalia	Bhil, Kunbi,	Kunbi, Varli
Total number of families	210	302	204	139
Total number of BPL families				
0–16 score	104	214	104	106
17–20 score	20	49	27	10
More than 20 score	120	39	77	29
Education facilities	Up to 5th Std.	Up to 8th Std.	Up to 10th Std.	Up to 5th Std.
Number of rooms in the school	4	8	6	3
Number of teachers in the school	4	11	5	3
Total number of school-going children				
Primary	135	327	201	127
Secondary	20	40	157	12
Higher secondary	08	14	10	04

College	07	06	12	08
Professional course like ITI, computers	10	10	10	03
Distance of secondary school from the village (in km)	8 km	15 km	-	7 km
Total number of children enrolled in anganwadi	48	156	100	70
Literacy Rate				
Male	25%	55%	78.48%	40%
Female	20%	36%	32.83%	30%
Religions practiced in the village	Hindu, Christian	Hindu, Christian	Hindu, Christian	Hindu, Christian
Distribution number of household as per religion				
Hindu	200	52	101	134
Christian	10	250	100	05
Total number of cultivators	86	64	60	65
Big farmers (more than 10 acres)	5	5	3	-
Marginal farmers (6 to 10 acres)	40	14	10	2
Small farmers (less than 5 acres)	36	45	47	63
Total land in the village (in hector)	398.8	300.8	1392.9	819.1
Cultivable land	165.5	265	226	182.3

(*Cont'd*)

TABLE 9.1 (*Cont'd*)

Details	*Villages*			
	Borigavtha	*Koshimda*	*Linga*	*Chokia*
Grazing land	66.9	40.4	62	39.3
Forest land	162	-	1,028.2	591
Total number of migrant families in the village	50	180	20	30
Total number families as agriculture labour	10	60	50	5
Daily wage of agriculture labour	Rs 40	Rs 50	Rs 35	Rs 35
Total irrigated land (in hector)	82	10	–	–
Total number of wells	9	35	6	2
Total number of borewells	22	47	6	5
Total number of oil engines	12	45	6	2
Major crops	Paddy, ragi, tuwer, udat, groundnut	Paddy, ragi, varai, tuwer, udat, javar, groundnut	Paddy, varai, ragi, tuver, udat	Ragi, paddy, varai, udattuver
Drinking water facility	Yes	Yes	Yes	Yes
Milk co-operatives in the village	Yes	Yes	No	No
Number of members in the milk co-operatives	64	92	No	No
Total milk collected in a day (in litres)	414	545	No	No

Total livestock				
Milch animal	128	250	–	–
Bullock	500	120	300	100
Goat	250	400	500	100
Hen	700	1,000	1,000	300
Total Number of shops	7	7	7	2
Number of tractors	5	3	–	1
Number of televisions	30	100	20	10
Number of motorcycles	35	60	9	5
Number of four- wheelers	–	Tempo: 2 Jeep: 6		3
Number of mobile holders	50	100	50	15
Total Number of RSBY beneficiaries	80	25	10	10
NGOs in the village	Yes	Yes	No	No
Pakka road connectivity	Yes	No	No	Yes
Pakka panchayat house	Yes	Yes	Yes	Yes
Places of migration	Sugar factory in South Gujarat and Grape labour work in Maharashtra	Sugar factory in South Gujarat	Sugar factory in South Gujarat and Grape labour work in Maharashtra	Sugar factory in South Gujarat
Minor forest produce in the village forest	Tendu leaves, gum, mahuva flower, bamboo	Tendu leaves, gum, mahuva flower, bamboo	Mahuva flower, tendu leaves, gum	Mahuva flower, gum, tendu leaves

(*Cont'd*)

TABLE 9.1 (*Cont'd*)

Details	*Villages*			
	Borigavtha	*Koshimda*	*Linga*	*Chokia*
Number of households having electricity connection	200	260	50	105
Medical facility	No	No	Yes	No

Source: Data collected by the field team from the Gram Panchayat Office of selected villages studied in August 2010.

it should be noted here that inadequacy of staff had seriously affected the implementation of the programme. For instance, presently there are only four technical assistants (TAs) in the district for 70 group Gram Panchayats (total villages 311). It is very difficult for a TA to supervise the work of 75–80 villages.

This is what one of the TAs told us:

> Every day I have to visit a minimum of 12 to 15 villages; I have 75 villages under me. When NREGS work is going on in all villages, it is next to impossible to visit all ongoing projects. As per rule, I have to visit each work site and once work is over, I have to sign on the muster book; then only will it go to the higher level. Many times I am not in a position to sign the muster for more than a week, which results in delayed payment.

Similarly, officials at the District Rural Development Agency (DRDA) office also repeatedly complained about staff shortage. Another problem was of GRS; as per NREGS website, a sevak had been appointed in all group Gram Panchayats in the district, but, in reality, this was not the case. In our sample villages, there had been no sevak for the last six months, and hence no one took up the responsibility. GRS was required to have a degree or diploma from a Government ITI, and had to work as data entry operator. He/she was paid Rs 1,000 per month, which was recently enhanced to Rs 4,000. Those employed as GRS had no job security, because they were hired on contract basis for 11 months. To implement the scheme, the district had the following staffing pattern (Figure 9.1).

PROFILE OF RESPONDENTS

We randomly selected a total of 100 respondents from four villages, and through prepared questionnaires, collected relevant information, which is presented below.

Out of the 100 respondents, 14 were women. Thirty-four respondents were below 40 years, while 32 were between 44–50 years. Others were above 50 years. Regarding education, 39 respondents were illiterate, while 35 had primary level education, and 25 per cent had secondary level education or more. Religion-wise, 88 respondents were Hindus and 12 Christian. Tribe-wise, Bhils constituted 30 of the respondents, Kokanis 60, and Gamits 10.

Agriculture was the main occupation of 95 respondents; the family income of 66 respondents was in the range of Rs 16,000

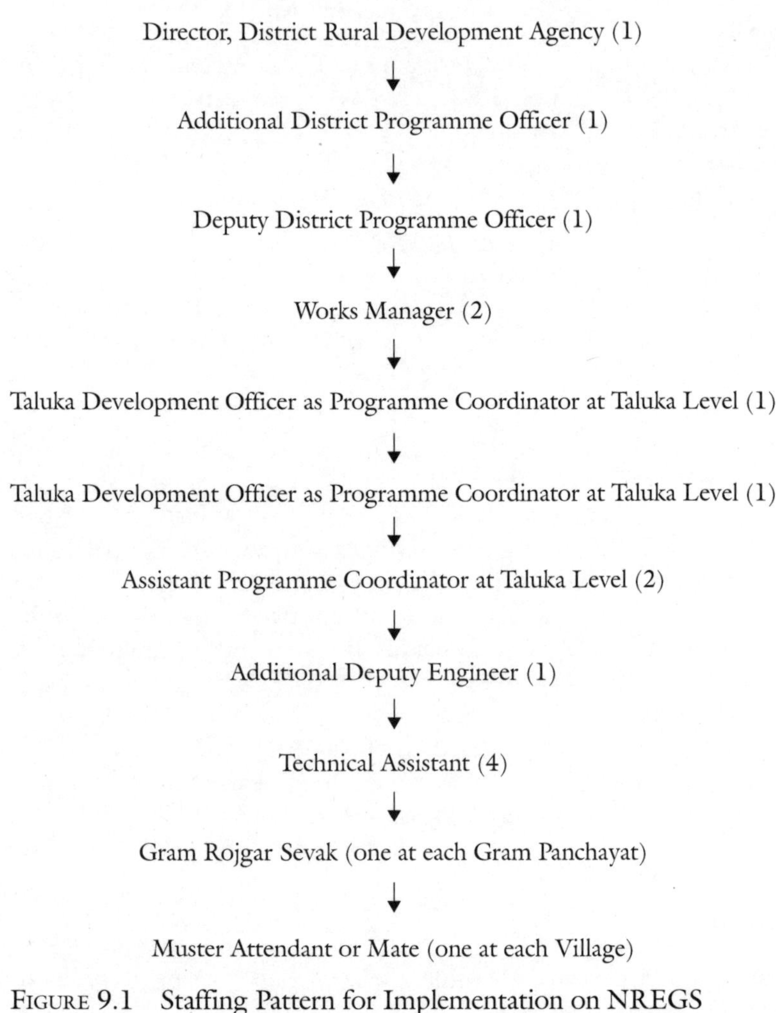

FIGURE 9.1 Staffing Pattern for Implementation on NREGS

Source: District Rural Development Agency, Dangs District, August 2010.

Note: Figures in bracket indicate the number of persons in the respective position.

to Rs 20,000, while that of 33 was in the range of Rs 6,000 to Rs 15,000. Regarding land, 21 respondents did not possess any, while 48 had less than three acres and 10 had less than five acres.

Due to its hilly terrain, irrigation was a big problem in Dangs. Only 13 respondents reported that they had any irrigation facility.

The percentage of BPL families in the sampled villages was 42, much less than the overall district percentage of 88. There were a lot of discrepancies in the BPL identification in these villages. Consequently, there were widespread complaints from the villagers that they did not benefit from the Government schemes because they were not in the BPL list. Only six reported that they had two-wheelers. Similar was the attitude in reporting other assets like TV and mobile phones.

JOB CARDS AND THEIR UTILIZATION

Our inquiry revealed that 98 respondents had job cards, largely through efforts of the Sarpanch. The GRS and the Sarpanch together were responsible for securing these cards for the villagers. In the sample village of Koshimda, however, 46 families belonging to the Kotvalia tribe did not have any job card. When asked, the GRS said that he was not aware why so many were left out. For their part, the families explained that they were not aware of the existence of the card and no official had bothered to educate them about it. Even the Sarpanch was unaware of the exclusion of so many families.

Another problem was the misuse of job cards. During our group discussion with Sarpanches and Taluka Panchayat representatives, some startling facts came to light about how some Taluka and District Panchayat representatives were misusing job cards. When NREGS was launched, the entire allocation of funds was given to the Gram Panchayat. However in the last two years, only 25 per cent of the allotted fund was given to the District and Taluka Panchayats. Even so, these Panchayats managed to complete the works using half of the budget, and produced work completion certificate that showed 100 per cent fund utilization, using faked muster books and payment receipts. The nefarious nexus between bureaucrats and politicians also helped them use funds for personal gains. Our inquiry further revealed that entries in job cards were not done regularly, and that many of them were in the possession of the Sarpanch or Elected Representative.

WORKS UNDERTAKEN

During the last three years, Dangs had been allocated Rs 39 crore, Rs 44 crore, and Rs 59 crore respectively. But last year, about Rs 3 crore remained unspent. This happened due to the slow pace of issuing the work order. The Sarpanch of Borigavtha explained thus:

> Once the Gram Sabha passes the resolution on the work to be undertaken for the Gram Panchayat, we submit the proposal to the Taluka Panchayat, which will approve it in its general body meeting and send it to the District Panchayat. After getting it sanctioned by the District Panchayat general body, it will go to the Technical Assistant for technical estimation, after which it will be again sent to the Taluka Panchayat for approval. After this, the work order will be issued to the Gram Panchayat concerned. The entire process takes three to four months. As per rules, every Gram Panchayat has to submit its work proposals by the end of December for the next financial year, but very few are able to submit it in time.

Beside this, there were many bureaucratic hurdles responsible for the delay in issuing the work order. According to one of the officials from NREGS Department, to get the work proposal approved at the Taluka level, Sarpanches often had to bribe the officers. Sarpanches, in turn, sought extra money from the people. Tables 9.2, 9.3, 9.4, and 9.5 give an idea about the extent of work done in our sample villages in the last two years.

In the last two years, payments made to laboureres and for materials in Borigavatha, Koshimda, Linga and Chokia were Rs. 4.34, Rs 3.68, Rs 7.84, and Rs 11.78 lakh, respectively. These disparities were due to several reasons. First, Borigavtha and Koshimda were prosperous villages with good irrigation facilities, which resulted into good agricultural production (see Table 9.1). Milk co-operatives were also functioning efficiently, which provided extra income to the people. The Sarpanches of the two villages said,

> There is labour shortage in our villages. Majority of the people are busy in their own fields. Those who do not have land prefer to work in the sugar factories in South Gujarat. There they get regular employment for six months. Under the NREGS, an individual hardly gets 20 days employment in a year. Hence we do not propose more funds in our villages under NREGS.

In contrast, Linga and Chokia do not have good irrigation facilities. Hence, more people were available for work. That apart, the Sarpanches of both the villages showed initiative in preparing programmes and getting them sanctioned using personal contacts with bureaucrats at the Taluka and District levels.

Often the sanctioning officials have to be bribed to get the necessary clearances for even NREG-related schemes. In fact, the

Table 9.2 Work Done under NREGS in Borigavtha for the Years 2009–10 and 2010–11

Type of Work	*Year 2009–10*				*Year 2010–11*			
	Amount Paid to Labour	*Amount Paid for Material*	*Total*	*Total Man Days Generated*	*Amount Paid to Labour*	*Amount Paid for Material*	*Total*	*Total Man Days Generated*
Digging of Check dam	10,58,23	–	10,58,23	1,876				
Digging of Pond	1,33,832	–	1,33,832	1,221				
Metal Road	30,885	–	30,885	172				
Well Construction	–	–	–	–	55,636	–	55,636	548
Well Construction					54,120	–	54,120	528
Well Construction					54,494	–	54,494	528
Total	2,70,041		2,70,041	3,269	1,64,250		1,64,250	1,604

Source: Project Coordinator, NREGA, District Rural Development Agency, Ahwa, Dangs.

TABLE 9.3 Work Done under NREGS in Koshimda for the Years 2009–10 and 2010–11

Type of Work	*Year 2009–10*				*Year 2010–11*			
	Amount Paid to Labour	*Amount Paid for Material*	*Total*	*Total Man Days Generated*	*Amount Paid to Labour*	*Amount Paid for Material*	*Total*	*Total Man Days Generated*
Metal Road	68,168	23,195	90,363	593				
Watershed Wall	1,33,832	–	1,33,832	1221	10,598	–	10,598	117
Watershed Wall					14,406	–	14,406	144
Watershed Wall					14,719	–	14,719	110
Watershed Wall					9,724	–	9,724	117
Watershed Wall					14,852	–	14,852	147
Watershed Wall					15,300	–	15,300	186
Metal Road					1,32,000	–	1,32,000	1,320
Total	68,168	23,195	90,365	593	2,77,599		2,77,599	2,801

Source: Project Coordinator, NREGA, District Rural Development Agency, Ahwa, Dangs.

TABLE 9.4 Work Done under NREGS in Linga for the Years 2009–10 and 2010–11

Type of Work	*Year 2009–10*				*Year 2010–11*			
	Amount Paid to Labour	*Amount Paid for Material*	*Total*	*Total Man Days Generated*	*Amount Paid to Labour*	*Amount Paid for Material*	*Total*	*Total Man Days Generated*
Digging of Check dam	1,27,027	–	1,27,027	1,368				
Digging of Check dam	62,330	–	62,330	585				
Digging of Check dam	64,845	–	64,845	605				
Watershed Wall	20,228	–	20,228	260	16,940	–	16,941	176
Metal Road					63,650	5,145	68,795	660
Metal Road					39,732	5,100	49,832	396
Metal Road					78,772	21,830	1,00,602	792
Metal Road					1,75,800	96,490	2,72,290	1,758
Total	2,74,430	–	2,74,430	2836	3,74,894	1,28,556	5,09,459	3,758

Source: Project Coordinator, NREGA, District Rural Development Agency, Ahwa, Dangs.

Table 9.5 Work Done under NREGS in Chokia for the Years 2009–10 and 2010–11

Type of Work	*Year 2009–10*				*Year 2010–11*			
	Amount Paid to Labour	*Amount Paid for Material*	*Total*	*Total Man Days Generated*	*Amount Paid to Labour*	*Amount Paid for Material*	*Total*	*Total Man Days Generated*
Metal Road	93,032	21,315	1,04,347	856	39,799	9,453	49,254	498
Watershed Wall	22,517	–	22,517	210				
Protection Wall	82,116	52,430	1,34,546	820	1,92,246	92,700	2,55,046	1,846
Watershed Wall	38,532	–	38,532					
Watershed Wall	29,873	–	29,873	272				
Protection Wall					3,20,019	1, 72,900	4,92,916	3,280
Metal Road					39,468	12,390	51,806	346
Total	2,56,070	73, 745	3,28,815	2,462	5,91,524	2, 57,485	8,49,009	5,972

Source: Project Coordinator, NREGA, District Rural Development Agency, Ahwa, Dangs.

confession of the President of the Sarpach Association of Dangs was quite revealing, 'At every level we had to pay a bribe. If we had not, the necessary sanction would have been refused. We also had to visit the district headquarters many times, which is expensive.'

EMPLOYMENT GENERATED

According to NREGA rules, up to 100 days of work needs to be guaranteed to rural people. Official figures for 2009–10 and 2010–11 showed that around 4,300 and 6,667 families respectively had been provided 100 days employment in Dangs district. This was well below the total number of job cards issued in the district (Table 9.6).

What went wrong? From our fieldwork observations and interviews with various stake holders this was the picture we got:

1. Due to the apathy of Sarpanches and Village Officials, work proposals from the Gram Panchayat seldom reached the higher offices on time. There was a shortage of TAs in Dangs. There were only four TAs as against 70 group Gram Panchayats, for 311 villages.
2. The sanctioning procedure is very cumbersome. The proposal goes through a minimum of five departments, which takes up to two to three months. By the time a sanction is obtained,

TABLE 9.6 Job Cards Issued and Employment Generated for the Years 2009–10 and 2010–11

Job Cards Issued	*Total*
SC	96
ST	45,008
Others	1,050
Total	46,151
Cumulative number of households provided employment	33,868
Number of households working under NREGS	20,566
Cumulative number of households completed 100 days	6,670

Source: www.nrega.nic.in.

people might not be available due to their own agricultural work or migration.

3. Allocation of funds is often inadequate. During the last financial year, about Rs 44 crore had been allocated to Dangs. Out of this, about Rs 7 crore was kept reserved for construction of Rajiv Gandhi Seva Kendra(s) at all Gram Panchayats. The remaining amount was distributed among three agencies, the District Panchayat (Rs 9 crore), the Taluka Panchayat (Rs 9 crore), and the Gram Panchayats (Rs 18 crore). If the Rs 37 crore was divided among the 70 Gram Panchayats, then it would amount to approximately Rs 50 lakh for each Panchayat. If it were divided among 311 villages, then it would come to Rs 11.57 lakh per village. If the mandatory 40 per cent material cost were deducted, then each village would get only Rs 6 lakh for wages. This would not be enough for an entire village to be provided with employment. Given the total job cards in the district (46,000) with 100 days of employment at the rate of Rs 100 per day, the total amount would come to about Rs 46 crore, plus Rs 30 crore on material cost, making it a total of Rs 76 crore.
4. People were told not to demand work. There was a tacit understanding between the Sarpanch and Government Officials in this regard; the explanation from the officials was that no work was available as there was no administrative clearance for any. This might be due to paucity of funds, they added.

It appeared that NREGS had not made much of an impact on employment generation in Dangs. Apart from paucity of funds, there were managerial hurdles which could have been removed at district and taluka levels.

MIGRATION AND ASSET BUILDING

One of the important objectives of the scheme was to reduce migration and improve the quality of life of the people through employment. If this scheme only generated 15 to 20 days of employment for an individual, as seen above, it would be difficult to percolate the benefits of employment to migration reduction and new asset creation. Out of 100 respondents, 82 reported that their family earned between

TABLE 9.7 Agriculture Production in the Dangs District (in kg per acre)

Crop	*Year 2001 (base year)*	*2007–8*	*2008–9*	*2009–10*	*2010–11*
Paddy	1,008	2,165	2,005	1,752	2,060
Ragi	649	1,009	1,210	856	712
Juvar	1,044	1,536	1,464	1,473	1,100
Tuver	–	–	1,088	727	–

Source: Agriculture Department, District Panchayat, Dangs.

Rs 1,500 and Rs 2,000 last year; as opposed to the previous year, where 84 respondents had reported that they earned Rs 700 and Rs 1,000. Migration from Dangs to South Gujarat for sugarcane cutting had come down by 10 to 12 per cent in recent years. This was due to several reasons.

NREGS might have influenced migration, but not on a big scale. However, many respondents said that if they got continuous employment for 100 days, they would not go to the sugarcane fields, as the work there was very hard and laborious. They only sought work there for the regular employment of six to seven months. Reduction in migration was also due to overall improvement in agriculture in the district. Data on the agricultural production in last 10 years suggested that production had increased two-fold (Table 9.7).

Apart from cereal crops, production of vegetables and cash crops, like sugarcane and groundnut, had also increased. This generated avenues for agricultural labour, thanks to better irrigation facilities. Consequently, reducing migration.

Another important factor for reducing migration has been the increase in the number of milk co-operatives, and the overall increase in milk production, which generated additional income for the people (Table 9.8).

A policy change by the State Forest Department in 1997 regarding tree felling also seemed to have helped reduce migration. Around 82 per cent of people were landholders in the Dangs. Till 1980, the owners could cultivate the land but were barred from felling the trees. In that year, the Forest Department allowed partial cutting of trees. During a three-year period, the landholder could cut 10 trees but had

TABLE 9.8 Dairy Development in Dangs from 2001–2 to 2007–8

Subject	*2001–2*	*2002–3*	*2003–4*	*2004–5*	*2005–6*	*2006–7*	*2007–8*	*2008–9*
Number of existing DCS on 15 April	09	17	34	50	56	-	-	145
Number of newly formed DCS	08	97	151	18	32	-	-	00
Number of DCS closed	00	54	01	03	00	01	05	06
Number of DCS running	17	34	50	65	97	150	147	147
Total annual milk procurement (in lakh)	2.28	11.36	18.79	31.24	42.87	76.88	82.16	74.60
Average daily milk procurement	626	3.113	5.150	5.558	11.747	21.058	22.415	20.441
Total annual income	22.87	113.68	187.94	312.48	428.48	828.99	985.07	995.8

Source: Office of the Registrar Co-operatives, Dangs District.

Note: DCS = Dairy co-operative society.

to grow 30 trees. Only after the newly grown trees attained a certain growth were the old trees allowed to be cut. The Forest Department auctioned the felled trees and 30 per cent of the amount was given to the land owner. But in 1997, this 70:30 formula was changed and a new 80:20 formula was implemented. This impacted income generated to a large extent, and was also one of the probable reasons for reducing migration.

With regard to asset creation, it should be noted that under NREGS, 748 private wells had been constructed. Indirectly that facilitated irrigation and agricultural production. Construction of a watershed wall in the field helped conserve water. Around 123 check dams were dug, which not only boosted irrigation, but also helped people generate additional income.

PEOPLE'S PERCEPTION OF NREGS

There was a perception among people, politicians and government functionaries that NREGS was a scheme to earn money through corrupt practices. Though unfair, it was not a baseless assumption. Detailed discussions with various officials and politicians revealed that at the local level—at the Sarpanch level—cash transaction of funds was taking place. For example the Sarpanch of Borigavtha showed us his diary which had a column for *kharchi*, or expenses, under which he had entered varied amounts ranging from Rs 700 to Rs 5, 000, with no details. He explained that each time he went to Ahwa to collect NREGS payments, he had to pay money to various officials. If the pending payment was about Rs 10,000, he had to pay at least Rs 500 to the officials concerned. They called this kharchi. Once they got the payment, they equally divided it among themselves. Even to get sanction for any work proposal the officials had to be paid.

However, there were allegations that some of the Sarpanches were also making money in the process. In several cases, the building contractors and material suppliers were related to the Sarpanches, while in other instances the Sarpanches themselves were contractors or material suppliers. An RTI query revealed that 47 contractors were related to Sarpanches. There are allegations that in all the cases, the Sarpanches themselves were the *benami* (undisclosed) owners of the contracting firms. In other words, out of a total 70 Sarpanches in Dangs, around 70 per cent were involved in corruption. It was also revealed that all these firms were registered after 2006. This had a direct correlation with NREGS.

At the Taluka and District levels, the *modus operandi* of corruption was unique, involving not only the highest level of officials and politicians, but the entire line department. As mentioned earlier, Taluka and District Panchayat representatives were misusing job cards. Since 2008, 25 per cent budget of NREGS had been allocated for Taluka and District Panchayat representatives equally—prior to this only the Sarpanches benefited by this scheme. Many Sarpanches believe that corruption began in NREGS after this reallocation of funds.

Owing to vested interests, many were very keen on becoming Taluka and District Panchayat representatives. During the recent elections (held in October 2010) to Taluka and District Panchayats, an average Rs 5 to Rs 6 lakh had been spent by each candidate. Take the case of the Sarpanch of Borigavtha, who contested the District Panchayat polls. The campaign style was unique as there were no public meetings, but a huge rally of around 30 jeeps and 75 motor cycles. All vehicles were decorated with the party symbol and the photos of the candidate. After visiting 4–5 villages, they all assembled at one particular place to have lunch. The entire expense was borne by the candidate. This exercise was explained by the candidate, saying,

> The number of vehicles in the campaign will impress the voters. They will think that the candidate has substantial influence, and he could help them once he gets elected. I had contested in the last Panchayat elections in 2005 as well. Then I spent Rs 2 lakh, but this time I have spent Rs 4 lakh already. The total figure would go to Rs 10 lakh.

Said Ghelubhai Nayak, who is a Gandhian,

> I have been working in Dangs from 1948. Now I am 83 years old. I have witnessed all levels of elections here since 1952. I myself had contested the District Panchayat elections in 1964 and 1970. The recent elections to Taluka and District Panchayat were the most expensive. My rough estimate is each candidate must have spent a minimum of Rs 10 lakh and a maximum of Rs 25 lakh. I am completely baffled as to where they get this money from. Surely they must be hoping to recover it by siphoning off funds from schemes like NREGS and BRGF (Backward Regions Grant Fund).

Interestingly, four big contractors who had done around Rs 2–3 crore worth of work under NREGS and other schemes in the last two years had contested the Taluka and District Panchayat polls, and all four won the elections.

In March 2011, NREGS auditors found irregularities in data entries of Keshabandh and Shingana villages. There were no muster roll entries in the computer, but payment had been made to both the Village Sarpanches of around Rs 9.5 lakh and Rs 53.75 lakh respectively. The irregularities were brought to the notice of the Collector, and in the course of the subsequent investigation it was found that no work had been carried out in either of the villages. People had not been paid any money. The entire line department was found to be involved in the corruption. The Sarpanch and Village Officials were suspended, and the contracts of Technical Assistants of that area and NREGS programme Co-ordinator were terminated. Two Class II officers in NREGS were transferred.

It was thus obvious that malpractices had been carrying on at every level, with people accepting money without any hesitation. The new generation of representatives did not have any problem with this system. They were fully convinced that it was there legitimate right to siphon off money for their personal use. Meanwhile, beneficiaries became increasingly skeptical about these schemes and the intentions of the state.

RASHTRIYA SWASTHYA BIMA YOJANA (RSBY)

The RSBY is one of the foremost health insurance schemes for rural poor. As mentioned earlier, 86 per cent of the families in Dangs fall in the BPL category. Hence, implementation of this scheme is very important for improving the health standard of the people. BPL family members have to register themselves first, and then collect the smart cards to avail of the cashless health benefits. The total number of BPL families in Dangs is 35,344 of which 26,590 have been enrolled under RSBY and have received smart cards. In other words, 75 per cent of BPL families have been enrolled. In 2009–10, four private and two government hospitals had been empanelled for this scheme.

However, the scheme faced severe criticism in the very first year, due to irregularities indulged in by private hospitals and the insurance company personnel. These hospitals were later blacklisted; however, the claims made by them have not been cleared till date. Our inquiry revealed that the irregularities were mainly in making false cases and issuing fake smart cards. Faking smart cards was found to be easy. Multipurpose health workers (female) had been asked to accompany insurance company personnel to issue the smart cards;

they had been given Field Key Authority (FKA) by the District Project Co-ordinator (DPC). As per this arrangement, the female health worker has the authority to issue the smart cards, as does the DPC. In connivance with DPC and female health worker, many fake smart cards had been issued in the first year of the scheme. These fake cards were inserted into hospital machines and false cases were registered, on the basis of which payments were made. Once this scandal became public, the authorities had to act against the erring officials. In fact, we met doctors of three private hospital, payments to whom had been stopped, and who were later blacklisted.

Dr P.D. Mehta of Sai Hospital, Wagai believed that 'The scheme is very good but there are also a lot of practical difficulties. In 2009–10, I treated 2,000 cases. Because of irregularities in Samarth Hospital at Ahwa, all payments were stopped. I am tired of this, and next year I am not going to accept this.'

However, health officials told us that Sai Hospital had been denied payment as it too had prepared fake claims, and an inquiry had been ordered against it. Major irregularities had, however, happened at the Samarth Hospital, Ahwa. Dr Sirsagar, an Ayurvedic doctor, had been practicing there for the last 10 years. As per RSBY norms, only those with MBBS degree could be empanelled. Dr Sirsagar informed us that he had employed an MBBS doctor. Hence his hospital was eligible. He alleged that he had been targeted due to political reasons. Till date, claims worth about Rs 32 lakh have not been settled.

The implementation of the scheme was better in 2010–11. Stern steps had been taken against the use of fake smart cards. The insurance company was also changed. The District Project Co-ordinator of Dangs said that not a single fake card was detected during 2010–11.

The above data indicated satisfactory progress of the scheme in 2010–11. Of the 1986 claims made, 1817 cases were settled, amounting to a total payment if Rs 20,68,050, which was made (Table 9.9). According to the District Heath Officer, Ahwa, the irregularities in the scheme and malpractices like smart card duplication had come down owing to strict vigilance. 'Normally,' he said, 'smart cards were issued in the July–August period. This year we were very strict and issued the cards on the spot, so that duplication was difficult. Even where we could not reach due to heavy rain, we issued the cards on the spot after the monsoon.'

TABLE 9.9 Hospital-wise Claims and Number of Settled Cases of Year 2010–11

Name of the Hospital	*Total Number of Claims*	*Total Amount*	*Total Settled Cases*	*Total Amount Paid*
Civil Hospital, Ahwa	323	5,38,373	296	4,89,375
Gaurang Nursing Home, Ahwa	824	8,21,675	757	7,47,675
Shradhadha Hospital, Ahwa	839	9,05,500	764	8,31,000
Total	1,986	22,65,548	1,817	20,68,050

Source: DPC, Health Department, District Panchayat, Ahwa-Dangs.

OLD AGE PENSION SCHEME

Old Age Pension was another social security scheme for the rural poor. There were two schemes for the old people in Gujarat. One was implemented by the Central Government and the other by the State Government. As per the Central scheme, those who belonged to the BPL category and had crossed 65 years of age would get Rs 400 per month. The State Government scheme, on the other hand, covered persons who were above 60 years, did not have a son of 21 years of age, and whose annual income did not exceed Rs 2,400, or whose family income was not more than Rs 4,500. They were eligible for Rs 200 per month. Once a person crossed the age of 65 and fell in the BPL list, he automatically became eligible for the national pension scheme that fetched Rs 400 per month as old age pension. In Dangs, there were 2,024 old age beneficiaries, of which 90 received the state pension. This scheme was implemented in Dangs in December 2008. Data given in the table below will indicate the progress of the scheme (Table 9.10).

The above table indicates that the number of beneficiaries has been continuously increasing, while many have still been left out. We found that in Chokia and Borigavtha villages, 30 and 40 people respectively were getting old age pensions, while in Linga only one person was the beneficiary, and in Koshimda, none. We found that Sarpanches of both the latter villages were not interested in

TABLE 9.10 Total Number of Beneficiaries under Old Age Pension Scheme in Dangs, 2008–11

Year	*Number of Beneficiaries*	*Number of Beneficiaries Added in the Year*
December 2008 to March 2009	682	
April 2009 to March 2010	1,136	545
April 2010 to March 2011	1,628	492
April 2011 to July 2011	2,024	396
Total as on July 2011	2,024	

Source: Office of the District Social Welfare Board, Dangs District.

enrolling people for the scheme. Many old people who had been left out complained that they were unaware of the procedures for enrollment.

In Koshimda village, three eligible pensioners told us that the Sarpanch of their village had not informed them about the scheme. 'We came to know only last month, from a neighbouring village, that old persons there were getting Rs 400 per month,' they said. When they complained to the Sarpanch, they were told that there were no forms available at the Collectorate, and that they would have to produce certain documents.

WIDOW PENSION SCHEME

The widow pension scheme is meant for providing security to destitute widows. According to the guidelines, the applicant must be between 18 to 60 years of age and should not have a son above 21 years. Her annual income should not exceed Rs 2,400 and family income should be below Rs 4,500. The eligible widow will get Rs 500 per month. A maximum of two minor children are also entitled to a benefit of Rs 80 each, per month, under this scheme.

Table 9.11 indicates that the number of widowed beneficiaries has been increasing. This is a positive sign as it implies an overall awareness about the scheme. This apart, it gave respectability to the widows. Some people in Linga and Borigavtha believe that:

We are now respected by our villagers. Even family members give us love and respect. We are no more dependent on any one. We do not have to succumb to any pressure for earning money. We take

TABLE 9.11 Total Number of Beneficiaries under Widow Pension Scheme in Dangs from 2006–7 to 2009–10

Sl. No.	*Year*	*Total Disbursement of Money*	*Total Number of Beneficiaries*	*Total Number of Trainee*	*Total Disbursed Amount to Trainees*	*Total Number of Kits Distributed*
1.	2006–7	9,92,875	175	25	1,41,050	25
2.	2007–8	11,72,500	226	25	1,29,375	25
3.	2008–9	13,50,360	256	25	2,12,000	25
4.	2009–10	15,89,000	350	25	1,75,018	19
5.	2010–11	20,94,320	421	25	1,85,112	22

Source: Collectorate office, Dangs district.

care of our health and also spend money on food. If there is a need, we can help our relatives. We have become self-sufficient. We are happy with this scheme.

***

The importance of social security schemes for the rural poor in a district like Dangs, with a heavy concentration of tribal population well below the poverty line, is revealingly evident. The study undertaken by us in the four selected villages in Dangs district was not hassle-free. We did undertake in-depth investigation and analysis, conduct in-depth interviews with various stakeholders of the schemes, social and political leaders and bureaucrats, and extensively tour the areas covered by the schemes. We faced great difficulties in collecting official data. In some cases, we had to file RTI petitions to get the data.

We found that except NREGS, other schemes like RSBY, Old Age Pension and Widow Pension were being implemented satisfactorily. However, there was a lack of support from elected representatives, particularly Sarpanches and government officials. For example, in the RSBY scheme, there was monetary provision for IEC (Information, Education and Communication) for beneficiaries, but this amount remained unspent as no effort was made to educate the people about it. The latter were also confused about the criteria for the schemes. Being illiterate, the prospective beneficiaries were totally dependent on outside help. The Sarpanches could have played an important role to help the poor avail of the benefits of these schemes. This was also true for the government officials. Those who got the benefits of Old Age Pension, or Widow Pension, felt that it had changed their lives and status in family as well as in society. They felt secure and were leading a respectable life. This was an important fallout of the schemes.

With regards to NREGS, our inquiry revealed that this scheme had not been implemented in its true spirit. There were many drawbacks. First and foremost was corruption. Elected representatives and government officials concerned were siphoning off money from this scheme for their personal benefit. In spite of many checks, they still managed to find loopholes in the scheme. There were also other problems in Dangs; as per the rules, the Gram Panchayat must provide work once it was demanded by the people. However our study indicated that while on the face of it there was no such demand by the people, but in reality people had demanded work but it was discouraged by officials and Sarpanches, because there was no work available. If these officials had considered their demand of work in such cases, they would have had to pay unemployment allowances, which had adverse impact the official's career. Our data suggested that on an average, only 15–17 days of employment was given to people. Out of 100 respondents, only three reported that they had got 50 days of work in two years. In other words, there is no regular employment available through NREGS. Those who are migrating need assurance of regular work. Besides this, income from migratory work is much higher than what the erratic NREGS employment would fetch. Non-availability of work under NREGS was due to total apathy of government machinery to provide work, and complicated procedure of sanctioning work. So households are left with no choice but to continue migrating to other places for economic reasons. Our inquiry also revealed that migration from Dangs had slowed down in recent years, but that was due to the increase in agricultural production and animal husbandry development. In short, NREGS had not provided any employment guarantee to Dangs. Rather, it had deliberately excluded masses and included the elite of the district into the scheme. Political representatives had started seeing this scheme as an important tool for making money, and thereby established their control over the people. Corruption had become an accepted practice in Dangs, which had serious ramifications in the region, with the masses being alienated from the socio-political system.

Social security for the marginalized rural people is one of the important components of human development. Various schemes have been introduced after Independence to achieve this. But their shoddy implementation confirms that providing meaningful security to the rural poor remains a distant dream. This also questions the political environment of rural India, particularly in the tribal region. Inclusion of rural poor in the development process requires political will and commitment, but free market economy has promoted individualism and consumerism, making the rural elite self-centered, and greedy for more wealth, at any cost. To achieve this, they have resorted to using government schemes for self-promotion. This, in our view, is a major road block hindering the poor from receiving benefits of various schemes, exclusively meant for them.

References

District Panchayat (Statistical Branch). 2008–9. *Samajik Arthik Samiksha, (District Statistical Profile of Dangs)*, Dangs District Panchayat.

Gaykwad, M. 2000. *Kokani Adivasioma Samajik Parivartan*, Unpublished Ph.D. Thesis (in Gujarati), April. Department of Sociology, South Gujarat University, Surat.

Hardiman, D. 1994. 'Power in the Forest: The Dangs 1820–1940', in D. Arnold and D. Hardiman (eds), *Subaltern Studies VIII*. New Delhi: Oxford University Press.

Hardiman, D. 1996. 'Farming in the Forest: The Dangs 1830–1992', in M. Poffenberger and B. McGean (eds), *Village Voices, Forest Choices: Joint Forest Management in India*. New Delhi: Oxford University Press.

Hirway, I and N. Shah. 2011. 'Labour and Employment Under Globalization: The Case of Gujarat', *Economic and Political Weekly*, 46(22), 28 May: 57–65.

Joshi, S. 1992. *Daxin Gujaratni Jungle Kamdar Sahakari Mandaliono Samajsastriya Abhyas*, Unpublished Ph.D. Thesis (in Gujarati), Centre for Social Studies, Surat.

———. 1999. 'Tribals, Missionaries and Sadhus: Understanding Violence in the Dangs', *Economic and Political Weekly*, 34(37), 11 September: 2667–75.

———. 2002, 'Development, Deprivation and Discontent: A Case of Dangs Tribals', in G. Shah, M. Rutten, and H. Streefkerk (eds), *Development and Deprivation in Gujarat: In Honour of Jan Breman*. New Delhi: SAGE Publications.

Kannan, K.P. 2010. 'The Long Road to Social Security', Paper 2, published under the series *The Challenges of Universal Coverage for Working Poor in India*. Trivandrum: Centre for Development Studies, Knowledge Programme, HiVOS, University of Amsterdam.

Mistry, P. and A. Jaswal. 2009. 'Study of Implementation of the NREGs: Focus on Migration', mimeo, Ahmedabad: Disha.

Punalekar, S. 1989. *Agricultural Profile of Dangs District*. Surat: Centre for Social Studies.

Shah, G. 1997. 'Growth of Group Identity among the Adivasis of Dangs, Gujarat', *Journal of the Gujarat Research Society*, 34(2), April: 28–59.

Skaria, A. 1996. 'Writing, Orality and Power in the Dangs, Western India, 1880s–1920s', in S. Amin and D. Chakraborty (eds), *Subaltern Studies, IX: Writings on South Asian History and Society*. New Delhi: Oxford University Press.

———. 1998. 'Timber Conservancy, Desiccations and Scientific Forestry: The Dangs 1840–1920', in R. Grove, V. Damodaran and S. Sangwan (eds), *Nature and the Orient: The Environmental History of South and Southeast Asia*. New Delhi: Oxford University Press.

Thakar, H.H. and R.L. Shiyani. 2009. 'Socio-Economic Development in Gujarat: Rosy Picture with Concerns', *Journal of Rural Development*, 28(4): 515–28.

Varghese, S. 1993. 'Women, Resistance and Development: A Case Study from Dangs, India', *Development Practice*, 3(1): 110–28.

V

ODISHA

10 STRUCTURAL LEGACY, INEFFICACY, AND WEAKENING SOCIAL SECURITIES

A STUDY OF NREGS IN A PANCHAYAT IN ODISHA

Rathi Kanta Kumbhar

The present study is an attempt to understand the implementation and working of the Mahatma Gandhi National Rural Employment Guarantee Act (NREGA) and how successfully it has helped promote a better livelihood for the rural poor in Odisha (formerly known as Orissa), the poorest state in India, with the highest incidence of income poverty and low human development index (HDI) (Planning Commission, 2010). With an impressive economic growth due to incessant flow of foreign capital and virtual stagnation in income of the poorer sections, and a high per capita net availability of food grains with high incidence of under nourishment, the state presents a stark paradox. The state's HDI has also remained at the bottom for more than three decades. The perennial problem of distribution stands like a wall, hampering poverty reduction. The laggardness of the state may have its roots in the social system, which is hierarchical, and in which the socially elite groups capture power and run local institutions to their advantage. This not only brings inefficiency into the system, but by exercising different discriminating policies, excludes the Schedule Castes/Schedule Tribes (SC/ST) and the poor from the system itself, thus depriving them of social security benefits provided by the state. This structural legacy, which denies the active participation of certain groups of people in the state, has also contributed to both economic backwardness and social exclusion, and hence is the root cause of low output and employment growth, and extreme poverty.

The distributional problem in the state reveals that the employment insecurity and incidence of poverty have remained high among the SC/STs. The National Sample Survey Organisation (NSSO) 61st Round data reflect that the incidence of poverty (as per the official poverty line) is the highest among the STs (75.25 per cent), followed by SC (52.63 per cent), and the Other Backward Classes OBCs (38.32 per cent), with the state average being 47 per cent. The proportion of below poverty line (BPL) population is lowest among the category of 'other' social group, or the higher castes (25.37 per cent). Further, the occupational distribution data show the highest incidence of poverty among agricultural labourers.

The severity of distributional problems can also be observed from the skewed distribution of land holdings. Eighty-six per cent of the total landholders belong to the marginal category (less than one acre).[1] They are mostly agricultural labourers. Among the SC/STs, 27 per cent are landless compared to the state average of 9.56 per cent. Further, among the STs, while 95 per cent are marginal farmers, among the SCs marginal farmers account for 82 per cent. Hence, they not only face class deprivation, but also caste deprivation.[2]

The existence of institutional norms in Odisha shapes the social hierarchy system, which determines the socio-economic power of a person and whether he will face employment or livelihood insecurity. In the social history of Odisha, the SC/ST group has been excluded from various mainstream activities, and hence their social exclusion reinforces them to face livelihood insecurity. The well-to-do section in the state, which manages the state's machinery, has least interest in the improvement of the masses as that will conflict with their interests. On the other hand, the socially disadvantaged lack economic as well as social power and awareness, and have failed to get organized to claim their right from the state's machinery.

Given this scenario, the role of the State Government becomes crucial in implementing developmental schemes like National Rural Employment Guarantee (NREG). Odisha is backward in terms of underdeveloped institutional systems, where there is existence of a passive civil society, a lack of social mobilization efforts, and interference of local power, and fragile unions of labour. To add to this is the lack of a proactive and innovative bureaucracy. But the labouring poor survive more by the mercy of the dominant and corrupt bureaucracy rather than the entitlement provided through NREG, on a right-based approach of the state. Hence, the study is located in the context of the overall backwardness and structural weaknesses like slow economic growth, low levels of literacy/education, lack of assets, high social disparity, supply side bottlenecks, and the absence of pro-poor organizations. Therefore, it is hypothesized that the structural legacy and the state's inefficacy are major barriers in the effective functioning of NREG in Odisha.

The study uses both secondary and primary data. The macro picture of the state with regard to NREG has been presented with the help of secondary data, extracted from the official website (www.nrega.ac.in), Panchayat Office, and various published reports. For assessing the ground realties of the scheme, the Sason Panchayat in Sambalpur district was selected. In terms of socio-economic parameters, Sambalpur district in Odisha is averagely developed, as we see mirrored in the Sason Panchayat, which we are familiar with due to our participation in an earlier study (Kannan and Pillai, 2008). 35 per cent of the total households of the Panchayat belong to the landless categories, who are victims of employment insecurity. The field survey was conducted through regular visits to different villages of the Panchayat, and to all the worksites. Group discussions were conducted with workers, and interviews were carried out with different stakeholders, including state government officials, the Sarpanch and the 'contractors', who took contracts of NREG work. Different households were also randomly selected to understand their perception of the scheme; meetings were arranged to know the problems and prospects of NREG at the grass root level.

REVIEW OF LITERATURE

Available literature dealing with social security schemes in Odisha showed that structural inequality (based on caste and class), existence of weak and malfunctioning institutions providing various social securities, and influence of local power groups accounted for the failure of schemes to reduce poverty, (Kannan and Pillai, 2011; Sarap and Sarangi, 2009; Kumbhar, 2010). The social inequalities, which had a legacy in the social history of the state, enabled the elite to control power at all levels, leaving the marginalized and socially backward groups with limited or no access to the entitlements provided by the Government.

The study by the Centre for Environment and Food Security (2007), conducted in the KBK (Koraput-Bolangir-Kalahandi) region of Odisha showed that many villages and households had not been covered by the social security schemes, and were denied not only jobs, but job cards as well.[3]

Drèze *et al.* (2007), who found some potential in NREGA to reduce poverty through employment, also noted ten loopholes in the schemes. They are (i) faulty design; (ii) erratic maintenance of job cards; (iii) incomplete distribution of job cards; (iv) wrong adjustments in the muster rolls and job cards; (v) lack of transparency in muster rolls; (vi) continued hold of contractors, vulnerability to local collusion and corruption; (vii) cryptic work measurement; (viii) shortage of staff; (ix) dormant Gram Sabhas; and (x) ritualistic vigilance procedures and lack of grievance redressal.

In 2008, the Comptroller and Auditor General of India conducted a survey on the implementation and functioning of the scheme in the 19 districts of Odisha during 2006–7. The report emphasized that 'the main deficiency in the implementation of the scheme is the lack of adequate administrative and technical manpower at the block and Grama Panchayat levels, especially the Programme Officer, Technical Assistants, and Employment Guarantee Assistants. The lack of manpower adversely affected the preparation of plans, scrutiny, approval, monitoring and measurement of works, and maintenance of the stipulated records at the Block and Gram Panchayat level'.

The National Institute of Rural Development (NIRD, 2007) study conducted in 40 Gram Panchayats across the state found that in the KBK region, only 26 per cent of the reported wage payments actually reached workers. The magnitude of bogus wage payments in different districts were as follows: Kalahandi, 88 per cent; Malkangiri, 89 per cent; Koraput, Keonjhar and Dhenkanal, 75 per cent each; Nawarangpur, 73 per cent; Nuapada, 59 per cent; Bolangir 57 per cent; and Rayagada 53 per cent. The NIRD Social Audit reports revealed that for the periods 2006–7 and 2007–8 'more than 58 per cent of the reported wage payments (in Odisha) are bogus'. Nayak, *et al.* (2010) conducted a thorough study to review and appraise the implementation of NREG processes and procedures in Odisha, and suggested some remedial actions for successful execution of the programme. The study, however, was content with merely identifying the diverse social structure and its impact on NREG, and did not elaborate further. Hence, like other earlier studies, it also found number of constrains in the schemes, such as lack of awareness, transparency, high transaction costs, time gap in wage payment and meticulous calculation of wage payment, inadequate manpower, seasonal problem, and custody of the job cards. The study also reported a number of good practices due to the functioning of the scheme, such as livelihood security, women's empowerment, social harmony, proximity of workplace, regular and institutionalized wage payment, employment that halted migration, asset creation, community participation, ensuring leadership at the ground level, and enhancement of the role of Sarpanch in effective implementation.

The literature reviewed above, and some others, have attempted to study the procedure and functioning of NREG in Odisha, both at the macro and grass root levels. Yet, it is required to find out as to why the poor in general, and SC/ST in particular, lacked voice to claim their full entitlements from NREGA.

NREGS IN ODISHA

In Odisha, NREG was implemented in three phases (see Table 10.1). In the First Phase (2 February 2006), it covered 19 districts, largely dominated by SCs/STs. On an average, around 52 per cent of the population of these districts belonged to SCs and STs. In Koraput, Malkangiri, Mayurbhanj, Nabarangpur, Phulbani and Rayagada districts, the share remained higher than 60 per cent. In the Second Phase (1 April 2007) the scheme was extended to another five districts and in the Third Phase (1 April 2008) to the rest of six districts.[4] The average SC and ST population in the districts covered under the second and third phases were 30.4 per cent and 20.5 per cent, respectively.

By August 2011, a total of 60.93 lakh households were provided job cards under NREG. Ganjam district topped in providing job cards to the highest number of households (4.46 lakh), followed by Nuapada (4.30 lakh), and Deogarh (58, 514). In Sonepur district, the percentage of job cards issued to the SC and ST remained lower than their population share in the district, whereas in the case of 'Others' (socially advantaged groups), job cards issued remained higher than their share in population. However, for the state as a whole, the share of job cards issued was higher than the share of both SC and ST in total population.

Work participation rate in the districts covered in the first phase was higher than in other districts, while literacy rate remained lower. The analysis also revealed that there was a marginal difference between the relative shares of job cards registered by SC/ST households and their respective share in population. The backwardness of the districts

TABLE 10.1 Socio-economic Profile of the Districts Covered under Different Phases of MGNREGA and Registration of Job Cards across the Districts of Odisha (up to August 2011)

	Districts	Cumulative Number of Households Issued Job Card	Share of Job Cards			Share of Population			% of Job Cards % of Population					
			SCs	*STs*	*Others*	*SCs*	*STs*	*Others*	*SCs*	*STs*	*Others*	*Literacy*	*WPR*	*HDI Rank*
1	2	3	4	5	6	7	8	9	*10*	*11*	*12*	*13*	*14*	*15*
Phase-I	Bolangir	2,54,224	18.04	22.96	58.97	16.92	20.63	62.45	1.12	2.33	−3.48	65.5	45.73	21
	Boudh	82,451	24.67	13.06	62.25	21.88	12.47	65.65	2.79	0.59	−3.40	72.51	33.92	23
	Debagarh	58,514	17.61	32.14	49.18	15.37	33.6	51.03	2.24	−1.46	−1.85	73.07	46.06	5
	Dhenkanal	1,73,625	22.11	15.22	62.63	18.49	12.79	68.71	3.62	2.43	−6.08	79.41	33.42	12
	Ganjam	4,45,682	22.50	5.61	71.89	18.57	2.88	78.56	3.93	2.73	−6.67	71.88	41.32	20
	Gajapati	1,24,158	8.46	55.01	36.18	7.5	50.78	41.72	0.96	4.23	−5.54	54.29	53.11	28
	Jharsuguda	72,677	22.55	41.72	35.67	17.07	31.34	51.59	5.48	10.38	−15.92	78.36	37.2	2
	Kalahandi	2,85,817	19.88	30.39	49.65	17.67	28.65	53.68	2.21	1.74	−4.03	60.22	46.5	11
	Kendujhar	1,54,408	14.75	42.89	42.16	11.62	44.5	43.88	3.13	−1.61	−1.72	69.00	39.77	24
	Koraput	3,04,835	16.50	53.98	27.32	13.04	49.62	37.34	3.46	4.36	−10.02	49.87	48.32	27
	Malkangiri	2,82,160	24.33	59.27	14.26	21.35	57.43	21.22	2.98	1.84	−6.96	49.49	49.11	30
	Mayurbhanj	1,25,750	14.31	54.10	31.56	7.68	56.6	35.72	6.63	−2.50	−4.16	63.98	46.23	9
	Nuapada	4,30,025	15.21	35.81	48.85	13.62	34.71	51.66	1.59	1.10	−2.81	58.20	46.05	14
	N.Rangapur	2,19,879	16.74	54.98	27.11	14.1	55.03	30.87	2.64	−0.05	−3.76	48.20	49.46	26

	Phulbani	110327	21.52	50.54	27.24	16.89	51.96	31.15	4.63	−1.42	−3.91	65.12	47.24	29
	Raygada	186172	17.49	57.47	24.47	13.92	55.76	30.32	3.57	1.71	−5.85	50.88	48.03	25
	Sambalpur	156390	21.31	35.80	41.30	17.04	34.5	48.46	4.27	1.30	−7.16	76.91	45.03	13
	Sonepur	103950	21.91	9.71	68.36	23.62	9.78	66.6	−1.71	−0.07	1.76	74.42	43.74	16
	Sundergarh	311542	11.68	64.88	23.35	8.62	50.19	41.19	3.06	14.69	−17.84	74.13	40.36	4
Phase-II	Angul	177069	18.95	14.61	66.44	17.2	11.67	71.13	1.75	2.94	−4.69	78.96	39.79	6
	Baleshwar	305174	18.79	10.52	69.40	18.84	11.28	69.88	−0.05	−0.76	−0.48	80.66	31.87	18
	Bargarh	253461	20.63	21.63	57.74	19.37	19.36	61.27	1.26	2.27	−3.53	75.16	44.08	17
	Bhadrak	201161	19.98	1.82	73.24	21.5	1.88	76.62	−1.52	−0.06	−3.38	83.25	28.87	8
	Jajpur	268411	26.43	8.75	64.82	22.99	7.76	69.25	3.44	0.99	−4.43	80.44	27.49	22
Phase-III	Cuttack	218825	25.16	5.95	68.89	19.08	3.57	77.34	6.08	2.38	−8.45	84.20	33.92	3
	Jagatsingpur	130671	25.19	0.70	74.11	21.05	0.82	78.13	4.14	−0.12	−4.02	87.13	31.2	19
	Kendrapada	185146	21.12	0.78	78.00	20.52	0.52	78.95	0.60	0.26	−0.95	85.93	29.82	10
	Khordha	103273	20.48	8.31	69.84	13.54	5.18	81.28	6.94	3.13	−11.44	87.51	30.63	1
	Nayagarh	150513	14.31	7.50	78.04	14.04	5.88	80.08	0.27	1.62	−2.04	79.17	33.32	15
	Puri	216516	20.26	0.75	75.96	18.23	0.3	81.47	2.03	0.45	−5.51	85.37	29.98	7
	Total	6092806	19.08	27.99	52.26	16.53	22.1	61.34	2.55	5.86	−9.08	73.45	38.88	

Source: Columns 1 to 6 are from www.nrega.ac.in; Columns 7, 8, 9, and 13 are from Census of India, 2011; WPR is from Census 2001; and HDI is from *Orissa Human Development Report*, 2004.

covered in different phases was also revealed from the rank of different districts in Human Development Index. Most of the low-ranking districts were covered in the first phase.

Table 10.2 reveals that there is a steady increase, both in the number of households issued with job cards (from 52.67 lakh in 2008–9 to 60.56 lakh by October 2011), and households provided with employment (from 12 lakh in 2008–9 to 20 lakh in 2010–2011). However, employment provided as a percentage of job cards issued remained at a low level (33 per cent in 2010–2011), which might technically be construed as demand for work. Employment generation in the state through NREG also showed steady increase from 433 lakh in 2008–9 to 977 lakh in 2010–11; but employment generated per job card remained low (around 16 days in 2010–2011). So far, less than 2 per cent of the workers had completed 100 days of work in a year.

The share of the marginalized group in NREG work suggests that women's participation had increased from 36 per cent in 2009–10 to 39 per cent in 2011–12, while participating workers belonging to ST showed a marginal decline. The share of SC workers declined noticeably, from 20.24 per cent in 2008–9 to 18 per cent in 2011–12.

The expenditure on NREG revealed that though there was an increase in aggregate expenditure, the share of wages in total expenditure not only declined from 62.48 per cent in 2009–10 to 60.85 per cent in 2010–11, the average wage cost per person per day had also declined from Rs. 106 in 2009–10 to Rs 96 in 2010–11.

Table 10.3 presents the percentage of job cards issued, man-days generated by their social group and gender for financial year 2011, across different districts of Odisha.[5] It was found that, on an average, 86.38 per cent of the rural households in the state had been issued job cards. The highest number of job cards (95.6 per cent) was issued in districts covered in the first phase. It was 84.7 per cent and 63.05 per cent, respectively, for districts covered in the second and third phases.

Among rural households, Gajapati district distributed the maximum job cards (118 per cent) among rural households and Khordha district the minimum (47 per cent). When the number of job cards issued exceeds 100 per cent, it means that there are more number of cards than the number of households, suggesting the existence of 'fake' cards.

District-wise analysis also showed that in Nabragpur out of the total households which were issued with job cards, 24 per cent demanded jobs, which was the highest. On the other hand, in

TABLE 10.2 A Macro-level Picture of MGNREGA in Odisha

	2008–9	*2009–10*	*2010–11*	*2011–12**
1. Number of Households Covered				
No. of Households issued Job Cards since inception (lakh)	52.67	58.02	60.25	60.56
Households demanded Employment annually (lakh)**	12.20	14.16	20.3	–
Households provided Employment annually (lakh)**	11.99	13.98	20	13.6
2. Person-days of Employment Generated				
Total per annum (lakh)	432.58	554.09	976.59	227.4
Per Job Card	8	10	16	–
Per Household Employed in MGNREGA	36	40	49	–
No. of workers completed 100 days of work	52,459	82,710	2,04,229	
3. Share of Marginalized Group in MGNREGA Employment (%)				
Women	37.59	36.25	39.40	39.23
Scheduled Tribe	35.81	36.26	35.55	34.54
Scheduled Caste	20.24	19.16	18.13	18.03
4. Expenditure on NREGS		**93,898**	**1,533.14**	
Total Expenditure (Rs in lakh)	–	93,898.37	1,53,314.26	–
Total wage Expenditure	–	58,671.56	93,293	–
Share of Wages in Total Expenditure (in per cent)	–	62.48	60.85	
Average Expenditure per Person Day (Rs)	–	169	157	–
Average Wage Cost per Person Day (Rs)	–	106	96	–

Source: www.nrega.ac.in.

Notes: * April to October 2011;

** April to March 2011, unless otherwise mentioned;

– incomplete data to calculate.

Table 10.3 Percentage Distribution of Job Cards Issued, Person-days Generated across Districts by Social Groups and Gender in Odisha, 2010–11

District	*% Job Card Issued to Rural Household*	*Employment Demanded as % of Job Card Issued*	*% of BPL Family*	*Person-days Distribution*				
				SCs	*STs*	*Others*	*Total*	*Women*
Bolangir	88.68	6.2	61.06	18.29	26.59	55.12	100	39.74
Boudh	95.94	3.6	80.2	24.47	12.85	62.68	100	44.84
Debagarh	105.23	1.7	78.79	16.77	38.41	44.81	100	40.85
Dhenkanal	79.81	9.8	62.63	21.35	14.05	64.60	100	34.87
Gajapati	118.68	11.9	61.38	7.359	65.77	26.87	100	46.84
Ganjam	80.49	11.7	55	24.8	6.586	68.62	100	50.29
Jharsuguda	99.16	8.2	49.02	20.9	48.16	30.94	100	35.59
Kalahandi	91.75	5.4	62.71	17.02	35.52	47.45	100	42.42
Kandhamal	102.21	22.8	78.42	20.6	58.65	20.75	100	45.78
Kendujhar	99.15	16.7	76.96	12.69	45.11	42.20	100	41.63
Koraput	111.19	7.3	83.81	13.27	61.73	24.99	100	42.04
Malkangiri	114.43	8.8	81.88	27.18	57.84	14.98	100	42.80
Mayurbhanj	94.54	15.6	77.74	13.98	53.28	32.74	100	46.67
Nabarangapur	95.32	23.9	73.66	13.55	61.92	24.54	100	41.36
Nuapada	91.3	4.2	85.7	14.11	44.49	41.40	100	46.07

Rayagada	106.78	10.7	72.03	16.05	60.25	23.70	100	47.07
Sambalpur	93.44	14.2	59.78	20.87	35.97	43.15	100	38.29
Sonepur	87.08	13.6	73.02	21.08	9.632	69.28	100	37.07
Sundargarh	111.39	6	65.22	10.39	73.24	16.37	100	36.25
Total, Phase I	**95.6**	**11.33**	**70.47**	**17**	**45.29**	**37.71**	**100**	**42.79**
Angul	87.88	7.2	59.36	16.24	16.76	67.00	100	38.65
Baleshwar	80.42	7.8	73.72	18.77	13.19	68.04	100	35.62
Bargarh	89.88	5.9	60.38	19.35	29.22	51.43	100	34.37
Bhadrak	85.18	8.7	66.7	21.17	2.55	76.28	100	26.04
Jajpur	82.73	19.4	60.4	28.38	6.952	64.66	100	22.95
Total, Phase II	**84.7**	**10.05**	**64.112**	**22**	**12.56**	**65.43**	**100**	**30.30**
Cuttack	58.48	16.5	52.38	24.12	6.047	69.83	100	32.22
Jagatsinghapur	58.12	16.3	52.75	22.66	0.654	76.69	100	34.27
Kendrapara	61.81	23.3	59.89	23.1	0.655	76.24	100	22.95
Khordha	47.12	4.6	59.17	21.44	11.62	66.93	100	20.84
Nayagarh	72.9	10	67.91	14.63	7.416	77.95	100	24.28
Puri	80.75	11.8	69.13	19.26	0.439	80.30	100	36.47
Total, Phase III	**63.05**	**14.45**	**60.205**	**18.13**	**35.55**	**46.32**	**100**	**39.40**
Odisha	86.38	11.56	-	18.13	35.55	46.32	100	39.40

Source: www.nrega.ac.in; www.orissa.gov.in/panchayat/bpl1.htm.

Debagarh district only 1.7 per cent job card holders demanded jobs, which was the lowest. On an average, only 11.6 per cent of households that were issued with job cards demanded employment under NREG. The districts covered in the third phase demonstrate higher demand for jobs compared to the districts covered in the first and second phases. The average percentage of households that demanded jobs in the districts covered in the first and second phases were 11.3 and 10.5, respectively. This might be due to lack of awareness among the workers.

Women's participation in NREG works was the highest (50 per cent) in Ganjam district, followed by Gajapati, Rayagada, and Mayurbhanj, at 47 per cent. It was the lowest in Khordha (21 per cent). As for social groups, Jajpur led the rest with 28 per cent of the total work being given to SC workers (highest). Sundergarh provided the highest (73 per cent) to ST workers.

However, the NREG scheme did not seem to have benefited the BPL category, who accounted for the lion's share of population. For instance, in Nuapada district, with its huge BPL population (85.7 per cent), only 4.2 per cent of households issued with job cards demanded work. Similarly, in Koraput, Malkangiri, and Boudh districts, which had more than 80 per cent of the total BPL population, only 7.3 per cent, 8.8 per cent, and 3.6 per cent, respectively, demanded work under the NREG programme. This might be due to lack of awareness among the beneficiaries of what they were entitled to under the programme. But the districts that were covered in the third phase, and where prevalence of poverty was relatively less as compared to the districts covered under the first and second phases, the demand for jobs was much higher.

The expenditure data (Table 10.4) revealed that the share of wages to total expenditure varied from 36 per cent in Khorda to 69 per cent in Ganjam district. However, Ganjam had the lowest wage rate per person per day (Rs 86.45).

The secondary data tended to show that the scheme ensured proportional representation to all social groups with no gender discrimination. It was a rosy picture, but the ground reality was different. Our study showed indications of social exclusion of SC/ST, especially in Sonepur district. The share of NREG work provided to SC category showed a decline. In brief, the state might have failed to create adequate awareness among the workers on how to demand works under the Act.

Table 10.4 Expenditure Details of NREGA in Odisha for the Financial Year 2010–11

Districts	*Man-days Generated (in lakh)*	*Cumulative Households Provided Employment*	*Wage Expenditure (in lakh) in FY**	*Total Expenditure (in lakh) in FY*	*Column 4/ Column 2*	*Column 5/ Column 2*	*Column 4/ Column 5*100*	*Per HH Wages Received in a FY*	*Per HH Expenditure in a FY*
1	*2*	*3*	*4*	*5*	*6*	*7*	*8*	*9*	
Bolangir	30.35	61,419	2,780.95	4,938.73	91.63	162.73	56.31	4,527.83	8,041.05
Boudh	12.22	26,008	1,163.71	2,025.01	95.23	165.71	57.47	4,474.43	7,786.10
Deogarh	7.81	16,840	774.19	1,334.89	99.13	170.92	58.00	4,597.33	7,926.90
Dhenkanal	33.67	61,554	3,078.47	4,903.61	91.43	145.64	62.78	5,001.25	7,966.35
Gajapati	32.75	67,950	2,935.49	4,874.03	89.63	148.83	60.23	4,320.07	7,172.97
Ganjam	62.1	1,25,069	5,368.61	7,832.2	86.45	126.12	68.55	4,292.52	6,262.30
Jharsuguda	14.64	24,821	1,368.9	2,226.04	93.50	152.05	61.49	5,515.09	8,968.37
Kalahandi	35.95	84,234	3,563.05	5,796.49	99.11	161.24	61.47	4,229.94	6,881.41
Kandhamal	45.63	88,562	4,336.96	6,344.76	95.05	139.05	68.35	4,897.09	7,164.20
Kendujhar	66.83	1,24,404	6,783.86	11,313.42	101.51	169.29	59.96	5,453.09	9,094.10
Koraput	45.81	97,510	4,479.12	7,094.62	97.78	154.87	63.13	4,593.50	7,275.79
Malkangiri	34.77	58,841	3,340.16	5,017.74	96.06	144.31	66.57	5,676.59	8,527.63
Mayurbhanj	74.7	1,48,146	7,325.14	11,687.08	98.06	156.45	62.68	4,944.54	7,888.89
Nabarangapur	59.5	1,01,398	6,039.99	9,081.03	101.51	152.62	66.51	5,956.72	8,955.83
Nuapada	10.7	24,469	1,012.45	2,252.68	94.62	210.53	44.94	4,137.68	9,206.26

(*Cont'd*)

Table 10.4 (*Cont'd*)

Districts	*Man-days Generated (in lakh)*	*Cumulative Households Provided Employment*	*Wage Expenditure (in lakh) in FY**	*Total Expenditure (in lakh) in FY*	*Column 4/ Column 2*	*Column 5/ Column 2*	*Column 4/ Column 5*100*	*Per HH Wages Received in a FY*	*Per HH Expenditure in a FY*
1	*2*	*3*	*4*	*5*	*6*	*7*	*8*	*9*	
Rayagada	48.4	75,826	4,650.42	7,481.22	96.08	154.57	62.16	6,133.02	9,866.30
Sambalpur	37.61	60,560	3,530.42	5,215.19	93.87	138.66	67.69	5,829.62	8,611.61
Sonepur	24.71	45,701	2,366.61	3,795.99	95.78	153.62	62.35	5,178.46	8,306.14
Sundargarh	44.85	95,516	4,247.75	7,528.48	94.71	167.86	56.42	4,447.16	7,881.90
1st Phase	**723**	**13,88,828**	**69,146.25**	**1,10,743.2**	**95.64**	**153.17**	**62.44**	**4,978.75**	**79,73.86**
Angul	23.03	54.169	2,125.54	4,080.72	92.29	177.19	52.09	3,923.90	7,533.31
Baleshwar	19.71	49,322	1,916.37	3,584.88	97.23	181.88	53.46	3,885.43	7,268.32
Bargarh	17.11	46,594	1,681.94	3,347.56	98.30	195.65	50.24	3,609.78	7,184.53
Bhadrak	16.86	37,841	1,606.74	3,151.01	95.30	186.89	50.99	4,246.03	8,326.97
Jajpur	40.13	94,086	3,672.65	6,110.77	91.52	152.27	60.10	3,903.50	6,494.88
2nd Phase	**116.84**	**2,82,012**	**11,003.24**	**20,274.94**	**94.17**	**173.53**	**54.27**	**3,901.69**	**71,89.39**
Cuttack	30.76	75,730	2,880.51	5,132.9	93.64	166.87	56.12	3,803.66	6,777.90
Jagatsinghpur	24.45	49,553	2,258.86	3,808.93	92.39	155.78	59.30	4,558.47	7,686.58
Kendrapara	25.97	76,885	2,671.03	3,968.57	102.85	152.81	67.30	3,474.06	5,161.70
Khorda	4.99	15,431	463.43	1,284.79	92.87	257.47	36.07	3,003.24	8,326.03

Nayagarh	30.07	57,272	2,995.72	5,204.82	99.62	173.09	57.56	5,230.69	9,087.90
Puri	20.51	59,104	1,874.02	2,896.1	91.37	141.20	64.71	3,170.72	4,900.01
3rd Phase	**136.75**	**3,33,975**	**13,143.57**	**22,296.11**	**96.11**	**163.04**	**58.95**	**3,935.50**	**66,75.98**
Odisha	976.59	20,04,815	93,293.06	1,53,314.3	95.53	156.99	60.85	4,653.45	7,647.30

Source: www.nrega.nic.in.

The field survey report conducted in the Sason Panchayat of Sambalpur district of Odisha is presented in the following section. First, it provides the descriptions of the Panchayat and analyses the role of Panchayat Officials (institutions) in executing the schemes; second, it analyses the panchayat level data available in the Panchayat Office and on the NREG website; third, it presents the responses of beneficiaries; and the last section provides the summary.

FINDINGS FROM FIELD SURVEY

INSTITUTIONAL INEFFICIENCY AT THE SURVEYED PANCHAYAT

Constituted in 1955, the Sason Gram Panchayat (GP) comes under the Dhankauda block in Sambalpur district of Odisha. Besides the Ward Members and Sarpanch (the President of the Panchayat), who are elected representatives, there are only two officials in the GP, the Panchayat Secretary and the Peon. The Panchayat Secretary is the only person to record all the official minutes of various meetings, maintain accounts, stores, and so on. During our recent visit, we observed that the two rooms of the Panchayat building had collapsed. Tables 10.5 and 10.6 provide detailed information of the Panchayat.

Presently, Sason Panchayat has eight revenue villages, with a population of 6,209, and covers an area of roughly 17 square kilometres. The eight villages have been further divided into 15 Wards in the Panchayat. 67 per cent of the total area of the GP is cultivable land, of which 58 per cent is irrigated. The principal crop of the region is paddy. The work participation rates for male and female are 57 per cent and 46 per cent, respectively. The main economic stay of the Panchayat is agriculture. A small share of population (mostly women) is engaged in other activities like *beedi* (thin, Indian cigarette) making. The service sector in the Panchayat is also cropping up, which is visible from the presence of a number of small hotels, other shops, public institutions like schools, anganwadi, post office and banks. However, recently, a number of small industries have come up within a 30 to 40 km radius of the panchayat, which is gradually providing alternative sources of livelihood to large number of households.

Landless labour constituted 35 per cent in the Panchayat. This huge reservoir of labour could be one of the reasons for low wages for agricultural labourers. Historically, farm labour belonged to a specific social group, the SC/ST, with a few exceptions. Brahmins

TABLE 10.5 General Details about the Panchayat

Name of the Panchayat	Sason
State	Odisha
District	Sambalpur
Block	Dhankauda
Area of the Panchayat	16.95 sq. km
Number of Revenue villages	8
Number of wards	15
Total population	6209
Population density	356
Scheduled Caste population	1691 (28 %)
Scheduled Tribe population	1872 (31 %)
Sex ratio	947
Number of Households	1324
Average household size	4.7
Number of members in the Panchayat	15
Literacy rate	Male – 77.0, Female – 51.6*
Work Participation rate	Total – 51.6, Male – 56.6, Female – 46.4*
Cultivable area under irrigation	59%
Major economic activities	Agriculture
Percentages of land less labour	35

Source: Field Survey at Sason, 2010.

Note: *Calculated from 2001 Census data.

owned most of the fertile lands of the region. Although in education and social status the ST population remained backward, they own a sizeable area of land, unlike the SCs, who were mostly farm workers.

The caste profile of the households in the Panchayat is very heterogeneous. People from a number of castes like Brahmin, Karana (Mohanty), Gauda, Dhuba, Kandha, Luhura, Ganda, Ghansi, Doomal, Kulta, Teli, and Munda live in this Panchayat. Among them, the SC (Ghansi, Ganda, Dhuba, Luhura, etc.) and ST (Munda and Kandha) households are the most backward, socially and economically. It is found that around 28 per cent of the population in Sason GP belongs to the SC and 31 per cent of population belongs to the ST category.

Table 10.6 Socio-economic Characteristics of the Panchayat Members of Sason Panchayat during 2010

Members	*Age*	*Sex*	*Religion*	*Caste*	*Education*	*Political Party*	*Actual Job/Occupation*
Secretary	52	M	H	OC	BA	BJD	Service
Sarpanch	37	M	H	ST	BA	BJD	Farmer
Member 1	50	M	H	GEN	Non Metric	NON	Business
Member 2	26	F	H	SC	7TH	NON	HW
Member 3	35	F	H	SC	5TH	NON	HW
Member 4	35	F	H	OC	+2	BJP	HW, Partially Business
Member 5	48	M	H	SC	5TH	BJD	Farmer
Member 6	40	M	H	OC	10TH	BJD	Farmer
Member 7	45	M	H	ST	7TH	BJD	
Member 8	39	M	H	SC	9TH	BJD	
Member 9	35	F	H	OC	7TH	BJD	HW
Member 10	45	M	H	OC	4TH	BJD	Farmer
Member 11	47	F	H	SC	5TH	BJD	HW
Member 12	48	M	H	OC	11TH	BJD	Social worker
Member 13	45	F	H	ST	4TH	BJD	HW
Member 14	32	M	H	OC	9TH	BJD	Farmer
Member 15	26	F	H	ST	4TH	BJD	HW

GRS	25	M	H	OC	BA		NON	Service
Peon	33	F	H	OC	+2		NON	Salary from GP income

Source: Panchayat office, Sason.

Notes: BJD stands for Biju Janata Dal, which is the ruling party in the state of Odisha.

BJP stands for Bharatiya Jananta Party.

NON stands for Non-party, meaning they do not belong to any political party.

Evidently, Sason was a fit case for NREG. Had there been equal rights for all in the Panchayat, one would hardly have required assistance from social security schemes. The level of education of the Panchayat members revealed that while most of the members of 'Other Castes' had college education, those belonging to the SC/ST category had either primary or secondary education. The former obviously set the rule. Further, though Panchayat as a local level institution existed, the manpower to run it had been insufficient.

Functioning of NREG in Sason Panchayat

As stated earlier, the implementation of NREG scheme is discussed in three stages (i) pre-work activity; (ii) work activity; and (iii) post-work activity.

Pre-work Activity

Pre-work activities at the panchayat level included creating awareness, registration and issue of job cards, conducting of Palli Sabha and Gram Sabha, and participating in the Samiti Sabha, to send the work proposal to Panchayati Raj Department through District Rural Development Agency (DRDA).

In Sason Panchayat, awareness about NREG was created by open publicity, by beating the drum and calling for registration, followed by issuance of job cards. Different agents—the Block Development Officer (BDO) at the block level, the Programme Officer from DRDA office, the District Project Coordinator, the Project Director, the Additional District Magistrate, the Commission from the Panchayat Raj Department and/or different Non-governmental Organizations (NGOs)—had been at work. However, the awareness created was not enough to include all the needy households into the system, and hence we found workers without job cards.

The panchayat level job cards were issued as per the BPL survey of 2002. In 2002, there was a survey to identify the BPL households, and the households with BPL cards were given job cards. The rest of the households, which were left out in the BPL survey, or the newly formed ones, did not get job cards. In 2007, a survey was conducted for those households which did not possess the BPL card, to provide job cards. But our recent visits to the field showed that many of the desiring households did not receive job cards, despite the fact that they had applied for the same. Most of these households belonged to SC/ST communities. Respondents from these communities said that historically they had been neglected and discriminated against. They wanted to meet the Collector to voice their grievances, but the Panchayat officials advised them against it, and even threatened that in the event of their meeting the Collector, they could stand to lose their work in the Panchayat.

Tables 10.7 and 10.8 present the percentages of households registered and persons covered under NREG, from each social group. From the total households of the Panchayat, 73 per cent had registered under the scheme. These can be deconstructed as 92 per cent each for SC and ST category and 51 per cent for 'other' groups. As far as the coverage of persons in the Act is concerned, it is 38 per cent, 47 per cent, 46 per cent and 28 per cent for total, SC, ST, and 'other' categories, respectively. Regarding job card, different field visits suggest that there are many households and persons who were interested in obtaining job cards, had even applied for them, but could not obtain one.

The villagers of S. Katapali reported that 50 per cent villagers had received their job cards. The remaining cards were kept by the Panchayat officials. When queried, the official said that they had kept the cards for affixing photographs on them. But our informal enquiry revealed that the cards had been retained for manipulation.

One general problem pointed out by the Programme Officer was that the people were neither aware of, nor conscious of NREG, and hence did not demand work in a written format or by verbal request. In such cases the official took interest and initiated the process. The officials explained that many workers not having job cards demanded work, and the concerned Programme Officer found it difficult to manage such situations.

The non-issue of job cards seemed to have led to renting out job cards. During our visit, one Mr Kshama (the ward member of Chhatargada) revealed that he had 'rented' out his job card to another family. Using his card, the other family got 14 days of work. He was, of course, paid approximately Rs 100 by the family. The renting out of the job card is done either by the card holder himself, or by the Secretary, or the Gram Rozgar Sevak (GRS), or by the Contractor. The demand for such cards generally came from SC/ST communities.

Different Palli Sabhas at the village level and Gram Sabhas at the Panchayat level were conducted rather ritualistically, being institutionally mandatory, but the decisions were taken by a few influential

TABLE 10.7 Distribution of Population and Households by Their Social Groups in Sason Panchayat

	Total		*SCs*		*STs*		*Others*		*Male*	*Female*
	HH	*Persons*	*HH*	*Persons*	*HH*	*Persons*	*HH*	*Persons*		
Chhatargada	46	231	15	75	22	112	9	44	116	115
Gurupali	32	164	0	0	11	55	21	109	92	72
N.khurigaon	258	1,191	67	311	112	516	79	364	605	586
Papali	142	679	26	123	23	112	93	444	365	314
Ranikhinda	373	1,769	91	431	79	377	203	961	915	854
S.Katapali	180	788	61	268	19	85	99	435	396	392
Sadasinghha	140	687	55	268	51	251	34	168	336	351
Sason	153	700	60	274	11	49	82	377	364	336
Total	1,324	6,209	375	1,750	328	1,557	620	2,902	3,189	3,020

Source: Census of India (2001).

TABLE 10.8 Percentage of Households Registered and Persons Covered under MGNREGA in Sason Panchayat

Villages	*Total*		*SC*		*ST*		*Others*	
	HHs	*Population*	*HHs*	*Population*	*HHs*	*Population*	*HHs*	*Population*
Chhatargada	124	55	27	7	195	90	111	45
Gurupali	22	8	0	0	0	0	33	12
N. Khurigaon	88	49	91	49	90	47	84	52
Papali	27	10	50	21	48	15	15	6
Ranikhinda	70	36	97	48	116	62	39	21
S. Katapali	86	50	97	54	58	32	85	51
Sadasinghha	80	38	116	53	67	32	41	21
Sason	73	39	95	54	100	47	52	26
Total	73	38	92	47	92	46	51	28

Source: Data collected from the Panchayat and cross checked from Census of India (2001); and www.nrega.ac.in.

persons, often belonging to the higher strata of society. If a person was not influential, then he had to pay some bribe.

Work Activity

NREG work started in Sason in 2006, in the village of Rani Khenda, and the project cost was Rs 5 lakh. There was hardly any demand for work from job card holders. Nonetheless, 22 projects were approved, of which only two had been completed. In the initial phase, in the absence of demand from the workers, it was the Block Officials (village level workers or village agricultural workers) who took initiatives in preparation of project. It was reported that these project works use almost 100 per cent labour. Two projects were executed during 2009–10—the road improvement work from Palsapali to Pandiapali (1 km), at a cost of Rs 4 lakh; and the road from Sadhasingha to Chhatargada (1 km) at a cost of Rs 3 lakh.

While workers belonging to SC/ST classes desperately wanted to work, there seemed to be an overall shortage of workers, resulting in projects being inordinately delayed. The shortage was partly because the wages offered under the programme were only marginally higher than the prevailing market rate. Further, there was substantial delay in the payment of NREG wage rate, which forced workers to drop out of NREG work. Many unskilled labourers from Sason Panchayat also migrated to other states like Gujarat, Kerala, and Tamil Nadu, in search of jobs.

Material cost and labour cost ratio The officially fixed labour-material cost ratio of 60:40 often created problems. For instance, the road leading to Chhatargada village was in a very bad condition, but the needed repair could not be undertaken as some of the inputs required—soil, for example—had to be brought from far, which pushed up the material cost, thereby upsetting the ratio.

Market wage rate and nature of work Another problem noted in Chhatargada was that the market wage rate (Rs 120 for male and Rs 100 for female) was almost equal to the NREGA wage rate. Those working in brick kilns earned even more—anything between Rs 150 and Rs 200—depending on the quantum of work. Also, farm operations demanded more workers because of the double crop the area practiced. Some households were also engaged in beedi making. However, what came out of the group discussion was that it was not so much the wage rate as the nature of work that mattered. Since NREGA programmes covered mostly road construction, or pond digging work, which involved hard labour under the scorching sun, there were fewer takers. Many preferred jobs that gave them the option to work under the shade. It was primarily the unskilled SC/ST workers who opted for NREGA works, as they were not allowed to work on the premises of the upper caste. Unfortunately, not many among them owned job cards. Hence, they borrow, of course for a price, the job cards from those who had them.

Report from S. Katapali During our visit to S. Katapali, a road construction work (clay) was going on. Many of the card holders opined that they were not interested to work because of the low wage rate (Rs 90 per day). It was the SC/ST card holders who were ultimately roped in. But the work sites were devoid of basic facilities. Discussion with the workers revealed that they had not received wages for three months. The workers complained to the village *Saathi* who, unfortunately, could do nothing. The workers did not even know the balance money available in their bank accounts. People were afraid of complaining against the Panchayat officials for fear of losing whatever little they were receiving. During our visit, there were 10 workers on site, and all of them belonged to either the SC or ST community. The workers were desperately waiting for their wage, which they had not received in the last three months, especially with the 'Nuakhai' festival approaching.

Post-work Activity

The post-work activities include payment of wages, assessment of the quantum of employment provided, accounting of unutilized fund and missing job cards, and social auditing. From a larger social point of view, it is also important to assess any impact on the bargaining power of rural labourers, as well as the functioning of local institutions.

Payment of wages The Programme Officer said that all the workers demand payment according to their days of work rather than the volume of work they do; for instance, the removal of a 10 cm length, 10 cm width and 1 foot depth of normal soil earns a worker Rs 125. But in such case, two workers finish that job and each of them demand Rs 125. So the Programme Officer faces problems. It was also reported that, the workers gets Rs 80 instead of Rs 125 per day per worker for earthwork. The reason provided by the Programme Officer is that the workers are not fully aware about the rules and regulations, and hence they are confused. For example, even if a small piece of work is done by a group of workers, the workers demand Rs 125 for each worker. But the problem the Programme Officer faces is that the work done by these workers was not worth Rs 125 per worker per day. Hence, the Programme Officer measures the volume of work, then finds out the average, and accordingly pays the workers; in the process, the average wage rate comes down. However, the workers stated that they finished the piece of work in a place and have surplus time in which they can do some additional work, but there is no additional work nearby. Therefore, it seems that the problem in coordination, arrangement and management persists.

Quantum of employment In the whole Panchayat, only 10 households completed 100 days of employment in the last financial year. Irregular payment and seasonality of work were said to be the reasons. As pointed out earlier, most of the households that worked in NREG belonged to extremely poor families, which needed wage payment on a daily basis for their basic necessities. But unfortunately the wage payment under the scheme took more than 15 days, or even longer. In such a context, the needy people got out of NREG work, and preferred to take up other works in the locality.

Misreporting and zero day work Our verification of job cards showed that in many cases the number of days listed in the cards was more than the actual number of days of employment provided to the beneficiaries. In other cases, no entry had been made regarding the work done by the people. On enquiring, the officials replied that they would enter such details only at the completion of the work.

Missing job card Many job cards were missing since the cards were usurped by Panchayat officials (contractor) in the name of entering the number of days of work into the card. Some of the workers had also lost their cards.

Unutilized Fund The Panchayat officials also reported that many a time, they failed to utilize the total amount of the fund they received. Labour scarcity was the main cause of underutilization of NREG fund.

Ritualistic social auditing In the surveyed Panchayat, social auditing was done ritualistically. The audit was carried out for record purpose with the help of a local person, who seldom remained neutral, and there was seldom anybody to complain against the official concerned.

Illusive right Though NREG is an Act, we found that people had no understanding of it. This was clear from the fact that many people had not got job cards. Similarly, wrong entry in the job cards, mismatch between the job demand and supply of job cards, and non-payment of unemployment allowance revealed that people had not become aware of their right to work, as provided under the scheme. This could be due to illiteracy, lack of awareness, and the feudal social relation between different social and economic groups. People felt scared to complain openly, even if they had been victims of discrimination.

Bargaining power of workers and workers' union Discussion with the workers brought to light the fact that their bargaining power had not improved under NREG. Two crucial reasons are first, many people worked with job cards of others' and hence did not have the legal entitlement to demand work under NREG. Second, there was no continuous works, and so they could not form a workers' union. However, there were instances of collective action; for example, some workers decided to meet the District Collector to bring to his notice certain malpractices. Such attempts, however, invariably got muffled by the elite officials of the Panchayat.

The social legacy in NREG One of the important observations from the field study was that many of the SC/ST households did not possess the job card, partly due to their own ignorance, and partly due to official negligence and discrimination. Ironically, most of the workers (to our observation it is almost 100 per cent) belonged to SC/ST communities. Those households which did not have job cards could still seek work under NREG by renting other's card (mostly of a member of an upper caste). In case they were unable to arrange a job card, the necessary arrangement was made by the contractor. Either way, the real workers had to pay some pre-determined amount of rupees to the card owner, as well as to the contractor. At the time of payment, the original card owner would go to the bank to draw the amount, and after taking his share and that of the contractor, the balance would be paid to the actual worker.

The solution, simple, would be to procure job cards for all SC/ST households. It will help a great deal to ameliorate poverty of these backward communities. The height of irregularity and corruption in the MGNREGA can be conceived from the case narrated in the Box 10.1.

Box 10.1 Irregularity and Corruption in the MGNREGA

After our work-in-progress workshop in November, we went back to the field to get some more insights. I also discussed some of the important findings with one of my colleagues at Sambalpur University, who happened to be the co-coordinator of National Service Scheme (NSS) unit of the University. He took the issue seriously, and made some enquiry in a nearby village where we had conducted the survey. It was found that under the MGNREGA scheme, wages were paid even in the name of persons who had died a decade ago, employees of public and private sectors (Sambalpur University, VSS Medical College, SBI, and Birla, etc.), school students and so on. Reports of such payments had been published in local newspapers. The fact was communicated to the Honourable Chancellor. Subsequently, officials of the Panchayati Raj Department visited the block (village) and found the complaints to be true. This led to the suspension of eight officials of the Dhankauda Block, including the BDO, Assistant Engineer, Junior Engineer, VLW, Sarpanch and three Contractors.

After a few days, I, along with my colleague, attended a social audit meeting in the same village (S. Katapali). The meeting was about to conclude by the time we reached the venue. As there was no incentive for the officials, or other members, to conduct the social audit meeting, everybody was in a hurry to wrap up the meeting without raising the issues, and discussing them in an in-depth manner. My colleague had a print out of a wage bill (2010–11 project at S. Katapali), downloaded from the MGNREGA official website. He read out the names of the persons to whom money had been paid. It was found that money had been paid in the name of a person who had died 15 years ago. Many of the workers present also objected that the amounts received were much less than what had recorded. Some of the card holders had also not received money.

Source: Field study, and reports in *The Samaja* (local newspaper).

The Story of 'Mo Pokhari' (My Pond) and Multipurpose Farm Pond

Under the 'Mo Pokhari' scheme, four work orders had been issued. These work orders were issued in the name of upper caste job card holders (one Brahmin and three OBCs). The reason behind this was that they were the influential people in the villages. Since the beneficiaries were financially resourceful, they started the work by spending from their own pocket and later got it defrayed from the Gram Panchayat. This would not have been possible had the work been given to SC/STs. Being poor, they would not have had the resources to finance the work; nor, for that matter would the Panchayat have been in a position to advance funds to them without upsetting their finances. In many cases, the GRS took Rs 200 from each applicant of 'mo-pokhari', which the poor among the SC/ST could not afford. Evidently, they were deprived of the 'Mo Pokhari' benefits (Box 10.2).

The multipurpose farm pond project in the state was also moving at snail's pace. During 2011–12, the fishery department had forwarded 8,923 proposals, of which 7,542 had been granted. Of this, 4,081 projects had been taken up and by October 2012, only 774 had been completed.

Enquiries with block officials revealed that since 'Mo Pokhari' projects did not involve middlemen and contractors, as the beneficiaries themselves initiated and executed the projects, there was no 'incentive' for the officials to promote them.

Box 10.2 Beneficiaries of 'Mo Pokhari'

Swarna Vainshal is one of the beneficiaries of 'Mo Pokhari'. He belongs to the OBC group. He received Rs 40,000 from the Panchayat to dig a pond. The pond water is used for paddy and vegetable cultivation. During summer, people from the village use the water for bathing purpose as well. We were told by the villagers that Mr Vainshal's nephew worked in the Panchayat Office, and that was the linkage through which he was able to get the benefit.

Nabin Dhar is another beneficiary, who received Rs 50,000 to dig a pond under the same scheme. Dhar belongs to the Brahmin caste and he is the brother of an ex-Panchayat Secretary. He spent some additional amount of money and increased the size of the pond. The pond irrigates at least 10 acres of paddy land owned by him and his relatives. Dhanu Vainshal and Prabhasini Nag also received Rs 40,000 each under the scheme of 'Mo Pokhari'. In both the cases, the pond water helps their agriculture operations.

In all the four cases, the main objective of the 'Mo Pokhari' scheme, to create additional man-days of work, was overlooked. The ponds were dug by machines, and workers were employed just for finer work. Hence, though 'Mo Pokhari' contributed to output, it did not generate employment.

Source: Field study.

***

Our study shows that the MGNREGA programme in Odisha does promote and improve the livelihood of the rural poor. However, there exist a number of shortcomings, which have social and institutional dimensions.

The socio-economic profile of the job card holders suggests that while the share of SC/STs among job card holders is high, a sizable section is kept out, despite their willingness to work. Hence, it is very important to ensure that job cards are issued to all rural households who demand it. In fact, getting the job card should form part of their legal right under the NREGA. In some cases it was pure official negligence.

Our study also shows that very rarely do the beneficiaries apply for employment. It is left to the officials and local politicians to get a project sanctioned and create employment. Ironically, the official websites give the impression of the beneficiaries demanding work. The contradiction remained unexplained.

One of the major weaknesses of the schemes is the delayed payment of wages. The poorest of the poor workers need daily wage payment to meet their basic necessities. Nevertheless, due to delay in the payment of wages, in some cases by more than two months, the workers prefer to take up non-NREG works. Although NREGA provides work as a right of the poor families, this has not been realized yet. Due to illiteracy and ignorance, poor families fail to claim their right through the Panchayati Raj Institutions.

Moreover, due to the prevalence of feudal social relations in the rural areas, the poorer section of society fails to protest against exploitation by Panchayat officials. Various media reports and research findings also have pointed out the massive irregularities in the implementation of the NREG scheme. Nevertheless, the effective implementation of NREGA will go a long way in promoting social security of rural poor by providing employment opportunities in the locality.

The functioning of the Act could have strengthened the bargaining power of the workers, but this has not happened. Third Party monitoring in social auditing could have helped the functioning of the Act better, but the social auditor, being a local man, is often caught in local power politics.

The Act also suffers from institutional bottlenecks. Shortage of manpower comes in the way of effective implementation of programmes. Meagre staffing of just three officials, including a Peon, run the Panchayat Office in Sason. In the absence of adequate manpower and meagre remuneration, the officials involved in NREG have little incentive to implement schemes properly, and hence often indulge in different dubious activities.

There is also the absence of a vigilant civil society in the Sason Panchayat to take up the grievances of people, and get them their due entitlements. As for the beneficiaries, they are too poor and illiterate to fight for their basic rights—job cards, payment of wages, and the quantum of employment.

Notes

[1] 14.4 per cent of total households in Odisha held 58.48 per cent of total land during 2002–3.

[2] The socio-cultural history of India is such that caste, as an institution, divides society into different groups in a social hierarchy, and that hierarchy determines the socio-economic status of a person. The higher the order in a social hierarchy, the higher is the wealth, education, occupation, income and well-being; hence lower order would mean hunger and deprivation.

[3] The study stated that Bilamal, which had lost four members to starvation in 2001, didn't receive job cards till the survey time. Large numbers of needy households were denied not only jobs but even job cards, and not more than five days of average wage employment had been given to a needy family. There continues to be poor job card maintenance, lack of transparency in muster rolls, and the continued involvement of contractors.

[4] Since the complete coverage of the Act took till April 2008, the data analysis is done only after that period.

[5] The data has been taken from www.nrega.ac.in website. However, it has shown certain unexpected findings; for instance percentage of job cards issued exceed 100 percent, which ideally should not have.

References

Centre for Environment and Food Security. 2007. *Rural Job Scam Survey Report on Implementation of NREGA in Orissa*. New Delhi: Government of India.

Drèze, J.P., R. Khera, and Siddhartha. 2007. NREGA in Orissa: Ten Loopholes and the Silver Lining, mimeo, Allahabad: G.B. Pant Social Science Institute. Also available at www.righttofoodindia.org.

Kannan, K.P. and V.M. Pillai. 2008. *In the Vacuum of Public Action—Social Security in Orissa: A Long Way to Go*, MPRA Paper No. 9692.

Kumbhar, R.K. 2010. *Political Economy of Hunger and Deprivation: A Study of Orissa in India*, Unpublished Ph.D. Thesis, awarded from JNU Thiruvananthapuram: Centre for Development Studies.

Nayak, N.C., B. Behera, and P. Mishra. 2010. *Appraisal of Processes and Procedures of NREGS in Orissa: A Study of Mayurbhanj and Balasore District*. Report submitted to Ministry of Rural Development, Government of India, New Delhi.

NIRD. 2007. *Some Studies on NREGA in Orissa—A Bird's Eye View*. Hyderabad: National Institute of Rural Development.

Planning Commission. 2010. *Report of the Expert Group on Methodology for Estimation of Poverty*. Chaired by Prof. Suresh D. Tendulkar, New Delhi, India. Also available at www.planningcommission.nic.in

Sarap, K. and T.K. Sarangi. 2009. 'Malfunctioning of Forest Institutions in Orissa', *Economic and Political Weekly*, 44(37), 12 September: 18–22.

11 SOCIAL HEALTH INSURANCE FOR THE POOR

A STUDY OF RSBY IN ODISHA

Amarendra Das

Social security measures have enormous relevance and crucial significance in a developing country like India, where a majority of its population languishes in poverty and vulnerability. Odisha (earlier known as Orissa) records the highest incidence of poverty, with around 57 per cent of its population below the official poverty line (GoI, 2009). The state is well known for its economic backwardness and low level of human development, with very high infant and maternal mortality rates, and low life expectancy. Although it has registered impressive economic growth in the last decade, a major share of its population suffers from malnutrition, health insecurity, and old age vulnerability. In such a context, state sponsored social security schemes assume paramount importance. Effective functioning of various social security schemes can play a pivotal role in supplementing the livelihood and health security of the poor. Governments at national and state levels have undertaken initiatives in this direction, but a number of questions arise on the effective implementation of the schemes. Are the benefits of social security schemes reaching the beneficiaries? Do the beneficiaries face any obstacles in availing those benefits for themselves? Are there any weaknesses existing in the present institutional set up for the effective implementation of social security schemes? What is the beneficiary's perception on these schemes?

OBJECTIVES AND METHODOLOGY OF THE STUDY

The objectives of the study are (i) to comprehend the institutional setup, designed for the implementation of various social security schemes, especially the Rashtriya Swasthya Bima Yojana (RSBY);

(ii) to assess the satisfaction of beneficiaries of social security schemes; and (iii) to examine the overall success of RSBY in Odisha.

The study has adopted a mix of qualitative and quantitative approaches for assessing the implementation of social security schemes, especially RSBY. We have used both secondary and primary data for this purpose. The secondary data were collected from the RSBY website, the insurance company linked to the scheme, and the nodal officer. The detailed information on the functioning of RSBY and other social security schemes has been collected through interviews and group discussions with the stakeholders, starting from the nodal officer to the beneficiaries of the schemes. To understand the ground realities of RSBY and other social security schemes, we have made a case study of Ghaduala village of Ghaduala panchayat in the Nayagarh district.

The chapter is organized as follows: it begins with a brief note on the functioning of various social security measures, other than RSBY, in the state. Then, it provides an overview of RSBY in India along with its functioning in Odisha. It moves on to the coverage of RSBY in Odisha, and the role of the hospitals in its implementation. It then explains the utilization of the benefits by the insured household under RSBY. Subsequently, it highlights the constraints faced in the state during the implementation of the scheme. Lastly, it provides the summary and conclusion of the study.

SOCIAL SECURITY SCHEMES OTHER THAN RSBY

Like any other welfare state, Odisha has been operating a few social security measures in the state. The Economic Survey of Odisha for the year 2009–10 (Government of Odisha, 2010) had listed three major social security measures, other than RSBY, in operation. This section provides a brief account of them.

Indira Gandhi National Old Age Pension Scheme (IGNOAP)

The National Old Age Pension Scheme, launched in 1995, provides social security to the poor and the destitute. It is entirely supported by the Union Government, under the National Social Assistance Programme (NSAP), later renamed as the IGNOAP, with revised selection criteria. All persons aged 65 and above, belonging to below poverty line (BPL) families as per the 2002 survey, are covered under the IGNOAP. The scheme covered 6,43,400 beneficiaries, each of whom are entitled to a monthly pension of Rs 200.

National Family Benefit Scheme (NFBS)

The National Family Benefit Scheme is the second component of NSAP and has been in operation in the state since 1995. Under this scheme, financial assistance of Rs 10,000 is given to a BPL family on the death of its primary bread earner, in the age group of 18–64 years. The assistance is paid to the head of the household, such as the spouse, minor children, unmarried daughters and dependent parent. In the case of an unmarried adult, the term household would include minor brothers and sisters. The scheme covered 33,384 beneficiaries in 2008–9.

Madhu Babu Pension Yojana (MBPY)

In 2008, the state introduced MBPY by merging two pension schemes, the Old Age Pension Rule of 1989 and the Disability Pension Rule of 1985. All the beneficiaries of these schemes came under MBPY. The target groups in this new programme included the old, widows, cured leprosy patients and the differently able. Pensioners were given Rs 200 per month, on the 15th day of every month, from the office of Gram Panchayats. The criteria fixed for these pensioners were as follows:

1. The annual income of the family should be less than Rs 32,000.
   a. The beneficiary should be over 60 years of age, for both male and female.
   b. Widows are eligible, irrespective of age factor.
   c. Disabled leprosy patients are eligible, irrespective of age factor.
2. The following target groups above the age of 5 years, whose annual family income is less than Rs 11,000.
   a. Completely blind people.
   b. More than 40 per cent physically challenged, male or female.
   c. More than 40 per cent mentally challenged, male or female.

Apart from this, those getting the state's old age pension and physically challenged pension were also to be considered as beneficiaries under the new scheme. During 2008–9, 12.08 lakh beneficiaries were covered under the scheme.

RSBY IN ODISHA

Since the main features of the RSBY are detailed in Overview, Chapter 3, we will not repeat them here. Taking up implementation of the scheme, the state governments engage in a competitive public-bidding process, and select a public or private insurance company, licensed to provide health insurance by the Insurance Regulatory Development Authority (IRDA), or enabled by a Central legislation. While more than one insurer can operate in a particular state, only one insurer can operate in a single district at any given point in time. Respective state governments need to convert their existing BPL data in the appropriate format for each district and send the same to the Union Government, which in turn checks the compatibility of the data with the standard format. Third Party Administrators (TPAs) are engaged to mediate between the BPL households and the insurer, and to issue the smart card. TPAs are paid by the government for rendering these services. The selected insurance company will empanel both public and private health care providers of the nearby district in the project, based on prescribed criteria. The insurer must also provide a list of RSBY empanelled hospitals to the beneficiaries at the time of enrollment. This list is revised at periodic intervals as more and more hospitals are added. When empanelment takes place, a nationally unique hospital ID number is generated so that transactions can be tracked to each hospital. The transaction process begins when the member visits the participating hospital. Upon release of the beneficiary from the hospital, the card is again swiped, along with fingerprint verification, and the pre-specified cost of the procedure is deducted from the amount available on the card. The beneficiary is also paid Rs 100 by the hospital as transportation expense at the time of discharge. After rendering the service to the patient, the hospital needs to send an electronic report to the insurer/TPA.

To assess the functioning of RSBY in Odisha, we used the secondary data obtained from the RSBY website (www.rsby.nic.in) and the insurance agency—New India Assurance. Besides, we interviewed various stakeholders of this programme—BPL families covered under RSBY, hospitals, TPA, Insurance Agency, and the state nodal officer.

An analysis of the functioning of RSBY in Odisha was done in two phases. The first phase was from September 2009 to March 2011, and the second phase was from April 2011 onwards. The reason for the two-phase analysis was the change in the empanelled insurance company during these two periods. According to Central Government guidelines, the State Government should delegate responsibility to the insurance company, on appropriate procedure, for providing health insurance for a minimum duration of one year. The agreement is renewed at the end of each year. Based on this principle, the New India Assurance (NIA) Company was selected to provide the health insurance in the first phase, covering six districts. The enrollment of BPL families in the six districts, nonetheless, started at different points of time. For example, enrollment commenced in the Nayagarh district in September 2009, followed by Kalahandi in October, and the remaining four districts of Puri, Jharsuguda, Nuapada, and Debagarh in January 2010. Depending on the commencement, the scheme was stopped after the completion of one year. Similarly, much time had lapsed between the enrollment of BPL families and provision of insurance benefits at hospitals. For example, in Nayagarh district, the official enrollment was started in September 2009; but the insurance benefits at hospitals were available only from July 2010. Keeping in view the delayed activation of the scheme, the Odisha Government asked NIA to provide the insurance benefits for an extended period, which it did. For instance, the scheme was supposed to expire by end of September 2010. But after negotiation with the insurance company, the scheme was extended up to December 2010. Similarly, in Puri district the scheme officially expired by January; but it was extended up to March 2011. The detailed information on the date of commencement and expiry of RSBY in six districts is given in Table 11.1.

In the second phase, the Odisha Government empanelled five new insurance companies namely, United India Insurance Company Limited, ICICI Lombard General Insurance, the Oriental Insurance Company Limited, Star Health Insurance, and IFFCO-TOKIO General Insurance. Meanwhile, NIA, which was not included in the second phase, lodged a complaint with the Odisha High Court, seeking an explanation from the State Government for its exclusion in the second round. As a result, the newly selected insurance companies are yet to begin enrollment of BPL families.

TABLE 11.1 Commencement and Expiry of RSBY in Different Districts

Districts	*Commencement Date*	*Closing Date Including the Extension Period*
Debagarh	30.1.2010	January 2011
Jharsuguda	8.1.2010	January 2011
Kalahandi	6.10.2009	November 2010
Nayagarh	10.9.2009	December 2010
Nuapada	8.1.2010	January 2010
Puri	4.1.2010	March 2011

Source: rsby.nic.in (accessed 3 July 2011).

CURRENT STATUS

The discussion with the nodal officer revealed that presently RSBY was in operation in three districts of Odisha, namely, Debagarh, Jharsuguda and Nuapada. In Puri, district enrollment of beneficiaries is going on. A new insurance company—ICICI Lombard General Insurance—was given license for providing insurance in these four districts. The insurance company had to carry out fresh registration of the beneficiaries. Therefore there was a discontinuity in providing insurance benefits for around five months, during this transition phase. The nodal officer also reported that in Debagarh, Jharsuguda and Nuapada districts, around 1,000 claims had already been made. IFFCO-TOKIO General Insurance Company was given the responsibility of Cuttack, Khordha, Raygada, Ganjam, Sambalapur, and Sundergarh districts. The other 20 districts were distributed among four insurance companies, namely, United India Insurance Company Limited, ICICI Lombard General Insurance, Oriental Insurance Company Limited, and Star Health Insurance.

ORGANIZATIONAL STRUCTURE

The organizational structure of RSBY in Odisha is outlined in Table 11.2. The State Government selected NIA through competitive bidding, to provide insurance to BPL families under RSBY. As per the rules framed by the Centre, the insurance company was to be paid a maximum sum of Rs 750 per family. However, NIA won the

TABLE 11.2 Coverage of RSBY in Odisha

Indicator	*Progress*
Total Districts selected	12
Districts selected in Phase-I	6
Districts selected in Phase-II	6
Enrollment Complete	6
Enrollment in Progress	6
Total BPL Families	7,54,942
BPL families Enrolled	4,22,929 (56%)
BPL Population	29,11,539
BPL Population Enrolled	11,86,796 (41%)
Number of Private Hospitals Empanelled	47
Number of Public Hospitals Empanelled	67
Total Number of Hospitals Empanelled	114

Source: Data collected from NIA up to December 2010.

competitive bidding at a premium of Rs 645 per family. Of this, the registered family paid Rs 30 at the time of registration. The balance Rs 615 was paid by the Centre and the State Governments in a 75:25 ratio. Thus, the former pays Rs 499 and the latter, Rs 116. The policy became effective for the registered BPL family from the first day of the succeeding month. For example, if a family registered on 3 July 2010, the policy would be effective from 1 August 2010, for one year.

The scheme allowed registration of a maximum of five family members. The master card carried the photo of the head of the family and other four family members. In case of a joint family having more than five family members, the head of the family decides the five members to be covered under the scheme. In case of split families (family members staying in more than one place), there was also the provision to issue maximum two dummy cards, with the same unique identification number. For this purpose the family was charged an additional Rs 30, which was also charged for the issue of a new card in case of the loss of or damage to the original smart card. However, an official of NIA stated that in Odisha no family availed of this provision.

The insurance agency was expected to create awareness about the scheme through advertisement. This was called 'information education communication'. This was advertised on TV, radio, in newspapers, and through distribution of leaflets, public announcements, and health camps, apart from hoardings and wall paintings placed at various locations, explaining the details of the scheme. The insurance company was also asked to create awareness at the time of registration, of how to avail of the benefit.

In order to comprehend the process through which smart cards were issued to the concerned BPL families, we interviewed the branch manager and field officer of E-Meditech, Bhubaneswar, the TPA engaged in this process.

It was found that there were many disputes while identifying the BPL households. On a few occasions there was tension among the villagers, TPA, and the Block Officials. Some of the families who did not possess the BPL card were found enlisted in the RSBY beneficiary list, and a few other households, who possessed the BPL card, were excluded from the RSBY beneficiary list. In such an event, the former started aspiring for other benefits provided to BPL households, like public distribution system, Indira Awas Yojana etc. The latter, on the other hand, were apprehensive of losing the existing benefits received from the Government. In one village it so happened that many of the households who did not find their name in the list went on a demonstration to the District Collectorate. Such confusion caused unnecessary delay in completing the enrollment. TPAs were given four months extension to finish the process. In extreme cases the period was extended by another two months. E-Meditech could, in effect, obtain only 20 days extension due to official delay in granting the extension. It started the enrollment process in September 2009, and finished in March 2010.

COVERAGE UNDER RSBY

In Odisha, RSBY was launched in 2009 and in the first phase, six districts, namely, Debagarh, Jharsuguda, Kalahandi, Nayagarh, Nuapada, and Puri, were brought under the scheme. For the geographical locations of these districts, refer to Figure 11.1. NIA officials stated that no criteria were followed in the selection of these districts. The State Government could provide the complete BPL list only for these six districts, and that was the only reason why these six districts were selected. The first enrollment of a BPL family under RSBY took place in the Nayagarh district. The data collected from NIA, which is yet to

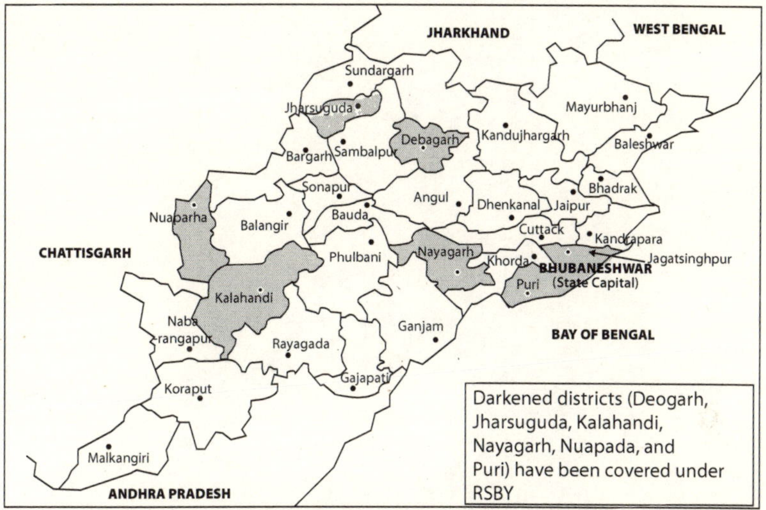

FIGURE 11.1 RSBY Coverage in Odisha

Source: rsby.nic.in (accessed 3 July 2011).

be updated on the website, showed that 4,22,929 BPL families had been enrolled under RSBY as on December 2010. Table 11.2 provides an overview of the coverage of RSBY in Odisha. In the state, a total of 114 hospitals had been empanelled for providing service under RSBY. Of these, 67 were public and remaining 47 hospitals were private.

Table 11.3 provides the district-wise progress of RSBY in Odisha. In absolute numbers, Kalahandi district had the distinction of having the highest number of BPL families enrolled under RSBY (1,03,083) and Debagarh the lowest (46,777). However, in percentage terms, the rate of enrollment in Debagarh was 66.87 per cent, while in Kalahandi it was 48 per cent. In these six districts, 56 per cent of families had been enrolled under RSBY, though only 41 per cent of the population came under RSBY.

The total number of hospitals empanelled in the six districts was 89, of which 22 are private and 67 public sector hospitals. Relatively, more public hospitals have been empanelled in all six districts. In the backward districts, even if there were some private hospitals, many of them were not eligible to get empanelled under RSBY due to lack of adequate infrastructure and services. In the advanced districts like

Table 11.3 Progress of RSBY in Six Districts of Odisha

District	*Given Data*		*Enrolled Data*		*% of Families Enrolled*	*% of Population Enrolled*	*Empanelment of Hospitals*		
	Families	*Population*	*Families*	*Population*			*Private*	*Public*	*Total*
Puri	1,98,123	8,30,808	1,17,355	3,20,048	59.23	38.52	9	17	26
Nayagarh	1,30,065	5,06,280	82,361	2,30,567	63.32	45.54	10	13	23
Kalahandi	2,14,889	7, 52,067	1,03,083	2,91,456	47.97	38.75	11	18	29
Debagarh	46,777	1,98,347	31, 281	1,02,732	66.87	51.79	–	05	5
Nuapada	1,08,408	4,10,999	53, 210	1,50,060	49.08	36.51	–	07	7
Jharsuguda	56,680	2,13,038	35, 639	91,933	62.88	43.15	02	07	9
Total	7,54,942	29,11,539	4,22,929	11,86,796	56.02	40.76	22	67	89

Source: Computed from the data obtained from NIA.

Puri, a number of private hospitals were equipped with good medical facilities, but at a high price. Most of the hospitals empanelled in the Nayagarh district were located in Bhubaneswar, which came under another district—Khordha. Since empanelment of hospitals is a continuous process, new hospitals would get empanelled under this scheme. The increasing number of hospitals being empanelled was clearly observable during our survey.

On 10 October 2010, the State Government decided to launch a state-wide public awareness campaign, to include optimum number of people in the ongoing RSBY. A. high-level meeting chaired by Chief Minister Naveen Patnaik decided to involve the representatives of the Panchayat Samiti, Self Help Groups (SHGs), Accredited Social Health Activists (ASHA), and Anganwadi workers in the campaign. The New India Assurance Company was selected, through the tender process, to implement the scheme in six other districts—Khurda, Cuttack, Ganjam, Rayagada, Sambalpur, and Sundergarh. As many as 435 public and 44 private hospitals were empanelled to provide health care facilities to the people covered under the scheme. Nevertheless, the proposal is yet to gain momentum.

ROLE OF HOSPITALS IN RSBY

The selected hospitals were empanelled under the scheme, to provide medical services to the registered beneficiaries. In aggregate, more public hospitals had been empanelled under the scheme than private hospitals.

To avail of the benefit, a beneficiary had to be admitted in the hospital for at least one day. Outdoor treatments were not covered under RSBY. The transaction process began when the member visited the participating hospital. After reaching the hospital, the beneficiary was required to visit the RSBY help desk therein, which verified the person's identity using the photograph and fingerprints stored on the smart card. If a diagnosis led to hospitalization, the assistant at the help desk checked whether the procedure was in the list of pre-specified packages. If so, the appropriate prescribed package was selected from the menu. If not, the help desk assistant would check with the insurer the cost of that procedure. While being discharged from the hospital, the card would again be swiped, along with the fingerprint verification, and the pre-specified cost of the procedure would be deducted from the amount available on the card. The beneficiary would also be paid Rs 100 by the hospital for travel expense at the time of discharge.

However, the total travel assistance could not exceed Rs 1,000 per year, and it was part of Rs 30,000 coverage. No proof was required by the beneficiary to get the travel allowance.

The Union Government had listed 725 diseases for treatment within one year, with the maximum payment of Rs 30,000. All these treatments were classified into surgical and non-surgical. For surgical treatments, the Government had fixed different rates. For non-surgical treatments, hospitals could charge a maximum sum of Rs 500 per day. In case the patient was admitted in the intensive care unit (ICU), the hospital could charge a maximum of Rs 1,000.

Hospitals had the incentive to provide treatment to a large number of beneficiaries, as it was paid per beneficiary treated. Even public hospitals had the incentive to treat beneficiaries under RSBY, as the money from the insurer would flow directly to the public hospital concerned, which it could use for its own purposes. The hospitals require to install necessary hardware and software to process smart card transactions. They also need to set up a special RSBY desk, with trained staff. The insurer provides a list of RSBY empanelled hospitals to the beneficiaries, at the time of enrollment. This list would be revised at periodic intervals, as more and more hospitals were added to the list. When empanelment took place, a nationally unique hospital ID number was generated, so that transactions could be tracked to each hospital.

During our interview with the E-Meditech officials—the TPA engaged in Nayagarh, Jharsuguda and Debagarh districts—it came to light that till the date of our interview in Nayagarh, the maximum patients had been treated under RSBY at the district hospital at Nayagarh. Most of the private hospitals empanelled for Nayagarh districts were located in Bhubaneswar, which is quite far away from Nayagarh district (at least 70–80 km). The distance became a hurdle to access the benefit from some of the specialty hospitals. The officer opined that many of the nearby private hospitals did not have the minimum infrastructure and facilities to be empanelled under RSBY. The officer also stated that in comparison to government hospitals, private hospitals, especially large private hospitals in Bhubaneswar, charged around three to four times higher fee.

Public Hospitals

In order to understand the functioning of RSBY in public hospitals, we visited the district hospital at Nayagarh. The hospital began dispensing treatment services under RSBY from 6 July 2010. Till November 2010, the RSBY counter used to run with the help of a TPA official and a few other staff of the hospital. In November 2010, contractual appointments were made to manage the desk.

On an average, 15–20 patients were treated daily. Our one day observation at the hospital revealed that people were using RSBY benefits for a wide range of non-surgical illnesses like fever, malaria, burns, filarial, and elephantiasis. Hospitalization ranged from 2–20 days, depending on the nature of the disease. The hospital carried out free diagnosis and provided free medicines. The amount claimed during one hospitalization ranged from Rs 3,500 to Rs 7,000. Even for general fever, the hospital claimed Rs 5,000, which seemed to be a little high, especially in a public hospital. All services were covered under RSBY. In a few cases, patients were asked to purchase small items like a sterilized syringe, or cough syrup, which beneficiaries did not mind. Most of the patients expressed happiness on the service provided under the scheme. Similarly, people travelled from near and far—around 50–60 km—for treatment under RSBY.

A few patients also expressed suspicion on the quantity of medicine provided by the hospital. They alleged that the medicine counter sometimes provided less medicine compared to what was prescribed. This could not be verified as the patients never bothered to look at the price of the medicine. Nor did the hospital provide a special bill for the medicine. The hospital only provided a printout, which mentioned whether the disease was surgical or non-surgical, the number of days of hospitalization, and amount blocked. The amount claimed by the hospital from the insurance company was based on the number of days. The number of hospitalization days was mentioned in advance, at the time of admission in the hospital. In case a patient was cured before the prescribed days of hospitalization, the hospital authority did not return the smart card; the hospital asked the patient to collect the card only after the completion of the prescribed days. In a few cases, it was observed that patients got their smart cards with an undertaking. In a few cases patients requiring additional days of hospitalization were asked to procure medicines from outside, when they exceeded their prescribed limit.

Lack of Awareness

It was observed that many people were not aware of the hospitals where RSBY benefits were available. In some cases, it was found that a patient did not know how and when to avail of the benefits under the scheme, though he had been issued with the master smart card.

Private Hospitals

To understand the functioning of private hospitals providing services under RSBY, we visited a private hospital and interviewed the officer at the special RSBY desk. The process of availing of the RSBY benefits in a private hospital remained the same as in a public hospital. The facilities and services available at the private hospitals were far better than public hospitals. However, the former charged more.

The major difference was in the case of hospitalization charges. Unlike public hospitals, private hospitals charged daily room fee, apart from expenses of medicine and diagnosis. Therefore, the aggregate bill became much higher, and additional money was collected from the patient. An official of a private hospital stated that many times the patients were not clear about the expenditures covered under RSBY. Therefore, when the hospital asked for additional fees, patients showed reluctance to pay. Similarly, some treatments were more expensive than the rates prescribed in the RSBY package. Thus hospitals were reluctant to treat the patient, fearing that the latter may refuse to pay the extra amount. The processing time for the payment by the TPA and the insurance company also took a longer time; some payments took more than two months, though of late the gap was getting reduced.

UTILIZATION OF RSBY

The data collected from NIA showed that as on 28 February 2011, as many as 7,484 claims had been made in the six districts, amounting to Rs 272.03 lakh (Table 11.4). It was pointed out that in Kalahandi district, 90 per cent of the claims were made by people suffering from malaria, and the range of claims varied from Rs 2,000 to Rs 7,000. In the other districts, 50 per cent of the cases were surgical in nature and the claims ranged up to a maximum of Rs 10,500 while the rest of the cases were of fever and diarrhea, with a maximum claim of Rs 2,000 (24duniya.com, 2010).

For a disaggregated and updated analysis, we collected data on the claim settlement from the NIA. District-wise claims made under RSBY in comparison with the individual family estimates, as given in Table 11.4, shows that as on 28 February 2011, a total number

TABLE 11.4 District-wise Comparison of the Claims Made under RSBY (as on 28 February 2011)

Districts	*Number of Claims Made by Males*	*Share of Males in Total Number of Claims*	*Number of Claims Made by Females*	*Share of Females in Total Number of Claims*	*Total Number of Claims*	*Total Amount Claimed in Lakh Rupees*	*Claim per Family in Rupees*	*Expenses per Claim*
Kalahandi	836	59.63	566	40.37	1,402	33.61	2,397.29	2,397.48
Puri	2,349	57.29	1,751	42.71	4,100	169.18	4,126.34	4,126.34
Nayagarh	613	77.79	175	22.21	788	35.27	4,475.89	4,475.51
Jharsuguda	63	70.79	26	29.21	89	4.69	5,269.66	5,266.85
Nuapada	131	58.22	94	41.78	225	6.66	2,960.00	2,961.33
Debagarh	483	54.89	397	45.11	880	22.62	2,570.45	2,570.45
Total	4,475	59.79	3,009	40.21	7,484	272.03	3,634.82	3,634.82

Source: Computed from the data collected from New India Assurance Company.

of 7,484 claims had been made under RSBY in the six districts of Odisha; out of these 4,475 claims were from males and 3,009 from females. In absolute number, the highest number of patients claims for medical expenditure under RSBY was from Puri district, followed by Kalahandi, Nayagarh, Debagarh, Nuapada, and Jharsuguda; the respective total number of claims being 4,100, 1,402, 788, 880, 225, and 89. Similarly, in monetary term, Puri district claimed the maximum amount, followed by Kalahandi, Nayagarh, Debagarh, Nuapada and Jharsuguda.

Since the quantum of BPL population varied widely across the six districts, it was not possible to make any comparison with regard to absolute number of claims. We have, therefore, calculated some ratios for comparison. Reimbursements per family (estimated as total Rs claimed/total BPL families enrolled) incurred by NIA across districts showed that the highest claim was made in Jharsuguda district (Rs 5,269.66), followed by Nayagarh (Rs 4,475.89), Puri (Rs 4,126.34), Nuapada (Rs 2,960.00), Debagarh (Rs 2,570.45), and Kalahandi (Rs 2,397.29). On an average, the amount of money claimed per hospitalization (total sum claimed / total no. of claims) was Rs 3,049.71. District-wise comparison showed that the claim made per hospitalization was highest in Jharsuguda (Rs 5,519.23), followed by Nuapada (Rs 4,862.22), Nayagarh (Rs 4,222.44), Puri (Rs 2,901.17), Debagarh (Rs 2,773.39), and Kalahandi (Rs 2,660.40).

On an average, a larger proportion (60 per cent) of claims under RSBY was by males. The share of males was disproportionately higher in Nayagarh (78 per cent) and Jharsuguda (71 per cent). For the remaining, the ratio was 60:40. The explanation for a higher proportion claimed by male population was said to be due to the imbalanced sex ratio and the male bias in accessing health care (Ganatra and Hirve, 1994). The sex ratios in these districts were as follows: Jharsuguda 931, Puri 924, Nuapada 971, Nayagarh 851, Kalahandi 947, and Debagarh 917.

The scheme provided opportunity to avail insurance benefits in other district and states as well. Table 11.5 shows district-wise claims made by beneficiaries in public hospitals of the district, and in other states. About 45 beneficiaries had claimed benefits in Chhattisgarh, neighboring Odisha. A maximum of 21 claims had been made from Nuapada district in Chhattisgarh, followed by Puri with 13 claims.

TABLE 11.5 Insurance Claimed in the Public Hospital of the District and Outside of the State

District	*Public Hospital of the District*				*In other State (Chhatisgarh)*				*Total Rs Claimed*
	Male	*Female*	*Total*	*Rs Claimed*	*Male*	*Female*	*Total*	*Rs Claimed*	
Jharsuguda	7	4	11	41,750	–	–	–	–	41,750
Puri	–	–	–	–	10	3	13	66,000	66,000
Nuapada	13	11	24	86,500	10	11	21	1,32,300	2,18,800
Kalahandi	41	44	85	2,32,000	0	1	1	4,000	2,36,000
Debagarh	93	78	171	4,74,250					4,74,250
Total				8,34,500				2,02,300	10,36,800

Source: Data collected from New India Assurance, Bhubaneswar.

Nuapada district's proximity to Chhattisgarh could well be the reason behind it.

CASE STUDY OF GHADUALA VILLAGE IN NAYAGARH DISTRICT

In order to understand the ground realities in the functioning of RSBY and other social security schemes, we undertook a case study of Ghaduala village of Ghaduala panchayat in Nayagarh district. The rationale for selecting this village was its proximity (3 km) to the district headquarters, as it enabled the villagers to access better information, and thus reap the benefit of the schemes. About 3 km east of Nayagarh district headquarters, Ghaduala is on the way to Khordha and Bhubaneswar.

Ghaduala Panchayat has 11 wards of which Ghaduala village is one. There was only one permanent government employee, a village level worker (VLW), and one contractual employee for the Mahatma Gandhi National Rural Employment Guarantee Scheme (MGNREGS) as Technical Assistant. The VLW was given additional responsibility of Gadadhar Panchayat, and hence could not perform his duty efficiently. The same situation was also observed in our study of NREGA in the Sason Panchyat of Sambalpur district. Shortage of staff in the Panchayat office often marred the effective implementation of various government schemes in Odisha.

FUNCTIONING OF PENSION SCHEMES

The number of beneficiaries of different pension schemes is presented in Table 11.6. There were 246 pension beneficiaries in the panchayat,

TABLE 11.6 Beneficiaries of Different Pension Schemes in Ghaduala Panchayat

Pension Scheme	*Number of Beneficiary*
Madhu Babu Pension Yojana (MBPY)	160
Pension for Handicapped Person (PHP)	31
National Old Age Pension (NOAP)	55
Total	246

Source: Data collected from the Ghaduala Panchayat office.

of which 160 were MBPY beneficiaries, 31 PHP beneficiaries, and 55 NOAP beneficiaries. We interviewed two beneficiaries from ward number 1 and one beneficiary from ward number 3. In the former, about 20 people were getting different pensions. There was only one physically handicapped, Duryodhan Pradhan, who received PHP. He was 36, married with a son (14 years) and a daughter (10 years). Duryodhan's family was landless and he used to work as a mason. About six years ago, he consumed poison in an attempt to commit suicide. In an attempt to save him, the doctors had to amputate both legs, and he was provided with artificial limbs. Since then, his mobility had been restricted. Three years ago, his father passed away. To support his family he started working as a labourer in a stone quarry. His widowed mother assisted him to carry stones. As a quarry labourer, Duryodhan could earn a monthly income of Rs 1,200–1,300, which was not sufficient to meet the family expenditure. At that time he approached the ward member, and applied to the Panchayat for PHP. Since then he had been receiving a monthly pension of Rs 200 under PHP. His widowed mother, Sulochana Pradhan, also receives a pension of Rs 200 under MBPY. Although the total amount of Rs 400 was insufficient to meet his family expenditure, it did contribute to the family budget to some degree. They used the money to purchase rice, kerosene and sugar from the public distribution system. Financial constraint, coupled with poor performance in studies (8th class), forced his son to drop-out of the school.

We interviewed another beneficiary of NOAP, named Ladu Barad of ward 3. He was 80 years old and a widower. 10 years ago, he approached his friend, Bhagirathi Sahoo (who was then the Block Panchayat Chairman), to enlist his name among the beneficiaries of NOAP. Being a Congress party worker, he did not face any problem. Barad's family had only one-fourth of an acre of agricultural land. Even so, he was not able to do anything. A few years ago he was treated for TB, but later became a chronic asthma patient. Every month he needed around Rs 700 to Rs 800 for medicines. His son, who had a petty business in his village, supported him. Barad spent the pension money on his medicines, although it was not sufficient. When we asked Barad whether he would ask for a hike in the pension amount, he replied that 'this is the mercy of the government that we are receiving this amount, so it is up to them. It will be definitely better if they hike the amount.' Barad also expressed satisfaction in the regularity of payment. Every month his grandson took him to the Panchayat office to collect the pension money.

We interviewed the Panchayat President Mr Akrura Barad, Vice-President Mrs Ashalata Swain, the VLW Mr Bichitra Pattnaik, and two ward Members, Mr Bijay Kumar Mallik of Ward 1 and Mrs Sailabala Das of Ward 3. There were 11 Ward Members in the Panchayat. Only Mr Bijay Kumar Mallik had studied up to Class 12; all other Ward Members had not even passed Class 10. Many of them were not even able to read and write properly. The Sarpanch, who had also attended Class 12, took all decisions unilaterally. Except Mr Bijay Kumar Mallik, there was nobody to oppose anything. As a result, the Sarpanch misappropriated the food supplied through Public Distribution System (PDS). There were many complaints of misappropriation of food supply and pension funds. The Ward Members, and also the people of Ghaduala, complained that they got sugar through PDS only once in six or seven months. Similarly, when some households failed to lift their PDS quota on time for want of money, the Sarpanch sold items like rice, sugar, or kerosene in the open market and made good profit. 'After frequent complaints, the Sarpanch has stopped this practice for rice,' said Mr Mallik, who also expressed that Ward Members lacked power. The Sarpanch played divisive politics. There were instances wherein the pension application from those in the opposition political party had been kept pending on the ground that they had not reached the cut-off age. Many illiterate people were not aware of their accurate age. Therefore, they had entered the wrong age in the voter ID card, which was used as the proof for identity and age. There was also provision that if the applicant could produce court affidavit for age proof, then his / her application would be considered. A few households had already done that. But even these applications were kept in abeyance. Mr Mallik alleged that this was done purposely, due to political rivalry. Mrs Sailabala Das also complained that the Sarpanch did not call meetings on a regular basis to discuss the problems of the Panchayat. Although they asked him to convene a meeting of all the office bearers time and again, he had not paid any heed to it. More than eight months had passed since the Panchayat had convened its last meeting.

Functioning of RSBY

We visited Sinduria, Brajabalhabapur, and Ghaduala villages to learn how the benefits of RSBY accrued to the beneficiaries. Besides three

Ward Members in the three villages, we also interviewed a Ward Member of ward 5, Mr Ashok Kumar, who explained that in Sinduria village where there were about 170 to 180 BPL families, none ever got a smart card under RSBY. The Vice President of the Panchayat explained that TPA officials had asked the Panchayat President to distribute the cards in the village, but the President refused to do so. In Brajabalhabpur village, the Ward Member and the people alleged that although they had completed all formalities (paid Rs 30 and had their photo taken by the government officials), no smart card was issued to them till March 2011. In Ghaduala village, we also interviewed the Sarapanch and Nayab Sarpanch (Vice President) to learn about the progress of RSBY in their village. At the outset we interviewed Mrs Ashalata Swain, Nayab Sarpanch of Ghaduala Panchayat. She was in no mood to have any interaction with us. She told that she did not know anything about the scheme and asked us to talk to the Sarpanch, Mr Akrura Barad. The latter guessed that around 78–80 households had received RSBY smart card. A large number of people who had BPL cards did not come under RSBY. He pointed out that although people had received the card, they did not know how to use this card. Similarly, they did not have any information about the hospitals empanelled under RSBY scheme, and how money was to be claimed using this card. Similarly, he complained of the non-renewal of the scheme.

Apart from this discussion with the office bearers of the Panchayat, we also met two families who possessed the RSBY smart cards. Only one family had availed of the benefits. Janardhana Behera, a 50 years old man, fell down from a bridge under construction and broke his leg. His family members rushed him to a hospital in Cuttack, about 100 km from the village. He was hospitalized for 19 days, and spent around Rs 55,000. At the time of his admission he did not have his smart card. After a few days, the smart card was produced at the hospital to avail of the insurance benefits, but not being an empanelled hospital under the scheme, the hospital refused to provide any benefit. His wife, Mrs Sukia Behera, pointed out that they had incurred a debt of Rs 30,000 to meet the hospital expenditure. Village people also had provided some financial support. Till the date of our interview Mr Janardana Behera was not able to walk properly. The poverty of Mr Behera's family was clearly visible from their thatched home with barely two rooms, and mud flooring and walls. Their ignorance about the empanelled hospital and benefits of smart card was the reason behind their inability to claim the benefits of RSBY.

Panchu Swain of the same village had similarly been injured when the same bridge collapsed. But his family took him to a different hospital, which was empanelled under RSBY. For his treatment an amount of Rs 30,000 was spent, of which only Rs 19,000 could be claimed. The reason for his inability to claim the full amount was that the smart card had expired in the course of his treatment. Panchu Swain's family also did not know whether the hospital was empanelled under RSBY. It was just that the hospital had the provision to claim the benefits of RSBY. Panchu Swain's family was equally poor. A part of the wall of his house was made of bamboo sticks and it had mud flooring and thatched roofing. His family was indebted after this accident.

RURAL POWER STRUCTURE AND GOVERNMENT SCHEMES

In a democratic country like India, the successful implementation of any government scheme would depend on the active participation of local level bodies, that is the Panchayati Raj Institutions, and the active participation of civil society. But this was sadly missing in Odisha. Most of the Panchayat Presidents and Ward Members were either poorly educated, or illiterate. A very low percentage of the rural population was highly educated. Apart from this, the caste/social hierarchy in the villages played an important role in the power structure. The career-oriented educated youth hardly played any role in the villages. Although the constitutional provision for the reservation of Panchayats for women, SC and ST had been met, real power was still concentrated with the traditional rural elite. The petty politicians in rural areas captured power by doing some favour for the influential families. For example, a large number of families which did not come under BPL list were recipients of BPL cards. Similarly, a number of other benefits stemming from schemes such as the Indira Awas Yojana and various government loans, with a very high subsidy, were extended to such families. By doing so, the political representative minimized the risk of any opposition. Realizing this nexus among the rural elites, the poor and illiterate families seldom gathered the courage to oppose, even though they were deprived of their rights and remained mute spectators. In most of the villages in Odisha, black marketing of PDS ingredients was a common phenomenon. Poor households, who struggled to eke out their livelihood from their daily wages, did not find the time and energy to enquire about misappropriation and protest collectively.

For their part, the elected representatives sought to maximize their own profit by misappropriating public funds. His / her coming back to power depended upon their vote purchasing power. Therefore, amassing wealth through unholy means became the sole objective after assuming office. The public who elected their representatives by receiving money hardly had the courage, or moral right, to oppose any kind of corruption by the former. So there was hardly any incentive for the Panchayat officials to create awareness among the villagers about various government schemes, or to assist them get these benefits. Rather, the competition was in extracting more and more profit through misappropriation of public money. These officials showed little concern for successful implementation of government schemes in which there was no scope for extracting some benefits. In the case of RSBY, the funds were being directly transferred to the poor. There was no scope for Panchayat officials to extract any rent. That probably explained the ineffective implementation of RSBY by Panchayat Officials.

CONSTRAINTS

During the interaction with the different stakeholders of RSBY, a number of constraints came to the fore.

BPL dataset: The success of the RSBY depended on the identification of BPL families, and their registration under the scheme. Like the poverty estimates, the identification of BPL families had been shrouded in controversies. In Odisha, only around 56 per cent of BPL families in the six districts had been covered under the RSBY. Due to the provision of registering only five members of a family in one smart card, the percentage of population covered under RSBY had been even lower as compared to the percentage of families covered under RSBY. Our study found that only 40 per cent of BPL population had been registered under the scheme. During our interview it was pointed out that during registration, many BPL families did not find their names in the RSBY list, and a few other households, who did not come under BPL category, were covered under RSBY. This created tension among the officials and the local community. Besides, it marred the main objective of providing insurance to the poor families.

The registration for RSBY was carried out on the basis of the 1997 BPL list. Although in 2002 the State Government carried out another round of the BPL survey, the same had not been released yet. As per the information of the NIA officials, the BPL list provided to NIA was made by amalgamating the 1997 and 2002 surveys. Therefore, there were many errors in the list. Since the list was around one-and-half decade old, many families were not covered under the BPL list. Similarly, a number of families might have come out of poverty or gone BPL in the interim. The slow progress of RSBY in Odisha could also be due to this.

Migratory population: In the backward districts, the BPL families frequently migrated from one place to other in search of work and other livelihood options. It became hard to include them in the BPL list, and hence provide insurance coverage. Similarly, many of the nomadic communities were not covered under the scheme due to lack of proper identity.

Poor health infrastructure: One of the most important reasons for the poor health standards in Odisha was its lack of adequate health infrastructure. Odisha has less than one hospital for one lakh of population, which is even less than the national average. Better performing states like Kerala and Arunachal Pradesh have 14 and 24 hospitals respectively for one lakh of population.

There were very few hospitals available in the locality with adequate infrastructure. Such hospitals were not eligible to be empanelled under RSBY. Even the available public hospitals did not have all the provisions. For example, the district hospital at Nayagarh did not have facilities for major surgery. Due to inadequate staff and poor infrastructure, these hospitals were unable to provide treatments covered under RSBY.

Lack of awareness: Another major obstruction in the spread of RSBY was lack of awareness about the scheme. Even the registered BPL households did not know how to avail of the services, which diseases were covered under the scheme, which hospitals were empanelled, and which hospitals had specialized facilities.

Discontinuity: A major drawback of RSBY in Odisha had been the discontinuity in the scheme. The functioning of RSBY in the six districts of Odisha had come to a standstill after the expiry of one year. The renewal of cards had not been carried out in a timely manner. Moreover, due to change in the insurance provider, things had become more complicated. The change in the insurance provider increased the transaction cost. For example, a new insurance company had to enroll the BPL families afresh, involving the same procedure. This involved extra monetary expenses and human power. A long-term contract to the insurance agency would minimize such transaction cost.

***

The study on the implementation and functioning of RSBY in Odisha suggested that it had enormous potential to provide health insurance coverage, and hence health care to the poorest of the poor. However, there were a number of loopholes in the scheme: (i) there were very few hospitals available in the locality with adequate infrastructure; (ii) RSBY had been implemented in only six out of the 30 districts in Odisha; (iii) the implementation of RSBY relied on a clearly defined BPL list, but in Odisha, the Government provided the BPL list which was prepared in 1997; and (iv) only 50 per cent of the BPL families, consisting only 40 per cent of the total BPL population, came under the scheme.

There were very few hospitals available in the locality with adequate infrastructure. Most of the BPL families who claimed the benefits under RSBY were satisfied with the scheme. People used the benefits for surgical and non- surgical purposes. There were also instances of beneficiaries from neighbouring states availing of the benefits. Lack of awareness, poor BPL dataset, lack of adequate health infrastructure were the major constraints in widely utilizing the benefits under the scheme. There were also numerous complaints about the administrative inefficiency of the State Government. So it could be said that the scheme might take a little longer to spread and get popular in the state. But the fact remains that the scheme has the potential to bring about a virtual revolution in the health sector in the state.

References

Ganatra, B. and S. Hirve. 1994. 'Male Bias in Health Care Utilization for Under-fives in a Rural Community in Western India'. *Bulletin of the World Health Organization*, 1994, 72(1): 101–4.

Government of India. 2009. *Report of the Expert Group to Review the Methodology for Estimation of Poverty*. November. New Delhi: Planning Commission.

Government of Odisha. 2010. *Economic Survey, 2009–2010*, Planning and Coordination Department, Directorate of Economics and Statistics.

24duniya.com. 2010. *Orissa to Launch Massive Campaign on RSBY.* http://www.24dunia.com/english-news/shownews/0/Orissa-to-launch-massive-campaign-on-RSBY/7589845.html (accessed 15 October 2010).

VI

PUNJAB

12 FUNCTIONING OF NREGS IN A PROSPEROUS STATE

A STUDY IN PUNJAB

Sucha Singh Gill, Sukhwinder Singh, and *Jaswinder Singh Brar*

Punjab is one of the foremost developed states in India. It is amongst the top four states in terms of per capita income, and is several notches above the rest in terms of Human Development Index (HDI) (GoI, 2002 and GoP, 2004) and per capita consumption expenditure (Jain, 2010). It has the lowest incidence of poverty (GoI, 2011). Its immense success in agriculture, rural development, small-scale industries, and business activities in the sixties and seventies created vast employment opportunities for its workforce and the migratory labour, which largely come from states such as Bihar and Uttar Pradesh.

Over the years, however, decelerating growth, over-mechanization of agriculture, and the consequent decline in employment opportunities seem to have reduced the labour absorptive capacity of the agriculture sector in the state. In fact, the ever growing nature of mechanization and automation of almost all agricultural operations (field preparation, harvesting, threshing, and even marketing) have greatly reduced the demand for labour, except in the case of paddy transplanting and cotton picking. Various estimates showed that the demand for agricultural labour declined significantly in Punjab since the late 1980s, from 47.9 crore man-days in 1983–4 to 42.2 crore man-days in 2000–01 (Sidhu and Singh, 2004). Further, it is estimated that an average farm in the state employs 104 man-days of labour per hectare in crop cultivation, annually. Of this, 37 man-days (35 per cent) are contributed by the family labour and the remaining 68 man-days (65 per cent) by the hired labour. Moreover, the number of man-days created also depends on the nature of cropping pattern. For instance, it is the highest in wheat-cotton (135 man-days) and the lowest in the wheat-paddy (77 man-days) rotation (Singh, 2010). It is to be noted that the wheat-paddy rotation constituted nearly 78 per cent of total cropped area of the state in 2009–10 (GoP, 2010). Thus, the total quantum of direct and indirect employment available in the state through the main cropping pattern is not enough to sustain the agricultural labour for the whole year (Gill, 2002).

Further, rural employment in the state, primarily based on the mechanized agriculture, is highly seasonal in nature. For example, during the paddy transplanting season, the state requires about 7.5–8.0 lakh labourers in order to transplant paddy on 27 lakh hectares of land. Out of this paddy area, 15 per cent is transplanted by local labourers and the rest (85 per cent) by the migrants from other states; approximately 3.5–4.0 lakh migratory labourers moved from other states to Punjab, for paddy transplantation alone. It is worthwhile to note that the paddy transplanting season is of very short duration since it lasts only about three to four weeks (Mann, 2012). Truly, demand for casual labour at the sowing and harvesting seasons is still high, but it is not enough to provide employment to rural labour for a major part of the year. Consequently, the state's existing rural workforce is unable to get adequate number of man-days in agriculture and its allied activities, not to speak of decent work. The worst sufferers are the poor who are illiterate, unskilled, lack mobility, and face other cultural barriers in finding adequate amount of work. The livelihood for these sections therefore continues to remain acute in the state, which necessitates the launch of special employment generation programmes.

Ironically, the state does not have an impressive record in initiating innovative and self-sustaining employment policy measures, or social security schemes for the working poor as compared to, for instance, the southern states of Kerala, Tamil Nadu, and Andhra Pradesh. In fact, Punjab had, passed through a serious politico-religious crisis in the past, in the form of terrorist violence, which severely affected its socio-economic fabric for a prolonged period of 14 years (1982–95). As a consequence, an increasing proportion of state funds were diverted to the security forces and their modernization for maintaining the rule of law. The state was forced to resort to public borrowings that, in this event, shifted its spending priorities from development programmes to debt servicing (Gill *et al.*, 2010). Consequently, even after the democratic process was restored in 1992 and militancy ended by 1995, subsequent elected democratic governments indulged more in populist and election-oriented gimmicks (free power, free water, abolition of land revenue and octroi) instead of following a sustainable development agenda, which played havoc with the scarce state finances.

The weak state finances also came in the way of attracting private investments in the aftermath of the new economic policy of 1991, adopted at the national level. In fact, all the policy packages failed to take the state to a higher growth rate in the 1990s and beyond (Gill *et al.*, 2010). Moreover, the terrorist movement had weakened the leftist and other progressive movements in the state, particularly in the rural areas. Eventually, the activities of organized workers' trade unions, civil society, and intellectual leadership touched a nadir. These developments reduced the pressure of masses on the State Government, to strengthen the pro-poor employment and social security schemes (Jain, 2010).

The study has critically examined the functioning of NREGS in the state. Its implementation has been analyzed in the larger context of the political economy and the compulsions of the state, if any. Theoretically, NREGS is rooted in the right-based approach, and has many good features (NCAER, 2009; and Reddy, 2011). It seems to be one of the best state interventions for enhancing livelihood security of the rural poor through the provision of at least 100 days of employment on asset creating public works programmes, with a statutory minimum wage rate, and a provision for the adult member(s) of a household, by application, to volunteer for unskilled manual work. Today, the NREGS has become the world's largest employment guarantee scheme, reaching out to 54 million rural households in India during 2010–11 (UNDP, 2011).

METHODOLOGY OF THE STUDY

The study utilized both the primary and secondary data. The secondary data were collected from the official websites and office records of the State and District level departments concerned. For collecting primary data, 16 villages (eight from each district; see Appendix A12.1) had been selected from Patiala and Sangrur districts of Punjab. Overwhelmingly, wheat-paddy is the dominating cropping pattern in these villages. Four villages from each district, where NREGS had been implemented during 2009–10, were selected. Another four villages where NREGS had not been initiated during the last three years were also identified for comparison. Among these villages, a list of households which worked as wage workers within and/or outside the village(s) was prepared. The primary survey was carried out during 2010–11. Overall, 240 rural households (120 households each from NREGS and non-NREGS villages) were chosen randomly from these villages. Each randomly selected household was approached personally through a well-structured questionnaire to generate reliable data.

Further, group meetings were conducted in each village with the beneficiaries, Sarpanch and/or Panchayat Members, and non-beneficiaries. Village elders and village-level officials were approached to discuss pro-poor schemes, to make them more inclusive and transparent. In group meetings, issues relating to livelihood (for example, employment, labour bondage), caste biases in selection, exclusion/bogus enrollments, pilferages, harassments, etc., were discussed. Well-structured interviews and meetings were arranged with the NREGS activists and union leaders involved in organizing rural labour.

IMPLEMENTATION OF NREGS

NREGS was launched in Punjab on 2 February 2006 in one district (Hoshiarpur). It was extended to three more districts, namely, Amritsar, Nawanshahar, and Jalandhar in 2007–8, and to all districts on 3 April 2008. Incidentally, Punjab did not have any earlier experience in implementing such a gigantic employment generation programme. In many districts, although clear-cut guidelines had been statutorily stipulated, the administration found it difficult to implement the programme. A way out was found by involving expert agencies (for example, Non-governmental Organizations (NGOs), institutions) in the preparation of district development plan for NREGS through open advertisements. From among the many applicants who applied for this work, the district administration picked the one it found most suitable for the job. In Patiala District, for example, the Progressive Youth Forum, Ghagga, was assigned this task (PYF, 2010). In other districts, the administration had involved either outside agencies, or prepared the district NREGS plans itself.

The agencies, for their part, constituted expert teams which interacted with the officials concerned, and assessed physical and financial requirements, problems, prospects, and challenges associated with the task. They were expected to visit each village in the district, consult representatives of PRIs, and participate in the Gram Sabha meetings also. By 31 October 2010, 10 districts (50 per cent) of the state had successfully prepared their plans. In six districts, such plans were prepared by the NGOs, and, in the other four districts, the administration undertook the task—in about 50 per cent of the districts, this task was yet to be completed. This involved estimation of village-wise number of job seekers, type of work to be done, coordination of work sites, facilities to be created at work sites, conversion of physical targets into monetary targets, and other associated requirements. The common activities identified in Punjab under NREGS revolved around digging/desilting of ponds, afforestation and land development (for example, levelling) of common and wastelands, drainage of water logged/flood affected areas, road connectivity, strengthening of roads, minor irrigation works, and provision of irrigation in land owned by Scheduled Castes (SCs) and beneficiaries of Indira Awas Yojana, to name a few.

The data showed that the pace of implementation of NREGS works gathered momentum during the last three years, that is, in 2008–9, 2009–10, and 2010–11. Not surprisingly, the number of completed works remained very low. Only 26.40 per cent of projects were completed in 2008–9. This increased to 53.28 per cent in 2009–10, and slipped to 45.47 per cent in 2010–11 (Table 12.1). One reason for this could be the adhoc selection of projects, which were not based on comprehensive and systematic planning. This is the main reason that a large number of NREGS works undertaken fell under the category of ongoing works during these three years.

An assessment of NREGS projects started in the state revealed that majority of them fell under the category of 'most productive' assets; that is that when completed, these works will certainly add to the productive base in the villages, apart from improving the quality

TABLE 12.1 Number of Completed and Ongoing Works under NREGS in Punjab

Year	*Number of Works*			*Percentage*		
	Ongoing	*Completed*	*Total*	*Ongoing*	*Completed*	*Total*
2008–9	3,878	1,391	5,269	73.6	26.4	100
2009–10	5,509	6,283	11,792	46.7	53.3	100
2010–11	8,146	6,793	14,939	54.5	45.5	100

Source: www.nrega.nic.in (accessed 22 September 2011).

of life of the villagers. For instance, works relating to improving rural road connectivity, flood control and protection, water conservation and water harvesting, drought proofing would add, directly and indirectly, to more productivity and tangible and non-tangible asset creation in rural areas (Table 12.2).

During 2008–9, more than half of the total projects were related to desilting/digging of ponds (54.13 per cent), followed by improving road connectivity (17.73 per cent), land development (10. 63 per cent), drought proofing (7.04 per cent), water conservation/harvesting (6.04 per cent), to name a few. In subsequent years, other works gained importance and preference. For instance, in 2010–11, rural road connectivity alone received a significant share (31.62 per cent), followed by de-silting/digging of ponds (26.36 per cent), drought proofing (14.18 per cent), land development (11.60 per cent), minor irrigation projects (7.93 per cent), flood control/protection (2.40 per cent), and water conservation/harvesting (2.07 per cent). Surprisingly, irrigation facility on land owned by SC/ST families got just 0.02 per cent share during these three years.

On the employment front, the record of NREGS was very low. In the first year of its implementation covering the entire state (2008–9), the total number of job cards issued to households was 5.25 lakh, but the number of households provided with employment was just 1.50 lakh (28.56 per cent). During 2009–10, the number of households getting employment rose to 2.72 lakh (38.49 per cent), as against 7.06 lakh job-seeking households. Again, in 2010–11, the total number of job card holders increased to 8.21 lakh, but only 2.78 lakh got employment, which reduced the proportion of eligible households getting employment to 33.87 per cent. Further, the average number of man-days a worker got employment under NREGS was much lower in Punjab—around 27–28 days per year—as compared to the guaranteed employment of 100 days per household (Table 12.3), and the all-India average of 54 days in 2009–10, up from 43 days in 2008–9 (Kannan and Jain, 2011).

Table 12.4 shows that a large majority of households received a very low quantum of work or employment. In 2009–10, as much as 55.02 per cent households got up to 20 days of work and they cornered 22.58 per cent of the man-days of employment created. Another one-fourth of households (25.66 per cent) got work in the range of 21–40 days and shared 29.21 per cent of man-days created. Only 1.61 per cent of households got stipulated days of employment (100 days and more),

Table 12.2 Distribution of Works/Activities (Completed and Ongoing) under NREGS in Punjab

Major Head	*Details of Work*	*2008–9*	*2009–10*	*2010–11*
Rural Connectivity	Roads, passages, etc.	934	3,603	4,723
Percentage		17.73	30.55	31.62
Flood control and protection	Drainage in water logged areas, construction and repair of embankment, others, etc.	170	420	359
Percentage		3.23	3.56	2.40
Water conservation and water harvesting	Digging of new tanks/ponds, percolation tanks, small check dams, others, etc.	318	332	309
Percentage		6.04	2.82	2.07
Drought proofing	Afforestation and tree plantation, etc.	371	1,401	2,118
Percentage		7.04	11.88	14.18
Micro irrigation works	Minor irrigation canals, distributaries, etc.	43	625	1,185
Percentage		0.82	5.30	7.93
Provision of irrigation facility to land Owned by SCs/STs, etc.	SCs/STs land reforms, Indira Awas Yojana, small/marginal farmers, etc.	1	1	3
Percentage		0.02	0.01	0.02

(Cont'd)

Table 12.2 (*Cont'd*)

Major Head	*Details of Work*	*2008–9*	*2009–10*	*2010–11*
Renovation of traditional water bodies	De-silting of tanks/ponds, de-silting of old canals, de-silting of traditional open well, others, etc.	2,852	3,761	3,938
Percentage		54.13	31.90	26.36
Land development	Land levelling, plantation, others, etc.	560	1,208	1,584
Percentage		10.63	10.24	10.60
Any other activity approved by MRD	Other MRD approved schemes including Bharat Nirman Rajiv Gandhi Sewa Kendra, etc.	20	441	720
Percentage		0.38	3.74	4.82
Total		5,269	11,792	14,939
Percentage		100.00	100.00	100.00

Source: www.nrega.nic.in (accessed 22 September 2011).

TABLE 12.3 Number of Households Issued Job Cards and Provided Employment in Punjab

Year	*Number of Households*		*Employment Generated*		*Best Performing Districts*
	Issued Job Cards	*Provided Employment*	*Man-days (in lakh)*	*Mean Days per Household*	
2008–9	5,24,928 (100.00)	1,49,902 (28.56)	40.27	26.9	Hoshiarpur, Amritsar, Bathinda, Sangrur, and Gurdaspur
2009–10	7,06,508 (100.00)	2,71,941 (38.49)	77.17	28.4	Hoshiarpur, Amritsar, Bathinda, Mukatsar, and Gurdaspur
2010–11	8,21,076 (100.00)	2,78,134 (33.87)	75.38	27.1	Hoshiarpur, Amritsar, Mukatsar, Firozepur, Ludhiana, and Sangrur

Source: www.nrega.nic.in (accessed 22 September 2011).

Note: Based upon the data given in NREGA Implementation Status Report (respective years).

and they shared 6.57 per cent of man-days of employment. Similarly, a little more than one-half of households (52.87 per cent) got up to 20 days of work and they cornered 20.81 per cent of man-days of employment created, and another one-fourth of households (25.79 per cent) got work in the range of 21–40 days and shared 27.54 per cent of man-days created. Just 2.04 per cent of households got the stipulated days of employment (100 days and more), and they shared 7.73 per cent of man-days of employment. One can easily visualize that as number of days of employment range rise, the proportionate share of households getting employment decreases drastically.

Under the scheme, 90 per cent of expenditure is financed by the Union Government and the remaining 10 per cent by the State Government. Being a demand-driven scheme, there is no upper cap

TABLE 12.4 Number of Households Getting Employment and Man-days Generated in Punjab

Employment Range	*Number of Households Getting Employment*		*Number of Man-days Generated*	
	2009–10	*2010–11*	*2009–10*	*2010–11*
1–20	1,36,348	1,52,276	14,20,162	16,19,106
%	55.02	52.87	22.58	20.81
21–40	63,597	74,275	18,36,516	21,43,325
%	25.66	25.79	29.21	27.54
41–60	26,486	31,133	13,00,559	15,33,824
%	10.69	10.81	20.68	19.71
61–80	11,671	13,407	8,08,112	10,72,446
%	4.71	4.66	12.85	13.78
81–99	5,707	9,041	5,09,877	8,11,797
%	2.30	3.14	8.11	10.43
100+	3,995	5,873	4,13,126	6,01,681
%	1.61	2.04	6.57	7.73
Total	2,47,804	2,88,005	62,88,352	77,82,179
%	100.00	100.00	100.00	100.00

Source: www.nrega.nic.in (accessed 22 September 2011).

Note: Based upon the data given in Employment Generation Report (respective years).

on allocation of financial resources. But there seemed to have been under-utilization of available funds. For instance, in 2008–9, out of the total available funds (Rs 114.85 crore), 63 per cent (Rs. 72.36 crore) was utilized. In 2009–10, as much as 71.69 per cent (Rs 149.96 crore) of the total available funds (Rs 209.17 crore) was utilized. In 2010–11, it was further improved to 73.86 per cent of the available funds (Rs 226.91 crore).

On its part, the state had not contributed its 10 per cent statutory share of total expenditure. Norms regarding expenditure incurred on unskilled wages, skilled or semi-skilled wages, and material costs were given the short shrift in most of NREGS works. The increasing share of material costs (from 28.56 per cent in 2008–9 to 29.00 per cent in 2009–10, and 33.86 per cent in 2010–11) was also a cause for concern (Table 12.5). This showed a tendency among the powerful implementing

Table 12.5 Availability and Utilization of Funds under NREGS in Punjab

Year	*Total Funds (Rs lakh)*			*State Share* (%)*	*Utilization of Funds (%)*				
	Available	*Utilized*	*Per cent Utilized*		*Unskilled Wage*	*Semi-Skilled/ Skilled Wage*	*Cost of Material*	*Adm Cost*	*Total*
2008–9	11,485.06	7,235.81	63.00	N/A	61.56	4.06	28.56	5.82	100.00
2009–10	20,916.90	14,995.90	71.69	7.29	63.55	2.72	29.00	4.73	100.00
2010–11	22,691.12	16,576.85	73.05	3.53	59.05	1.49	33.86	5.60	100.00

Source: www.nrega.nic.in (accessed 22 September 2011).

Note: *Share of total state funds to total available funds (Central and State shares together).

personnel to be extravagant with the cost of material, which in turn offered scope for pilferages. For instance, out of the 14,939 works started in 2010–11, 6, 518 works (43.63 per cent) violated the labour-material norms (60:40) stated in the Act (www.nrega.nic.in).

The employment benefits under NREGS had been extremely favourable to the weaker sections of Punjabi society. The most dominant group of beneficiaries consisted of SC families, their share being as high as 74.17 per cent of man-days of employment in 2008–9, 78.92 per cent in 2009–10 and 78.31 per cent in 2010–11 (Table 12.6). Incidentally, 33.04 per cent of rural population consisted of SC families in Punjab as per 2001 Census figures (GoP, 2007). The remaining employment went to non-SC families, especially the Backward Castes/ Other Backward Castes (BC/OBC) families. Most of the SC families living in rural areas were landless and worked as agricultural labour. The availability of additional employment to such labourers, especially during the lean seasons, was extremely useful in strengthening their livelihoods, and lifting them above the poverty line. Other major beneficiaries of NREGS employment were female workers; their share in total man-days of employment rose from 22.60 per cent in 2008–9 to 26.29 per cent in 2009–10, and was 37.87 per cent in 2010–11. It meant that increasingly more female workers were getting wage employment under this scheme, in or around their living locations.

To bring transparency in wage payments, the NREGS beneficiaries were paid wages either through bank accounts (between 74.69 per cent and 79.39 per cent) or post office accounts (between 25.31 per cent and 20.61 per cent). This removed the possibility

TABLE 12.6 Percentage Distribution of Man-days Generated by Caste of Beneficiary

Year	*Man-days (percentage shares)*				
	SC	*ST*	*Others*	*Total*	*Women*
2008–9	74.17	0.00	25.83	100.00	22.60
2009–10	78.92	0.00	21.08	100.00	26.29
2010–11	78.31	0.01	21.68	100.00	33.87

Source: www.nrega.nic.in (accessed 22 September 2011).

Note: Based upon the data given in NREGA Implementation Status Report (respective years).

of under-payments. And though there could always be scope for manipulation of wage payments, the chances were very less. There had been very few reports on that count when discussions were held with the beneficiaries, representatives of PRIs, researchers and activists involved in organizing workers, and evaluating this programme. Such complaints had also not come to our notice from the media, or any other source. The State Government had also appointed district-wise Ombudsmen to look into proper utilization of NREGS funds.

Group discussions with NREGS Workers' Unions, rural development experts, and women workers threw up the many advantages of NREGS works. It certainly increased female participation in gainful employment, and also helped generate a strong desire for women's empowerment in the state. There are many other advantages that arose out of this as well. First, there is no discrimination between male and female wage rate in this programme. Women are paid Rs 123 per day wage rate for the standard work defined for the day (10' × 10' × 1' in the case of digging earthwork). This is a first, when women are paid wage rate at par with men. Second, the women along with men are employed on community-based works, where they are not subordinate to any individual farmer / employer. Since women work together, or in groups at worksites, the chances of their harassment are also reduced. According to the young marriageable girls of Chharwar village, their parents did not allow them to work in the fields of individual farmers, but allowed them to work in groups at NREGS sites. Third, under this scheme, there is a major shift from working for individual farmers/ employers, to collective community work. This may rekindle a hope among women workers to have their own unions, which will fight for their rights. Fourth, in many NREGS and non-NREGS villages, the women workers have already organized themselves and led agitations (across Moga, Jalandhar, Mukatsar, and Firozepur districts) for their demands, particularly for raising NREGS wages, demanding at least 100 days employment, provisioning of crèche at work-sites, better provision of schooling for their children, and so on. It is expected that they may reap the benefits of collective bargaining in wage determination. Fifth, NREGS has also increased wage rates in non-NREGS activities, especially for women working/seeking employment within the village, both in agricultural as well as non-farm activities. Moreover, this programme is extremely useful for crisis-ridden farmers/peasants, who are in distress, and are facing 'de-peasantization' in the state (Singh *et al.*, 2009). A few households of such category are found to be working in NREGS works in sampled villages. Lastly, in many districts of Punjab, especially Barnala, Moga, Jalandhar, Mukatsar, Kapurthala, Gurdaspur, Ludhiana, and Firozepur, NREGS workers' unions have come into existence to take on issues such as low NREGS wage rate, non-fulfilment of statutory provisions of the Act, etc. Many research studies carried out in Punjab and elsewhere by different scholars support these findings (ISWSD, 2006; Ballan and Singh, 2009; Ghuman and Dua, 2008; Kannan, 2010; and IHD, 2010).

NREGS: Findings and Observations from Primary Survey

An analysis of 240 rural households (120 NREGS and 120 non-NREGS households) supplying labour force revealed many interesting results. For one, 82.08 per cent households belonged to the SC/ST categories, followed by 12.92 per cent of the BC/OBC, and just 5 per cent were general category households. The proportion of SC/ST category was higher in the NREGS households (85.83 per cent) as compared to non-NREGS households (78.33 per cent) (Table 12.7).

For another, going by the poverty and ration card status, 33.75 per cent households fell in the category of APL (Above Poverty Line) and another 41.67 per cent households enjoyed the Atta-Dal scheme (of Punjab). Further, 14.17 per cent households came under BPL (Below Poverty Line) facility, 9.17 per cent under BPL plus Atta-Dal scheme, and just 1.25 per cent under Antodaya Anna Yojana (AAY)

TABLE 12.7 Distribution of Households by Caste Status

Caste Status	*Type of Household*		
	NREGS	*Non-NREGS*	*Total*
SC/ST	103	94	197
%	85.83	78.33	82.08
BC/OBC	13	18	31
%	10.83	15.00	12.92
General	4	8	12
%	3.33	6.67	5.00
Total	120	120	240
%	100.00	100.00	100.00

Source: Primary survey, 2010–11.

TABLE 12.8 Distribution of Households by Type of Ration Card

Type of Ration Card	*Type of Household*		*Total*
	NREGS	*Non-NREGS*	
APL	37	44	81
%	30.83	36.67	33.75
Atta-Dal (Punjab)	47	53	100
%	39.17	44.17	41.67
BPL	21	13	34
%	17.50	10.83	14.17
BPL + Atta-Dal (Punjab)	13	9	22
%	10.83	7.50	9.17
AAY + Atta-Dal (Punjab)	2	1	3
%	1.67	0.83	1.25
Total	120	120	240
%	100.00	100.00	100.00

Source: Primary survey, 2010–11.

plus Atta-Dal scheme. More BPL households were observed across the NREGS households (17.50 per cent) as compared to non-NREGS households (10.83 per cent) (Table 12.8).

These households consisted of 1,101 persons, with 606 males (55.04 per cent) and 495 females (44.96 per cent). As expected, the educational level of the sampled population was very weak, with illiterates comprising 41.42 per cent, primary school pass 26.07 per cent, middle school pass 30.43 per cent, matriculate pass 1.45 per cent, and plus-two pass 0.64 per cent (Table 12.9). The educational level of females was lower than that of males. For instance, proportion of illiterate women (50.71 per cent) was higher than that of men (33.83 per cent). Similarly, women were found to be less qualified compared to men at every education level.

WORKFORCE AND WORK PROFILE

Among the rural labour households, work participation rate was quite high as each person tried to contribute his/her bit to the family's livelihood strategy. Overall, 52.23 per cent of population (54.30 per cent in NREGS and 50.09 per cent in non-NREGS households) was engaged

TABLE 12.9 Distribution of Sampled Population by Sex and Education Level

Education Level	*Type of Household*						
	NREGS		*Non-NREGS*		*Total*		
	M	*F*	*M*	*F*	*M*	*F*	*T*
Illiterate	103	118	102	133	205	251	456
%	33.12	47.77	34.58	53.63	33.83	50.71	41.42
Primary	87	56	85	59	172	115	287
%	27.97	22.67	28.81	23.79	28.38	23.23	26.07
Middle	117	69	98	51	215	120	335
%	37.62	27.94	33.22	20.56	35.48	24.24	30.43
High	4	3	5	4	9	7	16
%	1.29	1.21	1.69	1.61	1.49	1.41	1.45
Plus Two	0	1	5	1	5	2	7
%	0.00	0.40	1.69	0.40	0.83	0.40	0.64
Total	311	247	295	248	606	495	1,101
%	100.00	100.00	100.00	100.00	100.00	100.00	100.00

Source: Primary survey, 2010–11.

Note: No member studied beyond Plus-Two level of education.

in various types of works. Workers across the NREGS households were exclusively working as agricultural labour. However, some workers, both in NREGS and non-NREGS households, were found to be engaged as industrial workers, drivers, and artisans. (Table 12.10).

Quite expectedly, the educational level of rural workforce was very low. More than one-half of workers were illiterate (53.39 per cent), and two-fifth workers (41.04 per cent) had middle-level education. Just 4.35 per cent and 1.22 per cent were matriculates and plus-two pass, respectively. Ironically, nearly three-fourth of women workers was found to be illiterate (Table 12.11).

EMPLOYMENT, WAGES, AND EARNINGS

The average days of employment among the sampled NREGS workers equalled 42 days during 2009–10, with male workers getting work for 38 days and female workers for 45 days (Table 12.12). Since these days of employment were not sufficient for their livelihoods, they

Table 12.10 Distribution of Workforce by Occupational Status of Workers

Occupation	*Type of Household*		
	NREGS	*Non-NREGS*	*Total*
Agricultural Labour	294	243	537
%	97.03	89.34	93.39
Industrial Labour	2	7	9
%	0.66	2.57	1.57
Driver	2	5	7
%	0.66	1.84	1.22
Artisan	2	10	12
%	0.66	3.68	2.09
Any Other	3	7	10
%	0.99	2.57	1.74
Total	303	272	575
%	100.00	100.00	100.00
Work Participation Rate	54.30	50.09	52.23

Source: Primary survey, 2010–11.

Table 12.11 Distribution of Workforce by Gender and Education Level

Education Level	*NREGS*		*Non-NREGS*		*Grand Total*		
	M	*F*	*M*	*F*	*M*	*F*	*Total*
Illiterate	79	84	74	70	153	154	307
%	42.47	71.79	41.81	73.68	42.15	72.64	53.39
Primary	34	19	34	10	68	29	97
%	18.28	16.24	19.21	10.53	18.73	13.68	16.87
Middle	70	12	50	7	120	19	139
%	37.63	10.26	28.25	7.37	33.06	8.96	24.17
High	3	1	14	7	17	8	25
%	1.61	0.85	7.91	7.37	4.68	3.77	4.35
Plus Two	0	1	5	1	5	2	7
%	0.00	0.85	2.82	1.05	1.38	0.94	1.22
Total	186	117	177	95	363	212	575
%	100.00	100.00	100.00	100.00	100.00	100.00	100.00

Source: Primary survey, 2010–11.

TABLE 12.12 Number of Mean Days of Employment of NREGS Workers

Category of Work	*Mean Days of Employment*		
	Males	*Females*	*Wt. Mean*
NREGS Work	38	45	42
%	23.75	62.50	39.62
Non-NREGS Work	122	27	64
%	76.25	37.50	60.38
Total	160	72	106
%	100.00	100.00	100.00

Source: Primary survey, 2010–11.

had to seek employment in other vocations as well. On an average, a worker got employment for 64 days in non-NREGS activities.

For a male NREGS worker, estimated mean days of employment came to 122 days per year in non-NREGS activities, and for female workers, it was just 27 days per year. Interestingly, female workers got more days of NREGS work (45 days) than non-NREGS works (27 days). The former, in practice, was more women intensive.

Average wage rate in NREGS work during 2009–10 was Rs 123 per day (Table 12.13). It was gender neutral, being equal for both men and women workers. However, in non-NREGS work, average wage rate for male worker was considerably higher (Rs 182) than that for female worker (Rs 106). And yet, NREGS had contributed significantly to the earnings of female workers.

During 2009–10, mean earning of a worker from NREGS work came to Rs 5,207.25—Rs 4,625.19 for a male worker and Rs 5,570.32 for a female worker. But in the case of non-NREGS work, mean earning of the male worker was substantially higher (Rs 22,293.65) than that of female workers (Rs 3,882.18). Evidently, the NREGS had played a strong role so far as women's employment and earnings were concerned.

IMPACT ON MIGRATION AND WAGES

One of the intended benefits of NREGS is to arrest internal distress migration, that is migration from rural to urban areas, as well as

TABLE 12.13 Average Wage Rate and Earnings Generated by NREGS Workers, 2010–11

Wage Rate/Earnings	*Gender*		
	Male	*Female*	*Total*
Average Wage Rate (Rs)			
NREGS Work	123	123	123
Non-NREGS Work	182	106	157
Wt. Mean	168	115	144
NREGS Worker's Average Earnings (Rs)			
NREGS Works	4,625.19	5,570.32	5,207.25
%	17.18	58.93	32.22
Non-NREGS Works	22,293.65	3,882.18	10,954.88
%	82.82	41.07	67.78
Total	26,918.84	9,452.50	16,162.13
%	100.00	100.00	100.00

Source: Primary survey, 2010–11.

inter-state migrations. Truly, Punjab's agriculture, industry and services sectors are employing a large number of migrants. For instance, 21.65 lakh migrant workers were employed in these sectors during the late 1990s (GoP, 2004). During the group meetings, it was found that the number of migrant workers from other states like Uttar Pradesh, Bihar, etc., to rural Punjab certainly decreased (yet not stopped altogether), mainly due to the availability of NREGS works in their own states. The actual or imaginary shortage of migrants had pushed up the general/specific wage rates in the state. Availability of NREGS work within the sampled villages had also pushed up wage rates in agricultural activities. For instance, normal agricultural wage rate in four villages—Chharwar and Dulbha in Patiala district, and Ubhewal and Daulat Pur in Sangrur district—was raised by Rs 20–25 per worker after the introduction of NREGS activities in these villages. In Chharwar village, agriculture wage rate was just Rs 100–110 per day in 2008–9. With the starting of NREGS in 2009–10, wage rate of manual local labour rose to Rs 125–135 and, in 2010–11, was quoted at Rs 150–160 per day. Women workers were the real beneficiaries of the rise in wage rate.

On the question of arresting migration from the rural to the urban within the state, an analysis of sampled households indicated that the workforce in NREGS villages, particularly the women workers, had fewer tendencies to go outside their own village in search of jobs. However, in non-NREGS villages, many male workers were found working outside their villages. As a proxy measure, NREGS works positively arrested the distress migration among workers. Interestingly, the State Government had anticipated shortage of migrant workers in the coming years in the event of the NREGS experiment succeeding in UP, Bihar, etc. Hence, the state machinery had been working overtime to find suitable alternatives like mechanization of paddy transplantation, for instance, to meet labour shortage. Already, many power driven paddy transplanters had been imported at high costs and sold to the farmers at subsidized rates. Further, the state authorities had taken many effective steps to protect the interest of farmers and industrial lobbies. For example, the minimum NREGS wage rate had not been increased during 2009–10, largely due to the pressure of farmers and industrial lobbies, as noticed by the NREGS activists, policy makers and state academia.

ORGANIZING THE WORKFORCE

The organizational problems of rural labour are examined in the larger context of the political economy of the state. Though labour experts, and trade union leaders and activists involved in organizing labour have different perspectives regarding the problems of rural labour and how to organize them, they unanimously favoured implementation of various pro-poor welfare schemes, including the NREGS. Persons with leftist leaning are the front-runners in organizing NREGS workers in Punjab. Many radical elements are also organizing rural labour. Some of them are the Punjab Khet Mazdoor Sabha (Regd.), Chandigarh, with more than 1.50 lakh members; the All India Agricultural Workers Union, with 1.18 lakh members; and the Pendu Mazdoor Union Punjab, Jalandhar, with 9,000 member households. All of them are working for the welfare of rural labour, including the NREGS workers. But they are concentrated largely in few districts—Barnala, Moga, Jalandhar, Mukatsar, Firozepur, and some parts of Ludhiana, Amritsar, Kapurthala, and Gurdaspur.

These organizations agree that NREGS has opened up new opportunities and helped them to organize labour better, as so many workers are found to be working together at one place, creating common property assets and resources, and developing community feeling among the fellow workers. This environment has also helped to provide a platform for them to discuss their common problems, know about the benefits of 'strength-in-unity', and incline favourably to formulate own unions (Box 12.1).

However, because of illiteracy, a large proportion of NREGS workers are unable to visualize the benefits, like how to seek employment, and what facilities they are entitled to. The mindset of the rural dominant classes is also working against these workers. Although all sampled workers viewed NREGS work favourably, yet they did not know about the intricacies of demanding employment, and also how to demand unemployment allowance. Administrative apathy, non-effective role of Gram Sabhas, and illegal occupation of common property resources by influential villagers are other bottlenecks in the smooth functioning of NREGS (Gill, 2011) (Box 12.2).

On the question of low NREGS wage rate, the leaders of NREGS workers unions' argue that the lobbies of industrialists, Farmers' Unions (particularly a BKU group), and other local forces inimical to rural labour have been working overtime to scuttle the move to raise the minimum wage rate applicable in NREGS works in the state. For their part, the NREGS Workers' Unions have been organizing *dharnas*, blockades, strikes, hunger strikes and the like, to fights for the rights of workers. Workers are also being educated by highlighting the benefits of NREGS through expert lectures, pamphlets, and other educative measures.

At many places, NREGS works have been started, and employment given under pressure from these unions. This had happened in Chharwar village, where an elected Sarpanch, Darshan Singh, organized local labourers (mainly the women) to restart NREGS work during 2010–11. The elected Panchayat of Dulbha village, led by Sarpanch Raj Singh of the SC community, fought first with the influential landlords and then with the NREGS officials to get project funds. Besides garnering the support of local women workers, he also got the support of the district unit of the Congress party and cadre-based NREGS unions. In both villages, women workers were more articulate and progressive in nature. The cadre-based trade unions organized lectures by experts on the rights and responsibility of NREGS workers.

Box 12.1 NREGS' Best Practices

The best practices of NREGS can be seen in four villages—Chharwar, Dulbha and Fatehpur in Patiala district, and Ubhewal in Sangrur District. The Panchayat of Chharwar village recently took possession of village common land (about 270 acres) after a prolonged litigation with influential farmers. Half of this land lacked adequate irrigation facilities. Therefore, it could not fetch a high rent in an open auction across the competing farmers, who were willing to carry out cultivation, especially on the land earmarked for the SC families as one-third common land (*shamlat*) was reserved for SC families. Only those farmers who had adjoining farms with sufficient irrigation facilities of their own took it on rent. Many times collusion among such farmers deliberately depressed the rent value of *shamlat* land. The NREGS works started in Patiala district during 2008–09 proved a blessing in disguise for the village Panchayat and District Level Officials. The Village Panchayat, along with NREGS officials, innovatively designed a NREGS project at an estimated cost of Rs 30.50 lakh to create irrigation facility on this *shamlat* land by lift-irrigation from the Ghaggar river, flowing along the village boundary (1.5 km away), and by channelizing the lifted water through underground pipes. This increased the rental value of land as also the agricultural outputs. The most significant advantage of this scheme was that the SC families could now hope to carry out cultivation on this land by following the competitive bidding process, which was earlier not possible in the absence of irrigation facility. Further, the surplus water could be stored in a deep-dug pond by using NREGS funds on two acres common land in the vicinity of the *shamlat* land. In the lean season, this surplus water would provide regular supply of water to irrigate the fields. There was another proposal to convert it into an artificial lake for water sports and fishing. The perceived synergy among the local populace, Village Panchayat, Gram Sabha and NREGS officials is worth emulating.

Another best practice was seen in Ubhewal village in Sangrur District. The Panchayat headed by a young, enthusiastic Sarpanch, belonging to SC category, and consisting of other young *Panches* had given a pledge to the village people (at the time of election) to work for the welfare of the village. Taking advantages of his political connections with the ruling Siromani Akali Dal (SAD), the Sarpanch extracted maximum funds under the NREGS and other rural development schemes. The Panchayat, with the help of District Officials, also designed many development works under NREGS. An earth-filling project was the first to be taken up. Under this project, the area around the village water works constructed earlier by Public

Health Department was developed into a beautiful park by planting a variety of trees, shrubs and seasonal flowers. The second work related to leveling of three acres of low-lying Panchayat land that, in the event, enhanced the rental value of said land by Rs 1.10 lakh per year. De-silting of the village pond for improving the sanitation, the construction of a well-equipped gymnasium using NREGS funds and grants from other departments of the State Government were the other works. Similarly, the Panchayat constructed a shed at a village bus-stop, and a water tank on it for regular drinking water supply. All these proved how the synergy between NREGS and others rural development schemes could be achieved and used for the welfare of the villagers. The role of the youth and political backup were indeed added advantages.

The Dulbha's experiment is no less exciting. Here, an energetic Sarpanch belonging to the SC category was able to carry the entire Panchayat with him and use his political connection with the Congress party to extract maximum funds under NREGS. He was able to improve sanitation, and deepened an old pond, to store drainage water that often flooded the village streets. This not only provided employment to all those workers in the village who demanded work, but also to those in the nearby village, Partapgarh. The greening of the village elementary school with trees and flower-plants was yet another work undertaken by the Panchayat. In 2010–11, a large, eight-foot deep pond was excavated for breeding fish. More than 80 per cent of the total expenditure incurred on these projects went to the labourers of two villages.

In Fatehpur, an articulated and educated Sarpanch with large land holdings tried to translate his ideas about rural development into reality with the help of other members of the Panchayat. Aware of the significance of trade unionism, he used his BKU (a farmer's organization) connections to release more funds under the NREGS for improving village sanitation, flood control, and other protective measures. First, the Panchayat cleared the wild growth from a canal based water channel, which was a source of irrigation in the village. It increased the water speed and water carrying capacity of the channel. Second, widening and deepening of the village pond and filling it with clean water—a long standing demand of the villagers—were also taken up. Third, a centre, the Rajiv Gandhi Sewa Kender, for holding meetings and conducting training programmes was set up in the village at an estimated cost of Rs 10 lakh under the NREGS. Finally, thanks to the efforts of Sarpanch, four/five workers from his villagers got NREGS-related work in the adjoining village.

Source: Primary Survey, 2010–11.

Box 12.2 NREGS' Worst Practices

The worst forms can be seen in those villages where no NREGS work of any type was started in the last three years. Rural labour in these villages had been deprived of the benefits of 100 days of employment. Wage loss per annum on normative basis was Rs 12,300 per worker. The worst hit villages were Bhore (57 BPL families), Binjoki Kalan/Khurd (51 BPL families), and Dhindsa (36 BPL families), where a large number of BPL households were reported to be living. These BPL families, particularly the women workers, requested the study team to use influence to get them jobs under NREGS. In these villages, the Panchayats were faction-ridden or controlled by the landed aristocracy, and beneficiaries had not been unionized or did not have links with party in power. All these factors contribute to the unpleasant living conditions of rural poor households. In the absence of assured employment, the rural poor households were found to be living under sub-human conditions. Even the little common property resources at village level were put to commercial use, and yet could not provide much help to the rural poor.

Another group of three villages—Mithu Majra, Chamarheri and Rampur Bhindran—did not have enough common land to do any NREGS work, not to speak of Panchayat initiatives. The little common land available in these villages was under illegal occupation of influential adjoining households. District level officials turned a deaf ear to the voices of job seekers under NREGS because the Panchayats were faction-ridden and the labour class was not organized or articulated enough. Even, the resolutions passed in Gram Sabhas of these villages were of little use. The Panchayats did not have sufficient political links with the party in power to get any favour. Few other villages (Daulatpur and Amir Nagar) got only Rs 1.00 lakh each during 2009–10. With this paltry amount, the Panchayats were neither able to finish the digging work, nor were they able to provide sufficient employment (man-days) for rural labour, despite the fact that enough number of rural labour households had the job cards, and were willing to do work. Even, the NREGS works started in adjoining villages were not enough to get them employment.

Another worst practice was the non-payment of unemployment allowance to any worker in these villages, despite an overwhelming majority of job card holders having registered themselves for NREGS employment. Even when Panchayats of many villages passed resolutions through Gram Sabhas to identify the projects to be undertaken, there was no follow-up action. This grim reality was a poor reflection on the state's administrative machinery, civil society, and trade union movements in this progressive State. Among the non-NREGS villages, many unskilled workers were found going daily to nearby cities / towns in search of employment, but their women could not move outside the villages for employment. The women of these villages were deprived of NREGS employment opportunities. Class bias was also working against them.

In a nutshell, the worst forms of NREGS were observed in those village: (i) where no NREGS work was started yet; (ii) where adequate common property resources were not available, or grabbed by the influential villagers; (iii) where Village Panchayats were faction-ridden and not showing adequate dynamism; (iv) where Panchayats were controlled by influential classes; (v) where the beneficiaries were not adequately unionized; and (vi) where the Panchayats were not well-connected with the party in power.

Source: Primary Survey, 2010–11.

CONCEIVING NREGS WORKS

Group meetings made it clear that the Village Sarpanch and other elected members, on the advice of NREGS officials, played significant roles in identifying possible works to be undertaken in the village. The resolution to identify works had to be passed by the Gram Sabha. Since the institution of Gram Sabha was weak in the state, majority of villagers did not participate in its meetings. The common practice in most of the villages was that the first Gram Sabha meeting used to be adjourned for want of quorum. In subsequent meetings, as no quorum was required, the intended resolutions were easily passed by simple majority of members present. The experiences of sampled villages testified this. These resolutions in the form of work demands were sent to block level officials, to prepare technical details like estimated expenditure, demand for works, feasibility, etc. Then these resolutions of different villages were put to vote at the meetings of the Panchayat Samiti and the Zila Parishad. At both levels, new proposals, which benefited groups of villages, could be added. These proposed projects, complete in all respects, would be sent to the state agencies for onward journey to the central authority. At the central level, these proposals were subject to complete scrutiny. Only very few projects got the required sanction or money. Since the democratic process at village level was weak, the Sarpanch, Panchayat Members, NREGS officials, and other pressure groups played an important role in initiating works therein (Gill, 2011). State agencies also played an important role. On this count, the experience of Patiala district was depressing.

Here more than 95 per cent of Panchayats (891 village panchayats) passed resolutions in favour of NREGS works and estimates were sent for final approval to the central authority, but only 171 villages in 2009–10 and 391 in 2010–11 got the required grants to start work.

***

The analysis makes it clear that the NREGS in Punjab, like other state social security measures—except the old age pension and subsidized food (Atta-Dal) where political commitments are more pronounced—is operating much below expectations. The low performance was observed in terms of number of households which got employment, man-days of employment created, low allocation of funds by the state, delays in completion of works, and under-utilization of allocated funds during the last three years. Though it is true that a very high proportion of man-days created (around three-fourth share) was cornered by SC families, the share of female workers in man-days employment was still low but is rising (22.60 per cent in 2008–9, 26.29 per cent in 2009–10 and 33.87 per cent in 2010–11).

District level prospective plans under NREGS, on systematic and scientific lines, are yet to be prepared for all districts in the state. Social audit does not exist as yet in Punjab. The Vigilance Committees have not come into existence in villages. In spite of a large gap between the number of job card holding families, and those actually getting employment, no one has been paid unemployment allowance. Further, provisions of first-aid kit, arrangement of shade, drinking water facilities, provision of crèches for children of women workers, etc are not available at or near the work-sites. The implementation of NREGS in Punjab is subject to many constraints like lack of political will, administrative apathy, factional village polity, upper castes' dominance, and illiteracy among beneficiaries to name a few.

The village level ground realities highlighted by the primary survey show that most of the rural workers are not only poor, but also uneducated and unskilled. They lack mobility and prefer to work in their own village, or in the adjoining villages. Mono-cropping pattern, over-mechanization of agriculture, dwindling operational holdings, etc have adversely affected demand for the hired labour in these villages. The results also show that among NREGS households, an average male worker got 160 days of employment per annum (38 days in

NREGS works and 122 days in other works) and a female worker 72 days of employment (45 days in NREGS works and 27 days in other works) during 2009–10. Moreover, the NREGS wage rate is gender neutral, where men and women get equal wage rate for carrying out a stipulated work. It has been noticed that NREGS works in the state are being undertaken, mostly in those months when demand for labour is least in the agricultural sector. Thus, employment in NREGS activities has added to the income of agriculture labour households. Starting of NREGS works has also raised general wage rate in other forms of rural employment in these villages, as the rural wages were not rising sufficiently due to huge influx of migratory labour in the state. Hence, the local rural workforce who participated in NREGS works has benefitted from the employment under the scheme in the various ways, thus justifying the implementation of NREGS in a state that attracts migratory labour in large numbers from other states.

NREGS works also provides new opportunities for the rural labour to organize themselves. Persons with leftist leanings are the front-runners in organizing NREGS workers in the state. Rural workers, being illiterate and poor, cannot visualize the statutory provisions and intended benefits of NREGS works. The mindset of rural dominant classes is also working against these workers. Administrative apathy, ineffective role of the Gram Sabha, and illegal occupation of common property resources by influential villagers are other bottlenecks in the smooth functioning of NREGS. The lobbies of industrialists, farmers' union (particularly a BKU group), and other forces inimical to rural labour are working overtime to scuttle the move to raise minimum wage rate applicable in NREGS works. The NREGS workers unions have been organizing dharnas, blockades, strikes, hunger strikes, along with submitting memorandums, to fight for the rights of workers. They also arranged expert lectures, and prepared leaflets to educate the workers. At numerous places, NREGS works have been started under the pressure of these unions.

Among surveyed villages, there was no report of non-payment or under-payment of wages as wages were paid through banks or post office accounts. The programme is extremely useful for weaker sections (SCs and women), including the pauperized sections of peasantry. Several new avenues of employment, like horticulture, can be explored for gainful employment of labour for longer periods. Moreover, the NREGS is expected to arrest the flow of distress migration of rural labour to the urban centres in an appreciable way. Minimum wages must be revised at the earliest to make NREGS wage rate competitive.

Many works started in the surveyed villages, with NREGS funds, gave examples of best practices and must be emulated elsewhere. Truly, the power groups did influence decisions on the type of NREGS works, quantum of funds, inclusion of beneficiaries, etc. NREGS works were also not implemented on a rational basis. Instead, the whims and fancies of elites, bureaucracy, political forces, and local lobbies determined the granting of funds and works to be accomplished in the villages. For instance, more than two-third of the villages in the surveyed districts did not get any fund due to one reason or another. Truly, the state's political economy and short-sightedness of the present ruling combine have a lot to do with the low performance of NREGS in the state.

For its part, the state administration does not show much enthusiasm to take full advantage of Central funded schemes. Partly, this is due to the general apathy and indifferent attitude of state bureaucracy towards all government programmes. Partly, it is attributed to lack of political-will, as shown by the prevailing power structure in the state. The state power structure in the rural areas is largely controlled by the big and middle-level farmers. They are least interested in the implementation of any programmes that benefit the poor. They are only interested in implementation to the extent that these programmes help them in winning elections. The state can be made more responsive, if the beneficiaries organize themselves in the form of genuine associations or unions.

For better implementation, people's involvement, especially of the beneficiaries, is of utmost importance. The system of setting up of vigilance committees at the village level, introduction and faithful implementation of social auditing, and operation through the PRIs can make such programmes more successful. In fact, for getting better results, training of elected representatives of the PRIs is essential to make them aware of their powers and duties. The state and district administration need to be toned up where performance is below the average. There is also need to create better awareness among the elected representatives and beneficiaries about this programme. Uplifting the educational level and regular training of beneficiaries can generate better results. There is a need to increase the minimum wage rate and employment days under the NREGS. Utmost transparency and accountability in selecting beneficiaries and working of this scheme must be ensured.

APPENDIX A12

TABLE A12.1 List of Sampled Villages by Location

Name of Village	*Block*	*District*
Chharwar	Rajpura	Patiala
Dulbha	Sanaur	Patiala
Partapgarh	Sanaur	Patiala
Fatehpur	Patiala	Patiala
Dhindsa*	Rajpura	Patiala
Chamarheri*	Patiala	Patiala
Mithu Majra*	Patiala	Patiala
Bhore*	Nabha	Patiala
Ubhewal	Sangrur	Sangrur
Daulat Pur	Malerkotla	Sangrur
Jitwal Kalan	Ahmedgarh	Sangrur
Amir Nagar	Ahmedgarh	Sangrur
Ranwan*	Malerkotla	Sangrur
Binjoki Kalan/Khurd*	Malerkotla	Sangrur
Rampur Bhindran*	Malerkotla	Sangrur
Sherpur*	Dhuri	Sangrur

Source: Primary survey, 2010–11.

Note: *Non-NREGS villages.

APPENDIX A12.2

ADDITIONAL NOTE ON SAMPLED NREGS WORKERS

A brief analysis of additional view-points of NREGS workers about the scheme is as follows: (i) the Panchayats were found to be the major source of information for NREGS related employment across the sampled villages. Overall, 76.09 per cent of the workers got information from this source, followed by the radio, television, newspapers, apart from friends, relatives, or neighbours; (ii) a majority of NREGS workers (57.50 per cent) got NREGS work during the months of January, February and March (the lean season in Punjab agriculture), while another 37.50 per cent got work during the October, November and December; and (iii) 54.17 per cent of the NREGS workers received

TABLE A12.2 Percentage Distribution of NREGS Workers by Source of Information, Employment Months, and Wages Disbursal Time

Source of Information	*Percentage Shares*	*Employment Months*	*Percentage Shares*	*Wages Disbursal Time Within*	*Percentage Shares*
Panchayats	76.09	April, May, and June	0.00	Two Days	0.00
Radio/TV/ Newspapers	13.41	July, Aug., and Sept.	5.00	Seven Days	54.17
Friends/ Relatives/ Neighbours	8.70	Oct., Nov., and Dec.	37.50	Fifteen Days	41.67
Govt. Functionaries	1.81	Jan., Feb., and Mar.	57.50	One Month	4.17
Total	100.00	Total	100.00	Total	100.00

Source: Primary survey, 2010–11.

the wages within 7 days of the work and 41.67 per cent within 15 days of the work (Table A12.2).

Regarding presence of facilities at an NREGS workplace, the analysis shows a mixed picture (Table A12.3). All NREGS workers reported non-availability of a crèche at work place. The availability of drinking water was reported by 88.33 per cent workers, while 51.67 per cent workers complained about no arrangement of shade for rest. However, all workers reported 'rest time' (one hour) while doing work. 70 per cent reported that the work sites were free from the health hazards. Group insurance was completely missing, as no worker reported this facility.

The workers spoke highly about positive features of NREGS work, (Table A12.3). First, an overwhelming majority of workers were satisfied with the mode of work measurement. Second, about 79 per cent availed of one day leave per week. Third, as many as 68 per cent workers reported the presence of regular mate for day-to-day monitoring of work. About 59 per cent reported that the mate was one among the fellow workers. Fourth, 95 per cent reported the availability of NREGS work within a distance of 5 km from their residences. Fifth, level of awareness about accident benefits among the

TABLE A12.3 Percentage Distribution of NREGS Workers, Reported Facilities at Work Place, Satisfaction, and Impacts

Facility	*%age Shares*	*Features*	*%age Shares*	*Impacts on Income Level*	*%age Shares*
Crèche	0.00	One Day Leave per Week	79.17	Considerably Raised	30.00
Drinking Water	88.33	Satisfied with Work Measurement	96.67	Increased Somewhat	66.67
Shade for Rest	48.33	Regular Mate Availability	68.33	Not Increased/Same	3.33
Rest Time during Work	100.00	Mate amongst Workers	58.54	Decreased Somewhat	0.00
Free from Health Hazards	70.00	Mate Rotation System	15.00	Decreased Considerably	0.00
Group Insurance	0.00	Work within 5 km	79.17	Total	100.00
		Awareness about Accident/ Injury Benefit	0.83		

Source: Primary survey, 2010–11.

TABLE A12.4 Percentage Distribution of NREGS Workers' Responses

Characteristics	*Percentage Shares*	*Expenditure Items Witness Rise*	*Percentage Shares*	*Impacts on School Going Children*	*Percentage Shares*
Priority Given to NREGS Work	98.33	Food Items	86.67	Easy Purchase of Books, etc.	91.55
NREGS Improved Village Poor	98.33	Durables Items	25.83	No possibility of Drop-out	33.80
Other Household Members got Employment	30.83	Health Maintenance	63.33	Learning Increased	14.08
Children Attended School	59.17	Education	43.33	Hoping for Higher Education	9.86
Social Audit Committee	2.50	Loan Payment	30.83	No Visible Change	19.72
Involved in Work Selection	0.83	Social Ceremony	20.83		
Attended Gram Sabha Meetings	0.00	Land/House Improvement	3.33		
		Animal Purchase	0.83		
		Productive Assets	2.50		

Source: Primary survey, 2010–11.

NREGS workers was very low. Lastly, NREGS workers also reported many positive impacts on their livelihoods. Many workers (30.00 per cent) reported strong positive income impacts. Another 66.67 per cent workers mentioned positive income impacts to some extent.

These sampled workers, particularly the women, stated that they would like to be employed in NREGS works on a priority basis, as shown in Table A12.4. They opined that NREGS work has improved socio-economic conditions of the village poor. Surprisingly, as high as 99.17 per cent NREGS workers reported that they were not involved in the selection of the work at all, and no NREGS worker attended any meetings of the Gram Sabha. Nearly three-fifths of the workers (59.17 per cent) felt comfortable in sending their children in the schools. The NREGS income has rekindled a hope among these workers and households that their children would not have to drop out of school now. Moreover, it also enhanced the hope to obtain higher education, and helped in the purchase of books and stationery items. As many as 86.67 per cent of households reported that with the NREGS income, their consumption expenditure increased to a greater extent than before. Many others reported a rise in their expenditure on health maintenance (63.33 per cent), children's education (43.33 per cent), durable goods (28.83 per cent), loan repayments (30.83 per cent), and social ceremonies (20.83 per cent).

Most of the NREGS workers (91.67 per cent) felt that NREGS wage rate is very low compared to the prevailing wage rates in their villages, particularly during the busy agricultural seasons (Table A12.5). Other major problems that hindered the implementation of NREGS works in their villages, as stated by them, were upper

TABLE A12.5 Percentage Distribution of NREGS Households Reported Problems in Its Implementation

Main Problem	*Percentage of Households*
Less NREGS Wage Rate	91.67
Upper Castes' Dominance of Village Polity	60.83
Ignorance of Beneficiaries	47.50
Dominance of Bribery	11.67
No Common Land	9.17

Source: Primary survey, 2010–11.

TABLE A12.6 Village-wise Number of Job Cards Issued, and Eligible Persons Seeking NREGS Employment in Patiala and Sangrur Districts (Punjab), 2009–10 and 2010–11

Name of Village	*Name of Block*	*Number of Households Issued Job Cards*			*Persons Covered*		*Sex of Persons*			*BPL/AAY HH Covered*
		SC	*Other*	*Total*	*SC*	*Other*	*Male*	*Female*	*Total*	*%*
Patiala District										
Chharwar	Rajpura	56	35	91	78	42	47	73	120	1
%		61.54	38.46	100.00	65.00	35.00	39.17	60.83	100.00	1.10
Dulbha	Sanour	33	6	39	70	8	44	34	78	2
%		84.62	15.38	100.00	89.74	10.26	56.41	43.59	100.00	5.13
Partapgarh	Sanour	33	4	37	55	7	29	33	62	0
%		89.19	10.81	100.00	88.71	11.29	46.77	53.23	100.00	0.00
Fatehpur	Patiala	18	3	21	19	3	21	1	22	
%		85.71	14.29	100.00	86.36	13.64	95.45	4.55	100.00	0.00
Dhindsa*	Rajpura	27	6	33	27	6	18	15	33	1
%		81.82	18.18	100.00	81.82	18.18	54.55	45.45	100.00	3.03
Mithu Majra*	Patiala	13	0	13	13	0	13	0	13	2
%		100.00	0.00	100.00	100.00	0.00	100.00	0.00	100.00	15.38
Chamarheri*	Patiala	9	3	12	9	3	12	0	12	0
		75.00	25.00	100.00	75.00	25.00	100.00	0.00	100.00	0.00
Bhore*	Nabha	51	8	59	51	8	54	5	59	9
%		86.44	13.56	100.00	86.44	13.56	91.53	8.47	100.00	15.25
Total		240	65	305	322	77	238	161	399	15
%		78.69	21.31	100.00	80.70	19.30	59.65	40.35	100.00	4.92

District Sangrur										
Ubhewal	Sangrur	74	39	113	100	41	99	42	141	10
%		65.49	34.51	100.00	70.92	29.08	70.21	29.79	100.00	8.85
Daulat Pur	Malerkotla	25	0	25	30	0	12	18	30	2
%		100.00	0.00	100.00	100.00	0.00	40.00	60.00	100.00	8.00
Jitwal Kalan	Ahmedgarh	66	10	76	82	11	41	52	93	0
%		86.84	13.16	100.00	88.17	11.83	44.09	55.91	100.00	0.00
Amir Nagar	Ahmedgarh	59	6	65	59	6	24	41	65	0
%		90.77	9.23	100.00	90.77	9.23	36.92	63.08	100.00	0.00
Ranwan*	Malerkotla	32	5	37	35	5	21	19	40	0
%		86.49	13.51	100.00	87.50	12.50	52.50	47.50	100.00	0.00
Rampur Bhindran*	Malerkotla	15	7	22	16	8	13	11	24	7
%		68.18	31.82	100.00	66.67	33.33	54.17	45.83	100.00	31.82
Binjoki Khurd/ Kalan*	Malerkotla	32	35	67	33	35	53	15	68	0
%		47.76	52.24	100.00	48.53	51.47	77.94	22.06	100.00	0.00
Sherpur Sodhian*	Dhuri	30	1	31	49	1	28	22	50	2
%		96.77	3.23	100.00	98.00	2.00	56.00	44.00	100.00	6.45
Total		333	103	436	404	107	291	220	511	21
%		76.38	23.62	100.00	79.06	20.94	56.95	43.05	100.00	4.82

Source: Office of the Deputy Commissioners, Patiala, and Sangrur districts.

Note: *Non-NREGA villages.

castes dominance of village polity (60.83 per cent), followed by the ignorance of beneficiaries (47.50 per cent), dominance of bribery (11.67 per cent), and non availability of common land (9.17 per cent) in their villages.

References

Ballan, P.P. and S. Singh. 2009. *National Rural Employment Guarantee Scheme: Appraisal of Impact Assessment of NREGS in Selected District of Himachal Pradesh, Punjab and Haryana*. Chandigarh: Centre for Research in Rural and Industrial Development.

Ghuman, R.S. and P.K. Dua. 2008. *NREGA and Rural Employment in Punjab: An Evaluative Study of Hoshiarpur District*. Paper Presented in the Conference on Employment Opportunities and Public Employment Policy in Globalizing India, 3–5 April, Centre for Development Studies, Thiruvananthapuram.

Gill, S.S. 2002. 'Agriculture, Crop Technology and Employment Generation in Punjab', in S.S. Johl and S.K. Ray (eds) *Future of Agriculture in Punjab*, pp. 56–68. Chandigarh: Centre for Research in Rural and Industrial Development.

———. 'Why Punjab is Cold to Job Scheme', *The Tribune*, 3 September.

Gill, S.S., S. Singh, and J.S. Brar. 2010. *Globalization and Indian State: Education, Health and Agricultural Extension Services in Punjab*. New Delhi: Aakar Books.

GoI. 2002. *National Human Development 2001*. Planning Commission, New Delhi.

———. 2011. *Economic Survey 2010-11*. New Delhi: Oxford University Press.

GoP. 2004. *Human Development Report 2004 Punjab*. Chandigarh: Government of Punjab.

———. 2007. *Statistical Abstract of Punjab 2007*. Economic Advisor to Chandigarh: Government of Punjab.

———. 2010. *Statistical Abstract of Punjab 2010*. Chandigarh: Economic Adviser to Government, Economic and Statistical Organization of Punjab.

IHD. 2010. *National Rural Employment Guarantee as Social Protection*. New Delhi: Institute of Human Development.

ISWSD. 2006. *Monitoring and Evaluation of National Rural Employment Guarantee Scheme with special focus on Gender Issues*, Final Report based on Field Visits in June–August 2006, New Delhi: Indian School of Women's Studies Development.

Jain, V. 2010. *Affluence, Vulnerability and the Provision of Social Security: Assessing State's Concern for the Working masses in India*, HiVOS Knowledge

Programme, Paper 3. Amsterdam: University of Amsterdam, and Thiruvananthapuram: Centre for Development Studies.

Kannan, K.P. 2010. *The Long Road to Social Security: Challenge of Universal Coverage for the Working Poor in India*, HiVOS Knowledge Programme, Working Paper 2. Amsterdam: University of Amsterdam, and Thiruvananthapuram: Centre for Development Studies.

Kannan, K.P. and V. Jain. 2011. *Implementation of NREGA across Indian States: A Phase-wise Analysis*, A Paper Presented at Final Workshop under CDS-ASSR Project on Monitoring the Implementation of Social Security for the Working Poor in India's Informal Economy, 20–22 June, Centre for Development Studies, Thiruvananthapuram.

Mann, M. 2012. 'Cash Course for Bihar Migrants', *The Tribune*, Chandigarh, June 13, p. 4.

NCAER. 2009. *NCAER-PIF Study on Evaluating Performance of National Rural Employment Guarantee Act*. New Delhi: National Council of Applied Economic Research.

PYF. 2010. *Five Year Perspective Plan of District Patiala under Mahatma Gandhi National Rural Employment Guarantee Scheme (MGNREGS) 2010–11 to 2014–15*, Progressive Youth Forum, Ghagga, Punjab.

Reddy, D. Narasimha. 2011. *Functioning of National Rural Employment Guarantee Scheme (NREGS) in Andhra Pradesh*, A Paper Presented at Final Workshop under CDS-ASSR Project on Monitoring the Implementation of Social Security for the Working Poor in India's Informal Economy, 20–22 June, Centre for Development Studies, Thiruvananthapuram.

Sidhu, R.S. and Sukhpal Singh. 2004. 'Agricultural Wages and Employment in Punjab', *Economic and Political Weekly*, 39(37): 4132–5.

Singh, Sukhpal. 2010. 'The Status of Agricultural Resources in Punjab: Need for Alternatives', in R.S. Ghuman, Surjit Singh, and Jaswinder Singh Brar (eds) *Globalization and Change: Perspectives from Punjab*, pp. 257–74. Jaipur: Rawat Publications.

Singh, K., S. Singh, and H.S. Kingra. 2009. 'The Agrarian Crisis and Depeasantization in Punjab: Status of Small and Marginal Farmers who left Agriculture', *Indian Journal of Agricultural Economics*, 64(4), October–December: 585–683.

UNDP. 2011. *UNDP in India: Results from 2010*. Available at www.undp.ord.in (accessed 5 October 2011).

13 SOCIAL SECURITY IN PUNJAB

A BLEND OF STATE AND CENTRAL SCHEMES

Sucha Singh Gill, Sukhwinder Singh, and *Jaswinder Singh Brar*

The social security schemes in the state have evolved over a considerable period of time. These are the result of socio-economic and political processes, which led to the introduction of some schemes in the state before they began to be introduced at an all-India level by the Union Government. In fact, the state had witnessed a strong regional movement for the formation of a Punjabi speaking state during the late 1950s and early 1960s on one hand, and another strong peasant mobilization in 1959, against the betterment levy imposed on canal water in the wake of expansion of canal irrigation from the Bhakra project (Lyallpuri, 2010). These movements were followed by rise of the Naxalite movement, creating a strong base of the left forces amongst the youth and peasants in the state. In the wake of these mobilizations, the state government introduced an old age pension scheme in 1964, and financial assistance to widows and destitute women and dependent children in 1968. After the National Commission for Enterprises in the Unorganized Sector (NCEUS) Report of 2007 (NCEUS, 2007), the Union Government passed an Unorganized Workers' Social Security Act 2008, to provide social protection to the unorganized workers and their families (Kannan, 2010). Surging growth rate along with political commitment (CMP) during the past decade has led to the rapid expansion in public spending, which has created new possibilities for social protection in India (World Bank, 2011).

Passing of this act, in fact, is a revolutionary step, aimed solely to create a dedicated social protection environment for the unorganized sector's workforce. The Act mandates the Union Government to formulate and notify suitable welfare schemes, from time to time, for the welfare of workers of the unorganized sector, on matters relating to (i) life and disability cover; (ii) health and maternity benefits; (iii) old age protection; and (d) any other suitable benefit. This act empowers the Union Government to constitute a national social security board (for a term of 3 years) and state boards, to exercise the powers and functions conferred to them (Kannan, 2010). Lack of these provisions exposes the workers and their families to the adversities like food insecurity, loss of employment, old age, injuries/deaths, sickness, etc. It is indeed true that many progressive Indian states (like Kerala, Tamil Nadu, Andhra Pradesh, and Punjab) have enacted certain laws in the past, and initiated schemes to protect the interests of the poor and vulnerable sections of society. However, in the absence of legal entitlement, inadequate provisions of funds, and political commitment, true benefits of these schemes could not percolate down to the masses. Moreover, these schemes (transitional in character) are not enforceable by law, whereas the legislative acts are enforceable by the courts.

Punjab is one of the foremost states of India, in terms of development—ranked 2nd and 4th respectively in terms of Human Development Index (HDI) (after Kerala) and per capita income (after Haryana, Maharashtra, and Gujarat). The state also occupies a high position, consistently, on the basis of per capita consumption expenditure (Jain, 2010) and lowest incidence of poverty (GoI, 2011). The state, however, did not have an impressive record of initiating new and innovative social security measures for the working poor as compared to the southern states of Kerala, Andhra Pradesh, and Tamil Nadu. In the past, the state had faced a grave politico-religious crisis (terrorists violence) for 14 years (1982–95), when more state funds were diverted to maintain law and order, and the state was forced to resort to more public borrowings, which shifted the state's spending priorities from development purposes to debt servicing (Gill *et al.*, 2010). Though democratic process was restored in the state in 1992, and militancy ended by 1995, subsequent elected democratic governments indulged in populist and election-oriented gimmicks (free power / water, no land revenue/octroi, etc.) instead of following a sustainable development agenda, which played havoc with the scarce state finances.

Further, state economy had not been able to extract large benefits from the economic reforms initiated at the national level since 1991. In fact, all these policy packages completely by-passed the state economy's possibilities to grow fast in the 1990s and in the subsequent decade (Gill *et al.*, 2010). Further, the leftist and other progressive movements in the state became very weak, particularly in the rural areas as they were targeted by the terrorists. In fact, it was the left movements which were mobilizing the agricultural labourers, small and marginal farmers, before the terrorist movement emerged in the state. The weakening of progressive movements of the rural poor reduced the pressure on the state government in strengthening the pro-poor social security schemes (Jain, 2010).

METHODOLOGY OF THE STUDY

This research work concentrates on state and centre specific contingency social security schemes, operating in Punjab. These schemes include various pensionary benefits (old age, widow/destitute women, disabled persons, and dependent children)—Rashtriya Swasthya Bima Yojana (RSBY), and subsidized food (Atta-Dal scheme) operating in the state. The evolution of these schemes has been examined in context of the political economy, and compulsions of the state. The study used both the primary and secondary data. The secondary data were collected from the office records of the state/district level concerned departments. To collect primary information, group meetings were conducted in each village with the beneficiaries, Sarpanch and/or panchayat members, Anganwari workers, and non-beneficiaries in 16 villages (eight villages each) of Patiala and Sangrur districts of Punjab, selected purposively under the NREGS (see, the discussion on the functioning of NREGS in Punjab in Chapter 12). Village elders and officials, involved in the selection of beneficiaries, were approached to make these schemes more inclusive, transparent, and efficient in the future. In group meetings, issues related to regularity of pensions, caste biases in selection, exclusion, bogus enrollments, various local harassments, and pilferages of benefits were also discussed. Further, well-structured interviews and meetings were arranged with the NREGA activists and union leaders involved in organizing the rural poor.

The chapter has been organized in the following structure. First, besides introduction and methodology, the chapter briefly lays down the significance of social security schemes. Then, it examines the progress and working of various pensionary schemes in the state. It subsequently moves on to an analysis of the RSBY. The following section gives a vivid account of the state's Atta-Dal scheme. And lastly, it traces main conclusions and related public policy issues.

SOCIAL SECURITY SCHEMES

On the pension front, two types of social security schemes are operating in Punjab. One set comes under the exclusive domain of state government, consisting of old age pension, financial assistance to widows and destitute women, dependent children, and disabled persons. The second set consists of old age pension (since 15 August 1995), family benefits (since 15 August 1995), and pensions to widows and disabled persons (since February 2009), under the umbrella of central schemes. Interestingly, state social schemes have been operative in the state since a long ago—old age pension (1964); financial assistance to widows and destitute women and dependent children (1968); and assistance to disabled persons (1982).

Table 13.1 clearly, albeit briefly, outlines the eligibility conditions, the amount of pension or assistance, and sanctioning authority in case of the state social security schemes operating in Punjab. The first is the old age pension, for all women aged 60 years or more and men aged 65 years or more; individuals with a monthly income of up to Rs 1,000, or Rs 1,500 if both husband and wife are alive, are eligible to get a pension benefit of Rs 250 per month per person in the state. The second scheme is meant for widows and destitute women below the age of 60 years, who are (i) without a means of subsistence, or (ii) deprived of their husband's support due to continued absence from home, or (iii) suffering from chronic illness or similar condition, or (iv) unmarried women aged 30 years or above, living the life of destitution; all such women, whose monthly income from all sources is less than Rs 1,000, are eligible to get a monthly pension of Rs 250 per month per woman. The third is for dependent children below 21 years of age, whose mother, father, or both have passed away, or become incapacitated due to physical or mental disability, or are faced with loss of parental support, and whose grandparents or guardians' individual monthly income is not be more than Rs 1,000, and Rs 1,500 if both husband and wife are alive, are eligible to get a monthly pension of Rs 250 per children. The fourth scheme is for disabled persons where an eligible person gets monthly pension at Rs 250 per person, if he/she fulfills three conditions: (i) disability is permanent (blind, deaf and dumb, orthopedically handicapped and mentally retarded); (ii) he/she has at least 50 per cent disability; and (iii) his/her monthly income does not exceed Rs 1,000 per month in the case of individual and Rs 1,500 if both (husband and wife)

Table 13.1 Terms and Eligibility Conditions of Various National and State Level Social Security Schemes

Name of Scheme	*Starting Year*	*Eligibility Conditions*	*Contingent Security Benefits per Person*	*Sanctioned Authority (Same for all Schemes)*
Old Age Pension	1964	1. Applicant's age is 60 years or more for women and 65 years or more for men. 2. Applicant's Monthly income should not be more than Rs 1,000 in case of individual and Rs 1,500 if both husband/wife are alive. (Before 15.7.97, the limit of monthly income was Rs 500 and Rs 750 for individual and couple case respectively).	Rs 250 per month (Pension rate was Rs 150 per month before April, 1995 and Rs 200 per month before April, 2006)	**In Rural Areas** An applicant will submit the application duly attested and recommended by Sarpanch/ MLA to the Gram Sabha. Gram Sabha will identify the eligibility of the beneficiaries under the Scheme in General Ijlas and send the list along with application form to Gram Panchayat for onward transmission to Child Development Project Officer. CDPO after the approval of Panchayat Samiti will issue the sanction and will send the list of beneficiaries to the District Social Security Officer for updating the record and issuance of pension fund accordingly.
Financial Assistance to Widows and Destitute Women	1968	1. Women below 60 years age having no means of subsistence or deprived of her husband's support due to continued absence from home or chronic disease or any other reason, or Unmarried women aged 30 years or above living the life of destitution. 2. Applicant's Monthly income from all sources is less than Rs 1,000 (Before 15.7.97, the limit of monthly income was Rs 500).	Rs 250 per month (Pension rate was Rs 150 per month before April, 1995 and Rs 200 per month before April, 2006)	

Financial Assistance to Dependent Children	1968	1. Children below 21 years age through their parents/guardian, whose mother/father or both have passed away or become incapacitated due to physical/ mental disability or loss of parental support, etc. 2. Monthly income of the applicant should not be more than Rs 1,000 in case of individual and Rs 1,500 in couple case (Before 15.7.97, the limit of monthly income was Rs 500 and Rs 750 for individual and couple case respectively).	Rs 250 per month (Pension rate was Rs 150 per month before April, 1995 and Rs 200 per month before April, 2006)	**In Urban Areas** An applicant will submit the application in prescribed performa, duly attested and recommended by the MC/MLA to the Executive Officer of the Municipalities or Secretary of the Municipal Corporation. After processing applications, the Executive Officer and Secretary Corporation will submit the application to the Sub-Divisional Magistrate for sanction/rejection, then to District Social Security Officer for updating the record and issue of pension fund accordingly.

(Cont'd)

TABLE 13.1 (*Cont'd*)

Name of Scheme	*Starting Year*	*Eligibility Conditions*	*Contingent Security Benefits per Person*	*Sanctioned Authority*
Financial Assistance to Disabled Persons	1982	1. Applicant with permanently disabled like Blind, Orthopedically Handicapped, Deaf and Dumb, Mentally Retarded is eligible. The financial assistance is allowed from birth or from the first of the month in which the medical certificate issued by the Medical Officer in the prescribed form. 2. Now Govt. has decided that disabled persons who have at least 50 per cent disability would be eligible for financial assistance. 3. Applicant's Monthly income does not exceed Rs 1,000 per month in case of individual and Rs 1,500 if husband and wife are both alive. In case of the applicant is not earning the income of their parents does not exceed Rs 2,500 per month. In case a parent has more than two children, their income should not exceed Rs 3,000 per month. (Before 15.7.97, the limit of monthly income was Rs 500 and Rs 750 for individual and couple cases respectively).	Rs 250 per month (Pension rate was Rs 150 per month before April, 1995 and Rs 200 per month before April, 2006)	

Source: Constructed from information provided by the Office of the Department of Social Security Punjab, Chandigarh.

are alive. Further, if the applicant is not earning, and the monthly income of his/her parents does not exceed Rs 2,500, and Rs 3,000 in the case of parents with more than two children, they are eligible. The monthly pension to a disabled person is allowed from birth, or first day of month in which the medical certificate has been issued by the Medical Officer in the prescribed form.

Regarding the sanctioning authority of such pensions, there are some differences in rural and urban areas. For instance, in rural areas, an applicant has to submit his/her written application, duly attested and recommended by the Sarpanch/MLA, to the Gram Sabha. The Gram Sabha in its general meeting judges the eligibility of the beneficiaries and sends the list of applicants, along with relevant forms, to the Gram Panchayat for onward transmission to the designated block officer. This designated authority, after getting the approval of the Panchayat Samiti, issues the sanction letter and sends the names to the District Social Security Officer (DSSO) to update the record and issue pension benefits accordingly. The DSSO in turn, disburses the pensions to the beneficiaries through the village Sarpanch led committee (consisting of five members) in rural areas. In urban areas, an eligible applicant applies in prescribed performa, duly attested and recommended by the MC or MLA to the Executive Officer (EO) of the concerned municipality, or Secretary of municipal corporations. After processing applications, the EO or Secretary submits the list to the Sub-Divisional Magistrate for sanction or rejection, which then moves to the DSSO for him to update the record and issue pension to beneficiaries. In the case of urban areas, the DSSO directly transfers the pensionary amount to the beneficiaries' saving bank accounts opened in the commercial banks or post offices.

Further, responding to changing time, the income eligibility, and monthly pension and assistance were revised periodically across all schemes in the state. For instance, earlier monthly pension was fixed at Rs 150 per person until 31 March 1995, which was raised to Rs 200 per person till 31 March 2006, and to Rs 250 per person since April 2006, for all four schemes. Similarly, monthly income limit, wherever applicable, was updated from Rs 500 for an individual and Rs. 750 for the couple before 15 July 1997 to Rs 1,000 for an individual and Rs 1,500 for the couple, particularly in the case of old age pensions. Further, new applicants can enter into the list of beneficiaries twice a year, and there is no cap (fixed quota) on the maximum number of beneficiaries in Punjab. It is also true that the persons belonging to the creamy layers are kept out of these schemes.

On the other hand, however, two national social security schemes—old age pension and family benefit schemes—are operative in the state since 15 August 1995. Both these schemes have been named after the Mrs Indira Gandhi. Besides, two other schemes—Indira Gandhi National Widow Pension Scheme and Indira Gandhi National Disabled Persons Scheme—were introduced in February 2009. About eligibility conditions, to get the benefits of national old age pension, an applicant must be 65 years of age or more for both sexes, without an income source, and belongs to the Below Poverty Line (BPL) family. Further, disabled, issueless, widows, and destitute women (aged 65 years and above), belonging to a BPL family, within the monthly income limit, is eligible to get such pension. The national family benefit scheme of Rs 10,000 per family is available to the BPL family whose bread earner dies between the ages of 18–65 years. A person coming under the national old age pension gets a monthly pension of Rs 200 plus Rs 250 (state share), because he/she is also eligible for the state old age pension scheme. The eligibility conditions, amount of pension and assistance, and sanctioning authority of these benefits are reproduced in Table 13.2.

PERFORMANCE OF STATE PENSION SCHEMES

An analysis of the data showed that the number of beneficiaries of the four state pensionary schemes has almost doubled; it increased from 9,29,049 in 2002–3, to 18,02,806 in 2009–10 (Table 13.3). Yearly receipts per beneficiary also doubled; it rose from Rs 1,358 to Rs 2,508 during the same time period. However, the data on budgetary allocations, actual amount released and actual amount disbursed pointed out that in 2004–05, inadequate funds were allocated (Rs 5,874.43 lakh) and actual amount released and spent (Rs 3,791.84 lakh) was too low (64.55 per cent) compared to the allocated amount which was actually released (Rs 14,844.39 lakh) in 2003–4. In fact, 2003–4, the actual amount disbursed was Rs 14,789.60 lakh and the funds released equaled Rs 15,193.09 lakh; comparatively, and actual funds disbursed in 2002–3 was Rs 12,621.03 lakh. It means that inadequate budgetary allocations lead to the low release of funds. As a result, a large number of beneficiaries did not get pensionary

TABLE 13.2 Terms and Eligibility Conditions of National Social Security Schemes in Punjab

Name of Scheme	*Starting Year*	*Eligibility Conditions*	*Contingent Security Benefits per Person*	*Sanctioned Authority*
Indira Gandhi National Old Age Pension Scheme (IGNOAPS)	15.08.1995	1. Applicant's age must be aged 65 years and above, dependent without income and of BPL family. 2. Disabled, issueless, widow and destitute women (65 + aged) belong to BPL family are also eligible for the scheme.	Monthly pension of Rs 200 w.e.f. April 2006 and Rs 250 as state share	Same as per state procedure for all these schemes
Indira Gandhi National Family Benefit Scheme (IGNFBS)	15.08.1995	1. Available to families of deceased bread winner if the family lives below the poverty line and the bread winner dies at 18–65 years of age (Between 1995–2002 as the Central Government Scheme and 2002–3 onwards as State Government Scheme)	Rs 10,000	
Indira Gandhi National Widow Pension Scheme (IGNWPS)	February 2009	Available to widow women aged 40–64 years and above, and belong to BPL family (Yet to be operative in the state as Central Government Scheme)	Rs 200 per month	

(*Cont'd*)

Table 13.2 (*Cont'd*)

Name of Scheme	*Starting Year*	*Eligibility Conditions*	*Contingent Security Benefits per Person*	*Sanctioned Authority*
Indira Gandhi National Disabled Pension Scheme (IGNDPS)	February 2009	1. Available to persons aged 40–64 years and above. 2. Physical disability at least 80 per cent and belong to BPL family. (yet to be operative in the state as Central Government Scheme)	Rs 200 per month	

Source: Constructed from information provided by the Office of Department of Social Security Punjab, Chandigarh.

Table 13.3 Number of Beneficiaries and Expenditure of State Social Security Schemes in Punjab

Year	*Number of Beneficiaries*	*Figures in Lakh*				*Col. 4/Col. 2(%)*
		Budgetary Allocation	*Actual Released*	*Actual Disbursed*	*Per Year per Beneficiary Expenditure (Rs)*	
	1	*2*	*3*	*4*	*5*	*6*
2002–3	9,29,049	15,193.09	15,193.09	12,621.03	1,358.49	83.07
2003–4	9,64,330	14,844.39	14,844.39	14,789.60		99.63
2004–5	10,01,307	5,874.43	3,791.84	3,791.84	2,016.85*	64.55
2005–6	11,21,126	45,383.48	44,072.29	43,670.53		96.23
2006–7	14,27,962	40,757.24	36,681.93	36,631.77	2,564.6	89.88
2007–8	15,38,425	45,214.57	45,090.85	44,032.03	2,862.15	97.38
2008–9	16,38,562	47,154.91	46,972.91	46,474.01	2,836.27	98.55
2009–10	18,02,806	51,797.00	42,995.43	45,217.02	2,508.16	87.30

Source: Office of Department of Social Security Punjab, Chandigarh.

Note: *Average per year.

benefits in time (disbursing pensions after three–six months was a common phenomenon in 2004–5) and expenditures were spilled over to the next year, that is, 2005–6. During this period, media reports also highlighted the poor performance of these schemes. There was a huge hue and cry across the beneficiaries and ruling political class during this period. In order to streamline regular disbursement of pensions and assured flow of funds, under popular political pressure the state government set up a Dedicated Social Security Fund—an innovative way to generate adequate budgetary support (Box 13.1).

The composition of beneficiaries revealed (Table 13.4) that the old age pension scheme was the biggest scheme, as it constituted nearly three-fourths of the beneficiaries (74.78 per cent in 2009–10), followed by the widow and destitute women scheme (12.96 per cent), the disabled persons scheme (6.72 per cent), and the dependent children (5.54 per cent). The analysis also showed that the number of old age pensioners decreased relatively, from 79.09 per cent in 2002–3 to 74.75 per cent in 2009–10. The proportionate share of widow and destitute women increased marginally from 12.44 per cent in 2002–3 to 12.96 per cent in 2009–10. Consequently, the proportion of dependent children rose from 3.87 per cent in 2002–3

Box 13.1 Creation of *Dedicated Social Security Fund*

In order to streamline the disbursement schedule and a regular flow of funds to the pensionary schemes, state government set up a Dedicated Social Security Fund by (a) enhancing 3 per cent Stamp Duty on the registration of urban properties; and (b) imposing 5 per cent Extra Electricity Duty on the electricity consumption in the state. The dedicated fund came into existence w.e.f. 1 April 2005. Due to this single measure, regular flow of funds have become a reality and more funds are allocated to finance all pensionary schemes on a regular basis; the state, in turn, has begun to disburse these pensionary benefits regularly and, most of the times, on a monthly basis as compared to the earlier mechanism of delayed payments (three–six months late). After the creation of dedicated funds, approximately Rs 450–480 crore were added to the state treasury every year, and with this, disbursement of pensionary benefits has been streamlined in the state during 2005–6 and 2006–7. This fact was authenticated, to some extent, by the beneficiaries in the group and individual meetings with the study team.

TABLE 13.4 Number of Beneficiaries of State Social Security Schemes in Punjab

Year	*Name of Scheme*				*Total*
	Old Age Pension	*Widows and Destitute Women*	*Dependent Children*	*Disabled Persons*	
2002–3	7,34,749	1,15,603	35,943	42,754	9,29,049
Percentage	79.09	12.44	3.87	4.60	100.00
2003–4	7,60,217	1,20,774	38,268	45,071	9,64,330
Percentage	78.83	12.52	3.97	4.67	100.00
2004–5	7,81,433	1,27,915	40,297	51,662	10,01,307
Percentage	78.04	12.77	4.02	5.16	100.00
2005–6	8,50,412	1,50,542	53,316	66,856	11,21,126
Percentage	75.85	13.43	4.76	5.96	100.00
2006–7	10,78,848	1,84,520	72,463	92,531	14,28,362
Percentage	75.53	12.92	5.07	6.48	100.00
2007–8	11,56,129	1,99,689	80,357	1,02,250	15,38,425
Percentage	75.15	12.98	5.22	6.65	100.00
2008–9	12,28,924	2,14,103	84,568	1,10,967	16,38,562
Percentage	75.00	13.07	5.16	6.77	100.00
2009–10	13,48,170	2,33,630	99,914	1,21,092	18,02,806
Percentage	74.78	12.96	5.54	6.72	100.00

Source: Office of Department of Social Security Punjab, Chandigarh.

to 5.54 per cent in 2009–10 and of disabled persons from 4.60 per cent in 2002–3 to 6.72 per cent in 2009–10.

Caste composition of beneficiaries revealed that, on an average, more than half of them (52.59 per cent) belonged to the SC households, nearly one-fifth (19.20 per cent) to BC/OBC households, and the remaining 28.21 per cent were from the general category. However, there were certain differences across the location and caste composition of beneficiaries. For instance, 51.17 per cent beneficiaries in rural areas were from the SCs compared to 57.61 per cent beneficiaries in urban areas, who fell in the same category. Moreover, religious composition of beneficiaries was on expected lines. More than three-fourth beneficiaries (77.53 per cent) in rural areas belonged to the Sikh religion compared to a little less than three-fifth beneficiaries (59.26 per cent) in urban areas. Beneficiaries belong to the Hindu religion constituted 39.51 per cent in urban areas, whereas the Hindu beneficiaries formed only 17.56 per cent in rural areas. Muslim beneficiaries formed less than 1 per cent of total beneficiaries in the state. Other religions constituted just 3.63 per cent of total beneficiaries. Interestingly, overall nearly one-fourth beneficiaries (24.31 per cent) were from the BPL families. In rural areas, proportion of BPL beneficiaries was 23.86 per cent compared to 26.34 per cent in urban areas (Table 13.5).

During group meetings at the village level, the elders and a few beneficiaries were very vocal on the exclusion of deserving cases and inclusion of land owners into these schemes, particularly those getting old age pension. The press reports in the English and vernacular newspapers and discussions with state officials stated that at an operational level, bogus enrollment of old aged persons under the pension scheme was a very serious problem, as in the past. The verification carried out in 2002–3 by the Department of Social Security, Punjab found 1,14,780 ineligible old age pensioners out of 5,20,628 verified cases. The highest proportion of ineligible cases was reported in politically heavy-weight districts (nine in number), where nearly one-third cases (32.43 per cent) were found to be ineligible. This inclusion of non-deserving and exclusion of deserving cases highlights how the rural and urban power structure works; how by violating the norms, the PRIs and ULBs have selected the beneficiaries; and how the state officials succumb to the political pressure or whimsical dictates of political leadership in the state.

PERFORMANCE OF NATIONAL SOCIAL SECURITY SCHEMES

The data showed that 61,371 persons were getting the benefits under the IGNOAP scheme in Punjab during 2005–6, 2006–7 and 2007–8, and the number jumped to 159,292 persons during 2008–9 and 2009–10 (Table 13.6). This increase was largely due to widening of the scope with a revision of eligibility criteria from 'a person of 65 years old and a destitute' to 'a person of 65 years old and belonging to a BPL family', as prescribed by the Government of India. Similarly, number of Indira Gandhi National Family Benefit Scheme (IGNFBS) beneficiaries seems to be fixed—1,290 families during

TABLE 13.5 Caste and Religious Composition of Social Security Beneficiaries in Punjab, 2010

Caste Composition	*Location of Beneficiaries*			*Religious Composition*	*Location of Beneficiaries*		
	Rural	*Urban*	*Total*		*Rural*	*Urban*	*Total*
SC	438	140	578	Sikh	666	144	810
Percentage	51.17	57.61	52.59	Percentage	77.53	59.26	73.50
BC/OBC	166	45	211	Hindu	150	96	246
Percentage	19.39	18.52	19.20	Percentage	17.46	39.51	22.32
Others	252	58	310	Muslims	5	1	6
Percentage	29.44	23.87	28.21	Percentage	0.58	0.41	0.54
Total	856	243	1099	Others	38	2	40
Percentage	100.00	100.00	100.00	Percentage	4.42	0.82	3.63
BPL*	205	64	269	Total	859	243	1102
Percentage	23.86	26.34	24.41	Percentage	100.00	100.00	100.00

Source: Singh and Bansal (2011).

Note: *Beneficiaries belonged to the BPL category.

TABLE 13.6 Progress under IGNOAPS and IGNFBS

Year	*Funds Released by GoI*	*Actual Expenditure (in Rs Crore)*	*Estimated Beneficiaries*	
			IGNOAPS	*IGNFBS*
2005–6	15.71	15.71	61,371	1,290
2006–7	12.89	12.89	61,371	1,290
2007–8	12.29	12.29	61,371	1,290
2008–9	47.92	32.81	1,59,292	2,672
2009–10	37.69	54.43	1,59,292	4,823

Source: Office of Department of Social Security Punjab, Chandigarh.

2005–6, 2006–7 and 2007–8, which increased to 2,672 families during 2008–9 and 4,823 families during 2009–10. Naturally, the total expenditure on both schemes increased from Rs 1,571 lakh in 2005–6 to Rs 3,281 lakh in 2008–9 and Rs 5,443 lakh in 2009–10 in the state (Table 13.7). Interestingly, there is a provision to recover whole payments if a case of the wrong inclusion of pensioner is found to be true at a later stage.

INSIGHTS FROM GROUP MEETINGS

In group meetings, the main points of discussion were exclusion of deserving cases, bogus enrollments (wrong inclusion), disbursement problems, and quantum of benefit amount. In these group meetings, it was observed that (i) the monthly pensionary amount (Rs 250 per person) was too low in the present reality of rising cost of living. The beneficiaries favoured that there should be four-fold increase in the pensionary benefits granted to them; (ii) exclusion of many deserving families from these benefits, especially of old age pensions has occurred, largely due to divisive and factional politics played at the village level. There are reports of bogus enrollment and wrong inclusion of certain well-connected (certainly not poor) families. This was largely due to the administrative apathy, or nepotism practiced by the officials, and power politics involved in granting these benefits; (iii) late disbursement of pensions has become a routine matter. This fact was corroborated by the disbursement schedules followed in

TABLE 13.7 Number of BPL Families Enrolled under RSBY in Punjab

Year	*Population (2001)*	*Number of BPL Families (2002)*			*Number of Families Enrolled*		
		Rural	*Urban*	*Total*	*Rural*	*Urban*	*Total*
2008–9	1,34,50,975	2,01,737	70,503	2,72,240	85,952(42.61)	21,580 (30.61)	1,07,532 (39.50)
2009–10	2,43,58,999	3,30,534	1,03,816	4,34,530	1,31,336(39.73)	32,211 (31.03)	1,63,547 (37.64)

Source: Office of Punjab Health Systems Corporation (PHSC), Punjab, SAS Nagar (Mohali).

Patiala district during the last two years, that is, 2008–9 and 2009–10 (Appendix A13.1); and (iv) the beneficiaries, being illiterate and poor, are dependent for employment and the daily necessities (food, credit, etc.) on those people who largely belong to the richer sections of society in rural and urban areas. A clear-cut class bias was observed in sanctioning these benefits. Factionalism, political connections, etc. determine granting of pensionary and other benefits. The victims of 'wrong exclusion' are found to be cursed due to their poor living conditions, illiteracy, administrative apathy, and caste-dominated power structure in the villages, which is extremely exploitative in nature.

They also stated that, since most of pro-poor schemes are focused on BPL families identified during the 2002 BPL survey, which is too old and full of defects, there is now a need to carry out a fresh survey to identify BPL families in the state. In fact, their demand has a logic because after this survey, (i) many households who were not poor at that time may have been added to the poor's category because of vulnerable conditions against the market forces (rising prices, causal nature of employment, chronic illness); (ii) some households are sub-divided into two or more family units, largely due to emerging trend of nuclear families, or due to available PDS benefits, granted irrespective of family size (35 kg wheat given to a BPL and AAY household); (iii) few families have wrong or double names; (iv) household heads in many cases had died; and (v) some households had their name missing from the BPL list, indicating either the bogus entry or such households may have migrated.

IMPLEMENTATION OF RSBY

It is largely true that poverty and ill-health are closely correlated and reinforcing each other. For the poor people, an illness means a loss of work, a threat to income generating capacity, and an additional cost on seeking treatment. A serious illness of longer duration in a poor family means tremendous wage loss and additional expenditure, that may force the family to borrow money, and/or sell whatever little assets the household has to finance the rising cost of treatment (Singh, 1991; NCAER, 2002; Kumar and Singh, 2010; Kumar, 2011; and Singh, 2011).

These tragic outcomes of the poor's ill-health can be overcome either through free or low cost public health services, or through pro-poor health insurance. In the absence of subsidized public health services, alternately, a hassle-free and low premium health insurance with wider coverage is the right answer. In the past, the Union Government has tried to provide a health insurance cover on limited scale to a select group of beneficiaries at the national or state levels. Most of these schemes, however, failed to achieve their intended goals because of faulty designs and/or problems at the level of implementation. After examining all the existing and earlier health insurance schemes, with an view of learning from past mistakes and adopting good practices, the Union Government adopted the RSBY, which covers all BPL families.

On the basis of wide coverage and intended benefits, next to NREGA, the RSBY is a large scheme. Since the year 2008, it is being implemented enthusiastically across many states of India. As per the RSBY guidelines, it was to be implemented in Punjab in a phased manner (since 2008–9), and would have covered the entire state within five years (by 2012–13). Accordingly, the RSBY was to start in three districts each in the first three years (2008–9 to 2010–11), and four districts each in the next two years (2011–12 and 2012–13). Visualizing its intended benefits, the state government, however, introduced the scheme in eight districts in 2008–9 (the first year), and covered the remaining 12 districts in 2009–10 (the second year).

At the level of implementation, the performance of RSBY is very low, as nearly two-fifths of the BPL families (39.50 per cent) were enrolled under the RSBY during 2008–9. Enrollment of BPL families was higher in the rural areas (42.61 per cent) than that in the urban areas (30.61 per cent) in 2008–9. However, instead of rising, the enrollment ratio, declined to 37.64 per cent in the state (39.73 per cent in rural areas and 31.03 per cent in urban areas) in 2009–10 (Table 13.7).

Regarding patients treated under RSBY, the data elucidated that 2,698 persons and 4,603 persons received treatment in 2008–9 and 2009–10 respectively (Table 13.8). The total cost of treatment incurred by hospitals on such patients was Rs 174.43 lakh in 2008–9, and Rs 298.80 lakh in 2009–10. The average per patient cost was Rs 6,465 in 2008–9 and Rs 6,491 in 2009–10. Among the patients treated, a gender bias was observed as more male patients (61.75 per cent in 2008–9 and 73.00 per cent in 2009–10) were treated compared to female patients.

TABLE 13.8 Number of Persons Benefited and Amount Claimed under RSBY, 2008–9 and 2009–10

Year	*Number of Persons Benefited and Amount Claimed*			*Sex of Claimants*		
	Number of Claimants	*Amount Claimed (Rs)*	*Per Claimant (Rs)*	*Male*	*Female*	*Didn't Know*
2008–9	2,698	1,74,42,636	6,465	1,666 (61.75)	938 (34.77)	94 (3.48)
2009–10	4,603	2,98,79,600	6,491	3,360 (73.00)	1,187 (25.79)	56 (1.22)

Source: Office of Punjab Health Systems Corporation (PHSC), Punjab, SAS Nagar (Mohali).

Another important aspect of RSBY is the low bidding premium negotiated by the insurance companies compared to the maximum premium suggested by the Central Government (Rs 750 per household). Most of the bids on the premium amount across eight districts during 2008–9 (the first year) were Rs 670.30, but the premium bids were reduced considerably in the second year (Rs 446.72 in four districts, and Rs 561.80 in one district). Further, the data on hospitals empanelled revealed that out of 515 empanelled hospitals, 361 hospitals (70.10 per cent) belonged to the private sector and 154 hospitals (29.90 per cent) to the public sector (Table 13.9).

INSIGHTS FROM GROUP MEETINGS

Through group meetings, the study team tried to find out the political economy and low enrollment of BPL families under the RSBY in the state. Indeed, a low enrollment ratio could put a question mark on the long-term sustainability of the scheme because the RSBY is designed as a business mode, where maximization of beneficiaries' gains (cashless and quality treatment), insurance companies' business, and profits of hospitals (by attracting patients) are the hallmark of each entity. So, higher enrollment of BPL families is the necessary condition for its expansion and sustainability. On enquiry, the villagers cited many valid reasons for low enrollment of BPL families, which largely circled around the political set-up, administrative apathy, ignorance of

TABLE 13.9 Premium Rates per Household and Empanelled Hospitals under RSBY in Punjab

Policy Phase	*Premium (Rs) with Service Tax*	*Number of Districts*	*Hospitals Empanelled*		
			Private	*Public*	*Total*
First	670.30	9	133	63	196
Second	561.80	1	20	11	31
Second	446.72	4	110	36	146
	Not Available	5	98	44	142
Total		20	361	154	515

Source: Office of Punjab Health Systems Corporation (PHSC), Punjab, SAS Nagar (Mohali).

beneficiaries, illiteracy, non-suitability of enrollment timings (9 a.m. to 6 p.m.), limited publicity of enrolling dates, etc. Most of the BPL families that the study team met with did not know the benefits of RSBY. Village level factional politics and rural power structure again worked against them. Being poor and illiterate, nobody gave them information; officials did not come on the appointed date or time, and were generally dismissive of them. They feel that smart card-making should be propagated properly, and also suggested that the information must be addressed on the public address system available in the villages, Gurudwaras, and Temples. The Sarpanch, members of PRIs and ULBs, and other government functionaries associated with village or urban life should be involved in preparing smart cards, and their presence must be obligatory on the stipulated day and time, as well as on the day before.

Since the beneficiaries of RSBY are from the BPL list prepared in the year 2002, the list is largely outdated in the present context. It did not have the names of those persons who have been added to the 'poor' category after 2002. Further, over the last decade or so, many new born children have been added to the family list; many households have been sub-divided and partitioned into two or more family units; heads of many households have died; some households are untraced (may be migrated); a few families have wrong or double names, etc. Moreover, there are many instances of families who were not poor at that time, but have now become poor due to their vulnerable conditions against market driven forces like uncontrolled prices rise, loss of bread winner, serious illness, accidents, etc. Thus, many deserving individuals and families are excluded from the RSBY, and should be included in the BPL list.

Many BPL family heads who were more articulate and well informed sought the help of the study team to highlight their woes of unhealthy living conditions (lack of safe drinking water, stagnation of dirty water around their houses, poor sanitation, shortage of space, etc.). They also suggested that the academia of the state universities, with a pro-poor image, should be involved in the supervisory work during the next BPL survey which is likely to be conducted in 2011–12.

During the survey, only 14 patients utilized this facility in these sampled villages. Without bias, they praised the benefits of scheme. However, two cases were not paid any transport charges by the hospitals, and food was provided by their family members. When told that it should be given to them, both were ignorant about such benefits. This amounts to malpractice on the part of the hospitals. However, they were happy because they were at least able to access a certain quality of health services, necessary to live a decent life, and rejoin work to continue earning. They opined that RSBY should cover all family members, more illnesses and diseases (indoor and outdoor treatments), and hospitalization costs should be increased to Rs 50,000 per household.

A STATE INITIATIVE: *ATTA-DAL* SCHEME

Poverty Scenario in Punjab

In Punjab, the share of socially and economically poor and vulnerable sections is very large (Jain, 2010). Officially, 5.20 per cent of the state's population was categorized as BPL in 2004–5 (GoP, 2008–9a). Similarly, 5.23 lakh families (12.42 per cent of total families) were identified as BPL families in the state (GoP, 2008–9b). Moreover, in six districts of Punjab, the proportion of population living below the poverty line in the rural areas during 2004–5 was reported to be very high: Mukatsar (28.3 per cent), Moga (25.2 per cent), Faridkot (23.9 per cent), Bhatinda (23.1 per cent), Firozepur (17.9 per cent), and Mansa (16.6 per cent). These six districts constituted 26.40 per cent of total rural population of the state (Chaudhuri and Gupta, 2009).

This implies that the poor need basic social security measures in the form of employment and subsidized food in the state.

What is *Atta-Dal* Scheme?

The Atta-Dal Scheme (ADS), which was initiated in Punjab on 15 August 2007, happens to be one of the largest poverty alleviation programmes ever commenced in the state. In fact, providing subsidized food to the poor—35 kg wheat flour (atta) at Rs 4 per kg and 4 kg dal (pulse) at Rs 20 per kg—was the main poll promise of the present political set-up (the Akali–BJP coalition) during the State Legislative Elections of February 2007. The scheme is aimed at giving direct support to the poor families in the form of subsidized food through designated ration shops and depots. It supplies specified quantity of two items, wheat and dal (*moong* and gram), which form the core of the staple diet in the region.

ADS survey to identify eligible households was carried out under the direction and control of the Deputy Commissioners. The state followed a liberal criterion to identify the poor families; those whose income from all the sources was less than Rs 30,000 per annum on a household basis (GoP, 2008–9a). In order to assess the income of agricultural families, income from agricultural land was assessed at the rate of Rs 10,000 per acre for irrigated land and Rs. 5,000 for non-irrigated land. These income figures were taken as indicative, and the enumerators were authorized to assign higher values in particular cases while carrying out the survey. Some checks and balances were also introduced through (i) verification of land holdings by the state revenue department; and (ii) random checking of the surveyed cases and families. Moreover, the heads of households were made to submit affidavits regarding their overall sources and level of income. The families identified under ADS were issued the Blue Cards (Box 13.2).

PDS ALLOCATION FOR THE STATE

The working of ADS has been analysed in the background of certain peculiar features of the Public Distribution Scheme (PDS) in the state. The most important feature of the PDS at present is that the total allocation of food items are made under different heads—APL, BPL, AAY and ADS. The analysis makes it abundantly clear that the total allocations of wheat and dal made towards ADS declined

Box 13.2. ADS: Subsidized Food Initiative in Punjab

The ADS was initiated to fulfill one of the poll promises of present Akali–BJP coalition. The whole exercise was completed in a time-bound manner. The field work for inclusion of families was finished in 14 days (9 April to 22 April 2007). After cross-checking, 13.47 lakh eligible families were listed by 31 May 2007 under the ADS. Out of 43.48 lakh surveyed families and households, 30.98 per cent families (56,67,844 persons; 23.27 per cent of the 2001 population) were identified the poor (GoP, 2008–9a). These families were issued Blue Cards (the blue colour is associated with the turbans tied by the workers of Shiromani Akali Dal) and become eligible to get subsidized food equivalent to 7 kg of wheat (at the price of Rs 4 per kg) per person per month, to a maximum limit of 35 kg per family (5 or more members). The pulses are equivalent to 1 kg (at the price of Rs 20 per kg) per member per month, to a maximum limit of 4 kg per family (5 or more members). The estimated cost of ADS was estimated Rs 583 crore for the period of 10 months, at 2007–8 market prices. At present, allocation of wheat and pulses has reduced to maximum of 25 kg and 2.5 kg respectively, per family of 5 or more members.

considerably in the 'state flagship programme' of the Punjab government (Table 13.10). The amount of wheat declined from 31,998 MT to 25,793 MT; that is, a 19.39 per cent decline in March 2010 over March 2009. Similarly, the quantity of dal declined from 4,654 MT to 2,936 MT; that is 36.91 per cent decline in 2010 over 2009. This means that less supply of subsidized food (wheat and dal) is largely related to its financial sustainability. Due to this reason, the

TABLE 13.10 Allocations under *Atta-Dal* Scheme in Punjab, March 2009 and March 2010

Time Period	*Allocations of Wheat and Dal (in metric tons)*	
	Wheat	*Dal*
March 2009	31,998	4,654
March 2010	25,793	2,936
Percentage decline	19.39	36.91

Source: Office of District Controller, Food Civil Supply and Consumer Affairs, Patiala.

state government altered the Atta-Dal allocations to each family by reducing the amount of 'Atta' from 35 kg to 25 kg, and 'Dal' from 4 kg to 2.5 kg per family, on a monthly basis. This reduction in the quantity of atta and dal was planned due to the 'operational' difficulties, as claimed by the state government. In fact, this alteration reduced the financial burden on the state exchequer by Rs 150 crore per year.

Under the PDS in the state, the highest allocation of wheat was made under the APL category (84,782 MT; 66.78 per cent), followed by the ADS (25,793 MT; 20.32 per cent), the BPL (10,098 MT; 7.95 per cent), and the AAY (6,280 MT; 4.95 per cent) categories as on March 2010 (Table 13.11). In a nutshell, about one-third of total wheat (33.32 per cent) was earmarked for the poor in the state.

The working of PDS in the state becomes clearer with the case study of Patiala district, where the number of Ration Cards (all types) was 5,24,861 and 5,30,917 by the end of March 2009 and March 2010 respectively (Table 13.12). The subsidized food entitled for six categories—AAY, AAY plus Blue Card, BPL, BPL plus Blue Card, Blue Card, and APL. Out of these, APL cards constitute the largest share (79 per cent). The next important category, the Blue Card (ADS), exclusively comprised approximately a 15 per cent share. The Blue Cards also supplemented AAY and BPL categories. The number of cards under AAY, AAY plus Blue Card, and BPL declined marginally in March 2010 over March 2009. However, the remaining two categories—BPL plus Blue Cards and Blue Cards—increased during the corresponding periods.

TABLE 13.11 Monthly Allocation of Wheat under PDS in Punjab, March 2010

Category of PDS	*Allocation of Wheat (MT)*	*Per cent Share*
APL	84,782	66.78
BPL	10,098	7.95
AAY	6,280	4.95
ADS	25,793	20.32
Total	1,26,953	100.00

Source: Office of District Controller, Food Civil Supply and Consumer Affairs, Patiala.

TABLE 13.12 Number of Households Eligible for Public Distribution System in District Patiala

Type of Household	*Number of Ration Cards*			
	March 2009		*March 2010*	
	Number	*%*	*Number*	*%*
AAY	6,450	1.23	6,422	1.21
AAY + Blue Card	4,558	0.87	4,543	0.86
BPL	12,876	2.45	12,803	2.41
BPL + Blue Card	8,193	1.56	8,214	1.55
Blue Card	76,377	14.55	77,876	14.67
APL	4,16,407	79.34	4,21,059	79.31
Total	5,24,861	100.00	5,30,917	100.00

Source: Office of District Controller, Food Civil Supply and Consumer Affairs, Patiala.

Further, changed allocation norms under ADS were implemented in 2010. Under the Blue Card, wheat quota was reduced from 35 kg to 25 kg (by decreasing allocation from 7 kg to 5 kg per member), and of dal from 4 kg to 2.5 kg (by reducing allocation from 1 kg to 0.5 kg per member). An AAY household received a wheat quota of 35 kg as per the centre's norms (at the subsidized price of Rs 2 per kg). However, a household covered under AAY and a Blue Card got the additional entitlement of dal equivalent of 2.5 kg (at the price of Rs 20 per kg) with the overall quota of AAY wheat 35 kg in 2010 (Table 13.13).

EVALUATION OF *ATTA-DAL* SCHEME

The ADS appears to have begun with an objective of extending benefits of the scheme to large number of poor people. The whole process was designed to generate a list of beneficiaries in a shortest possible time, so that the poll promises of ruling coalition could be fulfilled. The inclusion of land holding families as the beneficiaries led to the exclusion of genuinely poor families. Theoretically, all AAY families should have been included in the ADS as they were the poorest of poor. However, all AAY holders (poorest of BPL) were not covered under the ADS, although eligibility norms to grant AAY status are

TABLE 13.13 Food Entitlement under PDS in Patiala District, March 2010

Type of Household	*Eligibility Norms (kg)*		*Rate per Kg (Rs)*		*Allocation Remarks*
	Wheat	*Dal*	*Wheat*	*Dal*	
AAY	35	Nil	2.00	Nil	Wheat per household irrespective of size
BPL	35	Nil	4.59	Nil	Wheat per household irrespective of size
AAY + Blue Card	35	2.5	2.00	20.00	Wheat per household irrespective of size, Dal @ 0.5 kg per member up to 2.5 kg maximum per household
BPL + Blue Card	35	2.5	4.00	20.00	Wheat per household irrespective of size, Dal @ 0.5 kg per member up to 2.5 kg maximum per household
Blue Card	25	2.5	4.00	20.00	Wheat 5 kg per member; 25 kg maximum for five and more members' family; Dal @ 0.5 kg per member up to 2.5 kg maximum per household
APL	Eligible for 30 kg Wheat Flour per month @ Rs 12 per kg				

Source: Office of District Controller, Food Civil Supply and Consumer Affairs, Patiala.

simpler than that of ADS. Contrary to the expectations of the poor, blue card families get their monthly wheat and dal quota regularly, and of good quality, as told by the beneficiaries across sampled villages.

However, ration depot-holders do not receive any remuneration or commission for disbursing these goods. They are forced to do this service free of cost, for the poor. In the absence of incentives, depot-holders are found to be charging more in the range of Rs 10–25, or supplying 2–5 kg wheat less than the prescribed quota, to recover the transportation and handing (loading and unloading) charges. When questioned, some depot-holders outright denied it, while others indirectly admitted to it by terming it as the cost of delivering the commodities at the beneficiaries' doorsteps. Many beneficiaries also complained about the poor quality of wheat given to them. But, both the quality and weight of gram (*dal*) were good. By not giving any incentive to depot-holders, the State Government indirectly allowed the pilferage of Atta-Dal.

Another important malpractice which is thriving in the state's PDS related to overlapping of various schemes (Blue Card, BPL, and AAY). For instance, the total number of eligible people covered under the PDS schemes (APL, Blue Card, BPL, and AAY) become much more than the total population of Patiala district in 2011. This implies that a large number of Ration Cards are falling under the category of bogus or are counted double. A case study of Patiala district concerning this practice is eye-opener (Box 13.3).

The field employees and other staff involved in food supply point out that many ration card holders, after shifting to other places (transfer or migration or any other exigency), are not deleting their cards; many others secured more ration cards under different household heads, by showing same family members to claim more ration goods and services. Out of the total cards in Patiala district, about 80 per cent falls under APL category. At meetings, it was brought to our attention that a good proportion of APL families do not purchase food items from the ration depots due to various reasons, largely due to poor quality of wheat flour, good economic conditions, etc. In fact, wheat allocated to APL families as central quota, at subsidized rates, is basically used to finance the Atta-Dal scheme in the state.

***

An evaluation of the performance of all social security schemes apart from the old age pension and subsidized food (Atta-Dal) schemes shows that other schemes fair much below the expectation. In fact, many social security schemes were started long ago, like pensions or financial assistance to old age persons (1964), widows and destitute women (1968), dependent children (1968) and disabled persons

Box 13.3 Problems of Bogus Ration Cards and Reduced Entitlement

In Patiala district, the total number of all types of Ration Cards was 5,30,917 as on March 2010. Of these, 79.31 per cent belonged to the APL category and the rest (20.69 per cent) consisted of Blue Cards, BPL and AAY categories. When the total number of ration cards were multiplied by the average family size of the state (5.5 persons), it becomes equal to 29.20 lakh persons (March 2010). However, the total population of the Patiala district is just 18,92,282 persons as on 31 March 2011, as per the latest Population Census (Office of Deputy Commissioner, Patiala). This means that a large numbers of ration cards were bogus in the district; thus indicating a lackadaisical attitude of state administration. This case of bogus ration cards has led to pilferage of benefits of PDS in the state.

Though the quality and weight of dal was good (many packets tested by the study team), high pilferage of wheat by depot-holders, as reported by the beneficiaries, has become an unbridled routine in the state and is a cause of concern. Further, village level group meetings highlighted the inclusion of many land-owned households and exclusion of many deserving labour households from the Atta-Dal scheme. This indicates how the benefits of Atta-Dal scheme are not allowed to trickle down to the deserving poor, but instead are usurped by the better-off households. Moreover, a planned programme / policy favouring the poor is allowed to suffer for want of adequate funds. Consequently, the amount of wheat was reduced from 35 kg to 25 kg and that of the Dal from 4 kg to 2.5 kg, to save Rs 150 crore per annum.

(1982); whereas the central schemes (pension for old age since 1995, widows and disabled persons, 2009) were instituted recently. While central schemes apply to BPL families, state pensionary schemes have much larger scope as the non-BPL persons and families are also eligible to get these benefits. Further, BPL families are entitled to get benefits of both central and state pension schemes. Rate of monthly pension in the state is higher than that of central pension, by Rs 50 per person.

In the state, disbursement of pensionary benefits has been streamlined since the creation of Dedicated Social Security Fund since 2005. The number of pensioners, under democratic pressures, also doubled in the state (from 9.29 lakh in 2002–3 to 18.03 lakh in 2009–10) and covered nearly 7.40 per cent of state population in 2009–10. As expected, most of pension beneficiaries belonged either to the SCs or the BCs/OBCs. Nearly one-fourth of them were from the BPL families. These pensions were directly deposited in beneficiaries' bank or post office accounts in urban areas, whereas in rural areas these were distributed in cash through the Sarpanch led committee, at the village level. It is heartening to note that the democratic bodies (Gram Sabha/Panchayat in the rural areas, and MCs/MLAs in the urban areas) are given key roles in sanctioning these benefits. The poor migrants face great problems in getting such recommendations and are often ignored. Taking advantage of soft state apparatus, local power pressures, factional approach, many non-eligible persons have succeeded in usurping pensionary benefits, as more than one-fifth of old age pensioners in 2002 (22.05 per cent) fell in the non-eligible category.

The working of social security schemes in the state highlights that there are provisions to include the poor as well as the non-poor sections of the society. These schemes, in fact, cover those sections of the population which come under the category of unorganized sectors of the economy. There has been a tendency towards greater coverage, but not universal coverage. In that sense, the schemes at the state level are broader than those at the national level. The national level schemes are strictly for the BPL families, but the state schemes cover not only the BPL families, but also the eligible APL households. In other words, the provision of subsidized food and old age pension have much larger coverage in the state than the proportion of population living below poverty line. This is not to negate the fact that there are still instances of exclusion of the poor and deserving cases, and inclusion of the non-poor or non-eligible cases, which need to be rectified. There is also poor coverage of BPL families under RSBY, depriving the majority (nearly 60 per cent) of the population from the benefits of assured health insurance upto the stipulated level. Unlike the Aarogyasri for BPL families (a unique health insurance scheme operating in Andhra Pradesh), where coverage is much larger and wider scope (Vijay, 2011), Punjab state does not think beyond the narrow financial constraints.

The state administration did not show enthusiasm to take full advantage of the centrally funded schemes. This is partly explained by a general level of apathy and the indifferent attitude of state bureaucracy towards all government programmes; and partly it is attributed to lack of political-will as shown by the prevailing power structure in the state. The present state government and administration is least interested in the implementation of any such programmes initiated the UPA government, albeit framed for the benefit of the poor. They are interested in minimal implementation of these programmes, to the extent that it may help them win the next elections. The state can be made more responsive if the beneficiaries organize themselves in the form of genuine associations or unions.

In fact, operation of contingent social security schemes in the state is largely governed by dynamics of electoral power politics between two political formations (SAD–BJP, and the Congress), which alternatively come to power. The ADS is the state's flagship scheme and the dearest to present political set-up, thus ensuring better implementation as compared to the performance of NREGS and RSBY in the state. For better implementation, therefore, people's involvement especially of beneficiaries, is of utmost importance. The system of setting up of vigilance committees at the village level, introduction and faithful implementation of social auditing, and operation through the PRIs and ULBs' elected representatives can make these programmes more successful.

There is also a need to create better awareness about these schemes among the elected representative and beneficiaries. Organization of beneficiaries and up-lifting their educational level will certainly bring efficiency at the level of implementation. The use of ICT will plug the leakages across the various schemes. There is need to enhance the amount of pensionary benefits at least four-fold, and double the treatment limit under the RSBY. Capacity building of state apparatus, utmost transparency, and accountability in selecting beneficiaries must be ensured.

APPENDIX A13

TABLE A13.1 Disbursement Schedule of Pensionary Benefits in Patiala District, 2008–9 and 2009–10

Pension Month	*2008–9*		*Pension Month*	*2009–10*	
	Budget Received Date/Month	*Disbursement Date/Month*		*Budget Received Date/Month*	*Disbursement Date/Month*
April–May–June 2008	30.07.08	07.08.08	April–May 2009	27.06.09	29.06.09
July 2008	08.10.08	21.10.08	June 2009	06.11.09	19.11.09
August 2008	18.11.08	27.11.08	July–August 2009	03.12.09	10.12.09
September 2008	08.12.08	18.12.08	September 2009	03.02.10	11.02.10
October 2008	08.01.09	19.01.09	October–November 2009	05.03.10	08.03.10
November 2008	16.01.09	19.01.09	December 2009	26.03.10	30.03.10
December 2008	29.01.09	31.01.09	January 2010	31.03.10	31.03.10
January 2009	09.03.09	18.03.09	February–March 2010	13.05.10	27.05.10
February 2009	31.03.09	20.04.09			
March 2009	27.06.09	29.06.09			

Source: Office of District Social Security Officer, Patiala (Punjab).

References

Chaudhuri, S. and N. Gupta. 2009. 'Levels of Living and Poverty Patterns—A District-wise Analysis for India', *Economic and Political Weekly*, 44(9): 94–110.

Gill, S. S., S. Singh, and J.S. Brar. 2010. *Globalization and Indian State: Education, Health and Agricultural Extension Services in Punjab*. New Delhi: Aakar Books.

GoI. 2011. *Economic Survey 2010–11*. New Delhi: Oxford University Press.

GoP. 2008–9a. *Annual Plan 2008–09, Vol. I*. Department of Planning, Chandigarh, Punjab.

———. 2008–9b. *Economic Survey of Punjab 2008–09*. Economic Adviser to Government, Economic and Statistical Organization, Chandigarh, Punjab.

Jain, V. 2010. *Affluence, Vulnerability and the Provision of Social Security: Assessing State's Concern for the Working masses in India*, HiVOS Knowledge Programme, Paper 3. Amsterdam: University of Amsterdam, and Thiruvananthapuram: Centre for Development Studies.

Kannan, K.P. 2010. *The Long Road to Social Security: Challenge of Universal Coverage for the Working Poor in India*, HiVOS Knowledge Programme, Working Paper 2. Amsterdam: University of Amsterdam, and Thiruvananthapuram: Centre for Development Studies.

Kumar, K. 2011. *State, Market and Utilization Pattern of Health Services: A Study of Punjab*, Unpublished PhD Thesis, Department of Economics, Punjabi University, Patiala.

Kumar, K. and S. Singh. 2010. 'Health Infrastructure and Utilization Pattern in Rural Punjab: Emerging Public Policy Issues', *Journal of Economic and Social Development*, 6(2): 79–96.

Lyallpuri, J.S. 2010. *My Life My Times: Journey of A Revolutionary*. Ludhiana: Unistar Books.

NCAER. 2002. *Who Benefits from Public Health Spending in India*. New Delhi: National Council of Applied Economic Research.

NCEUS. 2007. *Report on Conditions of Work and Promotion of Livelihood in Unorganized Sector*, Government of India, New Delhi.

Singh, M.M. and S. Bansal. 2011. *Evaluation of Social Security Schemes in Punjab*, A Research Project Sponsored by Department of Planning, Government of Punjab, Centre for Research in Rural and Industrial Development, Chandigarh.

Singh, S. 1991. *Development and Use of Health Care Services in Rural Areas: A Case Study of Punjab*, Unpublished PhD Thesis, Department of Economics, Punjabi University, Patiala.

Singh, V.J. 2011. *Financing of Health Expenditure in Rural Punjab: A Study of Indoor Patients*, Unpublished M.Phil. Thesis, Department of Economics, Punjabi University, Patiala.

Vijay, G. 2011. *The Business of Health Care and Challenges of Health Security: A Case of Arogyasri Health Insurance Programme in Andhra Pradesh*, A Paper Presented at Final Workshop under CDS-ASSR Project on Monitoring the Implementation of Social Security for the Working Poor in India's Informal Economy, 20–22 June, Centre for Development Studies, Thiruvananthapuram.

World Bank. 2011. *Social Protection for A Changing India, Vol. I*. Washington, D.C.: The World Bank.

EDITORS AND CONTRIBUTORS

K.P. Aravindan is Professor, Pathology, Calicut Medical College, Kerala. He has been an activist with the Kerala Sasthra Sahitya Parishath (KSSP) for more than two decades, spreading awareness on health and livelihood issues.

Jan Breman is Professor Emeritus, Comparative Sociology, and Fellow, Amsterdam Institute for Social Science Research, University of Amsterdam, The Netherlands. The themes of his research include past and present labour relations, and work and employment in rural and urban South and Southeast Asia. Most of his publications are empirical studies in which he contextualizes his fieldwork-based findings in macro settings. Among various others, he has authored *Outcast Labour in Asia: Circulation and Informalization of the Workforce at the Bottom of the Economy* (2009; paperback edition in 2012), *The Poverty Regime in Village India: Half a Century of Work and Life at the Bottom of the Rural Economy in South Gujarat* (2007), and co-authored (with Arvind Das; photographs by Ravi Agarwal) *Down and Out: Labouring under Global Capitalism* (2000), all published by Oxford University Press. He has also co-edited (with Isabelle Guérin and Aseem Prakash) *India's Unfree Workforce: Of Bondage Old and New* (Oxford University Press, 2009).

Amarendra Das is Assistant Professor, Post Graduate Department of Analytical and Applied Economics, Utkal University, Bhubaneswar, Odisha, India. He has an MA in Analytical and Applied Economics from Utkal University, an MPhil in Applied Economics, and a PhD in Economics from the Jawaharlal Nehru University (JNU), New Delhi. His teaching and research interests lie in public economics, natural resource management, and environmental economics. He received theGlobal Development Network award in 2008.

N. Jagajeevan is Programme Officer, Kerala State Poverty Alleviation Mission, Trinavdrum, and an activist of the Kerala People's Science Movement, an organization that aims to popularize science and scientific outlook among common people.

Varinder Jain is Assistant Professor, Institute of Development Studies, Jaipur. Prior to this, he worked as a research associate at the Centre for Development Studies (CDS), Trivandrum. He is interested in the questions of vulnerability and social security for the working poor, especially in the context of developing world. Along with this, he is also engaged in research in the areas of informal manufacturing, agriculture, and energy economics.

Satyakam Joshi is Associate Professor, Centre for Social Studies, Surat. He is a social anthropologist and has PhD in Sociology and MSW from Nirmala Niketan College of Social Work, University Of Bombay. He is engaged in conducting action research on caste and social resources, and in training elected representatives of local governance. He is currently working on Gandhian organizations and their role in peaceful co-existence, and the social and political history of Dangs after independence.

K.P. Kannan is Chairman, Laurie Baker Centre for Habitat Studies, Trivandrum, India, and Visiting Professor, Institute for Human Development, New Delhi. He is a development economist and a former director and fellow of the CDS, Trivandrum. He was a member of the erstwhile National Commission for Enterprises in the Unorganized Sector (NCEUS), 2004–9. He was conferred the V.V. Giri Memorial Award for his contributions in the area of social security, especially for the informal workers in 2008. He is a member of the editorial advisory boards of two international professional journals, *International Social Security Review* and *Globalizations*. His earlier books include *Of Rural Proletarian Struggles: Mobilisation and Organisation of Rural Workers in South West India* (Oxford University Press, 1988; reprint in 1989), and *The Plight of the Power Sector in India: Inefficiency, Reform, and Political Economy* (co-authored with N. Vijayamohanan Pillai) (CDS, 2002). His areas of specialization are labour and development, poverty and human development and environment and development.

Rathi Kanta Kumbhar is Lecturer, Department of Economics, Sambalpur University, Odisha, India. He obtained his MPhil and PhD degrees from CDS, Trivandrum, and JNU, New Delhi. His areas of research include political economy of poverty, employment, and social security. His writings have been published in various reputed journals.

T.P. Kunhikannan is Professor, Economics, Government College, Perambra, Calicut, Kerala. He is an activist and past President of the

KSSP, an organization that spearheads a people's science movements in Kerala. He has written extensively on various developmental issues in Malayalam published by the KSSP.

Darshini Mahadevia is Professor, Faculty of Planning and Public Policy, and Member Secretary, Centre for Urban Equity, Centre for Environmental Planning and Technology (CEPT) University, Ahmedabad. She obtained her PhD from the Centre for Study of Regional Development, JNU, New Delhi. Her research areas are urban development, and human and gender development. She has published widely in these areas. Recently, she co-authored the *Handbook of Urban Inequalities* with Sandip Sarkar (Oxford University Press, 2012).

D. Narasimha Reddy holds the S.R. Sankaran Chair in Rural Labour Studies, National Institute of Rural Development, Hyderabad. He was Head of Department, Economics, and Dean of Social Sciences, University of Hyderabad. He is also a member of the Indian Society of Labour Economics. His areas of interest are political economy of labour and development, agrarian distress and agricultural development, and employment and development in India.

Sukhwinder Singh is Professor of Economics, Punjabi University, Patiala. He has many books to his credit and has published research papers in national/international journals. His areas of interests are health economics, quantitative economics, and human capital.

Jaswinder Singh Brar is Professor of Economics, Punjabi University, Patiala. He has authored many books and published research papers in national/international journals. His areas of interest include international trade, economics of education, and agricultural economics.

Sucha Singh Gill is Director General, Centre for Research in Rural and Industrial Development (CRRID), Chandigarh. Earlier, he was Dean of Academic Affairs, Dean of Research, Dean of Social Sciences, and Head, Department of Economics, Punjabi University, Patiala. He has varied interests, particularly in development economics, labour economics, and macroeconomic theory. He has published various books and research papers in known national and international journals.

G. Vijay is Assistant Professor, School of Economics, University of Hyderabad. He is also an adjunct faculty, Centre for Human Rights, University of Hyderabad, and Secretary, Centre for Social Concerns,

Hyderabad. He has a doctorate from the Institute of Social Studies, The Hague. He received the Sanjay Thakur Young Labour Economist Award in 2008. He specializes in economics of labour, of business organizations, environmental economics, law and economics, and political economy of development, and has several publications in journals and books.

This publication is the outcome of the knowledge project, *The Long Road to Social Security: Assessing and Monitoring the Implementation of Social Security for the Working Poor in India's Informal Economy*. It is a result of a collaborative effort between the Humanistic Institute for Development Cooperation, The Hague, The Netherlands (HiVOS), Amsterdam Institute for Social Science Research, and the Centre for Development Studies, Trivandrum, India. For more information, see, www.hivos.net.